*Information-Processing
Approaches
to Visual
Perception*

Information-Processing Approaches to Visual Perception

Edited by RALPH NORMAN HABER

UNIVERSITY OF ROCHESTER

Holt, Rinehart and Winston, Inc.

NEW YORK   CHICAGO   SAN FRANCISCO   ATLANTA   DALLAS
MONTREAL   TORONTO   LONDON   SYDNEY

*This Book Is Dedicated
to All Scientists Who Study
Visual Perception.*

Preface

The purpose of making these readings available in book form is to show the power of information-processing analyses to the study of visual perception. This is a relatively new development, although it does have some antecedents in earlier theories. Nowhere, however, has a concerted effort been made to bring samplings of this approach together, and it is to repair this deficiency that the present volume has been compiled. I feel that the problems herein outlined, and the topics discussed, hold the principal operations for understanding the means by which human beings perceive, process, remember, and respond to visual stimulation. It is my hope that having these papers available in one place may suggest the fertility of this approach to other researchers working on visual perception.

The genesis of the present work grew out of a prior collection of research and theory papers spanning most of the major topics in visual perception (Haber, *Contemporary Theory and Research in Visual Perception,* 1968). In preparing that volume I became aware that whole sections of it were permeated with material on information-processing approaches. When the overall length became critical, it was decided to separate the information-processing material into a second volume rather than cut down the more traditional areas covered in the first. Since the first volume contains eighty readings and this one forty-seven, the magnitude of the size problem is apparent.

The Introduction to these readings attempts to define what I consider to be the current meanings of an information-processing approach to visual perception. In some respects, no fixed boundaries can be drawn between these approaches and what is often called temporal factors in vision. To this extent, the content of some of the chapters overlaps what might be included in a book on temporal factors; in fact, the chapter titles would probably be quite similar. Information-processing approaches, however, go well beyond the traditional topics of temporal factors in the types of analyses proposed and in the underlying models used to understand the functions being investigated. This point is discussed at some length in the Introduction and is explicit in many of the papers which follow. Even so, the book can be used as a reference or as a source by anyone interested in temporal factors generally without any great commitment to information-processing approaches to visual perception.

Forty-seven readings may seem an intensive as well as a broad sampling of this field, but the selections were made from more than one thousand papers that formed a subset of the four thousand which were the basis of choice for *Contemporary Theory and Research in Visual Perception.* There has been no need to maintain a bias toward recent publication; that comes naturally with this topic.

v

More than half of the papers were published within the two years prior to publication of this volume and ninety percent within five years. This rate of recency, unfortunately, implies that the collection may go out of date faster than the typical compilation of research and theory readings in a rapidly changing and developing science.

Advantage has been taken of many professional counselors in the organization of this book and decision on specific papers, and I would like to acknowledge their indispensable assistance. My thanks also are again extended to each of the authors and their publishers for permission to reprint their articles, and to Elsie Hayes, Elizabeth Whitehead, and Barbara Herr for their help in assembling the manuscript.

R.N.H.
Rochester, New York
January 1969

Contents

Information-Processing
Approaches
to Visual
Perception

Introduction*

The alliance of an information-processing approach to the study of visual perception is one of the newest areas in experimental psychology and is still not fully confirmed. I feel that the relationship should be encouraged, as it already establishes much earlier work and it will lead, I am convinced, to a very productive future.

Sensation, perception, memory, and thought must be considered on a continuum of cognitive activity. They are mutually interdependent and cannot be separated except by arbitrary rules of momentary expediency. Further, to understand how these processes function and interact, they should be subjected to an information-processing analysis, rather than be viewed as static structural systems. Such an analysis makes it clear that a proper explication of thought processes must begin with perceptual behavior, just as thought cannot prosper in the absence of stimulation. Equally as important, it is not possible to understand perception, especially recognition, identification, and perceptual memory, without understanding the whole range of cognitive activity.

Before getting deeply into this thesis, some basic definitions are needed. I call "perceptual" all those processes concerned with the translation of stimulus energy falling on a receptor surface (limited to visual for this discussion) into the reports of experience, responses to that stimulation, and memory persisting beyond the termination of that stimulation. "Perceptual experience" is a label for the perceiver's report of what he says the stimulus looks like. This experience may be reported as an introspection, or the perceiver may be required to follow specific rules and to use specific categories of report, as Postman (1963) discusses for the analysis of the introspective-like reports. As indicated in other places (e.g. Haber, 1966 and especially Natsoulas, 1967), attention to reports of what the perceiver says he has seen when a stimulus appears are crucial data for any theory of perception. All too often we attempt to find out something about perception by only asking what the perceiver thinks was presented, rather than asking him what, in fact, he does see. I am defining "detection," "reaction time," "recognition," and "identification" responses in the typical ways—realizing, of course, that many methodological variations exist, some of which intrude into theoretical interpretations. Memory or, in this case, "perceptual memory" is a report by the perceiver of a stimulus which is no longer impinging on the receptor surface. In this sense, most laboratory experiments of detection, recognition, or identification demand reports of perceptual memory, since the effective stimulus

* Adapted from a paper presented by the editor at a conference on "Approaches to Thought," sponsored by the Learning Research and Development Center, University of Pittsburgh, October 1966, and published in their proceedings (Haber, 1969). It was prepared with the assistance of research support from the U.S. Public Health Service (MH 10753; MH 03244) and the National Science Foundation (GB 2909, GB 5910). I want to thank Naomi Weisstein for her perceptive comments on an earlier draft, and my graduate students at the University of Rochester who have offered many critical suggestions and improvements.

has ended by the time the report is given. It is, of course, for this reason that many memory processes cannot be isolated from perceptual ones. I use the term "perceptual response" to apply to all of the above categories indiscriminately.

Processing models are not new to psychology (for example, Freud's personality development and motivational theories can be considered *energy* processing models since they are concerned explicitly with the transformation, fixation, and investment of psychic energy). However, only the last decade or so has seen the greatest development of *information-processing* models in cognitive activities, especially in the analysis of sensory and perceptual systems and behavior. Reitman (1965) has provided an excellent review and discussion of these advances in thinking and problem solving, and Broadbent (1965a) briefly indicates how this approach has been applied to perceptual processing.

Several trends have combined in this new direction—most notably those of microgenetic interests in temporal processes in vision, the application of communication theory in psychology, especially when viewing sensation-perception as a communication system, and some theoretical analyses based upon information theory and computer models as they apply to vision. Equally as important, information processing language permits us to talk about sensory-perceptual processes in a common vocabulary. As Broadbent (1965a) points out so clearly, one of the great impasses before has been, to use his example, trying to relate spectral energy falling on specific receptors on the one hand to the experience of perceiving red on the other. Information-processing analysis attempts to look for correlations between contents of the stimulus and contents of the responses measured at various times after the stimulation begins. By examining these correlations some notions can be gained of the properties of the flow of information on the nervous system, especially regarding the content of that information at any given point. It is not immediately concerned (though it can be ultimately) with the specific physiological-neurological units, or with the energy distribution of the information flowing through the nervous system.

What is assumed is that if the appropriate operations could be devised, it should be possible to sample and examine the contents of stimulation at every point in time, and at every level in the nervous system. Comparing those samples over time and location with the original stimulus and with the perceiver's responses (be they description of his perceptual experience, or his detection, recognition, reaction time, identification, or other discrete responses) would indicate the nature of the processing of that stimulus into perceptual experience and responses. This is analogous to what a verbal learning theorist does when he analyzes the changes in the contents of memory over time since initial memorization (e.g., Waugh and Norman, 1965). In doing this he attempts to make statements about the reorganization of memorial processes as a result of time, limited capacity of retention, interference, and other competing demands upon cognitive activity.

Only recently have such attempts as these been made for the study of perception itself, and for the translation of stimulation into experience, response, and memory. One of the purposes of this paper is to demonstrate the utility of looking at the processing of sensory information as it acts upon and is transformed by the nervous system.

Several basic assumptions have governed these new approaches. A perceptual response is assumed not to be an immediate consequence of stimulation, but one which has gone through a number of stages or processes, each of which take time to organize or transverse. Further, it is assumed that this processing is limited by the capacities of the information-handling channels, the information content of the stimulus, and the prior experiences and condition of the perceiver. In addition, it is assumed that perceptual processes cannot be studied or analyzed independent of memorial ones, since recoding and preservation of information occurs at all stages of information processing.

The assumptions apply to the typical laboratory recognition or identification situation, in which the stimulus is on view for a relatively short time, so that the responses to it occur at a time when the perceiver cannot continue to refer back to it. While a number of different issues have to be considered for a situation in which the stimulus continues in view, these same assumptions still apply.

In addition, problems arising from eye-movement scanning, from temporal summation, and from updating of processing arising from the continued presence of the stimulus have to be taken into account in ways that are elaborations and extensions of the assumptions being presented.

Before discussing these assumptions in detail, a theoretical concern regarding methodology needs to be underlined. Many experiments have reported effects that are consistent with a process analysis, but are little more than suggestive because of the many alternative interpretations open to their results. Garner, Hake, and Eriksen (1956) elaborated the concept of a converging operation specifically to limit interpretations of experimental results. They argue that, for every possible potential mechanism process or model that might be used to explain an empirical result, it is necessary to provide some operation in the experiment that will differentiate that mechanism from all others.

A processing approach such as the one being proposed here requires very careful attention to converging operations. Most specifically, whenever it is proposed that a process occurs between time t_0 and time t_1 (or locus L_0 and locus L_1), it is required not only that a measure of the information content be made at both t_0 and t_1, but also that some additional manipulation or measure be taken "to converge" on the changes observed between t_0 and t_1. For example, finding an information loss between t_0 and t_1 is open to many interpretations, such as interference, fading trace, selective encoding, and probably others. However, a poststimulus sampling cue introduced at various intervals of time between t_0 and t_1 could provide information about the time course of the loss of content. Hence, poststimulus sampling is one converging operation. Manipulating the stimulus content could provide another converging operation. For example, if two sets of stimuli were used, one composed of items known to be prone to interference and another known to be resistant to interference, and no differential loss between the two sets of stimuli occurred between time t_0 and t_1, then this converging operation would suggest that interference was probably *not* involved in the process accounting for the loss. Without these two converging operations, and probably several others as well, merely reporting the loss from t_0 to t_1 indicates relatively little about the underlying process. It is for this reason that information-processing analyses cannot usually be applied to old data. If the converging operations were not included at the time, it is usually impossible to differentiate possible interpretations or processes. Nor are such analyses often applicable to data collected for other reasons or within the context of other points of view.

The first assumption, that of the nonimmediacy of perceptual responses arising from stimulation, is the most important and far reaching. Until quite recently, perception, as an end product of sensation, was considered to be immediate (which was one of the several reasons James Gibson, 1959, objected to using these two concepts when he thought one would do). Gestalt theory also did much to advance this immediacy view. And, of course, nearly all introspection of percepts arising from stimulation supports immediacy because rarely can one have any sense of a time lag or of stages taking time. However, failing to be aware of elapsed time does not prove that time does not pass. It has taken rather elaborate experiments to demonstrate that the "sense of immediacy" means no more than that short durations of time are difficult to discriminate.

Microgenetic theory (see Flavell and Draguns, 1957, for a general review) has argued for a temporal developmental process of each percept of a stimulus, characterized primarily by a growing clarity over the first few hundred milliseconds after the onset of stimulation. However, while microgenetic theorists speak of stages, they usually imply continuous processes of growth rather than qualitatively different operations being performed on the percept. Kaswan and Young (1963) have reported recent work which also suggests a quantitative growth of contours, which until clear, makes it difficult for the subject to distinguish fine detail. But since they do not provide operations to separate slow continuous growth from distinct operations, it may be that the basic microgenetic theory can be subsumed under information-processing analyses. Werner and his co-workers at Clark University have been most influential in arguing for and demonstrating this form of nonimmediacy of perception. Their model has not been as productive as it could be, primarily, I think, because it fails to provide very many operations to examine the changes occurring between stimulation and response. This is one reason why I think information-processing analyses are in a position to make far more rapid advances.

Information-processing analyses assume that the total time from stimulus onset to the occurrence of a perceptual response can be divided into intervals, each characterized by a different operation. Using this assumption, we can create a block design of these intervals, labeling each block according to its operation, connecting the blocks to suggest the order that the operations are performed, and paralleling the blocks to suggest operations that are simultaneously performed. Then we can begin a careful program of experimentation derived from aspects of this design: have the intervals been divided up correctly, are the order of operations correct, is the overall organization of the processing of information correct, and so forth. These types of questions and the experiments derived from them represent the crux of information-processing analyses. A number of models have been constructed using such block designs, most notably those of Broadbent (1958), Sperling (1963), and Melton (1963).

The second assumption, regarding limited information-handling capacities, is also an important one. The problem of limited channel capacity has been clear in the study of perception for most of the history of experimental psychology: witness concepts such as selective attention, and immediate memory span. The nervous system is apparently just not large enough to maintain all aspects of stimulation permanently. What this suggests for information-processing analyses is that we should look for instances in which recoding of information takes place—recoding generally in such a way that some of the content is maintained more explicitly at the expense of the other aspects which are dropped out. The points in time where the recoding occurs should be particularly important ones in the study of information processing, and it is not surprising that most information-processing models refer to these points almost exclusively.

Boynton (1961) has argued that whenever channel capacity is exceeded, temporal information is sacrificed in favor of retention of spatial characteristics. While he was concerned with peripheral neural encoding mechanisms, his comments suggest operations by which the encoding and recoding processes could be studied and manipulated. Pollack (e.g., 1964) has been pursuing such an approach for several years now.

The third assumption underlying an information-processing analysis concerns the commonality of perception and memory. This theoretical assumption has grown out of an important methodological controversy affecting the design and interpretation of perceptual experiments—how is it possible to conclude whether or not a particular independent variable affected perception when the subject must use a response indicator, drawing primarily on his memory, to report what he thinks he saw? This concern is whether independent variables are affecting perception directly, or whether their effects are being mediated entirely by changes in the indicator system being employed by the subject. Thus, for example, do frequent words produce clearer percepts, or given the same adequacy of percept, is it easier to guess the word (Eriksen, 1962), or does it require less information to fill in the part-cues (Guthrie and Weiner, 1966) or do we have a lower criterion for reporting frequent words (Broadbent, 1967)? Each of these latter alternatives suggests an effect of word frequency acting upon the type of report required, quite independent of any perceptual effect. Garner, Hake, and Eriksen (1956) were the first to see this issue most clearly, in a paper that has great importance even twelve years after it was written. Many others have made this distinction in the course of interpreting individual experiments (e.g. Goldiamond, 1958; Eriksen, 1958, 1960, 1962; Haber, 1966), but judging from the mistakes still being made by current investigators the point has not entirely struck home.

It is obvious that as perceivers we can remember what we have previously seen, but as psychologists we tend theoretically to isolate the study of the processes that give rise to the perception from those that give rise to the memory. While it is likely that these processes differ, they also share a common antecedent—stimulation—and except in some unusual situations they both *always* occur as a result of stimulation. Thus, not only do we have a percept of stimulation while that stimulation lasts, but we also have a memory of that stimulation and percept persisting for from minutes to decades after the stimulation itself is terminated. Most of us (with perhaps the exception of Broadbent, Sperling, and Melton) have overlooked or played down this important theoretical implication present in the Garner, Hake, and Eriksen article.

Thus, it is not sufficient merely to worry as to whether the response indicator is an unbiased index of the perception. Since (at least in many natural and most research settings) the stimulus is either changed or is no longer present when the response is given, we must also worry about the content and organization that that stimulation has taken in memory. To say, therefore, that a particular response indicator does not give a fair picture of perception may also mean that most of the variance in the experiment was concerned with how the stimulus and percept were translated into memory and not with perception at all (see Haber, 1966, for a detailed discussion of this point). Information-processing analysis makes this quite explicit, since many, if not most, of the operations specified are concerned with recoding or translation. While some of these recodings are designed primarily to permit the information to travel through limited capacity channels, some of them, especially in latter stages, are designed for preservation of the information more permanently. This, of course, is the operation of memory.

I have reviewed these assumptions briefly to set the stage for more detailed examination of some of the theoretical issues and operations being employed in information-processing approaches to perception and cognitive processes. Before proceeding further, however, a few comments are in order regarding the relevance of physiological and neurological disciplines to this discussion.

Physiological psychologists have a clear referent for stages—that of referring to the neurological pathways marked off by different levels of synapses. Thus, we find an overriding distinction set up between peripheral and central mechanisms, corresponding usually to events taking place before or after the impulses enter the primary visual cortex. Within the peripheral events, they talk about events occurring at the primary receptor cells, combinations at the bipolar level, the ganglion cell in the optic nerve, and the synapses and crossings at the lateral geniculate body. What is clear, from a large mass of research, is that it takes time—a lot of time—for the train of pulses, and changes in resting levels, to travel from the receptor surface to the visual cortex and beyond. Further, the properties of those trains of pulses may be changed radically from level to level.

My interest in information-processing approaches to the study of visual perception has been to map out the stages that are required to process sensory information into perceptual experiences, perceptual memories, and perceptual responses. I am not concerned with information processing at the strictly neurophysiological level, nor with translating concepts between the two levels. I do not mean what the neurophysiological psychologist implies by stages—the different pathways, synapses, and centers that are involved in the neural transmission of impulses. No attempt is made to imply or deny that such stages correspond to the stages in an information-processing analysis.

A more interesting side question concerns the physiological correlates of information itself. It has been argued that we can talk about information impinging on the retina only insofar as we have a model or theory which gives the transfer function for such stimulus energies falling on the retina to be transformed into information. The most common and most developed of such models is one which considers patterns of active and inactive cells on the retina as the information in the stimulus. Nearly all theories of pattern recognizers (e.g., Rosenblatt, 1957; Uhr, 1963) use such a model quite effectively. Recently, however, quite different models have been suggested, following evidence that receptor fields of cells in the retina are arranged in such a way that impulses will arise from them only when the shape, or orientation, or movement of the stimulus energy corresponds to that specific arrangement of cells. Hubel and Wiesel (e.g., 1962) have provided the best documentation on this, although numerous publications now support this kind of peripheral information processing.

The discussions in this paper do not rest on any one model regarding how information or information processing is defined physiologically. All operations will either be in terms of the stimulus, or the response, or their correlation.

Before formally discussing the principal converging operations used in information-processing analyses of perception, I would like to select as an example the different theoretical attacks and methodological procedures that have been employed to study a specific aspect of this problem.

One important facet of information-processing analyses is often phrased in terms of asking whether information is transferred through stages in parallel or in serial order. In a typical visual stimulus, where the information is concentrated on or near the fovea, that information is seen at a glance. This can be thought of as being received in parallel—in that a large number of retinal units are stimulated simultaneously. However, it is possible to inquire whether these parallel inputs are also being processed in parallel or whether some mechanism treats them sequentially in a serial order. For example, Sperling (1963) has argued that arrays of letters are stored in a visual short-term storage lasting several hundred milliseconds, after which they fade and all information is lost. But during that time the contents of that storage are being translated item-by-item into a more permanent memory. He finds on that basis of several converging operations that the rate of serial processing of individual letters is about 10 milliseconds per letter. Broadbent (1958) used an auditory task to show that if a string of different digits arrived simultaneously to the two ears, the subject will report all of the ones from one ear and then report those from the other ear. This suggests that while we may think we can pay attention to two conversations simultaneously (in parallel), we actually listen to one and then to the other (in serial). It also suggests that a short-term storage is needed to hold those items whose report is delayed.

On the other hand, there is some evidence that doing two or three things at once takes no longer than doing one—suggesting that parallel operations are being performed. Neisser (1963) showed that it takes no longer to search for two items in a list than for one, thus implying that the two operations can be combined so as to be done at the same time, that is, in parallel. More will be said about his research design when reaction time as a converging operation is discussed.

It can be mentioned also that the interpretation of reading skills is usually viewed as a parallel process, such that each fixation brings in a block of information that is handled as a unit. This has led to the prediction that if larger block sizes are acted upon with fewer fixations thereby being needed, then reading speed could go up without sacrifice to comprehension. This seems to be true up to a point, as attested by the success of speed reading programs (see Miller, 1956; and Poulton, 1962, for two examples). Of course, without any converging operation on what happens during each fixation, such evidence can be no more than suggestive of major parallel operations.

As another example of the serial-parallel distinction, evidence with respect to the duration of stimulation needed for correct recognition as a function of stimulus content has been considered relevant. If it is true that a linear increase in duration is needed for correct recognition as a function of increases in stimulus information, serial item-by-item processing might be indicated. A parallel process might produce a step function, with no decrease in accuracy occurring as content increases up to a point, after which too many items would be present for a single parallel operation.

The evidence for recognition tasks generally supports the linear (serial) relationship between accuracy and information content. I have verified this in my laboratory when the number of letters in the stimulus array is increased. Weisstein (1966), in a task in which only one item is selected for report, showed that as the number of items displayed increases, the probability of correct recognition decreases. The result is somewhat confounded by the fact that the arrow telling the subject which item to report also produced some masking, but probably not sufficient to invalidate this particular conclusion. Hake (1957), and Estes and Taylor (1966) also report data suggesting that it takes longer for a complex stimulus to be perceived.

Evidence from counting tasks, however, in which the subject is asked to count the number of items in a briefly presented display, generally show a step function (Hunter and Sigler, 1940; Cheatham and White, 1952; and Averbach, 1963), with the first step occurring as items increase beyond five to eight per presentation. Further steps for each two to three items added were found by White (1963). This suggests that small groups of items can be taken in at a glance and counted in parallel, but as further items are presented, additional counting steps are added serially.

These last results suggest the difficulty of simply using the correlation between information content of the stimulus and response accuracy as an index of serial or parallel processes. Longer processing time may be needed with more complex stimuli because more serial operations are needed, or because a single parallel operation has to be performed over and over again serially. Weisstein (1964, 1966) has discussed this point carefully, and has argued that a converging operation—some other index over and above response accuracy alone—has to be used before the correlation between information and accuracy can be interpreted in terms of information processing successfully.

As a final general example of serial versus parallel processing, duration of presentation can be reduced without loss in accuracy if the items combine together to form a meaningful or familiar larger whole, as when letters form words. This would suggest that individual items can be processed as a group somewhat simultaneously. If the items are processed serially at a given rate and then synthesized, how could this latter combination permit a more rapid processing of the items to occur before the synthesis? Some theorists have argued that this is a response rather than a perceptual effect. For example, Eriksen (1958) has argued that perception is unaffected by meaning, but rather the perceiver is able to remember the items better or fill in a partial perception if they spell a word for him. I have attempted to refute this argument in a series of experiments on word-recognition processes (Haber, 1965, 1967; Haber and Hershenson, 1965; Haber and Hillman, 1966; Hershenson and Haber, 1965) where I have suggested that meaning is capable of acting upon the process of perceptual experience directly, rather than being mediated indirectly by response or memory effects. To the extent that this argument is correct then the recognition of meaning must be occurring at somewhat the same time as the perception in the individual items, and that this recognition of a superordinate meaning can be considered as parallel to that of the individual items.

On the the other side of this coin several lines of evidence exist that when sequential items are presented at high rates of speed, the order in which they came in often cannot be reported correctly— even when the names of the individual items are successfully reproduced (Crossman, 1960). This would suggest that item identification and order reconstruction are distinct processes, and are serial, in the sense that it takes longer to do both than it does to identify the items regardless of order. Kolers and Katzman (1966) have carried this one step further, since they have evidence suggesting that in addition to the separation of item and order information, there are certain rates at which the subject can reproduce the items in the correct order but may not be able to name the familiar word the items spell. This implies that synthesis of meaning is an even further serial process occurring after item and order information are extracted.

The serial-parallel distinction is illustrative of the theoretical fertility of information-processing analyses of perceptual and cognitive processes, and of the importance of converging operations in the research designs used in the manipulations. As has already been indicated, without such converging operations, it is nearly impossible to make justifiable statements about processing.

Next, I will review some of the major converging operations used in information-processing analyses, the data generated, and the theoretical interpretations and confusions created thereby.

The three principal research designs that have been employed to examine these kinds of temporal information processes in perception are those using reaction time, backward masking, and post-stimulus sampling.

Unfortunately, the reaction-time procedures, while vitally concerned with serial parallel distinctions in decision making (see Lindsay and Lindsay, 1966, for a brief review), have not been consistently used to study perception components. For example, in one typical reaction-time design—the one used by Neisser (1963)—the subject has to scan a large number of items, looking for a critical characteristic. When such is located or determined, he responds as rapidly as possible. Dividing reaction time into the number of items scanned, number of critical items presented, or other stimulus variables, yields various estimates of decision time per item. This then can be studied as a function of the number and characteristics of the items, the subject's strategy, his expectations, and the like. While this often has great relevance to an explication of decision processes, the perceptual aspects are not clearly represented. There is no control over the amount of time each item is stimulating the subject, nor on his scanning behavior itself (how many items are observed at one time, how many fixations are made per item, how fast is the scanning rate, and so forth, although in some research, scanning behavior is recorded (e.g., Gould and Schaffer, 1965). These tasks also involve relatively long search times so that multiple fixations are possible, thereby confounding eye movements with decision making. While it is possible to divide the total search time by the number of items being searched to arrive at a decision time per item, no converging operation is provided to show that, in fact, the decision time actually corresponds to the time it takes to decide whether an item is critical. It is possible that items may be searched in groups (parallel), a decision made, and then the next group taken, and so forth (serial). It is this lack of a converging operation that makes it difficult to draw firm conclusions from research in this area using a search procedure.

The specific problem with reaction-time research, with respect to the perceptual components of an information-processing analysis, is that it has yet been unable to separate the different processes that eventually result in a decision to respond. For example, when the task is to respond only if the item does *not* contain a critical element, several experiments have reported that it takes longer to process the elements of each item. A number of hypotheses are available to explain this—some stress processing steps after the elements are clearly perceived, others stress differential discriminability of the elements themselves, and still others stress different strategies the perceiver is using, especially whether he is processing more than is necessary. What is needed in order to separate more of these hypotheses is to specify the stimulus characteristics that are being processed—template matching, hierarchical testing of element by element, and so on—and to separate out registration of the stimulus, from processing of a short-term visual storage, from decisions about whether the items require a response. The latter could be started by controlling the exposure duration in a scanning task. While it is obvious that most of the time is needed to make decisions, no one knows how much time is needed to view the stimulus itself. If that viewing time interacts with the other variables, then the processing steps will become more apparent.

A second major converging operation has been the use of backward masking. It is relevant since it suggests that a later stimulus interferes with the processing of one that came before it. Crawford (1947) showed that a masking flash coming after a test stimulus will elevate the threshold for the latter up to one log unit, depending upon the luminance and the time between the target and mask. He thought the effect could be due to the overtaking of neural impulses somewhere in the visual system. This interpretation has some credence since this type of masking effect generally occurs only when the masking stimulus is of greater area and intensity, thereby producing a shorter latency of response. Donchin, Wicke, and Lindsley (1963) have shown with evoked potentials in humans that this type of masking effect occurs before the visual cortex, and Donchin (1966) reported a study using recording electrodes in the optic tract of cats, with results suggesting that the masking effect occurs before that point, since the response to the first stimulus is attenuated when the second one follows in the appropriate time intervals. Thus, in those studies in which the masking flash is usually one of high intensity and often in a considerably larger area than the target, a rather peripheral mechanism is suggested to explain the elevation of the threshold of the test spot by the subsequent masking flash.

However, there is also a large literature on metacontrast effects (see Raab, 1963; Alpern, 1952; and Kahneman, 1968) in which backward masking-like effects are found, but under circumstances when the masking stimulus is not a large bright flash, but a figure with adjacent contours to the target stimulus. Thus, Werner (1935) showed elevation of the threshold of a disc when an annulus followed it by the appropriate delay. He interpreted this as evidence for a microgenetic approach, due to the interference with the slow development of the contour of the disc. Numerous studies have shown this relationship—one that seems to stress the closeness of the contour between the two stimuli in space, even if different in time. For example, Weisstein and Haber (1965) found a U-shaped masking function for letters when followed by a ring, so that no loss in accuracy of recognition of the letters was observed for either simultaneous or short interstimulus intervals, or for very long ones. However, for intermediate intervals, a sharp loss in accuracy occurred. Weisstein (1964) showed that this effect was more pronounced when the shapes of the target and mask fit together most closely (e.g., when an O as compared to a D was masked by a ring).

This type of metacontrast effect cannot be adequately handled in the same way as the Crawford type of backward-masking demonstration. While the time relations are often similar, no requirement is necessary for greater area or greater intensity—only for adjacent contours. While contour interactions seem to be important, a number of studies have looked for central versus peripheral mechanisms of a more general nature. The most direct attack on this has been to demonstrate dichoptic masking, in which the target is shown to one eye and the mask to the other—such evidence strongly indicating at least some, if not an entire, central interaction. This has been shown by Kolers and Rosner (1960), Schiller (1965), and Kinsbourne and Warrington (1962 a,b). No one has been able to establish dichoptic masking using the Crawford-type masking paradigm. A second line of evidence in support of primary central involvement comes from studies in which reaction time is used as a converging operation for the effects of masking. When a stimulus is decreased in physical energy, reaction time to its onset is increased proportionately. However, the reaction time to masked stimuli, which appear phenomenally decreased in brightness, if not occluded altogether, is not affected (Fehrer and Raab, 1962; Schiller and Smith, 1966; Harrison and Fox, 1966) suggesting that the masking affect must be occurring at some center higher than that mediating reaction time.

The third line of evidence for central determination of masking is derived from data from certain kinds of metacontrast experiments. When the luminances of the target, mask, and adaptation fields are equal, then a U-shape function of masking is found as the time interval between target and mask is increased. Thus, when target and mask appear simultaneously or the mask follows by less than 15–30 milliseconds, no loss in accuracy occurs (as compared to presenting the target alone). Accuracy decreases to a minimum value at 50–100 milliseconds interval, and then returns to nearly the same level as for the very short intervals. Considerably more will be said about the U-shape function later on, but its relevance here is that it would be quite difficult to construct a peripheral model of masking to explain this shape, while a model employing a central mechanism can easily handle it.

Backward masking and metacontrast are relevant to information-processing analyses of perception and thought because a number of theorists recently have argued that both backward masking and metacontrast interfere with the processing of visual information by the nervous system. Before examining this argument, however, it is necessary to look at the third principal research design, that of poststimulus sampling, and at the general concept of short-term visual storage.

The first and most explicit of the models to stress the relationship between information-processing analyses to interference phenomena has been the one proposed by George Sperling (1963). Discussing his work on short-term visual storage and backward masking, Sperling argues that visual information processing can be thought of as first creating a short-term storage for stimulation lasting a fraction of a second. The content of that store is scanned, items being processed serially, item by item, until the store has either faded away, or has been erased by new information, or until all of the information is extracted. Thus, for Sperling, while the store is loaded by parallel inputs of information, it is processed serially. [It is unfortunate that Sperling chose to call this storage "short-term memory," because of the already extensive but quite different usage this concept has in studies of verbal learning. In the latter case it refers to accuracy of recall measured in the first few seconds to minutes after learning (see Broadbent, 1965b, for a review of methods). Even though other terms have been suggested, confusion is still prevalent. To avoid this, I shall refer to this general concept in perceptual information processing as a "short-term visual storage."]

Evidence for the concept of a short-term visual storage comes primarily from the work of Sperling (1960, 1963, 1967), of Averbach and Coriell (1961), and of Mackworth (especially 1963). The research designs generally have employed poststimulus sampling. The subject is presented with an array of information. Shortly after the offset of the array he is shown another stimulus which consists of a marker or indicator telling him which item in the array he should report. This technique is used on the assumption that the probability that the subject can report a single item at any moment is indicative of the percentage of the items of the stimulus available in a short-term visual storage at that moment.

In general, results using this procedure have shown that, with poststimulus sampling of a complex target, the subject is able to report individual items of information that were indicated by a marker for several hundred milliseconds after the termination of the target. Since this accuracy is far higher than that achieved when the subject has to report the entire stimulus, it is further concluded that the subject has this information available in a short-term visual storage for this brief time, but can only demonstrate it if he is asked for only one item at a time. Otherwise, by the time he can organize his memory for all of the items he has to report, some of them are forgotten. Averbach and Coriell found that accurate recognition of a single letter as a function of the interstimulus interval between a 16-letter array and an arrow indicator declined gradually for several hundred milliseconds, and then dropped more steeply until reaching the base line of accuracy equivalent to the percentage accuracy for the subject reporting all 16 letters (immediate memory span). It was this higher accuracy during the first few hundred milliseconds after the stimulus offset which Averbach and Coriell also referred to as a short-term (visual storage) memory.

The relevance of a concept of short-term visual storage to information-processing approaches is obvious. It suggests that an early process is one in which all (or nearly all) of the stimulus information is represented intact. Processing proceeds from that representation rather than from the stimulus, whether it is present or not and, of course, this provides a device to prolong the effective stimulus by several hundred milliseconds.

Despite the theoretical fertility of this concept, including a remarkable number of references to it, relatively little direct work has continued on the basic demonstration. Mayzner, *et al* (1964) report at least a partial replication, in that accuracy stayed invariant from 50 to 150 milliseconds of interstimulus interval. Since they did not employ either smaller or larger interstimulus intervals, no further evidence from their work is available. Because Averbach and Coriell found a decay in accuracy over the range of 50 to 150 milliseconds, this was considered by Mayzner to be somewhat negative evidence. However, since they used a different array size, visual angle, and probably luminance, it is possible that longer delays would have shown the drop.

Eriksen and Steffy (1964), using a modified forced-choice test, failed to find a short-term visual storage effect. Rather they found interference at short interstimulus intervals, with accuracy *increasing* to a maximum value after about 100 milliseconds. They argued that the indicator, coming rapidly after the stimulus, produced interference, mediated by brightness summation leading to contrast reduction (see also Eriksen, 1966). Only with delays longer than 100 milliseconds, in which the indicator cannot summate with the luminance of the target, will accuracy of the target be observed. These effects were obtained with dark pre-, post-, and interstimulus interval fields, so that the onset and offset of the target and the indicator represented abrupt shifts in illumination—conditions greatly facilitating luminance summation and in general producing interference of perception. For some reason they never ran the conditions similar to Averbach and Coriell's, in which the fields were all at the same luminance. They had a middle condition in which the indicator was a luminous arrow rather than a dark figure on a bright field. Here they find neither interference or short-term memory—the accuracy is essentially invariant over 700 milliseconds of delay. However, the sudden increase and decrease in the illumination of the target, especially its offset, could begin to contribute to the interference. Thus, the Eriksen and Steffy experiment is probably not related to tests of a short-term visual storage.

Sperling has elaborated his notion of a short-term visual storage extensively, particularly with respect to his information-processing model for visual memory tasks (1963, 1967). He has discussed masking operations in several ways. When specific letters are masked by a ring surrounding them (metacontrast), he views this as interfering with the processing of that item in short-term visual storage, or more explicitly, with the transfer of that item from short-term visual storage to a longer persistence storage. He has also used large masking flashes that are not specific to single items, either of the large intense field such as Crawford used, or a random noise grid with a random pattern of dots or lines, usually at lower overall intensity than the target (Sperling, 1965). In general, he assumes that this masking stimulus effectively halts all processing of short-term visual storage, so that whatever has not yet been transferred is now lost. No mechanism is proposed for how this occurs, though he does use a computer analogy or erasure of the short-term visual storage by subsequent masking stimulus.

Weisstein and Haber (1965) and Weisstein (1966) have used this similar kind of hypothesis, but adapted it to explain the U-shaped function obtained by themselves and others. Thus, simultaneous target and mask or a very short interstimulus interval between them has no effect on accuracy because the processing of the "masked" item has not yet begun. Likewise, very long interstimulus intervals will not interfere with recognition of the "masked" item since it has already been read out of the short-term visual storage, and after that, masking by subsequent noninformational stimuli has no effect. Only at the time when active transfer is under way can the masking interfere with that transfer.

It is clear that this kind of perceptual interference is quite different from the physiological interpretation offered by Crawford, Lindsley, Donchin, and others. I view masking as an interference with transfer of information that is already stably represented in the nervous system as a short-term visual storage. The latter theorists see it as an inhibition of neural transmission on the way to higher centers, presumably long before there is any stable representation of the target established anywhere in the nervous system. Viewing a short-term visual storage as a receptor phenomenon, perhaps analogous to an after-image, will not reconcile the two positions. An after-image model will not predict the U-shaped masking functions, since very short interstimulus intervals should produce even greater interference than longer ones. One would need to argue that a second flash, following close upon the heels of the first one, would not disturb the after-image of the first as much as if it were delayed 5 to 100 milliseconds. There seems to be no evidence for this assumption. Further, an after-image storage would suggest that no dichoptic masking would be found, an assumption contrary to data. Thus, while there may be data storage in the receptor or in other peripheral units, such storage does not seem to be the same as a short-term visual storage, nor can such storage be that which is obliterated by masking flashes.

Eriksen, in a number of recent experiments (especially 1966) has questioned the interpretation of masking as an interference with information processing. Basically, he has proposed that masking can best be understood as a brightness summation effect—such that as two stimuli are presented in close conjunction in time their brightness summates in the nervous system, effectively reducing the contrast of each. It is this reduction in contrast that would account for threshold elevations or losses of accuracy of recognition. His model thus predicts that forward masking would be as effective as backward masking, and that the point of maximum masking should occur with simultaneity of presentation of target and mask. He is able to demonstrate these predictions when the eyes are dark-adapted prior to either target or mask presentation and when the interstimulus interval also remains dark. However, under somewhat comparable conditions, Schiller and Smith (1965) find clear asymmetry between forward and backward masking, which raises some doubt as to the adequacy of the luminance summation-contrast model of Eriksen.

Further, when the eyes are light-adapted to the same luminance as the target and mask, as is the interstimulus interval, then the U-shape data already discussed is obtained. Thus, it would appear as if the luminance relationships are crucial (see Kolers, 1962) though perhaps not through luminance summation as Eriksen thinks. His model clearly would not predict any type of U-shaped function, only a monotonic one with maximum masking effects occurring at simultaneity of presentation, and decreasing as the interval between the target and mask changes in either direction. Some recent data by Kahneman (1966) offer a different type of negative evidence. He found that if a blanking field and a target are presented, far *less* masking is shown if the blanking field is presented simultaneously with the target than if it is delayed by one-tenth of a millisecond after the offset of the target. If the subject is adding the luminance of the blanking flash to that of the target and thereby reducing the contrast of the target, introducing any delay, even one this small, would attenuate this effect. This should reduce masking, not increase it as Kahneman found. This would imply that interference is occurring in this situation over and beyond any possible contrast reduction caused by luminance summation.

I have lingered on Eriksen's recent work because he has proposed a model to explain these interference phenomena peripherally, without any reference to an information-processing mechanism. For the reasons cited above, however, and because the peripheral models designed to account for metacontrast are also open to serious objections, I feel that these peripheral alternatives are not adequate, and that central events must be considered.

Backward masking, metacontrast, and short-term visual storage (poststimulus sampling) designs each involve the presentation of two stimuli, separated by some variable time delay. It is often difficult to specify criteria for which design should be called by what name. An important distinction, between short-term visual storage and the others, concerns whether the second (masking or indicator) stimulus is informational—for example, does it tell the subject what it is he is to report. In masking situations the second stimulus is usually a brighter flash of greater area than the target, or it is a patterned stimulus superimposed over the target or surrounding the target. In all of these cases, the subject has to detect the presence of the stimulus or estimate or match its brightness. However, just to complicate the distinction, Averbach and Coriell (1961), in one of their studies, and Weisstein (1966), and Weisstein and Haber (1965), used a ring surrounding part of the stimulus as a mask, so that the masking stimulus interfered with the recognition of an item of the target, but also signaled to the subject to attempt to report that item.

This review of the converging operations of reaction time, backward masking, and poststimulus sampling has been designed to show how it is possible to pinpoint transformation stages in the processing of visual information. In general, the data from the experiments discussed have been used to bolster a particular theoretical point of view—that is, of the existence of a relatively complete but unstable representation, from which information is extracted to be available for report, awareness, and subsequent perceptual memory. The emphasis in this paper has limited the general information-processing approach to the early stages of the overall perception-cognition continuum. I have done so because this emphasis is perhaps more novel, and less advanced, even though it is beginning to create excitement and activity among visual scientists and perception researchers.

Information-processing analyses do not stop here, however, nor do the models being developed on the basis of new experiments. The models of Broadbent, Sperling, and Melton are most explicit in looking beyond these early stages to the processes concerned with filtering or selective attention, encoding mechanisms, recognition processes, rehearsal or memory-maintenance processes, retrieval procedures, and the like. These other processes in this continuum between sensory registration and perceptual responses are currently receiving increased experimental interest as well: witness, for example, the interest in auditory rehearsal processes, and their interaction with stimuli that have high potential for auditory, visual, or semantic confusability; the interest in encoding strategies used to encode the content of the stimulus (or more likely the content of the short-term visual storage) into memory; the interest in the differences between long-term and short-term memory (the latter concept as used by verbal-learning theorists) as an attempt to look at recoding, interference, and decay effects; or the interest in simulating perceptual and cognitive activities, which demands an explicit information-processing analysis, since the computer program must be specified by discrete operations and stages.

I have not attempted to spell out the details of these latter stages, nor have I even made very concrete all of the implications of the earlier stages. I think our knowledge is changing too fast to do this well as yet. But I am quite convinced that it will be done very soon. My hope, in presenting this line of argument, is that the fertility of an information-processing analysis of perceptual behavior, and the power of converging operations, as for example, reaction time, masking, or metacontrast types of interference, or poststimulus sampling, will become more apparent. If my expectations are correct, the entire field of cognitive processes, which rest so heavily on concepts of perception and thought, will undergo a revolution in the next five years, due primarily to the application of these more recent ways of theorizing about the underlying processes.

In summary, I have attempted to discuss some of the general properties of information-processing analyses as they apply to the handling of visual stimulation. Three basic assumptions were presented: visual experience and responses are not immediate, but are built up as a result of the number of distinct successive and simultaneous operations; processing is limited by the capacities of channels and storage; and encoding and memorial processes cannot be divorced from sensory registration and experiential ones.

Following a discussion of these assumptions, some of the basic research designs in information-processing analyses of visual perception were reviewed, especially those using backward masking and those using poststimulus sampling. The concepts of short-term visual storage and of interference processes were discussed in detail, both in their own right and in relation to each other, in terms of a number of recent experiments. One theme running through this discussion and review of past work was the distinction between serial and parallel processes. This theme was used both to illustrate information-processes analyses, and to explore in some detail an important theoretical issue being posed and investigated in current research today.

My interest in these phenomena has been most explicitly concerned with the perceptual rather than the purely sensory or physiological levels of interpretation. A number of questions need immediate attention, with respect both to short-term visual storage, and to masking effects, since these two concepts have been almost inseparably intertwined both theoretically and operationally. Of primary concern is the assumption that masking interferes with the processing of information from a short-term visual store into a more permanent one. This assumption underlies much of the work in the field at the moment, and while it has been used to interpret data, it has itself not been explicitly examined. If some converging operations can be used to bolster the validity of these assumptions, then a major theoretical model of information processing can be more seriously advanced.

Perhaps an even more pertinent question concerns the concept of short-term visual storage itself. While the few references discussed do not cover all of the current work, still, relatively little direct attack has been made on it. This, plus the somewhat contradictory data obtained, certainly makes it necessary to continue a direct examination of the data and their underlying assumptions.

Both of these questions have been translated into many different kinds of specific experiments. This work, plus that being done on other parts of the information-processing analysis of a stimulation-perception-cognition continuum should help maintain this revolution.

References

Alpern, M. Metacontrast: historical introduction. *American Journal of Ophthalmology*, 1952, *29*, 631–646.

Averbach, E. The span of apprehension as a function of exposure duration. *Journal of Verbal Learning and Verbal Behavior*, 1963, *2*, 60–64.

Averbach, E., and Coriell, A. S. Short-term memory in vision. *Bell Systems Technical Journal*, 1961, *40*, 309–328.

Boynton, R. M. Some temporal factors in vision. In M. R. Rosenblith (ed.), *Sensory Communication*. New York: Wiley, 1961, 739–755.

Broadbent, D. E. *Perception and Communication*. New York: Pergamon Press, 1958.

Broadbent, D. E. Information processing in the nervous system, *Science*, 1965a, *150*, 457–462.

Broadbent, D. E. Techniques in the study of short term memory. *Acta Psychologica*, 1965b, *24*, 220–233.

Broadbent, D. E. The word frequency effect and response bias. *Psychological Review*, 1966, *74*, 1–15.

Bruner, J. S. On perceptual readiness. *Psychological Review*, 1957, *64*, 123–152.

Cheatham, P. G., and White, C. T. Perceived number as a function of flash number and rate. *Journal of Experimental Psychology*, 1952, *44*, 447–451.

Crawford, B. E. Visual adaptation to brief conditioning stimuli. *Proceedings of the Royal Society*, 1947, *B134*, 282–302.

Crossman, E. R. F. W. Information and serial order in human immediate memory. In C. Cherry (ed.), *Information Theory*. London: Butterworth, 1960.

Donchin, E. Personal communication, 1966.

Donchin, E., Wicke, J. D., and Lindsley, D. B. *Science*, 1963, *141*, 1285–1286.

Eriksen, C. W. Unconscious processes. In M. R. Jones (ed.), *Nebraska Symposium on Motivation*. Lincoln: University of Nebraska Press, 1958, 169–226.

Eriksen, C. W. Discrimination and learning without awareness: a methodological survey and evaluation. *Psychological Review*, 1960, *67*, 279–300.

Eriksen, C. W. Figments, fantasies, and follies: a search for the subconscious mind. In C. W. Eriksen (ed.), *Behavior and Awareness*. Durham: Duke University Press, 1962, 3–26.

Eriksen, C. W., and Steffy, R. A. Short-term memory and retroactive interference in visual perception. *Journal of Experimental Psychology*, 1964, *68*, 423–434.

Eriksen, C. W. Temporal luminance summation in backward and forward masking. *Perception and Psychophysics*, 1966, *1*, 87–92.

Estes, W. K., and Taylor, H. A. Visual detection in relation to display size and redundancy of critical elements. *Perception and Psychophysics*, 1966, *1*, 9–16.

Fehrer, E., and Raab, D. Reaction time to stimuli masked by metacontrast. *Journal of Experimental Psychology*, 1962, *63*, 143–147.

Flavell, J. A., and Draguns, J. A. A microgenetic approach to perception and thought. *Psychological Bulletin*, 1957, *54*, 197–217.

Garner, W. R., Hake, H. W., and Eriksen, C. W. Operationism and the concept of perception. *Psychological Review*, 1956, *63*, 317–329.

Gibson, J. J. Perception as a function of stimulation. In S. Koch (ed.), *Psychology: A Study of a Science.* New York: McGraw-Hill, Vol. 1, 1959, 456–501.

Goldiamond, I. Indicators of perception: I. Subliminal perception, subception, unconscious perception: an analysis in terms of psychophysical indicator methodology. *Psychological Bulletin*, 1958, *55*, 373–411.

Gould, J. D., and Schaffer, A. Eyemovement patterns during visual information processing. *Psychonomic Science*, 1965, *3*, 317–318.

Guthrie, G., and Wiener, M. Subliminal perception or perception of partial cue with pictorial stimuli. *Journal of Personality and Social Psychology*, 1966, *3*, 619–628.

Haber, R. N. The effect of prior knowledge of the stimulus on word recognition processes. *Journal of Experimental Psychology*, 1965, *69*, 282–286.

Haber, R. N. The nature of the effect of set on perception. *Psychological Review*, 1966, *73*, 335–351.

Haber, R. N. Repetition as a determinant of perceptual recognitive processes. In W. Wathen-Dunn, (ed.). *Symposium on Models for the Perception of Speech and Visual Form*. Cambridge, Mass.: MIT Press, 1967, 202–212.

Haber, R. N. Perceptual processes and general cognitive activity. In J. F. Voss (ed.), *Approaches to Thought*. Columbus: Merrill Publishing Co., 1969.

Haber, R. N., and Hershenson, M. The effects of repeated brief exposures on the growth of a percept. *Journal of Experimental Psychology*, 1965, *69*, 40–46.

Haber, R. N., and Hillman, E. R. Changes in single letter clarity with repetition. *Perception and Psychophysics*, 1966, *1*, 347–350.

Hake, H. W. Contributions of psychology to the study of pattern vision. *USAF WADS Technical Report* No. 57–621, 1957.

Harrison, K., and Fox, R. Replication of reaction time to stimuli masked by metacontrast. *Journal of Experimental Psychology*, 1966, *71*, 162–163.

Hershenson, M., and Haber, R. N. The role of meaning on the perception of briefly exposed words. *Canadian Journal of Psychology*, 1965, *19*, 42–46.

Hubel, D. H., and Wiesel, T. N. Receptive fields, binocular interaction and functional architecture in the cat's visual cortex. *Journal of Physiology*, 1962, *160*, 106–154.

Hunter, W. S., and Sigler, M. The span of visual discrimination as a function of time and intensity of stimulation. *Journal of Experimental Psychology*, 1940, *26*, 160–179.

Kahneman, D. Time-intensity reciprocity under various conditions of adaptation and backward masking. *Journal of Experimental Psychology*, 1966, *71*, 543–549.

Kahneman, D. Method and theory in studies of visual masking. *Psychological Bulletin*, 1968, 69.

Kaswan, J., and Young, S. Stimulus exposure time, brightness, and spatial factors as determinants of visual perception. *Journal of Experimental Psychology*, 1963, *65*, 113–123.

Kinsbourne, M., and Warrington, E. K. The effect of aftercoming random pattern on the perception of brief visual stimuli. *Quarterly Journal of Experimental Psychology*, 1962a, *14*, 223–234.

Kolers, P. A. Intensity and contour effects in visual masking. *Vision Research*, 1962, *2*, 277–294.

Kolers, P. A., and Rosner, B. S. On visual masking (metacontrast): dichoptic observation. *American Journal of Psychology*, 1960, *73*, 2–21.

Kolers, P. A., and Katzman, M. T. Naming sequentially presented letters and words. *Language and Speech*, 1966, 84–95.

Lindsay, R. K., and Lindsay, J. M. Reaction time and serial versus parallel information processing. *Journal of Experimental Psychology*, 1966, *71*, 294–303.

Mackworth, J. F. The duration of the visual image. *Canadian Journal of Psychology*, 1963, *17*, 62–81.

Mayzner, M. S., Abrevays, E. L., Frey, R. E., Kaufman, H. G., and Schoenberg, S. M. Short-term memory in vision: a partial replication of the Averbach and Coriell study. *Psychonomic Science*, 1964, *1*, 225–226.

Melton, A. W. Implications of short-term memory for general theory of memory. *Journal of Verbal Learning and Verbal Behavior*, 1963, *2*, 1–21.

Miller, G. A. The magic number seven, plus or minus two. *Psychological Review*, 1956, *63*, 81–97.

Natsoulas, T. What are perceptual reports all about? *Psychological Bulletin*, 1967, *67*, 247–272.

Neisser, U. Decision time without reaction time: experiments in visual scanning. *American Journal of Psychology*, 1963, *76*, 376–385.

Pollack, I. Interaction of two sources of verbal context in word identification. *Language and Speech*, 1964, *7*, 1–12.

Postman, L. Perception and learning. In S. Koch (ed.), *Psychology: The Study of a Science*, 1963, *5*, 30–113.

Poulton, E. C. Peripheral vision, refractoriness and eye movements in fast oral reading. *British Journal of Psychology*, 1962, *53*, 409–419.

Raab, D. H. Backward masking. *Psychological Bulletin*, 1963, *69*, 193–199.

Reitman, W. R. *Cognition and Thought: an Information-Processing Approach*. New York: Wiley, 1965.

Rosenblatt, F. The preceptron: a probabilistic model for information storage and organization in the brain. *Psychological Review*, 1958, *65*, 386–407.

Schiller, P. H. Monoptic and dichoptic visual masking by patterns and flashes. *Journal of Experimental Psychology*, 1965, *69*, 193–199.

Schiller, P. H., and Smith, M. C. A comparison of forward and backward masking. *Psychonomics Science*, 1965, *3*, 77–78.

Schiller, P. H., and Smith, M. C. Detection in metacontrast. *Journal of Experimental Psychology*, 1966, *71*, 32–39.

Sperling, G. The information available in brief visual presentations. *Psychological Monographs*, 1960, *74*, (11, whole No. 498).

Sperling, G. A model for visual memory tasks. *Human Factors*, 1963, *5*, 19–31.

Sperling, G. Temporal and spatial visual masking: I. Masking by impulse flashes. *Journal of the Optical Society of America*, 1965, *55*, 541.

Sperling, G. Successive approximations to a model for short term memory. *Acta Psychologica*, 1967, *27*, 285–292.

Uhr, L. "Pattern recognition" computers as models for form perception. *Psychological Bulletin*, 1963, *60*, 40–73.

Waugh, N. C., and Norman, D. A. Primary memory. *Psychological Review*, 1965, *72*, 89–104.

Weisstein, N. Temporal aspects of perceptual systems. Unpublished Ph.D. dissertation, Harvard University, 1964.

Weisstein, N. Backward masking and models of perceptual processing. *Journal of Experimental Psychology*, 1966, *72*, 232–240.

Weisstein, N., and Haber, R. N. A u-shaped backward masking function in vision. *Psychonomics Science*, 1965, *2*, 75–76.

Werner, H. Studies in contour: I. Quantitative analyses. *American Journal of Psychology*, 1935, *47*, 40–64.

White, C. T. Temporal numerosity and the psychological unit of duration. *Psychological Monographs*, 1963, *77*, (12, whole No. 575).

CHAPTER *1*

Short-Term Visual Storage Models and Evidence

1.1. A Model
for Visual Memory Tasks*

GEORGE SPERLING

Introduction

I shall be concerned with the apparently simple situation in which an observer looks briefly at a complex visual display and then attempts to reproduce part or all of it. Understanding this visual, immediate-memory task is important both in practical problems and in basic psychological problems. From the practical point of view, it is relevant to everyday situations such as a person looking at a number in a telephone book and then attempting to dial it, as well as to the esoteric problems that arise in matching complex visual displays to human capabilities. I shall not be concerned directly with specific applications; rather, some general principles will be evolved.

The brief visual exposure has a special theoretical significance. Normally, the eye moves in brief, quick motions between its steady fixations upon objects. These movements, called saccads, were first noticed by Javal (1878) and described by Erdmann and Dodge (1898). In such varied tasks as reading, looking at stationary objects and even in visually tracking most moving objects, the eye moves in saccads and takes in information only during the fixation pause between the saccads. As there are several fixations per second, the eye codes information

from the environment into a rapid sequence of still pictures. It is natural, therefore, that the problem of what can be seen in a single brief exposure has fascinated researchers for over 100 years.[1] My purpose is to describe some of the components and properties of a preliminary model for the information processing that begins with the observation of a brief visual stimulus and that ends with the observer's response.

Historically, most research in immediate-memory (or span of attention) has been confined to the problem of capacity. That is, experimenters usually have presented subjects with a great variety of stimuli and measured simply the number of items reported correctly. While such experiments reveal something about the capacity of a memory, they do not usually reveal much about its structure. For example, by structure I mean such properties as—to use computer terminology—whether a memory has random access or whether restraints limit the sequence in which items can be remembered or recalled. To ferret out structural details, the experimental technique requires the presentation of one kind of stimulus over and over to determine the various capabilities and limitations of the observer in dealing with this stimulus. In other words, one must determine the limits of the observer's ability to cope with this stimulus depending upon instructions and

* Invited address, "Symposium on Information Processing in Man: Research Frontiers," sponsored jointly by the Los Angeles Chapter of the Human Factors Society and the University of Southern California. Held at USC, June 23, 1962.

[1] Volkmann (1859) coined the word "tachistoscope" for a device he invented. It utilized falling shutters to replace the electric sparks which had been—up to that time—the primary means of producing brief exposures.

"irrelevant" stimuli such as various kinds of interference. In principle and in intent, this method has a precedent in the work of Kulpe (1904) and his followers.

THE MODEL

In order to facilitate the exposition, it is desirable at this point to give a brief sketch of the model as follows. (1) The observer sees the stimulus material for a short time. (2) He scans it, selecting certain information to rehearse. (3) He later reports what he remembers of his rehearsal. The experiments seek to clarify and quantify these three main aspects of the model. In the first place it will be established that even in a brief exposure the observer may have available much more information than he can later report. Because the duration for which he "sees" the stimulus normally exceeds the stimulus exposure duration, this component of the model is called visual information storage. The second concern is with the rate at which the observer can select and utilize the visual information. This is called scanning or read-out from visual storage. When it is not limited by the requirement of making muscular responses, the scan rate can be quite high.

The third component of the model deals with the subvocal and/or vocal rehearsal of the selected items and the memory for this rehearsal. The memory is called auditory information storage. It will be suggested that the auditory component may be the limiting factor in a wide range of both visual and auditory reproduction tasks. This single limiting process, common to many tasks, would help account for the item constancy of the so-called span of immediate-memory (cf. Pollack, 1953; Miller, 1956).

Visual Information Storage

Much of the material in this section has been published elsewhere (Sperling, 1960b; Averbach and Sperling, 1961) but it is presented briefly for completeness and because the results are needed for the model. Subjects are characteristically able to report about six or fewer items from brief stimulus exposures. This finding

dates to the last century (Cattell, 1885; Erdmann and Dodge, 1898). In my own experiments involving immediate memory for visual stimuli, this finding occurs with great consistency. For example, in one of my studies using five experienced subjects, it was found that the average number of symbols correctly reported was equal to the number of symbols in the stimulus when stimuli contained four or fewer symbols, and equal to about 4.5 symbols when stimuli contained five or more symbols. This held for various spatial arrangements of the symbols, and for mixtures of letters and numbers as well as for letters alone. There was, moreover, no change in the number of letters correctly reported within the entire range of exposure durations tested, from 15 to 500 msec. In these presentations the stimulus was preceded and followed by a dark field. With another apparatus capable of shorter exposures, I found no change in the number of letters reported correctly even for exposures as short as 5 msec and with light pre- and post-exposure fields.[2] At such short exposures the apparent contrast of the stimulus letters was greatly reduced (black letters appeared light grey) but this did not affect the number of letters reported correctly. These results taken together, define the invariant span of attention, or span of immediate-memory.

The span of immediate-memory, however, is not due to a limit on what the subject can see. This was first proved by using a partial report procedure in the following experiment (Sperling, 1960b). Subjects were presented stimuli consisting of 12 letters and numbers in three rows of 4 symbols each. The exposure duration was 50 msec. The stimulus exposure was immediately followed by a tonal signal. The subjects had been told to report only one row of letters and the signal indicated to the subject the particular row to be reported. Subjects were able to report correctly 76 percent of the called-for letters even though they did not know in advance which particular row would be called for. This result indicates that after termination

---

[2] Unpublished experiments conducted at the Bell Telephone Laboratories, 1958.

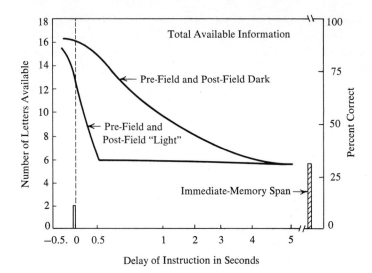

FIGURE 1   Information available to one observer from two kinds of stimulus presentation. The right ordinate is the average accuracy of partial reports; the left ordinate is the inferred store of available letters. Average immediate-memory span for both presentations and for 0.0 and 5.0 sec delay of report is indicated at right. Stimulus exposure is schematically indicated at lower left. (Redrawn from Averbach and Sperling, 1960)

of the exposure, subjects still had available (somewhere inside them) 76 percent of the 12 symbols, that is, 9.1 symbols. However, when the tonal signal was delayed for only one second, the accuracy of report dropped precipitously from 76 to 36 percent. Note that 36 percent of 12 symbols is 4.3 symbols; the previously measured memory span for this material was also 4.3 symbols.

The explanation for these results is that the visual image of the stimulus persists for a short time after the stimulus has been turned off, and that the subjects can utilize this rapidly fading image. In fact, naïve subjects typically believe that the physical stimulus fades out slowly.

The visual basis of this very short-term information storage can be demonstrated more convincingly by comparing two different kinds of stimulus presentation. In the first type, the pre- and post-exposure fields are dark; in the second, the pre- and post-exposure fields are light. It is well known that the first kind of presentation can produce persisting after-images of the stimulus and the second kind of presentation does not. Stimuli of 18 letters were exposed for 50 msec. After a variable delay following the exposure, any one of six different tonal combinations was presented to indicate the particular letters to be reported. The results of the partial report procedure applied to these stimuli are shown in Figure 1.

The reader will recall the procedure for estimating the number of letters available to the subject. The fraction of letters reported correctly in random samples (partial reports) of the stimulus is multiplied by the number of letters in the stimulus. These values are indicated by the ordinates of Figure 1. The abscissa indicates the time after the exposure at which the instruction calling for the partial report was given. Figure 1 shows that letters in excess of the memory span were available to the subject for one-half second when the pre- and post-exposure fields were light, and for nearly five seconds when the pre- and post-exposure fields were dark. The exposure itself was exactly the same in each case. The ability of noninformational visual fields occuring before and after the stimulus to control the accuracy of partial reports strongly suggests their dependence on a persisting visual image. Conversely, the number of letters given in the usual immediate-memory report is almost independent of the exposure conditions and does not change appreciably if the subjert is required to delay his report for five seconds (or longer) instead of being allowed to report immediately. Therefore, the number of letters given in memory reports can be presented by a single bar in Figure 1.

The short-term memory for letters in excess of the immediate-memory span will be called visual information storage (VIS). Some established properties and some hypotheses regarding VIS are listed below.

(1) The effective input for VIS is a local change in retinal light intensity. The contents of VIS depend on visual stimulation. Such factors as stimulus intensity, contrast, duration, pre- and post-exposure fields, etc., are particularly important.

(2) The contents of VIS can become available to subsequent components of the model as a sequence of items through "scanning" or "read-out."

(3) VIS is two-dimensional (for example, contents can be scanned either in a vertical or horizontal sequence).

(4) Maximum information in VIS is at least 17 letters when measured with stimuli containing 18 letters. Stimuli containing more than 18 letters would probably have yielded higher estimates. However, the resolution is disturbed when items that can be resolved individually are spaced too closely together.

(5) Subsequent stimuli can replace or interfere with the previous VIS contents (see below). This process is not the passive addition of a new stimulus to the fading trace of its predecessor but the active replacement of an earlier stimulus by a later one (Sperling, 1960a).

(6) Contents of VIS normally decay rapidly, decay times varying from a fraction of a second to several seconds.

(7) Long durations of visual storage can occur in the form of after-images which appear to move when the eye moves and therefore are probably localized in the retina. It has not been determined how the central nervous system is involved in the kind of VIS discussed here.

(8) It is tempting to speculate on the purpose of VIS because its properties seem so well suited to the requirements of a system like the eye, which processes information in temporally discrete chunks. The function of the persistence (the storage aspect of VIS) seems to be to maintain a visual image from one fixation of the eye to the next. The function of erasure is to permit the new image following a saccad to overwrite the trace of the previous one without interference to itself and also to "erase" the blur resulting during movement of the eye. The minimum duration of storage that has been recorded ($\frac{1}{4}$ sec) is still long enough to preserve the image between eye movements. The minimum time between saccads is typically too long to allow the image produced by the second saccad to interfere with more than the tail end of the image produced by the first. Thus VIS acts as a buffer which quickly attains and holds much information to permit its relatively slow utilization later. VIS also segregates and isolates from each other successive bursts of visual information (e.g., images).

Scanning

In order to determine the rate at which information can be utilized, it is necessary to gain precise control of actual stimulus availability, that is, the contents of VIS. This cannot be accomplished by controlling exposure duration alone. No matter how brief a *single* stimulus flash may be, if it is of sufficient contrast for easy legibility of letters, then it will be available for about a quarter of a second or longer.

The idea that stimulus duration does not determine stimulus availability is not new. For example, in 1868, Exner published a psychophysical study of the apparent duration of short flashes in which he found that short flashes exert their effect over a considerable time span.

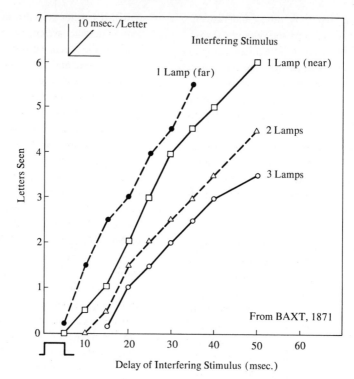

FIGURE 2   The number of letters seen as a function of the delay between the onset of a 5.0 msec lettered stimulus and a 120 msec blank interfering stimulus. The parameter is the intensity of the interfering stimulus. The time course of the lettered stimulus is indicated at the lower left. (Based on the protocols of Baxt, 1871)

Baxt (1871), also working in Helmholtz's laboratory, performed a logical sequel to this work. He followed the stimulus exposure after a delay with a bright second flash which was intended to obliterate the persisting after-image of the stimulus.[3] In one of his experiments he used a stimulus flash of 5.0 msec and a bright second flash of 120.0 msec duration. Observers viewed stimuli of 6 or 7 printed letters and reported the number of letters they could see with various time delays between the two flashes. Figure 2 contains a graph that I prepared from Baxt's tabular, introspective data. The abscissa represents the time from the onset of the stimulus to the onset of the "interfering" second flash; essentially, this is the time that the observer had to look at the stimulus. The ordinate represents the number of letters the observer said he could see. The parameter is the intensity of the interfering flash in terms of the arrangement that produced the intensity (three, two, or one lamps, one lamp far). The slope of the data points show that Baxt could see an additional letter for approximately each 10 msec of delay of the interfering flash.

The data of Figure 2 were obtained with dark letters on a white background. Baxt obtained similar results when viewing light letters on a dark surround. He himself did not notice the simple relation of constant slope, perhaps because he did not graph his results.

Baxt's results show that the minimum delay at which detection of a letter is first possible depends on the intensity of the interfering second flash. This flash exerts its interfering effect more rapidly when it is more intense. A similar situation occurs in masking experiments. An intense

[3] The method of Baxt was described by Ladd (1887) and James (1890) in their textbooks but it is no longer well known. Consequently, it has been rediscovered, recently by Lindsley and Emmons (1958), Gilbert (1959) and by the author.

masking flash can cause marked threshold changes for detection of a test flash even when the test precedes it by as much as forty msec. Had Baxt used hundreds of lamps instead of just three for his brightest interfering stimulus, the minimum delay necessary for detection of a letter might have been increased from 20 msec (with three lamps) to 40 msec or more.

The results of Baxt's 2-flash experiment are more reasonable than those of the single flash experiments. It will be recalled that reducing the duration of a single flash reduced the apparent contrast of the exposed letters but the number reported correctly did not change with exposure duration *per se* except at ridiculously short exposures. It does not make sense to conclude, for example, that if four letters can be read from a single exposure of one msec that the time for reading a letter is $\frac{1}{4}$ msec. Nevertheless, even the scanning rate of one letter per 10 msec (or 100 letters/sec) in Baxt's experiment seemed so remarkably fast that it seemed worthwhile to attempt to reproduce some of Baxt's conditions. With certain reservations, comparable results were obtained. Some minor changes intended to improve the procedure were also tried. Subjects were required to report letters and were scored for the number correct. (Baxt had asked his observer only to say whether or not he saw a letter.) The blank second field was replaced with a visual "noise" field, consisting of densely scattered bits and pieces of letters. The noise stimulus is much more effective interference than a homogeneous field. For example, letter detection is virtually stopped when the noise and letters are viewed simultaneously at the same intensity. Baxt's procedure requires a second flash many times more intense than the stimulus to achieve comparable interference.

The main objection to Baxt's procedure, however, is a surprising one: I found that the second flash may produce a clearly visible negative after-image of the first stimulus and thereby indirectly fail to stop its persistence. In fact, in certain conditions of presentation, the blank interference produced a negative after-image of the stimulus without a prior positive image being seen (Sperling, 1960c). Ironically, here is a case of simultaneous perfect interference (the positive stimulus is completely invisible) and of perfect persistence (all the stimulus information is available in the after-image). Use of the noise field as the interfering stimulus mitigated this problem somewhat since even an after-image of the stimulus is better hidden by the noise. However, such paradoxical effects as simultaneous interference with and yet persistence of information, certainly argue for caution in interpreting the results of Baxt-type experiments.

Using the noise technique, we sought further clarification of the Baxt procedure. Baxt's results were that the scan rate is the same no matter when the scan is ended. That is, bright flashes presumably ended visual availability of the stimulus sooner than dim flashes. One obvious question that needed to be answered was "is the scanning rate the same no matter when the scan begins." If it were, then this would provide more confidence in the method.

To delay scanning, we used two different pre-exposure fields. One was a dark field which presented no visual recovery problem and the other a noise field. Figure 3 illustrates the sequence in each of the two kinds of presentations. In the first, the pre-exposure field is dark. It is followed by an exposure of variable duration, which is then terminated by a noise post-exposure field. In the second kind of presentation, the pre-exposure field is noise; followed by an exposure of variable duration, which is then also terminated by a noise post-exposure field. The number of letters in the stimuli was varied from two to six in order to check for possible spatial location effects. Data were obtained with two subjects. Figure 4 illustrates the results for the less variable subject.

The data of Figure 4 indicate that the subject gained information from the various stimuli at the rate of one letter per 10 msec and that this rate was independent of the number of letters in the stimulus or of the pre-exposure field. When the pre-exposure field was dark, the subject began to gain information almost immediately upon stimulus exposure. It took this subject about 20 msec to recover from pre-exposure to visual noise. Once she was able to scan, the rate

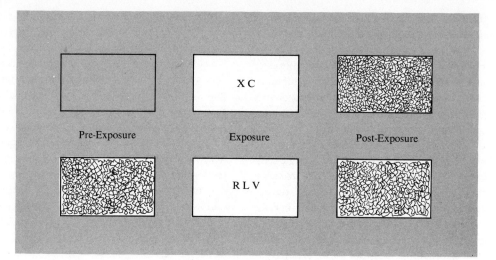

FIGURE 3   Two kinds of stimulus presentations modified from the method of Baxt. The sequence of stimuli on a trial is indicated from left to right. The luminance of the lettered stimulus was 31 Ft-L.; of the visual noise, 20 Ft-L.

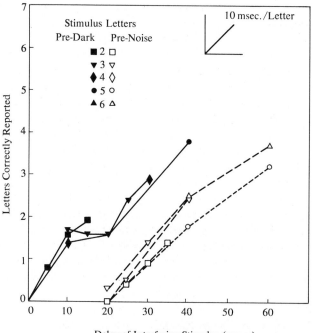

FIGURE 4   The number of letters correctly reported as a function of the delay between the onset of a lettered stimulus and an interfering visual "noise" stimulus. The number of stimulus letters was also varied. The pre-exposure field was either dark or "noise."

was still about one letter per 10 msec. These results support the hypothesis that pre-exposure could change the time at which a scan begins but not its rate.

Various other pre-exposure fields have also been tried. For example, with a pre-exposure field 100 times brighter than the stimulus field, scanning may be delayed for over 100 msec.

Once the stimulus letters become legible, they are scanned at comparable rates. A serious problem in this kind of experiment is that it is very difficult to insure that all letters fall upon retinal locations which recover sensitivity at the same rate. This particular procedure therefore has not been pursued in detail. Preliminary data also indicated that rate of scanning was but slightly reduced when the stimulus intensity was reduced to $\frac{1}{100}$ of its prior level. Other factors such as stimulus size, geometry, and contrast have not yet been studied to see how they affect the scan rate.

The point of all these experiments is that, under a variety of conditions, random letters of good contrast are scanned at the same rate; typically, about one letter per 10 msec. However this holds true only for the first three or four letters to be scanned. Figure 5 shows data obtained with the same two subjects viewing a dark pre-exposure field and a noise post-exposure field. One subject reported three, the other four letters in the first 50 msec of exposure. Additional stimulus exposure from 50 msec to 100 msec accounted for about one or two additional letters. Beyond 100 msec the rate of acquiring additional letters is so low as to be virtually indistinguishable from zero on this time scale. Additional data points would have shown the critical break in the curve to occur well before 100 msec.

This kind of experiment perhaps more clearly than any other defines an immediate-memory span for visual materials. Letters up to the immediate-memory span can be scanned at a rate of one letter per 10 or 15 msec. This is so rapid that the rate of acquiring additional letters beyond the immediate-memory span is negligible by comparison.

Rehearsal and Auditory Information Storage

In the last two sections it was shown (1) that letters are visually available to an observer during and after a brief exposure and (2) that they need not be visually available for more than 10 to 15 msec per letter in order to be reported correctly. Yet, the observer usually does not begin his report until several seconds after the exposure, long after his visual store of letters is depleted. In fact, he can delay his report for an additional 30 seconds or more without any loss of accuracy. What are the characteristics of this later, long term memory?

One important clue is obtained from the kinds of errors subjects make. In writing down symbols from a brief stimulus, subjects frequently make auditory confusions; that is, writing D for T, T for 2 and so on. On questioning, subjects assert that they indeed do "say" the letters to themselves prior to report. This kind of behavior is represented in the model by rehearsal (saying the letters to oneself) and by auditory information storage (hearing the rehearsal letters). The properties of auditory information storage (AIS) are in some respects similar to those of VIS. The main functional difference between AIS and VIS in these experiments is the possibility of feeding information already in AIS back into storage again by rehearsal.

The various components of the model and their interactions are represented in Figure 6.

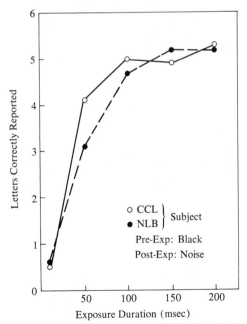

FIGURE 5 The number of letters reported correctly as a function of the exposure duration or equivalently, the delay of the post-exposure visual "noise" interfering stimulus. The pre-exposure field was dark.

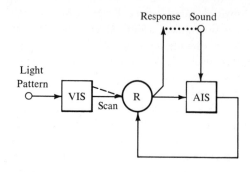

FIGURE 6 A schematic model for short-term memory tasks. VIS = visual information storages, R = rehearsal component, AIS = auditory information storage. See text for details.

The model illustrates that a visual stimulus is first stored in VIS, then scanned and rehearsed. The rehearsal component has two inputs: items scanned from VIS and those heard in AIS. Only one input is rehearsable at any one time and it probably takes a short time to switch from one input modality to the other (cf. Broadbent, 1956, 1958). The rehearsal component produces a verbal response "audible" in AIS or a vocal response audible to another person and indirectly also in AIS.

It will be suggested below that rehearsal cannot proceed faster than about ten syllables per second. Scanning itself may initially be ten times faster, 100 items per second. The difference between the rates of scanning and rehearsal poses a real problem. To account for this difference, it tentatively will be assumed that items may accumulate very briefly in the scan path or rehearsal component until they can be rehearsed.[4] Two scan arrows are drawn from VIS

[4] Another possible assumption is that there is an error in the interpretation of scan experiments using a Baxt type of stimulus presentation. Two attempts were made to measure directly the stimulus persistence (availability). In the first attempt, the partial report procedure was applied to a Baxt presentation. It was not successful because subjects' performances tended to deteriorate in all respects. In the second procedure, the apparent duration of the visual stimulus was compared to the duration of various simultaneous acoustic signals. For example, a Baxt stimulus presentation from which four letters could usually be read (letter duration = 50 msec) was matched to acoustic stimuli of roughly comparable duration. In such comparisons, it is quite obvious that the apparent duration of the visual letters is a small fraction of a second. Although this is a subjective judgment, it has strong face validity. The result only affirms that the scan rate can be much more rapid than rehearsal.

to Rehearsal to represent the assumed temporal overlap in the scan of successive items.

The rehearsal items are maintained in AIS at least for several seconds during which time they are usually rehearsed again. Finally, when a response is required, the letters are either rehearsed again as they are being written or, if they are spoken aloud, the feedback loop may be closed externally as well as internally—the spoken sound re-entering AIS.

In summary, there are at least three sources of information for auditory storage: (1) an actual acoustic stimulus, (2) rehearsal of information already in AIS, (3) the scanning process —it is assumed that observers hear themselves make a verbal response as they scan.

EVIDENCE

In this model, the auditory components assume the major burden of short term visual memory. Data relevant to the auditory part of the model are difficult to obtain because audition involves higher order processes. There are some data, however, which come from three kinds of experiments: (1) experiments that measure AIS directly by using auditory stimuli, (2) experiments that seek to measure rehearsal by instructing subjects with regard to rehearsal, and (3) experiments that use interfering stimuli to interfere selectively with some aspects of the process and thereby reveal others. I shall consider these approaches in order.

(1) *Auditory Information Storage.* Our common experience leave little doubt of the fact that there is auditory information storage. If, for example, one is spoken to while occupied with another task, one may continue working for a few moments and yet still be able to recover the message later. Two kinds of recent experiments illustrate this type of auditory storage especially well. In the first kind of experiment the subject is presented with several stimuli at once. For example, Broadbent (1957a) produced a spoken sequence of digits at the subjects' ears, with different digits being spoken simultaneously into each ear. When digits were spoken rapidly, subjects could not shift their

attention back and forth from one ear to the other with each pair of spoken digits. Rather, they could only report all the digits heard at one ear first and then attempt to report the digits—if any—that were still audible at the other ear. This ingenious procedure excludes the possibility of any simultaneous recoding of the inputs at both ears. It thereby forces the subject to rely directly upon AIS.

The second kind of experiment (Anderson, 1960) was a direct application to audition of the partial report procedure previously used to measure visual storage. A list of 12 letters in three groups of four each was read to subjects. At various times later, an instruction signal was given the subjects to indicate the particular group to be reported. Anderson's results can be interpreted in terms of auditory storage to mean that initially subjects had about 10 letters available. Accuracy of report deteriorated most rapidly during the first five seconds after the presentation and slowly thereafter. Other factors, such as unlimited opportunity for rehearsal and differential recall for certain groups of letters indicate that more than simple AIS was probably involved. All in all, both experiments demonstrate an auditory information storage capable of retaining information before it has been acted upon and whose contents decay during a period of many seconds.

(2) *Rehearsal.* The role of rehearsal in memory is a problem that psychologists—with a few exceptions—have hoped would solve itself if only they ignored it sufficiently. Rehearsal is not quite so intractable to measurement as many of us were brought up to believe. For example, subjects may be asked to say a particular sequence of letters as fast as they can and to use a stop-watch to time themselves for the task. They may also be asked to say the letters to themselves without producing any sound and to time themselves as before. Subjects understand this second instruction without difficulty. Elapsed times are about three syllables per second for unfamiliar letter sequences spoken aloud. Silent rehearsal is slightly faster. The maximum rate for highly familiar sequences is about 10 syllables per second.

More controlled and somewhat similar studies of rehearsal were conducted by Brown (1958), Peterson and Peterson (1959) and by Murdock (1961). In the Petersons' experiment, subjects were initially presented with a sequence of letters. They were then told to rehearse them out loud in time with a metronome at two letters per second. Other subjects were given an equivalent time duration that could be used for silent rehearsal. The length of time allowed for rehearsal was varied. Following the initial rehearsal period, the subjects were put to a task intended to interfere with further rehearsal, such as counting backwards. Those subjects who had most time for initial rehearsal—aloud or silent—recalled best, accuracy being proportional to rehearsal time. Spoken rehearsal was more effective than silent rehearsal, a result that will be encountered again below.

These experiments indicate that a short period of rehearsal after an auditory stimulus presentation facilitates later recall. An interpolated period of non-rehearsal interferes with recall as does the competing auditory stimulus of hearing oneself saying irrelevant material.

(3) *Interference.* Brown (1958) sought to interfere with rehearsal by requiring his subjects to read digits aloud. Peterson and Peterson (1959) made their subjects count backwards between stimulus presentation and recall. These interpolated tasks produced a decrease in accuracy of recall which was interpreted as due to the interference of counting with rehearsal. The longer the period of counting, the less accurate the recall, presumably because of the fading of the rehearsed letters in auditory storage and the accumulation of interfering auditory stimuli. Brown had previously noted that interpolated silence (which permits rehearsal) does not have a comparable destructive effect on recall.[5]

To a certain degree, even when he is counting backwards, the subject's cooperation is needed for interference with his rehearsal. He is in effect asked to devote himself fully to the task of counting and to neglect completely the

---

[5] Brown, J. *Immediate Memory.* Doctoral thesis, University of Cambridge, 1955. Cited in Broadbent (1958), p. 225. See also Averbach and Sperling (1960).

task of recall. It would be desirable to find a method of interference whose success did not depend upon the subject's cooperation—a method comparable to Baxt's method of eliminating visual persistence. Towards this end, I constructed two different acoustic stimuli which might interfere with rehearsal by providing a competing input to AIS. The first of these was a loud noise at 90 dB SPL, analogous to Baxt's interfering field. The second interfering stimulus was a recording of the subject's own voice speaking letters at a rate of 6/sec, also at 90 dB. This stimulus is analogous to visual noise. At each trial, either silence or one of these extremely loud stimuli was played into the subject's ears, beginning before stimulus exposure and continuing until after report.

The number of letters subjects reported correctly was the same in noise and in silence, and only very slightly lower for the speech interference although the difference was statistically significant (Sperling, 1962). Two supplementary observations were made which elucidate the failure of the interpolated stimuli to interfere with recall. First, the subjects described the task as one of selective listening, that is, of hearing the speech interference as localized at the ears and their rehearsal as localized inside the head. The speech interference accentuates the subjective aspect of listening to rehearsal so that even subjects who are not normally cognizant of the auditory aspect become so.

The second observation was that normally silent subjects, when listening to speech interference, frequently mouthed or even spoke the letters out loud during the period between the stimulus exposure and writing down the response. This overt behavior reflects an effort to accentuate and emphasize the rehearsal. The conclusion therefore is that speech and perhaps also noise do interfere but that subjects can accentuate their rehearsal in order to cope successfully with the interference.

SUMMARY OF HYPOTHESES ABOUT AUDITORY INFORMATION STORAGE (AIS) AND REHEARSAL

(1) The primary input to AIS is sound. The contents of AIS probably depend on sound intensity, complexity, background,

etc.[6] A secondary and possibly less effective input is by rehearsal.

(2) AIS is locally one-dimensional and directional. That is, a string of letters is stored in sequence and it can be recovered only in that sequence. However, one string of letters may be localized at the left ear and another simultaneous string of letters may be localized at the right ear. Thus, although each stored string of letters is individually one-dimensional, the simultaneous imbedding of many strings in storage implies a very complex overall structure for AIS.

(3) At least 10 non-rehearsed items can be maintained momentarily in AIS. They are probably grouped into several strings.

(4) The contents of AIS decay slowly relative to VIS. Rehearsal of items appears to lengthen their subsequent decay times but it also brings into play more complex mechanisms for long term memory via association which are beyond the scope of this paper.

(5) The contents of AIS, VIS, and of any comparable system in other modalities may be rehearsed. That is, a verbal response is made to items in the storage and this verbal response, which may or may not be audible to another person, is an input to AIS. When a stimulus consists of a number of clearly identifiable items, then the characteristics of the AIS-Rehearsal loop will probably be the limiting factor in the immediate-memory span for this stimulus.

(6) Rehearsal usually proceeds at a rate of about 3 syllables per second and cannot proceed faster than about 10 syllables per second.

(7) Only one item may be rehearsed at a time. The interval between the rehearsal of

---

[6] Wundt (1912) provides an insightful and provocative analysis of auditory memory for patterns of metronome beats. Wundt could maintain in his consciousness 8 groups of two beats each or 5 groups of eight beats each. (This material was presumably not rehearsed verbally. Wundt's introspections would suggest that the contents of AIS are limited most directly by subjective grouping itemizing) and only to a lesser extent by their duration of complexity (information content).

successive items is longer if they are not taken from the same sense modality.

(8) Subsequent acoustic stimuli can interfere with the contents of AIS beyond what might be expected from passive decay. So far, only self-produced verbal stimuli have shown the effect. The interference is most effective against items that have not been rehearsed and diminishes with the number of rehearsals. If rehearsal is permitted during the presentation of interfering stimuli (recorded, in this case) then the interference is barely measurable.[7]

Discussion

The model is perhaps more useful for organizing data and experiments than for precise prediction because it consists of complex and only partially specified components. In this respect it reflects the complexity of its human subject matter and the limitations of its human designer.

TRANSIENT VERSUS STEADY-STATE INFORMATION FLOW

The model was derived only from the "transient" response of a human to information; that is, the situation in which he is given a single burst of information and much time to process it. The responses to a "steady-state" or continuous information input undoubtedly involve

---

[7] Broadbent (1957b, 1958) has suggested several models for immediate-memory. While a brief discussion cannot do justice to his ingenious and stimulating proposals, it is worthwhile to indicate some of the major similarities and differences. The obvious, basic similarities are the possibility of storage of unrecoded information and the recognition of a rehearsal loop. The differences lie in the nature and subdivision of these functions and are undoubtedly due in part to the different sets of data which each account seeks to explain. In the present model, items (or stimuli) circulate in the rehearsal loop while Broadbent specifically states that information (not items) circulates. The present account assumes one rehearsal loop and one store for rehearsed material, not several of each. Here VIS and AIS are identified in detail from introspective and direct experimental data while in Broadbent's models, storage of unrecoded information is of a more inferential and hypothetical nature—it can even be by-passed entirely. Broadbent is especially concerned with the case of simultaneous or conflicting inputs. He does not consider the special problem of scanning in vision nor make comparable distinctions between the processing of visual and of acoustic stimuli; etc.

further complications and new processes. For example, following a brief stimulus exposure, the auditory feedback loop from AIS through Rehearsal was of primary significance in recall. Visual processes in recall may come to be of importance only with longer exposures. Perhaps this is because following a brief stimulus exposure, most people cannot create in themselves a visual feedback loop, but they can in effect do so during a continuous stimulus exposure by looking repeatedly at certain aspects of the stimulus. This example emphasizes another difficulty in the understanding of steady-state observation conditions. Namely, the sequential flow of information into the observer may depend on his own actions so that every complexity and nuance of human judgment and decision making must be considered in a complete steady-state model. On the other hand, some complex tasks have been devised so that a continuous verbal protocol is available—the subject thinks out loud so-to-speak (e.g., Newell and Simon, 1961). In such tasks, the knowledge of how many and for how long the subject's past utterances are available to him in AIS may well be of significance in the understanding of the process of decision making or "thinking."

Keeping in mind the restriction of the model to "transient" responses, it is still possible to make some hypotheses about the mechanisms underlying humans' response to complex displays and some tentative suggestions on how to improve their response.

(1) *Independence of the Immediate-Memory Span.* Because of verbal rehearsal, humans transmit items, not bits. The limit on the number of items depends on such factors as the code (e.g., syllables per item) and upon the individual characteristics of the AIS-Rehearsal loop (e.g., AIS decay time). In so far as these are independent of the input modality of the stimulus, the information limitations in human responding will be independent of sense modality.

(2) *High Information Requirements.* Even in a brief exposure a human can take in much more information than he can ultimately transmit. By scanning and rehearsal he effectively

samples an uncoded form of the input in VIS and AIS. In many practical situations one cannot dictate to the observer what aspects of the stimulus to sample. For example, in order to provide customer satisfaction, a television picture may have to contain information to match the enormous capacity of VIS and not merely the small amount of information transmitted in a sample from it. On the other hand, in other contexts it may be economical to keep the displayed information at the transmission (and not the storage) level.

(3) *Rapid Reading.* Observers can extract small numbers of items very quickly from visual stimuli; 10 to 15 msec per letter is a typical rate for the first three or four items. In the absence of interfering stimuli, even a microsecond flash, if it is seen clearly, will usually be visually available for many times the length of time needed to extract the items up to the immediate-memory span. To transmit the maximal information from a brief exposure of a visual display, therefore, the display should be coded into about four symbols (e.g., digits) to take advantage of the rapid scan capability. Of course, other considerations such as the kind of errors may indicate other kinds of displays. In steady exposures, the rate of item utilization is usually not limited by visual factors but by the rehearsal process to a rate of 10 syllables per second or slower.

(4) *Non-Susceptibility to Auditory Interference.* One useful if obvious result is that properly motivated subjects can perform visual memory tasks during extreme auditory interference and show almost no performance decrement. Specifically, subjects can perform without loss in 90 dB noise and almost without loss when barely tolerable levels of speech (recorded letters spoken by themselves) are being "shouted" into their ears. For practical purposes, therefore, it may be assumed that the number of letters reported from a brief exposure will be the same under optimal or adverse conditions.

(5) *Auditory Simplification.* In order to facilitate performance and to avoid errors in visual monitoring tasks, telephone dialing, etc., it is necessary to consider the task from the auditory point of view as well as the purely visual. All possible outcomes should be given names that are easy to rehearse and not likely to be confused. The *laissez-faire* practice of allowing the operator to develop his own terminology is not recommended. When only numerals are involved, there is no problem as these are quite distinct. But we have found, for example, that subjects required to memorize sequences of the letters B,P,D,T, etc., do not do as well as when confronted with an equivalent sequence of letters which do not sound so much alike. Frequently, complex tasks which do not appear to involve audition can be simplified and made less susceptible to errors by means of an appropriate code that will ease the auditory memory load (in syllables) and help to avoid auditory confusions.

Summary

A model for visual recall tasks was presented in terms of visual information storage (VIS), scanning, rehearsal, and auditory information storage (AIS). It was shown first that brief visual stimuli are stored in VIS in a form similar to the sensory input. These visual "images" contain considerably more information than is transmitted later. They can be sampled by scanning for items at high rates of about 10 msec per letter. Recall is based on a verbal recoding of the stimulus (rehearsal), which is remembered in AIS. The items retained in AIS are usually rehearsed again to prevent them from decaying. The human limits in immediate-memory (reproduction) tasks are inherent in the AIS-Rehearsal loop. The main implication of the model for human factors is the importance of the auditory coding in visual tasks.

References

Anderson, Nancy S. Poststimulus cuing in immediate-memory. *J. exp. Psychol.,* 1960, *60,* 216–221.
Averbach, E., & Sperling, G. Short term storage of in-

formation in vision. In C. Cherry (Ed.), *Information theory*. London: Butterworths, 1961, pp. 196–211.

Baxt, N. Ueber die Zeit welche nötig ist, damit ein Gesichtseindruck zum Bewusstein kommt und über die Grösse (Extension) der bewussten Wahrnehmung bei einem Gesichtseindrucke von gegenbener Dauer. *Pflüger's Arch. ges. Physiol.*, 1871, *4*, 325–336.

Broadbent. D. E. Successive responses to simultaneous stimuli. *Quart. J. exp. Psychol.*, 1956, *8*, 145–152.

Broadbent, D. E. Immediate memory and simultaneous stimuli. *Quart. J. exp. Psychol.*, 1957a, *9*, 1–11.

Broadbent, D. E. A mechanical model for human attention and immediate memory. *Psychol. Rev.*, 1957b, *64*, 205–215.

Broadbent, D. E. *Perception and communication*. New York: Pergamon Press, 1958.

Brown, J. Some tests of the decay theory of immediate memory. *Quart. J. exp. Psychol.*, 1958, *10*, 12–21.

Cattell, J. McK. Ueber die Zeit der Erkennung und Benennung von Schriftzeichen, Bildern und Farben. *Philos. Stud.*, 1885, *2*, 635–650.

Erdmann, B., & Dodge, R. *Psychologische Untersuchung über das Lesen*. Halle, M. Niemeyer, 1898.

Exner, S. Ueber die zu einer Gesichtswahrnehmung nöthige Zeit. *S. B. Akad. Wiss. Wien.*, 1868, *58*, 601–633.

Gilbert, L. C. Speed of processing visual stimuli and its relation to reading. *J. educ. Psychol.*, 1959, *50*, 8–14.

James, W. *The principles of psychology*. New York: Holt, 1890.

Javal, L. E., Essai sur la physiologie de la lecture. *Ann. Oculist. Paris*, 1878, *82*, 242–253.

Külpe, O. Versuche über Abstraktion. In *Bericht über den I. Kongress für experimentelle Psychologie, 1904*. Leipzig: Barth, 1904, pp. 56–68.

Ladd, G. T. *Elements of physiological psychology—a treatise of the activities and nature of the mind*. New York: Charles Scribner's Sons, 1887.

Lindsley, D. B., & Emmons, W. H. Perception time and evoked potentials. *Science*, 1958, *127*, 1061.

Miller, G. A. The magical number seven, plus or minus two: some limits on our capacity for processing information. *Psychol. Rev.*, 1956, *63*, 81–97.

Murdock, B. B., Jr. The retention of individual items. *J. exp. Psychol.*, 1961, *62*, 618–625.

Newell, A., & Simon, H. A. Computer simulation of human thinking. *Science*, 1961, *134*, 2011–2017.

Peterson, L. R., & Peterson, Margaret J. Short-term retention of individual verbal items. *J. exp. Psychol.*, 1959, *58*, 193–198.

Pollack, I. Assimilation of sequentially encoded information. *Amer. J. Psychol.*, 1953, *66*, 421–435.

Sperling, G. Bistable aspects of monocular vision. *J. opt. Soc. Amer.*, 1960a, *50*, 1140–1141. (Abstract.)

Sperling, G. The information available in brief visual presentations. *Psychol. Monogr.*, 1960b, *74*, No. 11 (Whole No. 498).

Sperling, G. Negative afterimage without prior positive image. *Science*, 1960c, *131*, 1613–1614.

Sperling, G. Auditory interference with a visual memory task. Paper read at Eastern Psychological Association, Atlantic City, New Jersey, April, 1962.

Volkmann, A. W. Das Tachistoscop, ein Instrument, welches bei Untersuchung des monentanen Schens den Gebrauch des electrischen Funkens ersetzt. *S.B. Kgl. Sächs. Ges. Wiss. Lpz., math-phys.*, 1859, *11*, 90–98.

Wundt, W. *An introduction to psychology*. Tr. from 2nd German ed., 1911, by R. Pintner. New York and London: Macmillan, 1912; reprinted London: Allen & Unwin, 1924.

1.2 Successive Approximations to a Model for Short-Term Memory*

GEORGE SPERLING

Introduction

One major difficulty in studying human memory is that we have not yet learned how to obtain systematic physiological information. This means that the only technique available for the study of human memory is to present the subject with a variety of memory tasks, and then to record his actions and the accuracy of his performance. From these observations, we try to abstract the functions or operations that the subject performs on the to-be-remembered stimulus in order to produce the observed performance.

Because of the complexity and subtlety of human behavior, it seemed desirable to us to confine ourselves initially to a simple memory task. A subject looks at a row of random letters and then writes them down. If this situation were understood, perhaps the principles could be generalized to more complex tasks.

Models

MODEL 1

When a row of letters is exposed briefly, i.e., for 1/20th sec, an adult subject can reproduce

about 4 or 5 of the letters (Cattell, 1885). The simplest model for the action of reproducing visually presented letters might be organized into two main components: (1) a visual memory containing the letters (called visual information storage) and (2) a translation component, which can translate a visual image of the letters into a series of motor actions; namely, copying the letters onto a piece of paper (Figure 1). The limited memory span of the subject might be represented in the model by progressive deterioration—a fading into illegibility—of the contents of visual storage. While the subject is writing, the contents of his visual memory are decaying, so that when he finally comes to write the fifth or sixth letter his visual memory of the stimulus no longer is legible.

Without elaborating further on the difficulties of Model 1, we can reject it immediately for one basic reason: before the subject begins to write the letters, his visual image of the let-

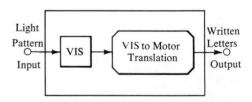

FIGURE 1 Model 1. The large box represents the subject. Arrows indicate the direction of information flow. The components are visual information storage (VIS) and a translator. The translator converts an input (the memory of a letter) into an output (a series of motor actions) which result in a written representation of the letter.

* Originally presented at the symposium on "Memory and Action," XVIII International Congress of Psychology, Moscow, 1966. It was published in *Acta Psychologia,* 1967, vol. 27, pp. 285–292. The first person plural is used to refer at various times to Mrs. Susan A. Speeth, Mrs. Mary W. Helms, and Dr. Roseanne G. Speelman, whose able assistance is acknowledged thereby.

ters has already disappeared. (The measurement of the duration of visual storage is described below.) Having shown that letters are not stored visually until they are reproduced, we must now determine the form in which they are stored.

MODEL 2

Occasionally a subject, when he is writing down letters, can be heard to mumble the letters as he is writing them. His tendency to say the letters aloud can be emphasized by playing loud noise into his ears. Noise itself does not seem to alter performance in any other significant way. We have used this technique, together with a microphone placed near the subject's mouth, to record the actual letters the subject is saying. We also recorded automatically whenever the subject was writing. The most interesting results with this technique are obtained when the subject is required to wait (e.g., for 20 sec) after the stimulus exposure before writing the letters. He repeats (rehearses) the entire letter sequence several times with a pause between each repetition during the interval. Then, at the time of writing each letter, he also may speak it simultaneously.

Rehearsal suggests an obvious memory mechanism. The subject says a letter, hears himself saying it, and then remembers the auditory image. As the auditory image fades, he repeats it to refresh it. Most of our subjects do not vocalize during recall, but they all concur in stating that they rehearse subvocally. Therefore, we assume that the sound-image of a letter can enter auditory memory directly from subvocal rehearsal without the necessity of actually being converted into sound and passing into the external world. These relations are illustrated in Figure 2.

The auditory nature of subvocal rehearsal can be emphasized by playing distracting speech into one's ears during rehearsal. The speech seems to emanate from one set of locations in space (the ears) while one's rehearsal is heard as an internal voice speaking from the center of the head. External sound also can be used as a clock against which to measure the rate of subvocal rehearsal. Another method of measuring the rate of subvocal rehearsal is to ask subjects to rehearse a sequence of letters subvocally 10 times and to signal when through. This may be compared to a vocal rehearsal of the same sequence. All these indirect measures of the rate of subvocal rehearsal indicate that, while it may be slightly faster than vocal rehearsal, it is basically the same process (cf. Landauer, 1962). The maximum possible rate is about 6 letters per second but, in memory experiments, maximum rates of about 3 letters per second are more typical.

The existence of auditory memory in visual reproduction tasks also may be inferred from the deterioration in performance which occurs when the stimulus letters sound alike (B, C, D, etc.) We have studied a large variety of tasks in which stimuli were presented visually or auditorily and found almost the same rule to apply to both modalities of presentation. When the memory load is small (about 2.5 letters in an auditory task, 3 letters in a visual task) it

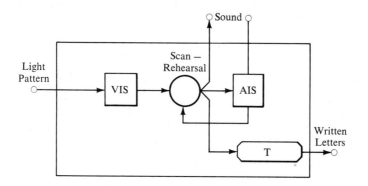

FIGURE 2   Model 2. VIS = visual information storage, AIS = auditory information storage, T = translator.

makes little difference to performance whether the stimulus letters sound alike or sound different. Additional letters beyond the minimal number are remembered only about half as well when they sound alike as when they sound different. This dependence of performance on the sound of letters—even in a task which nominally involves only looking and writing—is of practical as well as of theoretical importance (Conrad, 1963; Sperling, 1963).

According to Model 2, stimulus letters first are retained in visual storage. They are rehearsed, one at a time (i.e., converted from a visual to an auditory form), and then remembered in auditory storage. Subsequently they may be rehearsed again and again as required until they are written down. The limits on performance may arise either from the limited duration visual storage (so that some letters decay before they can be rehearsed) or from the limited capacity of the rehearsal-auditory storage loop, depending on the stimulating conditions.

Attractive as Model 2 seems, it is inadequate for the following reason: it is possible to generate an image in visual storage which has a duration of definitely less than .1 sec and from which 3 letters can be reported. This would require a rehearsal rate of over 30 letters per second, which clearly is completely beyond the capabilities of the rehearsal processes described for Model 2. Before considering Model 3, we need to examine in more detail some properties of visual information storage.

SHORT DURATION VISUAL IMAGES

When the contents of an image in visual storage exceed four or five items, they can be measured by a sampling technique which requires the subject to report only a part of the contents (Sperling, 1960). For example, by this technique it was shown that the visual image induced by a ½0th sec exposure may contain as many as 18 unrelated letters, and that as many as 10 items may still remain 2 sec after the exposure. The visual image of shortest duration that we have measured by this technique was produced by a stimulus exposure of ½0th sec,

preceded and followed by bright white fields. Immediately after the exposure, 14 letters were contained in visual storage; within 1/2 sec they had vanished (Averbach and Sperling, 1960). To produce and to measure really short duration images, however, different methods are required.

In a letter-noise stimulus sequence, a second, interfering, stimulus (visual "noise") is exposed immediately on termination of the letter stimulus. The duration of the letter images can be estimated by comparing them to an auditory signal. Two different methods were used. In the first method two clicks were produced at the ears of the subject. He then adjusted the interval between the clicks until the auditory interval was judged equal to the visual duration. In the second method, the subject heard only one click at a time. He adjusted this click to occur so that it coincided subjectively with the onset of the visual image. After this judgment was complete, he made another adjustment of the click to coincide with the termination of the visual image. The measured interval between clicks—taken to be the duration of the visual image—was the same by both methods. The apparent image duration of the letters in a letter-noise sequence is zero for extremely brief exposures (e.g., less than 10 msec) and then increases linearly with increasing exposure duration for durations exceeding about 20 msec (Figure 3a).

When stimuli of 5 letters, followed by noise, are exposed for various durations, the accuracy of report increases with exposure duration as shown in Figure 3b. The most interesting aspect of these data is revealed by analyzing separately the accuracy of report at each of the 5 locations (Figure 3c). The accuracy of report at each location reported increases continuously as a function of exposure duration. For this subject, the order of the successive locations which are reported correctly is generally left-to-right (I to V), except that location V is reported correctly at shorter exposures than location IV. Other subjects have different idiosyncratic orders, e.g., I, V, III, II, IV. By definition, in a purely serial process the nth location is not reported better than chance until the exposure duration at

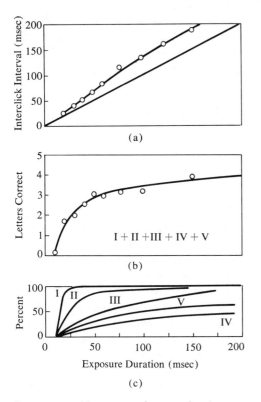

(a)

(b)

I + II + III + IV + V

(c)

Exposure Duration (msec)

FIGURE 3 (a) The apparent duration of the letters in a letter-noise presentation. Abscissa is the exposure duration of the letters. Ordinate is the duration of an interval between clicks which was judged equal to the visual letters. Data for one typical subject. (b) The total number of letters reported correctly. Five letters were presented, one in each location, I to V. (c) The percent of letters reported correctly, shown individually for each location, I to V.

sures, may be interpreted as evidence of an essentially parallel process for letter-recognition.[1] This process gives the illusion of being serial because the different locations mature at different rates (cf. Glezer and Nevskaia, 1964; Sperling, 1963). These findings are taken into account in Model 3 (Figure 4).

MODEL 3

In Model 3, the scan-rehearsal component of Model 2 is subdivided into three separate components. The first of these is a scan component which determines—within a limited range—the sequence of locations from which information is entered into subsequent components. The extent to which the subject can vary his order of scanning is a current research problem. In very brief exposures, the variation in scanning may be limited to changing the rate of acquisition at different locations—information processing beginning simultaneously at all locations. On the other hand, the overall rate of information flow through the scanner must be limited.

The second new component is the recognition buffer-memory. It converts the visual image of a letter provided by the scanner into a "program of motor-instructions," and stores these instructions. This program of motor instructions, when it is executed by the rehearsal component, constitutes rehearsal. The impor-

which the n-1th location is reported with maximum accuracy is exceeded. The observation that all locations begin to be reported at better than chance levels even at the briefest expo-

[1] An alternative interpretation is that the scan is serial but the order varies from trial to trial and/or there is great variability in the processing time per item. We tentatively consider that interpretation to be unlikely because (a) the modal scan pattern is highly repeatable from session to session and (b) parallel processing of other aspects of the stimulus is occurring, e.g., of its orientation, overall length, brightness, etc.

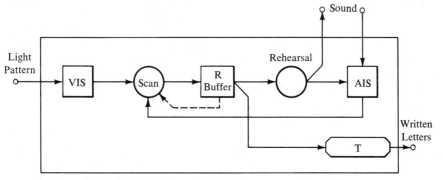

FIGURE 4 Model 3. (See Figure 2) R-buffer = recognition buffer-memory.

tant idea embodied in the recognition buffer-memory is that the program of motor-instructions for a rehearsal can be set up in a very short time (e.g., 50 msec for 3 letters) compared to the time necessary to execute it (e.g., 500 msec for 3 letters).

The recognition buffer is efficient partly because the programs for rehearsing several letters can be set up in it simultaneously. However, the major gain in speed derives from the assumption that setting up a program to rehearse a letter is inherently a faster process than executing the program, i.e., rehearsing the letter. In fact, the biological organization of motor systems is extremely hierarchical. Thus the program in the recognition buffer could be a program to call a program, etc., and the ultimate representation at the top of such a pyramid could be called quickly.

The rehearsal component executes the rehearsal, which then is entered and remembered temporarily in auditory storage. The memory of the rehearsal in auditory storage is scanned, the auditory image is converted to motor-instructions in the recognition buffer, and a second rehearsal is executed. This loop continues until the response is called for and the letters are written down. I know almost nothing about the translation of the memory of a letter to its written representation except that it occurs, and therefore must be represented in the model. It has been represented in parallel with rehearsal because writing a letter so often is accompanied by vocalization.

Consciousness in the Memory Models

One can know the contents of the consciousness of another individual only insofar as they are expressed by his behavior, particularly by his verbal behavior. In the models, this structure would induce us to look for evidence of consciousness at the level of the rehearsal unit. However, one also must admit that a person who is unable to speak or act may still retain consciousness. The critical aspect of the contents of consciousness is that they normally are

capable of being verbalized or acted upon. Within the limits of the tasks for which Model 3 was proposed, we can identify the contents of the scan component with the contents of consciousness. This is because the scan component contains the information upon which actions are performed.

There are several inferences to be drawn from this identification. When contents of visual memory are not scanned before they fade away, they never become conscious. And, we are unconscious of all contents of our auditory memory except those being scanned. Another inference is that if the contents of a memory cannot be scanned, they are not accessible to consciousness.[2] The untransformed contents of the recognition buffer-memory are not accessible to scanning and therefore never the objects of consciousness. This makes it indeed a mysterious component; it cannot be observed directly either from within or from without! However, this inaccessibility should not surprise us. It is axiomatic that in any system which examines itself there ultimately must be some part of the mechanism which is inaccessible to examination from within. The recognition buffer-memory is such a part in the human memory mechanism.

Summary

Experimental data are considered from a simple task in which an observer looks at letters and then writes them down. Three models are proposed. Model 1 consists of only two components: a visual memory for the letters and a motor translation component to enable copying a visual memory onto paper. Model 1 is inadequate because the visual image is shown not to persist until the time of reproduction. Model 2 corrects this deficiency by incorporating the

[2] In conceptualizing Sternberg's experiments, it is useful to assume that the recognition buffer-memory can be scanned for a minor aspect of its content, e.g., whether it contains an item which was entered much more recently than the others. A dotted line has been drawn from the recognition buffer to the scan component to indicate the possibility of this kind of scan.

possibility of subvocal rehearsal of the stimulus letters and an auditory memory for the rehearsal. However, Model 2 cannot account for performance with extremely short duration images because of the limit on the maximum rehearsal rate. The critical improvement in Model 3 is a more detailed specification of scanning, recognition and rehearsal, including a form of memory which is inherent in the process of recognition itself. Model 3 accounts for these data and incidently gives rise to some interesting inferences about the nature of consciousness.

References

Averbach, E. and G. Sperling, 1961. In C. Cherry (Ed.), *Information theory,* London: Butterworth, 196–211.

Cattell, J. McK., 1885. *Philos. Stud., 2,* 635–650.

Conrad, R., 1963. *Nature, 197,* 1029–1030.

Glezer, V. D. and A. A. Nevskaia, 1964. Doklady Academy of Sciences USSR, *155,* 711–714.

Landauer, T. K., 1962. *Percept. Motor Skills, 15,* 646.

Sperling, G., 1960. *Psychol. Monogr., 74,* No. 11, (Whole No. 498).

Sperling, G., 1963. *Human Factors, 5,* 19–31.

1.3 The Relation between the Visual Image and Post-perceptual Immediate Memory[*]

JANE F. MACKWORTH

Several authors have suggested that incoming stimuli are stored in two different ways: a preliminary very brief storage followed by a selective process leading to a somewhat more durable storage (e.g., Broadbent, 1958; Mackworth, 1959; Sperling, 1960). Sperling called the preliminary storage of visual information the visual image, but did not clearly distinguish between this and the classical concept of immediate memory. He showed that much more information was originally contained in the visual image than the S could completely report, and Averbach and Sperling (1961) suggested that the duration of the visual image was about 0.25 sec. Mackworth (1963) showed that the duration of report from the visual image was constant at about 1–2 sec so that the number of items reported depended on the rate at which they could be identified.

* *Journal of Verbal Learning and Verbal Behavior,* 1963, vol. 2, pp. 75–85. This work was supported by the Defense Research Board under PCC No. D77–94–20–46 (H.R. No. 247).

It appeared from previous experiments that there should also be a relation between the immediate memory span and the rate of reading items. Brener (1940) has shown that the immediate memory span is largest for digits; letters come next, then colors, and finally shapes show the shortest memory span. Mackworth (1963) has reported that the rates of reading digits, letters and colors fell in the same order, digits being read fastest. Sampson and Spong (1961) showed that when conventional and unconventional digits were used as visual stimulus material, more of the conventional digits were recalled and they were also read faster. The first aim of the experiments described below was to show that there was a relation between the visual image report, the rate of free reading, and the immediate recall for different materials. A hypothesis is suggested to account for these relationships, and experiments are described which investigate the relationship between the interference effects of excess material on recall of the different materials.

The amount recalled from materials presented for brief periods is closely dependent on the duration of the presentation as well as on the number of items shown simultaneously (Mackworth, 1962a, b). Therefore, in order to compare immediate recall for different materials it is necessary to examine the effect of these factors. The length of message also plays an important part, since messages which are longer than the span give a smaller recall. Hence the experiments also consider recall from messages of equal length, recall from messages which are near the optimum length for each material and recall from messages which are too long.

Experiment I

METHOD

Experiment I was designed to give a broad view of the relation between types of material, exposure time per item, method of presentation, and amount recalled. Motion-picture films were used, each film showing only one of the four types of material, namely digits, colors, letters, or shapes. The letters were B, C, D, F, G, H, J, K, L, M. The colors were black, white, and the following Munsell colors: blue (5 PB 5/10), purple (5 P 5/10), brown (10 YR 5/4), yellow (5 Y 9/14), red (5 R 5/10), pink (10 R 8/4), orange (2.5 YR 6/14), and green (10 G 16/8). The ten shapes were square, cross, circle, star, wheel, triangle, heart, spade, club, and diamond.

Each film showed 24 messages of randomly selected members of one of the above vocabularies, each message being nine or ten items in length. The structure of the films has been described (Mackworth, 1962a). There were two methods of presentation: (i) the Single presentation, in which items were shown one at a time successively from left to right; and (ii) the Block method, in which all items in the message were displayed simultaneously. The total message times were the same for both presentations, i.e., 0.25, 0.50, and 1 sec per item, allowing up to 9 or 10 sec per message.

Eight housewives served as Ss; these Ss will be referred to as Group 1. Each S was shown a practice film first, and then, in Latin square order, two films of each material. After each message had disappeared, the S repeated aloud as much of it as she could, reporting the items in the order in which they appeared. The results were scored by the number of items mentioned in the correct order, whether or not wrong items were included among them.

After the memory test, Ss were asked to read aloud displays of ten items as fast as they could while the display remained visible. The answers were recorded on tape so that the duration of response could be measured.

RESULTS

Figure 1 shows for Group 1 the results for the Single and Block presentations, the three durations of exposure and the four kinds of material; Table 1 shows selected points from Figure 1 together with data for a second group to which reference will be made later. Performance for the digits is clearly much better

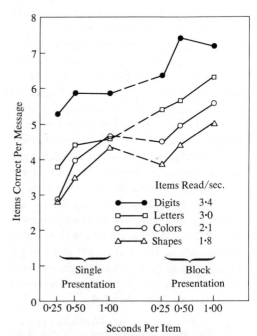

FIGURE 1   Amount recalled from messages of different materials following Single or Block presentation at three speeds.

TABLE 1

Response Characteristics for Different Materials

	DIGITS	LETTERS	COLORS	SHAPES
Group 1				
Reading Speed				
Items/sec	3.4	3.0	2.1	1.8
Items Correct Per Message				
Block (5 sec message)	7.6	5.7	5.0	4.4
Single (10 sec message)	5.9	4.7	4.7	4.4
Group 2				
Reading Speed				
Items/sec	3.6	3.1	2.2	1.9
Items Correct Per Message				
Block (4 sec message)	7.9	6.6	5.3	4.9*
Single	5.8	5.0	4.6	4.1
0.1 sec Exposure	4.7	3.5	3.1	2.6

* Critical difference ($p < 0.01$) = 0.5 items.

at all levels of presentation. Analysis of variance on all the recall data (Table 2) showed that although the S interactions were somewhat inflated, the main effects, tested against the S interactions, were highly significant. In recall, each kind of material was significantly different from the others. An effect will be called significant throughtout this paper when it differs from chance at the level of $p < 0.01$ or better. The interaction among presentation, material, and time is inflated but not significant. In particular the difference between the letters and the colors disappears at the one sec Single presentation.

TABLE 2

Analysis of Variance, Data from Experiment I

	df	MS	F
Presentation (P)	1	618.0	51.5*
Time (T)	2	160.5	88.8*
$P \times T$	2	1.0	
Material (M)	3	406.7	73.9*
$P \times M$	3	7.3	
$T \times M$	6	6.0	3.3*
$P \times T \times M$	6	3.2	2.1
Subjects	7	111.7	
$P \times S$	7	12.1	
$T \times S$	14	1.8	
$P \times T \times S$	14	3.6	2.4*
$M \times S$	21	5.5	3.7*
$P \times M \times S$	21	3.0	2.0
$T \times M \times S$	42	1.8	
$P \times T \times M \times S$	42	1.5	
Residual	1344	1.5	
Total	1535		

*$p < 0.01$.

TABLE 3

Individual S's Correlation Coefficients (r) *for the Various Measures, Groups 1 and 2*

	READING SPEED × RECALL					BLOCK 4-SEC RECALL BY	
	GROUP 1		GROUP 2				
Ss	BLOCK 5 SEC.	Ss	BLOCK 4 SEC.	0.1 SEC.	SINGLE	0.1 SEC.	SINGLE
1	0.81	9	0.96	0.94	0.75	0.97	0.71
2	0.96	10	0.83	0.70	0.76	0.96	0.98
3	0.92	11	0.97	1.00	0.78	0.96	0.85
4	0.83	12	0.98	0.89	0.75	0.99	0.84
5	0.71	13	0.94	0.96	0.91	0.93	0.99
6	0.90	14	0.98	0.99	0.87	0.97	0.91
7	0.98	15	0.89	0.98	0.95	0.96	0.95
8	0.64	16	0.92	0.75	0.98	0.98	0.97
Correlations across Ss							
Group 1	0.61	Group 2	0.50	−0.03	0.69	0.51	0.82

The differences among the reading speeds for different materials (as shown in Table 1) were significant. For each *S* correlation coefficients (*r*) were calculated between the Block recall at 0.50 sec per item and the speed of reading; all were positive (first column in Table 3) giving a significant probability that for individual *S*s a positive correlation exists between material recall and reading rate.

Experiment II

METHOD

In view of the significant interactions found in the previous experiment it was necessary to study the effects of presentation rate and message length.

This experiment was undertaken to study the recall for the different materials with the Single presentation. Different lengths of message were used to determine the optimum. For the digits, a film showing eight or nine digits in a message was used. These messages appeared for durations of 0.75, 1, and 1.50 sec per digit. One film was prepared for each of the other three types of material. Messages were five, seven, or eight items long, shown for durations of 1, 1.50, and 2 sec per item.

The vocabulary of letters was C, F, H, J, K, M, Q, R, S (these were more distinguishable by name than the previous set). Vocabularies of nine colors (omitting orange from the colors used in Experiment I) and shapes (omitting wheel) were used.

Eight housewives (Group 2) served as *S*s in this experiment and in Experiment III. Each received the four materials in a different order.

RESULTS

Table 4 shows the results for the various materials at the different presentation rates and the different message lengths. Analysis of variance was carried out on the data for letters, colors, and shapes and is shown in Table 5. While the *S* interactions were somewhat inflated, the effect of the material was still significant. Seven *S*s recalled more letters than colors, and seven *S*s recalled more colors than shapes. The effect of rate of presentation was not significant, nor was the message length. A significant *S* × Message Length interaction is to expected, since the optimum length would differ with the different abilities of the *S*s. Eight items per message gave the best average recall for all the materials. It can therefore be concluded that the recall of digits, letters, colors, and shapes will be in that order when they are presented as separate items.

Experiment III

It has been reported (Mackworth, 1962b) that when eight or twelve digits are shown simultaneously for varying lengths of time, the curve representing the relation of the amount reported for each message to the exposure duration can be divided into two sections; the first represents the increase in the amount that the S can name to herself as the exposure duration is increased, while in the second part the amount reported increases with duration at a much slower rate, and is presumably limited by the memory of what has been named. Since different kinds of material are read aloud at different rates, it was of interest to determine the precise effects of the exposure duration on recall for the different materials with the Block or simultaneous display. Experiment III was therefore undertaken to prepare curves relating recall to exposure duration in greater detail, and also to examine "the visual image report" which is measured by the number of items that the S reports from an exposure duration of 0.1 sec. It has been shown (Mackworth, 1963) that the visual image report is proportional to the rate of reading items aloud, because the duration of the report is approxi-

TABLE 4

Average Number of Items of Various Types of Materials Recalled When Presented Singly in Message Sets of Different Length (Group 2)

MATERIALS	NUMBER OF ITEMS PRESENTED PER MESSAGE			
	5	7	8	9
Digits			5.8	5.7
Letters	4.5	4.9	5.1	
Colors	4.2	4.4	4.6	
Shapes	4.0	4.1	4.1	

TABLE 5

Analysis of Variance of Data from Experiment II Single Presentation of Three Materials (Items) at Different Speeds (Times) and Message Lengths

SOURCE	df	MS	F
S	7	33.1	
Item (I)	2	41.2	15.0*(I/SI)
Time (T)	2	1.7	
Message (M)	2	9.8	
IT	4	2.3	
MI	4	1.2	
TM	4	3.2	
ITM	8	3.4	6.2*
SI	14	2.7	4.8*
ST	14	2.1	3.6*
SM	14	2.4	4.1*
STI	28	0.4	
SMI	28	3.0	5.4*
SMT	28	0.9	
STIM	56	0.55	
Residual	662	0.58	
Total	863		

* Significant $p < 0.01$.

mately constant. Therefore, it was expected that there would be significant correlations between the Block span, the rate of reading the different materials aloud, the visual image report as measured in Experiment III, and the Single span as measured in Experiment II.

METHOD

The method employed has been described (Mackworth, 1963). Briefly, sets of ten, eight, six, and four items were prepared, each set containing only one of the four kinds of material. The Ss were shown a set in a tachistoscope for a certain duration of exposure and, after the display had disappeared, reported as many as they could remember in the correct order. Each S was tested for five sessions. In the first they were shown five sets of each kind of item at each of five exposure durations, ranging from 0.1 sec to 3 sec. This was the practice session. The Ss were told the names of the colors and shapes beforehand. In each of the other four sessions each S received two of the four kinds of material. Ten messages were shown for each

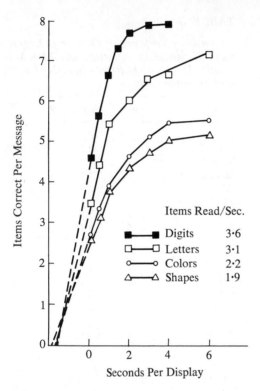

FIGURE 2 Amount recalled from messages of different materials following Block presentation at various durations of exposure.

kind of material at each of seven exposure durations, ranging from 0.1 sec to 6 sec as shown in Figure 2. The message lengths employed were those which gave optimal recall for that S at each duration, as indicated in the practice sessions. This procedure was repeated with the same material in a later session. The eight Ss received the four kinds of material in two different Latin square orders. First each S received the four materials in one order, and then in the reverse order, in an attempt to balance the effect of order for each S. The exposure durations were given systematically, with two messages at each duration in descending followed by ascending order.

In the last session Ss were shown five sets of ten items for each kind of material, and were asked to read them aloud as fast as possible while the display remained visible. These reports were recorded on tape and later the duration of each response was measured to obtain the reading speed of each S.

The Ss were the same as those employed in Experiment II (Group 2) so that the Single span measure also could be correlated with the others.

RESULTS

Figure 2 shows the amount reported for the different kinds of material after the different durations of exposure. These data suggest [as discussed previously (Mackworth, 1962b)] that for the short exposures, reports were limited by the amount that could be read, but for exposures of 4 sec or more the limit was set by the quantity that could be remembered of what had been read, since an additional 2 sec exposure adds very much less than the four or more extra items that could be read by the S in this time. Therefore, the recall score for the Ss at this exposure duration has been selected as a measure of the Block verbal memory. It can also be seen from Figure 2 that the increase in exposure duration from 2 to 4 sec for digits makes very little difference to the recall score, so that the fact that digits can be read nearly twice as fast as the colors or shapes has little effect on the amount recalled at 4 sec.

Figure 2 also shows that the time-axis intercepts for all curves are about −1.6 sec. This supports the idea that the S can continue to recognize material from a visual image which remains for 1–2 sec after the display has disappeared (Mackworth, 1963). Table 1 shows various measures obtained from Figure 2 in relation to the free reading speed. The Single recall figures are averages from Table 4. It can be seen that the four kinds of material fall into the same order on all these measures.

The next step was to determine the correlations between these measures within Ss. Correlations within each S in Group 2 (Table 3) were all positive; the lowest correlation coefficient (r) was 0.70. By the most conservative estimate the probability of obtaining this value by chance as the lowest of eight estimates for each comparison of a pair of measures is less than 10^{-5} when the hypothesis predicted a positive correlation a priori. Thus it can safely be said that for individual Ss a high correlation may be expected between any of the different kinds of measures shown in

Table 1. The position was different, however, when correlations were determined between the totals for different Ss. Table 3 shows the various correlations that were calculated, and the only significant correlation between Ss was that between the Block (6 sec) recall and the Single recall for Group 2.

DISCUSSION

The absence of any correlation between the 0.1 sec measures and the speed of reading across Ss was particularly striking. On examination it was found that at the 0.1 sec exposure duration the Ss fell into two groups. In one group the four Ss gave mean rates of errors per message of 0.1, 0.1, 0.2, and 0.2, respectively. The other four Ss showed error rates of 1.0, 1.4, 1.5, and 1.6 errors per message. It appeared that Ss adopted different levels of certainty for their replies. The four Ss who gave the more accurate answers were ranked in the same order for both speed of reading and amount reported from 0.1 sec exposure, but the others showed an average speed of reading which was slower than that of the first group, while their report from the 0.1 sec exposure was longer. Some of the errors seemed obviously related to a partial fading of the trace; for instance, when the last mentioned shape was a heart it was often identified as a diamond, and a pale color such as sky-blue might be identified as pink, while an eight might be called a three. Thus Ss who were prepared to give answers with lower certainty not only got more answers correct, but conveyed some information even in their wrong guesses. The 4 sec recall for these Ss, however, was slightly lower than for the more accurate Ss, suggesting that the fading of the visual trace was no longer a factor in limiting the report.

As mentioned in the introduction, it is thought that the amount reported from the visual image is directly limited by the rate of recognizing the materials, since the trace is believed to fade at the same rate regardless of the material. This recognition rate is believed to set the limit for the reading rate also, since even digits can be named much faster than 3 per sec when there is no uncertainty about them.

On the other hand, the immediate memory recall appears also to be related to the rate of reading, but there is evidence that this is not a direct limitation. An extra 2 sec, beyond sufficient time to read the whole message, has very little effect on the recall. It is thought that the immediate memory is limited by the same factor that limits the rate of free reading. This factor may be strength of association between the picture and its name, or the difficulty of discriminating within members of a set, which is particularly evident with colors, or the strength of the links between various members of a set due to past experience, e.g., almost all digits are equally likely to be next to any other (with certain exceptions such as dates) but the consonants chosen have a very low association value. Thus the difficulty may lie either in the naming of particular items or in the forming of links between them.

When the pictured items are read into the memory store, they must be named in the same way as when they are read aloud. The S recalls the names rather than the pictures in immediate memory, whereas when reporting from the visual image he is probably naming aloud directly from a pictorial representation of some kind. Thus it seems desirable to draw a distinction between the visual image report and the immediate memory report. The immediate memory span might be defined theoretically as the longest message which can be completely recalled after only one hearing or reading. Such a definition is not operational, but a method of obtaining this value theoretically will be described.

It is proposed that the process of immediate memory can be divided into four parts: (a) reading into store; (b) storing; (c) other intervening activities; and (d) reporting. It is suggested that for the usual brief period over which immediate memory is measured there is a constant quantity of some factor which is used for all these processes. This is called the A-factor, because it is believed to be related to attention. Then if a' is the total A-factor used for process (a) and so on, $a' + b' + c' + d'$ A-units are used for all these processes involved between presentation of the first and recall of the last of a set of items. This total, which is constant, is arbitrarily taken as 100 A-units.

It is quite likely that the relation between successive items is exponential, as suggested by the data of Peterson and Peterson (1959), and Hellyer (1962). For simplicity, however, it will be considered that at least the initial loss can be represented by a straight line, and the following experiments were designed to see how far this simplification is reasonable.

Suppose that M items are read into store, each item taking a A-units to read. Then the total A-units for reading into store are Ma, leaving $100 - Ma$ for storage and report, if there is no other intervening activity. Since no distinction will be drawn between storage and report in this paper, the two processes will be treated as one and called recall. It is assumed that each item requires s A-units for recall, so that when N items are recalled, they use Ns A-units. Thus $Ma + Ns = 100$. If the memory span represents the longest message which can be repeated correctly, then for the span M and N are both equal to the length of the span, M' items. Thus $M' (a + s) = 100$, so that the total number of A-units per item is the reciprocal of the memory span.

If the length of the message is increased beyond the memory span, items will be forgotten, so that by comparing the recall from different message lengths it should be possible to obtain values for the terms in these equations. If $a = Ks$, so that both a and s are linearly related to the reciprocal of the memory span, then the lines relating M and N for different materials and different Ss should be parallel. It is necessary to be sure that Ss actually read the whole message in order to obtain accurate readings.

Experiment IV

METHOD

This experiment was designed to investigate the effect of the message length on the recall of letters. It resembled one by Brown (1958). Capital letters were typed in rows of two letters each and shown on a memory drum at a rate of one pair every sec. The message lengths ranged from 5 letters to 20 letters, an extra single letter being shown to obtain lengths of 5, 7, and 9 letters. The eleven different message lengths (shown in Figure 3) were presented in random order, followed by three other random orders. In the second session another four sets of messages were presented. Each S received the same material. The Ss read the letters aloud as they were presented. At the end of the message they were required to repeat the letters in the order in which they were presented. It was emphasized that they had to begin at the beginning, and that they would obtain no score for repeating only the last few. This procedure was adopted in order to prevent the development of a running memory span technique, by which Ss deliberately forget earlier material when the number of letters presented is greater than the span. The 12 Ss were high-school girls, ranging in age from 15 to 17 years. The letter vocabulary was the same as that used in the previous experiment.

RESULTS

There was a great range in the ability of the Ss, some having a maximum recall nearly twice as long as others. Figure 3 shows the results. The center line represents the mean values for all Ss together. Letters were scored as correct if they occurred in the correct order, up to the first consecutive double error. Thus the recall scores represent a measure of how much of the beginning of each message Ss could recall. The figure also shows the means for the four best and the four poorest Ss.

DISCUSSION

One of the sources of irregularity appeared to be the extra single letter that occurred in the seven- and nine-letter messages. However, it seems that there is a range immediately after the maximum which can be reasonably fitted with a straight line. There also appears to be an abrupt change in slope when all but about two letters have been forgotten. It is clear that the theory is inadequate to explain the whole curve. It does, however, appear to fit the initial loss of most of the message.

Applying the equation $Ma + Ns = 100$, where M is the message length and N the

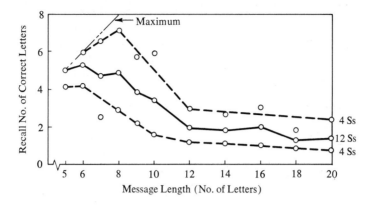

FIGURE 3   Effect of message length on the recall of letters presented at a rate of one pair per second.

number recalled, to the three initial slopes shown in Figure 3, the following values are obtained. For the mean of 12 Ss, from the values for 8 and 12 letters presented it was calculated that $a = 7.0$ A-units per item read into store, and $s = 9.3$ A-units per item stored and reported, giving a theoretical memory span of 6.2 letters from the equation: memory span $= 100/a + s$. For the best four Ss, $a = 6.6$ and $s = 6.5$, with a span of 7.5 letters. For the worst four Ss (from the values for 6 and 10 letters) $a = 8.0$ and $s = 12.5$, with a memory span of 4.9 letters. Thus the worst Ss have more difficulty with both the reading into store and the storage and report than the best ones do. These calculations will be discussed further in connection with the next experiment. They may be compared with those calculated from the experiment by Brown (1958) mentioned above. His Ss recalled 5.4 letters from 8 presented and 2.0 from 14 presented, giving values of $a = 5.75$ and $s = 10.0$. A slightly lower value of a is to be expected, since recall for a message length of 14 letters is found, on the second, flatter part of the curve.

Experiment V

METHOD

Since it had been determined that the initial slope could reasonably be regarded as linear, even with a detailed analysis, the following experiment was designed to examine the same range of message lengths in a more general way with the four materials. Cards were prepared each carrying one message of one of the four materials, digits, letters, colors, and shapes, using the same vocabularies as in Experiment III. The message lengths were 6, 8, 10, 15, or 20 items per message. The letters and digits were shown with message lengths of 8 to 20 items, while the shapes and colors were shown with 6 to 15 items per message. This was done because it was desired to obtain the maximum score and also the most information about the range.

The cards were shown in a tachistoscope, and Ss were asked to read the messages aloud. As they reached the last item but one, the message disappeared. This was an attempt to prevent the Ss from observing the beginning of the message while they were naming the end, since the technique does permit this possibility. It is necessary to be sure, however, that the S has read the whole message at least once, and the use of the memory drum is not suitable for studying the Block presentation. As soon as the message had disappeared, Ss were required to repeat the message from the beginning, giving the items in the same order as they were read. Two messages for each condition were given consecutively. The 16 conditions (4 message lengths × 4 materials) were given in 4 random orders in 1 session, followed by another 4 random orders in another session. Each S was given different random orders. The Ss were high-school girls as before.

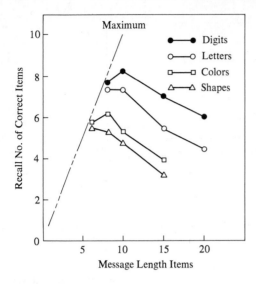

FIGURE 4 Effect of message length on the recall of different materials, with Block presentation long enough to allow the message to be read aloud once.

RESULTS

The results are shown in Figure 4. Analyses of variance were carried out on the appropriate sections of the data as follows: (1) the results for the 10, 15, and 20 items per message for the digits and letters (the 8-item length was omitted since it was submaximal); (2) the results for the 8-, 10-, and 15-item messages for the colors and shapes; and (3) the results for the 10- and 15-item messages for all four materials. The analyses showed in each case that there were significant main effects of the material (tested against S interactions) and the message length, while the interaction between these effects was extremely small. This indicated that the curves of Figure 4 were effectively parallel for the four materials. The S interactions were not significant in the data for the letters and digits, nor in the pooled data for all four materials. They were significant in the data pooled for shapes and colors, but sufficient evidence is presented in this paper to indicate that the differences between colors and shapes for group recall are reliable.

DISCUSSION

The same calculations can be applied to these data as before, and are shown in Table 6. It can be seen that reading into store takes approximately a quarter of the total A-units. It is interesting to compare these results with the previous experiment. There the storage value for the letters was 9.3 for the group, almost identical to that found here, while the reading value was much higher, i.e., 7.0 A-units, about twice as great as the value of 3.4 for reading letters presented simultaneously. It was shown

TABLE 6

Calculation of Constants for Memorizing and Forgetting Four Kinds of Materials (Ma + Ns = 100 A-units, Memory Span = 100/(a + s) Items)

MATERIAL	MESSAGE LENGTH (M) (NUMBER OF ITEMS)	RECALL (N) (NUMBER OF ITEMS)	READING (a) (A-UNITS/ ITEM)	RECALL (s) (A-UNITS/ ITEM)	a + s (A-UNITS/ ITEM)	THEORETICAL MS (ITEMS)
Digits	10 15	8.3 7.0	2.5	9.0	11.5	8.7
Letters	10 15	7.2 5.4	3.4	9.2	12.6	8.0
Colors	8 15	6.3 3.9	3.8	11.2	16.0	6.3
Shapes	8 15	5.3 3.1	4.0	13.0	17.0	5.9

in Experiment I that the presentation of items one at a time had a marked effect on recall as compared with presentation in Block form. It seems possible that difficulties of reading into store, which probably includes the formation of links between successive items, is increased as items are presented in smaller groups.

An example of the application of these calculations to another experiment may be given. An experiment was reported (Mackworth, 1962c) which studied the effect upon recall of searching for digits on a manual switchboard (manual recall). The mean number of digits reported from Block dictating recall was 7.8, from Block manual recall 6.3, from Single dictating recall 6.6, and from Single manual recall 5.5. The method of presentation was the same as used in Experiment I in this paper. By making a few reasonable assumptions the following results are obtained. First, it is assumed that Block s (A-units per item stored and verbally reported) $= 3a$, as suggested in Table 6.

Thus for Block verbal report

$$10a + 7.8s = 100, \text{ and } 3a = s$$

For Single verbal report

$$10a' + 6.6s = 100$$

For Block manual report

$$10a + 6.3 \, (s + x) = 100$$

where x is the extra A-units per item to locate a digit on the board.

These calculations give

$$a = 3.0, s = 9.0, a' = 4.0, \text{ and } x = 2.0$$

For Single manual report

$$10a' + 5.5 \, (s + x) = 100$$

and again, $x = 2.0$.

Thus it seems that the number of extra A-units used to find a digit on the board is independent of the number of digits recalled.

General Discussion and Conclusions

It was suggested in the introduction that a relation exists between the number of items reported from very brief exposures (visual image report), the rate of reading the items, and the length of the memory span for the items. In fact, there is a relation between recall from all durations of exposure and both kinds of presentation (Single and Block) and speed of reading, as tested within each S. It has also been suggested that recall of visual material can be divided into a number of different processes. First there is a very brief store, the visual image, from which materials may be recognized. The amount that can be recognized is limited by the rate of recognition, if the duration of the visual image is constant. Items are recognized and named either from the visual image or, more commonly, from the display, and read into store. It is suggested that there is a constant quantity of A-factor available for short periods of testing, arbitrarily fixed at 100 A-units, some of which is employed to read the material into store and some for storing and reading out of store. The difficulty of reading into store is similar to the difficulty that limits the rate of free reading, and it appears that the difficulty of reading into store, as calculated in A-units from the loss due to reading longer messages, is related to the reciprocal of the memory span. Hence, there is a relation between the memory span or recall under various conditions and the rate of reading. Therefore, since the visual image report is dependent on the rate of reading, it is also related to the memory span for a particular S and a particular material.

Summary

These experiments investigated the relations between immediate recall of visually presented digits, letters, colors, and shapes and various methods of presentation, in order to illustrate the use of a simple equation which gave a quantitative analysis of the factors involved. This analysis was based on the assumption that the whole of the recall task involved a constant amount of a quantity called the A-factor.

Experiment I compared Single and Block presentation at three speeds (0.25 to 1 sec/item); Experiment II studied Single presentation at slower speeds (1 to 2 sec/item) with shorter messages. Experiment III studied Block presentation at exposures from 0.1 to 6 sec. Eight Ss, housewives, were used for each experiment. The speed of reading the materials was measured. There was a positive correlation for each S between the various measures. Experiment IV examined the effect of message length up to 20 letters upon the recall of letters. The Ss were 12 schoolgirls. The relation between message length and recall could be regarded as a rapid loss of most of the message, followed by a slow loss of the last few items. A linear equation seemed to be a reasonable fit for the first part of the curve. This was $Ma + Ns = 100$, where M = number of items given, and N = number of items recalled.

Experiment V examined the effect of message length upon recall of the four materials. The Ss were ten schoolgirls. The recall loss due to excess material was approximately linear and parallel for the four materials.

It was concluded that report from the 0.1 sec exposure was made from a rapidly decaying pre-perceptual visual image, and was limited by the speed of recognition, which itself was limited by the same difficulties that affect the postperceptual immediate recall.

References

Averbach, E., and Sperling, G. *Information theory.* London: Butterworths, 1961. Pp. 196–211.

Brener, L. R. An experimental investigation of memory span. *J. exp. Psychol.,* 1940, *26,* 467–482.

Broadbent, D. E., *Perception and communication.* New York: Pergamon Press, 1958.

Brown, J. Some tests of the decay theory of immediate memory. *Quart. J. exp. Psychol.,* 1958, *10,* 12–21.

Hellyer, S. Supplementary report: Frequency of stimulus presentation and short-term decrement in recall. *J. exp. Psychol.,* 1962, *64,* 650.

Mackworth, J. F. Paced memorizing in a continuous task. *J. exp. Psychol.,* 1959, *58,* 206–211.

Mackworth, J. F. The effect of display time on the recall of digits. *Canad. J. Psychol.,* 1962, *16,* 48–56. (*a*)

Mackworth, J. F. The visual image and the memory trace. *Canad. J. Psychol.,* 1962, *16,* 55–59. (*b*)

Mackworth, J. F. The effect of the response upon the immediate memory span. *Canad. J. Psychol.,* 1962, *16,* 120–127. (*c*)

Mackworth, J. F. The duration of the visual image. *Canad. J. Psychol.,* 1963, *17,* 62–81.

Peterson, L. R., and Peterson, M. J. Short term retention of individual verbal items. *J. exp. Psychol.,* 1959, *58,* 193–198.

Sampson, H., and Spong, P. Handedness, eye dominance and immediate memory. *Quart. J. exp. Psychol.,* 1961, *13,* 173–180.

Sperling, G. The information available in brief visual presentations. *Psychol. Monogr.,* 1960, *74,* No. 498.

1.4 Short Term Memory Systems in Human Information Processing*

MICHAEL I. POSNER

Introduction

All human information processing requires keeping track of incoming stimuli and bringing such input into contact with already stored material. In the most general sense, short term memory (STM) systems refer to the storage capacity available to perform these functions within ongoing serial activity.

I believe that the study of STM has been ambiguous because one mechanism has been used to refer to three reasonably distinct features of such systems. The most common definition of STM relates to the interval between presentation and recall. That is, STM refers to the retention of new information over relatively brief periods of time, for example, up to one minute (Melton, 1963). The empirical feature which makes this temporal period distinct is that under proper conditions information can be lost so rapidly. This notion of STM closely fits some of the psychological theories which have been suggested relating to activity traces and consolidation processes (McGaugh, 1965).

The second sense in which STM has been used is a relatively direct representation of the stimulus, as opposed to memory systems, which involve symbolic recoding, such as storing the name or description of the stimulus. Broadbent (1958) certainly had this in mind when he placed his S system prior to his filtering mechanisms. This direct representation of information without verbal encoding is required to explain the learning and retention of many skills, such as tracking, which involve complex patterns of input and sequences of movement. Some such ability is also present in nonverbal organisms when they perform tasks like delayed matching from sample (Knorski, 1961). It is commonly agreed that such representational storage exists, at least in the form of visual after-images, for very short periods of time (Melton, 1963). It has been typical, however, to identify representational storage as a very early stage in information processing which decays in the order of a second or two unless coded into verbal form (Sperling, 1963). The present paper suggests that the degree to which a memory system involves direct representation or imagery is a question which is separable from the temporal course of information storage. Although it is true that the early stages of information processing involve more direct representation, it can be shown that images persist over intervals at least as great as those usually considered in STM studies.

There is still a third use to which a short term memory mechanism has been put (Hunter, 1964). This is the concept of an "operational memory" for information stored in long term memory which has been activated in the process of solving a particular problem. Suppose I ask you to add together the digits of your

* Reproduced by permission of *Acta Psychologica,* 1967, vol. 27, pp. 267–284. © North-Holland Publishing Co., Amsterdam. This research was sponsored by the National Science Foundation under grant GB 3939 to the University of Oregon.

telephone number. It is necessary to keep available the stored digits of the phone number during the course of producing their sum. The limitations of such operational memory are of considerable importance to the analysis of complex information processing, particularly that involved in many intellectual tasks. Despite much speculation (Alexander, 1965; Hunter, 1964), there is no reason to believe that the characteristics of the system involved in this process will be identical with those found in the usual STM studies.

In this paper I consider each of the uses of STM. First is the question of representational memory or imagery. Second is the temporal course of forgetting for verbal material. Third is the problem of reactivating information from long term store (operational memory). Each area presents its own peculiar problems, experimental analysis and empirical results. Fortunately, a general information processing model (Broadbent, 1958) provides a broad framework within which the analysis and comparison of these various STM systems can proceed.

Representational Memory

Some authors (Mackworth, 1964; Pollack, 1959; Sperling, 1963) have distinguished between memory systems which conserve most of the information present in the stimulus and those which involve verbal recoding of the stimulus properties. In the areas of motor skills (Adams and Dijkstra, 1966; Bilodeau and Bilodeau, 1961; Poulton, 1963) and thinking (McKeller, 1957) there is wide acceptance of the notion of information storage in the form of images. In this sense, an image is a relatively direct representation of the stimulus which might include spatial position and other detailed information which would not appear in a verbal description of the stimulus. One of the reasons imagery has been less well accepted in theories of memory is that it has not lent itself to exact specification and experimental control. In this section I shall review the experimental evidence for such representational memory systems and shall try to show how they can be tied in closely to a general analysis of human memory systems.

VISUAL

Sperling (1963) and Mackworth (1964) have presented evidence for the persistence of a visual image during the first one or two seconds after the off-set of a complex visual stimulus. Their results indicate that a common method by which the human subject operates is to encode visual material from a peripheral representational store to a central symbolic store by the operation of naming. These results suggest that the encoding and storage of letters and other forms involves an audio-speech system.

Sternberg (1963) and Neisser et al. (1963) have studied the processes of searching memory. In these studies the subject has stored an array of items and must report when some new target item is a member of that array. Sternberg found a linear relationship between the number of items in store and the time required to search them. This result is quite compatible with the idea of an auditory recoding of the visually presented information. Neisser, however, found that after considerable practice subjects showed no increase in the length of time to search memory as a function of the number of stored items. This finding is difficult to understand on the basis of a search through an orally encoded set of stimulus items. However, the level of practice necessary for the Neisser result suggests the importance of the array being well integrated as a unit within long term memory and, therefore, the experiment does not provide a test of the question of the energy form of material in STM. It does suggest limitations to the concept of serial search of memory for highly overlearned material.

Chase and I (1965) attempted to provide a more direct analysis of the question of auditory storage of recent information. We compared two different search tasks. In one task, called *Visual Comparison* Search, the array, consisting of one to four items in a circle, and the test, consisting of a single letter at the circle's center, were presented simultaneously. In a second condition, *Memory-Search,* the subjects had 10 sec to memorize the array, which consisted of one to four items. At the end of the 10 sec they received a one-second warning signal and then a single test letter. In both conditions they were required to respond as rapidly as possible, indicating whether or not the test letter was a member of the array. We recorded the latency between test letter presentation and the pressing of a yes or no key. Three populations of letters were used: neutral, high acoustic confusing, and high visual confusing. Our expectation, in accordance with the Sperling (1963) model, was to find that the rate of search in the visual comparison task was solely a function of visual confusability and was unrelated to auditory confusability, while in the memory search the reverse would be true. By allowing sufficient time to enunciate the array on each trial, we expected to produce favorable conditions for finding an acoustic confusion effect. We hoped we could then fractionate the interval between the simultaneous presentation of target and array (visual comparison) and the 10-second delay (memory search), and, by a psychophysical procedure, observe successive stages of acoustic encoding of the stimuli. The results are shown in Table 1. In the first place, the rate of search per item for the visual comparison and memory search tasks was similar when neutral letters were used. Moreover, the visual comparison search was greatly affected by visual confusability. However, the memory search task showed no effect of acoustic confusability and a small effect of visual confusability.

TABLE 1

Search Rates (msec/item) for Visual and Memory Search Tasks Using Letters of Neutral, High Auditory and High Visual Similarity[*]

TASK	LETTER POPULATION		
	NEUTRAL	VISUAL	AUDITORY
Visual comparison search	62	130.1	57.7
Memory search	53	70.8	59.7

[*] After Chase and Posner, 1965

These results seem to indicate that the storage of the letters of the array did not involve an acoustic recoding.

Gibson and Yonas (1965) have reported findings similar to ours in that search of visual material was shown to be unrelated to factors which would be expected to interrupt or reduce the ability to search an acoustically encoded stimulus.

These findings do not refute the Sperling-Mackworth results. It is still to be expected that in many tasks, information which is taken in visually is then encoded in a verbal form. However, they do raise serious doubt as to whether such recoding is a necessary condition for the storage of information in STM.

AUDITORY

The representational storage of auditory stimuli has not been as frequently considered. Broadbent (1958) explored a paradigm in which digits were presented in pairs, one to each ear, with the time between successive pairs varying. Under some conditions, clarified later by a series of experiments (Bryden, 1964; Yntema and Trask, 1963), performance was best when information was reported ear by ear rather than in temporal order. In most cases, the subjects chose this method in free recall. Recall by ear is not always superior, particularly when information content is varied. However, those conditions in which ear order is superior seem to suggest that the digits presented to one ear are being held in a peripheral system during the period of time that the information presented to the other ear is being processed and stored. This phenomenon is similar to the old idea of prior entry, but extends over a temporal period of 1 to 2 sec.

Support for the direct representation of auditory information comes from the study of the time error in auditory psychophysics. Koester (1947) has shown that for both loudness and pitch the variability of subjects' judgments is a direct function of the time between the presentation of the standard and the comparison stimulus. In these situations, if a verbal encoding of the original standard were used, one would expect to find no forgetting over a brief unfilled interval. Bachem (1954) has shown that the increase in variability may continue over an entire week, thus suggesting that representational storage of material of this type need not be only short term.

Pollack (1959) has varied independently the number of alternatives from which a message (single word in noise) could be drawn and the number of alternative responses which are later provided to the subject. Pollack found that the accuracy of recall was independent of the message uncertainty but varied inversely with the response uncertainty. He suggested that subjects were storing a representation of the stimulus which could be used for categorization up to fifteen minutes later. Similarly, Crossman (1958) reports a study in which a single word was played at half-speed on a tape recorder. Providing subjects with reduced response alternatives, improved performance out to 40 sec.

Warren and I sought to compare delay of auditory information with comparable delay of visual information, using a method of presenting simultaneous audio-visual digits adapted from Broadbent and Gregory (1961). The interval between the onset of successive digit pairs was varied from 2 to ¾ sec. The visual simulus followed the onset of its auditory pair by less than 30 msec and remained on during the 300 to 400 msec necessary to present the various audio-digits. Three orders of recall were used: temporal order, that is, pair by pair; ear followed by eye; and eye followed by ear. The results are shown in Table 2. Broadbent's

predictions concerning the advantage of channel order over pair by pair are borne out and this advantage tends to increase as the speed increases. In addition, delaying the report of auditory information resulted in much less error than delayed reporting of visual information.

Of course, these results do not indicate that the subject is storing a pure representation for either modality. However, if Broadbent's hypothesis of successive attention to the two channels is correct for this situation, the data do suggest that it is the auditory rather than the visual information which can best survive a delay in a peripheral storage system.

REPRESENTATION IN SKILLS

Perhaps the best place to look for representational memory is in the area of skill learning. Research in simple motor tasks has been an exception to the general verbal emphasis in STM. Bilodeau et al. (1962) developed a lever positioning task in order to study retention of simple motor movements. Adams and Dijkstra (1966) using a similar task, obtained rapid forgetting for blind positioning movements over unfilled intervals from 5 to 120 sec. Both the overall level of accuracy and the large forgetting with brief unfilled intervals led them to suggest that information was not stored in the form of verbal labels. The image showed a strong tendency to become fixed or consolidated over successive trials.

TABLE 2

Percentage of Digits Recalled in Error for Simultaneous Audio-Visual Presentation

ORDER OF RECALL	MODALITY	INTER-STIMULUS INTERVAL (SEC)			
		2	1	¾	AVE.
Temporal order	Audio	17.9	16.6	19.2	17.9
	Visual	36.3	38.7	40.9	38.7
Delay auditory	Audio	18.8	14.6	10.9	14.7
	Visual	14.2	11.3	15	13.5
Delay visual	Audio	10.9	10.9	11.7	11.1
	Visual	27.1	20.8	22.1	23.3

Broadbent (1958) contrasted retention of motor movement with information processed through other sensory modalities and suggested that the former might be shown to require less central processing capacity since it gave rise to fewer reports of conscious rehearsal.

Konick and I (Posner, 1966; Posner and Konick, 1966) attempted to explore this proposition. We used two tasks which seemed to differ in degree of conscious involvement and which were important components of many skills. The two tasks were the retention of a position on a line (visual-location) and the retention of the distance of a motor movement conducted without visual information (kinesthetic-distance). In our study we varied not only the length of time in which the information was to be stored but also the processing capacity available to the subject during the interval. Processing capacity was controlled by interpolated tasks of differing levels of difficulty, as measured by the amount of information reduction which the task required. All the interpolated tasks involved manipulation of digit pairs, varying from a simple recoding, writing down the digits, to a complex transformation, in which the subject simultaneously classified each pair as to whether it was high or low and odd or even. Retention intervals varied from 0 to 30 sec.

The results were confirmed in several replications and bore up under statistical analysis. Both visual-location and kinesthetic-distance showed orderly forgetting as measured by changes in accuracy of reproduction over the delay intervals. However, the conditions under which they showed forgetting were dramatically different. Kinesthetic-distance showed forgetting even when the subject did nothing during the interpolated interval. Moreover, the rate of forgetting was completely independent of the complexity of the information processing interpolated between presentation and recall. Visual-location showed no forgetting at all if the subject was at rest, and rather dramatic increases in forgetting as the difficulty of the interpolated activity increased. The introspections of the subjects suggest that the position of the circle on the line gave rise to rather vivid imagery which could be maintained with great accuracy, provided the subject was free to concentrate during the interval. However, once his attention was distracted by complex processing, the image was lost. The justification for considering imagery in these tasks is clearest for kinesthetic-distance, where forgetting occurs even over an unfilled interval. For visual-location tasks, the argument for imagery rests upon the extreme accuracy of the subjects' recall, plus the rather striking introspective reports.

More recently, I have replicated this difference in retention of visual and kinesthetic images, using two otherwise similar tasks. Four different groups were used: visual-location, visual-distance, kinesthetic-location and kinesthetic-distance. All groups used one lever box to make the movement and another to reproduce it. However, in the visual condition subjects could see their hand, while in the kinesthetic, they could not. Our previous work (Posner and Konick, 1966) showed that adding kinesthetic information to visual information did not modify the effect obtained with pure visual information. The location conditions involved reproducing the movement from a starting position identical to the initial movement, while the distance conditions always involved reproducing from a new starting position. Only two levels of interpolated processing, rest and classification, and two delay intervals, 0 and 20 sec, were used.

For all conditions, regardless of interpolated task, there were significant changes over the 20-second interval. In every case (except the visual-location with interpolated rest) these were in the direction of increased error. Visual-location with interpolated rest showed *improved* retention after 20 sec. The finding of improved retention over time in the visual-location task may seem strange at first, but it also occurred in our previous work and is probably due to the consolidation of the image over time which allows it to resist the interference effects of the reproduction. It seems to me evidence for the non-verbal character of the image in the visual-location condition, since any simple verbal encoding would be to show either forgetting or improvement over an unfilled interval.

The changes in error over time (forgetting scores) are shown for each condition in Table 3. In general, the previous findings are replicated both for visual-location and for kinesthetic-distance. The classification task clearly increases forgetting for visual-location, and does not for kinesthetic-distance; in fact, the trend is opposite. Collapsing across type of movement, the visual tasks show clear effects of interpolated task difficulty, while the kinesthetic tasks do not. An analysis of the forgetting scores shows a significant ($p = .025$) modality by interpolated task interaction. The location conditions tend to show more effect of interpolated task than do the distance conditions, but this is not significant ($p = .1$).

TABLE 3

Mean Increases in Error (mm) over 20 Second Delay Interval for all Conditions with Interpolated Rest and Classification

Movement Condition	Interpolated Task	
	Rest	Classification
Visual-location	−2	9.1
Visual-distance	2.4	6.7
Kinesthetic-location	4.1	6.3
Kinesthetic-distance	6.7	2.5
Visual (combined)	.2	7.9
Kinesthetic (combined)	5.4	4.4
Location (combined)	1.0	7.8
Distance (combined)	4.5	4.6

The evidence indicates that representational storage exists for all modalities. It is, perhaps, most closely associated with the very early stages of processing of information, but we certainly cannot reject the hypothesis that permanent storage can be in this form. It is clear that retention functions for images may be rather different, depending upon their sensory source. The ability to control the attention of the subjects during the retention interval appears to be one fruitful method of relating the retention of images to more general theories of information processing.

Temporal Effects in Short-Term Memory

The temporal course of forgetting is best understood for materials which are in verbal form. Most materials studied in the laboratory are coded by the subject in words. Certainly the data from the study of visual materials (Conrad, 1964; Sperling, 1963) and the data previously presented from simultaneous audio-visual presentation argue strongly for the importance of verbal encoding if visual information is to survive in the presence of continued input. This section will be confined to materials stored in verbal form and to the factors which govern retention over brief intervals.

ENCODING

The first stage in the memory process involves getting external stimulation into some sort of internal code. Sperling (1963) suggests that both visually and aurally presented information is read into an auditory information storage system at a very rapid rate. This basic notion has received support from studies of acoustic confusion errors in recall of visual material (Conrad, 1964), correlations between overt reading rates and memory span (Mackworth, 1964), and correlations between recall errors and the description lengths for nonsense patterns (Glanzer and Clark, 1963).

The idea of an auditory information storage system suggests that storage of information presented aurally is subject to simpler encoding than visually presented information. This prediction receives support from two findings. First, increasing rate of presentation tends to improve auditory immediate memory performance (Conrad and Hille, 1958; Posner, 1964) and to depress visual performance (Mackworth, 1965). Since encoding or acquisition strategies require time, this indicates that visual storage involves more of such strategies. Moreover, the facility with which subjects can delay one channel in a dichotic listening study (Broadbent, 1958; Bryden, 1964) contrasts markedly with their inability to do so when simultaneous material is presented separately to the two eyes (Sampson and Spong, 1961). The data on bi-sensory stimulation presented earlier reveals this same asymmetry.

The degree to which encoding differences affect studies of memory varies with the task. Haber (1964) has shown that retention of pairs of visual forms varying in several dimensions depends upon whether a dimension or object code is used. Norman (1966) has argued that differences in rate of presentation affect only acquisition and not retention in memory. How-ever, Norman only required single responses from his subjects for each stimulus list pre-sented. It is not clear how recall of single items is related to memory span studies in which sub-jects must recite all that they can remember from a just previously presented list. In auditory memory span studies, increased rate of presenta-tion actually improves performance. While it is certain that when complex encoding is in-volved, acquisition effects must be separated from memory effects, it is less clear how a strict separation can be made in the usual memory span or delayed recall tasks.

REHEARSAL

Once material has been encoded by the sub-ject it may then be practiced by him. In this sense rehearsal may be thought of as being re-lated to learning. In fact, it has been shown that the total time spent in learning a list of items is much more important than the way the time is divided between length of trial (rehearsal) and number of trials (Bugelski, 1962; Murdock, 1965). However, rehearsal may be less effective than a new learning trial since rehearsal usually implies repetitions. Peterson (1966) has shown that spacing repetitions leads to better retention than massing them for all but the shortest recall intervals. Thus massed rehearsal may be of less value than well spaced trials.

According to some memory models (Waugh and Norman, 1965), the effect of rehearsal is to present an opportunity for information to be sampled from the short to the long term store. The effectiveness of a period of rehearsal de-pends most extensively upon the amount of information present in STM at the time. When

the number of items in store are well below the memory span (Brown, 1958) a period of free rehearsal will prevent any loss during a subse-quent period of rehearsal prevention. However, when the amount of information in store ap-proaches the memory span, considerable op-portunity for free rehearsal (Conrad, 1960) does not necessarily lead to any improvement in recall score.

In most analyses of STM, rehearsal is equated with repeating things to oneself. From an in-formation processing viewpoint, it may be useful to consider rehearsal as demanding a portion of the limited information processing capacity of the subject (Broadbent, 1958). Thus in verbal tasks it may involve covert speech while in other situations (Posner and Konick, 1966b) something more akin to concentration may be appropriate. Such a view of rehearsal reduces the necessity of relying upon introspec-tive accounts or instructions to determine if a subject is rehearsing. Moreover, it allows the comparison of memory systems, both human and animal, which are clearly verbal with those which are not. It has been shown that the amount of capacity required for interpolated tasks is systematically related to the amount of forgetting (Posner and Rossman, 1965). This holds true whether or not the information in store is similar to that of the interpolated ac-tivity (Posner and Konick, 1966a). This is not to say that the similarity of the interpolated task cannot vary the rate of forgetting, but simply that it is not the only determinant, and that one must take into consideration the diffi-culty or attention value of the interpolated activity.

LOSS OF INFORMATION

Many investigators have found a rapid loss in correct recall of subspan series over brief periods when rehearsal is prevented (Brown, 1958a; Peterson and Peterson, 1959). Whether or not such losses can be interpreted as evi-dence of a basic decay mechanism has been disputed. I believe that the evidence from the non-verbal memory systems reviewed in the last section support the utility of decay notions for these systems. The improved retention with rapid presentation in studies of the auditory memory span (Conrad and Hille, 1958; Howe, 1965; Mackworth, 1965; Posner, 1964) suggests that a decay factor is also appropriate for verbal materials.

There are also, however, compelling empirical reasons for postulating an important role for interference factors in governing the level of retention. Despite deep and prolonged distraction, forgetting is not an inevitable consequence of rehearsal prevention. For example, Keppel and Underwood (1962) have shown that on the very first trial of a memory experiment there may be only small, if any, differences in retention between 3 and 18 sec of counting backwards. It is not until the subjects have had two or three trials that preventing rehearsal causes a rapid fall-off in performance. Indeed, it has been shown that if a subject is switched to a new type of material after a number of trials, the probability of error on the first trial after the switch is greatly reduced (Wickens et al., 1963). In addition, varying the similarity of information between presentation and recall has also been shown to affect performance (Wickelgren, 1965). These findings indicate the importance of retroactive and proactive inhibition in the study of short term memory. These interference phenomena have been used by some to suggest that short term memory and long term memory do not differ (Melton, 1963; Postman, 1964). Such interpretations suggest that no information would be lost from short term memory in the absence of specific retroactive and proactive effects. The data, however, do not force such a position. For example, Brown (1958b) and Conrad (1966) have suggested that interference effects found in short term memory are the result, rather than the cause, of forgetting. In the next two sections I would like to examine some of the theoretical implications of the interference effects which have been found.

RETROACTIVE INHIBITION (RI)

Wickelgren (1965) found highly significant increases in RI when he varied the phonemic similarity of the interpolated material to that in store. He has also shown that such RI increases systematically with number of inter-

polated items up to 16 letters. Wickelgren (1966) interprets his results as indicating that RI effects are of two kinds. First, they cause loss of information from the stored items due to their prevention of subsequent rehearsal. Second, the similarity of the RI items has a specific effect upon the trace.

It should be noted that specific RI effects due to similarity, have not been easy to demonstrate using dimensions of similarity other than acoustic confusability. Kennelly (1941) showed that increasing the number of common elements or the number of items of a common class (formal similarity) did not lead to increase in RI. More recent studies (Dale and Gregory, 1966) have shown very small, if any, effects of varying formal and semantic similarity upon the amount of RI. Such findings argue that the short term memory coding system depends upon acoustic properties, at least for letters, words, and other verbal material. In order to understand the role of similarity in causing forgetting, it will be helpful to turn to the phenomenon of proactive inhibition.

PROACTIVE INHIBITION (PI)

In many ways, the study of proactive inhibition provides a better opportunity to observe specific interference due to similarity, since proactive materials do not act to prevent rehearsal. A few facts about PI are different than those found in RI. First, PI effects build up to a maximum quite rapidly (Melton, 1963; Peterson and Gentile, 1965). Intrusions in recall occur primarily from the last two or three trials. Even within a single list, Wickelgren (1966) found that PI effects increased only up to a total of four items prior to the critical item. Second, PI effects occur more easily over a wider variety of material than do RI effects. Effects of varying semantic (Loess, 1965) and formal similarity (Brown, 1958a), as well as acoustic similarity, have been readily demonstrated.

What are the mechanisms by which PI operates? The two general, theoretical positions which have developed are decay theory (Brown, 1958b; Conrad, 1965) and interference theory (Melton, 1963; Postman, 1964). Though these theories are usually thought to be in conflict, they provide a similar mechanism for PI. They both argue that PI occurs as the result of competition between traces at the time of recall. However, their reasons for the increase in competition over the recall interval are quite different. Decay theory suggests that the stored trace decays over the interval, thus allowing less discrimination between it and similar traces. Interference theory suggests two alternative explanations of increased PI over time. First, the correct trace might be unlearned or extinguished due to the intervening activity. This hypothesis applies directly only when the intervening activity involves learning, and only when the S–R relationships between the original and intervening learning can be specified as obeying the A–B, A–C paradigm. If unlearning is postulated to occur much more generally, it becomes operationally equivalent to decay. Interference theories place more stress on a second mechanism which postulates the spontaneous recovery of competing associates which were inhibited at the time of presentation of the new material. This mechanism accounts for increased PI over time but has been difficult to demonstrate directly (Koppenaal, 1963).

Several recent findings shed some light upon the possibility of accounting for PI by response competition. Peterson (1966) presents evidence from a study of recall of trigrams after intervals of up to 18 sec. Subjects were informed as to the correctness of their first responses and were allowed to make subsequent guesses. They were able to improve their recall slightly after an initial error, but were by no means able to find the correct responses in all of the trials. Peterson suggests that in some cases the correct responses were simply not available.

Conrad (1966) also presents evidence on response competition at the time of recall. He used series of four visually presented consonants, followed by a period of digit reading, which was either 2 sec (6 filler digits) or 7.2 sec (18 filler digits). He compared the error matrix at the two intervals. Essentially, Conrad found that the error matrix at the short interval was predictable from acoustic confusions and that errors at the long interval were significantly more random than those at the short interval.

These two results pose considerable problems for a theory of PI based solely on competition at the time of recall. It is difficult for an interference account to handle the lack of availability at recall and the predominance of acoustic confusion errors at the short interval. Moreover, Conrad (1966) suggests a modification in decay theory so that loss of information occurs along the dimensions which are used to discriminate among items stored in STM. This view will be discussed again shortly.

All the models proposed so far rely on competition at the time of recall to account for the effectiveness of PI. I have presented some experiments (Posner, 1966; Posner and Konick, 1966a) which challenge this assumption. These experiments show that the effectiveness of PI, as measured by the degree of acoustic similarity between letters, is a function of the time an item is in store and is independent of the item's strength. In order to vary the strength of the stored items, the capacity available for rehearsal was controlled. In contrast to this, all trace comparison views predict that effectiveness of interference depends upon the strength of the stored item in comparison with the competing items. The results of these studies suggest that the rate of decay of the stored trace is a function of the similarity of items presented within a short temporal period. This view, in which similarity of stored materials affects the rate of decay, is called the "Acid Bath" view.

The "Acid Bath" idea is in accord with most (Posner, 1963; Postman, 1964) of the evidence usually adduced to support both decay and interference theories. Since it is a decay theory, it predicts loss of information over time, but the amount of interference governs the rate of such loss. The "Acid Bath" notion seems to demand that information be coded, upon entry, into dimensions of similarity, and that similar items be related in storage so that they interact more strongly. This implies an associative STM system. Wickelgren (1966) has presented the strongest arguments for such an associative STM memory system rather than one in which information is stored, based only on temporal order. His studies showed that memory for items repeated within a series was different than would be predicted by two independent stored representations. This suggests that incoming information is sorted and stored, based on important input dimensions. Many recent studies of STM have also provided direct evidence for such a position (Rudov, 1966; Yntema and Trask, 1963). Moreover, this sorting or dimensionalization at the time of input is in accord with the filtering principles which have played an important role in recent studies of attention (Broadbent, 1958). The "Acid Bath" suggestion is also related to Conrad's view that decay exists along the dimensions used to store and discriminate items in STM. Presumably, both the likelihood and the rate of decay depend upon the encoding rules used to describe the stimuli.

Operational Memory

The previous sections have emphasized the capacity for retaining information in STM. Recently, investigation of retrieval mechanisms have received increased attention (Norman, 1966; Reitman, 1965). These studies raise the problem of an "operational memory" or the capacity available for the active reinstatement of permanently stored information. Many authors have suggested that a basic factor in problem solving is the difficulty of grasping several things actively at the same time. This is true when the items are permanently available within the long term store or in a static display. For example, Simon and Kotovsky (1963) in studying serial completion problems, suggest that the basic limitation in solving such problems is the number of items which must be processed together in order for the subject to infer the correct generating rule. In that study the problems were present in a static display. Nevertheless the limitations of operational memory remain.

Broadbent (1958) gives some recognition to the area of retrieval by providing feedback from the rehearsal system to the peripheral memory. However, his model does not indicate whether material permanently stored in long term memory is temporarily returned to STM during a mental operation. Hunter (1964) does suggest this possibility by indicating that operational memory may have the same limits as the more conventional STM system. He says, "Limitations of short-term memory also raise difficulties for highly accomplished thinkers. The solving of a complex problem in, say scientific research, involves novel combination of ideas, that is, the bringing together of various items of evidence into a unitary pattern of unaccustomed relationships. Now this coherent pattern may comprise a large number of component relationships which must, so to speak, all be brought to mind together and at nearly the same time. Such holding together of components—comprehending—requires the collective recalling of the components. In other words, the activity of comprehending may be limited by short term memory."

This represents the third sense in which STM has been used. In this sense, it has profound implications for many areas of human information processing. However, operational memory limitations have not been shown to be identical or even closely related to those discussed in the previous section. The operations which define the STM systems for incoming information all involve the empirical fact that with rehearsal prevented, information will be lost over time. Operational memory limitations surely are not of the same type. One does not permanently lose his address even if he is interrupted immediately after reciting it. Thus, the hypothesis that operational memory is like STM with respect to *recall errors* is clearly false. That is, stored information is not removed from LTM and transferred lock, stock and barrel to STM when it is activated. However, there might still be some tendency for recently activated information to be more susceptible to interference than if it had been dormant in long term memory.

Ellen Rossman and I set about to test this hypothesis. We taught four groups of subjects an identical list of nonsense items by a standard paired associate method. Two days later, when about 60% of this material was still available in their long term memories, we brought them back to the laboratory. At this time, one group received a single presentation of the original stimuli, while a second group received a single anticipation learning trial on the original material. These two reinstatement groups then learned an interfering list and finally relearned the original list. A third group learned the interfering list and relearned the original list, but had no reinstatement trial, and a fourth group only relearned the original list without any interpolated learning. The results are shown in Table 4. They are quite simple. There is no evidence that the reinstatement groups are any worse on the first trial of relearning (in fact, they are better) than the group which had interpolated learning without reinstatement. Since the group which had only the stimuli reinstated did as well as the group which had both the stimuli and responses reinstated the results do not appear to be due entirely to additional learning during reinstatement. There is clearly no support for the notion that making the original learning active immediately before the interpolated learning, increases the effectiveness of interference.

TABLE 4

Mean Number of Correct Responses on First Trial of Relearning

GROUP	NO. CORRECT
I.L. No reinstatement	1.9
I.L. S reinstatement	3.4
I.L. S-R reinstatement	3.0
Control (No I.L., No reinstatement)	4.5

Although this experiment is not definitive, it is certainly in agreement with many findings (Postman, 1961) that the position of interpolated learning relative to original learning is not an important variable in memory studies. Thus, it does not seem that having a memory recently active, or reinstated, leads to a greater susceptibility to interference.

I have yet to find anyone, even the most devoted believer in the limitations of operational memory, who is surprised by my results. They are inclined to argue that information lost from an "operational store" does not show up in error because it can still be recalled from the long term store where it is also present. I agree that this must be the case; but it should be recognized that this suggestion requires defi-

nitions of what is meant by "operational memory" which are fundamentally different from those used to define STM. It calls for techniques of experimental analysis which are not identical with the measurement of recall errors typical of the experiments cited in the last section.

There has been relatively little experimental work which details the function of operational memory during the problem solving. Many of the experiments which have been conducted, such as on the role of memory in concept learning (Hunt, 1964), have involved memory for new incoming information as well as retention of previous hypotheses. One way to determine the limitations of operational memory is to study differences in the rate and quality of problem solving, concept learning or other tasks while varying the amount of material required from long term store. There have been some promising starts in this direction (Hayes, 1966). At present, however, operational memory has not been shown to be equivalent to STM.

Summary

In this paper, three aspects of the role of memory in information processing have been considered. Retention of images, preservation of verbal information over brief periods, and reactivation of material from long term store represent different senses in which the term STM has been used. The assumption that all of these involve a single system may be fruitful for some purposes, but may also lead to inappropriate generalizations. For example, it does not appear that imagery need be short term or that reactivated information is especially susceptible to interference. Nevertheless, a considerable amount is now known about each of these systems and both comparisons and contrasts may prove useful.

References

Adams, J. A. and S. Dijkstra, 1966. *J. Exp. Psychol., 71,* 314–318.

Alexander, C., 1964. *Notes on the synthesis of form.* Cambridge, Mass.: Harvard Univ. Press.

Bachem, A., 1954. *J. Acoust. Soc. Amer., 26,* 751–753.

Bilodeau, E. A. and I. McD. Bilodeau, 1961. *Ann. Rev. Psychol., 12,* 243–280.

Bilodeau, E. A., J. L. Sulzer and C. M. Levy, 1962. *Psychol. Mongr., 76,* 20.

Broadbent, D. E., 1958. *Perception and communication.* London: Pergamon Press.

Broadbent, D. E. and M. Gregory, 1961. *Quart. J. Exp. Psychol., 13,* 103–109.

Broadbent, D. E. and M. Gregory, 1964. *Quart. J. Exp. Psychol., 16,* 309–317.

Brown, J. 1958a. *Quart. J. Exp. Psychol., 10,* 12–24.

Brown, J., 1958b. In *The mechanization of thought processes.* Nat. Phys. Lab. Sympos. No. 10. London HMSO.

Bryden, M. P., 1964. *Canad. J. Psychol., 18,* 126–137.

Bugelski, B. R., 1962. *J. Exp. Psychol., 63,* 409–412.

Chase, W. G. and M. I. Posner, 1965. Paper presented at Midwestern Psychological Association Meeting.

Conrad, R., 1960. *Quart. J. Exp. Psychol., 12,* 45–47.

Conrad, R., 1964. *Brit. J. Psychol., 55,* 75–84.

Conrad, R., 1965. *J. Verb. Learn. Verb. Behav., 4,* 161–169.

Conrad, R., 1966. *J. Verb. Learn. Ver. Behav.* In press.

Conrad, R. and B. A. Hille, 1958. *Canad. J. Psychol., 12,* 1–6.

Crossman, E. R. F. W., 1958. Discussion on the paper by J. Brown. In *The mechanization of thought processes.* Nat. Phys. Lab. Sympos. London HMSO.

Dale, H. C. A. and M. Gregory, 1966. *Psychonomic Science, 5,* 75–76.

Gibson, E. J. and A. Yonas, 1966. *Psychonomic Science, 5,* 163–164.

Glanzer, M. and W. H. Clark, 1963. *J. Verb. Learn. Verb. Behav., 2,* 75–85.

Haber, R. N., 1964. *J. Exp. Psychol., 68,* 257–262.

Hayes, 1966. In B. Kleinmuntz (Ed.), *Problem solving: research, method theory.* New York: Wiley and Sons.

Howe, M. J. A., 1965. *Quart. J. Exp. Psychol.,* 338–342.

Hunt, E. B., 1962. *Concept learning.* New York: Wiley and Sons.

Hunter, I. M. L., 1964. *Memory.* Baltimore: Penguin Books.

Kennelly, T. W., 1941. *Arch. Psychol., 37,* No. 360.

Keppel, G. and B. J. Underwood, 1962. *J. Verb. Learn. Verb. Behav. 1,* 153–161.

Knorski, J., 1961. In J. F. Delafresnaye (Ed.), *Brain mechanisms and learning.* Oxford: Blackwell. 115–132.

Koester, T., 1945. *Arch. Psychol.*

Koppenaal, R. J., 1963. *J. Verb. Learn. Verb. Behav., 2,* 310–329.

Loess, H., 1965. Paper presented to Psychonomics Society.

McGaugh, J. L., 1965. In D. Kimble (Ed.), *The anatomy of memory.* Vol. *I,* 240–291.

McKellar, P., 1957. *Imagination and thinking.* London: Cohen and West.

Mackworth, J. F., 1963. *J. Verb. Learn. Verb. Behav., 2,* 75–85.

Mackworth, J. F., 1965. *Canad. J. Psychol., 19,* 304–315.

Melton, A. W., 1963. *J. Verb. Learn. Verb. Behav., 2,* 1–21.

Murdock, B. B., Jr., 1965. *J. Exp. Psychol., 69,* 237–240.

Neisser, U., R. Novick and R. Lazar, 1963. *Percept. and Motor Skills, 17,* 955–961.

Norman, D. A., 1966. Paper presented at XVIII International Congress of Psychology, Moscow.

Peterson, L. R., 1966. *Psychol. Rev., 73,* 193–207.

Peterson, L. R., 1966. Paper presented at the Symposium on Cognition, Carnegie Institute.

Peterson, L. R. and A. Gentile, 1965. *J. Exp. Psychol., 76,* 473–478.

Peterson, L. R. and M. J. Peterson, 1959. *J. Exp. Psychol., 58,* 193–198.

Pollack, I., 1959. *J. Acoust. Soc. Amer., 31,* 1500–1508.

Posner, M. I., 1963. *Psychol. Bull., 60,* 333–349.

Posner, M. I., 1964. *Brit. J. Psychol., 55,* 303–306.

Posner, M. I., 1966. *Science 152,* 1712–1718.

Posner, M. I. and A. F. Konick, 1966a. *J. Exp. Psychol.* In press.

Posner, M. I. and A. F. Konick, 1966b. *J. Org. Behav. Human Perf.* In press.

Posner, M. I. and E. Rossman, 1965. *J. Exp. Psychol., 70,* 496–505.

Postman, L., 1961. In C. H. Cofer, (Ed.), *Verbal learning and verbal behavior.* New York: McGraw-Hill.

Postman, L., 1964. In A. W. Melton (Ed.), *Categories of human learning.* New York: Academic Press.

Poulton, E. C., 1963. *Ergonomics, 6,* 117–132.

Reitman, W. R., 1965. *Cognition and thought.* New York: Wiley and Sons.

Rossman, E., 1965. *The effects of interference on a reinstated memory trace.* Unpublished Honors Thesis, Univ. of Wisconsin.

Rudov, M. H., 1966. *J. Exp. Psychol., 71,* 273–281.

Sampson, H. P. and P. Spong, 1961. *Quart. J. Exp. Psychol., 13,* 173–180.

Sperling, G., 1963. *Human Factors, 5,* 19–31.

Sternberg, S., 1963. Paper presented at the Psychonomics Society.

Simon, H., and K. K. Kotovsky, 1963. *Psychol. Rev., 70,* 534–546.

Waugh, N. C. and D. A. Norman, 1965. *Psychol. Rev., 72,* 89–104.

Wickelgren, W. A., 1965a. *J. Verb. Learn. Verb. Behav., 4,* 53–61.

Wickelgren, W. A., 1965b. *Quart. J. Exp. Psychol., 17,* 14–25.

Wickelgren, W. A., 1966. *J. Exp. Psychol., 71,* 396–404.

Wickens. D. D., D. G. Born and C. K. Allen, 1963. *J. Verb. Learn. Verb. Behav., 2,* 440–445.

Yntema, D. B. and F. P. Trask, 1963. *J. Verb. Learn. Verb. Behav., 2,* 65–74.

1.5 Short-Term Visual Storage*

STEVEN W. KEELE   WILLIAM G. CHASE

A series of experiments by Sperling (1960) and by Averbach and Coriell (1961) suggested a short-term visual store. Their tasks involved brief tachistoscopic exposures of information followed after a variable interval by some indicator signalling S to report a specific part of the information. Sperling presented his Ss with two or three rows of letters for 50 msec followed at various intervals by one of two or three tones indicating which row to report. He found that over delays between the array and tone ranging from 0 to 500 msec, report accuracy fell from about 9.1 items to memory span accuracy of about 4.3 items. The memory span was determined by asking the S to report all the items he could regardless of the row they occurred in. Thus, with the probe technique, Sperling was able to demonstrate that Ss have much more information available than can be reported by the memory span technique. Since this information is available only for about ½ sec, the memory span technique is too slow to demonstrate this storage. Averbach and Coriell (1961) in a similar experiment using a visual marker found the same sort of decay function.

In a recent study by Eriksen and Steffy (1964), a circular arrangement of six Xs and Os was presented briefly and followed after a delay by an arrow pointing at one of the six positions. They found no evidence for a decline

* Reproduced by permission of *Perception & Psychophysics,* 1967, vol. 2, pp. 383–386. This experiment was supported by PHS fellowship to S. W. Keele.

in the number of correct reports as the delay between the stimulus array and the indicator increased from 10 to 700 msec. Consequently, they questioned the concept of a short-term visual store.

There are at least two possibilities for the apparent discrepancy between the results of Eriksen and Steffy (1964) and those of Sperling (1960) and Averbach and Coriell (1961): (a) Sperling varied the number of stimulus items from three to 12. There was no decline in the percent correct when a partial report technique was used unless the number of items exceeded the memory span. Thus, there is no reason to expect that Eriksen and Steffy would find a decline with six items, especially when it is considered that binary items have a slightly larger memory span than a population including all the letters of the alphabet (Miller, 1956). (b) As pointed out by Eriksen and Steffy, the intensity of their stimulus arrays (3.7 ft-L) was much less than that of Averbach and Coriell (70 ft-L). It may be that the amount of information in store and the rate of decline of the amount in store is a function of stimulus intensity.

Preliminary investigations indicated that with a 6-item binary array, Ss could greatly reduce the number of positions attended to by using a simple coding strategy. By attending to the positions of one of the symbols, say the Xs, the S could remember the other positions by elimination. Thus, if the indicator arrow did not point to one of the attended positions, the S simply reported that the other symbol

61

was indicated even though he had not attended to it. It is therefore apparent that in order to exceed S's memory span, the information content of the arrays must be increased.

The present experiment replicates the main features of Experiments II and III of Eriksen and Steffy (1964). The information content of the arrays is greatly increased, however, by using 10 items rather than six and by using digits and letters rather than Xs and Os. In addition, the luminance of the stimulus array is varied over three levels.

Method

SUBJECTS

Three women and one man served as paid Ss in this experiment.

MATERIALS

Forty-two white stimulus cards were prepared with 10 black letters and digits arranged in a circle. The circle subtended a visual angle of approximately 2.5° and individual letters and digits subtended a visual angle of approximately .30°. Each of the 26 letters of the alphabet and the digits 1 through 9 occurred an equal number of times over the set of 42 arrays, but otherwise the items and order of items appearing on a stimulus were randomly determined.

A separate indicator card with a white arrow on a black background was constructed for each of the 10 positions. The arrow originated from a fixation point and pointed at one of the 10 positions. The distance between the head of the arrow and the position at which it was pointed was approximately .12°. The fixation point was a back-lighted pin hole in opaque black poster-board.

The three channels of a Scientific Prototype Tachistoscope were used to present the array, the indicator arrow, and the fixation point.

DESIGN

On the first day, Ss practiced on the high luminance with a 0 msec delay for 126 trials. On the following days there were three levels of stimulus intensity (3.7, 16, and 70 ft-L) and seven delays between the offset of the stimulus array and the onset of the arrow (0, 50, 100, 250, 500, 1000, and 5000 msec). A given delay was run in blocks of six trials and each of the seven delays was run at one level of intensity before shifting to another intensity. The order of the six-trial blocks for delay intervals was randomized for each luminance, and the order of intensities over the nine experimental days was counterbalanced by means of 3 by 3 Latin squares for each S. Thus there was a total of 54 trials for each S at each of the 21 delay by luminance conditions.

PROCEDURE

The Ss viewed the stimuli from a dark chamber that was screened from outside light sources. Prior to beginning each experimental session, Ss were dark adapted in the chamber for 4–5 min.

Upon a signal from E, the S looked into the tachistoscope, and when he could clearly see the fixation point he initiated a trial by pushing a microswitch. A stimulus array was exposed for 100 msec, followed by a blank interval of 0 to 5000 msec, and then exposure for 150 msec of an arrow pointing at one of the stimulus positions. The pre-exposure and delay fields were dark with the exception of the dim fixation point. The Ss were asked to report the letter or digit that the arrow had pointed at. Approximately 10 sec elapsed between report and the following trial.

At the end of 42 trials with one luminance, an independent estimate of the memory span was obtained. Each of five arrays was presented for 100 msec, and S reported as many letters as he could.

The Ss knew the delay and luminance conditions in advance but no feedback on the correctness of their responses was given until after all the trials at one luminance.

Results

The percent correct reports as a function of delay and luminance is plotted in Figure 1 along with the percentage of the 10 items cor-

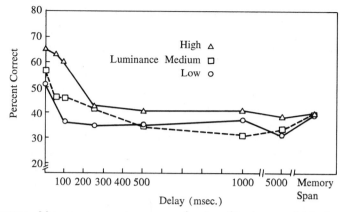

FIGURE 1   Mean percent correct reports as a function of luminance and delay interval.

rectly reported in the memory span condition. For each level of luminance the percent correct shows a monotonic decline from 0 to 250 msec. For delays of 250 msec or longer, performance has deteriorated to memory span accuracy of about four items. The amount of decline is greater for the high luminance than for the medium luminance, and the latter shows a greater decline than the low luminance. Large sample approximations of the 95% confidence intervals for each point in Figure 1 vary from ±5.7% to ±6.5%. An analysis of variance showed delay, luminance, and the delay by luminance interaction to be significant (F = 7.92, df = 6/18, error MS = .0071, p < .001; F = 14.65, df = 2/6, error MS = .0123, p < .005; and F = 2.21, df = 12/36, error MS = .0076, p < .05, respectively).

Figure 2 shows the mean percent correct for Ss as a function of delay interval. Large sample approximations of the 95% confidence intervals for each point vary from ±5.8% to ±7.7%. Both Ss 1 and 4 show large effects of delay whereas Ss 2 and 3 show only a slight effect of delay. The marked individual differences in these tasks thus limit the generality of the results.

A further analysis was performed only on the errors. To get enough error data, the errors were pooled for all Ss and all luminances and were further summed over 0, 50, and 100 msec delays (short), 250 and 500 msec delays (medium), and 1000 and 5000 msec delays (long). From the resulting three 35 by 35 stimulus-response tables were taken the three 26 by 26 submatrices of letter contingency tables. These

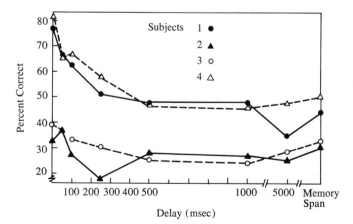

FIGURE 2   Mean percent correct reports for each S as a function of delay interval.

tables yielded approximately equal error distributions for the three delays: 582, 506, and 534 errors for short, medium, and long delays, respectively. These matrices were then converted to error proportion matrices by dividing the errors for a particular stimulus-response combination by the number of occurrences of that stimulus. Then the two error proportions for two letters when one was the stimulus and the other the response and vice versa were averaged, resulting in triangular matrices. These confusion matrices were then correlated with a triangular matrix giving the percent overlap in the contours for each possible pair of letters. This percent overlap matrix is a measure of the structural similarity of the letters. The resulting Pearson product-moment correlations were .37, .17, and .17 for the short, medium, and long delays, respectively. Two-tailed z-tests showed each of the correlations to be significantly greater than zero ($p < .01$). In addition, the correlation at the short delay was significantly greater than at the longer delays ($p < .01$).

Similar correlations were obtained between the present confusion matrices and an auditory confusion matrix reported by Conrad (1964). Those correlations were .02, −.04, and .09 for the short, medium, and long delays, respectively. None of these correlations were significantly different from zero.

Discussion

The present experiment demonstrated a large decrease in the accuracy of identification of visually presented information over short delays following the visual exposure. This rapid decline in accuracy was found even with luminance conditions similar to those used by Eriksen and Steffy (1964). It appears, therefore, that their failure to find a similar decline was a result of using a small number of binary items that could be rapidly processed before the information was lost from a short-term visual store.

The visual nature of this storage system is indicated by the fact that luminance interacted with delays producing better performance for higher intensity arrays at short delays. In addition, there were more visual confusions at short delays since the correlation between letter confusions and the overlap between letter forms was greater at short delays.

Conrad (1967) has recently shown that errors in the short-term recall of visually presented quadrigrams involved a large number of acoustic confusions. The number of acoustic confusions declined as the retention interval was lengthened over a period of several seconds. This finding is consistent with other recent evidence indicating that acoustic similarity is a potent source of interference in short-term memory tasks (Conrad, 1964; Wickelgren, 1965, 1966; Posner and Konick, 1966.)

The fact that there was no evidence of acoustic confusions in the present experiment suggests that short-term visual storage is a separate system from that studied in short-term memory experiments where retention of material is studied over longer intervals. These findings are consistent with Sperling's (1963) model which postulates two systems: (1) a very brief visual storage system which holds a great deal of information for a short time (up to ½ sec) until it can be attended to, and (2) an auditory short-term memory where a limited amount of information is held for several seconds after it has been processed. Visual variables such as visual similarity and luminance would have their effect while material is still in the visual storage system, whereas acoustic and associative variables would have their effect after the information is processed and is in a short-term auditory store or more permanent memory.

Summary

The delay between the offset of a briefly exposed array of letters and digits and the onset of an arrow pointing at one of the array positions was varied from 0 to 5000 msec. In addition, the luminance of the stimulus array was varied over three levels. The Ss reported the item in the position indicated by the arrow. Luminance, delay, and the luminance by delay interaction were all significant. Performance monotonically decreased from a delay of 0 msec to a delay of 250 msec, but the percent correct remained fairly constant from 250 msec to 5000 msec. With delays shorter than 250 msec, high luminance arrays showed better performance.

References

Averbach, E., & Coriell, A. S. Short-term memory in vision. *Bell Sys. Tech. J.,* 1961, *40,* 309–328.

Conrad, R. Acoustic confusions in immediate memory. *Brit. J. Psychol.,* 1964, *55,* 75–84.

Conrad, R. Interference or decay over short retention intervals. *J. verbal Learn. verbal Behav.,* 1967, *6,* 49–54.

Eriksen, C. W., & Steffy, R. A. Short-term memory and retroactive interference in visual perception. *J. exp. Psychol.,* 1964, *68,* 423–434.

Miller, G. A. The magical number seven, plus or minus two: Some limits on our capacity for processing information. *Psychol. Rev.,* 1956, *63,* 81–97.

Posner, M. I., & Konick, A. F. On the role of interference in short-term retention. *J. exp. Psychol.,* 1966, *72,* 221–231.

Sperling, G. The information available in brief visual presentations. *Psychol. Monogr.,* 1960, *74,* No. 11 (Whole No. 498).

Sperling, G. A model for visual memory tasks. *Hum. Factors,* 1963, *5,* 19–31.

Wickelgren, W. Acoustic similarity and retroactive interference in short-term memory. *J. verbal Learn. verbal Behav.,* 1965, *4,* 53–61.

Wickelgren, W. Phonemic similarity and interference in short-term memory for single letters. *J. exp. Psychol.,* 1966, *71,* 396–404.

1.6 Decay of Visual Information from a Single Letter[*]

MICHAEL I. POSNER   STEVEN W. KEELE

A number of studies have found that information from complex arrays of visually presented items shows rapid decay in the 1st second after presentation (1). Such studies have led to the notion of a storage system for visual information which holds material for a brief period during the process of naming the stimuli (2). In this paper we present a technique which makes it possible to observe the decay of visual information from a single letter which has already been named.

In previous work (3), pairs of letters were exposed simultaneously within the fovea. The subject was instructed to respond, as rapidly as possible, whether the letters had the same name

* *Science,* October 6, 1967, vol. 158, pp. 137–139. Copyright © 1967 by the American Association for the Advancement of Science. This work was supported in part by NSF grants GB 3939 and GB 5960 to the University of Oregon.

or different names. The time to respond "same" depended upon whether the particular letter pair was physically identical (for example, AA) or whether it was not physically identical but had the same name (for example, Aa). The results indicated that subjects are able to respond to physical identity 70 to 100 msec more rapidly than to name identity, even for highly overlearned figures such as letters of the alphabet.

The present paper takes advantage of the differences in speed of response to physical identity and name identity. The first letter is always in memory while the second letter is present in the foveal field. If the differences in speed still obtain, it is possible to infer that visual information of the first letter, as distinct from the name, is in store. Changes in the relative speeds of physical and name identity over time can then be used to infer the availability of visual information from the first letter.

The stimulus population consisted of capital and lower case typewritten letters, A, B, F, H, and K. The letters were typed on a tape and viewed from a distance of about 46 cm on a Stowe Memory Drum. The ambient lighting approximated normal reading light and did not vary during the experiment. The first letter was exposed on the left side of the tape and remained present during the entire trial. Either simultaneously or 0.5, 1, or 1.5 seconds later a shutter was automatically raised and the second letter appeared at the right side of the tape. The first letter was always capital while the second letter could be either upper or lower case. The distance between the letters was 8.4 cm, subtending a visual angle of about 10°.

The subjects were 12 right-handed males who participated for 1 hour on each of 2 successive days. They were positioned in front of the drum with the index fingers of each hand resting upon microswitches. They were instructed to respond as quickly as possible after the second stimulus appeared. They were to respond "same" if the two stimuli had the same name and "different" if they did not. The "same" key was always assigned to the left hand.

Each trial began with the word "ready" presented verbally by the experimenter. About 0.5 second later the first stimulus appeared and was followed, after the indicated interval, by the second stimulus. The experimenter recorded the response, elapsed time, and provided feedback concerning errors and reaction time. The time between trials was about 6 seconds.

On each of the 2 days subjects received 160 trials each. The trials were divided into blocks of ten. For each block a given time interval between the first and second letter was used. The list of 160 trials consisted of 80 different letter pairs, 40 physically identical pairs, and 40 pairs which were not physically identical but had the same name. Within each session, subjects responded to 40 pairs at each interval. Each subject was assigned to one line of a random Latin square so that for a group of four subjects each particular pair was used once with each interval.

TABLE 1

Mean Reaction Time (msec) and Standard Errors (S.E.) for Responding to Letters Which Are Physically Identical (P), Have the Same Name (N), or Are Different (D), as a Function of Time Interval between Letters (Data are shown for performance on the second day only.)

MEAN AND S.E.	INTERVAL (SEC)			
	0	0.5	1	1.5
Type P				
Mean	879	505	582	609
S.E.	23	22	20	21
Type N				
Mean	966	563	629	628
S.E.	25	26	22	22
Type D				
Mean	928	558	615	629
S.E.	24	18	14	22

Mean and median reaction times for correct responses were calculated for each subject. Table 1 shows the overall means and standard error of the means for the second day's performance. Values are shown for each type of letter pair (physically identical, name identical, and different) at each delay interval. The data of Table 1 are based on ten letter pairs per subject at each time interval for physical identity and for name identity and twenty letter pairs for the "different" condition. Since error responses are excluded, these numbers vary slightly from subject to subject, depending on the number of errors which they made. However, overall error rate on the second day was only 4.8 percent. The general trend was for more errors to occur with the longer times. Results for the first day and for data based on medians are quite similar to those shown in Table 1.

In order to analyze the loss of visual information over time, two subtractive methods can be employed. The first involves subtraction of the time for physical identity responses from the time for name identity responses. This same-same method eliminates any differences between the time to respond with the same versus the different key. Another subtractive method is to subtract the physical identity "same" responses from the "different" responses. This subtraction is based on the assumption that the time to respond "different" includes time to check both physical and name identity. However, this method does involve differences between the time to use the left and right hand and other things that differ between the two responses (4). Figure 1 shows the results of these two subtractive methods. In both cases there is the steady decline in the relative advantage of the physical identity response over the name identity or different response.

The data for the same-same method seemed to be somewhat more orderly than for the same-different method, but both provide roughly similar functions. At time zero, the difference between physical identity and name identity is approximately 80 msec, which was about equal to that obtained with simultaneous foveal presentation.

The orderly subtractive data are obtained despite wide fluctuations in the absolute levels of the times obtained with different intervals. The mean time to respond to a physically identical pair when the two stimuli are simultaneous is nearly 900 msec. Of course, this must include the time for an eye movement from the first stimulus at the left side to the second stimulus at the right side of the tape. The time for the eye movement is removed when there is a delay period. Thus the delay conditions have mean times for physical identity which are close to half as long as that for the zero condition. There is also a tendency for all times to increase between 0.5- and 1.5-second delays. This increase in the absolute level of the times presumably reflects the increasing temporal uncertainty when subjects are required to wait for the second stimulus. This is a frequent finding in studies of reaction time (5).

The results described in the preceding paragraph are borne out by statistical analyses. An analysis of variance was performed on the data presented in Table 1. The analysis showed that the effects of interval (0, ½, 1, and 1½ seconds) and of type of stimulus pair (physical identity, name identity, and different) were both significant $P < .01$. A linear trend analysis was

run on the interaction between intervals and type of pair. This interaction is the curve displayed in Figure 1. The results showed a significant linear interaction between types and interval $(.025 > P > .01)$.

Not all subjects showed the orderly linear relationship reflected in the means. This may be owing to the relatively little data obtained from individual subjects and the local effects of order which were different for different subjects. There is, however, considerable uniformity, since out of 24 comparisons of name identity minus physical identity at zero and 0.5 second, 22 show a positive sign and only one shows a negative sign. A similar comparison of 12 subtractions of name minus physical identity at 1 second gives nine positive and three negative, and at 1.5 second, seven are positive and five negative.

It seems reasonable to conclude from the functions shown in Figure 1 that the visual information from the first letter shows a significant decay over time. The statistical analysis indicates that under these conditions the ad-

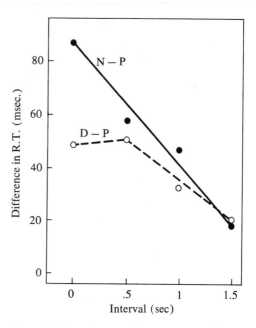

FIGURE 1 Decay functions for visual information obtained by use of two different subtractive methods: $N-P$ is name identity minus physical identity, and $D-P$ is different minus physical identity (see text). R.T., reaction time.

vantage of physical identity is lost after 1 to 1.5 seconds' delay.

Two objections might be raised to this conclusion. In the name identity condition the second letter is always lower case, and it could be that lower case letters are processed more slowly. This suggestion seems unlikely in view of the decay found over time. Moreover, there is no tendency for different responses which involve a lower case letter to be slower than those involving capitals only. The second objection concerns the fact that the first letter is present in the periphery of the visual field during the whole trial. It could be that subjects look at the first letter for a variable time as the interval increases. Subsequent studies have employed intervals which varied randomly over trials and conditions in which the first letter does not remain present. They have generally confirmed the findings presented here. It should be possible, however, to obtain much more accurate determinations of the decay functions than presented in this study.

The study reported in this paper differs considerably in methodology from previous reports concerning decaying visual information. Two differences appear to be crucial. All previous studies have used bright tachistoscopic flashes and have presented large amounts of information which cannot be encoded immediately. This study used reading light and only a single letter. The low error rate suggests that the subject has ample time to encode the letter. In view of these differences it is somewhat surprising that the decay rate obtained is so high and so closely resembles that in previous studies (1).

We believe that this rapid decay occurs only when the subject does not attempt to preserve the visual information from the first letter. In this experiment, the subject was given little or no incentive for preserving the visual information. He never knew whether he would receive a capital or small letter as the second stimulus. Thus, as the subjects report, the major way of preserving information seemed to be by way of verbalizing the letter and retaining the name during the interval. This should not be taken to mean that subjects would be unable to preserve the visual information of the first letter if, in fact, they desired to do so.

Summary

If the trace of a letter can be matched more rapidly with a physically identical letter (as in the pair AA) than it can be with a letter having only the same name (as in the pair Aa), then the trace must preserve the visual aspect of the letter. The visual information from a single letter decays in about 1.5 seconds if the task provides little incentive for preservation.

References

1. E. Averbach and A. S. Coriell, *Bell System Tech. J.* 40, 309 (1961); G. Sperling, *Psychol. Monogr.* 74, (whole No. 498) (1960); S. Keele and W. Chase, *Perception and Psychophysics* 2, 383 (1967).
2. D. E. Broadbent, *Perception and Communication* (Pergamon Press, New York, 1958); G. Sperling, *Human Factors,* 5, 19 (1963).
3. M. I. Posner and R. F. Mitchell, *Psychol. Rev.,* in press.
4. D. Bindra, J. Williams, S. S. Wise, *Science* 150, 1625 (1965).
5. E. T. Klemmer, *J. Exptl. Psychol.,* 54, 195 (1957).

1.7 Some Temporal Characteristics of Visual Pattern Perception*

CHARLES W. ERIKSEN   JAMES F. COLLINS

The visual perceptual system under certain circumstances is unable to resolve short time differences. Bloch's law relates to the fact that the perceived brightness of the stimulus is dependent not only upon its luminance but its duration. Recent work indicates that this critical duration over which time intensity reciprocity holds is valid not only for perceived brightness but also for form identification. In the latter case the values of the critical duration are somewhat longer than those found for luminance summation (Kahneman & Norman, 1964). These findings would imply that the visual perceptual system sums or integrates energy over the critical duration prior to the occurrence of the perception of a form or of a brightness magnitude.

Experiments upon perception of simultaneity and of perceptual rate have indicated a perceptual time unit generally in the region of 50–100 msec (see White, 1963, for an excellent review of these studies). These and the reciprocity studies have proven difficult to conceptualize.

* From: Charles W. Eriksen and James F. Collins, "Some Temporal Characteristics of Visual Pattern Perception," *Journal of Experimental Psychology*, 1967, vol. 74, pp. 476–484. Copyright 1967 by the American Psychological Association, and reproduced by permission. This investigation was supported by Public Health Service Research Grant MH-1206 and a Public Health Service Research Career Program Award K6-MH-22,014. This paper was presented in part at the Symposium on Temporal Factors in Vision and Visual Perception, June 1966, sponsored jointly by National Science Foundation and the Center for Visual Science, University of Rochester.

Attempts to deal with these temporal factors in perception have led to the conception of a psychological moment (Pièron, 1952; Stroud, 1956; White, 1963; White & Cheatham, 1959) that has many of the characteristics that have been ascribed to psychological time units by the philosophers Bergson (1913) and James (1890). Renewed interest in a psychological moment has come from research on backward and forward masking in visual perception. At least certain masking effects can be interpreted as a temporal summation of test and masking stimuli into a composite perception (Eriksen, 1966; Eriksen & Collins, 1965), and Boynton (1961) has suggested an explanation for temporal summation in vision and of masking phenomena in terms of a psychological moment.

Studies of temporal factors in visual perception, including the masking experiments, typically have dealt with brightness and acuity tasks and less frequently with form identification. However, Kahneman (in press) has suggested that the latter task as generally employed is essentially also an acuity task. In the present experiments we have employed a technique of stimulation that permits the study of the temporal development of organizational or integrational components in pattern perception. The first two lines in Figure 1 show what appear to be two random dot patterns. When these dot patterns are superimposed they yield the perception of the nonsense syllable VOH. Each of the dot patterns, hereafter designated

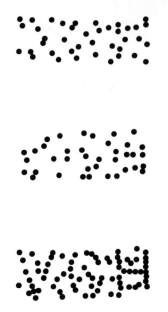

FIGURE 1   The upper two dot patterns when super-imposed result in the bottom stimulus pattern in which the nonsense syllable VOH can be read.

as a stimulus half, can be placed in the separate field of a tachistoscope and when the halves are properly aligned and exposed simultaneously at an appropriate luminance and duration, they yield the perception of the nonsense syllable. By introduction of systematic delays between presentation of the halves the temporal distribution of an organizational component in perception can be studied.

This task has several advantages. Not only does it permit the study of the temporal course of organizational components in perception similar to those that underlie perception of imbedded and street-gestalt figures, but it permits the study of a possible perceptual memory as suggested by Averbach and Coriell (1961) and Sperling (1963). As the reader can verify for himself, the two dot patterns are not such that they can be cognitized and/or remembered in such a manner as to yield the contained nonsense syllable. The nonsense syllable would seem to be capable of being perceived only if the two halves are perceived as psychologically simultaneous or the perceptual trace of the first half is still present when the second stimulus half occurs.

Experiment I

Subjects. Five male graduate students with normal or corrected to normal vision served as paid *O*s.

Procedure. A Scientific Prototype Model GA three-field tachistoscope was used for stimulus presentation. The "complete" stimuli consisted of 20 three-letter nonsense syllables. The first letter was always a T, V, or X, the second A, O, or U, and the third H, M, or W. As seen from the sample stimulus in Figure 1, the letters were composed of dots. The dots making up the forms of the letters were divided over two cards so that the dots contained on either card alone yielded minimum information as to the nature of the nonsense syllable. To reduce cues further and to minimize the possibility that the nonsense syllable could be guessed from the dots on only one stimulus card, slightly smaller camouflaging dots were distributed over each card. This technique yielded stimulus halves from either of which alone it was impossible to perceive the imbedded nonsense syllable. These stimulus cards were originally made up of India ink dots on white cardboard. Before use they were photographed to yield high-contrast negatives. The photographic negatives of the stimulus halves were presented in separate fields of the tachistoscope which had been carefully aligned so as to superimpose properly the corresponding halves thus permitting the nonsense syllable to be perceived.

As presented in the tachistoscope the stimulus halves subtended 2° of visual angle in length and 1° in height. They were backlighted with a luminance of 5 mL. in each field. The third tachistoscopic field was dark but contained a faintly luminous cross .3° of angle and positioned .5° below the center letter of the nonsense syllable.

The *S*s were instructed to fixate the cross and to trigger a stimulus presentation when the cross appeared sharp and clear. An experimental trial consisted of the presentation of both stimulus halves either simultaneously or at an experimentally varied interstimulus interval (ISI). The Ss had available in their dimly illuminated booth a list of the 20 possible nonsense syllables from which they selected their response following each trial. On the average, a 5-sec interval occurred between trials. Prior to beginning the experimental sessions each S served two practice sessions during which the corresponding stimulus halves were presented simultaneously for a duration of 6 msec. All Ss obtained an accuracy level of at least 85% but less than 100% for identification of the nonsense syllables during the second practice session (average 93%). Following the practice sessions Ss were run for five additional experimental sessions in which the stimulus halves were separated in time with ISI values of 0, 25, 50, 75, and 100 msec between the offset of the first half and onset of the second stimulus half. In each session a block of 20 trials was run for each delay. The delays were counterbalanced over sessions and Ss to cancel any order effects.

Following completion of the five experimental sessions, examination of the data failed to reveal a definitive asymptote in identification as the ISI was increased. To determine whether some temporal summation was still occurring at the 100-msec ISI, Ss returned for three additional experimental sessions during each of which they were run on ISIs of 100, 300, and 500 msec.

Results and Discussion

In Figure 2 mean percentage of correct nonsense-syllable identification is plotted as a function of ISI between the offset and the onset of corresponding halves. The average function is shown by a heavy line and the data for the five Ss is shown in the lighter lined functions. The three additional sessions at ISIs of 100, 300, and 500 msec that Ss served following the counterbalance experimental sessions are plotted separately in Figure 2. For three of the five Ss there is little if any drop in performance when the halves are presented over the range of simultaneity to an ISI of 25 msec. For all Ss performance decreases at an accelerated rate between ISI values of 25 and 75 msec. It appears clear that an asymptote in identification is approached at somewhere between an ISI of 100 and 300 msec.[1]

Phenomenal reports obtained from Ss indicated that nearly all were detecting the double stimulation or the separate halves by ISI values of 75 msec. At this separation Ss reported a

---

[1] With 20 nonsense syllables the a priori probability of a correct identification by guessing is .05. However, the inability to completely eliminate the partial cues in the separate stimulus halves required the determination of an empirical guessing accuracy level.

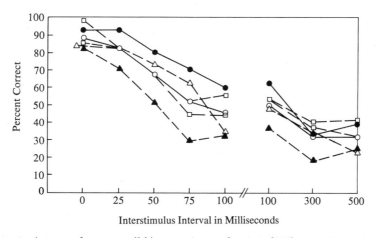

FIGURE 2   Accuracy of nonsense-syllable perception as a function of ISI between the corresponding stimulus halves. (The open circle function represents the average while the other functions are for the individual Ss.)

twinkling effect in the stimulation due to apparent movement of the dots toward adjacent dots. By 100-msec ISI most Ss could perceive the two halves as separate stimulations.

The decreasing identification performance as a function of increasing ISIs is similar to the masking effect produced by a second-field luminance upon identification of a form stimulus (Eriksen, 1966). However, the present function as well as many masking functions can be interpreted in either of two ways. Since these functions are obtained by averaging performance over a large number of trials, it is impossible to determine whether there is a constant effect on every trial, the magnitude of which varies inversely with ISI, or the effect is constant whenever it occurs but the proportion of trials upon which it occurs varies inversely with the ISI. For the present data the first alternative might be phrased in terms of a decaying trace of the first stimulus half. The longer the ISI the more the trace or "perceptual" memory of the first half has decayed. When the second half is presented S must put together or organize the decayed or less intense trace of the first half with the brighter second-half pattern in order to perceive the nonsense syllable. Thus at any ISI over the range where some integration occurs the difficulty of the organizational task is essentially constant for that given ISI on each trial. This would assume that the integration of the nonsense syllable from the two dot patterns is impaired if the halves are of unequal brightness.

In terms of the second alternative the obtained function is generated by an underlying process by which both halves are perceived simultaneously on some proportion of the trials. In this case performance is unimpaired. But on the remaining trials they are perceived as two separate dot patterns and integration is not possible. This second possibility would be commensurate with a concept of a psychological moment (Boynton, 1961; Murphree, 1954; Stroud, 1956; White, 1963).

If one postulates that experience and/or perception occurs in chunks or quanta of somewhere in the neighborhood of 50–100 msec duration, the present data would be interpreted in the following manner. At short ISI values the probability that both stimulus halves would occur in the same psychological moment and therefore be perceived as though presented simultaneously is quite high. However, as the ISI value increases the probability decreases that both halves would enter the same psychological moment. By the time the separation of the two halves is greater than the duration of the psychological moment, identification performance would have reached an asymptote since under these circumstances the probability is zero that they could enter the same moment.

Other explanations are of course possible and the present data do not provide even a choice between the decaying perceptual trace or memory explanation and the psychological moment concept. Experiment II was designed to test the appropriateness of a decay interpretation and also the possibility that the integration over time effects in the above study were due to subtle afterimages. This latter possibility is operationally difficult to distinguish or disentangle from a perceptual memory or a decay process and in the present paper no attempt is made to draw a distinction.

Experiment II

Design. One of the stimulus halves is given a longer duration than its corresponding half. The energy of the longer duration half is thus greater and in keeping with Bloch's law would be expected to constitute a brighter or more intense stimulation. In the present experiment one of the stimulus halves was always presented at a 25-msec duration at 5-mL. luminance while the corresponding stimulus half was presented at either 50-, 100-, or 150-msec duration at 5-mL. luminance. A second variable was whether the longer duration stimulus half preceded or followed the corresponding 25-msec duration half. Each combination of these two variables was presented at three ISIs: immediately successive (less than 1 msec apart); 20 msec; and concurrently. In the concurrent condition, due to the inequality of the duration of the stimulus halves, they were actually concurrent only for the 25-msec duration of the shorter half. The order variable was manipulated by having the corresponding halves have a concurrent onset or a concurrent offset. Thus, under the concurrent condition when the long duration half occurred first its onset preceded the short duration half by the amount of the time difference in their duration but they shared concurrently the last 25 msec of the duration of the longer half. For the reverse order both halves had a concurrent onset but after 25 msec the short-duration half terminated and the long-duration half continued for the length of its remaining duration interval. In addition to these conditions control observations were systematically obtained for the conditions where both of the corresponding halves had a 25-msec duration which was presented either concurrently, immediately successive, or at 20-msec ISI.

This design should permit answers to the following questions raised by the preceding experiment. First of all, a decaying trace interpretation of the above data requires that integration of the nonsense syllable from the corresponding stimulus halves is more difficult if the halves are of unequal energy than if the halves are of comparable energy. In the present experiment this assumption would lead to the expectation that identification performance should decrease as the duration of one of the stimulus halves varies from 25 msec to 150 msec and the other half remains constant at 25-msec duration. The decaying trace explanation is tested most directly by the order variable. It seems reasonable to expect that the absolute energy in a decaying perceptual memory (or for the clarity of an afterimage) at some succeeding moment in time would be greater for a high-energy stimulation than for a low-energy stimulation. For example, at an ISI of 20 msec, identification of the nonsense syllable should be easier if the first stimulus half had a longer duration since there would be a more persistent trace to integrate with the following short-duration half. The reverse order should lead to much worse performance, not only due to less persistence from the low-energy half having occurred first, but also because under

these circumstances there would be a greater absolute difference in energy of the corresponding halves. Further, the decaying perceptual memory explanation would expect an interaction between long-half duration and ISI since as ISI increases, high-identification performance could be maintained by increasing the energy in the first half presentation and therefore the amount of persistence of the memory trace.

Subjects. Six undergraduate students (four males) served as paid volunteers. All had normal or corrected to normal visual acuity and none had served in Exp. I.

Apparatus and stimuli. Apparatus and stimuli were essentially the same as those employed in Exp. I with these exceptions. Previously the dot patterns of the stimulus halves had been backlighted thus presenting a view of illuminated dots against a black ground. In this experiment the figure-ground relationship was reversed. The stimuli were made using India ink on white cards and were frontlighted in the tachistoscope at a luminance of 5 mL. To prevent luminance summation-contrast reduction effects that would vary as a function of ISI (Eriksen, 1966), the adapting field which contained a small black fixation cross also had 5-mL. luminance. To maintain contrast reduction due to luminance summation as a constant overall ISI and other experimental conditions, the adapting field was left on continuously except where the conditions required that both stimulus halves be on concurrently. Then the adapting field was off while the stimulus halves were concurrently presented but when either half terminated the adapting field came on instantaneously. As constructed on the white cardboards the black dots had a contrast of 95% but due to "veiling glare" arising from superimposition of adapting and stimulus fields or of the two stimulus fields at the eye the effective contrast was 47.5% (Kåhneman, 1966).

Procedure. The procedure was also essentially the same as in Exp. I. Each S served two practice sessions in which the 20 sets of corresponding stimulus halves were presented simultaneously for 25 msec. All Ss who were subsequently used in experimental sessions attained an accuracy level of at least 85, but less than 100% during the last practice session. Several potential Ss had to be dismissed because of their inability to achieve this criterion. Following the two practice sessions each S served for 12 experimental sessions. During these sessions each S had 40 trials under each combination of the 18 experimental conditions (three durations of the long stimulus half, 50, 100, and 150 msec; two orders, long half first or second; and three ISIs, concurrent, 0- and 20-msec delay between halves). In addition, 80 trials were run under the control conditions at each of the three ISI values where both stimulus halves were 25-msec duration.

Results

The number of correct nonsense-syllable identifications was analyzed in a four-way classification analysis of variance (three durations of the long-stimulus half, order of occurrence of long- and short-duration stimulus halves, ISI, and Ss). All main effects and interactions were significant beyond the .01 level except the main effect due to order of occurrence of long and short half, and the following interactions: Long-half duration with Ss; ISI, long-half duration and Ss; ISI, order and Ss; and long-half duration, order and Ss. The control condition for the equal duration halves at the three ISI values were analyzed separately and a significant effect ($p < .001$) was obtained for the effect of ISI.

In Figure 3 average percentage of correct nonsense-syllable identification is shown as a function of the duration of the long-stimulus half. The parameters in Figure 3 are the three ISI values; concurrent, 0, and 20 msec. For each of these ISI values the effect of order (whether the long duration-stimulus half preceded or followed the short-duration half) is also shown. The points at the extreme left of Figure 3 are for the control condition where the corresponding stimulus halves each had a duration of 25 msec and were obtained under each of the three ISI values.

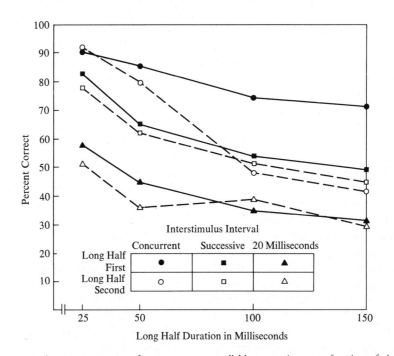

FIGURE 3   Average percentage of correct nonsense-syllable perception as a function of the duration of long-stimulus half, ISI, and sequence of long- and short-stimulus halves.

The data of Figure 3 may be summarized as showing that the ability to organize the nonsense syllables from the separate stimulus halves is: (a) greatest when the stimulus halves are concurrent and decreases as the halves are separated in time; (b) highest when the stimulus halves are of equal energy (duration) and decreases in a negatively accelerated function as the mismatch in energy increases; and (c) indifferent to the order of occurrence of unequal energy-stimulus halves except when the occurrence of the stimulus halves overlap in time (concurrent). In this latter instance performance is best if the unequal duration stimulus halves share a common offset rather than a common onset, and the greater the inequality in durations the greater is this effect.

Discussion

The above data support the assumption that inequality in energy between stimulus halves reduces integration or organization of the imbedded nonsense syllable. This assumption is basic to a decay explanation. However, a simple decay explanation is countermanded by the fact that, (a) when the stimulus halves are not concurrent, there is no performance gain when the high-energy stimulus half occurs first rather than after the low-energy half, and (b) there is a progressive decrease in performance when the occurrences of the stimulus halves are varied from concurrent to successive to 20-msec ISI for all duration or energy inequalities.

It seems reasonable that if a perceptual memory process exists, the greater the intensity or energy of the stimulation, the greater the intensity of the trace or memory at a succeeding point in time. Thus in the present study when a long duration half is presented first, there should be a more intense memory trace to integrate with the short-duration half when it occurs later in time. The reverse order should lead to inferior integration, not only because the short-duration trace is less intense but also because the energy inequality between the stimulus halves will also be greater. Since integration is best when the halves are of equal energy it also follows that an interaction of first-half

duration with ISI should occur. This would represent the instances where the decay of the more intense first-half stimulus now matches more closely the intensity of the succeeding short-duration half.

As was seen, there were no indications in the above data to support these deductions. The only case where order of occurrence of long- and short-duration halves made a difference was when the halves were on concurrently for the duration of the short half. For example, if the long-stimulus half had a duration of 100 msec and the short half 25 msec, perception of the nonsense syllable was more accurate if the 100-msec stimulus half was turned on first and the short-duration half turned on 75 msec after the onset of the long-stimulus half. If both stimulus halves were turned on simultaneously and 25 msec later the short-duration half terminated but the long half continued for an additional 75 msec, perception of the nonsense syllable was much inferior.

This finding is in itself puzzling. It does not fit a memory decay process since both halves always share a common 25-msec duration. Performance under either order is poorer than if both halves had been presented for only 25 msec concurrently. The inequality of the energy in the stimulus halves would seem to account for the decreased performance except that this inequality should be the same for either order of the halves occurrence. When the halves share a common onset there is a 25-msec period when they are of the same energy but it is apparent that perceptual integration does not occur that rapidly.

The interaction also is not readily interpretable in terms of a simple conception of a psychological moment. Since both halves always share a common 25-msec duration, at least this much would be included in the same psychological moment, and perception of the imbedded nonsense syllable would be expected to be quite accurate. Some deterioration in performance could be attributed to the variability of the beginning of the psychological moment such that on some trials more than 25 msec of the energy of the long stimulus-half duration might be included in the same moment with the 25-msec duration half. This would lead to some energy mismatch between the two halves with a corresponding decrease in identification performance. However, the operation of such a process would be independent of the order of occurrence of the long- and short-duration halves and would not be commensurate with the obtained interaction.[2]

Those who have discussed the concept of the psychological moment (Boynton, 1961; Murphree, 1954; Stroud, 1956; White, 1963) have not been sufficiently specific in describing its characteristics. To determine whether the concept has theoretical value in handling phenomena such as produced in the present experiments we need greater explication. Does an arriving stimulation enter an ongoing psychological moment or is it stored and then represented in the succeeding moment? In the latter case when it's stored does any deterioration occur in its trace or intensity during the period of storage? Does the duration of the moment vary with intensity of stimulation. Specifications such as these are essential if the moment concept is to be applied to the interpretation of the present data. Failure of the theorists to deal with these details of the nature of the concept is undoubtedly attributable to the paucity of experimental data on temporal factors in perception.

The results of the present experiments are most likely a product of several different processes in the visual perceptual system. It seems apparent from the present data alone that perception lags at least 25 msec or more behind the onset of stimulation in physical time. Differential latencies in transmission of stimulation from sense organ to higher brain centers may well be one factor in the present results. Perhaps most important is the consideration that a system which has the summative and persist-

ing characteristics of visual perception would seem to require other mechanisms to detect discontinuity or interruptions in stimulation. The "off" response recorded at the level of the retina (Granit, 1947) would seem to be one such mechanism. It is possible that this mechanism or similar mechanisms that detect discontinuity in stimulation have an inhibiting effect on the summative or the integrative process underlying performance in the present experiments. This would be commensurate with the finding that any discontinuity or interruption of stimulation was found to have a deleterious effect on perceptual integration of the imbedded nonsense syllables.

Summary

Visual stimuli were constructed so that any given stimulus by itself appeared to be a random collection of dots. However, when 2 corresponding stimuli were superimposed by means of a 2-field tachistoscope, a 3-letter nonsense syllable was perceived. Temporal organization in perception was studied in Experiment I by varying the interval between the presentation of the 2 corresponding patterns over 300 msec. Identification accuracy of syllables was a decreasing function of interstimulus interval over a range in excess of 100 msec. Experiment II used unequal energy levels for the 2 corresponding patterns and also varied the sequence of occurrence of the high and low energy members of corresponding sets. The relevance of such concepts as perceptual memory, afterimages, and psychological moments to the data was considered. It was suggested that mechanisms in the visual system such as the "off" response that detect the termination of a stimulus may be responsible for inhibition of integration over time.

---

[2] Fred Attneave (personal communication) has suggested that the interaction of order of occurrence with the long and short-duration halves might be attributable to apparent movement. When the stimulus halves have a common onset but terminate 75–125 msec apart, the short-duration half is assimilated into the long-duration half via apparent movement. This process would account for the unidirectional effect since if the halves have an asynchronous onset but common termination the conditions for apparent movement would not obtain.

References

Averbach, E., & Coriell, A. S. Short-term memory in vision. *Bell Sys. tech. J.,* 1961, *40,* 309–328.

Bergson, H. *Creative evolution.* New York: Holt, 1913.

Boynton, R. M. Temporal factors in vision. In W. A. Rosenblith (Ed.), *Sensory communication.* New York: Wiley, 1961. Pp. 739–756.

Eriksen, C. W. Temporal luminance summation effects in backward and forward masking. *Percept. Psychophys.,* 1966, *1,* 87–92.

Eriksen, C. W., & Collins, J. F. A reinterpretation of one form of backward and forward masking in visual perception. *J. exp. Psychol.,* 1965, *70,* 343–351.

Granit, R. *Sensory mechanisms of the retina.* New York: Oxford Univer. Press, 1947.

James, W. *The principles of psychology.* Vol. 1. New York: Holt, 1890. Pp. 605–642.

Kahneman, D. Time-intensity reciprocity under various conditions of adaptation and backward masking. *J. exp. Psychol.,* 1966, *71,* 543–549.

Kahneman, D. Temporal factors in vision: Some comments on terms and methods. *Psychol. Bull.,* in press.

Kahneman, D., & Norman, J. The time-intensity re-

lation in visual perception as a function of observer's task. *J. exp. Psychol.,* 1964, *68,* 215–220.

Murphree, O. D. Maximum rates of form perception and the alpha rhythm: An investigation and test of current nerve net theory. *J. exp. Psychol.,* 1954, *48,* 57–61.

Piéron, H. *The sensations: Their functions, processes and mechanisms.* London: Frederick Muller, 1952.

Sperling, G. A. A model for visual memory tasks. *Hum. Factors,* 1963, *5,* 19–31.

Stroud, J. M. The fine structure of psychological time. In H. Quastler (Ed.), *Information theory in psychology.* Glencoe, Ill.: Free Press, 1956. Pp. 174–207.

White, C. T. Temporal numerosity and the psychological unit of duration. *Psychol. Monogr.,* 1963, 77 (12, Whole No. 575).

White, C. T., & Cheatham, P. G. Temporal numerosity: IV. A comparison of the major senses. *J. exp. Psychol.,* 1959, *58,* 441–444.

1.8 Integrative Processes in Central Visual Pathways of the Cat*

DAVID H. HUBEL

An image falling upon the retina exerts an influence on millions of receptors. It is the task of the central nervous system to make sense of the spatial and temporal patterns of excitation in this retinal mosaic. Unless we know something of how the nervous system handles the messages it receives, we cannot easily come to grips with the problems of perception of form, movement, color, or depth.

For a study of integrative sensory mechanisms the visual system of mammals offers the advantage of a comparatively direct anatomical

pathway. At each stage, from bipolar cells to the striate cortex, we can compare activity of cells with that of the incoming fibers, and so attempt to learn what each structure contributes to the visual process. In this paper I summarize a series of studies on the cat visual system made by Torsten Wiesel and myself. I concentrate mainly on experiments related to form and movement.

It is often contended that in studying a sensory system we should first learn to understand thoroughly the physiology of receptors, and only then proceed to examine more central processes. In the visual system one should presumably have a firm grasp of rod and cone physiology before looking at bipolar and retinal ganglion cells; one should thoroughly under-

* Reproduced by permission of the *Journal of the Optical Society of America,* 1963, vol. 53, pp. 58–66. Originally presented as invited paper at the "Symposium on Physiological Optics," Joint Session of the Armed Forces-NRC Committee on Vision, the Inter-Society Color Council, and the Optical Society of America, 14–15 March 1962, Washington, D. C.

stand retinal mechanisms before taking up studies of the brain. Unfortunately it is not always possible to be so systematic. In the case of the visual system, orderly progress is impeded by the great technical difficulties in recording from single retinal elements, especially from the rods and cones and from bipolar cells. At the single-cell level, knowledge of the electrophysiology of these structures is consequently almost entirely lacking. If we wish to learn how the brain interprets information it receives from the retina we must either struggle with retinal problems of formidable difficulty or else skip over the first two stages and begin at a point where the appropriate single-unit techniques have been worked out, i.e., the retinal ganglion cell.

The subject of retinal ganglion-cell physiology is complicated by the fact that studies have been made in a wide variety of vertebrates and under a number of different experimental conditions. Here I only describe the receptive field organization of retinal ganglion cells in the cat. This is necessary for an understanding of the integrative function of the lateral geniculate body since the geniculate receives its main visual input directly from the retina.

Because there is convergence of a number of afferent fibers onto each cell, both for bipolar cells and for retinal ganglion cells, we are not surprised to learn that a single ganglion cell may receive its input ultimately from a large number of rods and cones, and hence from a retinal surface of considerable extent. At first glance it might seem that a progressive increase in the size of receptive fields as we follow the visual pathway centrally must lead to a wasteful and pointless blurring of detailed information acquired by the exquisitely fine receptor mosaic. To understand why fineness of discrimination is not necessarily blunted we must realize that all retinal connections are not necessarily excitatory. The existence of inhibitory connections means that when we shine a spot of light on the receptive field of a given cell we may decrease, rather than increase the cell's rate of firing. The effect of the stimulus will depend on the part of the receptive field we illuminate. The fineness of discrimination of a cell is deter-

mined not by the over-all receptive field size, but by the arrangement of excitatory and inhibitory regions within the receptive field.

With the experiments of Kuffler (1953) it became apparent that in the light-adapted cat, retinal ganglion cells did not necessarily respond uniformly throughout their receptive fields: their discharges might be activated or suppressed by a spot of light, depending upon where on the retina the spot fell. The receptive field of a ganglion cell could thus be mapped into distinct excitatory and inhibitory regions. Two types of cell were distinguished by Kuffler: those with fields having a more or less circular excitatory center with an annular inhibitory surround, and those having the reverse arrangement. These two concentrically arranged field types were called "on"-center and "off"-center fields. The terms "off" center and "off" response refer to the empirical finding that when a spot of light suppresses cell's firing, turning the spot off almost always evoked a discharge, termed the "off" response. Conversely when we see an "off" discharge we usually find that during the stimulus the maintained firing of a cell is suppressed.

Within the excitatory or inhibitory region of a receptive field one can demonstrate summation, i.e., for a given intensity of stimulus the response increases (number of spikes and frequency of firing increase, latency and threshold decrease) as the area stimulated is increased. On the other hand, when both types of region are included in a stimulus their separate effects tend to cancel. If the entire receptive field is illuminated, for example by diffuse light, a relatively weak response of the center type is usually obtained: an "on"-center cell thus gives a weak "on" response, and an "off"-center cell a weak "off" response. I shall use the term "peripheral suppression" to refer to this antagonistic interaction between center and periphery.

Retinal ganglion cells differ from one another in several ways besides those related to field-center type. Obviously they vary in the location of their receptive fields on the retina. In the cat (Wiesel, 1960) and the monkey (Hubel and Wiesel, 1960) there are considerable differences in the sizes of receptive-field centers, receptive fields near the area centralis or fovea showing a marked tendency to have smaller centers than fields in the peripheral retina. Even for a given region of the retina there is a large variation in the size of field centers. In the monkey the smallest field center so far measured had a diameter of 4 minutes of arc; this was situated 4° from the fovea. It is likely that the centers of foveal fields are much smaller than this. The total extent of a field is more difficult to determine, since the effect of a spot of light upon a cell decreases gradually with increasing distance from the field center. Measurements made by constructing area-threshold curves (Wiesel, 1960) suggest that receptive fields may not greatly differ in their total size despite wide variations in center sizes.

Retinal ganglion cells differ also in the effectiveness with which the receptive-field periphery antagonizes the center response. This may be measured by determining the difference between the threshold intensity of a spot covering the receptive-field center and that of a large spot covering the entire field. The difference tends to be greater for cells with small field centers (and hence large peripheral zones) than for cells with large field centers. Since cells with small field centers are especially common in the area centralis, this ability to discriminate against diffuse light is particularly pronounced in that part of the retina.

In the cat we know of no functional retinal ganglion cell types besides the "on"-center and "off"-center cells described by Kuffler. Occasionally diffuse light evokes a discharge both at "on" and at "off." This may occur in either "on"-center cells or "off"-center cells. It depends to some extent on the state of light adaptation, stimulus intensity, and other variables. The receptive fields of cells showing "on-off" responses to large spots do not seem to differ in any fundamental way from ordinary "on"-center or "off"-center cells. There thus seems to be no reason for regarding "on-off" retinal ganglion cells of cat as a distinct type.

In the cat the arrangement of excitatory and inhibitory regions within a given receptive field remains the same for all effective stimulus wavelengths. The fields thus seem to be very different from the more complex opponent-color fields described by Wolbarsht, Wagner, and MacNichol (1961) for goldfish retinal ganglion cells (see discussion of Barlow, in Wolbarsht et al., 1961, p. 176). In the monkey optic nerve and lateral geniculate body there are two types of neurones, one resembling cells of the cat in having receptive-field characteristics that are independent of wavelength, the other showing color-specific responses in many ways similar to those seen in the goldfish (Hubel and Wiesel, 1960; DeValois, 1960).

In the frog, Maturana, Lettvin, McCulloch, and Pitts (1960) have described retinal ganglion cells with highly complex response properties. Their records were made from unmyelinated axons or their terminal arborizations. If such axons exist in the optic nerves of cats, they have probably escaped detection in physiological studies. Unfortunately cat optic nerves have not yet been examined with the electron microscope, and it is not known whether or not they contain unmyelinated fibers.

Lateral Geniculate Body

Anatomically, the dorsal lateral geniculate body differs from most other structures in the central nervous system, and certainly from the retina and cortex, in its relative simplicity. In a sense it is a one-synapse way station, since its cells receive their major input directly from the optic tract, and since most of them send their axons directly to the visual cortex. It has often been asked whether the lateral geniculate body serves any integrative purpose besides that of relaying incoming messages to the cortex for further elaboration. Although in some ways the lateral geniculate body is a simple structure, an anatomist would hardly contend that it is nothing but a one-to-one relay station. The existence of convergence and divergence, complex dendritic arborizations, and, in the cat at least, cells with short axons terminating within the nucleus itself, all seem to be against such a supposition.

A strong case was made for the presence of one-to-one synapses in the geniculate by the microelectrode studies of Bishop, Burke, and Davis (1958). By electrically stimulating the severed proximal stump of the optic nerve and recording extracellularly from lateral geniculate cells they were able to record excitatory post-synaptic potentials (or the associated extra-cellular currents) and show that they were not continuously graded, but, at least for two of the cells they studied, were all-or-nothing. Most excitatory postsynaptic potentials were followed by geniculate spikes. The authors concluded that some lateral geniculate cells can be excited by one impulse in a single optic-nerve fiber. They were inclined to attribute the fact that the lateral geniculate cell occasionally failed to fire to the effects of anaesthesia, rather than to variation in possible additional inputs not detected by their electrode. Since both Bishop, Burke, and Davis (1958) and Freygang (1958) observed lateral geniculate cells for which the excitatory postsynaptic potentials were graded in several discrete steps, it is clear that not all geniculate synapses are of a simple one-to-one type. At least some must have several excitatory inputs.

If there is a "straight through" connection between some optic-nerve fibers and lateral geniculate cells, as Bishop's findings suggest, there should be no differences in receptive fields at the two levels. A study of lateral geniculate cells in the cat (Hubel and Wiesel, 1961) showed that lateral geniculate fields indeed have the same concentric center-periphery organization, and like retinal ganglion cells, are of two types, excitatory center and inhibitory center. It is clear enough, then, that in the lateral geniculate body there is no very profound reorganization of the incoming messages. Nevertheless, there was a suggestion that the ability of a receptive-field periphery to antagonize the center response was more marked in geniculate cells than in optic-nerve fibers. This was true even when variations in peripheral suppression with position of receptive fields on the retina (referred to above) were taken into account.

The fact that one can record geniculate spikes together with excitatory synaptic potentials of an all-or-none type suggested the possibility of making a more delicate test of geniculate function, namely, a comparison of the responses and receptive fields of a particular geniculate cell with those of its own excitatory post-synaptic potential (Hubel and Wiesel, 1961). When this was done for cells with all-or-none synaptic potentials, it was found that while almost all lateral geniculate spikes were triggered by an optic-nerve impulse, the converse was not true; each synaptic potential did not necessarily trigger a postsynaptic spike. The success rate of the optic-nerve impulse varied widely, depending on how the retina was stimulated. The receptive field centers of the optic nerve fiber and the lateral geniculate cell were, as far as one could judge, precisely superimposed. If one shone a restricted spot of light over the common receptive-field center, the likelihood that an impulse would trigger a postsynaptic spike was very high. If, on the other hand, the entire receptive field including the periphery was illuminated, very few of the synaptic potentials were followed by geniculate-cell spikes. For small spots in the center portion of the field the thresholds of the two units were apparently identical, but for large spots, including diffuse light, they were often several log units apart. Sometimes the geniculate cell would not respond to diffuse light at any intensity.

It was thus possible not only to confirm the impression that peripheral suppression is enhanced by lateral geniculate cells, but to obtain some notion of how the change is brought about.

This result shows clearly that even when we record a single all-or-none excitatory synaptic potential along with a geniculate cell spike, the synaptic potential we observe does not represent the only input to the cell. There must be other inputs which are influenced by illuminating the periphery of the common receptive field. Illuminating the periphery might activate retinal ganglion cells whose "on" centers were distributed over this annular region; if these neurons made inhibitory synaptic connections with the geniculate cell we could explain the cell's failure to be triggered when diffused light was used. We might equally well suppose that lighting the periphery suppressed the firing of a set of "off"-center retinal ganglion cells making *excitatory* connections with the geniculate cell. Now inclusion of the receptive-field periphery would suppress these cells removing the tonic asynchronous activation needed to enable the geniculate cell to follow the triggering impulses. The important point is that the geniculate cell must be receiving input from not one, but a large number of optic-nerve fibers. In a cell bound to an optic nerve fiber by a synapse having a "straight through" property, the property is a conditional one, depending on activity of other optic nerve fibers.

I have mentioned the possibility of suppressing a cell's firing by withdrawal of tonic excitation rather than by direct synaptic inhibition. The synapse that we are discussing gives us a vivid example of just that, for in illuminating the field center of an "off"-center geniculate cell we suppress firing by suppressing activity in the main optic-nerve fiber feeding into it. Of course the cell may at the same time be actively inhibited by other optic-nerve fibers (we have no evidence for or against this), but this inhibition would not be the main reason for the cessation of firing. To suppress the firing of any cell in the visual system there need only be one inhibitory link in the entire chain beginning with and including the receptor. In the case of the center of an "off"-center cell in the lateral geniculate we do not know at what stage this inhibitory link occurs. It is apparently not in the geniculate, and there is no evidence for or against its being at the retinal ganglion-cell level.

We may sum up the implications of these experiments as follows: (1) all cat geniculate cells apparently have multiple visual inputs; (2) there is often a particular relationship between a cell and one optic-nerve fiber with which it makes a powerful excitatory synapse; (3) when such a relationship exists, the receptive-field centers of the incoming fiber and the geniculate cell are of the same type, i.e., both are "on" center or both are "off" center; (4) the lateral geniculate body has the function of increasing the disparity, already present in the retinal ganglion cell, between responses to a small centered spot and to diffuse light.

The lateral geniculate body may have other functions besides that of increasing the effects of the receptive-field periphery. Cells in which the synaptic potential is graded in several steps must have more than one excitatory afferent. This kind of convergence might produce a geniculate receptive-field center larger than any of the field centers of the afferents. So far this has not been tested experimentally.

Some electrophysiological studies have suggested that the lateral geniculate body receives afferent fibers besides those of the optic tract (Hubel, 1960; Widén and Ajmone-Marsan, 1960; Arden and Söderberg, 1961). Nauta and Bucher (1954) have observed a cortico-geniculate projection in the rat, and recently Nauta (personal communication) and Beresford (1961) have found in the cat a topographically precise reciprocal pathway from the striate cortex to the lateral geniculate body of the same side. So far we have found no geniculate cells with the complex properties typical of cortical cells, but fibers with these properties are frequently recorded just dorsal to the lateral geniculate body. A knowledge of the presence of a reciprocal pathway is important if we are to avoid including these units in a study of geniculate cells, particularly if there is any chance that the recording electrode is not in the geniculate but just above it.

A problem that has attracted considerable attention concerns the amount of binocular interaction in the lateral geniculate body (Bishop, Burke, and Davis, 1959; Erulkar and Fillenz, 1960; Grüsser and Sauer, 1960; Hubel and Wiesel, 1961). While there is evidence that some geniculate cells can be influenced from the two eyes, it seems to be agreed that the proportion of binocularly influenced cells in the lateral geniculate body is small. This is certainly in keeping with the anatomical findings (Silva, 1956; Hayhow, 1958). We have so

far not succeeded in mapping out, for any geniculate cell, two receptive fields, one in each eye.
The marked contrast between the scarcity of
binocular interaction in the cat's geniculate
and its preponderance in the visual cortex does
not argue for any major role of the geniculate
in binocular vision.

On anatomical grounds it is well established
that alternate layers of the lateral geniculate
body receive their input from alternate eyes.
This has been confirmed in the cat by physiological methods (Cohn, 1956); cells in a
given layer can be driven from one of the two
eyes, but not from the other. A precise topographical representation of the contralateral
half-fields of vision on each geniculate layer,
the maps in the different layers being in register, has been established anatomically for the
rhesus monkey (Polyak, 1957) by noting trans-
synaptic atrophy following small retinal lesions.
Although a similar anatomical study in the cat
has not been made, the physiological evidence
for a precise topographical representation in
this animal is clear (Hubel and Wiesel, 1961).
The receptive fields of simultaneously recorded
cells are near to one another and often overlap
almost completely. The receptive fields of cells
recorded in sequence by an electrode passing
normal to the layers are close together or almost superimposed, whereas in an oblique or
tangential penetration, fields of successively recorded cells move systematically along the
retina. Finally, the maps in successive layers
are in register.

From what I have said about the lateral
geniculate body it will be apparent that the
physiological properties of even that simple
structure are far from simple. The fact that a
number of incoming optic-tract fibers converge upon one cell presents us with a number
of possibilities. Any particular geniculate cell
will have its own receptive field with center
and surround. Each fiber converging upon the
cell will have its own center located in the
center or surround of the geniculate cell's field:
the incoming fiber may have an "on"-center or
an "off"-center; the synapse it makes may be
excitatory or inhibitory. If excitatory, the
synapse may be powerful, capable of setting up

a spike in the geniculate cell; or it may be
weak, contributing to the summed effects of a
large number of other incoming fibers. Somehow these and perhaps other possibilities are
made use of, to produce a mechanism in which
individual incoming impulses may trigger individual postsynaptic impulses, but in which the
coupling between the incoming and outgoing
signals is varied. Such an ingenious piece of
machinery would surely have great appeal to
a mechanical or an electrical engineer. It may
be worth stressing how different this synapse
seems to be from that of the anterior horn cell
of the spinal cord, which, because it has been
so extensively studied by modern electrophysiological methods, is apt to be taken as a prototype of synapses in the central nervous system.

Visual Cortex

If the lateral geniculate body is anatomically
a structure of relative histological simplicity,
the primary visual cortex is in contrast one of
very great complexity. There is considerable
order to the architectural plan of the cortex,
yet our knowledge of the connections between
cells gives us very little notion of how this
structure functions. Of course, it has been
known for years that the striate cortex is concerned with vision, and that in most mammals
it is indispensible for form vision. What we
have not known is how cortical cells handle
the messages they receive from the lateral geniculate body. We have had insufficient evidence
even to decide whether the messages are modified at all, or just handed on to some still higher
centers for further elaboration (cf. Brindley,
1960, p. 122).

As long as methods for single-cell recording
were not available to neurophysiologists, this
question of integrative cortical mechanisms
could only be approached in a limited way.
Since gross electrodes record only synchronous
activity one could only examine attributes
shared by all or most cells in a relatively large
volume of tissue (the order of 1 mm³). We
know now that the one important psysiological
quality shared by cells over such a large area

of striate cortex has to do with the regions of visual field from which cells receive their projections. It is therefore not surprising that topography was one aspect of visual cortical function to be extensively explored with gross electrodes.

In a series of studies by Talbot and Marshall (1941), Talbot (1942), and Thompson, Woolsey, and Talbot (1950) the cortex was mapped in the cat, rabbit, and monkey according to the retinal areas projecting to it. These authors were able to go well beyond what was known from anatomical studies by showing that in the cat and rabbit there is a double representation of the visual half-field on the cortex of the contralateral hemisphere. The two maps lie adjacent to each other, bounded by a line which Talbot and Marshall termed the "line of decussation." This line receives projections from the vertical meridian. Any retinal region (besides the vertical meridian) projects to two regions on the cortex, one medial to the line of decussation and the other lateral to it. There has been some tendency to assume that the medial representation, called Visual Area I, is the classical striate cortex, whereas Area II is nonstriate. There is nothing in the literature to support the latter assumption, though to my knowledge it has never been questioned except by Bard (1956).

The mapping experiments of Talbot and Marshall and of Thompson, Woolsey, and Talbot have since been confirmed for the cat by single-unit techniques. We have confirmed the topographical projection scheme in the cat (Hubel and Wiesel, 1962), including the presence of a second visual representation lateral to the first. Daniel and Whitteridge (1961) have repeated the experiments in the monkey and have extended the map to buried parts of the cortex. Although Talbot and Marshall did not describe a second visual area in the monkey, Wiesel and I have recently found electrophysiological evidence for a precise retinotopic projection to nonstriate visual cortex.

The introduction of microelectrodes supplies us with a powerful means of studying properties of individual cortical cells, especially those properties that are not common to cells in a large volume of nervous tissue. To learn what kinds of transformations the visual cortex makes on the incoming visual signals we may compare responses of single cortical cells with those of afferent fibers from the lateral geniculate body. If we were to find no differences in receptive fields of cells in these two structures we would indeed be disappointed, for it would mean either that in spite of its anatomical complexity the striate cortex did virtually nothing, or else that our present microelectrode techniques were not equal to the problem. The second alternative is a possible one, since the elaborative functions of the cortex might be discernible only by examining simultaneously large numbers of cells and comparing their firing patterns, perhaps with the help of computers. As it turns out, there *are* differences in receptive fields, differences which give us a fair idea of some of the functions of the cortex. Here I only attempt to summarize some of our own work (see Hubel and Wiesel, 1959, 1962); for other microelectrode investigations of the visual cortex the reader may refer to several recent symposia (Rosenblith, 1961; Jung and Kornhuber, 1961).

In the striate cortex we have found no cells with concentric "on"- or "off"-center fields. Instead there has been an astonishing variety of new response types. These differ one from another in the details of distribution of excitatory and inhibitory regions, but they have one thing in common: that areas giving excitation and inhibition are not separated by circles, as in the retina and geniculate, but by straight lines. Some cells, for example, have receptive fields with a long narrow excitatory area flanked on either side by inhibitory areas, whereas others have the reverse arrangement, an inhibitory area flanked on the two sides by excitatory areas (Hubel and Wiesel, 1962, Text-Figure 2). Some fields have only two regions of opposite type separated by a single straight line. Summation occurs just as in the retina and geniculate, and the most effective stationary retinal stimulus for a cortical cell is one falling on either the excitatory parts of a receptive field or the inhibitory parts, but not on both simultaneously. Consequently stimuli such as long narrow dark or light rectangles, or boundaries with light to one side and darkness to the other ("edges"), are likely to be the most potent for cortical cells. Each cell will have its own optimal stimulus. Moreover the stimulus that works best in influencing a cell, exciting or inhibiting it, will do so only when shone on the appropriate part of the retina and in the correct orientation. Some cells prefer one inclination, vertical, horizontal, or oblique, others prefer another; and all inclinations seem to be about equally well represented. We have termed the inclination of the most effective stimulus the "receptive-field axis orientation" and have come to realize that this is one of a cell's most important properties. For example, if a stimulus such as a long narrow rectangle of light is shone at right angles to the optimum orientation it has little or no effect. Here the light covers portions of both the excitatory and inhibitory regions, and the two effects oppose each other.

We have already seen that turning on or off a diffuse light is not an ideal stimulus for a retinal ganglion cell. It evokes a response, but a much weaker one than that produced by a centered circular spot of just the right size. I have described how cells in the lateral geniculate body are influenced even less than retinal ganglion cells by diffuse light. In the cortex the process is apparently carried a step further. Here many cells give no response at all when one shines light on the entire receptive field. How the cat detects diffuse light and distinguishes different levels of diffuse illumination is something we do not know. Perhaps the mechanism is subcortical; it is known that the cat can make discriminations of intensity of diffuse light even when it lacks a visual cortex (Smith, 1937). The information that a large patch of retina is evenly illuminated may be supplied only by cells that are activated by the boundaries of the patch; the fact that cells with fields entirely within the illuminated area are uninfluenced presumably signals the absence of contours within the patch of light—in other words, that the region is diffusely lit.

One may ask why a diffuse flash of light evokes such a large cortical slow wave, if only a small proportion of cells respond to the stimulus, and these only relatively weakly. Too little is known about slow waves to permit an entirely satisfactory answer. It is possible that a large slow wave may be produced by a small proportion of cells firing weakly but synchronously. It is interesting, however, that the visual evoked response is maximal *outside* the cortical area commonly accepted as striate (Doty, 1958), and that within the primary visual area it is maximal well in front of the area centralis representation. Indeed, the area representing central vision gives only a relatively feeble response to a diffuse flash (Doty, 1958). We have not thoroughly explored cortical areas representing the far periphery of the retinas: it may be that compared with cells receiving projections from centralis, those with receptive fields in the far periphery respond more actively to diffuse light. This is, in fact, the case with retinal ganglion cells (Wiesel, 1960) and with geniculate cells (Hubel and Wiesel, 1961).

The amazing selectivity with which cortical cells respond to a highly specific stimulus and ignore almost anything else is explained by the existence of excitatory and inhibitory receptive-field subdivisions. While these mechanisms clearly make use of inhibition, it must be stressed that we have no direct evidence that the cortex contains inhibitory synapses, just as we have none in the case of geniculate or retinal ganglion cells (see discussion of Bremer, in Jung, 1960, p. 233). Whenever we suppress firing by turning on a stimulus, the effect may be produced by withdrawing tonic excitation as easily as by directly inhibiting, and so far the appropriate methods of distinguishing the two possibilities have not been used in the visual system.

In their behavior cells whose receptive fields can be divided into excitatory and inhibitory regions are probably the simplest of the striate cortex. It is therefore reasonable to suppose that at least some cells with simple fields receive their projections directly from the geniculate (Hubel and Wiesel, 1962). In the striate cortex we find cells of a second type whose properties we have called "complex." Cells with complex receptive fields do not respond well to small spots of light, and it has not been possible to map their fields into separate excitatory and inhibitory regions. They behave as though they received their afferents from a large number of cortical cells with simple fields, all of these fields having the same axis orientation, but varying slightly from one to the next in their exact retinal positions. A complex cell thus responds to an appropriately oriented slit, edge, or dark bar, not just when it is shone in one highly critical retinal position, as we find with simple cells, but over considerable regions of retina, sometimes up to $5°–10°$ or more. Presumably whenever the properly oriented stimulus is applied within this area, it activates some cells with simple fields (different ones for different positions of the stimulus) and these in turn activate the complex cell. For example, a typical complex cell might be activated by a horizontal slit of light regardless of its exact position within a region several degrees in diameter. For such a cell changing the orientation by more than $5°–10°$ renders the stimulus ineffective, as does making it wider than some optimum width (e.g., more than $\frac{1}{4}°$). It is as though such a cell had the function of responding to the abstract quality "horizontal," irrespective of the exact retinal position.

The idea that a complex cell receives its input from a large number of simple cells all having the same receptive-field axis orientation has a remarkable parallel in the functional anatomy of the cat striate cortex. Cells that are close neighbors almost always have receptive-field axis orientations that are, as far as one can tell, identical. By making long penetrations in the manner of Mountcastle (Mountcastle, 1957; Powell and Mountcastle, 1959) one can show that the regions of constant axis orientation extend from surface to white matter, with walls perpendicular to the cortical layers (Hubel and Wiesel, 1962). Within one of these regions, or "columns," there occur all functional types of cell, including simple and complex. All the cells in a column have their receptive fields in the same general region of retina, but there is a slight variation in exact receptive-field position from one cell to the next. If we assume

that a complex cell receives its input from cells with simple fields in the same column, this constancy of receptive-field axis orientation together with the slight differences in position of fields is sufficient to account for all of the complex cell's properties. A column is thus considered to be a functional unit of cortex, to which geniculate axons project in such a way as to produce simple cortical fields all with the same axis orientation, and within which simple cells converge upon complex ones.

From the standpoint of cortical physiology it is interesting that these visual columns are in many ways analogous to the columns in the cat somatosensory cortex, described in 1957 by Mountcastle, and confirmed for the monkey by Powell and Mountcastle (1959). A columnar organization may be a feature of many cortical areas. It seems surprising that this type of organization, which must depend primarily on anatomical connections, should have no known anatomical correlate.

As far as we know all striate cortical cells in the cat can be categorized as simple or complex; there do not seem to be still higher orders of cells in this part of the brain. We are inclined to think of complex cells as representing a stage in the process of form generalization, since we can displace an image by several degrees on the retina, as long as we do not rotate it, and the population of complex cells that is influenced by the borders of the stimulus will not greatly change. The same is true if we distort the image, for instance by making it smaller or larger. As far as we know, this is the first stage in the mammalian visual pathway in which such an abstracting process occurs.

It is important to realize again that the size of a receptive field does not have any necessary bearing on a cell's ability to discriminate fine stimuli. In the cat a typical cortical receptive field in or near the area centralis may have a diameter of $1°–2°$, and complex fields range in size from $2°–3°$ up to $10°$ or more. Nevertheless the optimum stimuli for these cells are likely to be of the order of 10 minutes of arc in width. In a simple field this corresponds to a dimension such as the width of a long narrow receptive-field center. The presence of convergence at each stage of the visual pathway does lead to increased receptive-field size, but not to a loss of detail. This is the result of an interplay between inhibitory and excitatory processes.

So far I have not made any reference to one of the most important aspects of vision, namely movement. A moving stimulus commands attention more than a stationary one; clinically, movement is generally one of the first types of visual perception to return after a cortical injury (for references, see Teuber, Battersby, and Bender, 1960, p. 19); even for the perception of stationary objects, eye movements are probably necessary (Ditchburn and Ginsburg, 1952; Riggs, Ratliff, Cornsweet, and Cornsweet, 1953). It is not surprising, then, to find that a moving spot or pattern is in general a powerful stimulus for cortical cells. To understand why this is so we must return for a moment to a consideration of cells with simple fields. If we bring a spot from a neutral region of retina into a cell's excitatory area we produce an "on" response; if we remove a spot from the "off" region of a cell we evoke an "off" discharge. If we combine the two maneuvers by moving a spot from an "off" area into an "on" area, the two mechanisms work together to produce a greatly enhanced response. Of course, the cortical cell is most efficiently activated by the stimulus if it is a slit, dark bar, or edge, and if it is oriented in the direction appropriate for the cell. If the receptive field of the cell is not symmetrical (if one flank is smaller or produces less powerful effects than the other), the responses to two diametrically opposite directions of movement may be different. For example, a cell may fire when a spot is moved from left to right across the retina, but not when it is moved from right to left.

Now let us consider how a moving stimulus influences a complex cell. According to the scheme proposed above, a cell with complex properties receives its input from a number of cells with simple fields whose positions are staggered. Because of these differences in field position, a moving stimulus will activate first one simple cell and then another. The complex cell will thus be continuously bombarded and will fire steadily as the stimulus moves over a

relatively wide expanse of retina. A stationary stimulus shone into the receptive field of a complex cell evokes as a rule only a transient response because of the adaptation which presumably occurs at the receptors and at subsequent synapses. The moving pattern would bypass much of this adaptation by activating many cells in sequence.

The same mechanism may play a part in the perception of stationary objects by making use of the saccadic eye movements which, at least in man, seem necessary for the persistence of a visual impression. A visual image as it passes across the moving retina presumably activates numbers of simple cells briefly and in sequence leads to a more steady activation of a much smaller number of complex cells.

From what has been said so far it will be apparent that the striate cortex has a rich assortment of functions. It rearranges the input from the lateral geniculated body in such a way as to make lines and contours the most important stimuli. Directionality of stimuli must be accurately specified; the presence of a columnar system based on receptive-field axis orientation testifies to the importance of this variable. What appears to be a first step in the process of perceptual generalization results from a cell's responding to a property of a boundary (its orientation) apart from its exact position. Movement also becomes an important stimulus parameter, whose rate and direction both must be specified if a cell is to be effectively driven.

To this list one more function must be added, that of combining the pathways from the two eyes. In contrast to the lateral geniculate body, most cells in the cat cortex (probably at least 85%) receive input from the two eyes (Hubel and Wiesel, 1962, Part II). By mapping out receptive fields in each eye separately and comparing them we can begin to learn about the mechanisms of binocular vision, and perhaps ultimately something about binocular depth perception and binocular rivalry.

The primary visual, or striate, cortex is probably only an early stage of the visual pathway. Yet, unfortunately, we have very little knowledge of the pathway from this point on. Except in the rat (Nauta and Bucher, 1954) and cat (Beresford, 1961) the points to which the striate cortex projects are not known. Even less is known about the connections of the neighboring nonstriate visual cortex, called 18 and 19, or parastriate and peristriate; we have no accurate description of what areas project to them, or of where they send their projections. There even seem to be doubts as to the validity of the distinction between the two areas (Lashley and Clark, 1946). Clearly, more will have to be learned about the anatomy before neurophysiologists can make much progress in parts of the pathway beyond the striate cortex.

The work I have described may help to show how visual messages are handled by the brain, at least in the early stages of the process. The analysis takes us to what are probably at least sixth-order neurons in the visual pathway. Our understanding of cells with complex fields will be incomplete until we know how these properties are used at the next stage of integration, just as our grasp of the significance of retinal and geniculate receptive-field organization was incomplete without a knowledge of cortical receptive fields. There is no way of foreseeing what the next transformations will be, but to judge from what we have learned so far one would guess that the process of abstraction will go on, and that response specificity will increase. But it is well to remember that central nervous physiology is in a descriptive and exploratory phase. Our ignorance of CNS processes is such that the best predictions stand a good chance of being wrong.

Summary

One may study the visual system by stimulating the retina with spots or patterns of light and recording from single cells at successive stages in the visual pathway. By comparing response properties of the cells in a given structure with those of the fibers feeding into it we can attempt to learn something of how the structure modifies the visual information it receives. A description is given of responses of single cells in the optic nerve, the lateral geniculate body, and the visual cortex of the cat.

References

G. Arden and U. Söderberg, "The Transfer of Optic Information through the Lateral Geniculate Body of the Rabbit," in *Sensory Communication,* edited by W. A. Rosenblith (MIT Press and John Wiley & Sons, Inc., New York, 1961), pp. 521–544.

P. Bard, *Medical Physiology* (C. V. Mosby Company, St. Louis, Missouri, 1956), p. 1176.

W. A. Beresford, "Fibre Degeneration following Lesions of the Visual Cortex of the Cat," in *Neurophysiologie und Psychophysik des visuellen Systems,* edited by R. Jung and H. Kornhuber (Springer-Verlag, Berlin, 1961).

P. O. Bishop, W. Burke, and R. Davis, "Synapse Discharge by Single Fibre in Mammalian Visual System," Nature *182,* 728–730 (1958).

——, "Activation of Single Lateral Geniculate Cells by Stimulation of Either Optic Nerve," Science *130,* 506–507 (1959).

G. S. Brindley, *Physiology of the Retina and the Visual Pathway* (Edward Arnold, Ltd., London, 1960).

R. Cohn, "Laminar Electrical Responses in Lateral Geniculate Body of Cat," J. Neurophysiol, *19,* 317–324 (1956).

P. M. Daniel and D. Whitteridge, "The Representation of the Visual Field on the Cerebral Cortex in Monkeys," J. Physiol. (London) *159,* 203–221 (1961).

R. L. De Valois, "Color Vision Mechanisms in the Monkey," J. gen. Physiol. *43,* Pt. 2, 115–128 (1960).

R. W. Ditchburn and B. L. Ginsborg, "Vision with Stabilized Retinal Image," Nature *170,* 36–37 (1952).

R. W. Doty, "Potentials Evoked in Cat Cerebral Cortex by Diffuse and by Punctiform Photic Stimuli," J. Neurophysiol. *21,* 437–464 (1958).

S. D. Erulkar and M. Fillenz, "Single-Unit Activity in the Lateral Geniculate Body of the Cat," J. Physiol. (London) *154,* 206–218 (1960).

W. H. Freygang, Jr., "An Analysis of Extracellular Potentials from Single Neurons in the Lateral Geniculate Nucleus of the Cat," J. gen. Physiol. *41,* 543–564 (1958).

O.-J. Grüsser and G. Sauer, "Monoculare und binoculare Lichtreizung einzelner Neurone im Geniculatum laterale der Katze," Pflüg. Arch. ges. Physiol. *271,* 595–612 (1960).

W. R. Hayhow, "The Cytoarchitecture of the Lateral Geniculate Body in the Cat in Relation to the Distribution of Crossed and Uncrossed Optic Fibers," J. comp. Neurol. *110,* 1–64 (1958).

D. H. Hubel, "Single Unit Activity in Lateral Geniculate Body and Optic Tract of Unrestrained Cats," J. Physiol. (London) *150,* 91–104 (1960).

D. H. Hubel and T. N. Wiesel, "Receptive Fields of Single Neurons in the Cat's Striate Cortex," J. Physiol. (London), *148*, 574–591 (1959).

——, "Receptive Fields of Optic Nerve Fibres in the Spider Monkey," J. Physiol. (London), *154*, 572–580 (1960).

——, "Integrative Action in the Cat's Lateral Geniculate Body," J. Physiol. (London), *155*, 385–398 (1961).

——, "Receptive Fields, Binocular Interaction and Functional Architecture in the Cat's Visual Cortex," J. Physiol. *160*, 106–154 (1962).

R. Jung, "Microphysiologie corticaler Neurone: Ein Beitrag zur Koordination der Hirnrinde und des visuellen Systems," in *Structure and Function of the Cerebral Cortex,* edited by D. B. Tower and J. P. Schadé (Elsevier Publishing Company, Amsterdam, 1960).

R. Jung and H. Kornhuber, Editors, *Neurophysiologie und Psychophysik des Visuellen Systems* (Springer-Verlag, Berlin, 1961).

S. W. Kuffler, "Discharge Patterns and Functional Organization of Mammalian Retina," J. Neurophysiol. *16*, 37–68 (1953).

K. S. Lashley and G. Clark, "The Cytoarchitecture of the Cerebral Cortex of Ateles: a Critical Examination of Architectonic Studies," J. comp. Neuro. *85*, 223–305 (1946).

H. R. Maturana, J. Y. Lettvin, W. S. McCulloch, and W. H. Pitts, "Anatomy and Physiology of Vision in the Frog (*Rana pipiens*)," J. Gen. Physiol. *43*, Pt. 2, 129–176 (1960).

V. B. Mountcastle, "Modality and Topographic Properties of Single Neurons of Cat's Somatic Sensory Cortex," J. Neurophysiol. *20*, 408–434 (1957).

J. H. Nauta and V. M. Bucher, "Efferent Connections of the Striate Cortex in the Albino Rat," J. comp. Neurol. *100*, 257–286 (1954).

S. Polyak, *The Vertebrate Visual System,* edited by H. Klüver (The University of Chicago Press, Chicago, 1957).

T. P. S. Powell and V. B. Mountcastle, "Some Aspects of the Functional Organization of the Cortex of the Postcentral Gyrus of the Monkey: a Correlation of Findings Obtained in a Single Unit Analysis with Cytoarchitecture," Johns Hopkins Hospital Bull. *105*, 133–162 (1959).

L. A. Riggs, F. Ratliff, J. C. Cornsweet, and T. N. Cornsweet, "The Disappearance of Steadily Fixated Visual Test Objects," J. Opt. Soc. Am. *43*, 495–501 (1953).

W. A. Rosenblith, Editor, *Sensory Communication* (MIT Press and John Wiley & Sons, Inc., New York, 1961).

P. S. Silva, "Some Anatomical and Physiological Aspects of the Lateral Geniculate Body," J. comp. Neurol. *106*, 463–486 (1956).

K. U. Smith, "Visual Discriminations in the Cat: V. The Postoperative Effects of Removal of the Striate Cortex upon Intensity Discrimination," J. genet. Psychol. *51*, 329–369 (1937).

S. A. Talbot, "A Lateral Localization in the Cat's Visual Cortex," Federation Proc. *1*, 84 (1942).

S. A. Talbot and W. H. Marshall, "Physiological Studies on Neural Mechanisms of Visual Localization and Discrimination," Am. J. Ophthalmol. *24*, 1255–1263 (1941).

H. L. Teuber, W. S. Battersby, and M. B. Bender, *Visual Field Defects after Penetrating Missile Wounds of the Brain* (Harvard University Press, Cambridge, Massachusetts, 1960).

J. M. Thompson, C. N. Woolsey, and S. A. Talbot, "Visual Areas and II of Cerebral Cortex of Rabbit," J. Neurophysiol. *13*, 277–288 (1950).

L. Wildén and C. Ajmone-Marsan, "Effects of Corticipetal and Corticifugal Impulses upon Single Elements of the Dorsolatera Geniculate Nucleus," Exptl. Neurol. *2*, 468–502 (1960).

T. N. Wiesel, "Receptive Fields of Ganglion Cells in the Cat's Retina," J. Physiol. (London) *153*, 583–594 (1960).

M. L. Wolbarsht, H. G. Wagner, and E. F. MacNichol, Jr., "Receptive Fields of Retinal Ganglion Cells: Extent and Spectral Sensitivity," in *Neurophysiologie und Psychophysik des visuellen Systems,* edited by R. Jung and H. Kornhuber (Springer-Verlag, Berlin, 1961).

CHAPTER 2

Visual Masking

2.1 Method, Findings, and Theory in Studies of Visual Masking*

DANIEL KAHNEMAN

The study of visual masking is currently one of the most active fields of experimental psychology; more studies of visual masking have appeared since the most recent review of the field (Raab, 1963) than were cited in that review. Although the major theoretical issues in visual masking are yet to be resolved, an additional review may be timely. The present review is divided into five main parts. The first introduces terms and classifies various paradigms in the study of masking. The second part is concerned with measurements of the strength of masking effects. The third and fourth respectively review the effects of masking on the detection of flashes and on the identification of forms. Finally, theoretical interpretations of masking are briefly reviewed.

The coverage of the literature has been selective, and no attempt was made to compile a comprehensive list of titles in the field. Additional references may be found in Raab (1963) where masking effects in other modalities are

* Reprinted from the *Psychological Bulletin,* 1968, 69 (December), by permission of the American Psychological Association. Part of the material of this paper was presented at the Conference on Temporal Factors in Vision, conducted by the Center for Visual Science at the University of Rochester in June, 1966. The preparation of the manuscript was supported in part by the National Science Foundation, Contract No. GS–1153 to Harvard University, Center for Cognitive Studies, and in part by the National Institute of Mental Health, Grant No. 1 PO1–MH 12623, to Harvard University, Center for Cognitive Studies. An excellent review of the field of masking (Norman, 1965) facilitated the author's task. The very detailed comments of D. Aaronson, R. M. Boynton, and J. Norman are acknowledged with special thanks.

also described. Alpern (1952) reviewed early work on metacontrast, and Sperling (1965) provides a comprehensive discussion of the detection of light flashes under masking.

Paradigms of Visual Masking

TERMINOLOGY

The term *visual masking* appears to have been introduced by Pieron (1925) and was revived by Boynton & Kandel (1957). It covers the class of situations in which some measure of the effectiveness of a visual stimulus (the test stimulus, TS) is reduced by the presentation of another (the masking stimulus, MS) in close temporal contiguity to it.

1) When MS follows TS, the situation is one of backward masking. Forward masking is the case when MS precedes TS.

2) When TS and MS do not spatially overlap, the cases of backward and forward masking are respectively termed metacontrast and paracontrast (Stigler, 1910). However, the term *metacontrast* is often applied generically to masking by a non-overlapping figure, regardless of the temporal order of TS and MS.

3) In the case of spatial overlap between TS and MS, a distinction is drawn between masking by light and masking by pattern (Sperling, 1964). In masking by light, MS consists of a flash of homogenous illumination over an area that completely contains the contours of TS. The pattern in masking by pattern may be regular (Schiller & Wiener, 1963), or else it

may consist of a random array of white and dark areas (Sperling, 1963). Kinsbourne and Warrington (1962a, 1962b) termed the latter condition *masking by visual noise* and that usage will be followed here.

The presentations of TS and MS are usually separated by an interval. The inter-stimulus-interval (ISI) is the interval between the end of the first stimulus and the onset of the second. We shall use the term *stimulus-onset-asynchrony* (Kulli, 1967) and the initials SOA to refer to the interval between the onsets of the two stimuli.

Some idiosyncratic usages should be mentioned. Conditioning stimulus has been used for MS by several investigators (e.g., Boynton & Kandel, 1957; Battersby & Wagman, 1959), following Crawford (1947). In backward masking of course, TS actually precedes the conditioning stimulus that affects its detectability.

The term *erasure* was introduced by Averbach & Coriell (1961) to describe backward masking of a letter (black-on-white) by a black ring surrounding its position. In the present terms, the paradigm is one of metacontrast. More recently, Alpern and Rushton (1965) have used *after-flash effect* to denote the rise of absolute thresholds under conditions of metacontrast.

Mayzner and his colleagues (Mayzner, Tresselt, Adrignolo & Cohen, 1967; Mayzner, Tresselt & Cohen, 1967; Mayzner, Tresselt & Helfer, 1967) have studied a phenomenon that they term sequential blanking. The letters that make up a word are successively presented in their appropriate positions on a computer-controlled oscilloscope face, and the display is repeated indefinitely. With certain sequences of letter exposures, some of the letters are not seen at all, whereas the others remain relatively steady in the field; the word CHAIR may be seen as C A R, and this percept is maintained as long as the stimulus sequence is shown. This is sequential blanking. We shall treat the effect as a special case of metacontrast, since the interacting elements of the pattern appear in adjacent areas.

Lindsley (1961; Lindsley & Emmons, 1958) had previously introduced the term *blanking* for the masking of a patterned stimulus by a flash of light. He has also used the highly sug-gestive *clearing time* to denote that interval between onsets of TS and MS beyond which masking is no longer found. The temporal masking function where TS threshold is plotted as a function of SOA has been called an *on-response* (Boynton & Kandel, 1957; Boynton & Siegfried, 1962; Onley & Boynton, 1962). The absence of any reference to masking in the titles of Boynton's papers probably caused them to be missed by many potential readers.[1]

LIMITING CASES OF MASKING PARADIGMS

In the general limiting case of visual masking, TS and MS are presented together for an indefinite period. Different limiting sub-cases illustrate the great variety of situations that are grouped under the common label of masking:

1) The metacontrast and paracontrast paradigms reduce to conditions of simultaneous contrast, or to contour interference, depending on whether the effect under study is a change of apparent brightness or a reduction of acuity for TS.

2) When TS is a flash of light and MS is an overlapping larger flash, their simultaneous presentation is appropriate to a study of brightness discrimination.

3) When TS is a form and MS is a field of homogeneous illumination, their simultaneous presentation reduces figure-ground contrast for TS.

4) When TS is a form and MS is a field of visual noise, their joint presentation results in a general degrading of the image.

Masking paradigms are related to other designs in which visual stimulation is systematically varied over time. Thus, temporal integration may be viewed as a special case of masking —in which TS and MS are identical, and in which the usual result is facilitation rather than interference.[2]

Experimental conditions are identical in studies of forward masking by light and in

---

[1] *Psychological Abstracts,* for example, failed to see the connection, and do not list this work under masking.

[2] The *Broca-Sulzer effect,* in which a longer stimulus is less effective than a shorter stimulus of equal luminance (Boynton, 1961; Raab, 1962) will not be discussed in this review.

investigations of the onset of dark adaptation. It was in a study of light adaptation that Crawford (1947) discovered the *Crawford effect* of backward masking of a flash by a subsequent larger and more intense stimulus. Baker's work on masking (e.g. Baker, 1953, 1955, 1963) is consistently presented as a study of light and dark adaptation and Battersby & Wagman (1959), as well as Boynton & Miller (1963) have used these terms.

Finally, the stimulus conditions which produce metacontrast are closely related to those which produce apparent motion (Fehrer & Smith, 1962; Fehrer, 1966; Kahneman, 1967b; Mayzner, Tresselt & Cohen, 1966; Mayzner, Tresselt & Helfer, 1967; Toch, 1956). For example, apparent motion is seen when a pattern is shown first in one location and then in another; metacontrast suppression is obtained when the original pattern is simultaneously repeated in two different locations on the second exposure.

There is an important theoretical conclusion to be drawn from the list of associations between masking phenomena and other visual effects; the different variants of masking almost certainly involve different mechanisms, as their limiting cases do. It is therefore highly unlikely that a single theoretical concept can account for the different cases of masking.

Measurement of Masking Effects

The present section reviews different dependent variables which have been used as measures of visual masking.

DURATION THRESHOLDS

Duration thresholds have sometimes been used in the measurement of metacontrast (e.g. Fehrer, 1966; Kolers, 1962), and masking (e.g., Schiller, 1965b). The independent variable in these studies was ISI, and duration thresholds were plotted as a function of this variable.

When the duration of TS is varied, with ISI constant, the onset asynchrony between TS and MS, SOA, is completely confounded with the duration variable. The implicit assumption in this design is that ISI is the main determinant of masking effects, but the evidence indicates that SOA is the more important variable in both masking by light (Donchin, 1967) and metacontrast (Kahneman, 1967b). The confounding of SOA with duration is therefore undesirable.

LUMINANCE THRESHOLDS

In the standard design for investigations of the masking of light flashes, luminance thresholds for TS are determined as a function of SOA (e.g., Baker, 1963; Boynton, 1961; Sperling, 1965). Luminance thresholds have also been measured for the detection of a flash masked by metacontrast (Alpern, 1965; Alpern & Rushton, 1965). Schiller & Smith (1965) determined luminance thresholds for the identification of letters under several conditions of masking.

We shall use the term *masking function* for the display of threshold TS luminance against SOA (*See* Figure 1). Details of the shape of this function have been of considerable theoretical interest. The peak of the masking function defines the maximal masking effect of a particular MS.

In the masking function, TS luminance is plotted against the physical SOA between TS and MS. However, it should be noted that conduction speed is usually a function of stimulus intensity. Consequently, the asynchrony between the arrival-times of the two sensory messages to the locus where they interact is not necessarily the same as SOA (Baker, 1963; Crawford, 1947; Donchin, 1967). Variations of the luminance of TS and MS presumably affect the *effective* asynchrony between them, and thereby introduce a milder version of the complexities which were described above in the context of duration thresholds (Boynton & Siegfried, 1962).

PROBABILITY OF SUCCESS

Many experimenters have displayed masking effects by plotting probability of detection or identification of a target against SOA or ISI. The method is very often used in studies of the masking of letters and words. There is no confounding of dependent and independent variables in this method. However, it suffers from the important drawback that the probability variable is sensitive only over a narrow range. The rule of thumb, in many visual situations, is that detection of a target varies from chance to absolute certainty with a 10-fold variation of target luminance. By the normal standards of visual experimentation, this is a small range. One study of letter recognition in which luminance thresholds were determined (Boynton & Miller, 1963) included conditions where TS threshold varied by a factor of 10,000. Thus, any masking effect which can be measured by probability of success would be considered minute by most visual scientists.

The physical characteristics of TS, including size, luminance, and duration, are usually kept constant or treated as parameters when masking is measured by probability of success. Other variables are manipulated such as the luminance of MS or ISI. The investigator faces the problem of selecting targets for which probability of success will be neither as high as 100% nor as low as chance performance, over the range of conditions which are to be studied. Normally, different Ss will require different targets if this requirement is to be met.

In Eriksen's laboratory the difficulty of the identification task is equated for different Ss by manipulating the duration of TS. For each S, a duration is found at which he is successful on, say, 80% of the trials in the absence of masking. The duration of TS is maintained at that value under all conditions of masking, and the probability of success is most often plotted as a function of ISI (e.g., Eriksen & Collins, 1964; Eriksen & Lappin, 1964; Eriksen & Steffy, 1964). In this procedure, different Ss experience different values of SOA, in precise correspondence with their original duration thresholds. The variable of duration is ignored when probability of success is finally displayed against ISI. However, Eriksen always ascertains that the variations of treatment for the different Ss have no effect, by testing the significance of the Subject x ISI interaction.

Kahneman (1966) used a similar procedure in a study of the effects of masking on acuity, but he adjusted target size rather than duration of exposure to make the task equally difficult

for different subjects. The likelihood of undesirable confounding may be somewhat smaller in this case than when exposure durations are allowed to vary.

BRIGHTNESS MATCHING

Two studies measured metacontrast effects in terms of the reduced brightness of TS. Alpern's subjects (1953) adjusted the luminance of TS to make its brightness match a standard. Such a procedure introduces major variations in the strength of the masking effect that is ostensibly under study (Fehrer & Smith, 1962). Schiller & Smith (1966) used the more appropriate method of manipulating the luminance of a comparison stimulus to match the changing brightness of TS, at different values of SOA. However, they encountered another difficulty; in the most critical range of masking, TS is not seen, and its brightness cannot be judged.

RATING METHODS AND PHENOMENOLOGICAL REPORTS

Ratings have recently been used in studies of metacontrast. Blanc-Garin (1965) obtained ratings of apparent contrast for a black target which was masked by metacontrast. A different rating method has been introduced by Kahneman (1967b). A perceptual effect, such as metacontrast or apparent motion, is described to S in some detail. S is then shown various displays, and he rates each of them for their correspondence to the effect that was described to him. The work of Mayzner's group, most recently reviewed by Mayzner, Tresselt, & Helfer (1967) relies on a particularly simple type of phenomenological report. A sequence of adjacent symbols is repeatedly presented on a computer-controlled scope face, and the observer merely reports which symbols he can see. Different observers show essentially perfect agreement in their reports, and these vary systematically with such parameters as exposure duration, SOA, and the order of appearance of the symbols.

ACUITY MEASURES

Visual acuity, the ability to resolve details of form, is the single most important dimension of visual effectiveness. Acuity is operationally defined by the minimal size of detail that can still be resolved. Standard tests of acuity are available, which are equally applicable to the calibration of stimulus conditions and to the measurement of individual differences (Boynton, 1962; Luckiesh, 1944).

Since masking operations reduce S's ability to recognize forms it is true by definition that these procedures reduce visual acuity. However, because the reduction of acuity was not explicitly recognized as such, masking effects have never been assessed in terms of critical size.

The failure to conceptualize the masking of form as a reduction of acuity has had an important methodological consequence. It is standard practice for each investigator to select the targets that are to be resolved under masking, and thus to construct his own test of acuity. Consequently, results obtained in different laboratories are often difficult to compare. In assessing the effects of a masking ring on letter recognition, for example, one laboratory has used the letters A, T, and U, presented at low energy (Eriksen & Collins, 1965; Eriksen, Collins, & Greenspoon, 1967). Another (Weisstein, 1966; Weisstein & Haber, 1965) used the letters O and D, and a higher stimulating energy. The two conditions can hardly be considered equivalent tests of acuity.

The technical difficulties of preparing a large number of stimuli which differ only in size may discourage the investigator from using target size as the dependent variable in studies of masking. However, it is sometimes advisable to use a standard acuity target for all conditions, and to measure masking by some variable other than critical size. Boynton & Miller (1963) used the Sloan-Snellen letters, and measured the contrast threshold for correct identification of the letters, under various masking conditions. Kahneman (1966) used a Landolt ring, and determined the probability of successful recognition with and without masking. The use of a standard acuity target such as the Landolt ring or the Snellen E has an important advantage. It provides an immediately interpretable index of the severity of the basic viewing conditions. We recognize at a glance

that the conditions which produce an acuity of 0.04 are extremely severe, whereas conditions are optimal if an acuity of 1.5 is attained. The present custom of reporting letter size and viewing distance in inches is hardly a satisfactory substitute, as it precludes adequate comparisons among studies.

Detection of Target Flashes under Masking

MASKING BY LIGHT

The Masking Function. A standard design has been used with few modifications in a large number of studies of flash detection under masking. TS is a brief flash which illuminates a small circular patch. MS is a more intense flash, illuminating a larger area. The two flashes are often superposed on a larger adapting field. Detection thresholds are obtained for TS at a series of values of SOA, almost always by short-cut psychophysical methods. The parameters that are most often varied in studies of masking are the luminances of MS and the adapting field (Baker, 1953, 1955, 1963; Battersby & Wagman, 1959, 1962; Crawford, 1947; Onley & Boynton, 1962; Sperling, 1965; Wagman & Battersby, 1959). For additional references *see* Sperling, (1965).

Figure 1 shows a schematic masking function, which illustrates the main features that have been reported by many experiments in the past. When TS precedes MS by 100–150 msec, its threshold is paradoxically lowered. The phenomenon of "backward sensitization" has been described by Sperling (1965); backward sensitization is also apparent in the data of Boynton & Miller (1963). When TS precedes MS by less than 50–100 msec, the threshold for its detection rises steeply. This is backward masking, also known in this context as the Crawford effect. Masking effects are usually most severe at SOA $= 0$, and the threshold for detection of TS gradually declines with further increases in SOA, until it finally reaches a stable light-adapted value (Baker, 1963). A slight rise in threshold is sometimes reported when TS just precedes the termination of MS, or coincides with it (Battersby & Wagman, 1962).

Masking as a Measure of On-Response. Boynton (1958, 1961; Boynton & Kandel, 1957; Boynton & Siegfried, 1962; Onley & Boynton, 1962) was impressed by the similarity between the masking function of Figure 1 and the temporal course of the on-discharge to a sudden increase of illumination. In his view, MS occasions a massive discharge; the visual system is overloaded by this response, and therefore fails to respond to the smaller and weaker TS. The masking function (Figure 1) is a measure of the on-response to MS. Baker (1955, 1963) has outlined a similar position.

In an elegant derivation from this theory, Boynton (1958; Boynton & Kandel, 1957) reasoned that pre-adaptation to light should deplete the store of available photochemical material, and thereby reduce the on-response to MS and its ability to interfere with TS. Thus, a high state of light adaptation should result in a *lower* threshold for the detection of TS under masking. This prediction was confirmed. The luminance threshold for TS at SOA = 0 was

the measure of the on-response (to MS) in these analyses. Thresholds were obtained under three conditions:

$$B_o = \text{threshold for TS under dark adaptation, without masking}$$
$$B_p = \text{threshold for TS under light adaptation, without masking}$$
$$B_{mp} = \text{threshold for TS under light adaptation, with masking}$$

The net masking effect of MS, with adaptation effects removed, is $B_m = B_{mp} (B_o/B_p)$, where the expression within parentheses is assumed to measure the reduction of visual sensitivity by light adaptation. Related subtraction procedures were employed by Battersby & Wagman (1959) and by Sperling (1965).

In subsequent studies of the on-response, Boynton & Siegfried (1962) showed essentially identical masking effects of two brief stimuli that differed in luminance and duration but were equal in total energy. The two on-responses differed only in latency; the response to the briefer and more intense stimulus was faster. Onley & Boynton (1962) used different

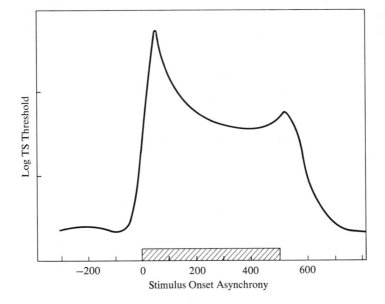

FIGURE 1 Schematic masking function. The threshold for detection of a brief TS is plotted against SOA. The duration of MS is 500 msec. Plotted values are characteristic but arbitrary.

levels of light adaptation to vary the apparent brightness of the masking flash independently of its luminance. They concluded that masking flashes which are equal in brightness often have identical masking effects.

Sperling (1965) defines the masking effect as $(B_{mp} - B_p)$. In several sets of data, including those of Onley & Boynton (1962), Weber's law applies. The difference $(B_{mp} - B_p)$ is linearly related to the energy of MS, and is independent of the adapting luminance on which TS and MS are superimposed.

Contour Effects. Battersby & Wigman (1959) used a subtraction procedure to estimate the relative contribution of photochemical and neural factors to the masking effect. They agreed with other investigators (Baker, 1963; Boynton, 1961; Sperling, 1965) that masking effects are mainly neural, but went further than others in suggesting that much of the interaction of TS and MS may occur at a central locus. The suggestion is supported by the occurrence of backward masking at SOA's of 50–100 msec. At these SOA's the sensory message elicited by TS has already reached the cortex when MS is shown. Further support for central effects in masking is derived from studies of dichoptic masking, where TS is shown to one eye and MS to the other (Battersby & Wagman, 1962; Battersby, Osterreich & Sturr, 1964; Boynton, 1961; Wagman & Battersby, 1959). Dichoptic masking is pronounced only when the contours of TS and MS are adjacent, which also defines the condition for severe binocular rivalry (Kahneman, 1967a). The evidence indicates that dichoptic interaction is almost exclusively a contour effect. Adjacent contours also favor masking in the monoptic case, but less dramatically.

Robinson (1966) has reported a phenomenon of disinhibition in which contour processes are probably involved. TS is a 0.23° circular patch, 5 ml in luminance and 20 msec in duration. MS, which follows after an ISI of 25 msec, is a circular patch of similar luminance and duration, 0.46° in diameter. TS is never seen. However, when MS is followed in turn by a larger flash (0.92° diameter) the first circle is seen on 80% of trials and the second is never seen! The disinhibition effect was subsequently confirmed by Dember & Purcell (1967).

Observer's Criterion and the Masking Function. Sperling (1965) has offered an analysis of the masking effect which illustrates the central importance of the observer's criterion, although Sperling himself does not emphasize the term. An explication of the concept of criterion may facilitate the discussion of Sperling's views, and will be useful later in our description of metacontrast.

The term *criterion* has at least two distinct meanings. Specification of *criterion level* answers a quantitative question: how reluctant is the subject to give a particular response? Criterion in this sense is used in detection theory. Experiments within that theoretical framework have repeatedly shown that criterion level may be made to vary over a wide range by suitable manipulations of payoffs and expectancies (Green & Swets, 1966; Swets, 1964). When S is allowed only the two responses "yes" and "no", the criterion is said to be low if yes-responses are relatively frequent. By specifying *criterion content*, one answers such questions as "can S maintain a stable criterion in judging the brightness of flashes that vary in duration?" or "what criterion does S apply when he reports a failure to see TS in a metacontrast display?" These questions concern phenomenology. They request a fuller description of the code that S uses in mapping his private experience onto responses to E's questions.

Detection theory has emphasized the lability of criterion level and has generally ignored the issue of criterion content. However, an important fact must be noted: in many situations, different subjects apparently gravitate towards the use of criteria that are highly similar in both content and level, and each subject appears capable of maintaining such a criterion over many sets of observations. In the following discussion, a criterion that meets the requirements of within-subject reliability and intersubject agreement is called a *natural criterion*.

The data reviewed by Sperling (1965) demonstrate that a natural criterion exists in studies of the masking of one flash by another. Different observers in different laboratories, all using yes-no responses as a semantic indicator (Goldiamond, 1958) provide essentially identical masking functions (Baker, 1963; Battersby & Wagman, 1959; Crawford, 1947; Onley & Boynton, 1962). Further, the *level* of this natural criterion is low: Sperling (1965) confirmed this conclusion by requiring confidence ratings in series of trials, including catch trials on which TS was not shown. However, the *content* of the criterion appears to vary systematically with SOA in the masking experiment.

Sperling's analysis of the masking function in Figure 1 relies heavily on hypothesized variations of criterion content. Thus, the threshold is highest at SOA = 0 because the observer is forced to rely exclusively on spatial contrast between the brightness of the target, which is illuminated by both TS and MS, and that of the surround, which is illuminated by MS alone. However, S is capable of using temporal contrast as well, when MS precedes TS: the central area increases in brightness when TS is superimposed on it, then becomes dimmer again. This additional information leads to lower thresholds. The backward masking effect when TS precedes MS is explained by a lack of temporal resolution. Backward sensitization, the slight decrease of threshold for TS when it precedes MS by 100 msec (*see* Figure 1) is explained as follows: even a sub-threshold TS may noticeably reduce the brightness of MS, and observers use this information in reporting that TS has been presented. Finally, Sperling reanalyzes the data of an earlier experiment (Battersby & Wagman, 1959) and notes that a 500 msec MS is much more effective than a 50 msec MS of equal luminance. Sperling believes that the longer flash more effectively prevents the perception of an after-image of TS (Sperling, 1960b). Similarly, he interprets the paradoxical decrease of thresholds with increases of background luminance (Boynton & Kandel, 1957) as due to the elimination of after-images of MS.

The long list of variations of criterion-content is not the main point of Sperling's paper. Rather, Sperling relies on these variations to justify his exclusive concern with the peak of the masking function, and to explain aberrant findings. His main intent is to show that the threshold at SOA = 0 is a pure contrast discrimination, and that the masking effect (B_{mp} − B_p) follows Weber's law and is largely independent of background luminance and of MS brightness. These conclusions are contrary to Boynton's analysis. In addition, we may note that the entire approach to the masking function differs sharply from Boynton's interpretation of that function as an on-response to MS. The phenomenological effects that Sperling describes deserve much further study.

DETECTION UNDER METACONTRAST

Metacontrast Paradigms. In metacontrast (Alpern, 1952; Stigler, 1910) the brightness of TS is reduced when its presentation is followed by that of MS to an adjacent area. Under many conditions, the effect of metacontrast is more radical than mere dimming; TS is reported to be phenomenally absent (Alpern, 1952, 1965; Alpern & Rushton, 1965; Fehrer & Raab, 1962; Fehrer & Biederman, 1962; Kahneman, 1967b, Kolers, 1962; Kolers & Rosner, 1960; Schiller, 1965a; Toch, 1956; Werner, 1935). We shall refer to the phenomenal disappearance of TS as metacontrast suppression.

Metacontrast suppression has been demonstrated under a variety of spatial arrangements of TS and MS (Alpern, 1952; Mayzner, Tresselt, & Cohen, 1966; Mayzner, Tresselt, Adrignolo, & Cohen, 1967; Mayzner, Tresselt, & Helfer, 1967; Toch, 1956; Werner, 1935, 1940). However, most research has been done with two particular displays. These are closely related to well known displays which produce two types of apparent motion (Kahneman, 1967b):

a) In the three-object display, a pattern is shown, and its presentation is followed by that of two similar patterns which flank it on either side (Alpern, 1953; Fehrer & Biederman, 1962; Fehrer & Raab, 1962; Fry, 1934; Kahneman, 1967b). All one need do in order to produce *beta* motion is remove one of the flanking objects. The complex displays that Mayzner

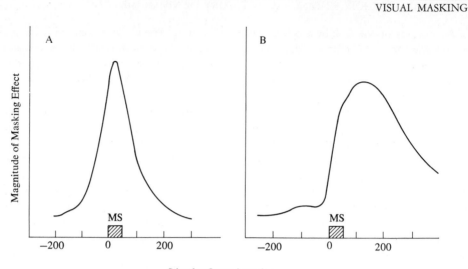

FIGURE 2   Two types of masking functions in metacontrast.

and his colleagues have investigated belong to this group.

b) In the disk-ring display, TS is a disk and MS is a ring; the inner contour of this ring is adjacent to, or coincident with the outer contour of the desk (Heckenmueller & Dember, 1965a, 1965b; Kolers, 1962; Kolers & Rosner, 1960; Schiller, 1965a; Schiller & Smith, 1966; Werner, 1935). The display is related to one in which a disk followed by another larger disk produces expansion-motion.

Masking Functions in Metacontrast. Two types of masking functions which have been obtained in metacontrast experiments are illustrated in Figure 2. The ordinate of Figure 2 is labelled *magnitude of masking effect* with deliberate ambiguity, because the two functions are usually obtained by different operations of measurement. The two types of masking functions have been called type A and type B by Kolers (1962). In A, the peak masking effect occurs at SOA = 0, and there is much forward masking (Battersby, Osterreich & Sturr, 1964; Fehrer & Smith, 1962; Kietzman, 1962). In B, there is little or no masking at SOA = 0, forward masking is weak or absent, and the peak masking effect is found at an SOA of 50–100 msec (Alpern, 1953; Fehrer & Smith, 1962; Kahneman, 1967b, Kolers, 1962; Mayzner, Tresselt, & Cohen, 1966; Mayzner, Tresselt,

Adrignolo & Cohen, 1967; Schiller & Smith, 1966; Toch, 1956; Weisstein, 1968; Werner, 1935).

The conditions that determine whether masking follows a function of type A or type B are reasonably well understood. A most important determinant is the observer's criterion. Metacontrast suppression can be obtained even when TS and MS are identical in intensity and duration (Kahneman, 1967b); it then follows a type B function. Most observers agree, in a three-object display, that there is nothing where the central object ought to be. However, the appearance of the display is easily discriminable from the presentation of MS alone (Fehrer & Raab, 1962; Fehrer & Smith, 1962; Schiller, 1965a; Schiller & Smith, 1966). The two objects that are seen in the three-object display are often seen to move away from the center. That impression of motion is of course absent when the two flanking objects are not preceded by MS, and the difference is easily available to the observer if he is to discriminate between a three-object and a two-object display. Similarly, Mayzner's display in which some letters of a word are never *seen* is easily distinguished from a display in which these letters are in fact not shown. The use of a semantic indicator will therefore indicate that masking occurs under conditions in which an accuracy indicator would show perfect discrimination.

The conclusion follows that the level of the natural criterion is high when a semantic indicator is used in metacontrast. Criterion-content is such that S says "yes" only when a well-formed image of definite contour is visible in the center of the display. The motion of the masking figures is ignored, since the observer confines his report to the presence or absence of the central object.

Type A masking functions can be obtained even with a semantic indicator, but only when MS is a much stronger visual stimulus than TS in terms of duration, luminance, or figure-ground contrast (Fehrer & Smith, 1962; Kolers, 1962). The dependent variable in these studies was the probability of reporting seeing MS, which was plotted as a function of ISI. Type A functions are also obtained when the detection threshold of MS is determined by varying its luminance (Battersby, Osterreich, & Sturr, 1964, Kietzman, 1962). The low criterion-level that this type of experimental situation tends to induce necessarily results in a very marked imbalance between the energy levels of TS and MS.

The conclusion of this section must be that type B masking functions do not represent absolute detection thresholds in any sensible use of that controversial term. The suppression of TS in type B functions is not complete. Thus, the well-known experiment of Fehrer & Raab (1962) demonstrated that Ss in a simple reaction-time situation respond to the initial TS, which they never *perceive*. This important result has been replicated several times (Fehrer & Biederman, 1962; Harrison & Fox, 1966; Schiller & Smith, 1966). In addition, Schiller & Chorover (1966) have shown that the evoked potential to TS is essentially intact in metacontrast, even when TS appears extremely dim, or fails altogether to be seen. The situation is different in the masking of a small flash by a larger overlapping flash; in that case, the correlation between the perceived brightness of TS and the evoked potential is quite close (Donchin & Lindsley, 1965b).

It is also significant in this context that type A and type B metacontrast can be obtained dichoptically. Battersby, Osterreich, & Sturr (1964) presented an illuminated disk to one eye, and a ring to the other, and determined the masking function for the detection of the disc. The function is very similar to that of masking by light (Figure 1). Schiller (1965a) obtained a type A function in dichoptic metacontrast with black targets. Werner (1940), Toch (1956), Kolers & Rosner (1960), and Mayzner, Tresselt, Adrignolo, & Cohen (1967) obtained type B metacontrast dichoptically with several different stimulus arrangements. In summary, the evidence is not consistent with an interpretation of metacontrast suppression in terms of retinal interaction (Alpern, 1965; Alpern & Rushton, 1965). Such an interpretation is particularly inappropriate to data which apparently conform to a type B function, since this function is typically associated with a high criterion-level.

Metacontrast Suppression—Two Types or One? The preceding section described the two types of results that may be obtained in a metacontrast experiment: the type B function, which occurs when TS and MS are similar in energy, and can only be obtained with a semantic indicator and at a high criterion level; the type A function, which is characteristically observed when MS is markedly longer or more intense than TS. Do the two functions represent different types of suppression processes? Is there a simple comprehensive theory that may explain the two?

Several partial theories have recently been advanced to account for type B functions. One theory was first proposed by Fehrer (1965; 1966; Fehrer & Smith, 1962) and further developed by Kahneman (1967b). The essential idea in this view is that type B functions are closely related to the phenomenon of apparent motion, whereas type A functions are not. The similarity of the type B masking function to the temporal parameters of apparent motion was noted incidentally by several authors Fehrer & Raab, 1962; Kolers & Rosner, 1960; Toch, 1956; Schiller & Smith, 1966; Werner, 1935). In fact the temporal parameters of the two effects are virtually identical (Kahneman 1967b). In that study, complete metacontrast suppression occurred at an SOA of about 100 msec, which also produced most reports of optimal motion. Kahneman (1967b) noted that the three-object display provides cues for an *impossible motion* of the central object in two directions at once, much in the way that the drawings of Penrose & Penrose (1958) provide cues for impossible three-dimensionality. The disk-ring sequence is similarly impossible in that the disk is made to grow and disappear at the same time. These observations suggest that metacontrast suppression may result from a failure of perceptual synthesis.

The most compelling evidence of a link between metacontrast suppression and impossible motion has been offered by Mayzner and his colleagues (Mayzner, Tresselt, & Cohen, 1966; Mayzner, Tresselt, Adrignolo, & Cohen, 1967), although they prefer another interpretation (Mayzner, Tresselt, & Helfer, 1967). When the letters of a word are shown in irregular succession in their computer-controlled display, the letters that are presented first fail to be seen. Even the two extreme letters of a word may be suppressed when they cannot be incorporated in a coherent percept of motion. The suppression is invariably a U-shaped function of presentation speed. On the other hand, all letters are seen in the many different sequences that permit the perception of a regular flow of motion.

There are other indications that backward masking and apparent motion may be closely related. Kahneman (1967b; Kahneman & Wolman, 1968) has noted that optimal motion involves an apparently retroactive suppression and modification of the percept of the first object to be shown. In addition, the effects of a value of SOA that is too short for optimal motion (or suppression) are strikingly similar in the two-object and three-object displays: the first object is seen as dimmer than the others. The dimming effect was noted by Wertheimer (1912) in the motion display; it depends very little on whether TS is followed by one object or by two.

Another theory of type B masking functions was proposed by Mayzner, Tresselt, & Helfer (1967). The authors note that the effects of a stimulus S_1 are particularly susceptible to interference by a subsequent stimulus S_2 that follows S_1 after an SOA of 100 msec. They suggest that the visual input is delayed at a gate prior to entry into subjective experience, and is especially vulnerable at the instant of entry. The model is constructed specifically to account for the large quantity of data collected by these authors on various types of sequential blanking and displacement.

The partial theories that have been listed so far are obviously inapplicable to type A masking functions. Alternative mechanisms have been mentioned to account for the latter result. Fehrer & Smith (1962) and Kahneman (1967b) noted that those conditions of imbalance between TS and MS which produce type A functions also favor the occurrence of lateral inhibition and simultaneous contrast. It is therefore possible that the two types of masking functions are due to two distinct suppression processes: type A is akin to masking by overlapping light (Kolers, 1962; Schiller, 1965a) and involves lateral inhibition; type B is an interaction that can occur only between successive stimuli, as is the case in apparent motion.

There has been one attempt to deal with both types of masking functions by a single set of processes (Weisstein, 1968). Weisstein showed that a process of lateral inhibition can produce type B masking functions. She assumes that the detection of TS depends on whether, at any time, the algebraic sum of an excitatory process (generated by TS) and of an inhibitory process (generated by MS) is sufficient to activate a central decision unit. She further assumes that the inhibitory activity produced by MS has a shorter latency than the excitatory activity due to TS, when the two stimuli are equal in duration and luminance. Therefore, if the two stimuli are presented simultaneously (SOA = 0) inhibition will be past its maximum when excitation builds up to its peak; inhibition thus *misses* excitation and there is little masking. The presentation of TS must consequently be delayed in order to increase the temporal overlap between the excitation and inhibition processes; this yields a type B masking function. Now consider the effect of making MS longer than TS; at SOA = 0, the rise of inhibition still precedes that of excitation, but inhibition is now maintained during the entire excitatory response to TS, and total suppression occurs. The masking function now belongs to type A, since TS is seen only when the SOA is so long that the excitation produced by TS occurs earlier than the inhibition produced by MS. Similar considerations explain the effect of the luminance ratio on the shape of the masking function.

Weisstein (1968) constructed a five-neuron model incorporating this basic idea, and simulated on a computer the results of a number of metacontrast studies. The model elaborates Landahl's (1967) conception of neural nets. It is generally successful in separating conditions leading to type A and to type B functions, but the success of predictions concerning the shape of masking functions is less impressive.

Weisstein's formulation has an advantage of specificity and parsimony over all its predecessors. However, the relation between type B metacontrast and apparent motion is too compelling to be ignored, as it is in her theory. It now appears likely that a comprehensive theory may be able to account for both these effects by the operation of a single mechanism. Weisstein's work indicates that variations of quantitative parameters of that mechanism may yield type A functions on some occasions and type B functions on others. Her model would have to be further elaborated to account for the fact that *creative* effects such as *beta*-motion are sometimes the counterpart of the suppressive effects of metacontrast. The function of perceptual synthesis should be added to the functions of excitation and inhibition that the model presently considers.

A PLEA FOR PHENOMENOLOGICAL DESCRIPTION

The studies that were reviewed in preceding sections illustrate the importance of phenomenological reports. Even informal reports may serve to illuminate complex results, as in Sperling's (1965) analysis of the masking function. Further, reports of subjective experience may become a source of data, as in the studies of metacontrast by Mayzner's group and by Kahneman. The high level of within-subject and between-subject reliability that is easily attained by naive observers justifies the use of this approach in studies of masking.

In the context of more *objective* studies of detection thresholds, the crucial role of the observer's criterion deserves special emphasis. Detection theory has emphasized one aspect of the problem, the necessity for control and specification of criterion level. The present treatment emphasizes the necessity of adequate specification of criterion content. The literature is notably deficient in this respect, perhaps because the description of criterion content involves phenomenological reports and sometimes requires detailed introspection. Whether we like it or not, however, the content of the subject's criterion determines his performance, and should therefore be described with the same care that is customarily devoted to specifying the stimulus. It is common practice, in visual science, to devote pages of text to the independent variable and to dismiss the dependent variable in a sentence.

The literature on masking consists very largely of threshold studies, where a low criterion level is presumably desirable. It should be emphasized, however, that a high criterion level may be quite valuable, provided only that it is a natural criterion. Type B metacontrast is just as real as type A, even if it is obtained only when criterion is high. In fact, a low criterion level may produce results which are hard to interpret. Sperling's (1965) analysis of the masking of flashes suggests that a criterion level which is consistently low may be associated with a criterion content which is highly variable over conditions; the observer uses all available cues in attempting to maintain a high rate of detection.

Identification of Forms under Masking

Identification of forms has been studied under three modes of masking: by an overlapping field of homogeneous luminance (masking by light); by a contour-rich overlapping field (masking by noise); and by contour surrounding the target (masking by metacontrast). The three paradigms are examined in subsequent section.

MASKINGS OF FORMS BY LIGHT

The Masking Function. Boynton & Miller (1963) report the only study in which a standard masking function was obtained for an identification task. They determined the contrast required for the identification of Sloan-Snellen letters of four different sizes, projected in positive contrast, under several conditions of sudden increase or decrease of background illumination. The masking functions that they obtained for identification are identical in shape to the functions reported for detection (Figure 1). In fact, Boynton & Miller report that the same contrast is required for a letter to be read and for a circular patch of similar size to be detected. The most plausible interpretation of this important result may be that the detection of the light patch was itself limited by contour processes under the conditions that Boynton & Miller studied.

Two characteristics of the masking function have been confirmed in a number of experiments:

1) A masking flash interferes with the identification of TS, both when it precedes TS (forward masking) and when it follows TS (backward masking).

2) Forward and backward masking effects are both most severe when TS and MS follow one another immediately (ISI = 0) (e.g., Eriksen & Hoffman, 1963; Eriksen & Lappin, 1964; Schiller, 1965b, 1966; Schiller & Smith, 1965).

Eriksen & Lappin (1964) found that the dependence of masking on ISI is very similar in forward and in backward masking. Mowbray & Durr (1964) masked target words by a black rectangle and also found forward and backward masking to be similar. However, other evidence indicates that the temporal range of forward masking is larger than that of backward masking (Kietzman, 1962; Schiller & Smith, 1965; Smith & Schiller, 1966).

Masking of forms by an unpatterned MS cannot be obtained dichoptically (Mowbray & Durr, 1964; Schiller, 1965a; Schiller & Wiener, 1963, Smith & Schiller, 1966). This result is to be expected on the general principle that dichoptic effects in masking correspond to dominance effects in binocular rivalry, (Kahneman, 1967a). When contours are presented to one eye, and a homogeneous field of light to the other, the contours are always perceived with little or no interference.

The time-intensity reciprocity law does not apply to the resolution of form under conditions of masking by light; a brief and intense exposure of TS is less effective than one that is weaker and prolonged (Kahneman, 1966; Kaswan & Young, 1963; Scharf, Zamansky, & Brightbill, 1966). The interpretation of this result must be qualified by Donchin's comment (Donchin, 1967) that duration of exposure is confounded with SOA in these experiments.

Interpretations of Masking by Light. Consider the limiting case of masking by light in which MS (a homogeneous field of light) and TS (a contoured pattern) are presented simultaneously; light from MS is spread over both the figure and the background of TS and reduces the contrast between them. Eriksen and his students (Eriksen, 1966; Eriksen & Hoffman, 1963; Eriksen & Lappin, 1964; Eriksen & Steffy, 1964; Thompson, 1966) have presented a theory of masking by light which reduces that effect to its limiting case of reduced figure-ground contrast. The physical asynchrony of TS and MS is assumed to be bridged by temporal integration of luminance. This is the luminance summation theory of masking by light.

Luminance summation theory entails that there should be little difference between forward and backward masking: temporal integration occurs in either case. In fact, the similarity between functions for forward and backward masking is often quite impressive (Eriksen & Lappin, 1964; Kahneman, 1966, Mowbray & Durr, 1964; Schiller & Smith, 1965). Eriksen (1966) has presented support for several other qualitative predictions derived from the theory, and Thompson (1966) has shown that the interfering effects of masking by light and of contrast-reduction are generally similar. There is no reason to doubt that luminance integration of TS and MS reduces the contrast of TS and thereby impairs its resolution. However, there are effects of masking by light for which luminance summation theory cannot account. Other factors are involved.

A study by Kahneman (1965) indicated that masking by light reduces the apparent contrast of a figure in two ways: directly, by luminance summation; indirectly, by preventing or retarding the formation of bounding contours. A matching method was used to measure the apparent contrast of a black square that was presented under standard tachistoscopic conditions, i.e. with pre- and post-exposure fields matching the luminance of the background on which the square was shown. Luminance summation theory entails that apparent contrast should be a linear function of exposure duration in this situation, reaching maximal contrast at the critical duration for brightness. In fact, the results indicate the existence of a definite duration threshold for the appearance of bounding contours, which is as high as 40 msec at very low luminances. Only flicker is seen below that threshold, but apparent contrast rises rapidly when contours are finally seen, and soon rejoins the function predicted by luminance summation. The presentation of a thin outline of the target square in the adapting field, which provides the target with prefabricated contours, yields a good fit to the linear function predicted by luminance summation theory.

Contour effects may be responsible for other results that luminance summation theory cannot explain:

(1) The disinhibition effects reported by Robinson (1966) and by Dember & Purcell (1967).
(2) The superior acuity for a target that is superimposed on a steady adapting field, compared to the case in which the adapting field is briefly turned off during target presentation (Kahneman, 1966).
(3) The transient reduction of acuity when target and mask are presented simultaneously, compared to the light-adapted acuity when MS precedes TS, which is later superimposed on it (Boynton & Miller, 1963).

Transient *on* and *off* responses occur in all these instances (Boynton, 1961; Dember & Purcell, 1967; Schiller, 1968). The technique of making contours of TS available in the adapting field could be used to discover whether transient interference acts directly on the apparent brightness and contrast of TS, or whether the effect is mediated by retardation of contour formation.

MASKING BY NOISE

Masking by noise is much more effective in reducing form recognition than is masking by light (Scharf, Zamansky, & Brightbill, 1966; Sperling, 1963; Schiller, 1965b; Schiller & Wiener, 1963; Smith & Schiller, 1966). The most important difference between the two types of masking is that masking by noise or pattern occurs in dichoptic presentation (Kinsbourne & Warrington, 1962b; Schiller, 1965b; Schiller & Wiener, 1963; Smith & Schiller, 1966) whereas masking by light occurs only when TS and MS are both shown to the same eye.

All investigators agree that masking by pattern is most severe at ISI = 0, but they usually fail to include a case of temporal overlap of TS and MS (SOA = 0). Kinsbourne & Warrington (1962a, 1962b) reported evidence for a simple relation between threshold TS duration and ISI in masking by noise: Duration × ISI = Constant. Surprisingly, there have been no further investigations of this result. The same function applied to both forward and backward masking, but forward masking was consistently more severe. The greater severity of forward masking has been confirmed for the monoptic case (Schiller, 1966; Schiller & Smith, 1965; Smith & Schiller, 1966). However, Smith & Schiller (1966) and Greenspoon & Eriksen

(1968) report that dichoptic forward masking by pattern is quite weak.

Interpretations of Masking by Noise. Two competing conceptions have been proposed for masking by noise. Following Baxt (1871) Sperling (1963, 1967; Averbach & Sperling, 1960) concluded that the presentation of MS interrupts the process of reading out parts of the primary visual image onto a more permanent storage. On the other hand, Kinsbourne & Warrington (1962a, 1962b) concluded that MS and TS are effectively simultaneous in masking by noise; the reduction of performance is due to a degradation of the primary visual stimulus. Their interpretation of masking by noise is precisely analogous to Eriksen's interpretation of masking by light.

Sperling's treatment is restricted to the case of backward masking. Two lines of evidence support it:

(1) When an array of letters was shown, the number of items retrieved was a linear function of exposure duration prior to masking (Baxt, 1871, Sperling, 1963). Most compelling, the number of items retrieved was independent of the number of items shown: for several sizes of array, letters were acquired at a rate of one letter for every 10 msec of exposure, up to a maximum of about 4.5 letters which represents a limitation of short-term memory. Such results strongly support a process of sequential reading-out from a visual image, and the masking experiment was proposed (Sperling, 1963) as a means of measuring reading-rate. A similar interpretation was advanced by Averbach (1963) to account for the linear rise of the span of apprehension with exposure duration under conditions of masking by noise. Sperling (1967) subsequently amended his view and proposed that items may be read in parallel from the visual image, but he did not modify his interpretation of masking by noise.

(2) The reduction of visual persistence by masking is quite obvious, in both masking by light (Dodge, 1907, Sperling 1960a) and by noise. The observer often reports the impression that a clear visual stimulus was there to be read, but time did not suffice. Sperling (1967) has attempted to quantify directly this effect of masking by noise on visual persistence. Ss were required to adjust the timing of clicks to apparent simultaneity with the onset or disappearance of a visual target, which was preceded by light and followed by a field of visual noise. By this measure, the apparent duration of the visual stimulus under masking by noise is only slightly longer than its physical duration, and the correlation between physical and apparent duration is close, even in the range 20–100 msec.

The arguments for the interpretation of masking by noise in terms of interrupted processing of TS appear strong. However, the counter-arguments are equally compelling.

1) Sperling's theory rests on the assumption that a complete visual representation of TS is briefly available for processing under conditions of masking by noise. This crucial assumption is never tested directly. The basic finding, that the number of items retrieved rises with exposure duration prior to masking, is more parsimoniously explained on the claim that exposure duration controls the quality of the visual image that S is required to read, and not only the time in which he may read it (Eriksen and Hoffman, 1963; Eriksen & Steffy, 1964; Kinsbourne & Warrington, 1962a, 1962b).

2) Sperling's finding (1963) that the number of items read is independent of the number shown was not obtained by Kinsbourne & Warrington, (1962a), who reported that all the letters in an array become legible at about the same SOA between TS and MS. The specific conditions under which one or the other effect is obtained have not been determined.

3) Sperling's (1967) study of the duration of the visual image is also open to question. In informal attempts to apply Sperling's technique, the author has found that an observer can adopt one of two different sets: the click may be matched either to the disappearance of the letters, or to the sudden appearance of the masking pattern. The results that Sperling reported are easily obtained when the latter set is adopted, but the subject himself is often unsure

of whether the onset of the noise and the disappearance of the letters are in fact simultaneous.

4) Finally, the similarity of results for forward and for backward masking appears to be a serious embarrassment for the interruption theory, and provides the strongest support for the simultaneity theory proposed by Kinsbourne & Warrington (1962b). However, further discussion below will show that an interruption theory of backward masking may be compatible with a simultaneity theory of forward masking.

The interruption theory promotes masking by noise as the tool of choice with which to study the speed of perceptual events, and thereby makes masking a central topic in cognitive psychology (Haber, 1966; Neisser, 1967). However, the evidence at hand is not sufficient to conclude that interruption of processing is always the limiting factor whenever masking by noise is used. There may be conditions of very high luminance, large target size, and high contrast where a legible image is formed that S has too little time to read; under other conditions, masking may preclude identification by disrupting the formation of a legible image. Finally, the hypothesis may be considered that the image itself is formed by a rapid sequential process (P. Liss; R. N. Haber, personal communications) instead of instantaneously, as Sperling (1960a, 1963, 1967) suggests. This hypothesis suggests a distinction between *seeing* items and reading them, both sequential processes. The conditions under which these various effects may occur are yet to be studied in detail.

MASKING BY METACONTRAST

Averbach & Coriell (1961) presented an array of letters, and shortly thereafter a ring surrounding the position of one of the letters. The ring was originally intended to serve as an indicator of which letter to report. Instead, presentation of the ring at certain ISI's resulted in complete masking of the letter. The phenomenon was termed *erasure*. Other studies have confirmed the effectiveness of a ring as a masking stimulus, but there is no agreement on the shape of the masking function.

We noted earlier that the *detection* of a target under metacontrast may follow either a type A or a type B masking function (Figure 2). The two types of function have also been obtained with *identification* as criterial response. Averbach & Coriell (1961) reported that backward masking by a ring is a U-shaped function of ISI (type B). Weisstein (1966; Weisstein & Haber, 1965) confirmed this result. Fraisse (1966) and Mayzner and his colleagues (Mayzner, Tresselt & Cohen, 1966; Mayzner, Tresselt, Adrignolo, & Cohen, 1967) have also reported U-shaped functions when different parts of a word are presented in sequence. Other studies (Eriksen & Collins, 1964, 1965; Eriksen, Collins & Greenspoon, 1967; Norman, 1965; Schiller & Smith, 1965) report functions in which masking decreases monotonically with increasing ISI. In several of these studies forward masking by the ring is also observed (Eriksen & Collins, 1965; Schiller & Smith, 1965).

The review of metacontrast effects on the detection threshold in an earlier section suggested that two distinct processes are involved under different experimental situations (Fehrer & Smith, 1962; Kahneman, 1967b; Kolers, 1962). The presence of contours in close proximity to an acuity target strongly interferes with the resolution of that target, in both monoptic (Flom, Weymouth, & Kahneman, 1963) and dichoptic presentation (Flom, Heath, & Takahashi, 1963), a lateral inhibition effect. In addition, the suggestion was made that impossible motion is sometimes involved. The relation between suppression and motion is clearly illustrated in studies of sequential blanking (Mayzner, Tresselt, & Cohen, 1966; Mayzner, Tresselt, Adrignolo, & Cohen, 1967). With the appropriate sequencing of the presentations of individual letters, the word CHAIR is normally read as C A R, even when the presentation is repeated indefinitely. Certainly, any measure of acuity would reveal impaired performance in the two critical positions. Fraisse (1966) has used a related mode of presentation in which two interlaced halves of a six-letter word are presented in succession. Recognition was impaired for the three letters that were shown first and the masking function was U-shaped.

The conditions under which masking by a surrounding ring will produce masking functions of type A or type B remain unclear. It is a plausible conjecture that investigators have obtained type B functions by inadvertently optimizing conditions for a motion effect, but the parameters of that effect are obscure. So far, no study of target recognition has been reported in which a U-shaped function is reliably obtained under some conditions but not under others. Eriksen, Collins, & Greenspoon (1967) noted several flaws in the design of Weisstein's (1966) experiment, but their comments do not explain why she obtained a U-shaped function and they do not. It is probably significant, however, that TS was presented at a higher energy in studies which yielded U-shaped functions (Averbach & Coriell, 1961; Weisstein & Haber, 1965; Weisstein, 1966) than in studies which yielded monotone functions (Eriksen & Collins, 1964, 1965; Eriksen, Collins, & Greenspoon, 1967; Norman, 1965; Schiller & Smith, 1965).

Averbach & Coriell (1961) obtained masking by a ring only when several letters were simultaneously presented in the target array. Weisstein (1966) obtained type B masking functions even with a single target, but masking effects were more pronounced with larger arrays; also, the peak of the masking function was displaced to higher ISI's when the array was large. Eriksen, Collins & Greenspoon (1967) confirmed the finding that masking is more severe when the array is larger, with a type A masking function.

Effects of array size may require different interpretations depending on the shape of the masking function. A relevant observation, where motion is involved, is that apparent motion may be inhibited by an *analytic* attitude Neuhaus, 1930), when attention is sharply focused on the initial object shown. Informal observations of the author suggest that apparent motion is most compelling when one part

of a cluttered array is set into motion. This would account for the failure of Averbach & Coriell (1961) to obtain masking of a single letter by a surrounding ring.

In the data of Eriksen, Collins, & Greenspoon (1967), the masking functions are monotonic. The effect of array size on masking is slight at short ISI's and increases steadily thereafter. The authors' interpretation is in the spirit of earlier work (Averbach & Coriell, 1961; Sperling, 1960a, 1963). When the size of the array exceeds S's capacity, items must be processed serially from a decaying perceptual trace. At any time after exposure, the probability that a given item has been processed is inversely related to the number of items in the array. The ring cannot be effective as an indicator of which item to report if it indicates an item which has not been processed, and has already decayed. In addition, the ring has a masking effect. The weaker items in the larger array are more vulnerable to this masking effect and their relative vulnerability increases with the decay of the perceptual trace.

Theory

All current theories of backward masking share a central idea: the visual response to a brief stimulus lasts much longer than did the stimulus that caused it; consequently, the responses to two successive stimuli may overlap in time. Further, there is general agreement that overtake effects may contribute to masking: when MS is more intense than TS, the difference in latencies increases the temporal overlap of the responses (Baker, 1963; Crawford, 1947; Donchin & Lindsley, 1965a, 1965b; Donchin, 1967). However, perfect overlap is not a necessary condition for the occurrence of masking, since all varieties of masking have been observed with TS and MS equal in intensity (e.g. Averbach & Sperling, 1960; Boynton, 1961, Greenspoon & Eriksen, 1968; Kahneman, 1966, 1967b; Schiller, 1968).[3] Because of tem-

---

[3] Partial overlap is a necessary condition for the occurrence of apparent motion and type B metacontrast (Kahneman, 1967b; Weisstein, 1968).

poral overlap of responses, backward masking is not a retroactive effect; it is an interaction between responses that are at least partly concurrent. While agreeing on this general position, theories of masking diverge on the nature of the interaction between the response to TS and to MS. Two modes of interaction have been described most often: integration and interruption.

INTEGRATION THEORIES

The simplest version of integration theory assumes that TS and MS are linearly summed and that the response to their presentation in sequence is the same as would be evoked by their joint simultaneous presentation. Visual masking becomes a special case of temporal summation of heterogeneous stimuli. The temporal range of masking corresponds to the range of temporal summation.

Kinsbourne & Warrington (1962a; 1962b) first proposed that TS and MS are effectively simultaneous in masking by noise. Eriksen (1966; Eriksen & Hoffman, 1963) has been a vigorous champion of this view in explaining masking by light in his luminance summation theory. The theory accounts for forward as well as for backward masking. It also fits the general observation that dichoptic interactions follow the same rules for simultaneous and for successive interactions.

Boynton's theory of masking (Boynton, 1961; Boynton & Kandel, 1957) may also be described as a summation theory. However, it assumes a nonlinear summation of response rather than a linear summation of stimuli. To the extent that the system is overloaded by the massive response to MS, it is less capable of conveying information about TS, and a more intense TS is required to pierce this barrier. The masking function (Figure 1) describes the time-course of the response to MS. Schiller (1968) has provided a striking illustration of this concept in single-cell recordings in the LGN of the cat: cells that respond at their maximal level to MS fail to register the earlier presentation of TS. The concept of response summation provides an elegant explanation of the masking function; it also accounts for some transient effects of masking that simple stimulus integration cannot explain.

Weisstein's (1968) theory of metacontrast represents a further level of complexity. The responses to the two stimuli are now broken down into excitatory and inhibitory components, each with a time course of its own, and these components are continuously summed by a *decision* neuron. The theory explains both type A and type B functions in metacontrast. It also offers promise of an explanation for the disinhibition effects reported by Robinson (1966) and by Dember & Purcell (1967).

INTERRUPTION THEORIES

Interruption theories emphasize the idea that the normal perception of a TS requires time, and that the process may be stopped by a stimulus presented during that time. There are different versions of what requires time and of what is interrupted.

One version of interruption theory simply states that MS interrupts the consolidation of the percept of TS (Lindsley, 1961; Lindsley & Emmons, 1958; von Noorden & Burian, 1960). A rather different conception assumes that a visual image of TS is formed, but the observer is interrupted before he can read the information contained in that image into a more permanent store (Averbach, 1963; Averbach & Coriell, 1961; Averbach & Sperling, 1960; Haber, 1966; Smith & Carey, 1966; Sperling, 1960a, 1963, 1967; Weisstein, 1966). The concept of erasure (Averbach & Coriell, 1961) implies that the presentation of MS immediately relegates TS to the psychological past. Similarly, Sperling (1963, 1967) equates the duration of the visual image with the SOA between TS and MS. The main difference between the two versions of interruption theory is that, in Lindsley's view, the percept of TS is not formed under masking, whereas it is formed and quickly destroyed according to Averbach and to Sperling.

Interruption theories do not account for forward masking, but this is not a fatal flaw. MS is a more intense visual stimulus than TS in most studies of masking. It is therefore conceivable that TS fails to be perceived in backward masking because MS interrupts the process; TS fails to be seen in forward masking because it is too weak a stimulus to interrupt the continued processing of MS. An interruption theory of backward masking is not incompatible with an integration theory of forward masking.

When coupled with a view of reading-out as a serial process, interruption theory entails that the number of items read should be independent of the number shown (Sperling, 1963). However, Sperling (1967) has recently concluded from an analysis of error data that various items may be processed in parallel, although at different rates. This hypothesis no longer entails the result that Sperling (1963) had obtained earlier. It is not obvious, in fact, that an interruption theory is capable of generating specific hypotheses about target identification, without the additional assumption of serial processing.

Interruption theory accounts for a compelling experience that observers sometimes report under conditions of masking. Many different operations cause failures of identification, but masking may be unique in producing the conviction that "given more time, I certainly could have read it!" However, backward masking does not always yield that experience, and the conditions under which it occurs have not been isolated. Even when it occurs, of course, such an experience does not necessarily indicate that a lack of processing-time actually caused the failure of identification.

MASKING AND PSYCHOLOGICAL TIME

It is generally agreed that the temporal sequence of perceptual events does not correspond strictly to the temporal sequence of stimulation. Perception lags after stimulation, and integrates successive stimuli into composite chunks, or moments (Boynton, 1961; Eriksen & Collins, 1967; Stroud, 1956; White, 1963), in which some elements may be obliterated and others altered. The rules that relate the sequence of percepts to the sequence of stimuli define the problem of psychological time, and it has long been hoped (Monjé, 1928; Piéron,

1925) that masking methods could contribute to its solution. The fulfillment of this hope is tardy, but some promising concepts have emerged.

Clearing time (Lindsley, 1961) and perception time (von Noorden & Burian, 1960) are defined by the range of delays over which backward masking can be obtained. An event that has already occurred cannot be prevented, and the range of the masking function therefore corresponds to the time required for the consolidation of the percept of TS. An unequivocal measurement of perception time requires that TS and MS be equal in intensity and spatial extent, so as to preclude overtake effects. Perception time is at least 130–150 msec long, by this measure (Mayzner, Tresselt, & Helfer, 1967): some metacontrast effects only reach their peak at $SOA = 100$ msec.

The significance of the high value of perception time is that we *live in the past* at least to its extent (Efron, 1966). This fact may have important implications for the function of subjective visual experience. Mayzner, Tresselt, & Helfer (1967) consider that the delay of visual experience is consistent with the value of simple RT to light. However, the more radical conclusion appears warranted that subjective visual experience is not causally involved in triggering a simple response, since the two occur at about the same time. Indeed, a response can occur when the stimulus that triggered it is not represented at all in experience (Fehrer & Raab, 1962).

Another significant parameter of masking is the duration of the exposure of the masked target. What is the exposure duration beyond which a target may not be masked by a stimulus of equal intensity? There is a convergence of evidence that a state of stimulation which is maintained for more than 100 msec without any significant change will be registered as a separate perceptual event. Mayzner, Tresselt & Helfer (1967) and Kahneman (1967b) noted that metacontrast suppression is not obtained with longer durations of exposure. Kahneman (1967b; Kahneman & Wolman, 1968) described changes in the experience of apparent motion when the first object is shown for more than 100–120 msec: with brief exposures, the object is seen to be moving as soon as it appears; with longer exposures, the object is seen as stationary before it moves. Michotte (1963) reported that interruptions of real motion for less than 100 msec are seen as *stumbling* within a continuous movement. Longer interruptions produce two separate impressions of motion. Similarly, the causality effect is no longer experienced when the launching figure and its target are stationary side by side for more than 100 msec (Michotte, 1963). Again, two distinct and unrelated movements are seen.

There are other indications of a discontinuity in the effects of exposure duration at 100 msec. Kahneman (1967b; Kahneman & Wolman, 1968) suggested that the duration of the visual response begins to represent the duration of the stimulus only when the latter exceeds 100–120 msec. All briefer stimuli are treated as if they were 100 msec long. The assumption explains the strict dependence of several perceptual effects on SOA, rather than on the duration of TS or on ISI. This rule applies to masking by light (Donchin, 1967), to metacontrast and to apparent motion with brief identical stimuli (Kahneman, 1967b; Kolers, 1962; Mayzner, Tresselt, & Helfer, 1967) and to the identification of letters that are presented in rapid succession on the same spot (Haber & Nathanson, 1968). For motion, an abrupt transition to a strict dependence on ISI occurs at a duration of 100 msec (Kahneman & Wolman, 1968). This pattern of results is to be expected if seemingly retroactive effects in perception depend on temporal overlap of responses: the duration of TS is irrelevant to masking if it is not represented in the duration of the response, and we have assumed that it is not.

There appears to be a convergence of evidence for the conclusion that only brief stimuli can be masked, and that all stimuli below 100 msec may be considered brief. Mayzner, Tresselt & Helfer (1967) singled out the same value in their estimates of the central component of perceptual delay and of the duration of an instant of subjective visual experience. The idea that psychological time is quantized at a basic rate of 10/sec is of course not new (Stroud,

1956). It is encouraging that this parameter appears significant in studies of masking which were not available to Stroud.

Summary

The various paradigms in the study of visual masking are classified, and related to cases of interference among cotemporaneous stimuli. The dependent variables in masking studies are described. A distinction between criterion content and criterion level is introduced in the discussion of detection under masking and metacontrast. Various conceptions of identification of forms under masking and the contributions of masking effects to the study of psychological time are reviewed.

References

Alpern, M. Metacontrast: Historical introduction. *Amer. J. Optom.*, 1952, *29*, 631–646.

Alpern, M. Metacontrast. *J. opt. Soc. Amer.*, 1953, *43*, 648–657.

Alpern, M. Rod-cone independence in the after-flash effect. *J. Physiol.*, 1965, *176*, 462–472.

Alpern, M., and Rushton, W. A. H. The specificity of the cone interaction in the after-flash effect. *J. Physiol.*, 1965, *176*, 473–482.

Averbach, E. The span of apprehension as a function of exposure duration. *J. verb. Learn. verb. Behav.*, 1963, *2*, 60–64.

Averbach, E., and Coriell, A. S. Short-term memory in vision. *Bell System Tech. J.*, 1961, *40*, 309–328.

Averbach, E., and Sperling, G. Short-term storage of information in vision. In: *Information Theory*, C. Cherry (Ed.). London: Butterworth & Co., 1960. Pp. 196–211.

Baker, H. D. The instantaneous threshold and early dark adaptation. *J. opt. Soc. Amer.*, 1953, *43*, 798–803.

Baker, H. D. Some direct comparisons between light and dark adaptation. *J. opt. Soc. Amer.*, 1955, *45*, 839–844.

Baker, H. D. Initial stages of light and dark adaptation. *J. opt. Soc. Amer.*, 1963, *53*, 98–103.

Battersby, W. S., Oesterreich, R. E., and Sturr, J. F. Neural limitation of visual excitability. VII. Non-homonymous retrochiasmal interaction. *Amer. J. Physiol.*, 1964, *206*, 1181–1188.

Battersby, W. S., and Wagman, I. H. Neural limitations of visual excitability. I. The time course of monocular light adaptation. *J. opt. Soc. Amer.*, 1959, *49*, 752–759.

Battersby, W. S., and Wagman, I. H. Neural limitations of visual excitability. IV. Spatial determinants of retrochiasmal interaction. *Amer. J. Physiol.*, 1962, *203*, 359–365.

Blanc-Garin, J. Quelques problemes posés par l'étude du phenomène de metacontraste visuel. *Psychologie Française*, 1965, *10*, 147–154.

Boynton, R. M. On-responses in the human visual system as inferred from psychophysical studies of rapid adaptation. *A. M. A. Arch. Opthal.*, 1958, *60*, 800–810.

Boynton, R. M. Some temporal factors in vision. In: W. A. Rosenblith (Ed.), *Sensory Communication*, New York: Wiley, 1961, Pp. 739–756.

Boynton, R. M. Spatial vision. *Annual Rev. Psychol.*, 1962, *13*, 171–200.

Boynton, R. M., and Kandel, G. On responses in the human visual system as a function of adaptation level. *J. opt. Soc. Amer.*, 1957, *47*, 275–286.

Boynton, R. M., and Miller, N. D. Visual performance under conditions of transient adaptation. *Illum. Engr.*, 1963, *58*, 541–550.

Boynton, R. M., and Siegfried, J. B. Psychophysical estimates of on-responses to brief light flashes. *J. opt. Soc. Amer.*, 1962, *52*, 720–721.

Crawford, B. H. Visual adaptation in relation to brief conditioning stimuli. *Proc. Roy. Soc. Lond.*, 1947, *134B*, 283–302.

Dember, W. N., and Purcell, D. G. Recovery of masked visual targets by inhibition of the masking stimulus. *Science*, 1967, *157*, 1335–1336.

Dodge, R. An experimental study of visual fixation. *Psychol. Rev. Monogr. Suppl.*, 1907, *8*, (No. 35).

Donchin, E. Retroactive visual masking—the effect of test flash duration. *Vision Research*, 1967, *7*, 79–89.

Donchin, E., and Lindsley, D. B. Retroactive brightness enhancement with brief paired flashes of light. *Vis. Res.*, 1965a, *5*, 59–69.

Donchin, E., and Lindsley, D. B. Visually evoked response correlates of perceptual masking and enhancement. *Electroenceph. clin. Neurophysiol.*, 1965b, *19*, 325–335.

Efron, R. The duration of the present. Paper presented at Conference on Interdisciplinary Perspectives on Time. New York Academy of Sciences. January, 1966.

Eriksen, C. W. Temporal luminance summation effects in backward and forward masking. *Perception and Psychophysics*, 1966, *1*, 87–92.

Eriksen, C. W., and Collins, J. F. Backward masking in vision. *Psychon. Sci.*, 1964, *1*, 101–102.

Eriksen, C. W., and Collins, J. F. A reinterpretation of one form of backward and forward masking in visual perception. *J. exp. Psychol.*, 1965, *70*, 343–351.

Eriksen, C. W., and Collins, J. F. Some temporal characteristics of visual pattern perception. *J. exp. Psychol.*, 1967, *74*, 476–484.

Eriksen, C. W., Collins, J. F., and Greenspoon, T. S. An analysis of certain factors responsible for non-monotonic backward masking functions. *J. exp. Psychol.*, 1967, *75*, 500–507.

Eriksen, C. W., and Hoffman, M. Form recognition at brief duration as a function of adapting field and interval between stimulations. *J. exp. Psychol.*, 1963, *66*, 485–499.

Eriksen, C. W., and Lappin, J. S. Luminance summation-contrast reduction as a basis for certain forward and backward masking effects. *Psychon. Sci.*, 1964, *1*, 313–314.

Eriksen, C. W., and Steffy, R. A. Short term memory and retroactive interference in visual perception. *J. exp. Psychol.*, 1964, *5*, 423–434.

Fehrer, E. Contribution of perceptual segregation to the relationship between stimulus similarity and backward masking. *Percept. mot. Skills*, 1965, *21*, 27–33.

Fehrer, E. Effect of stimulus similarity on retroactive masking. *J. exp. Psychol.*, 1966, *71*, 612–615.

Fehrer, E., and Biederman, I. A comparison of reaction and verbal report in the detection of masked stimuli. *J. exp. Psychol.*, 1962, *64*, 126–130.

Fehrer, E., and Raab, D. Reaction time to stimuli masked by metacontrast. *J. exp. Psychol.*, 1962, *63*, 143–147.

Fehrer, E., and Smith, E. Effect of luminance ratio on masking. *Percept. mot. Skills*, 1962, *14*, 243–253.

Flom, M. C., Heath, G. G., and Takahashi, E. Contour interaction and visual interaction: contralateral effects. *Science*, 1963, *142*, 979–980.

Flom, M. C., Weymouth, F. W., and Kahneman, D. Visual resolution and contour interaction. *J. opt. Soc. Amer.*, 1963, *53*, 1026–1032.

Fraisse, P. Visual perceptive simultanity and masking of letters successively presented. *Percept. and Psychophysics*, 1966, *1*, 285–287.

Fry, G. A. Depression of the activity aroused by a flash of light by applying a second flash immediately afterwards to adjacent areas of the retina. *Am. J. Physiol.*, 1934, *108*, 701–707.

Goldiamond, I. Indicators of perception: I. Subliminal perception, subception, unconscious perception: an analysis in terms of psychophysical indicator methodology. *Psychol. Bull.*, 1958, *55*, 373–411.

Green, D. M., and Swets, J. A. *Signal Detection Theory and Psychophysics.* New York: John Wiley and Sons, Inc., 1966.

Greenspoon, T. S., and Eriksen, C. W. Interocular non-independence, *Perception & Psychophysics*, 1968, *3*, 93–96.

Haber, R. N. Perceptual processes and general cognitive activity. Paper presented at the Conference on Learning Processes and Thought. Pittsburgh, 1966.

Haber, R. N., and Nathanson, L. S. Processing of sequentially presented letters. *Perception and Psychophysics,* 1969, 5.

Harrison, K., and Fox, R. Replication of reaction time to stimuli masked by metacontrast. *J. exp. Psychol.,* 1966, 71, 162–163.

Heckenmueller, E. G., and Dember, W. N. A forced-choice indicator for use with Werner's disc-ring pattern in studies of visual masking. *Psychon. Sci.,* 1965a, 3, 167–168.

Heckenmueller, E. G., and Dember, W. N. Paradoxical brightening of a masked black disk. *Psychon. Sci.,* 1965b, 3, 457–458.

Kahneman, D. Exposure duration and effective figure ground contrast. *Quart. J. exp. Psychol.,* 1965, 17, 308–314.

Kahneman, D. Time-intensity reciprocity under various conditions of adaptation and backward masking. *J. exp. Psychol.,* 1966, 71, 543–549.

Kahneman, D. Temporal effects in the perception of light and form. In: J. C. Mott-Smith, W. Wathen-Dunn, H. Blum, and P. Lieberman (Eds.), *Symposium on Models for the Perception of Speech and Visual Form.* Cambridge: MIT Press, 1967a.

Kahneman, D. An onset-onset law for one case of apparent motion and metacontrast. *Percept. and Psychophysics,* 1967b, 2, 577–584.

Kahneman, D., and Wolman, R. Stroboscopic motion: effects of duration and interval. *Percept. and Psychophysics,* 1968, in press.

Kaswan, J., and Young, S. Stimulus exposure time, brightness and spatial factors as determinants of visual perception. *J. exp. Psychol.,* 1963, 65, 113–123.

Kietzman, M. L. *The perceptual interference of successively presented visual stimuli.* Ph.D. thesis, University of California at Los Angeles, 1962.

Kinsbourne, M., and Warrington, E. K. The effect of an aftercoming random pattern on the perception of brief visual stimuli. *Quart. J. exp. Psychol.,* 1962a, 14, 223–234.

Kinsbourne, M., and Warrington, E. K. Further studies on the masking of brief visual stimuli by a random pattern. *Quart. J. exp. Psychol.,* 1962b, 14, 235–245.

Kolers, P. A. Intensity and contour effects in visual masking. *Vision Research,* 1962, 2, 277–294.

Kolers, P. A., and Rosner, B. S. On visual masking (metacontrast): dichoptic observation. *Amer. J. Psychol.,* 1960, 73, 2–21.

Kulli, J. C. *Metacontrast and evoked potentials: a possible neural substrate.* Honors thesis, Harvard University, 1967.

Landahl, H. D. A neural net for masking phenomena. *Bull. math. Biophys.,* 1967, 29, 227–232.

Lindsley, D. B. Electrophysiology of the visual system and its relation to perceptual phenomena. In: M. A. B. Brazier (Ed.), *Brain and Behavior,* Vol. I.

Washington, D.C.: American Institute of Biological Sciences, 1961, Pp. 359–392.

Lindsley, D. B., and Emmons, W. H. Perception time and evoked potentials. (abstract) *Science,* 1958, 127, 1061.

Luckiesh, M. *Light, Vision and Seeing.* New York: Van Nostrand, 1944.

Mayzner, M. S., Tresselt, M. E., Adrignolo, A. J., and Cohen, A. Further preliminary findings on some effects of very fast sequential input rates on perception. *Psychon. Sci.,* 1967, 7, 281–282.

Mayzner, M. S., Tresselt, M. E., and Cohen, A. Preliminary findings on some effects of very fast sequential input rates on perception. *Psychon. Sci.,* 1966, 6, 513–514.

Mayzner, M. S., Tresselt, M. E., and Helfer, M. S. A provisional model of visual information processing with sequential inputs. *Psychon. Monog. Suppl.,* 1967, 2, 91–108, (Whole No. 23).

Michotte, A. *The Perception of Causality.* London: Methuen, 1963.

Monjé, M. Die Empfindungzeitmessung mit der Methode des Löschreizes. *Z. Biol.,* 1928, 87, 23–40.

Mowbray, G. H., and Durr, L. B. Visual masking. *Nature,* 1964, 201, 277–278.

Neisser, U. *Cognitive Psychology.* New York: Appleton-Century-Crofts, 1967.

Neuhaus, V. Experimentelle Untersuchung der Scheinbewegung. *Arch. f.d. ges. Psychol.,* 1930, 75, 315–348.

Norman, J. *Visual Retroactive Interference Phenomena: A Review and Experimental Study.* Unpublished MA dissertation, Hebrew University of Jerusalem, 1965.

Onley, J. W., and Boynton, R. M. Visual responses to equally bright stimuli of unequal luminance. *J. opt. Soc. Amer.,* 1962, 52, 934–940.

Penrose, L. S., and Penrose, R. Impossible objects: a special type of visual illusion. *Br. J. Psychol.,* 1958, 49, 31–33.

Piéron, H. Recherches experimentales sur la marge de variation du temps de latence de la sensation lumineuse (par une methode de masquage). *Année Psychol.,* 1925, 26, 1–30.

Raab, D. H. Backward masking. *Psychol. Bull.,* 1963, 60, 118–129.

Robinson, D. N. Disinhibition of visually masked stimuli. *Science,* 1966, 154, 157–158.

Scharf, B., Zamansky, H. S., and Brightbill, R. F. Word recognition with masking. *Perception and Psychophysics,* 1966, 1, 110–112.

Schiller, P. H. Detection in metacontrast as determined by a method of comparisons. *Percept. mot. Skills,* 1965a, 20, 47–50.

Schiller, P. H. Monoptic and dichoptic visual masking by patterns and flashes. *J. exp. Psychol.,* 1965b, 69, 193–199.

Schiller, P. H. Forward and backward masking as a function of relative overlap and intensity of test and masking stimuli. *Percept. & Psychophysics*, 1966, *1*, 161–164.

Schiller, P. H. Single unit analysis of backward visual masking and metacontrast in the cat lateral geniculate nucleus. *Vision Res.*, 1968, *8*, 855–866.

Schiller, P. H., and Chorover, S. L. Metacontrast: its relation to evoked potentials. *Science*, 1966, *153*, 1398–1401.

Schiller, P. H., and Smith, M. C. A comparison of forward and backward masking. *Psychon. Sci.*, 1965, *3*, 77–78.

Schiller, P. H., and Smith, M. C. Detection in metacontrast. *J. exp. Psychol.*, 1966, *71*, 32–39.

Schiller, P. H., and Wiener, M. Monoptic and dichoptic visual masking. *J. exp. Psychol.*, 1963, *66*, 386–393.

Smith, F., and Carey, P. Temporal factors in visual information processing. *Canad. J. Psychol.*, 1966, *20*, 337–342.

Smith, M. C., and Schiller, P. H. Forward and backward masking: a comparison. *Canad. J. Psychol.*, 1966, *20*, 191–197.

Sperling, G. The information available in brief visual presentations. *Psych. Monogr.*, 1960a, *74*, 1–29.

Sperling, G. Negative afterimage without prior positive image. *Science*, 1960b, *131*, 1613–1614.

Sperling, G. A model for visual memory tasks. *Human Factors*, 1963, *5*, 19–31.

Sperling, G. What visual masking can tell us about temporal factors in perception. *Proceedings of the Seventeenth International Congress of Psychology*. Washington, D.C., 1963. Amsterdam: North-Holland Publ. Co., 1964. Pp. 199–200.

Sperling, G. Temporal and spatial visual masking: I. Masking by impulse flashes. *J. opt. Soc. Amer.*, 1965, *55*, 541–559.

Sperling, G. Successive approximations to a model for short-term memory. In: *Proceedings of the Eighteenth International Congress of Psychology*. Amsterdam: North-Holland Publ. Co., 1967.

Stigler, R. Chronophotische Studien über den umgebungskontrast. *Pflüg. Arch. ges. Physiol.*, 1910, *134*, 365–435.

Stroud, J. M. The fine structure of psychological time. In: H. Quastler (Ed.), *Information Theory in Psychology*. Glencoe, Ill.: The Free Press, 1956, Pp. 174–207.

Swets, J. A. (Ed.) *Signal Detection and Recognition by Human Observers*. New York: Wiley and Sons, 1964.

Thompson, J. H. What happens to the stimulus in backward masking? *J. exp. Psychol.*, 1966, *71*, 580–586.

Toch, H. H. The perceptual elaboration of stroboscopic presentations. *Amer. J. Psychol.*, 1956, *69*, 345–358.

von Noorden, G. K., and Burian, H. M. Perceptual blanking in normal and amblyopic eyes. *Archives of Opthalmology*, 1960, *64*, 817–822.

Wagman, I. H., and Battersby, W. S. Neural limitations of visual excitability: II. Retrochiasmal interaction. *Am. J. Physiol.*, 1959, *197*, 1237–1242.

Weisstein, N. Backward masking and models of perceptual processing. *J. exp. Psychol.*, 1966, *72*, 232–240.

Weisstein, N. A Rashevsky-Landahl neural net: simulation of metacontrast. *Psychol. Rev.*, 1968, in press.

Weisstein, N., and Haber, R. N. A U-shaped backward masking function in vision. *Psychon. Sci.*, 1965, *2*, 75–76.

Werner, H. Studies on contour strobostereoscopic phenomena. *Amer. J. Psychol.*, 1940, *53*, 418–422.

Werner, H. Studies on contour: I. Qualitative analyses, *Amer. J. Psychol.*, 1935, *47*, 40–64.

Wertheimer, M. Experimentelle Studien über das Sehen von Bewegung, *Z. Psychol.*, 1912, *61*, 161–265.

White, C. T. Temporal numerosity and the psychological unit of duration. *Psychol. Monog.*, 1963, *77*, 1–37, (Whole No. 575).

2.2 Metacontrast: Its Relation to Evoked Potentials*

PETER H. SCHILLER   STEPHAN L. CHOROVER

When two equally intense visual stimuli with adjacent contours are presented in rapid succession, the brightness of the first stimulus appears greatly reduced. This type of brightness suppression, generally referred to as metacontrast (1), is one of several visual phenomena showing that brightness can be modified by a temporal interaction between stimuli.

Metacontrast has been extensively studied by psychophysical methods (2). It is readily observed under these conditions: A disk is presented very briefly and is followed, after a variable interval, by a surrounding ring of equal area, intensity, and duration. When the interval between disk and ring is short (0 to 10 msec), both are clearly seen. As the interval is increased, the brightness of the disk diminishes. At interstimulus intervals between 40 and 100 msec, metacontrast suppression becomes maximal and the disk virtually disappears. With further increases in the interstimulus interval the disk becomes progressively brighter again. When the two stimuli are separated by 200 to 250 msec, the disk appears to have regained its original brightness. Throughout a sequence of such presentations, the appearance of the ring remains relatively unchanged.

Several different theories have been proposed to explain metacontrast suppression in terms

* *Science*, September 16, 1966, vol. 153, pp. 1398–1400. Copyright © 1966 by the American Association for the Advancement of Science. We thank Richard E. Doherty for technical assistance. Supported by PHS grant 5-RO1-MH-07923 and the John A. Hartford Foundation.

of retinal (3), sub-cortical (4), and cortical (5) interactions between neural responses to the two stimuli. In order to evaluate such interpretations, one should be able to specify the neural correlates of brightness perception. This is not yet possible, but recent work with evoked potentials recorded from the scalp in man has shown that evoked potential amplitude increases and latency decreases as stimulus intensity (and therefore brightness) is increased (6). Are these covariations due to the altered stimulus intensity, or to the change in brightness, or both? In attempting to answer this question we wished to know whether the brightness reduction observed under metacontrast conditions (where brightness changes but intensity does not) is accompanied by evoked potential changes comparable to those that normally occur when stimulus intensity is varied. The finding that metacontrast suppression (like intensity reduction) is accompanied by a decrease in amplitude and increase in latency of the evoked potential to the initial stimulus would suggest that these aspects of the cortical evoked response correlate with the psychological variable of brightness perception rather than with physical variations in stimulus intensity per se. However, the finding that evoked potentials change only when brightness and intensity covary, and not when brightness alone is reduced (as in metacontrast), would suggest that, while the amplitude and latency of the evoked response may correlate with physical aspects of the stimulus, they do not

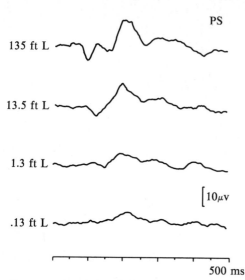

PS

135 ft L

13.5 ft L

1.3 ft L

$[10\mu v$

.13 ft L

500 ms

FIGURE 1 Averaged evoked potentials to disk presented alone at four intensity levels. Sweep (500 msec) starts at onset of light flash. Negativity down.

necessarily correlate with the perceptual response of the subject.

The same procedure was followed for each of five subjects. The subject was seated with his head on a chin rest facing the stimulus display unit 150 cm away. He was instructed to fixate binocularly on a faint red light 12 cm to the right of the center of the stimulus display. The experiment was carried out in a darkened room. Each subject was dark-adapted for at least 10 minutes before the beginning of a session.

The stimulus display consisted of a disk, 10 cm in diameter, surrounded by a ring with an inner diameter of 10 cm and an outer diameter of 14 cm. The face of the display assembly was machined from 1/4-inch (2/3-cm) opal Plexiglas. The disk and ring could be separately transilluminated by mercury-argon cold cathode lamps mounted behind them (7). A tachistoscopic programmer[1] was used to trigger the lamps and to control the sequence and duration of stimulus presentations. On all trials, exposure durations for the disk and the ring were equal and constant at 5 msec. On all metacontrast trials the intensity of each stimulus

[1] Sky Instrument Co., Syosset, N.Y.

was 135 ft-lam (1453 lu/m²). The following conditions of presentation were employed: disk alone; disk followed by ring at interstimulus intervals of 3, 30, 60, 100, 150, and 200 msec; ring alone, with equivalent delays. In order to compare evoked potential changes produced by metacontrast suppression with those produced by stimulus intensity reduction, we also presented the disk alone at 13.5 and 1.35 ft-lam. For each subject 100 consecutive trials were run under each condition; the recycling time was 2.1 seconds.

For recording the evoked potentials we used a conventional electroencephalographic machine, a tape recorder, and an average-response computer[2] (8). A midsaggital area of the subject's scalp, 4 cm above the inion, was cleaned with acetone and treated with a paste composed of bentonite and saturated $CaCl_2$ solution. A single, 0.5-cm-diameter disk electrode was taped to the scalp at this point. An ear lobe, similarly cleaned and treated, served to locate the indifferent electrode.

Figure 1 shows changes in the averaged evoked potential recorded from one subject as stimulus intensity was decreased. The characteristic reduction in amplitude and increase in latency are consistent with previously reported findings (6). Initial observations showed that during optimal metacontrast suppression a disk at 135 ft-lam actually appears less bright than a disk presented alone at 1.35 ft-lam.[3] Therefore, if the brightness reduction occurring during metacontrast suppression is accompanied by evoked potential changes like those that occur when stimulus intensity is reduced, the

[2] The recording equipment included a Schwartzer electroencephalograph (with amplifier bandpass between 1 and 30 cy/sec), a Mnemotron computer of average transients (CAT), and a tape recorder employing a four-channel multiplexed pulse-duration modulation and demodulation system. The tape system, which was designed and built under the supervision of S. K. Burns and J. McDonald of the Electrical Engineering Department at M.I.T., permits recording of bioelectric potentials on a conventional two-track audio tape recorder. The modulated pulses are recorded on one tape track and a stimulus marker signal is recorded on the other. The stimulus marker is read by a switching circuit that supplies the data to the CAT. The demodulated signals have a bandwidth from d-c to 250 cy/sec.

[3] This observation is consistent with psychophysical data obtained at lower luminance levels. See reference (9).

amplitude and latency of the averaged evoked response to the 135-ft-lam disk under metacontrast conditions should be similar to the amplitude and latency of the evoked response to the 1.35-ft-lam disk presented alone.

Figure 2 shows data obtained from two subjects during paired presentations, together with the averaged evoked response to the disk and ring presented separately. At all interstimulus intervals (including those at which metacontrast suppression is maximal), the initial negative wave of the evoked response to the disk remains essentially unchanged.[4] At interstimulus intervals of 60 and 100 msec the disk is virtually invisible, yet the amplitude and latency of the evoked response do not vary as they do when stimulus intensity is reduced (Figure 1).

The finding that the evoked response to the first stimulus is relatively unchanged, at interstimulus intervals producing maximal metacontrast suppression, helps to explain two observations that have previously been made in metacontrast experiments: (i) Reaction time to the first stimulus is not affected by metacontrast suppression (although reaction time normally increases as stimulus intensity is decreased); and (ii) in a forced-choice paradigm, the first stimulus is equally detectable at all interstimulus intervals (9).

It has been suggested (10) that in some cases cortical evoked potentials to paired stimuli are additive (that is, are the resultant of evoked responses to the two stimuli presented singly). In order to test whether or not this is the case in the metacontrast situation, we selected appropriate delay intervals and artificially combined evoked responses that had been recorded during presentations of the disk and ring alone.[5] Synthetic averages produced in this way are shown in Figure 3 (dotted lines) superimposed upon the directly recorded averaged evoked responses (solid lines) obtained during paired presentation of the stimuli. Since the initial negative response to the ring is clearly present in all of the synthetic tracings and since there are many other notable differences between the directly recorded and synthetically produced records, there appears to be little support for the view that later components of the evoked response to paired stimuli under metacontrast conditions represent a summation of evoked responses to the individual stimuli.

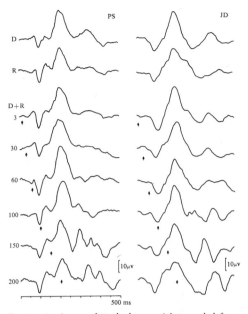

FIGURE 2   Averaged evoked potentials recorded from subjects PS and JD: D, disk alone; R, ring alone; D + R, paired presentations. Numbers at left indicate the interval between D and R (paired) in msec. Sweep (500 msec) starts with onset of first stimulus. Arrows show onset of second stimulus.

The results obtained for the paired presentations (Figure 2) also show that the wave form of the evoked potentials to the ring are considerably modified by the disk preceding it. Some effect is observable even with an interstimulus interval of 200 msec.[6] These results

---

[4] For two of the five subjects, evoked potentials were also recorded from additional scalp placements. Although the overall response patterns were slightly different for the various placements, the general relationships described in the report were obtained for all electrode locations.

[5] This procedure was patterned after the one described by Donchin, Wicke, and Lindsley.

[6] An analysis similar to one reported by Schwartz and Shagass was performed in which responses to a single disk were subtracted from responses evoked by paired presentations. The results confirmed the observation that the wave form of the second stimulus is altered by the first, with the effect diminishing with increasing interstimulus interval.

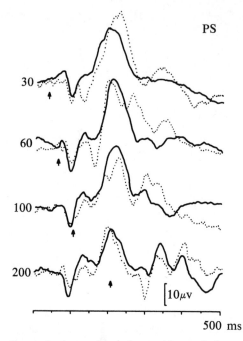

PS

30

60

100

200

$[10\mu v$

500 ms

FIGURE 3   Averaged evoked potentials to paired presentations (solid lines) compared with synthetic averaged evoked potentials obtained by summing responses to single stimuli (dotted lines). Sweeps are 500 msec.

sions obtained in masking and metacontrast experiments are mediated by different neural mechanisms.

In summary, the initial negative wave of the average cortical evoked potential manifests an increased latency and decreased amplitude when brightness is reduced by lowering stimulus intensity (Figure 1). However, comparable latency and amplitude changes do not occur under metacontrast conditions when brightness is reduced without lowering stimulus intensity (Figure 2). These findings suggest that a direct correlation between psychophysical indices and evoked potentials cannot always be assumed (13). Although metacontrast provides rather special conditions of stimulation, dissociation between brightness and intensity occurs commonly in normal visual perception (14). Further work is needed to determine the extent to which our findings are applicable to such situations.

Summary

Electrophysiological correlates of metacontrast were studied by means of averaged evoked potentials recorded from the scalp in man. Under conditions in which the brightness of the first of two successive stimuli appears diminished there is no accompanying attenuation of the evoked potentials to that stimulus. The results suggest that the amplitude and latency of evoked potentials correlate with stimulus intensity but not with brightness.

seem to be analogous to those observed with paired overlapping stimuli (11).

Comparison of our results with those obtained by Donchin and Lindsley (12) for visual masking reveals an interesting contrast. In visual masking, which has frequently not been distinguished from metacontrast, two stimuli of unequal intensity fall successively on the same retinal locus. At certain interstimulus intervals, the second, brighter flash (BF) masks perception of the initial test flash (TF). Under these conditions, Donchin and Lindsley found no detectable evoked response to the initial stimulus. They concluded, in part, that ". . . the masking phenomenon is due to a displacement of the neural response to the TF by the response to the BF and that this interaction occurs prior to the stage at which the evoked potential is elicited" (12, p. 334). That no such displacement occurs under metacontrast conditions is clear from Figures 2 and 3. The disparity in results suggests that the perceptual suppres-

References

1. R. Stigler, Arch. Ges. Physiol. 134, 365 (1910).
2. D. H. Raab, Psychol. Bull. 60, 118 (1963).
3. M. Alpern, J. Opt. Soc. Amer. 43, 648 (1953).
4. G. A. Fry, Amer. J. Physiol. 108, 701 (1934); H. Piéron. J. Psychol. Norm. Pathol. 32, 5 (1935).
5. H. Werner, Amer. J. Psychol. 47, 40 (1935); E. Baumgardt and J. Segal, Année Psychol. 43–44, 54 (1942).

6. D. I. Tepas and J. C. Armington, *Vision Res., 2,* 449 (1962); H. G. Vaughan, Jr., and R. C. Hull, *Nature 206,* 720 (1965).

7. P. A. Kolers, *MRL-TDR-62-33.* Wright-Patterson Air Force Base (1962).

8. T. S. Paxton and B. A. Sidelnik, "A time-multiplexed pulse duration modulation tape recording system," unpublished thesis, Massachusetts Institute of Technology (1964).

9. P. H. Schiller and M. Smith, *J. Exp. Psychol. 71,* 32 (1966).

10. E. Donchin, J. D. Wicke, D. B. Lindsley, *Science 141,* 1285 (1963).

11. M. Schwartz and C. Shagass, *Ann. N.Y. Acad. Sci. 112,* 510–525 (1964).

12. E. Donchin and D. B. Lindsley, *Electroencephalog. Clin. Neurophysiol. 19,* 325 (1965).

13. W. R. Uttal, *Psychol. Bull. 64,* 377 (1965).

14. J. L. Brown and C. G. Muller, in *Vision and Visual Perception,* C. H. Graham, Ed. (Wiley, New York, 1965), pp. 208–250; D. Jameson and L. M. Hurvich, *Science 133,* 174 (1961).

2.3 Reaction Time to Stimuli Masked by Metacontrast*

ELIZABETH FEHRER   DAVID RAAB

The experiment to be described below is concerned with the relation between (*a*) phenomenal characteristics and (*b*) an objective behavioral measure of metacontrast suppression. If a brief light flash is followed, after a suitable interval, by stimulation of adjacent retinal areas, its apparent brightness is reduced. The extent of such retroactive masking has been shown to be a U-shaped function of stimulus onset asynchrony, with the maximum suppression occurring at asynchronies of 70 to 100 msec (e.g., Alpern, 1953). At such asynchronies, the first stimulus may be phenomenally absent (Kolers & Rosner, 1960; Toch, 1956; Werner, 1935). It is not, however, without effect on perception since under these conditions there is an awareness of movement involving the second stimulus. (Such asynchronous stimulation of adjacent retinal areas is, of course, the condition for producing apparent movement.)

* From: Elizabeth Fehrer and David Raab, "Reaction Time to Stimuli Masked by Metacontrast," *Journal of Experimental Psychology,* 1962, vol. 63, pp. 143–147. Copyright (1962) by the American Psychological Association, and reproduced by permission. This research was supported by Grant G-6456 from the National Science Foundation.

The problem of the present experiment was to determine whether the phenomenal masking of the first stimulus is associated with a decrease in its capacity to elicit a simple overt response. Specifically, we hoped to determine whether reaction time (RT) is correlated with the apparent brightness of a flash of light subjected to various degrees of metacontrast masking. The question becomes of especial interest at those stimulus onset asynchronies at which the first flash is phenomenally absent and only the masking stimuli (flashed second) are perceived.

The present problem is related to that raised in a previous study (Raab, Fehrer, & Hershenson, 1961) which dealt with the relation between RT and the apparent brightness of light flashes as contingent on their duration. It was shown that RT depended on stimulus characteristics rather than on the phenomenal appearance of the stimulus.

RT is a convenient measure of retroactive masking since the masked stimulus is the one presented first. If the RT chronoscope is started when the first stimulus is presented, it is possible to compare the RT to this stimulus when it is presented alone with the RT to it when it is followed by masking stimulation. Any lengthening of RT can then be attributed to the masking procedure.

Method

APPARATUS

The stimulus lights and S were located in one room; E's control panel and the RT chronoscope were in another room.

The stimulus lamps were placed behind a 6×2 in. rectangular box divided by two partitions into three 2×2 in. square cells arranged horizontally (see Figure 1). The top, bottom, sides, and septa of the box were made of sheet aluminum, $\frac{1}{32}$ in. thick. The front of the array (as seen by S) was covered with a sheet of diffusing tissue pressed against the cell walls by a 18.5×8.5 in. pane of $\frac{1}{8}$-in. polished plate glass mounted in a 2-in. wooden frame. The entire assembly was placed at eye level and was viewed binocularly by S from a distance of 15 ft. The horizontal visual angle of the array was $2°$. For foveal stimulation, two pin-point red lights were placed at the locations marked F (Figure 1), and S was instructed to fixate between them. Autokinetic movement of these fixation lights

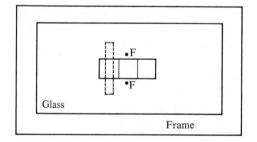

FIGURE 1 The stimulus array as seen by S. (The three light cells are covered by a sheet of diffusing tissue. The position of the fluorescent tube in each cell is indicated by the dashed outline in the left-hand cell. F and P are fixation points. For dimensions, see text.)

in the otherwise dark test room was eliminated by dimly illuminating the frame surrounding the plate glass. This illumination was too faint to be measured. The frame did not become visible to S until after 5 min. of dark adaptation.

For peripheral stimulation, a single fixation light, P (Figure 1), was placed 8.75 in. (i.e., $2°$ $50'$) above the top center of the central light cell.

A cold cathode fluorescent lamp was placed at the rear of each of the three light cells with phosphored portion $7\frac{1}{4}$ in. behind the diffusing tissue viewed by S. The lamps are of the mercury vapor type and are coated with a calcium halo phosphor. Luminance, measured at the diffusing tissue, was approximately 18 ft-L.

The lamps were pulsed by a "hard tube" high-voltage circuit. The vacuum tubes in series with each lamp were driven by a Tektronix 161 pulse generator. For all the work reported here, the lamp in the center cell was pulsed by one circuit and the two flanking cells were flashed together by an independent circuit. Regulated power supplies were employed throughout. When flashed, the lamps provide reasonably rectangular pulses of light. The chief departure occurs at offset and results from phosphor persistence.

Only two durations of flash, 5 and 50 msec, were used in this experiment. Since the light output from a lamp increases slightly with durations beyond 5 msec, the luminances of the two pulses at offset were not equal. The 50-msec pulse reached a level 0.076 log units above that of the 5-msec flash.

Timing of the stimulus pulses was accomplished by means of a set of Tektronix pulse and wave form generators. All critical timing voltages were regulated and the times themselves were monitored on a Westport WE-210 counter.

RT trials were presented once every 15 sec. Each trial began with a 1-sec warning tone. The stimulus pattern was presented (and the counter started) 2.9, 3.2, or 3.5 sec after the onset of the tone. The three foreperiods were switch selected and were presented in random order. The counter was stopped when S depressed a normally closed telegraph key.

RTs to the center light alone and to the center-plus-flanks could be read directly from the counter. RTs to the flanks alone were computed by subtracting the stimulus asynchrony from the counter readings.

PROCEDURE

Preliminary exploration indicated that good metacontrast suppression could be obtained with various durations of the center and flanking lights. It was arbitrarily decided to limit the present investigation to the following combinations: (*a*) center, 50 msec; flanks, 50 msec (50-50-50); (*b*) center, 5 msec; flanks, 50 msec (50-5-50). Each combination was studied in foveal and in peripheral vision.

Preliminary. Systematic variation of stimulus onset asynchrony (Δt) yielded the following perceptual correlates of asynchrony for the 50-50-50 sequence with foveal vision. The first perceptible darkening of the center light (as compared with the flanks) appears at a Δt of 4 to 6 msec. The darkening progresses with increases in Δt to about 35 msec. At this asynchrony, the center field is no longer homogeneous in color nor phenomenally a square, but appears as a faint, shapeless flash of light in the center of an extremely dark field between the flanks. Maximum suppression occurs with a Δt of approximately 75 msec. With increases in Δt beyond about 90 to 100 msec, depending on S, the center flash brightens again. At approximately 120 msec, it appears as a square preceding the flanks and of the same brightness as the flanks. Its apparent duration, however, is less than that of the flanks. With a Δt of about 150 msec, both brightness and duration of the center seem the same as those of the flanks.

With the 50-5-50 lights in foveal vision, the center square does not appear homogeneous even with a Δt of zero. Instead, only its center appears light. Maximum darkening and reappearance occur at about the same Δt's as for the 50-50-50 lights.

In peripheral vision, the phenomenal correlates of asynchrony differed from those described above for foveal vision only in that the apparent darkening of the center light was more pronounced than with foveal vision. With Δt's from 50 to 100 msec, the entire center square area appeared completely dark.

On the basis of the above findings, the following asynchronies were selected for systematic study: 0, 10, 25, 50, and 75 msec. It was assumed that, if RT parallels apparent brightness of the center light, RT, measured from the onset of the center light, should increase with Δt, reaching a maximum at a Δt of 75 msec, and that here, especially in peripheral vision, it might well be the same as RT to the flanks.

Foveal Vision. The authors and a graduate student served as Ss. All had had extensive previous experience with RT. Each S served in 50 sessions, 25 with the 50-50-50 durations and 25 with the 50-5-50. Of the 25 sessions at a given duration of the center light, 5 were assigned to each of the 5 stimulus onset asynchronies.

Thirty-six RTs were recorded at each session, 12 to the center light alone, 12 to the flanks alone, and 12 to the combination. Random presentation prevented S from knowing which stimulus pattern would be presented at a given trial. Foreperiod duration was also randomized.

The longest and the shortest RT of each 12 were eliminated before the three means for each session were computed. Since there were five sessions for each asynchrony, the means for each S are based on 50 RTs.

Two sessions were run on each experimental day, one with the 50-50-50 and one with the 50-5-50 durations. Sessions at the various Δt's followed each other in random order.

After 5 min. of dark adaptation, three practice trials were given. Then the recorded trials were run. A 1-min. rest period separated each 18 trials.

Perhipheral Vision. For the 50-50-50 durations, two graduate students and one undergraduate major served as Ss. For the 50-5-50, one author and one undergraduate major were Ss. Each served in 20 sessions, 5 each at the following four Δt's: 0, 10, 25, and 75 msec. The procedure was otherwise identical with that employed for foveal vision.

Results and Discussion

Since all Ss showed the same trends, only the group means are presented in Tables 1 and 2. The individual SDs were of the order of 12 msec and did not differ with stimulus conditions. The data in both tables show that RT to the center light was never *increased* by the addition of the masking stimuli. A series of *t* tests of the difference between each individual center and center-plus-flanks means showed that in no case was the RT to center-plus-flanks reliably longer. It follows, therefore, that decreases in apparent brightness produced by the

metacontrast procedure are not reflected in RT increases. This is true even for peripheral vision where, with a Δt of 75 msec, the center flash is phenomenally absent. Under all our conditions, RT seemed to be determined only by the *stimulus* characteristics of the light flashed first.

The fact that the stimulus does evoke a normal RT even when completely "masked" is not, perhaps, entirely unexpected. Since the metacontrast procedure is also the procedure for producing *phi* movement, it is obvious that the light flashed first does affect the total perception. Even though the center light appears "blanked," its prior occurrence is a necessary condition for the perception of movement involving the flanks, and such movement was apparent to all our Ss. Our data have shown clearly that RT to a light is the same when (*a*) it is presented alone and perceived as a bright flash, and when (*b*) it is followed by later stimulation of adjacent retinal areas and is "perceived" only through the apparent movement of these lights.

Our results do not depend on knowledge of stimulus conditions. RTs of 6 naive Ss were measured to the center light alone and to the center followed after 75 msec by the flanks. The 50-50-50 lights and peripheral fixation were used. Although the RTs were longer than those appearing in our tables (Ss were unpracticed), they were the same under both stimulus conditions. When these Ss were asked to describe what they saw, all reported seeing either a single square of light or two squares separated by a dark area about the size of one of the squares. Movement of the two squares was never spontaneously reported until at least 20 RT trials had been run.

The Ss were then tested to see whether they could learn to distinguish phenomenally between the appearance of the flanks alone and the center-plus-flanks. All but 1 learned to do so but not until 10 to 20 trials (with correction) had been run.

In other words, these Ss' RTs were from the beginning a reliable index of the presence of the "masked" center light whereas their phenomenal reports became adequate only after some specific training.

TABLE 1

Mean Reaction Times with Foveal Stimulation

Δt in Msec.	50-50-50			50-5-50		
	CENTER	FLANKS	ALL	CENTER	FLANKS	ALL
0	165.9	163.3	161.1	167.3	162.3	162.6
10	164.6	162.3	161.9	166.2	162.6	161.3
25	167.1	163.4	164.9	169.6	166.6	167.1
50	167.2	166.6	167.5	166.5	162.5	166.5
75	162.4	160.3	164.5	165.4	161.9	165.1
Mean	165.4	163.2		167.0	163.2	

TABLE 2

Mean Reaction Times with Peripheral Stimulation

Δt in Msec	50-50-50			50-5-50		
	CENTER	FLANKS	ALL	CENTER	FLANKS	ALL
0	159.6	155.2	153.4	167.6	160.2	160.9
10	162.3	155.6	158.9	164.4	160.0	163.5
25	163.2	160.5	164.1	164.8	159.6	164.3
75	161.8	158.1	161.5	165.7	160.0	165.0
Mean	161.8	157.3		165.6	159.9	

The data provide some information concerning the effect of stimulus duration on RT. The center stimulus was presented alone on one-third of the trials in each session. Since both 5-and 50-msec flashes were employed, RTs to these can be compared directly. With foveal vision (Table 1), the mean RT to the 50-msec flash was 165.4 msec; the mean RT of the same Ss to the 5-msec pulse was 167.0 msec. The absence of any marked difference in RT is in line with the results of a previous study (Raab et al., 1961) in which RT was found to be independent of stimulus durations between 10 and 500 msec. A similar comparison cannot be made with the present peripheral data since the 5- and 50-msec flashes were presented to different Ss.

That stimulus size affects RT (e.g., Froeberg, 1907) is shown by our data. Reactions to the single 50-msec center flash were slower than to the two 50-msec flanks. Of the 15 possible individual comparisons between center and flank means for foveal vision (3 Ss × 5 asynchronies), 13 show faster RT to the flanks than to the center ($P = .01$). Of the 12 comparisons (3 Ss × 4 asynchronies) in peripheral vision, 11 show faster RT to the flanks ($P < .01$). For foveal vision, the overall mean of 165.4 msec for the center light differs significantly ($P < .01$) from the mean of 163.2 for the flanks (Table 1, last row). The comparable difference for the peripheral data is also significant.

When the center and flanks are pulsed simultaneously ($\Delta t = 0$), the stimulus area is, in effect, three times that of the center alone. RT to this largest stimulus was in all cases faster than RT to the flanks.

It is interesting to note that RT to the center-plus-flanks is also faster than RT to the center alone when the flanks are delayed by 10 msec. Of the 11 differences between individual means at this asynchrony (6 for foveal and 5 for peripheral vision), 10 show this effect ($P = .01$). There is some indication that this effect persists up to the 25-msec Δt for foveal vision, since in the six possible comparisons under this condition, RT to the combined stimulation was faster in all cases than RT to the center alone. The finding of "facilitation" at these two asynchronies is the opposite of what would have been found if phenomenal brightness governs RT since, at these asynchronies, the center flash is appreciably darkened. The finding is similar to an intersensory facilitation of RT recently reported by Hershenson (1960).

Summary

This study was designed to determine whether metacontrast suppression of a light flash affects RT to the flash. Masking of a square target was achieved by subsequent flashing of two adjacent squares. Stimulus onset asynchronies were studied over a range from 0 to 75 msec. Phenomenal suppression of the first flash varied from none (0 asynchrony) to maximum (75 msec asynchrony).

With both foveal and peripheral vision, the results showed no effect of phenomenal brightness on RT. RT to the target, flashed alone, was never faster than RT to the target followed by masks. It was therefore the physical dimensions of the stimulus rather than its phenomenal characteristics that determined RT.

References

Alpern, M. Metacontrast. *J. Opt. Soc. Amer.*, 1953, 43, 648–657.

Froeberg, S. The relation between the magnitude of stimulus and the time of reaction. *Arch. Psychol., NY*, 1907, 16, 1–38.

Hershenson, M. Reaction time as a measure of intersensory facilitation. Unpublished master's thesis, Brooklyn College, 1960.

Kolers, P. A., & Rosner, B. S. On visual masking (metacontrast): Dichoptic observation. *Amer. J. Psychol.*, 1960, 73, 2–21.

Raab, D., Fehrer, E., & Hershenson, M. Visual reaction time and the Broca-Sulzer phenomenon. *J. exp. Psychol.*, 1961, 61, 193–199.

Toch, H. The perceptual elaboration of stroboscopic presentations. *Amer. J. Psychol.*, 1956, 69, 345–358.

Werner, H. Studies on contour: I. Qualitative analysis. *Amer. J. Psychol.*, 1935, 47, 40–64.

2.4 Temporal Luminance Summation Effects in Backward and Forward Masking*

CHARLES W. ERIKSEN

If a briefly presented visual stimulus is followed by a second stimulus within a short time lag, typically 100 msec or less, there are circumstances under which the two stimulations interact. Impairment in perception may occur for the first stimulus (backward masking), the second stimulus (forward masking) or for both stimuli. Eriksen and Hoffman (1963) have advanced a luminance summation-contrast reduction hypothesis to account for certain instances of these forward and backward masking effects. Noting the evidence that the visual system integrates luminances over intervals of the order of 100 msec (Clark & Blackwell, 1959; Matin, 1962) or perhaps even longer (Kahneman & Norman, 1964), Eriksen and Hoffman suggested that masking effects under certain experimental arrangements could be attributed to a reduced effective contrast for the stimulus figures arising from luminance summation between the two stimulations.

Backward and forward masking effects typically have been studied in Dodge-type tachistoscopes. A stimulus is presented to the eyes from one stimulus field and by means of a beam splitter the second stimulation comes from an independent field. If the stimuli consist of black figures on white grounds and the two figures do not fall on the same retinal areas, luminance summation-contrast reduction would

occur in the following way. For the purposes of illustration assume the luminance from the ground is 10 mL and from the figure, 1 mL giving a contrast ratio of 10:1. If the first stimulus is presented for 10 msec and followed immediately by the 10 msec presentation of the second stimulus, the retinal areas on which the ground of the first stimulus falls would receive a stimulation equivalent to that from a source of 20 mL. The retinal area corresponding to the figure would receive stimulation from 1 mL for the 10 msec exposure, but since the second stimulation now presents ground on the area that had received figure in the first stimulation, this retinal area will have a stimulation from 10 mL added to the previous 1 mL stimulus. In terms of effective stimulation the contrast ratio of the figure in the first stimulus with its ground has been reduced from a ratio of 10:1 to less than 2:1. Essentially the same luminance summation effects would occur for the second stimulus.

This explanation of certain instances of masking effects has received strong support in several experimental studies (Eriksen & Lappin, 1964; Eriksen & Steffy, 1964; Thompson, 1966). It was the purpose of the present experiments to provide more definite tests of the luminance summation-contrast reduction hypothesis, and specifically to test its ability to predict circumstances under which backward and forward masking effects would and would not be obtained.

The luminance summation-contrast reduction explanation of forward and backward

* Reproduced by permission of *Perception & Psychophysics,* 1966, vol. 1, pp. 87–92. This investigation was supported by Public Health Service research grant MH-1206 and a Public Health Service research career program award K6-MH-22,014.

masking effects requires two assumptions about the visual perceptual system.

Assumption I. The accuracy of form detection or identification at brief exposure durations is, within limits, a function of the luminance contrast of the form with the ground; the higher the contrast the more accurate the detection or identification.

Assumption II. The visual system sums luminance from two or more successive stimulations distributed within a brief time interval of the order of 100 msec, with the completeness of the summation inversely proportional to the time interval between successive stimuli.

In the two following experiments six predictions have been deduced from these two assumptions and experimentally tested.

Experiment I

The validity of Assumption I has been well established for both long (Connor & Ganoung, 1935) and for short exposure durations (Cobb & Moss, 1928). Experiment I, however, was designed to assess the magnitude of the effect that contrast reduction has on a form identification task using luminance values in the range of those employed in masking studies and where the contrast reducing luminance is produced by one of the fields of the tachistoscope (veiling glare). In this sense Experiment I serves as a calibration for Experiment II.

Prediction: If black forms on white grounds are presented at brief durations in one field of a tachistoscope and the second field simultaneously presents an empty white ground, then form identification will be impaired with the amount of impairment directly proportional to the luminance of the second field.

Method

SUBJECTS

Subjects were four undergraduate students (two females) who were paid volunteers. All Ss were highly practiced on perceptual recognition tasks and were run in this experiment following their completion of a very similar perceptual recognition experiment in which they had served 22 sessions.

APPARATUS AND PROCEDURE

A three-field Dodge-type tachistoscope, previously described (Eriksen & Hoffman, 1963), was used. Two fields, F I and F II, were used as stimulus fields and a third field (FA) as an adaptation field containing the fixation point. The stimulus forms consisted of the capital letters A, T and U, presented singly and requiring a forced-choice recognition response from S after each presentation. The letters occurred randomly on the corners of an imaginary square of 1.25° of angle centered on the fixation point. Previous research had indicated that these three letters were approximately equally discriminable and equally confusable one with another when presented at brief durations. Each letter subtended 0.2° of arc on its maximum dimension. The letters had luminance of 0.009 mL and their ground 0.20 mL yielding a contrast ratio of 22:1. The adapting field, FA, was dark except for a faint glowing "x" fixation point, subtending 0.2°.

The S was instructed to fixate the x and when it appeared sharp and clear to press a trigger which presented the stimulus. This stimulus consisted of one of the three letters in F I presented simultaneously with a blank stimulus card which was illuminated for the same duration in F II. Four levels of F II luminance were employed, 0.00. 0.09, 0.20 and 0.40 mL. Within an experimental session all four F II luminance levels occurred equally often and were presented in a counterbalanced order. During two experimental sessions each S made 50 judgments at each of the four F II luminance levels with 100 judgments being made in each experimental session. Prior to beginning the experimental sessions an exposure duration had been determined for each S that yielded between 80 and 85% forced-choice identification accuracy under the condition of the dark adapting field and no second field luminance. The exposure durations necessary for the four Ss to achieve

80 to 85% recognition accuracy under the condition of no second field luminance were 24, 26, 32, and 35 msec.

Results and Discussion

The test of the prediction is provided by the data in Figure 1 which show the average percent identification of the three letters as a function of the log of contrast ratio. The function as a whole is negatively accelerated. When the contrast has reached a ratio of approximately 3:1, identification accuracy shows relatively little further increase with increases in contrast.

The data for each of the four Ss was consistent with the average results. Each S had a progressive increase in identification accuracy as the luminance of the F II stimulation decreased from 0.40 to 0.00 mL, a result significant beyond the 0.001 level.

This result supports the experimental prediction. Strictly speaking, the data in Figure 1 do not show the relation between form identification and contrast ratio per se since in these data total luminance is confounded with contrast ratio. This confounding, however, was deliberate. It is identical to the confounding which occurs in typical tachistoscope studies of masking. A demonstration of the effect of contrast ratio on form identification holding total

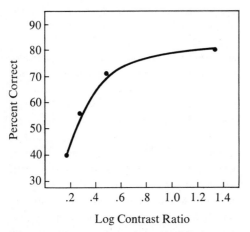

FIGURE 1   Percent correct form identification as a function of the log of the ratio of the luminance of the ground to luminance of the figure.

luminance constant would not have been as germane to the luminance summation-contrast reduction explanation of masking effects.

Experiment II

The two assumptions underlying the luminance summation-contrast reduction explanation of masking effects were used to deduce the following five predictions:

1. The exposure duration necessary to achieve a given criterion of form identification will be least when the form stimulation is preceded and followed by at least 100 msec of dark adapting field and greatest when the form stimulation is preceded, superimposed upon, and followed by an illuminated adapting field. A stimulation sequence in which the form is preceded by an illuminated adapting field which terminates with the onset of the stimulus and returns 100 msec or more following termination of the stimulus will require an intermediate exposure duration to achieve the identification criterion.

2. Form identification will show little change as a function of the interstimulus interval (ISI) between form presentation and masking stimulus for either backward or forward masking sequences when the form and masking stimulations are superimposed upon a continuously illuminated adapting field whose luminance is relatively greater than those of the two stimulation fields. Under these conditions luminance summation is already occurring between adapting and form stimulation fields preceding, during, and following the form occurrence and the relatively small luminance of the masking field contributes little to further reduction of effective contrast.

3. Form identification will improve with increases in ISI between form and masking stimulus for the forward masking sequence and will tend to remain constant with the backward masking sequence when an adapting field whose relative luminance is greater than that of form and masking fields

is employed in the following stimulation sequence: Adapting field terminates with onset of the first stimulation and remains off until 100 msec or longer after termination of the second stimulation. Under this arrangement a form presented in the second stimulation (forward masking) will become increasingly more identifiable as the dark ISI between the masking flash and the onset of the form stimulation becomes greater. The longer the ISI the less luminance summation occurs between the form stimulus in F II and the luminance of the adapting and masking fields. A form presented in F I, however, (backward masking) is always preceded by the greater adapting field luminance and increasing delays of the masking flash in F II does little to increase identification since its relatively lesser luminance makes only a small contribution to effective contrast reduction for the F I form even at short ISIs.

4. Both forward and backward masking effects will be marked when a dark adapting field and ISI are employed.

5. With a dark adapting field and ISI, forward masking will be greater in effect than backward masking. This prediction is deducible in part from the above two assumptions but it is in addition based upon the consideration that a form stimulation preceded by a masking flash has its contrast impaired right from its initial onset at short ISIs. On the other hand, a form stimulation followed by a masking flash has the full period of its duration plus the time of the ISI to act upon the visual system before its contrast is reduced by luminance summation from the masking flash.

Method

SUBJECTS

Six practiced Ss (three males) aged 19, 20, 22, 27, 39 and 44 years served as paid volunteers. All had normal or corrected to normal visual acuity.

APPARATUS AND PROCEDURE

The tachistoscope and stimulus forms were the same as employed in Experiment I. All Ss were run under three experimental conditions. Under all three conditions two stimulus presentation sequences were employed. Under the first sequence (backward masking), one of the three letters was presented in F I followed at ISIs of 0, 25, 50, 75 or 100 msec by the presentation of a uniform adapting field in F II. Under the other sequence (forward masking), the letter form appeared in F II preceded by a flash of a uniform adapting field in F I at one of the five ISIs. After a stimulation sequence, S was required to make a forced-choice response as to which of the three letters had been presented. The test letter of 0.009 mL was, as in Experiment I, associated with a ground of 0.20 mL.

The three experimental conditions differed in terms of whether the adapting field was light or dark and whether the ISI was lighted or dark. In Condition L the adaptation field with a luminance of 0.58 mL remained on continuously. A black x served as fixation point, 0.2° in size, and the stimulations from F I and F II were superimposed upon the adaptation field luminance.

Condition L-D also had a lighted adaptation field of 0.58 mL but here the adaptation field luminance terminated with onset of stimulation in F I and remained off until 300 msec after the termination of stimulation in F II. Thus F I was always preceded by a luminance of 0.58 mL and F II, except at zero delay, was always preceded by a dark ISI and followed by a dark interval of 300 msec duration.

In Condition D the adapting field was dark except for a faint glowing x which served as a fixation point and was the same size as that employed in the other conditions. The ISI was also dark containing only the faintly luminous fixation point.

The Ss were run in a counterbalanced order through the three conditions. Prior to undertaking the experimental sessions each S received two 1-hr. practice sessions during which he identified the three stimulus letters at brief exposure durations. Each S devoted six suc-

TABLE 1

Summary of Luminance Values in Millilamberts for the Three Experimental Conditions

Sequence		FA	FI	FII	Complete Summation	Summation at Longest ISI	Difference in Contrast Ratios (CR)
Condition L							
Forward	Ground	.58	.20	.20	.98	.78	
					CR = 1.24		CR = 1.32 .08
	Figure	.58	.20	.01	.79	.59	
Backward	Ground	.58	.20	.20	.98	.78	
					CR = 1.24		CR = 1.32 .08
	Figure	.58	.01	.20	.79	.59	
Condition L-D							
Forward	Ground	.58	.20	.20	.98	.20	
					CR = 1.24		CR = 20.0 18.76
	Figure	.58	.20	.01	.79	.01	
Backward	Ground	.58	.20	.20	.98	.78	
					CR = 1.24		CR = 1.32 .08
	Figure	.58	.01	.20	.79	.59	
Condition D							
Forward	Ground	.00	.20	.20	.40	.20	
					CR = 1.90		CR = 20.0 18.1
	Figure	.00	.20	.01	.21	.01	
Backward	Ground	.00	.20	.20	.40	.20	
					CR = 1.90		CR = 20.0 18.1
	Figure	.00	.01	.20	.21	.01	

cessive sessions to the L and the L-D conditions and 11 sessions to Condition D. The first session under a condition was devoted to obtaining a base level duration for that S in that condition that would lead to approximately 55% identification accuracy of the three letters. This base level condition was run under the adapting field conditions obtaining for that condition but no masking flash occurred. To assure comparability of F I and F II, half of the trials in random order contained the stimulus in F I and the other half in F II. Thus for Condition D, as an example, there was a dark adaptation field followed by the presentation of one of the three letters in either F I or F II and a return to the dark adapting field. In Condition L the S was confronted with the illuminated adapting field and a letter appeared in F I or

F II superimposed upon the adapting luminance and then returned to only the adapting luminance. In Condition L-D the base level stimulation sequence consisted of the adapting luminance which terminated with the onset of a stimulus in F I or F II and 300 msec after termination of this form a return to the adapting luminance. The exposure duration determined during the base level session was then used for a particular S for the F I and F II durations in the remaining experimental sessions under that condition.

In each of these five sessions S received six forward and six backward masking sequences or trials at each of the five ISIs. This resulted in a total of 30 identification trials for each S for the forward and 30 for the backward masking sequence at each of the five delay intervals per condition. An exception was Condition D where S served a total of 11 experimental sessions in order to provide greater sensitivity for detecting differences in backward and forward masking conditions. Here the number of identification trials was double that in the other two conditions. The beginning of each experimental session was preceded by a 10-min. dark adapting period and practice session.

The relation of the three experimental conditions to the predictions under test can be seen with the aid of Table 1. This table presents the figure and ground luminances by experimental condition for the different tachistoscopic fields and for the backward and forward masking sequences. The column labeled complete summation, shows the figure and ground luminances and contrast ratios that would obtain for the figure and ground if FA, F I and F II were activated simultaneously in the particular experimental condition. The next column, labeled minimum summation at longest ISI, shows the figure ground luminances and contrast ratios that would obtain for a condition if the ISI between form and masking flash was greater than the interval necessary for summation effects. (For simplicity in exposition, it is assumed that summation is complete if successive stimulations are separated by less than 1 msec. The last column shows the difference in contrast ratios between optimum summation and minimum summation. This difference between contrast ratios within a condition provides an index of how much change in identification of the forms can be obtained by manipulating ISI. Alternatively stated, it provides an index of how much evidence of masking can be obtained for the condition.

From Table 1 it can be seen that the maximum reduction in contrast that can exist for the retinal image would occur when all three tachistoscope fields were simultaneously illuminated. Here the contrast ratio would be approximately 1.24. In Condition L, which tests prediction 2, the stimulation is always superimposed upon the adapting field luminance. If the form occurs in F I, the retinal areas receiving the ground will be stimulated by a luminance of 0.78 mL and the areas receiving the figure will receive 0.59 for a contrast of 1.32. Even if the F II masking flash occurs at zero ISI, it changes the contrast ratio only to 1.24. From Figure 1 of the previous experiment it can be seen that such a slight decrease in effective contrast would have only a very slight effect upon form identification accuracy. In Condition L-D delaying the form stimulus in F II beyond the summation interval can lead to a marked increase in contrast ratio. Here if all three fields were simultaneously activated the ground would have a stimulation value of 0.98 mL and the form would have 0.79, yielding a contrast ratio of 1:24. However, delaying the presentation of the form in the F II stimulation beyond the summation interval results in an effective stimulus where the ground has 0.2 mL and the form image 0.01—a contrast ratio of 22:1. Under the backward masking sequence in this condition even with long ISIs between masking and form presentation there is little change in effective contrast ratio. Here the luminance relations remain essentially as in Condition L. It can also be seen that in Condition D contrast ratio will vary markedly for both the forward and backward masking sequence as the ISI between F I and F II varies.

Results

The first prediction pertained to the exposure duration required for 55% recognition accuracy of the forms when no masking stimulus was used. The base level data for the three conditions provide a test of this prediction. Condition L would be expected to require the longest duration since the forms were presented superimposed upon a brighter luminance from the adapting field. Condition D would require the shortest duration since the form was preceded and followed by a dark adapting field. An intermediate duration would be predicted for Condition L-D since the form followed immediately after the termination of the relatively brighter adapting field but was followed by 300 msec of dark interval. In Condition L the mean exposure duration for the six Ss was 75 msec, in

Condition L-D, 42, and in Condition D, 21. The data for each of the six Ss followed the same ordering across conditions as the means, a result significant beyond the .001 level.

Before examining the remaining predictions in detail, the number of correct form identifications were analyzed in a four-way classification analysis of variance (Ss, ISIs, forward and backward masking sequence, and experimental conditions). Of the four main effects only conditions failed to achieve significance at the .01 level. All the two-way interactions except those involving the S variable were significant at or beyond the .01 level. There was, however, a significant S by condition interaction and the triple interaction between ISIs, backward and forward masking and conditions was significant beyond the .05 level. The significant S effect and S by condition interaction, was anticipated due to inability to match Ss exactly at a base level of 55% identification accuracy within and across conditions.

The nature of these significant effects and interactions can be seen in Figure 2. Here identification accuracy is shown as a function of the backward and forward masking sequence and ISIs for each of the experimental conditions. The graphs also show the base level performance by stimulus fields which was obtained under the adapting field specifications for the experimental condition but without the masking flash.

The data from Condition L provide information on prediction 2 that for both forward and backward masking sequences, form identification would remain relatively constant as ISI varied. The data from this condition support the prediction. There is none of the usual evidence of masking. Form identification remains at essentially the base level irrespective of whether the form is preceded or followed by the relatively dim flash of the masking field.

The data from the L-D condition provide a test of prediction 3. For the backward masking sequence the form presented in F I is always immediately preceded by the relatively brighter adapting field. The relatively dimmer masking stimulus in F II, as was seen in Table 1, has little effect on further reducing the effective

contrast for the form presented in F I even at zero ISI. As a consequence, form identification for the backward masking condition was expected to remain at the base level condition. As is seen in Figure 2, this result essentially obtains although there is an unexplained decrease in form identification under this sequence at the ISIs of 75 and 100 msec.

For the forward masking sequence in Condition L-D the form stimulus appears in F II preceded by the relatively brighter adapting field and the masking stimulus in F I. As ISI increases, there is an increasing dark period preceding the occurrence of the form in F II. With the longer dark ISIs luminance summation from the adapting and F I masking stimulation decreases and there is an increase in effective contrast for the F II form with a corresponding increase in correct identification. In the graph identifiability of the form under the forward masking sequence rises from the base level to an asymptote in the neighborhood of 75 to 100 msec of ISI.

Prediction 4 stated that both forward and backward masking effects would be evident where the adapting field and ISI were dark, the arrangement that obtained in Condition D. As is seen in Figure 2, pronounced masking effects are found for both the forward and backward sequence out to an ISI of at least 75 msec. For both sequences identification drops from the base level with the introduction of the masking flash and then rises gradually to an ISI in the neighborhood of 75 msec.

Prediction 5 stated that forward masking effects under the circumstances obtaining in Condition D would be more extensive than backward masking effects. The functions shown in Figure 2 are consistent with this prediction. Identification is poorer with the forward masking sequence at all ISIs less than 75 msec.

As was pointed out in the procedure, twice as many observations were taken under this experimental condition, D, in order to provide a more sensitive test of differences between forward and backward masking sequences. To determine whether the differences between these sequences in this condition were statistically reliable, the data for this condition, using

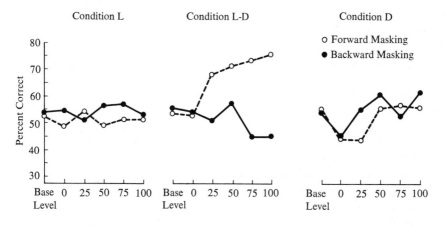

FIGURE 2 Percent correct form identification as a function of forward and backward masking sequence and experimental conditions.

only the ISI intervals of 50 msec or less, were subjected to a three-way classification analysis of variance (Ss, ISIs, backward and forward masking sequence). Significant at or beyond the .01 level were the main effects due to Ss, to lags and, of major interest, the interaction of lags by backward and forward masking sequence.

Discussion

The results of these two experiments provided rather striking confirmation for the six predictions derived from the assumptions underlying the luminance summation-contrast reduction hypothesis. The validity of these two assumptions is attested to not only by their ability to predict the circumstances under which masking effects will occur and the shapes of the particular functions but also from a much broader range of visual perceptual research. The summing of luminances over short time durations is indicated not only in the work on critical flicker fusion but in the well established Bunsen-Roscoe law. Directly relevant to luminance summation and the effect of contrast reduction on form recognition is the recent work of Thompson (1966). He found that lumi-

nance summation occurred over an interval of nearly 100 msec and he was able to directly relate form recognition to the attendant contrast reduction that occurred from the summation. Also, Zuercher (1965) found that the identification of letter forms was a direct function of the amount of light energy that occurred within an 80 to 100 msec interval, irrespective of whether the light energy was divided into from 2 to 12 separate pulses distributed over the interval.

While luminance summation with attendant contrast reduction for forms would seem to be a basis for certain backward and forward masking effects, there is also evidence that other processes may be involved in visual masking. For example, Alpern (1953), Averbach and Coriell (1961), and Eriksen and Collins (1964; 1965) have obtained masking effects under circumstances where luminance summation was eliminated or greatly reduced. But the luminance summation-contrast reduction effect seems well enough supported so that careful experimenters should insure that in future experiments it is not confounded with other masking effects they are attempting to study. Other masking processes can be more easily confirmed and identified if experiments are designed to eliminate or reduce luminance summation.

While the present experiments used black figures on white grounds and a blank white field as a masking stimulus, it is to be noted that luminance summation effects are not limited to these stimuli and masks. One can readily deduce the patterns of luminance summation and attendant contrast changes when overlapping stimuli and patterned stimuli are used as the masking stimulus. As Schiller and Smith (1965) have found, masking effects are apt to be much more extensive when a black and white patterned masking stimulus is employed. When a masking stimulus consisting of a pattern of black dots or squares on a white field is employed, the parts of the test form or letter that overlap black areas in the masking field come through to the eye with unimpaired contrast. Those parts that do not overlap have their contrast reduced. As a result one gets a very irregular random-type form in perception which can lead to confusions with other alternatives in the stimulus set. This would appear to pose a more difficult identification problem than when a blank white mask field is used and the test form appears only more faint but relatively undistorted.

Summary

Two experiments tested six predictions derived from the assumptions underlying the luminance summation-contrast reduction explanation for certain instances of forward and backward masking effects. The predictions concerned the circumstances under which masking would occur and also that forward masking would be more extensive than backward masking under specified luminance arrangements. All six predictions were confirmed.

References

Alpern, M. Metacontrast. *J. Opt. Soc. Amer.,* 1953, *43,* 648–657.

Averbach, E., & Coriell, A. S. Short-term memory in vision. *Bell Sys. tech. J.,* 1961, *40,* 309–328.

Clark, W. E., & Blackwell, H. R. Relations between visibility thresholds for single and double pulses. *U. Mich. Engng. Res. Inst. Proj. Mich. Rep.,* 1959, No. 2144-343-T.

Cobb, F. W., & Moss, F. K. The four variables of the visual threshold. *J. Franklin Inst.,* 1928, *205,* 831–847.

Connor, J. P., & Ganoung, R. E. An experimental determination of the visual thresholds at low values of illumination. *J. Opt. Soc. Amer.,* 1935, *25,* 287–294.

Eriksen, C. W., & Collins, J. F. Backward masking in vision. *Psychon. Sci.,* 1964, *1,* 101–102.

Eriksen, C. W., & Collins, J. F. A reinterpretation of one form of backward and forward masking in visual perception. *J. exp. Psychol.,* 1965, *70,* 343–351.

Eriksen, C. W., & Hoffman, M. Form recognition at brief durations as a function of adapting field and interval between stimulations. *J. exp. Psychol.,* 1963, *66,* 485–499.

Eriksen, C. W., & Lappin, J. S. Luminance summation—contrast reduction as a basis for certain forward and backward masking effects. *Psychon. Sci.,* 1964, *1,* 313–314.

Eriksen, C. W., & Steffy, R. A. Short-term memory and retroactive interference in visual perception. *J. exp. Psychol.,* 1964, *68,* 423–434.

Kahneman, D., & Norman, J. The time-intensity relation in visual perception as a function of observer's task. *J. exp. Psychol.,* 1964, *68,* 215–220.

Matin, L. Binocular summation at the absolute threshold of peripheral vision. *J. Opt. Soc. Amer.,* 1962, *52,* 1276–1286.

Schiller, P. H., & Smith, M. C. A comparison of forward and backward masking. *Psychon. Sci.,* 1965, *3,* 77–78.

Thompson, J. H. What happens to the stimulus in backward masking? *J. exp. Psychol.,* in press.

Zuercher, J. D. Visual recognition as a function of an intermittent stimulus varied over time. Unpublished doctoral dissertation, University of Illinois, 1965.

2.5 Backward Masking and Models of Perceptual Processing[*]

NAOMI WEISSTEIN

A visual stimulus produces a large number of discrete points of stimulation on the retina. After this stimulation, operations occur which transform the stimulus energies into the information which an O has available for report. This sequence, from input to report, may be called perceptual processing.

Certain studies have supported the idea of simultaneous operations, or parallel processing, for at least some parts of this process (Neisser, 1963). Other studies suggest that the operations in perceptual processing are in serial order, i.e., fully carried out on one part of the visual array before proceeding to another part. The current formulation of short-term memory (Averbach & Coriell, 1961; Sperling, 1963) assumes that operations are carried out on each item of a visual array in turn, that is, serially.

For both of these formulations, the decision between parallel and serial processing has been made on the basis of whether or not there is a

* From: Naomi Weisstein, "Backward Masking and Models of Perceptual Processing," *Journal of Experimental Psychology*, 1966, vol. 72, pp. 232–240. Copyright (1966) by the American Psychological Association, and reproduced by permission. Parts of this research were submitted in the form of a doctoral dissertation to the Department of Social Relations, Harvard University; the research was completed at Yale University and supported in part by a United States Public Health Service Grant, MH-03244 to R. N. Haber, principal investigator; and in part by a National Science Foundation Terminal Predoctoral Fellowship to the author. The author wishes to thank R. N. Haber and Brendan Maher for their invaluable assistance in every phase of this research, and to express gratitude to the Psychology Department of Yale University for making facilities available to her while she was a student at Harvard.

total increase in response time with an increase in the size of the array. In other words, if the time between presentation and report increases for larger arrays, then serial processing has been assumed. On the other hand, if the time between presentation and report remains the same as array size increases, then parallel processing has been assumed. However, this type of design, which measures a total increase in the time between presentation and report (Sperling, 1963) does not unequivocally suggest one formulation or the other. An increase in processing time may mean either that more operations are being performed simultaneously for each part of an array (parallel), or, equally likely, that the set of operations is repeating itself in turn for additional parts of the array (serial).

A technique which can help decide between these two formulations is one which can identify an operation occurring within the sequence from presentation to report. If such an operation can be identified, then its duration can be measured for arrays of different sizes. If duration is constant as array size increases, parallel processing can be assumed; if duration increases in certain regular ways as array size increases, serial processing can be assumed.

Certain types of backward-masking designs generate data which provide direct measures of operations occurring within the perceptual processing sequence. Backward masking refers to the power of certain stimuli, the masking stimuli, to disrupt or mask the processing of other stimuli, the target stimuli, which have been presented *earlier*. (See Raab, 1963, for a general summary.) When the amplitude of this disruption is a U-shaped function of the delay between offset of the target stimulus and onset of the masking stimulus, then this indicates an operation or set of operations which is distinct from other operations within the processing sequence. (See Weisstein, 1964; Weisstein & Haber, 1965, for a fuller discussion.) Moreover, the minimum duration of the processing sequence itself may be inferred to be at least the time between the onset of the earlier, target stimulus and the greatest delay at which the onset of the masking stimulus still has an effect. It is convenient to bound the operation by considering only the delays between target and mask at which maximum masking, or complete occlusion from perception occurs. These maximum masking ranges can be observed for arrays of different sizes and their durations compared; such a comparison will provide an indication of the type of processing occurring.

General Method

Target stimuli were presented in either 1-, 2-, 4-, or 8-item arrays. The array was presented tachistoscopically for a fixed, brief duration. Following its offset, a lighted blank field was presented, equal in intensity to the preexposure field, for a variable length of time. Then, a ring was presented, in a location which would have been encircling one of the letters in the array, had the array still been present. The time between offset of the array and onset of the ring is designated as the interstimulus interval (ISI).

Experiment I

Method. One-letter and four-letter arrays were presented. Each array was constructed from the letters O, D, or blanks. These were presented in a three-channel mirror tachistoscope (Scientific Prototype Manufacturing Corporation, Model G). The visual field was 5 in. horizontally × 7 in. vertically, 47 in. from S.

Accuracy for all ranges of duration was ±2%. Duration and intensity of the target field was monitored by an oscilloscope. In the target and masking channel, a tape of 140 rows of one- or four-letter displays and a tape of one ring per row, respectively, were displayed. After each presentation both tapes were advanced 2 in. and the next array and ring combination was aligned.

Each of five Ss, four males and one female, were tested individually; each had at least 10 hr. of previous practice. Sixteen sessions were run for each S. In each session, S first dark adapted for 1 min. and then light adapted to a blank preexposure field, illuminated, as were the target and mask fields, at 9.4 ftl. A black fixation point of less than 2′ was present in the center of the field. All fields were viewed binocularly. The array was presented for 20 msec in one field, and then, after a variable delay during which the preexposure field was viewed, the ring was presented for 50 msec in another field. The Ss responded by designating what was inside the ring: O, D, or blank. The location of the target letter and the subsequent ring was varied in one of four positions in the fields. For each of the seven ISIs per tape, there were 64 instances when a target letter was presented, and 16 instances when a blank was presented. A ring was presented where the target letter had been or where the target letter would have been, in the case of a blank. There was one ISI for which the ring was drawn directly on the target tape. ISIs were presented in two sets of seven randomized orders. The first set (containing ISIs of −20, 30, 40, 60, 80, 90, and 100 msec) was run on all Ss before the second set (containing ISIs of −20, 5, 10, 20, 35, 50, and 70 msec). Time between individual presentations was no less than 5 sec. All variables for a particular size-array location of target letter (one of four positions), ISIs (seven values), kind of target (O, D, or blank), were randomized within each session. One four-letter array and one-letter array were presented in each session, in ABBA order over sessions. Two controls were run. The first used arrows as indicators (instead of rings) but was in all other respects identical to the experimental condition, for the four-letter arrays. For the one-letter array, only concurrent presentation of arrow and letter was used. The second presented the one-letter array alone without indicators; 90 instances of these were run.

Each letter subtended .30° horizontal × .62° vertical with a thickness of .08°. The angular distance between the fixation point and the center of a letter was .61° for the letters appearing in the two middle positions, and 1.73° for those in the two outside positions. The masking ring had an inner diameter of .61° and a thickness of .051°. The angular separation be-

tween the outer edge of the letter and the inner edge of the ring was about .083°. All figures were done in black India ink with a Leroy scriber and template, and had a contrast of about .95.

Results. Figure 1 presents the errors made as a function of ISI for each array size and indicator separately. The two sets of ISIs are combined. The dotted line shows errors made with the arrow indicator for the four-letter array; no arrow indicators were run in the one-letter condition. All curves appear to be U shaped;

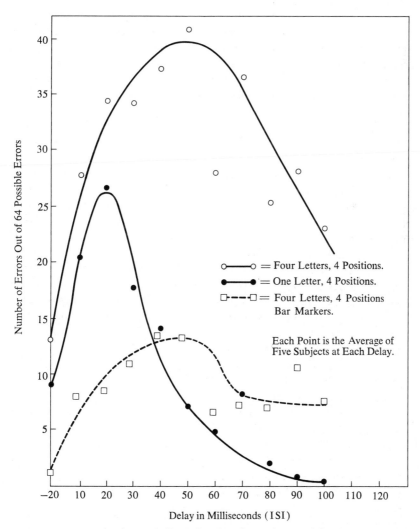

FIGURE 1   Ring and arrow indicator functions for one-letter and four-letter arrays.

and the maximum masking range for four letters appears much larger than the range for one letter. The Ss are combined.

It was first of all established that both the one-letter error function for rings and the four-letter error functions for *both* rings *and arrows* were U shaped, that is, were increasing in the early part of the delay range (0–30 msec) and decreasing in the later part (50–100 msec) by testing each part of each array-condition combination separately across Ss by a Friedman two-way analysis of variance (Mosteller & Bush, 1954). In all cases, $p < .05$.

When one letter was presented alone, without a subsequent indicator, there was perfect accuracy. Thus the one-letter error function is clearly a masking function. In order to get some estimate of masking for the four-letter array, independent of a base rate of error, the magnitude of errors made with rings was compared with the magnitude for arrows, and was greater by $p < .001$. Arrow indicators yield U shapes which rise and fall at the same delays as do the ring functions (χ^2 Arrow vs. Ring for each ISI, for each S, $p > .05$); thus a subtraction procedure will not give an accurate picture of the four-letter masking function. But they establish the presence of masking insofar as the masking amplitudes obtained are much less than those obtained for the rings.

Finally, there was more masking with four letters, than with one letter ($p < .001$). This was tested by taking the difference in error between rings and arrows for the four-letter condition, and comparing this difference to the one-letter ring functions.

The measure used to test the width of maximum masking ranges should be independent of the amplitude of masking at the maximum. Within certain limits, this may be done by taking the proportion of error to total error which occurs within a 20-msec range of highest error. This proportion will be designated, depending on the array, as P1 or P4. This treatment of the data allows two or more maxima, if they exist, to be accounted for, whether they occur contiguously or at a separation of a number of intervals. Notice that the relationship between P and the width of maximum masking is inverse: the smaller the proportion the wider the masking range.

The major question asked was whether the width of maximum masking was greater for the four-letter arrays than for the one-letter arrays. Ranges restricted to 20 msec of highest error could be considered since it was established that the functions for the two arrays, for each S, differed generally from each other beyond $p = .01$ (χ^2: ISI vs. array). A comparison of differences in maximum ranges by differences in proportion of error under a 20-msec range (P1 vs. P4) for each S, gives $p < .01$. An expression for the increase in masking range for the four-letter array is the ratio P1/P4. From this, the maximum masking range for the four-letter array was, on the average, about 1.54 times the range for the one-letter condition.[1]

Since the maximum masking range for the four-letter array is bigger than the maximum masking range for the one-letter array, no strict parallel processing can be assumed.

Similarly, since the maximum masking range for the four-letter array is not four times the maximum masking range for the one-letter array, there is a strong indication that the processing is not proceeding serially, item by item. However, this indication is not conclusive, since there remains the possibility that there are more than one maxima which are separated from each other by a certain range of delays. With the addition of other array sizes, and longer delay intervals this possibility can be checked. Thus, Exp. II repeated the basic design of Exp. I, adding four additional array sizes and longer delay intervals.

Experiment II

Method. The method here was the same as Exp. I with these exceptions. Each of four new Ss was tested individually for 30 sessions; each

---

[1] It is obvious that the ceiling for the ratio P1/P4 depends both upon the time at which the latter maxima would begin (if there are, in fact, later maxima), and on the number of ISIs tested. If maxima followed each other immediately, discounting -20 msec, the maximum range would be represented by the minimum proportion obtainable, 3/10. All Ss are below this range.

had 8 hr. of previous practice. One-letter, two-letter, four-letter, and eight-letter arrays were run. Two types of one-letter arrays were run: eight positions for the target and ring pair, and four positions for the target and ring pair. This provided a means of comparing directly the eight-letter results while holding possible spatial effects constant. The arrays will be designated 1-4, 1-8, 2-4, 4-4, and 8-8, where the first number designates the number of letters in the entire array and the second, the number of positions at which the target letter occurred. ISIs were combined into one set, yielding 13 intervals from −20 to 120 msec in 10 msec steps from 10 to 120 msec and in one 30-msec step from −20 to 10 msec. ISI presentation and order was automatically programmed and controlled by a stimulus programmer (Haber, Hershenson, & Schroeder, 1962) so that the

delay intervals were presented in random order in every session for every S. There were 64 trials for each S at each delay interval. No blanks were presented, and only a response of O or D was allowed. Controls were arrows as indicators instead of rings; only four tapes for each array size (32 instances per ISI) were run as compared with eight tapes for each array size on the rings (64 instances per ISI); otherwise, the control conditions were in all respects identical to the experimental conditions.

Results. Figure 2 presents the errors made with ring masks as a function of ISI for each array size separately, averaged over Ss. A comparison of the ring functions with those of Figure 1 shows that magnitudes differed by a greater amount in the first experiment; this is a result of the response indicator change. Re-

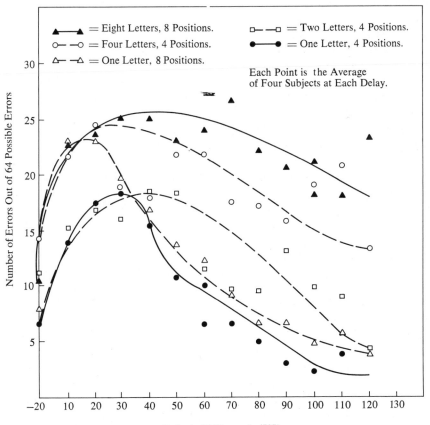

FIGURE 2   Masking (ring indicator) functions for each array size.

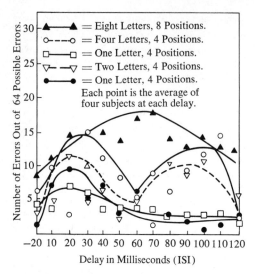

FIGURE 3   Arrow indicator functions for each array size.

call that in Exp. I errors were scored on the basis of S errors when there was a target present and this includes calling "blanks" when there is a letter present; thus the amount of errors could go much higher than the chance line. Other than this, there was no change in the data as a result of using a forced-choice response indicator. Most importantly, all ring-indicator functions obtained were U shaped—Friedman two-way analysis of variance gives $p < .05$ for increases for each array in the first part (0–30 msec) of the delay range and for decreases for each array in the last part (60–120 msec) of the delay range.

Figure 3 presents the errors made with arrow indicators for each array size separately, averaged over Ss. The magnitude of error again, as in Exp. I, was significantly greater for rings than for arrows, $p < .001$, z test on proportions. Arrow indicators yielded U shapes which rise and fall at the same delays as do the ring functions in 13 out of 20 cases (χ^2 ISI vs. indicator, $p > .05$). Thus again, as in Exp. I, a subtraction procedure will not give an accurate picture of the masking functions, but arrows do establish, by their reduced amplitude, the presence of masking. If the arrows had shown any consistent rise at the later ISIs, then a correction for memory decay would have been considered.

There was no consistent error pattern in the seven arrow functions which were not U shaped; thus the measure of masking used was, as in Exp. I, the number of errors S made at each delay interval.

Finally, an analysis of variance shows that difference in error scores between arrows and rings differed significantly from each other in strict ascending order by $p < .001$. This means that ring masking increases as array size increases, relative to arrow masking.

A general 13 × 5 χ^2 test of the differences in frequency distributions at each ISI for each S gives all Ss differences between arrays at $p < .05$. Thus a closer analysis of the differences between functions is justified.

The major question asked was whether the width of maximum masking was an exact multiple of the number of items in the array. Thus, the first phases of the statistical treatment are the same as in Exp. I. First, each array was compared with every other array, by 2 × 13 χ^2s, arrays vs. ISIs. For three out of four Ss, 1–4 differed significantly from both 2–4 and 4–4; for all Ss 1–8 differed significantly from 8–8 (p in all cases $< .05$); and in no case did 1–4 differ significantly from 1–8. Next the width of maximum masking was investigated: The measure of maximum masking is again the proportion of error to total error which occurs this time within a 30-msec range of highest error. This will be designated as $Pn\text{-}m$, n = the number of letters in the array, m = the number of positions the target letter was presented at. $Pi\text{-}j$ is a typical proportion. Within a 30-msec range, *all* $Pi\text{-}j$ differed from each other by $p < .001$ (1 × χ^2s, S vs. $Pi\text{-}j$ for all i). When each $Pi\text{-}j$ is tested against $Pk\text{-}l$, all Ss differ on P1–4 vs. P4–4 and P1–8 vs. P8–8; three Ss differ on P1–4 vs. P2–4; two Ss differ on P2–4 vs. P4–4 and on P2–4 vs. P8–8 (p in all cases $< .05$); and no Ss differ on P4–4 vs. P8–8, or on P1–4 vs. P1–8.

Whether or not individual pairs of proportions differed significantly, all arrays produce an increase in masking range, measured as the proportion of error to total error under a 30-msec range, for each increase in the number of items in the array. (Friedman analysis of variance, Pi-j × Ss, $p < .01$.) Thus Exp. II corroborates Exp. I: all ranges increase with increase in the size of the array. A significant difference was found between arrays for all Ss in general and for all Ss in terms of rank order. Thus it is reasonable to look at the precise differences in width of masking ranges. It is first of all apparent that the linearity of the increase in range cannot be precisely determined, since the measurement used to describe width of masking range is sensitive to errors outside this range, and there is no way of separating out errors due to short-term memory and errors due to the persistence of masking. However, some comparisons can be validly made. Recall that serial processing which is proceeding one item after another implies that masking ranges for N-sized arrays would be N times as large as masking ranges for one-letter arrays. With the measurement used in this study, errors outside the range of maximum masking tend to increase the estimate of width of range; thus it would be likely that masking ranges for N-sized arrays would appear to be N times as large, even when they were not. If the finding is in fact that they are not N times as large, then, there would be strong reason to conclude that the processing is not proceeding serially one item after another. If maximum masking ranges were N multiples of the range for one letter alone, then for these data, by two letters, the proportions would have reached their ceiling in all but one case; and the proportions for larger arrays would have been steady around this ceiling. Likewise, if there were one peak per letter, all functions above two letters would resemble the two-letter functions. It was established by comparing masking widths that all proportions differed from each other; moreover, a t test shows that all P1–4/Pn-m differ significantly from the ceiling ratio by $p < .01$. Thus it can be concluded that the increase in masking range is not N times the masking range for one item alone.

There exist two possibilities; one that the masking widths are underestimated; the other, that the masking widths are overestimated. The first has been shown unlikely. The second possibility, more specifically, is that due to memory decay, masking widths are overestimated to such an extent that if there had been some way to correct entirely for memory, the widths would not have differed at all from each other. But this is unlikely for the following reasons. If short-term memory decay were to explain the increase in masking range, then there should be no difference between the one-letter and the two-letter ranges, i.e., between arrays well within the span of immediate memory. However, the combined χ^2 differences (Mosteller & Bush, 1954) between the ranges of these arrays are less than $p = .001$. Second, an analysis performed on the data in Exp. I restricted the total number of delay intervals considered from 0 to 60 msec; maximum masking ranges still differed between arrays by $p < .01$. Finally, there was no consistent *effect* due to memory decay; that is, the errors did not significantly and consistently rise at the later ISIs. Thus, although there may be some overestimation due to memory effects and higher error rates, these do not account entirely for the increase in masking ranges with increase in array sizes.

Discussion

One-letter and N-letter arrays were presented, and one letter out of these arrays was subsequently masked by the presentation of a ring which encircled the position where the letter had been. Two types of response indicators were used: yes-no and forced-choice. As was to be expected, the magnitude of error decreased when forced-choice indicators were used; other than that, the change to forced-choice procedure had no effects on the data. For both, the amplitude of masking was U shaped with respect to the delay between offset of the target and onset of the ring. It was argued that since this kind of backward-masking function identifies an operation or a distinct set of operations within perceptual processing, then the duration over which maximum masking occurred would reflect the type of processing occurring. If the maximum masking ranges between one-letter and N-letter arrays did not differ, then parallel processing could be assumed; if they differed as an exact multiple of the number of items in the array, then the short-term visual memory formulation of item-by-item processing could be assumed.

Backward-masking data, in these experiments, yielded partial answers to these processing alternatives. The processing is in no strict sense parallel, since on both experiments, masking ranges increased with increase in the size of the array. However, this increase for an N-letter array was not N times the range for the one-letter array; thus processing is not proceeding serially, item by item, as has been assumed in some recent models. (See Sperling, 1963.)

If the maximum masking ranges indicate the occurrence of some perceptual operation or set of operations, as has been proposed in this study, then there are some important questions left to be answered. For instance, it is possible that the duration of occurrence of this set increases linearly with respect to items, that is, there is the possibility that serial processing is proceeding with respect to some feature of each item, although not item by item. In order to answer this question, analytic expressions for the masking functions are needed so that their width at maximum masking may be given in a precise manner. Such a procedure, in addition, would be able to test a serial vs. a parallel formulation with respect to other units besides items, such as the various types of contours in the target and masking stimuli. This analysis is underway.

In addition to the question of serial vs. parallel processing, this study bears directly on some questions within the general area of visual backward masking.

First, it will be noticed that U shapes are obtainable both with yes-no and with forced-choice response indicators. Thus, this shape cannot be explained solely on the basis of a change in criteria for detection as delay interval changes. In general, the obtaining of U shapes is at some variance with an explanation which sees masking as due merely to reduction in discriminability of the target due to the contrast reduction from luminance summation. (Eriksen & Collins, 1964). If discriminability of

the target gets better and better the longer the time between target and mask, or if discriminability of the target is impaired during a certain constant time interval after initial reception, then only monotones or shapes of zero slope should be obtained for masking functions. But monotones are only some of the functions that can be obtained. The conditions under which U shapes may be obtained have been fairly well investigated, and thus were expected in this study. (See Raab, 1963.) However, U shapes appeared also where they were not expected at all, namely, where arrows were used as indicators. The only exception previously noted to the contour rule for U shapes, that is, the rule that states that the inner contour of the mask should be quite similar to the outer contour of the target, is the work of Averbach and Coriell (1961). However, they obtained no masking when there was one letter alone in the target stimulus field; nor, paradoxically, did their bar indicators give masking shapes. Yet in the present study, not only were masking shapes obtained for one letter alone, but also, masking shapes occurred with arrow indicators for five out of eight conditions in which there was only one letter in the stimulus field.

The failure to obtain masking with one letter in the target field prompted Averbach and Coriell (1961) to propose that for masking, the target material had to be too complex in number to be dealt with all at once: items had to be put in temporary visual storage. The storage was unstable and hence items appearing later could replace those already in the storage. It is interesting that they did not question the absence of masking shapes for their bar indicators with such a formulation, since their distinction between maskable and nonmaskable did not depend on the characteristics of the stimuli but on the control system operating. The data in this study indicate that whatever the nature of the initial 100 msec or so of perceptual processing, one item can be affected as well as more than one item, and the amplitude of masking varies with the characteristics of the stimuli. Notice that the masking amplitudes in this study for the forced-choice data are not extremely high; none go so high as chance. Also, even though arrow indicators frequently give masking shapes, their amplitude is well below that of the ring indicators.

However, error amplitudes of the functions in this study increase when the stimulus size increases; it is probable that this accurately reflects an increase in masking amplitudes also, although the determination of this was not possible in this study since arrow-ring differences reflect a differential increase in masking width as well as in masking amplitude. In light of these considerations, it is suggested that the masking effect with 1 letter out of 26 was too weak to be noticed in S performance; as Averbach and Coriell increased their display, error amplitudes increased to such an extent that the U-shaped effect could be noticed. But it is the duration of the effect, rather than its presence, that varies with the number of items presented. It is suggested that, given the general conditions under which U shapes will obtain, this statement probably applies generally to a wide range of masks and targets; failure to obtain masking may be due simply to the weakness of the effect, rather than its absence in processing operations.

Summary

The decision between parallel and serial operations in perceptual processing has always been made on the basis of whether or not, as a visual array size increases, there is a total increase in time from presentation to report. The results from this type of design are ambiguous: no operation within the perceptual processing sequence itself is measured, thus it is equally likely that additional operations are being added or that the operations are repeating themselves. A design using U-shaped backward-masking function provided a measure of an operation occurring within the processing sequence; the duration over which this operation occurred for arrays of different sizes reflected the type of processing occurring. There was an increase in masking range as array size increased; thus, no strict parallel processing occurs. Since these increases were not whole multiples of the increase in array size, the processing is not serial, item-by-item. These results have some general implications for visual backward masking.

References

Averbach, E., & Coriell, A. S. Short-term memory in vision. *Bell Sys. tech. J.,* 1961, *40,* 309–328.

Eriksen, C. W., & Collins, J. F. Backward masking in vision. *Psychon. Sci.,* 1964, *1,* 101–102.

Haber, R. N., Hershenson, M., & Schroeder, D. Apparatus note: The use of an IBM 924 or 026 card punch for simultaneous stimulus programming and response recording. *Percept. mot. Skills,* 1962, *15,* 627–630.

Mosteller, R., & Bush, R. Selected quantitative techniques. In G. Lindsey (Ed.), *Handbook of social psychology.* Cambridge, Mass.: Addison Wesley, 1954, Pp. 289–334.

Neisser, U. Decision time without reaction time: Experiments in visual scanning, *Amer. J. Psychol.,* 1963, *76,* 376–385.

Raab, D. H. Backward masking. *Psychol. Bull.,* 1963, *60,* 118–129.

Sperling, G. A model for visual memory tasks. *Hum. Factors,* 1963, *5,* 19–31.

Weisstein, N. Temporal aspects of perceptual systems. Unpublished doctoral dissertation, Harvard University, 1964.

Weisstein, N., & Haber, R. N. A U-shaped backward masking function in vision. *Psychon. Sci.,* 1965, *2,* 75–76.

2.6 An Onset-Onset Law for One Case of Apparent Motion and Metacontrast*

DANIEL KAHNEMAN

The following sequence of visual stimuli often elicits reports of apparent motion: A square patch of light is briefly exposed; shortly after that exposure, a similar patch is briefly presented in another location. With appropriate values of spatial and temporal separation, a single illuminated square appears to be moving smoothly to right or left. Now consider a slight modification of this display: a single square, followed by two others, simultaneously presented to the right and left of it. These are conditions for metacontrast suppression; the initial square often fails to be seen and the two flanking squares are seen in motion away from the center. The present article is concerned with the relation between apparent motion and metacontrast suppression, and with some important regularities which they share.

Metacontrast is usually defined (Alpern, 1952, 1953) as the reduction in brightness of a stimulus caused by subsequent stimulation of an adjacent area. Alpern (1952) has reviewed several experimental arrangements in which such reductions are observed. Metacontrast suppression is the extreme case in which the first stimulus is reported to be phenomenally absent. Metacontrast suppression, so defined, has been observed in several variants of the three-object display described above (Alpern, 1952; Fehrer & Raab, 1962; Fehrer & Smith, 1962). The sequence of exposures is obviously similar to the two-object display which elicits reports of beta motion.

Werner (1935, 1940) introduced another arrangement which produces metacontrast suppression: a disk followed by a surrounding ring. The disk often fails to be seen (Kolers, 1962; Schiller, 1965; Schiller & Smith, 1966). The disk-ring sequence is related to the conditions which elicit report of expansive motion; such motion is seen, for example, when a small disk is followed by a large concentric disk.

In spite of the similarity between the conditions which elicit metacontrast and apparent motion, metacontrast effects are traditionally grouped with phenomena of backward masking (Kahneman, 1968; Raab, 1963), and are not even mentioned in recent surveys of apparent motion (Spigel, 1965). This classification ignores several points of similarity between apparent motion and metacontrast:

(1) When metacontrast suppression is complete, the two squares in the terminal display are usually seen in motion away from one another. Experiences of motion in the metacontrast situation have often been noted (Fehrer & Raab, 1962; Fehrer & Biederman, 1962; Schiller & Smith, 1966; Toch, 1956).

* Reproduced by permission of *Perception & Psychophysics*, 1967, vol. 2, pp. 557–583. This study is an outgrowth of an extensive series of pilot observations carried out in collaboration with Dr. J. S. Bruner. Kenneth Ledeen did the programming work, and the assistance of Ruth Wolman and Linda Onuska was most valuable. The study was supported in part by grant No. P 01-MH-12623 from the National Institute of Mental Health and in part by grant No. GS-1153 from the National Science Foundation to Harvard University, Center for Cognitive Studies.

(2) When the first and second segments of the metacontrast display are similar in energy and contrast, metacontrast suppression is a U-shaped function of the temporal separation between them (Fehrer & Smith, 1962; Kolers, 1962; Kolers & Rosner, 1960; Schiller & Smith, 1966; Werner, 1935). Optimal motion is also a U-shaped function of temporal separation.

(3) At temporal separations which are too short for complete suppression and for optimal motion, the initial stimulus is seen, but its brightness and contrast are much reduced. This reduction of brightness is not specific to metacontrast; it has also been noted in descriptions of apparent motion (Wertheimer, 1912; Korte, 1915). It is easy to demonstrate that the dimming effects which accompany partial motion are not much different from those which define partial metacontrast. In the three-square display, an interval may be selected at which the first square appears distinctly dimmer than its neighbors. The central square will remain dim even when one of its neighbors is removed from the display.

In general, students of apparent motion have paid little attention to the dimming of the first stimulus, as well as to other suppression effects of motion that will be discussed later. Several writers have mentioned movement in their discussions of metacontrast suppression (Fehrer & Raab, 1962; Kolers & Rosner, 1960; Mayzner, Tresselt, & Cohen, 1966; Toch, 1956; Werner, 1935), but the idea that the two phenomena may follow the same rules is recent (Fehrer & Smith, 1962; Fehrer, 1965, 1966; Pollack, 1966).

The hypothesis of the present study was that metacontrast suppression represents an anomalous type of apparent motion, at least when it occurs between targets that are similar in energy and figural characteristics (Fehrer & Smith, 1962; Kolers, 1962). The perceptual system is unable to resolve the simultaneous motions of a single object in two directions, and suppression results. In the three-square display, a single object is set into apparent motion in two directions at once; in the disk-ring sequence, a stimulus is presented which would cause the original disk to grow in size even as it disappears. The metacontrast display provides cues to "impossible motion," much in the way that the well known drawings of Penrose and Penrose (1958) provide cues for impossible three-dimensional figures.

If metacontrast is impossible motion, it follows that the quality of metacontrast and of apparent motion should depend on the same variables. Presumably, suppression is maximal when the opposing tendencies to motion are strongest. In order to test this hypothesis, the dependence of apparent motion and of metacontrast on the temporal parameters of stimulation was studied.

In most studies of apparent motion, the durations of exposure of the first and the second stimuli are equal. The fourth law of Korte (1915) states that as the duration of exposure (D) is increased, the interval between the end of the first stimulus and the beginning of the second (ISI) must be decreased to obtain optimal motion. Subsequent studies have confirmed Korte's fourth law (Kolers, 1964; Neuhaus, 1930; Sgro, 1963), though the results of these studies differ in many particulars.

Pilot observations of both motion and metacontrast in our laboratory suggested that the complementarity between D and ISI is very nearly perfect: D + ISI = Constant, for the perception of any degree of apparent motion. The sum of D and ISI defines the stimulus-onset asynchrony (SOA) between the two exposures.

Previous studies of Korte's fourth law reported systematic deviations from a strict onset-onset law, but they did not agree on the direction of the discrepancy. For example, the optimal SOA for motion is a monotonically increasing function of D in the data of Kolers (1964), and varies complexly with D in the data of Neuhaus (1930). However, these and other parametric studies of apparent motion and metacontrast are difficult to interpret because the experimental set of the subject is rarely specified in sufficient detail. Apparent motion and metacontrast are labile phenomena, which depend critically on the observer's criterion. Some investigators (Kolers, 1962; Neuhaus, 1930) have responded to the criterion problem by using highly experienced and knowledgeable observers. This procedure may improve reliability, but it suffers from a crippling defect: The instructional set which an experienced observer finally adopts is unique and idiosyncratic, and cannot be reproduced at will in another laboratory. Consequently, discrepancies among different sets of results cannot be resolved.

In the present study, naive subjects served as observers, and an attempt was made to establish their set by the instructions, which are reproduced in full below.

Method

SUBJECTS

Three Harvard and two Radcliffe undergraduates served for two 1-h sessions on consecutive days. The first session was devoted to metacontrast, the second to apparent motion.

APPARATUS AND STIMULI

The S was comfortably seated, with the back of his head supported at a distance of 130 cm from a Fairchild slave scope on which the stimuli appeared. The stimuli were three illuminated outline squares, 14 mm large, subtending 37 minutes of visual arc at the viewing distance. The distance between neighboring sides of the central and flanking squares was 7 mm. A fixation cross was presented 7 mm above the middle of the central square. The S initiated the display sequence by pressing a key. The fixation cross appeared, and was followed after 800 msec by the middle square, then by either the two flanking squares in the case of metacontrast, or the square on the right in the case of motion. The fixation cross remained in view until the sequence was completed.

The Fairchild scope was slaved to a DEC Type 340 scope, which was in turn controlled by a PDP-4 computer. Approximately 750 μsec were required for a single complete cycle, during which every point of the display was illuminated once. The durations and intervals could be controlled to the nearest msec. The persistence of illumination on the Fairchild scope is negligible. The luminance of the display at an indefinite duration of exposure was approximately 1 mL.

PROCEDURE

The following instructions were read to the S; the metacontrast instructions were given on the first day and the motion instructions (in parentheses) on the second day:

> Our experiment today is concerned with an effect in perception which is called metacontrast (apparent motion). I shall be showing you three (two) squares on this scope, first one in the middle, then two others flanking it (then another beside it). Metacontrast (apparent motion) is sometimes obtained under these conditions.
>
> Perfect metacontrast is the case when you see only the two flanking squares and the middle square is not seen at all. Partial metacontrast is when the middle square is seen, but it is dim, faint, or incomplete.
>
> (Perfect apparent motion is the case when you see only one square which moves smoothly from one position to the other, without changing in brightness along the way. Partial motion is the case when the starting and arrival positions can be seen as two squares, but there *is* motion between them.)
>
> Your task is to rate each presentation according to how well what you see corresponds to this description of metacontrast (apparent motion). Use numbers for your ratings, as follows: The number 5 indicates that this was perfect metacontrast (apparent motion). The number 3 indicates that metacontrast (apparent motion) is only partial, but still quite marked. The number 0 indicates that what you see bears no resemblance at all to metacontrast (apparent motion). Use the other numbers to indicate various degrees of correspondence between the description and what you see.

Five exposure durations were studied: 25, 50, 75, 100, and 125 msec. The duration of exposure was the same for the first and for the second stimulus in the sequence. In a series of consecutive trials, devoted to a particular duration, the S rated metacontrast or apparent motion at 11 values of stimulus-onset asynchrony (SOA): 2, 25, 50 . . ., 250 msec. The interval between successive trials was approximately

5 sec. The sequence of SOAs during a series was random. Five series of trials, one for each exposure duration, constituted a block. During the experimental session, four blocks were run, with a different random order of durations within each block. Altogether, there were 55 different conditions of exposure, and the S rated each condition four times.

Unknown to S, the first series of trials, conducted at a duration of 50 msec, was considered practice. Altogether, S was dark adapted for at least 10 min before data collection began. S communicated his ratings by intercom. E did not speak during the session except to announce short breaks between blocks and to answer direct questions, which were rare. All questions were answered by repeating relevant parts of the instructions.

After the termination of the main part of the second session, the instructions for ratings of motion were repeated, and three series of ratings were obtained with an exposure duration of 800 msec and ISIs ranging between −100 and +200 msec (SOAs of 700 msec to 1000 msec).

Results

Figure 1 presents average ratings of the quality of metacontrast and apparent motion as a function of SOA, for five values of D. The curves in each graph would diverge if either the duration (D) or the interstimulus interval (ISI) separately determined the perceptual effect. However, the curves overlap almost perfectly, with the exception of the function for D = 125 msec in metacontrast. This curve is lowest in average level for four of the five Ss, and next to lowest for the remaining S ($p < .01$). In accord with the major hypothesis of this study, results for motion and metacontrast are essentially identical. The only discrepancy was observed at SOA = 25 msec where, for three Ss, ratings of motion were consistently higher than ratings of metacontrast. In both metacontrast and apparent motion, an onset-onset law fits the data very well. Good metacontrast and apparent motion are obtained even at negative values of

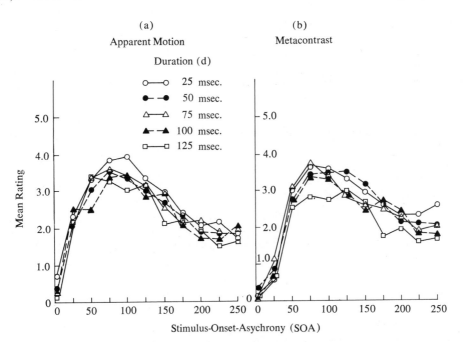

FIGURE 1   Mean ratings of displays of two squares (a) for apparent motion and three squares (b) for metacontrast, as a function of stimulus-onset asynchrony. Exposure duration is the parameter. Five observers rated each display four times.

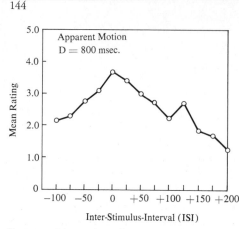

FIGURE 2 Mean ratings of apparent motion as a function of inter-stimulus interval at an exposure duration of 800 msec. Five observers rated each display three times.

ISI, when the second stimulus is shown before the first is removed. Both conclusions are confirmed within the separate data of each S.

When the temporal overlap (negative ISI) of the two stimuli exceeds a critical value, motion is not seen. S sees a single square, then two squares, and finally the second square alone, in accord with the physical sequence of stimulation. Consequently, the onset-onset law breaks down at high values of D, when the duration of overlap becomes too long. Optimal motion can be obtained when D is long, but only if the second stimulus is presented near the time at which the first is removed. The S sees a square, which is stationary for a while, then moves to another location. Figure 2 shows the dependence of the quality of apparent motion on ISI, for D = 800 msec. Adequate apparent motion is obtained over a large range of ISIs, including negative values for which the onset of the second stimulus precedes the physical disappearance of the first. The peak of the function is at or near ISI = 0, where the two events are simultaneous.

Discussion

METACONTRAST

An interpretation of metacontrast has been advanced, in which suppression in the three-square display is the counterpart of optimal motion in the two-square display. The hypoth-

esis is supported by the similarity between the functions that relate the two effects to temporal parameters of stimulation. The present view of metacontrast is most similar to that of Fehrer, who has stressed the similarities between meta-contrast suppression and apparent motion (Fehrer, 1965, 1966; Fehrer & Raab, 1962; Fehrer & Smith, 1962).

Mayzner and his colleagues (Mayzner et al, 1966, 1967) have reported observations which directly implicate motion in metacontrast suppression. They successively present at rapid rates the various letters of a word (e.g., SOM-ERSAULT), recycling the exposure repeatedly. At very fast rates of succession, the whole word is seen; at slower rates, the outcome depends on the sequencing of letters within the word. If the sequence permits a coherent organization of motion (leftward, rightward, inflowing or outflowing), that motion is perceived and the whole word is seen. When the letters are presented in an incoherent order, the letters that are presented first in the sequence disappear, and are not seen even over many cycles of presentation. Thus, the word CHAIR may be seen as C A R. These data provide the most direct support for the interpretation of metacontrast suppression as a case of impossible motion.

Apparent motion is always a U-shaped function of SOA. Consequently, a theory which views metacontrast as a motion effect cannot explain those cases where suppression is maximal at SOA = 0 and decreases monotonically with SOA (Eriksen & Collins, 1964, 1965; Schiller, 1965; Schiller & Smith, 1966). Other mechanisms must be invoked to account for these monotone functions (Fehrer & Smith, 1962). Kolers (1962) concluded from a series of experiments with disks and rings that monotone functions are obtained when a large difference of duration, intensity, or contrast favors the masking ring over the target disk. U-shaped functions are obtained when the target and the mask are more similar. Fehrer and Smith (1962) obtained comparable results in a three-square display, by varying the ratio of luminances of the target and masking squares. U-shaped functions were obtained when the ratio was near unity, and monotone functions when the ratio was low. Fehrer and Smith (1962) pointed out that the low ratios are favorable to the occurrence of simultaneous contrast.

Simultaneous contrast is a special case of lateral interaction between neighboring visual stimuli. The outcome of these interactions is a reduction of the brightness or contrast of the weaker stimulus (Heinemann, 1955), an elevation of difference thresholds in the vicinity of contours (Fry & Bartley, 1935), and a reduction of acuity (Flom, Weymouth, & Kahneman, 1963). Lateral inhibition disproportionately affects the weaker of two interacting stimuli (Hartline & Ratliff, 1957), and its effects increase with increasing imbalance between them. When a strong and a weak stimulus are presented at about the same time, the response to the weaker stimulus may be completely suppressed (Ratliff, Hartline, & Miller, 1963). On the other hand, suppression is primarily a motion effect when stimulus energies are more nearly equal. U-shaped functions are then obtained, and the extent of masking depends on the figural relations between the figures (Fehrer, 1965, 1966).

Since apparent motion can be obtained dichoptically (Smith, 1948), it must be determined fairly late in the sequence of visual processing. A theory which explains metacontrast in terms of motion is therefore consistent with the finding that a stimulus which is perceptually suppressed by metacontrast may nonetheless elicit a behavioral response (Fehrer & Raab, 1962; Fehrer & Biederman, 1962; Harrison & Fox, 1966; Schiller & Smith, 1966) and an essentially intact cortical evoked response (Schiller & Chorover, 1966). The occurrence of metacontrast suppression in dichoptic presentations was amply demonstrated by Kolers and Rosner (1960), and has been confirmed in another display by Mayzner *et al* (1967). There is no justification for the assumption that metacontrast suppression is a retinal effect (Alpern, 1965; Alpern & Rushton, 1965).

APPARENT MOTION

Our discussion of suppression in metacontrast has related that effect to the phenomenon of apparent motion. It is of some theoretical importance that this relation is mutual. Suppression effects are intimately involved in the perception of apparent motion. The following observations support that statement:

(1) The reduction in brightness and contrast of the first object in a motion display was mentioned earlier. This reduction is obtained at values of SOA which are too short for optimal motion. The effect is included in Wertheimer's description of partial motion (Wertheimer, 1912). When the objects are dark on a lighter background, the contrast of the first object is markedly reduced.

(2) With brief exposure durations (up to 100–150 msec in many conditions) the experience is not of a stationary object that moves to a new location, but of a moving object. Of course, the first object would be perceived as stationary if presented alone, but that percept is entirely suppressed when motion is seen.

(3) Excellent apparent motion is obtained even for negative values of ISI, when the two objects are in fact present side by side for as long as 50–75 msec. The percept that would correspond to the simultaneous presence of two objects in the field is suppressed.

(4) The following demonstration is easily arranged: Two squares are presented together for 800 msec. After an SOA of 750 msec, a third square is presented near one of the original squares, which is then seen in motion. When observers are required to judge which of the two initial squares was the first to disappear, they consistently select the one that was set into motion. Thus, motion curtails the normal persistence of the perceived stationary square.

(5) Suppression is directly observable when a homogeneously illuminated rectangle is shown twice in rapid succession with a slight lateral shift in position between the first and second exposures. The central area where the two exposures overlap should appear brighter than the two lateral areas which are illuminated only once, by temporal summation of bright-

ness. This is indeed observed at very short SOAs. At slightly longer SOAs, which are still too brief for optimal motion, the forward edge of the "moving" rectangle is seen as markedly brighter than both the area of overlap and the trailing edge.[1] This distribution of apparent brightness does not correspond to the distribution of stimulating energy, and obviously involves considerable suppression.

In these examples, the perception of motion is not merely a filler for the "dead time" between two successive percepts (Koffka, 1935). A radical alteration of the perception of the first object is caused by the presentation of the second. The percept which the first object would normally elicit is suppressed and replaced by another. Thus, apparent motion probably represents the most common type of retroactive interaction in visual perception.

How are such retroactive effects to be explained? The main theories which have been advanced to account for metacontrast and backward masking cannot be applied to motion.

Metacontrast suppression has sometimes been explained (Kolers, 1962; Werner, 1935) on the assumption that contour formation takes time; the contour that is shared by target disk and masking ring is appropriated by the ring before the disk is formed. This interpretation is inapplicable to the suppression effects which accompany beta motion between two squares that do not share a contour.

Another common interpretation of backward masking and metacontrast suppression attributes these effects to overtake (e.g., Crawford, 1947; Donchin, 1967). It is said that the response to the second stimulus overtakes the response to the first stimulus and interferes with it. However, the idea of different latencies is not applicable when the stimuli are equal in luminance, as they are in most studies of motion. In addition, it is easy to produce cascading of apparent motion with a series of stimuli, and the notion that the latencies of successive responses are progressively shorter is clearly untenable.

Although complete overtake of the first response by the second is very doubtful as an explanation of motion, there is certainly much *overlap* between the perceptual responses to the two stimuli. The response which a brief visual stimulus elicits lasts much longer than does the stimulus. This conclusion has been confirmed for the ERG (e.g., Johnson, 1958), the evoked potential (e.g., Wicke, Donchin, & Lindsley, 1963), and conscious visual experience (e.g., Mackworth, 1963; Sperling, 1960). At these various levels of visual response, the duration of the response appears to be approximately the same for brief stimuli (less than 100–150 msec), regardless of their duration.

If the response to a brief stimulus lasts longer than the stimulus, the responses to two stimuli which follow one another in quick succession must overlap in time, unless one makes the doubtful assumption that the first response is sharply interrupted as soon as the second begins. The apparently retroactive effects of suppression and motion are not retroactive at all, if the responses to successive stimuli occur side by side at some level of analysis, though one of them may have started earlier and the other is the last to cease. In order to account for the effects of temporal parameters on perceived motion, the further assumption is required that the amount of temporal overlap between successive responses at one level of analysis is itself the effective stimulus for the response of a subsequent level. In these terms, motion is seen when a period of response to the first stimulus alone is followed by a period of overlap—provided that the overlap is of intermediate duration—and the overlap is itself followed by a period of response to the second stimulus alone. Figure 3 is a schematic illustration of such a model. The levels at which the responses are parallel and the level at which they interact are not specified, and the relative values of response latency and response persistence are arbitrary. In spite of these limitations, Figure 3 illustrates that the response of "motion" cannot be initiated until information is received that the first stimulus has been re-

---

[1] The author thanks Dr. David N. Lee for this demonstration.

moved while the second is still present. The model is consistent with the well known fact that the duration of the second stimulus is essentially irrelevant to the perception of motion, unless that duration is very brief. As was mentioned earlier, the responses to brief stimuli are relatively prolonged, and the duration of response overlap therefore depends mainly on SOA and on the duration of the first stimulus.

The suggestion that the duration of response to brief stimuli is largely independent of the duration of exposure entails a similar independence for response overlap. Overlap depends only on SOA, as Figure 4 illustrates. This is the onset-onset law which the present study confirmed for both motion and metacontrast. There is evidence (Donchin, 1967) that SOA is also a most important variable in backward masking by a flash of light over the area of the target, and a similar model could be invoked to account for that result. SOA is the same for all conditions of Figure 4. In (A), (B), and (C), the stimuli are brief and the responses to them are assumed to be equal in duration. Response overlap is also constant, and any consequences of overlap, such as motion or suppression, would be equally evident in the three cases. In (D), stimulus duration is longer in the range where duration of the response increases with that of the stimulus. Consequently, response overlap is greater in (D) than in the other cases, perhaps long enough for an observer to report that the two objects were present together in his field of view.

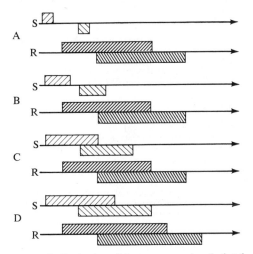

FIGURE 4   Derivation of the onset-onset law for brief stimuli. In A, B, and C, the responses (R) to brief stimuli (S) are identical in duration and overlap to the same extent. The response is longer in D, and overlap is correspondingly prolonged.

Figure 5 summarizes in terms of response overlap the conditions for the occurrence of simultaneity, motion, and successiveness, with stimuli of different durations. An arbitrary value was assumed for the persistence of long stimuli. The figure makes it clear that response overlap depends on SOA for brief stimuli and on ISI for longer ones. As a heuristic model, Figure 5 adequately summarizes the stimulus conditions under which motion is seen. The model also incorporates a plausible solution to the vexing question of retroactive effects in perception. However, a profound gap still separates such a descriptive model from an adequate theory of apparent motion.

Summary

Ss rated the quality of apparent motion and of metacontrast in computer-controlled sequences of two or of three outlined squares. For brief stimuli, the dependence of the two effects on temporal factors of stimulation is virtually identical. Motion and metacontrast depend solely on the asynchrony of onsets between the two exposures (SOA) over a wide range of duration and interstimulus intervals

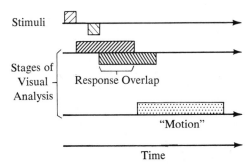

FIGURE 3   Responses to brief stimuli at two stages of visual analysis. Possible intermediate stages are not indicated.

Simultaneity

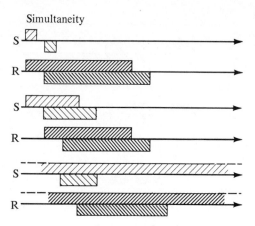

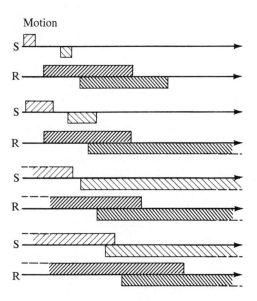

Motion

Successiveness

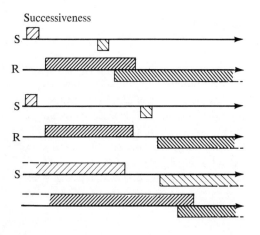

FIGURE 5   Schematic summary of conditions for apparent simultaneity (long response overlap), motion, and successiveness (overlap brief or absent) for both brief and more prolonged stimuli.

(ISI). Metacontrast suppression is interpreted as a case of impossible motion. The temporal determinants of apparent motion are summarized in a model in which the effect occurs when the temporal overlap between the perceptual responses to the successive stimuli is intermediate in value.

References

Alpern, M. Metacontrast: historical introduction. *Amer. J. Optom.,* 1952, *29,* 631–646.

Alpern, M. Metacontrast. *J. Opt. Soc. Amer.,* 1953, *43,* 648–657.

Alpern, M. Rod-cone independence in the after-flash effect. *J. Physiol.,* 1965, *176,* 462–472.

Alpern, M., & Rushton, W. A. H. The specificity of the cone interaction in the after-flash effect. *J. Physiol.,* 1965, *176,* 473–482.

Crawford, B. H. Visual adaptation in relation to brief conditioning stimuli. *Proc. Roy. Soc. Lond.,* 1947, *134B,* 283–302.

Donchin, E. Retroactive visual masking: effects of test flash duration on masking interval. *Vision Res.,* 1967, *7,* 79–89.

Eriksen, C. W., & Collins, J. F. Backward masking in vision. *Psychon. Sci.,* 1964, *1,* 101–102.

Eriksen, C. W., & Collins, J. F. A reinterpretation of one form of backward and forward masking in visual perception. *J. exp. Psychol.,* 1965, *70,* 343–351.

Fehrer, E. Contribution of perceptual segregation to the relationship between stimulus similarity and backward masking. *Percept. mot. Skills,* 1965, *21,* 27–33.

Fehrer, E. Effect of stimulus similarity on retroactive masking. *J. exp. Psychol.,* 1966, *71,* 612–615.

Fehrer, E., & Biederman, I. A comparison of reaction and verbal report in the detection of masked stimuli. *J. exp. Psychol.,* 1962, *64,* 126–130.

Fehrer, E., & Raab, D. Reaction time to stimuli masked by metacontrast. *J. exp. Psychol.,* 1962, *63,* 143–147.

Fehrer, E., & Smith, E. Effect of luminance ratio on masking. *Percept. mot. Skills,* 1962, *14,* 243–253.

Flom, M. C., Weymouth, F. W., & Kahneman, D. Visual resolution and contour interaction. *J. Opt. Soc. Amer.,* 1963, *53,* 1026–1032.

Fry, G. A., & Bartley, S. H. The effect of one border in the visual field upon the threshold of another. *Amer. J. Physiol.,* 1935, *112,* 414–421.

Harrison, K., & Fox, R. Replication of reaction time to stimuli marked by metacontrast. *J. exp. Psychol.,* 1966, *71,* 162–163.

Hartline, H. K., & Ratliff, F. Inhibitory interaction of receptor units in the eye of Limulus. *J. gen. Physiol.,* 1957, *40,* 357–376.

Heinemann, E. G. Simultaneous brightness induction as a function of inducing and test-field luminances. *J. exp. Psychol.,* 1955, *50,* 89–96.

Johnson, E. P. The character of the B-wave in the human ERG. *A.M.A. Arch. Ophthal.,* 1958, *60,* 565–591.

Kahneman, D. Method, findings and theory in studies of visual masking. *Psychological Bulletin.* In press.

Koffka, K. *Principles of gestalt psychology.* New York: Harcourt, Brace, 1935.

Kolers, P. A. Intensity and contour effects in visual masking. *Vision Res.,* 1962, *2,* 277–294.

Kolers, P. A. The illusion of movement. *Scient. American,* 1964, *211,* 98–106.

Kolers, P. A., & Rosner, B. S. On visual masking (metacontrast): dichoptic observation. *Amer. J. Psychol.,* 1960, *73,* 2–21.

Korte, A. Kinematoskopische Untersuchungen. *Z. Psychol.,* 1915, *72,* 193–296.

Mackworth, J. E. The duration of the visual image. *Canad. J. Psychol.,* 1963, *17,* 62–81.

Mayzner, M. S., Tresselt, M. E., & Cohen, A. Preliminary findings on some effects of very fast sequential input rates on perception. *Psychon. Sci.,* 1966, *6,* 513–514.

Mayzner, M. S., Tresselt, M. E., Adrignolo, A. J., & Cohen, A. Further preliminary findings on some effects of very fast sequential input rates on perception. *Psychon. Sci.,* 1967, *7,* 281–282.

Neuhaus, V. Experimentelle Untersuchung der Scheinbewegung. *Arch. f.d. ges. Psychol.,* 1930, *75,* 315–458.

Penrose, L. A., & Penrose, R. Impossible objects: a special type of visual illusion. *Brit. J. Psychol.,* 1958, *49,* 31–33.

Pollack, R. H. Initial stimulus duration and the temporal range of apparent movement. *Psychon. Sci.,* 1966, *5,* 165–166.

Raab, D. H. Backward masking. *Psychol. Bull.,* 1963, *60,* 118–129.

Ratliff, F., Hartline, H. K., & Miller, W. H. Spatial and temporal aspects of retinal interactions. *J. Opt. Soc. Amer.,* 1963, *53,* 110–120.

Schiller, P. H. Detection in metacontrast as determined by a method of comparisons. *Percept. mot. Skills,* 1965, *20,* 47–50.

Schiller, P. H., & Chorover, S. L. Metacontrast: its relation to evoked potentials. *Science,* 1966, *153,* 1398–1401.

Schiller, P. H., & Smith, M. Detection in metacontrast. *J. exp. Psychol.,* 1966, *71,* 32–39.

Sgro, F. J. Beta motion thresholds. *J. exp. Psychol.,* 1963, *66,* 281–285.

Smith, K. R. Visual apparent movement in the absence of neural interaction. *Amer. J. Psychol.,* 1948, *61,* 73–78.

Sperling, G. The information available in brief visual presentations. *Psychol. Monogr.,* 1960, *74,* 1–29.

Spigel, J. M. (Ed.) *Readings in the study of visually perceived movement.* New York: Harper and Row, 1965.

Toch, H. H. The perceptual elaboration of stroboscopic presentations. *Amer. J. Psychol.,* 1956, *69,* 345–358.

Werner, H. Studies on contour: I. Qualitative analyses. *Amer. J. Psychol.,* 1935, *47,* 40–64.

Werner, H. Studies on contour: Strobostereoscopic phenomena. *Amer. J. Psychol.,* 1940, *53,* 418–422.

Wertheimer, M. Experimentelle Studien über das Sehen von Bewegung. *Z. Psychol.,* 1912, *61,* 161–265.

Wicke, J. D., Donchin, E., & Lindsley, D. B. Visual evoked potentials as a function of flash luminance and duration, *Science,* 1964, *146,* 83–85.

CHAPTER *3*

Simultaneity

3.1 Excitability Cycles and Cortical Scanning: A Review of Two Hypotheses of Central Intermittency in Perception[*]

M. RUSSELL HARTER

When considering the problem of how the brain processes incoming sense data, two assumptions appear reasonable. First, if the brain utilizes its finite number of components in the most efficient manner, it should not operate continuously by processing all sensory information at all points in time, but should operate discontinuously by taking successive samples of sensory information at different points in time. Such sampling would be parsimonious since any one component could alternately perform many functions instead of continuously performing one, and the total amount of information processing would be reduced.

Second, the brain must code or label incoming sense information in terms of its time of occurrence. Such coding is necessary for events to be cognitively placed in proper temporal sequence and for the sensory, associative, and motor cortical functions to operate on a common time basis.

Some kind of cortical mechanism which divides and groups incoming sensory information into discrete temporal units is implied in both of the above assumptions. The effect of such a mechanism on perception would be that information could not be processed at a rate faster than the frequency of the discrete temporal units. A wide range of experimental findings may be offered in evidence that such a limit exists in perception: (*a*) events occurring within a critical period of time were perceived simultaneously (Blackwell, 1963; Hirsh & Sherrick, 1961; Lichtenstein, 1961; Lichtenstein, White, & Harter, 1963; Schmidt & Kristofferson, 1963; White & Lichtenstein, 1963); (*b*) subjective counting and rate judgments were not directly related to objective number and rate of presented stimuli (Cheatham & White, 1952, 1954; Forsythe & Chapanis, 1958; Lichtenstein, White, Siegfried, & Harter, 1963; White & Cheatham, 1959; White, Cheatham, & Armington, 1953); (*c*) the intermittency of corrective movements during tracking (Bertelson, 1966; Craik, 1948); (*d*) masking and retroactive brightness enhancement of a test stimulus followed by a conditioning stimulus (Boynton, 1961; Don-

* From: M. Russell Harter, "Excitability Cycles and Cortical Scanning: A Review of Two Hypotheses of Central Intermittency in Perception," *Psychological Bulletin,* 1967, vol. 68, pp. 47–58. Copyright (1967) by the American Psychological Association, and reproduced by permission. The concept of central intermittency was introduced by Craik (1948) and has recently been reviewed by Bertelson (1966). Although this concept has been based primarily on data from motor tasks (tracking and reaction time tasks), it depicts the phenomena under study in the present paper which were based primarily on data from perceptual tasks.

This paper was supported by funds received from the United States Navy Electronics Laboratory, San Diego, and from the National Aeronautics and Space Administration under a predoctoral fellowship. This manuscript was submitted with the understanding that a right of reproduction for governmental purposes is reserved for the United States Navy Electronics Laboratory. The opinions and assertions contained herein are the private ones of the writer and are not to be construed as official, or as reflecting the views of the Navy Department or the Naval service at large.

The author wishes to express appreciation to Robert W. Lansing, Neil R. Bartlett, Robert G. Eason, and Carroll T. White for their contributions in the preparation of this manuscript.

chin & Lindsley, 1965; Donchin, Wicke, & Lindsley, 1963); (*e*) the discontinuous nature of voluntary and evoked motor behavior (Bates, 1951; Callaway, 1962; Kibbler & Richter, 1950; Lansing, 1957); (*f*) the perception of apparent movement with intermittent stimuli (Lichtenstein, 1961; Murphree, 1954); and (*g*) the limit of temporal information processing of intermittent stimuli (Bach, 1957; Harter, Eason, & White, 1964). The critical periods of time at which the above phenomena occurred ranged from 50 to 200 milliseconds, the most common value being 100 milliseconds. These and other findings which illustrate the discontinuous nature of perceptual and motor processes have been comprehensively discussed elsewhere (Barlow, 1964; Ellingson, 1956; Lindsley, 1952; McReynolds, 1953; White, 1963).

Although the discrete nature of temporal perception may be the result of both peripheral and central neurophysiological processes, the present paper is concerned with central explanations of this limit. Two central hypotheses proposing a coding and how it affects temporal perception have recently gathered increasing interest. One assumes "cortical excitability cycles" which serve as a gating or timing device for incoming sense data, and the other proposes a "central scanning mechanism" which temporally groups sense data into "psychological moments."

Although these concepts have been referenced frequently as explanations of many diverse empirical findings, their exact nature remains somewhat vague and ambiguous. The necessity is evident for a critical review which clearly states the nature and implications of these hypotheses of central intermittency and compares them in light of their deductions. Such a review possibly would clarify the relationships between these concepts and indicate the relative explanatory power of each. The present paper attempts this task.

Cortical Excitability Cycles

The concept of cortical excitability cycles rests principally on amplitude measures of cortical potentials evoked by a sensory stim-
ulus or by direct cortical stimulation, although other criteria could be used (rate of neuron firing, thresholds of single neural units, convulsive threshold). Typically it has been based on the observed phenomenon that when a stimulus is presented to the nervous system, the amplitude of its resulting evoked cortical potential varies as a function of the temporal relationship between the stimulus and the spontaneous potentials or previously evoked potentials in the brain.

Lindsley (1952) was one of the first to review the development of the concept that the spontaneous alpha rhythm (10 cps in humans and 5 cps in rabbits) reflects cyclic fluctuations in cortical excitability. He wrote:

> The next assumption is that the alpha activity cycle represents for the individual cell or the aggregates of cells with which it is associated, an alternating excitability cycle. This conception was first proposed by Bishop (1933). . . . Bishop demonstrated that impulses initiated in the optic nerve of the rabbit found access to the cortex in the form of evoked responses only at certain intervals corresponding to the spontaneous rhythmic or alpha activity cycle at about 5 per sec. Accordingly Bishop interpreted this as evidence of a cortical excitability cycle.

Recovery time studies using paired stimuli also show temporal periodicities. The cyclic activity of evoked cortical potentials (ECPs) in anesthetized cats elicited by direct cortical stimulation (Chang, 1951) and by afferent stimulation (Chang, 1950) reflected changes in excitability in terms of the amplitude of a second ECP elicited by a second stimulus. Such recovery cycles have also been found when nonanesthetized animals were used (Evarts, Fleming, & Huttenlocher, 1960; Palestini, Pisano, Rosadini, & Rossi, 1965).

Cortical excitability cycles have also been demonstrated in humans in association with both the alpha rhythm and the time between light flashes. When light flashes were presented at various phases of the alpha rhythm, the amplitude of the ECP elicited by the flashes fluctuated as a function of alpha phase (points of maximum and minimum excitability occurring 180° out of phase of one another; Callaway & Layne, 1964). When the interval of time between light flashes was varied, the amplitude of ECPs (secondary responses) elicited by the second flash showed the greatest enhancement when presented approximately 100 milliseconds and 200 milliseconds after the first flash and the least enhancement when presented approximately 150 milliseconds and 250 milliseconds after the first flash (Cigánek, 1964; Gastaut, Roger, Corriol, & Naquet, 1951; Schwartz & Shagass, 1964). When the second flash followed the first by more than 100 milliseconds, it tended to replace or "reset" the ECP of the first. It may be noted that the ECPs were very complex and did not necessarily reflect the excitability-cycle period.

Evidence generally indicates that cortical excitability and cortical surface potentials are regulated by subcortical (brainstem) systems. Gastaut proposed that cortical excitability may be regulated locally by nonspecific projection systems and generally by the diffuse projection system—the level of excitability or the duration of the excitability cycle depending on the synchrony of elements within these systems. A continuum of EEG patterns and syndromes indicating cortical excitability have been suggested: (a) activated EEG pattern and hyperexcitability characterized by desynchrony of elements and cortical excitability cycles of short duration, (b) resting EEG pattern and hypoexcitability characterized by synchrony of elements and cortical excitability cycles of long duration, and (c) instability of EEG pattern characterized by variable synchrony and excitability cycle duration (Gastaut, 1953; Lindsley, 1952).

In light of the above findings, the question arises if cortical excitability cycles might serve as a temporal coding system for incoming sense data. Lindsley (1952) considered this possibility as an explanation of how letters and words are kept from smearing and running together when reading. He wrote:

Meister (1951) has proposed . . . the manner in which voluntary eye movements, initiated from the motor eye fields of area 8, may simultaneously and momentarily inhibit or block incoming impulses through connections with the occipital cortex. The exact manner in which this may occur remains to be demonstrated, but the psychological effect implies that some type of neuronic shutter mechanism is operating. Conceivably this could be through simultaneous discharges from area 8 to the extraocular muscles and the occipital cortex, the latter in effect inhibiting reception momentarily by resetting the alpha activity cycle in the given aggregate of cortical neurons involved in the perception. On the other hand it could arise through a timing mechanism which would permit activation of the eye muscle only in synchrony with the inexcitable phase of the alpha activity of the occipital cortex. In either case a kind of neuronic shutter effect would take place during the movement of the eye, in much the same fashion that a shutter in a movie projector permits two successive discrete exposures without smearing [pp. 448–449].

The idea of cortical excitability cycles serving as a temporal coding mechanism has been presented in a number of more recent papers (Callaway & Alexander, 1960; Ellingson, 1956; Gastaut, 1953; Lindsley, 1958; Surwillo, 1963). It was suggested that individual neurons have an excitability cycle which determines their accessibility (probability of being fired) to incoming neural pulses. When neurons in an aggregate have synchronous excitability cycles, the transmission of afferent impulses through them could be gated by their excitability cycle. Therefore, if the frequency of the excitability cycle was 10 cps, pulses could not be transmitted faster than 10 times per second.

It should be noted that alpha activity is not necessarily the result of an aggregate of neurons firing in synchrony. Brazier (1960, pp. 197–198) noted that an individual action potential has a duration of less than 1 millisecond, and, therefore, a large number of slightly asynchronous action potentials would be required for the 100-millisecond duration of the alpha wave. She suggested that the slow fluctuating alpha rhythm is the result of fluctuating cell membrane potentials and is determined by the membrane characteristics of the cell.

OBSERVATIONS AND DISCUSSION

1. The question has been raised that if the alpha frequency reflects a cortical excitability cycle, how can there be a cortical excitability cycle in the absence of alpha activity as recorded from the scalp? Lindsley (1952) noted that

there may be alpha activity within a particular aggregate of neurons in the absence of a recordable alpha rhythm as measured from the scalp. The alpha rhythm is evident only when a large number of neurons have synchronous alpha activity. On the basis of the brightness enhancement effect (Bartley, 1939), which occurred in the absence of recordable alpha rhythm, Lindsley concluded that only alpha activity must be present in the aggregate of cells participating in the response for an excitability cycle to occur. This conclusion has been supported in that excitability cycles measured by ECPs to paired flashes were found when the time period of the excitability cycle was not evident in the wave form of the ECP (Cigánek, 1964). This may be explained by the finding that the amplitude of ECPs measured on the scalp surface has been shown to be a poor indication of the number of neurons involved in the potential (Amassian, Waller, & Macy, 1964).

2. The delay in perceptual and motor processes can only partially be explained in terms of cortical excitability cycles. Even when afferent impulses are in synchrony with the excitatory phase of the cycle, the impulses having maximum accessibility to cortical neurons, considerable delay exists in the nervous system in addition to afferent and efferent conduction times. From this perspective, cortical excitability cycles account only for variability of central delay and not necessarily for the total period of delay. From another point of view, excitability cycles may account for the delay if afferent impulses are assumed to summate with the excitability cycle aggregate and become a part of the corticothalamic reverberations which, in turn, could serve as a short-term memory device. This assumption suggests an explanation of the many different time intervals cited as necessary for temporal order discrimination. This might well be the case since these time intervals have been found at harmonics and multiples of the alpha frequency (Stroud, 1949).

3. The concept of a cortical excitability cycle implies that the accessibility of an aggregate of neurons to afferent impulses is a function of both the phase of the aggregate excitability cycle and the frequency and intensity of the afferent impulses. Depending on the absolute amount of change in excitability during the cycle, the gating effect of the cortical excitability cycle could be altered by increases in stimulus intensity.

Callaway and Layne (1964) found that maximum excitability, as measured by presenting flashes at various alpha phases, occurred earlier in the phase with a brighter flash than with a dimmer one. This indicates that afferent impulses would be gated faster with high stimulus intensity than with low stimulus intensity. This would occur only when a single stimulus was being presented, variations in its intensity resulting in variations in when it would become effective in the excitability cycle. As discussed below, different results may be expected during continuous or rapid intermittent stimulation.

4. Excitability cycles have been hypothesized for both evoked and spontaneous brain activity. The question arises as to the relationship between these two potentials. They could occlude, summate, or interact with one another. Some of the observations that have been made on this point are: (a) the amplitude of ECPs was correlated with the energy in all frequency ranges of spontaneous activity, especially in the alpha range (Kooi & Bagchi, 1964; Rodin, Grisell, Gudobba, & Zachary, 1965); (b) rhythmic afteractivity (ringing) sometimes observed in ECPs occurred in the alpha frequency range and appeared to be dependent on the occurrence of spontaneous alpha activity (Barlow, 1960; Cohn, 1964); (c) the extent to which spontaneous activity was blocked or added to evoked activity depended in part on the intensity of the evoking stimulus (Callaway & Layne, 1964); (d) when paired stimuli were separated by less than 100 milliseconds their resulting ECPs appeared to interact, but when separated by more than 100 milliseconds the ECP resulting from the second stimulus appeared to "reset" the first potential (Chang, 1951; Cigánek, 1964; Schwartz & Shagass, 1964); (e) during rapid intermittent stimulation, ECPs were regular and cyclic in nature after an initial synchronization period (White & Eason, 1966); and (f)

evoked and spontaneous potentials were found to have some common neural elements (Barlow, 1960). On the basis of these observations, evoked and spontaneous potentials apparently are not two completely independent phenomena and may share some common central neural elements.

The following model may serve as an explanation of how excitability cycles are affected by evoked and spontaneous cortical activity. In the resting or stable state, the alpha rhythm reflects the fluctuating excitability of the system. The effect of afferent impulses on the alpha excitability cycle depends on the initiating stimulus intensity and the relative excitation of the cortex. Assuming that evoked sensory potentials use elements engaged in the resting rhythm, intense afferent stimulation suppresses the alpha excitability cycle by monopolizing the majority of available neurons. If afferent stimulation is weak and falls in a period of low cortical excitation, the alpha excitability cycle is only slightly affected. During rapid stimulation (stimuli separated by less than 100 milliseconds), neurons participating in the ECP progressively summate with the spontaneous activity of the cortex over time, resulting in an excitability cycle similar to the original spontaneous one (this might be the cause of the ringing afteractivity observed in some ECPs which is similar in frequency to alpha activity).

5. There is an apparent logical inconsistency between the concepts of generalized cortical excitability cycles and generalized cortical activation if they are assumed to exist simultaneously. An aggregate of neurons cannot be both highly activated (asynchronous) and show a rhythmic potential change (synchronous) at the same time. By excitability cycle is meant that aggregated neurons are in synchrony and attain their maximum level of excitation simultaneously, afferent impulses having maximum access to the aggregate only at that time. By activation is meant a desynchronization of cortical neural activity and that "incoming pulses would find access to some aggregate at almost any point in time. . . . [Impulses] might participate at one point in time with one aggregate and at another time with another [Lindsley,

1958, p. 521]." In the latter situation, generalized cortical excitability cycles are functionally nonexistent and, therefore, cannot serve as a gating mechanism which codes all incoming sense data on a common time base. This does not exclude the possibility of an excitability cycle existing in a particular aggregate of cortical neurons when generalized cortical activation exists.

6. The concept of cortical excitability cycles has been based entirely on paired-stimuli experiments. One can only speculate as to the nature and effects of excitability cycles during continuous stimulation. The nature of information received from a single stimulus (a), two stimuli (b), and intermittent or continuous stimulation (c) in temporal discrimination tasks may be quite different. As stated by White and Lichtenstein (1963):

(a) shows the response of a "resting" system; (b) shows the effect of the first stimulus on the second, or shows how long it takes the system to return to normal; and (c) gives information regarding the rate-handling capacity of the system and may involve very complex interactions at various stages in the system.

Cortical Scanning and Psychological Moments

In contrast to the concept of cortical excitability cycles, which arose primarily from electrophysiological recordings of brain activity, the scanning hypothesis arose primarily as an explanation of the discrete nature of behavior and on logical grounds, since such a scanning mechanism would also be a parsimonious way for the central nervous system to process incoming sense data. Pitts and McCulloch (1947) introduced the concept of cortical scansion to perception. This concept was part of a hypothesized neural net proposed as an explanation of how universals and forms can be identified regardless of size and spatial position. For present purposes, only the model itself is reviewed, noting that Pitts and McCulloch cited a substantial amount of histological and neurophysiological evidence in the model's support.

The model essentially consists in the cortex containing two main layers of neurons, each layer being divided into a number of horizontal sublayers. Impulses from the outer main layer descend to the inner main layer where they are averaged or combined over time during each cycle of scansion. Pitts and McCulloch (1947) described the scansion mechanism as follows:

> To complete the parallel with our general model, we require adjuvant fibers to activate the various levels M_a successively. It is to the non-specific afferents that modern physiology attributes the well known rhythmic sweep of a sheet of negativity up and down through the cortex—the alpha rhythm. If our model fits the facts, this alpha rhythm performs a temporal "scanning" of the cortex which thereby gains, at the cost of time, the equivalent of another spatial dimension in its neural manifold [p. 133].

"Scanning" meant an activation or excitation of successive layers of the cortex by nonspecific afferents causing a lowered threshold of those layers to their respective incoming specific afferents. That is, the afferents are capable of exciting the cortex only through summation with the excitation of the scan. The nonspecific afferents have their origin in the thalamus and their sweep of excitation is associated with the alpha rhythm. Temporal scanning and grouping result from the excitations of the outer cortex descending to the inner averaging layer, where they are averaged over the period of each scan. The summed excitations are then released periodically from the inner averaging layer by the descending wave of excitation.

Wiener (1948), while discussing a similar model, proposed a "group-scanning assembly" whereby all the transformations of a figure may be represented and summed during the course of a scan. He described the nature of group scanning and how it might affect perception as follows:

> A group-scanning assembly thus has well-defined appropriate anatomical structure. The necessary switching may be performed by independent horizontal leads which furnish enough stimulation to shift the thresholds in each level to

just the proper amount to make them fire when the lead comes on. . . .

> The scanning apparatus should have a certain intrinsic period of operation which should be identifiable in the performance of the brain. The order of magnitude of this period should show in the minimum time required for making direct comparison of the shapes of objects different in size. . . . When direct comparison seems to be possible, it appears to take a time of the order of magnitude of a tenth of a second. This also seems to accord with the order of magnitude of the time needed by excitation to stimulate all the layers of transverse connectors in cyclical sequence.

> While this cyclical process then might be a locally determined one, there is evidence that there is a wide-spread synchronism in different parts of the cortex, suggesting that it is driven from some clocking center. In fact, it has the order of frequency appropriate for the alpha rhythm of the brain, as shown in electroencephalograms. We may suspect that this alpha rhythm is associated with form perception, and that it partakes of the nature of a sweep rhythm, like the rhythm shown in the scanning process of a television apparatus. It disappears in deep sleep, and seems to be obscured and overlaid with other rhythms, precisely as we might expect, when we are actually looking at something, and the sweep rhythm is acting as something like a carrier for other rhythms and activities [Wiener, 1948, pp. 165–166].

In the first paragraph of the above statement, Wiener suggested a scan of excitation similar to the one proposed by Pitts and McCulloch. Yet, in the last paragraph, he introduced a different meaning in drawing an analogy between group scanning and the operation of television. Pitts and McCulloch proposed that scanning serves only as an excitatory mechanism and is not directly involved in the transmission of information. The television analogy suggests that the scanning mechanism serves as an actual carrier of information.

Stroud (1949) proposed the term "moment" as the period of time representing the duration of each scan. He described the properties of moments and how they might affect perception in the following statement:

> Physical time t is represented in the experience of man as psychological time T. . . . T is not a continuous variable. . . . [This] can be interpreted as a result of a scanning process. Each scan process . . . reduces the number of dimensions of representa-

tion. It loses all information contained in the order of the dimension eliminated by the scan over the period of the scan. The only order of information left in this dimension lies in the order of the elements of the series of representations produced by the scanning process.

The properties of moments, so far defined, could not contain movement as a property of the content of the moment, for movement is change with respect to time. . . . Psychological movement (apparent movement) . . . is in the nature of an inference based upon differences between moments.

Seen physical events, which differ from one another only by the dates of their occurrence, are differentiated in psychological time at a maximum rate of one per moment [Stroud, 1955, pp. 177–181].

Stroud's main contribution to the scanning concept was in relating it to perception. His emphasis on the temporal limitations of perception imposed by moments suggests a rich area of experimental investigation. Of particular interest is his emphasis of the discrete nature of the moment. "Therefore there is a boundary between the content of the moments which is pretty sharp. As nearly as I could determine, information is either in one moment or another moment [Stroud, 1949, p. 37]."

Stroud did not overtly identify the moment with any physiological mechanism. He only assumed that moments refer to events which are situated in the central nervous system. Yet, the possibility of electrocortical rhythms underlying moments was implied when he made the important point that the frequency of moments may vary an octave or more, and that the electrical activity of the brain can be driven over a comparable range. In regard to the alpha rhythm, he wrote:

I look at the alpha in this light: here I have a system which works on a fundamental periodicity. I must somewhere have a period generator; regardless of whether or not I am running a computer, I keep the motor running. I am inclined to look upon alpha rhythms as what might be called no-load current, the no-load signal of the system. Immediately you load it, it is like an over-modulated carrier. The carrier practically disappears. One might find that the characteristic requirements of the computer in use will tolerate quite a wide range of operating frequencies whereas the unloaded system may respond only at the frequencies

for which it is initially designed to operate [Stroud, 1949, p. 51].

Stroud implied a function for the alpha rhythm similar to that suggested by Wiener in his television analogy—that of an information carrier. This similarity holds only when the system is "unloaded" or the alpha rhythm is predominant. While Wiener implied that the alpha rhythm reflects the time period of a scanning device regardless of whether it is visible or obscured by other rhythms, Stroud implied that it reflects such a time period only in the resting system, the scan period being variable over a wide range of frequencies in the working system.

The scanning model drawn by analogy with the operation of television—the alpha rhythm analogous with the scan of the electron beam —was most explicitly stated by Walter (1950):

Applying the principle of parsimony then, we should expect to find in the space receptor sections of a brain, mechanisms whereby the sensory fields could be scanned continuously in such a way that the detailed bits of information they contain could be conveyed to a central assembly by only a few channels, there to be related one with another for appropriate action to be taken. . . . The characteristics of such a scanning mechanism would be that its range or amplitude of activity would be greatest in the absence of a signal, when it would be regular and rhythmic, sweeping over the featureless central projection of the sensory organ as smoothly as the electron beam of a television camera scans the image screen for the picture elements. But on the instant that a signal appeared on its beat it would be halted, and its position at the check would convey to all other regions the relative position of the detail of sensation. When a complex pattern appeared, the succession of runs and checks would repeatedly convert a spatial pattern which was constant during the time of a single sweep—a frame, as the television engineers call it—into a series of signals on a base of time, so that all the information contained in a single parameter of sense can be conveyed on a single channel in a code of pulses.

A special mechanism must be devoted entirely to the generation of the scanning sweep, and also, if action is to be taken on the basis of information received from the field scanner, to ensuring that executive orders are transmitted to effectors only at such moments as the sensory data are complete . . . [Walter, 1950, pp. 5–6].

Walter proceeded to identify the alpha rhythm as the most probable mechanism of scanning.

The models proposed by Pitts and McCulloch and by Walter are quite different as to how information arriving within scans is treated. In Pitts and McCulloch's model, the scan serves as a time-summing device. Incoming sensory information is grouped into moments, information within each moment being summed. This may be compared to motion picture film which is divided into frames, temporal information within each frame being summed. In Walter's model, the scan serves as a transmitting device, sensory information being sampled and coded for transmission. Due to the sampling nature of the scan, only sensory information arriving in temporal and spatial synchrony with the scan is processed. This mechanism has already been compared with the operation of television, the electron beam sampling, coding, and transmitting information.

Although the above models differ somewhat in their scanning characteristics, they have two common underlying assumptions. Moments are assumed to be discrete periods of psychological time containing no temporal information. With the exception of Stroud's model, moment duration is assumed to be relatively constant and to be reflected in the period of the alpha rhythm.

It should be noted that the term "moment" has been used in a number of other senses, two of which are discussed briefly.

McReynolds (1953) conceived of moments as a unit of information in contrast to a unit of time. He wrote:

> We assume, then, a succession of neural discharge patterns as underlying transient mental functions. I will refer to these successive patterns as *moments* (*M*'s . . . The phenomenal counterpart of an *M* may be termed a *percept,* and *moment sequence* will be used to refer to any number of *M*'s which occur successively [p. 320].

In this sense, moments do not reflect a time base on which the central nervous system functions. Moments may vary in duration and may temporally overlap and interact with one another. They do not represent discrete units of time but discrete units of information. Therefore, events are not temporally in one moment or another, as Stroud proposed, but may be in two or more moments. Furthermore, motion is not an inference based on differences in successive moments but "is itself a perception, and therefore would itself have to be represented in an *M* [McReynolds, 1953, p. 324]."

Shallice (1964) proposed a "perceptual moment" hypothesis asserting that sensory input is summated over discrete periods of time. This hypothesis is similar to that of Pitts and McCulloch, except they assumed that the duration of the perceptual moment varies with stimulus intensity. The following model was proposed:

> Consider a general accumulator, which receives input from all sense receptors, and assume that as soon as its contents reach a fixed level it will discharge and the discharge can act as a timing signal which will trigger the discharges of the specific accumulators. After the discharge it will start accumulating again and the cycle will repeat indefinitely. Thus, we have a very simple mechanism which produces a discharge at regular intervals under steady stimulus conditions, but if the stimulus intensity is increased the rate of discharging increases. This increase would not be as great as the increase in the rate of firing of the nerve fibers upon which the stimulus acts, since the vast majority of the input channels into the general accumulator will be unchanged. The general accumulator will be known as the reticular accumulator, since the obvious place for such a mechanism is in the reticular system where impulses from all sensory pathways converge [Shallice, 1964, pp. 131–132].

In summary, moments and cortical scanning mechanisms have been conceived in a number of different ways. Moments have been defined as the unit of time required between successive events for them to retain their temporal representation, information arriving within a single moment being summed across time (Pitts & McCulloch, 1947; Shallice, 1964; Stroud, 1949; Walter, 1950; Wiener, 1948); and as a unit of information or a percept (McReynolds, 1953). In the former case, moments are assumed to reflect an absolute time base on which the central nervous system functions, information falling in one moment or another. In the latter case, moments are not necessarily assumed to reflect an absolute time base and may overlap and interact with one another in time. The duration of psychological moments was proposed both as being relatively constant at 100 milliseconds (Callaway & Alexander, 1960; Pitts & McCulloch, 1947; Walter, 1950; Wiener, 1948) and as being variable, ranging from 50 to 200 milliseconds (McReynolds, 1953; Shallice, 1964; Stroud, 1949). It was hypothesized that psychological moments result from a cortical scanning mechanism, the alpha rhythm either directly or implicitly assumed to reflect the periodicity of the mechanism and therefore to reflect the temporal nature of successive moments. Two types of scanning models were proposed: vertical scanning of the cortex resulting in spatial representations being summed across time (Pitts & McCulloch, 1947); and horizontal scanning of the cortex resulting in spatial representations being sampled and coded on a time base (Callaway & Alexander, 1960; Walter, 1950; Wiener, 1948).

OBSERVATIONS AND DISCUSSION

1. Cortical scanning, as reflected by the periodicity of the alpha rhythm, is a speculative explanation of psychological moments. The scanning concept has been based primarily on a posteriori evidence, experimental results being related to it when appropriate. Of the the direct tests of this hypothesis, only three measured alpha frequency (MacKay, 1953; Murphree, 1954; Walsh, 1952); the others inferred it on the bases of past work (Callaway & Alexander, 1960; Harter *et al.,* 1964; Lichtenstein, 1961; Stroud, 1949; White, 1963).

2. The scanning hypothesis has seldom been considered in relation to how incoming sensory data might interact with the scanning process itself (as reflected by the periodicity of the alpha rhythm) and how this interaction might affect temporal discrimination. Walter (1950) and Wiener (1948) acknowledged that the alpha rhythm "blocks" during sensory stimulation but failed to discuss how this might be related to temporal perception. Shallice (1964) suggested that moment duration varies as a function of stimulus intensity but neglected to discuss this relationship in terms of brain rhythms. White (1963) was one of the few proponents of the moment hypothesis who discussed changes in temporal discrimination in relation to spontaneous and evoked brain rhythms.

3. Two types of cortical scanning have been proposed: horizontal and vertical. In Pitts and McCulloch's model, vertical scanning mediates the expansion and contraction of stimulus representations in the cortex and the summation of these representations over the period of the scan. On the basis of the mechanism, the prediction was made that perceptual distortion will occur if a visual image is expanded and contracted on the retina in synchrony with the scan rate, the imposed and spontaneous representations interacting. This prediction has been tested with negative results (Callaway & Alexander, 1960; MacKay, 1953). The temporal and spatial characteristics assumed with horizontal scanning have been directly tested by toposcopic analysis (Cooper & Mundy-Castle, 1960). The alpha rhythm did not "sweep" across the cortex in any constant manner; therefore, these types of scanning are questionable. Although Pitts and McCulloch's model does not seem plausible as an explanation of form perception, some type of vertical scanning appears to be most probable in relation to temporal discrimination.

4. If the alpha rhythm is assumed to reflect or serve as a scanning mechanism, two problems arise. Since moments are assumed to serve as an absolute time base on which the central nervous system functions—each moment temporally independent—it is difficult to conceive how the desynchronized alpha activity occurring during EEG activation could underlie such a concept. This problem was previously discussed in terms of the alpha rhythm reflecting an excitability cycle. Also, this assumption has not been supported empirically, cited moment durations ranging from 50 to 200 milliseconds and the alpha period ranging from approximately 77 to 125 milliseconds.

5. If the alpha rhythm or some other measurable periodicity is not assumed to reflect the frequency of the hypothesized scanning mechanism, the predictive power of the scanning hypothesis is considerably reduced. In order to make predictions as to rate-handling capacities of the nervous system other than simply stating that it is limited, some known scan duration is necessary, preferably tied to measurable periodicities in the brain.

Summary and Conclusion

The present paper has reviewed two hypotheses or models frequently referenced as explanations of the discrete nature of temporal discrimination. Although investigators differed considerably in their interpretation of the scanning model, it was usually identified with the operation of television. The model suggests that the sensory projection areas are scanned by some kind of central scanning mechanism, sensory information being sampled and coded in terms of psychological moments with each successive scan. The extent to which this model was identified with physiological processes varied widely. Usually the hypothesized scanning mechanism was associated with the alpha rhythm of the cortex.

The cortical excitability cycle hypothesis is more solidly based on empirical evidence. The cortex is assumed to vary rhythmically in threshold so that the effect of incoming sensory data on the cortex is a function of when it arrives at the cortex in reference to the excitability cycle. No scanning mechanism is assumed. Rather, the variations in cortical threshold are assumed to serve as a gating mechanism of incoming sensory and outgoing motor pulses. Considerable evidence was cited indicating that evoked and spontaneous cortical potentials reflect such excitability cycles. The rhythmic nature of the excitability cycle is assumed to be the result of a large number of cortical neurons having synchronous membrane potentials, the time period of the cycle being a function of the electrochemical nature of the neurons involved.

The excitability cycle and scanning models may be distinguished on three dimensions: time base, frequency of operation, and effect of incoming sensory impulses within a cycle of operation.

1. *Time Base Assumed.* The excitability cycle model assumes no particular time base. A cycle may involve the entire cortex, all sensory information being grouped on a common time base, or it may involve a particular neural aggregate, sensory information unique to that aggregate being grouped on its own time base. In the scanning model, an absolute time base is assumed—the entire cortex is scanned, all sensory information being grouped into discrete temporal units.

2. *Operation Frequency.* In the scanning model, scanning frequency is assumed to remain fairly constant at or near the frequency of the alpha rhythm. In the excitability cycle model, cycle frequency may vary considerably depending on the state of alertness of the organism and the nature of incoming neural impulses.

3. *Within-Operation Effects.* Although both models predict that the temporal order of incoming impulses is lost within a single operation (within scans or excitability cycles), they predict different within-operation effects as to the central nervous system's responsiveness to those impulses. Variations in the magnitude and latency of a response to a given stimulus would be expected within excitability cycles but not within scans.

In the present discussion, psychological moments were associated with the cortical scanning model, the between-scan interval delineating moment duration. The possibility of cortical excitability cycles underlying psychological moments appears equally probable. The moment concepts discussed may be classified into three groups on the bases of the time base and operation frequency assumed (within-operation effects were not considered extensively in the papers reviewed): those compatible with the scanning model, those compatible with the excitability cycle model, and those partly compatible with both models. Moments as conceived by Pitts and McCulloch and Walter may be identified with the scanning model—the alpha rhythm is assumed to sweep the cortex, temporally coding all sense data on an absolute time base of successive moments, the duration of each moment determined by the duration of each sweep. Moments as conceived by McReynolds fit into the excitability cycle model—no particular time base or frequency of operation is assumed.

The majority of moment concepts suggest underlying mechanisms which are contained in part within both models. Stroud and Shallice claimed that moments reflect an absolute time base which operates over a range of frequencies depending on the state of the system (resting vs. active) and on stimulus intensity. Wiener considered moment frequency to be relatively constant, approaching that of the alpha frequency, but also acknowledged that moments may be the result of local processes (alpha activity) or group processes (alpha rhythm) depending on the synchrony of the various sensory systems.

Although considerable evidence was presented indicating that the scanning and excitability cycle models suggest a plausible explanation of psychological moments, a number of problems were discussed which arise when these models are considered in relation to the effects of stimulus intensity and duration on moments, and when an attempt is made to reduce such models to neurophysiological processes. Perhaps the above discussion reified and interpreted the models far beyond the intention of their respective originators. If so, it was done to clarify differences and similarities. In light of our present knowledge and understanding of what the electrical activity of the brain signifies, the major contributions of such models are offering an explanation of behavior, and the mechanics of such models are of secondary importance. As stated by Walter (1962):

> Comparisons with familiar artificial scanning mechanisms—television and radar, for example—though illustrative, need not be taken too seriously, since there is ample evidence that within

the brain the intrinsic and evoked rhythms, whatever their functions, are extremely complex in their interactions with signals, with one another, and with brain topology.

Summary

A review of hypotheses frequently referenced as explanations of the discrete nature of temporal perception—i.e., the tendency for incoming sense information to be perceptually grouped in time. Hypotheses were divided into 2 categories: those assuming "cortical excitability cycles" which serve as a gating or timing device, and those assuming a "central scanning mechanism" which temporally groups sense data into "psychological moments." These concepts are discussed in relation to evoked and spontaneous cortical activity, effects of stimulus intensity and frequency, cortical activation, and perception. The concepts reviewed differ along 3 major dimensions: (a) time base assumed, (b) operation frequency assumed, and (c) within-operation effects.

References

Amassian, V. E., Waller, H. J., & Macy, J., Jr. Neural mechanism of the primary somatosensory evoked potential. *Annals of the New York Academy of Sciences,* 1964, *112*(Art. 1), 5–32.

Bach, L. M. (Chm.) ERDL-Tulane symposium on flicker. New Orleans, April 6, 1957.

Barlow, J. S. Rhythmic activity induced by photic stimulation in relation to intrinsic alpha activity of the brain in man. *Electroencephalography and Clinical Neurophysiology,* 1960, *12*, 317–326.

Barlow, J. S. Evoked responses in relation to visual perception and oculomotor reaction times in man. *Annals of the New York Academy of Sciences,* 1964, *112*(Art. 1), 432–467.

Bartley, S. H. Some factors in brightness discrimination. *Psychological Review,* 1939, *46*, 337–358.

Bates, J. A. Electrical activity of the cortex accompanying movement. *Journal of Physiology,* 1951, *113*, 240–257.

Bertelson, P. Central intermittency twenty years later. *Quarterly Journal of Experimental Psychology,* 1966, *18*, 153–162.

Bishop, G. H. Cyclic changes in excitability of the optic pathway of the rabbit. *American Journal of Physiology,* 1933, *103*, 213–224.

Blackwell, H. R. Neural theories of simple visual discriminations. *Journal of the Optical Society of America,* 1963, *53,* 129–160.

Boynton, R. M. Temporal factors in vision. In W. A. Rosenblith (Ed.), *Sensory communication.* New York: Wiley, 1961. Pp. 739–756.

Brazier, M. *The electrical activity of the nervous system.* New York: Macmillan, 1960.

Callaway, E. III. Factors influencing the relationship between alpha activity and visual reaction time. *Electroencephalography and Clinical Neurophysiology,* 1962, *14,* 674–682.

Callaway, E. III, & Alexander, J. D., Jr. The temporal coding of sensory data: An investigation of two theories. *Journal of General Psychology,* 1960, *62,* 293–309.

Callaway, E. III, & Layne, R. S. Interaction between the visual evoked response and two spontaneous biological rhythms: The EEG alpha cycle and the cardiac arousal cycle. *Annals of the New York Academy of Sciences,* 1964, *112*(Art. 1), 421–431.

Chang, H. T. The repetitive discharges of cortico-thalamic reverberation circuit. *Journal of Neurophysiology,* 1950, *13,* 235–258.

Chang, H. T. Changes in excitability of cerebral cortex following single electric shock applied to cortical surfaces. *Journal of Neurophysiology,* 1951, *14,* 95–112.

Cheatham, P. G., & White, C. T. Temporal numerosity: I. Perceived number as a function of flash number and rate. *Journal of Experimental Psychology,* 1952, *44,* 447–451.

Cheatham, P. G., & White, C. T. Temporal numerosity: III. Auditory perception of number. *Journal of Experimental Psychology,* 1954, *47,* 425–428.

Cigánek, L. Excitability cycle of the visual cortex in man. *Annals of the New York Academy of Sciences,* 1964, *112*(Art. 1), 241–253.

Cohn, R. Rhythmic after-activity in visual evoked responses. *Annals of the New York Academy of Sciences,* 1964, *112*(Art. 1), 281–291.

Cooper, R., & Mundy-Castle, A. C. Spatial and temporal characteristics of the alpha rhythm: A topo-scopic analysis. *Electroencephalography and Clinical Neurophysiology,* 1960, *12,* 153–165.

Craik, K. J. Theory of human operators in control systems: I. The operators as an engineering system. *British Journal of Psychology,* 1948, *38,* 56–61.

Donchin, E., & Lindsley, D. B. Retroactive brightness enhancement with brief paired flashes of light. *Vision Research,* 1965, *5,* 59–70.

Donchin, E., Wicke, J. D., & Lindsley, D. B. Cortical evoked potentials and perception of paired flashes. *Science,* 1963, *141,* 1285–1286.

Ellingson, R. J. Brain waves and problems in psychology. *Psychological Bulletin,* 1956, *53,* 1–34.

Evarts, E. V., Fleming, T. C., & Huttenlocher, P. R. Recovery cycle of visual cortex of the awake and sleeping cat. *American Journal of Physiology,* 1960, *199,* 373–376.

Forsyth, D. M., & Chapanis, A. Counting repeated light flashes as a function of their number, their rate of presentation, and retinal location stimulated. *Journal of Experimental Psychology,* 1958, *56,* 385–391.

Gastaut, H. J. P. Electroencephalographic records as an aid to the study of the action of the reticular system of the brain-stem on the electrical activity of the cerebral cortex in relation to states of consciousness. In, Laurentian symposium Ste. Marguerite. Symposium presented at University of California, Los Angeles, 1953.

Gastaut, H., Roger, A., Corriol, J., & Naquet, R. Étude électrographique de cycle d'excitabilité cortical. *Electroencephalography and Clinical Neurophysiology,* 1951, *3,* 401–428.

Harter, M. R., Eason, R. G., & White, C. T. Effects of intermittent visual input disruption, flicker-rate, and work time on tracking performance and activation level. *Perceptual and Motor Skills,* 1964, *19,* 831–848.

Hirsh, I. J., & Sherrick, C. E., Jr. Perceived order in different sense modalities. *Journal of Experimental Psychology,* 1961, *62,* 423–432.

Kibbler, G. O., & Richter, D. Alpha rhythm and motor activity. *Electroencephalography and Clinical Neurophysiology,* 1950, *2,* 227.

Kooi, K. A., & Bagchi, B. K. Observations on early components of the visual evoked response and occipital rhythms. *Electroencephalography and Clinical Neurophysiology,* 1964, *17,* 638–643.

Lansing, R. W. Relation of brain and tremor rhythms to visual reaction time. *Electroencephalography and Clinical Neurophysiology,* 1957, *9,* 497–504.

Lichtenstein, M. Phenomenal simultaneity with irregular timing of components of the visual stimulus. *Perceptual and Motor Skills,* 1961, *12,* 47–60.

Lichtenstein, M., White, C. T., & Harter, M. R. Note on estimation of short inter-flash intervals. *Perceptual and Motor Skills,* 1963, *17,* 677–678.

Lichtenstein, M., White, C. T., Siegfried, J. B., & Harter, M. R. Apparent rate of flicker at various retinal loci and number of perceived flashes per unit time: A paradox. *Perceptual and Motor Skills,* 1963, *17,* 523–536.

Lindsley, D. B. Psychological phenomena and the electroencephalogram. *Electroencephalography and Clinical Neurophysiology,* 1952, *4,* 443–456.

Lindsley, D. B. The reticular system and perceptual discrimination. In H. H. Jasper *et al.* (Eds.), *Reticular formation of the brain.* Boston: Little, Brown, 1958. Pp. 513–534.

MacKay, D. M. Some experiments on the perception of patterns modulated at the alpha frequency. *Electroencephalography and Clinical Neurophysiology,* 1953, *5,* 559–562.

McReynolds, P. Thinking conceptualized in terms of interacting moments. *Psychological Review,* 1953, *60,* 319–330.

Meister, R. K. A hypothesis concerning the function of the occipital alpha rhythm in vision with special reference to the perception of movement. Unpublished doctoral dissertation, University of Chicago, 1951.

Murphree, O. D. Maximum rates of form perception and the alpha rhythm: An investigation and test of current nerve net theory. *Journal of Experimental Psychology*, 1954, *48*, 57–61.

Palestini, M., Pisano, M., Rosadini, G., & Rossi, G. F. Excitability cycles of the visual cortex during sleep and wakefulness. *Electroencephalography and Clinical Neurophysiology*, 1965, *19*, 276–283.

Pitts, W., & McCulloch, W. S. How we know universals: The perception of auditory and visual forms. *Bulletin of Mathematical Biophysics*, 1947, *9*, 127–147.

Rodin, E. A., Grisell, J. L., Gudobba, R. D., & Zachary, G. Relationship of EEG background rhythms to photic evoked responses. *Electroencephalography and Clinical Neurophysiology*, 1965, *19*, 301–304.

Schmidt, M. W., & Kristofferson, A. B. Discrimination of successiveness: A test of a model of attention. *Science*, 1963, *139*, 112–113.

Schwartz, M., & Shagass, C. Recovery functions of human somatosensory and visual evoked potentials. *Annals of the New York Academy of Sciences*, 1964, *112*(Art. 1), 510–525.

Shallice, T. The detection of change and the perceptual moment hypothesis. *British Journal of Statistical Psychology*, 1964, *17*, 113–135.

Stroud, J. Psychological moment in perception. In H. V. Foerester (Ed.), *Conference on cybernetics*. New York: Josiah Macy, Jr., Foundation, 1949. Pp. 27–63.

Stroud, J. M. The fine structure of psychological time.

In H. Quastler (Ed.), *Information theory in psychology*. Glencoe, Ill.: Free Press, 1955. Pp. 174–207.

Surwillo, W. W. The relation of simple response time to brain-wave frequency and the effects of age. *Electroencephalography and Clinical Neurophysiology*, 1963, *15*, 105–114.

Walsh, E. G. Visual reaction time and the *alpha* rhythm, an investigation of the scanning hypothesis. *Journal of Physiology*, 1952, *118*, 500–508.

Walter, W. G. The functions of the electrical rhythms of the brain. *Journal of Mental Science*, 1950, *96*, 1–31.

Walter, W. G. Spontaneous oscillatory systems and alternations in stability. In R. G. Grenell (Ed.), *Neural physiopathology*. New York: Harper & Row, 1962. Pp. 222–257.

White, C. T. Temporal numerosity and the psychological unit of duration. *Psychological Monographs*, 1963, *77*(12, Whole No. 575).

White, C. T., & Cheatham, P. G. Temporal numerosity: IV. A comparison of the major senses. *Journal of Experimental Psychology*, 1959, *58*, 441–444.

White, C. T., Cheatham, P. G., & Armington, J. C. Temporal numerosity: II. Evidence for central factors influencing perceived number. *Journal of Experimental Psychology*, 1953, *46*, 283–287.

White, C. T., & Eason, R. G. Evoked cortical potentials in relation to certain aspects of visual perception. *Psychological Monographs*, 1966, *80*(24, Whole No. 632).

White, C. T., & Lichtenstein, M. Some aspects of temporal discrimination. *Perceptual and Motor Skills*, 1963, *17*, 471–482.

Wiener, N. Gestalt and universals. In N. Wiener, *Cybernetics*. New York: Wiley, 1948. Pp. 156–167.

3.2 Perception of Temporal Order and Relative Visual Latency[*]

RUTH RUTSCHMANN

When a person is stimulated by two spatially discriminable flashes of light and is asked to

report which flash appeared first, his choice of one or the other alternative is generally determined by the temporal relationships between the onsets of the two stimuli. Physical changes in the direction and magnitude of the onset asynchrony between two flashes are likely to produce concomitant changes in perceived onset asynchrony, thus influencing judgments

[*] *Science*, May 20, 1966, vol. 152, pp. 1099–1101. Copyright © 1966 by the American Association for the Advancement of Science. This work was supported in part by PHS grant MH 03616, and conducted at the Department of Psychology of the New York State Psychiatric Institute, Columbia University Medical Center. I thank Jacques Rutschmann for his assistance and the subjects for volunteering their services.

Foveal — Nasal Flash Pairs

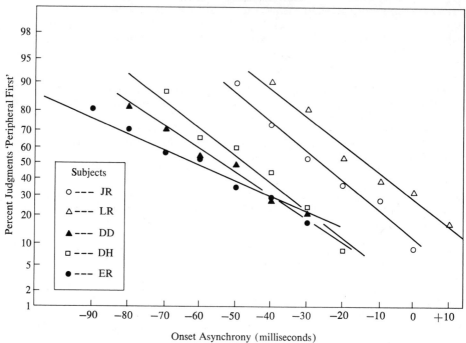

FIGURE 1   Proportion of responses "right first" to foveal-nasal flash pairs as a function of the
time interval between onsets (negative asynchrony indicates that the peripheral flash was
physically first).

of temporal order. Maximal uncertainty about temporal order is reflected by an equal probability of a subject's choosing between the two alternatives under a given condition of stimulation. A report by Hirsh and Sherrick (1) presents data to the effect that maximal uncertainty regarding the temporal order of two flashes at different eccentricities obtains when they are physically simultaneous, regardless of the retinal positions of, and spatial separation between, the two stimuli. These authors concluded that a relatively fixed onset asynchrony of 20 msec is required for 75-percent-correct detection of the temporal order of two events, independent of sense modality employed and stimulus conditions.

This study was conducted on the initial assumption that the temporal interval between the onsets of two visual simuli which yields maximal uncertainty about their temporal order represents an estimate of the average amount of latency difference to the two flashes. The ex-

periment was designed to investigate the dependency of judgments of temporal order on the location of the flashes on the retina. Within the framework presented here, Hirsh and Sherrick's generalization is questioned in the light of both existing reaction time (2) and psychophysical (3) measures of latency differences across the retina, and evidence that judgments of temporal order are a function of attributes of the stimulus (4).

The stimuli were pairs of light flashes generated by Sylvania R1131C glow modulator tubes. Each target subtended 1°12′. The flashes were delivered to the subject's right eye against a spherical background of uniform luminance (0.5 millilambert). Flash luminance was 125 mlam; flash duration was 500 msec. On each trial, one flash stimulated the fovea and the other a point on the horizontal meridian either 30° to the right of center (nasal retina) or 30° to the left (temporal retina). The sequence of fovea-right and fovea-left pairs was randomized.

The onset asynchrony between the flashes was varied in 10-msec interval steps according to the method of constant stimuli. Taking the onset of the foveal flash as $t = 0$, asynchronies were positive (foveal flash delivered first), negative (foveal flash delivered second), or zero (physical simultaneity). The subject fixated the center target and, after the presentation of each flash pair, gave a forced-choice judgment as to which appeared first, "foveal" or "peripheral." No knowledge of results was given. The five subjects tested were given approximately 800 trials with each of the two flash pairs.

The data of all sessions for each subject were pooled and plotted on a probability grid relating proportion of responses "peripheral first" to the onset asynchrony between the flashes. Foveal-nasal (Figure 1) and foveal-temporal (Figure 2) proportions were plotted separately, and straight lines were fitted to the data points by the method of least squares. The onset asynchronies associated with 50 percent re-

TABLE 1

Onset Asynchronies Required for Maximal Uncertainty of Temporal Order Judgments (50 Percent Response) and Corresponding Probable Errors (PE) (Negative asynchrony indicates that the peripheral flash occurred first.)

SUBJECT	FOVEAL—30° NASAL PAIR		FOVEAL—30° TEMPORAL PAIR	
	50% (MSEC)	PE	50% (MSEC)	PE
LR	−12	16	−34	20
JR	−25	14.5	−34.5	16
ER	−60	27	−75	16
DH	−46	15.5	−57.5	17
DD	−52.5	18.5	−31	21

sponse and the corresponding probable errors (denoting the slope of the functions) are presented in Table 1. All subjects require negative onset asynchronies (peripheral flash physically

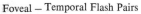

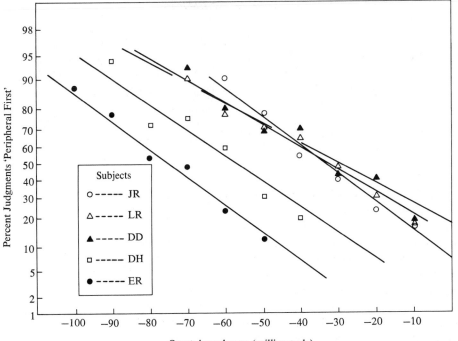

Foveal — Temporal Flash Pairs

FIGURE 2 Proportion of responses "left first" to foveal-temporal flash pairs as a function of the time interval between onsets (negative asynchrony indicates that the peripheral flash was physically first).

first) for maximal uncertainty about temporal order, and the data show that four of the subjects report "foveal first" 75 percent of the time when the foveal flash was in fact physically second. With a single exception, the negative asynchronies are greater with the foveal-temporal than with the foveal-nasal flash pair. The functions shown, however, do not exhibit a systematic difference in slope between flash pairs, indicating that the variability of judgments of perceived temporal order was comparable under the two conditions. It should be noted that, although there are individual differences in the absolute magnitude of the time intervals yielding indeterminancy of temporal order, the slopes of the five individual functions under both conditions of stimulation are similar. In all cases, the range of asynchronies required to bracket the psychometric functions was of the order of 60 to 80 msec.

These results are clearly at variance with those of Hirsh and Sherrick (1). Physical simultaneity does not produce uncertainty regarding the temporal order of two flashes stimulating the retina at two different places: Furthermore, given the large proportions of "foveal first" responses to flash pairs whose actual sequence was peripheral-foveal, the data cannot be discussed in terms of "correct" detection of temporal order. The findings indicate longer latencies to peripheral flashes than to foveal flashes of equal luminance; this result is on the whole consonant with the measures of latency variations as a function of locus of stimulation reported in the literature (2, 3). An interpretation of the effect in terms of the apparent brightness or sensory magnitude of the stimuli appears circular at this point, given the possibility that apparent brightness itself varies as a function of retinal location. None of the subjects here, however, reported perceiving systematic brightness differences between the foveal and peripheral flashes. The difference obtained in the onset asynchronies producing maximal uncertainty between the foveal-nasal and foveal-temporal flash pairs indicates greater latency to a stimulus applied to the temporal side of the retina. This finding presents a trend similar to the average differences between foveal and peripheral reaction times reported by Poffenberger (2).

In Poffenberger's study, the excess of peripheral reaction times over foveal reaction times at 30° on the nasal retina was of the order of 9 msec; at 30° on the temporal retina, of the order of 13 msec. By comparison, the estimates of relative latency obtained here show greater latency differences both between the fovea and periphery and between the nasal and temporal positions. These latency differences are apparently a function of the specific retinal location of stimuli and therefore cannot be attributed to the amount of spatial separation (angular distance) between the stimuli. This conclusion is lent support by the finding (5) that the perceived temporal order of foveal-peripheral flash pairs is dependent on both the laterality (right or left eye) and eccentricity of the peripheral flash.

Summary

Judgments of temporal order to monocular pairs of flashes of equal luminance delivered at various onset asynchronies to the light-adapted fovea and periphery show that uncertainty of temporal order results when the onset of the foveal flash is delayed. Relative latencies vary as a function of peripheral (nasal vs. temporal) locus stimulated.

References

1. I. J. Hirsh and C. E. Sherrick, *J. Exp. Psychol.* 62, 423–432 (1961).
2. M. Lichtenstein and C. T. White, *J. Opt. Soc. Amer.* 51, 1033–1934 (1961); J. D. Rains, *Vision Res.* 3, 239–251 (1963); A. T. Poffenberger, *Arch. Psychol.* 3, 1–73 (1912).
3. A. L. Sweet, *Amer. J. Psychol.* 66, 185–198 (1953).
4. H. Babkoff and S. Sutton, *J. Acoust. Soc. Amer.* 35, 574–577 (1963); R. Efron, *Brain* 86, 261–284 (1963); J. Rutschmann and R. Link, *Perceptual Motor Skills* 18, 345–352 (1964).
5. R. Rutschmann, in preparation.

3.3 Attention and Psychophysical Time[*]

A. B. KRISTOFFERSON

Introduction

The topic of this group of papers is Theory of Central Intermittency and I will address that topic directly by proposing a rather specific hypothesis concerning it and by summarizing some of the experiments which persuade me that it is worthy of consideration. I will also be discussing attention because I find that attention and time are intimately linked and that both can be clarified by considering them together.

The intermittency hypothesis which I am considering suggests that temporal integration of the data processing activities of the human central nervous system is achieved through the control of a "clock" which generates a succession of equally-spaced points in time. These time points occur at the rate of one point every 50 msec, approximately, and under normal conditions this rate is fixed although it differs to a small extent for different individuals. Since the points are generated by an internal mechanism their times of occurrence are independent of the time of occurrence of an external signal.

At least two major functions are performed by the time points. They determine when attention can, but need not, switch fron one input channel to another. And they also determine when messages which are in one stage or state of central processing can be transmitted into a subsequent stage. Thus, the clock is concerned with the time flow of data within the central nervous system and I do not assert that it also controls the flow within afferent channels.

Certain features of attention are implied by these remarks; let me be more explicit about that and indicate how the intermittency hypothesis fits into a more general structure. Attention is thought of here as the result of a gating mechanism which controls the flow of information from the sensory display areas into a central data processor. The gating is all-or-none, the central processor being open to one and only one display area, or channel, at any instant.

This central processor is a single-channel postulate and I must stress that I do not believe that it is part of every information route through the nervous system. It seems to be necessary also to recognize the existence of parallel pathways which by-pass the central processor and its associated attention mechanisms (Kristofferson, 1965). Whether a message may by-pass the central processor probably depends upon the use which must be made of the information content of the message and this, in turn, depends upon the nature of the experimental task. One and the same signal may or may not involve attention, depending

* Reproduced by permission of *Acta Psychologica*, 1967, vol. 27, pp. 93–100. North-Holland Publishing Co., Amsterdam. This research was supported in part by Grant No. NGR-52-059-001 from the National Aeronautics and Space Administration (US) and by Grant No. APB-112 from the National Research Council of Canada.

upon the task and the amount of practice the subject has received.

Information is fed into the central processor from the display areas associated with the various sensory input channels. These channels, and their display areas, are thought of as functionally independent channels and their boundaries are defined in terms of attention. *A channel is a set of all possible messages which can be admitted simultaneously into the central processor.* In different words, it consists of all signals which can be attended at the same instant. We know very little at the present time about the organization of channels defined in this way. It seems likely that there are many of them within each sensory modality although I have chosen to begin with the inter-modality case in the experiments which we have done to date. Once a valid theory of attention switching has been developed, we will then be in a position to use its quantitative power to enable us to map out the boundaries of channels defined by their relation to the central processor.

If attention is aligned with a particular input channel then messages arriving over that channel enter the central processor without delay. A message arriving over an unattended channel will be delayed by the time required to switch attention. It is necessary to assume that an unattended signal can attract attention; that each sensory channel has a name which is known to the attention mechanism and that a gross sorting of inputs occurs at a stage prior to attention. A consideration of brief signals will probably reveal the existence of short term storage at this level also but that is beyond the present argument. It is necessary to assume, however, that a clearly supra-liminal signal can instruct attention to switch to its channel when the next time point occurs and that such a switching operation can occur reliably, at least under ideal conditions.

Finally, something must be said about afferent latency. The problem is to infer the time required to switch attention from one channel to another. To do this it is necessary to know something about the relative times of arrival of messages in the display areas of the two channels. Since afferent latency differs between channels the latency difference itself must be a quantity represented in the theory. I am becoming convinced that one can make no strong assumptions about this. It seems that the afferent latency associated with a particular external signal is not a fixed value (Kristofferson, 1966a). It too depends upon the nature of the task and upon practice and it is necessary to provide experimental operations which allow it to be extracted from the data.

To summarize: there are three major assumptions in the above paragraphs. It is assumed that there are independent channels which are gated one at a time into a central processor. Further, an unattended input can signal the attention mechanism to open its gate. And finally, on occasions when attention must switch channels an increment of time is added to the time required to process the message. The intermittency hypothesis is a specific form of a third assumption which states that the added increment of time is the result of the need to wait until the next time point occurs.

Experimental Results

Next let us turn to some experimental results which have recently been published in greater detail (Kristofferson, 1966b). There are three principal behavioral measurements to consider. One of these is obtained from experiments on *successiveness discrimination* and the other two are derived from *reaction times*. The same two signals, a centrally-fixated spot of light two degrees in diameter and a 2000 cps pure tone, are used in all experiments and the critical events are always signal offsets.

SUCCESSIVENESS DISCRIMINATION

Successiveness discrimination functions are obtained with a two-alternative forced-choice procedure. On each trial two light-sound pairs are presented one after the other. For one pair the offsets are simultaneous. For the other pair the light offset occurs before the sound offset by a duration *t*. The subject must decide whether the light offset preceded the sound offset in the first or in the second pair. The probability of a correct identification of the asynchronous pair increases, of course, as t increases and the resulting function is the successiveness discrimination function.

Successiveness functions are described quite well as linear functions, a finding consistent with the intermittency hypothesis (Kristofferson, 1965), and the data for single individuals are summarized by fitting a straight-line segment to them. The value of t at which the line intersects the $P(C) = .5$ or chance level is called x and the distance spanned by the function as it rises from x to its intersection with $P(C) = 1.0$ is called M. The first quantity, x, is interpreted as the difference in afferent latency between the two channels and it is typically found to be small, averaging about 10 msec in the variation of the experiment under discussion here, and positive, implying more rapid conduction in the auditory channel. The second parameter, M, is the one of particular relevance here. Table 1 shows a value of M for each of eight subjects. The smallest value is 39 and the largest is 77. The mean for the group is 54 msec.

Thus, for the conditions of this experiment when the light offset precedes the sound offset by about 10 msec the auditory and visual messages arrive in the display areas simultaneously. When the time separation is increased from 10 to about 65 msec, the two messages can be discriminated as successive on every trial.

REACTION TIME

The second measurement is derived from the effect of uncertainty as to which channel will contain the next signal upon discrimination reaction time. On some trials the subject is informed of channel beforehand; on the remaining trials he knows that the signal may occur in either channel. By comparing reaction times to a given signal under uncertainty with those obtained under certainty some information can be obtained about the increments of time, δ, which are added by uncertainty.

Defining δ as an increment added by uncertainty on some proportion P of the trials, and assuming nothing about the distribution of δ but designating its mean as Δ, the means and variances under uncertainty (T) and certainty (t) will be related as follows:

$$\bar{T} = \bar{t} + P\Delta$$

$$\sigma_T^2 = \sigma_t^2 + P\sigma_\delta^2 + \left[\frac{1 - P}{P} \right] (\bar{T} - \bar{t})^2.$$

Combining these two equations to eliminate P gives

$$\sigma_\delta^2 = K\Delta - \Delta^2, \qquad (1)$$

in which

$$K = \frac{\sigma_T^2 - \sigma_t^2}{\bar{T} - \bar{t}} + (\bar{T} - \bar{t}). \qquad (2)$$

TABLE 1

Summary of Experimental Results. The Symbols are Explained in the Text. All in msec.

SUBJECT	M	K	Q	q	Alpha
NG	47	78	66	63.7	51.2
NC	61	73	53	62.4	49.8
PM	63	36	65	54.7	49.0
JC	77	62	55	64.4	47.8
KQ	59	33	46	45.7	47.3
GK	46	49	43	46.2	46.2
DC	39	40	45	41.3	45.3
JH	42	52	53	48.7	40.2
Mean	54	53	53	53.4	47.1

Eq. (1) shows the theoretical meaning of a coefficient K: it mediates a relation between the mean and the variance of the distribution of increments added by uncertainty. And K can be calculated from data as shown in eq. (2). K is a most useful quantity since it is independent of the distribution of δ and also of the probability that uncertainty will add an increment to reaction time.

To eliminate long term sources of variance, K is calculated for each session and, since it is based upon relatively few responses it is highly variable. Accordingly, the median value over many sessions is determined for each subject. And, of course, it is obtained for each of the two channels separately.

The two channels do not differ. For the eight subjects the median of K is 49.2 for the visual channel and 50.5 for the auditory channel. For each subject the median of all values of K is shown in Table 1. They range from 33 to 78 and average msec. Further, there is a significant correlation between the two channels over individuals.

The third temporal parameter is Q and it is obtained by modelling the distributions of reaction times for the certainty condition. Many of these distributions are described quite well by a three-stage quantal model. The stages are of two kinds: in one kind the message is delayed for a time equally-likely to be any value from zero to Q while the other kind introduces a delay which is always Q. This analysis is described more fully elsewhere (Kristofferson, 1966b, c); for the moment it is sufficient to state that it generates a reaction time distribution which spans three Q-units and it is from that reasoning that the values of Q in Table 1 were derived for each subject.

Again, a value of Q is gotten for each channel and they are very nearly the same for the two channels, the visual being 56 and the auditory 50 msec. Table 1 shows that Q is the same as K and M on the average for these subjects and that it varies perhaps slightly less over subjects than they do. Also, the values of Q for the two channels are highly correlated over subjects.

In summary, the three behavioral parameters are equal in average absolute value and vary to a similar extent over individuals. They do not differ for the two input channels and they are correlated between channels. While the inter-correlations among the three are insignificant for the data in Table 1, I have found M and K each to be correlated with Q in other studies (Kristofferson, 1966c). Altogether, the evidence strongly suggests that these three behavioral parameters directly reflect the action of a single, central timing mechanism.

For two signals in separate channels most efficiently to be discriminated as successive it is necessary that the subject attend to the channel which contains the first signal at the moment the first signal occurs. He must then switch attention to the second channel, completing the switching in the interval between the two signals. Since, under the intermittency hypothesis, switching can occur only when a time point is generated, it follows that the probability of discriminating two signals as successive is equal to the probability that a time point will occur in the interval between them. Thus, when the interval is x performance is at a chance level and when it is $(x + M)$ the probability is unity and M is the interval between time points. This implies that the time which must elapse between a signal and the next attention switching opportunity is equally-likely to be any value between zero and M.

Uncertainty affects reaction time because the subject is less likely to be attending to the correct channel than he is if he is certain. If this were the sole effect of uncertainty then δ in the above equations would be the time required to switch attention to the correct channel and P would be the proportion of trials on which attention is misaligned. But why should K be numerically equal to the other quantities? The simplest interpretation of K is that δ is a fixed value equal to K. Thus, the variance of δ is zero and eq. (1) is satisfied. This is, of course, a sufficient but not a necessary conclusion. Stated differently, the conclusion is that exactly K msec are added by uncertainty on *P* of the trials and exactly zero on the remaining trials. If the added time is in fact due to switching time then it would seem to follow that exactly 50 msec are required to switch attention from the moment of occurrence of a signal, a conclusion inconsistent with the conclusion of the preceding paragraph.

However, this inconsistency is resolved when one considers the meaning of *Q*. Messages pass through a series of stages within the central processor and they may go from one stage to the next only when a time point occurs. We need discuss only the time required for the message to travel from its display area to the output of stage 1 within the central processor. On trials when attention is aligned with the correct channel the message will travel immediately into stage 1 and be delayed there for some duration (d) equally-likely to be any value in the interval ($0 - Q$). But when attention is misaligned, d msec will be consumed in switching whereupon the message will enter stage 1 at the beginning of a quantum of time. The total time will then be ($d + Q$) and exactly one quantum will be added to reaction time even though the time required for switching is d. This argument assumes that the same clock controls both the switching of attention and delay in stage 1.

The assumptions about attention including the intermittency hypothesis provide a simple and integrated interpretation of all three behavioral time parameters.

ALPHA RHYTHM AND
HYPOTHETICAL CLOCK

Can the functioning of the hypothetical clock be discerned by direct neurophysiological means? With the above results in hand an obvious possibility is the alpha rhythm of the electroencephalogram which has a half-period of about 50 msec. The half-period or interval between zero-crossings might be the relevant measure since one might expect gating to occur at the zero-crossings. Table 1 shows the alpha half-periods for each of the subjects. These figures are averages for two sessions spaced a week apart. Within each session the reliability

of the measurement was satisfactory (.89 and .98) but between sessions it was less adequate (.79). Column *q* in Table 1 gives the mean of the behavioral parameters for each subject. The correlation between *q* and alpha is statistically significant, the four subjects highest on *q* also being highest on alpha.

TABLE 2

Summary of All Data with Eight Subjects Divided at Alpha Median

	Low ALPHA	HIGH ALPHA
M	46.7	62.0
K	43.1	62.1
Q	46.7	59.8
Mean	45.5	61.3
Alpha	44.8	49.5

The analysis in Table 2 adds some information. It indicates that *M, K* and *Q* each may be related to *alpha* to about the same extent, a finding which would be additional support for the conclusion that *M, K* and *Q* are identical, if it bears replication. The data also suggest that *q* and *alpha* are very close in absolute value for subjects on the low end of the scale but that there probably is a significant difference between them for the high subjects. Hence, we must conclude that *q* and *alpha* are probably different for some subjects.

Time does not allow me to bring this account fully up to date. The points discussed above fit together into a coherent structure, at least to my mind, and I offer them as a manageable first step toward an understanding of time and attention. We have done a number of other experiments, most of them on successiveness discrimination, and most of the results agree with the theory set forth here (Kristofferson, 1965, 1966a, c). However, some of the more recent findings, such as the lack of effect of uncertainty about which signal will occur first upon successiveness discrimination (Kristofferson, 1966a), do make the theory seem forced in its present form and I rather expect that we will soon have to revise it in major ways.

Summary

A theory of central intermittency is proposed in which a central temporal process is assumed to control both the switching of attention between input channels and the transfer of information between central stages. Three very different behavioral measurements are integrated by these assumptions and lead to the conclusion that the temporal process can be thought of as a succession of equally-spaced points in time occurring at a rate of approximately twenty points per second.

References

Kristofferson, A. B., 1965. NASA Contract Report, NASA/CR-194.

Kristofferson, A. B., 1966a. NASA Contract Report, NASA/CR-454.

Kristofferson, A. B., 1966b. NASA Contract Report, NASA/CR-427.

Kristofferson, A. B., 1966c. NASA Contract Report, NASA/CR-455.

3.4 Evoked Potentials and Correlated Judgments of Brightness as Functions of Interflash Intervals*

NEIL R. BARTLETT   CARROLL T. WHITE

Bloch's law (the reciprocal relation of luminous flux and duration) applies for visual thresholds for detecting a flash, so long as the duration remains below a critical value. At least for durations less than 1.5 msec Brindley (1) has demonstrated its applicability also to the judgment of brightness of suprathreshold flashes. However, in a study in which flashes of various durations were matched for brightness with a standard 200-msec flash, Katz (2) noted an apparent departure from reciprocity as the duration of the test flash was increased from 8 to 25 msec. Wicke, Donchin, and Lindsley (3)

published records of evoked potentials for foveal stimulation as luminance and duration of the stimulus flash were varied; in commenting on their records they emphasize that, although the latency appeared to be determined largely by the luminance, the wave form and amplitude of the average evoked potentials appeared to depend instead on the product of luminance and duration. Thus, by inference from Bloch's law, wave form and amplitude are closely related to perceived brightness when duration is varied below the critical value. In our study the effects on specific components of evoked cortical potentials were determined for stimuli comprised of pairs of brief flashes (10 μsec) of the same light energy but with different intervals between the flashes in each pair. We further determined whether such changes

* *Science*, May 14, 1965, vol. 148, pp. 980–981. Copyright © 1965 by the American Association for the Advancement of Science. We thank J. A. Hoke for technical assistance. Study supported in part by NSF (grant GB-231) and in part by the Navy Electronics Laboratory.

in the evoked response resemble those found with change in flash flux alone. Over the range of intervals studied there was no obvious difference in the apparent brightness of the fused flash pairs, but forced-choice judgments revealed the brightness order in which they fell.

The recording apparatus is described in detail elsewhere (4). Briefly, a Mnemotron computer of average transients was fed directly by an Offner type R dynograph equipped with a type 9806A input complex. Occipital cortical potentials were recorded with monopolar electrodes. The active electrode was 2.5 cm above the inion and 25 cm to the left of the midline. The reference electrode was attached to the left ear lobe. The computed average potentials from a set of stimulus presentations was recorded on graph paper with a Moseley X-Y plotter, model 2D2. The gain settings on all components of the recording system remained fixed during the study.

Flashes were presented to the right eye by a Grass photostimulator, model PS-2, mounted flush against a window (7.5 cm square) of an electrically shielded room. The subject sat inside the room with his eye approximately 90 cm from the window. One-half of a table-tennis ball was secured over his eye, its edges taped to the skin, thus rendering the flash stimulus a ganzfeld—that is, filling the entire field of vision. A low-level prevailing ganzfeld was provided by light from a projector, with filters, coming through a second window immediately below the first. The constant background was such as to raise the flash threshold about one-tenth logarithmic unit above the level found with full dark-adaptation. The photostimulator was operated at scale 1 (the lowest level) with no filters in some trials and with a 90 percent neutral-density filter for others. With no filters, stimuli were approximately four logarithmic units above threshold. All tests were run with a background of white noise well above the level required to mask clicks from the photostimulator.

Each subject was dark-adapted before being tested. Three subjects served in both phases of the experiment, and another was used only in the psychophysical judgments.

Tests were conducted in two phases. In the first, a train of three pairs of flashes, each pair having a different interflash interval, was presented after a "ready" signal. The subject indicated which pair was brightest, even though he may have felt that he was merely guessing. Intervals between pairs of flashes were approximately 2 seconds. Interflash intervals within pairs were 9, 16, and 25 msec; the order of the pairs in a trio was varied from trial to trial, according to a balanced design for a block of 27 trios. Two blocks, or 54 judgments, were recorded for each of the two flash luminances in a day.

In the second phase, evoked potentials were recorded for pairs of flashes having interflash intervals of 9 or 16 msec; no filter was used over the photostimulator. All four channels of the computer were used, two for the 9-msec condition and two for the 16-msec condition; thus we could check the reliability of the findings. Responses were recorded for 25 flash pairs, all of a set having one interflash interval (separation); 25 were then recorded for the other interval, in *A-B-B-A* order, until 100 responses were obtained for each channel. (For example, if channels 1 and 3 were used for 9-msec separations and channels 2 and 4 for 16-msec separations, the recording sequence would be 1-2-4-3, repeated four times.) The computer stored and averaged the output of the Offner over the 0.5-second interval initiated by the first flash of each pair. Flash pairs followed one another at intervals of 1.1 seconds. Six to eight flash pairs were presented before each set was recorded. Four complete sessions as described were run with each subject.

The data for the first phase (Table 1) show that pairs of flashes with 9-msec interflash intervals were most frequently judged to be brightest, pairs with 25-msec interflash intervals were judged as brightest least frequently. Simple statistical tests (chi square) show the finding to be significant for each of the four subjects at each of the two luminances. Thus, although the subjects were "guessing," forced judgments indicate that the sensory response varied as a function of flash separation. For this method of stimulus presentation, wherein light

TABLE 1

Judgments of the Brightest Pair of Flashes in a Trio.

SUB-JECT	INTERFLASH INTERVAL (MSEC)			N
	9	16	25	
With filter				
E	76	23	9	108
H	72	32	4	108
L	175	35	6	216
S	67	29	12	108
Without filter				
E	84	14	8	106
H	63	30	15	108
L	147	42	27	216
S	65	25	18	108

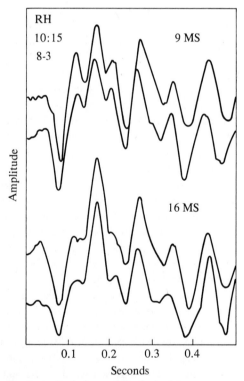

FIGURE 1 Evoked potentials obtained in response to fused flash pairs with interflash intervals of 9 and 16 msec. Onset at start of trace, each trace representing the summation of 100 flash pairs in one channel of the computer. All four records obtained during a single session, in counterbalanced order, as described in text. Negativity downward. Equal gain-setting in all four channels.

is not continuously present for a given interval of time, Bloch's law seems to be valid only as a first approximation.

Figure 1 illustrates the nature of the differences in the evoked potentials obtained with the 9-msec and the 16-msec interflash intervals during a typical recording session. The two top tracings represent the 9-msec condition, while the two bottom tracings represent the 16-msec condition. Differences in the overall wave forms, representing differences in the relative amplitudes of the various components of the complex response pattern, are evident for the two conditions.

The records were analyzed by measuring amplitudes at certain points in time following the onset of stimulation. Three such indices of response amplitude were agreed upon before the experiment was performed, this choice being based on the results of previous studies in our laboratory in which flash luminance was varied systematically. One index was the trough-to-peak amplitude between the large negative peak at a latency of about 80 msec and the positive peak at about 120 msec; a second was the trough-to-peak amplitude for the positive peak at about 210 msec; and the third was the sum of the ordinates, again from the 80-msec trough as a baseline, as measured at 20-msec intervals from 60 to 240 msec. Thus the last was the sum of 10 ordinates specified by latency. Then each index was compared with the corresponding index for each of the two recordings of the evoked potential for the alternative interflash interval in the same block. Thus four comparisons were made in each of the four blocks for each subject. For most of the

TABLE 2

Number of Times (of 16 Comparisons) the Pairs of Flashes with 9-msec Interflash Intervals Produced Amplitudes Greater Than Those with 16-msec Intervals.

SUB-JECT	ORDINATE		MEASURED (SUM OF 10)
	120	210	
E	12	15	15
H	14	14	16
L	15	15	15

comparisons (Table 2), the pairs with the shorter interflash interval show the larger index. Application of the sign test shows that the differences found are statistically significant at a high level of confidence.

These findings, obtained with the average-response computer, attest to the power of this technique for studying the relation between neural and sensory events; it was necessary to employ what is probably the most sensitive psychophysical technique available in order to establish the relative brightness of the various fused flash pairs.

Summary

Computer-averaged evoked potentials were recorded from subjects presented with pairs of flashes having equal light energy but differing in duration of the brief interval separating the flashes. For the experimental conditions studied, the pair was always subjectively fused. Although the brightness did not change noticeably as the interval was varied, the use of the forced-choice psychophysical technique showed that apparent brightness declined with increase in the interval. Analysis of the evoked potentials revealed a correlated change in amplitude and wave form previously demonstrated for changes in flash flux alone.

References

1. G. S. Brindley, *J. Physiol. 118,* 135 (1952).
2. M. S. Katz, *Vision Res.,* in press.
3. J. D. Wicke, E. Donchin, D. B. Lindsley, *Science 146,* 83 (1964).
4. R. G. Eason, L. R. Aiken, C. T. White, M. L. Lichtenstein, *Perceptual Motor Skills 19,* 875 (1964).

3.5 Perceived Number and Evoked Cortical Potentials[*]

M. RUSSELL HARTER   CARROLL T. WHITE

The perceived number of flashes has been compared to the actual number of flashes presented (1–4). In these studies, short trains of flashes (0 to 1000 msec) were presented at a rapid rate (20 to 50 flashes/sec) under conditions where the flashes appeared to be flickering but where each presented flash could not be counted individually. The flashes were somehow grouped into perceptual units of approximately 100 msec, the perceived number of flashes being

* *Science,* April 21, 1967, vol. 156, pp. 406–408. Copyright © 1967 by the American Association for the Advancement of Science. We thank R. G. Eason for assistance. Supported in part of NSF grants GB-4067 and in part by the Navy Electronics Laboratory.

much less than the actual number of flashes presented. For example, when 14 flashes were presented at 30 flashes/sec (a flash-train duration of 430 msec) subjects most frequently reported seeing four flashes, a perceived flash being added for approximately each 100 msec of stimulation (1, 2).

In working with averaged cortical potentials evoked by stimulus conditions similar to those used in the above experiments, we noted (i) that the temporal nature of visually evoked cortical potentials appeared to be related to the number of flashes perceived, and the occurrence of each successive perceived flash appeared to correspond with the occurrence of the successive components of the evoked response pattern, and (ii) that the temporal characteristics of cortical responses evoked by trains of flashes appeared to be similar to those evoked by single flashes. These observations suggest that "the onset of stimulation in some way initiates a process (or processes) which can have a marked influence on the perceptual response to any succeeding stimulation" (3). We investigated the relation between the temporal nature of evoked cortical potentials initiated by single flashes and trains of flashes and the number of flashes that were perceived.

Four subjects were presented trains of flashes containing from 1 to 14 flashes. Longer trains were not used because the variability in judgment becomes too great for our present purposes. The flashes were presented at 33.3 flashes/sec (there was an interval of 30 msec between flashes) and, therefore, the flash-train duration varied from 0 to 390 msec. Since the subjects did not always report the same perceived number of flashes to a given number of flashes presented, the subjects reported their perceptual response after each flash-train presentation. Each subject participated in three experimental sessions; in every session each of the 14 flash-trains was presented 50 times. A given flash-train was randomly selected and presented 25 times; then, another flash-train was randomly selected from those remaining and presented 25 times; this procedure was continued until all the flash-trains were presented. Therefore, the three sessions, four subjects, 14 flash-trains, and 50 flash-train presentations resulted in a total of 7000 observations.

The light flashes (4 mm in diameter and 10 μsec in duration) were viewed binocularly with the subject's eyes 60 cm from the flash source. The subjects fixated a point 5 mm above the flash source. The number (1 to 14) and frequency (33.3 flash/sec) of flashes within each flash-train, as well as the time interval between flash-trains (1.5 second), were controlled with an American Electronic Laboratory model 104A laboratory stimulator which triggered a model PS-2 Grass photostimulator set on intensity 2. The flashes were approximately 2.5 log intensity units above threshold and were surrounded

by a white homogeneous field (18.3 mlam). These conditions elicited a simple sinusoidal evoked cortical potential wave form and a clear perception of flicker.

Evoked cortical potentials were obtained in response to the same flash-trains used to elicit the perceptual judgments. The procedure used for recording evoked cortical potentials has been described (5). Briefly, potentials were recorded monopolarly from the occipital region of the scalp, the active electrode being placed 2.5 cm above the inion and 2.5 cm to the right of the midline. The reference electrode was attached to the right ear lobe. The potentials were amplified by an Offner type R dynograph and averaged with a Mnemotron model 400C computer of average transients. The averaged potentials were recorded on graph paper with a model 135C Moseley autograph (X-Y plotter).

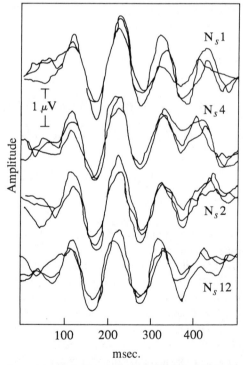

FIGURE 1   Evoked cortical potentials elicited by flash-trains containing 1, 4, 8, and 12 flashes. Flashes were presented at 33.3 flash/sec. Background illumination 602.6 mlam and fixation point directly on flash source. Each of the three superimposed evoked cortical potential traces represents the summation of responses to 100 flash-trains. Negativity downward. Subject is C.W.

The effects of the number of flashes in the flash-train on the resulting evoked cortical potential are illustrated in Figure 1. Consistent with past findings (3), the number of flashes of this size and intensity had no apparent differential effect on the evoked potential wave form. Although Figure 1 contains data from only one subject (C.W.) and four flash-trains (containing 1, 4, 8, and 12 flashes), these data are typical of all the flash-trains and subjects investigated. Therefore, in the remaining figure, the responses elicited by all the flash-trains are combined into a single average potential for each subject and each session.

The relation between evoked potential wave form and the number of flashes perceived is illustrated in Figure 2. The solid lines show the oscillations in the averaged evoked cortical potential wave form and the dotted lines show the frequency that each perceived number of flashes (N_8) was reported. For example, subject C.W. most frequently reported seeing one flash when one to four flashes were presented, two flashes when four to seven flashes were presented, three flashes when seven to ten flashes were presented, and so forth.

The results indicate that there was an initial fusion period, after the onset of stimulation, when the short flash-trains were perceived as fused (the subjects most frequently reported seeing one flash). The duration of the fusion period varied between subjects, ranging from 50 to 100 msec (flash-trains containing three to five flashes). In all cases, this period ended after

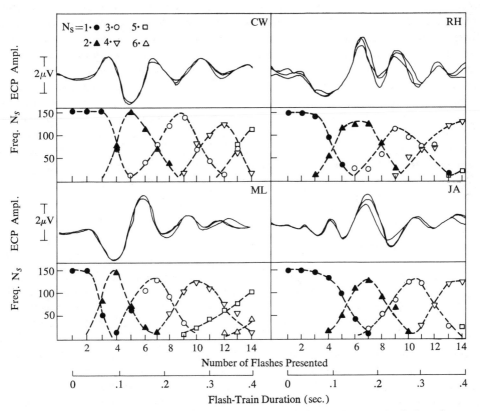

FIGURE 2 Effects of number of flashes presented on evoked cortical potentials (*ECP*) and perceived number of flashes (N_8). Flashes were presented at 33.3 flash/sec. Each of the three superimposed evoked cortical potential traces represents the summation of responses to all flash-trains within a single session (700 flash-trains consisting of 1 to 14 flashes). Negativity downward. Frequency of N_8 reflects the number of times each flash-train was perceived as 1, 2, 3, 4, 5, or 6 flashes, each flash-train being presented 150 times. Due to conduction time-lag, flash-train onset is displaced 35 msec after trace onset.

the first major deflection in the evoked cortical potential wave form. Otherwise, there was no apparent relationship between the evoked potential wave form and the perception of number during this period.

After the initial fusion period, that is, when the subjects most frequently reported seeing two or more flashes, the periodicity of the averaged evoked potentials appears to reflect the rate at which the successive perceived counts were added up to 350 msec after the onset of the flash-train. This relationship did not hold for subjects M.L. and R.H. when flash-trains longer than 350 msec were presented. To compare the rates at which the successive evoked potential components and the successive perceived counts were added, the average interval between the points in time when each N_8 was maximally perceived was compared to the average interval between the corresponding evoked cortical potential peaks or troughs (whichever the case may be). The respective average between count and between component intervals for each subject (in msec) were 103 and 107 (C.W.), 95 and 102 (M.L.), 97 and 90 (R.H.), and 102 and 103 (J.A.). If the similarity of these two average periods is a coincidence, it is indeed a striking one. Furthermore, the fact that both measures have 10 counts per second has considerable generality in view of the number of studies which have reported evoked potential data (3, 6) and perceptual data (1–4) similar to that reported here.

Our results may be summarized as follows: (i) the temporal nature of averaged evoked cortical activity was similar for potentials evoked by both single flashes and trains of flashes; (ii) the first large deflection in the averaged evoked cortical potential wave form appeared to reflect the minimal period of time required for the perception of two flashes, assuming a conduction-time latency of 35 msec; and (iii) after the initial fusion period, the periodicity of the averaged evoked cortical potential wave form appeared to reflect the frequency at which additional perceptual flashes were added for flash-trains up to 350 msec in duration. (Sufficient data were not collected to speculate on this relationship for longer flash-train durations.) These and other results suggest that the onset of stimulation initiates a central process which may have a marked effect on both the cortical and perceptual response to subsequent stimulation.

In conclusion, the findings of our study possibly are related to those of other studies concerned with cortical excitability cycles in humans (7, 8). In these studies, the excitability of the cortex was shown to fluctuate rhythmically after stimulation by a brief flash of light; when a pair of flashes was presented, the amplitude of the evoked cortical potential resulting from the second flash varied as a function of the time between the two flashes. The evoked cortical potential wave form elicited by the first flash may reflect the periodicity of the excitability cycle (8). In humans, a complete excitability cycle had a duration of approximately 100 msec, which is in accord with the duration of each perceived flash and evoked potential oscillation in our experiment. Apparently the flashes presented within a single excitability cycle (possibly reflected by the periodicity of the evoked cortical potential wave form) were grouped into a single perceptual unit and were perceived as a single flash. These findings are relevant to the current theoretical interest in the concept of central intermittency in perception (2, 9).

Summary

Evoked cortical potentials and the number of flashes perceived were compared when subjects were presented with short trains of flashes under conditions where each presented flash could not be counted individually, but the train of flashes appeared to be flickering (1 to 14 flashes at 33.3 flashes per second). The rate at which each successive perceived flash was added appeared to correspond with the rate at which the successive components of the evoked response pattern were added. The temporal nature of this pattern was similar for both single flashes and trains of flashes. The results suggest that the onset of stimulation triggers a process which has a marked effect on both the cortical and perceptual response to subsequent stimulation.

References

1. Forsyth, D. M. and A. Chapanis, *J. Exp. Psychol. 56*, 385 (1958).
2. White, C. T., *Psycholog. Monogr. 77*, Whole No. 575 (1963).
3. White, C. T. and R. G. Eason, *Psycholog. Monogr. 80*, Whole No. 632 (1967).
4. Cheatham, P. G. and C. T. White, *J. Exp. Psychol. 44*, 447 (1952); C. T. White and P. G. Cheatham, *J. Exp. Psychol. 58*, 441 (1959).
5. Eason, R. G., L. R. Aiken, C. T. White, and M. Lichtenstein, *Perceptual Motor Skills 19*, 875 (1964).
6. Eason, R. G., D. Oden, and C. T. White, *Electroencephalog. Clin. Neurophysiol.*, in press.
7. Ciğănek, L., *Ann. N.Y. Acad Sci. 112*, Art. *1*, 241 (1964).
8. Gastaut, H., A. Roger, J. Corriol, and R. Naquet, *Electroencephalog. Clin. Neurophysiol. 3*, 401 (1951).
9. Bertelson, P., *Quart. J. Exp. Psychol. 18*, 153 (1966); M. R. Harter, *Psychol. Bull.*, in press; D. B. Lindsley, *Electroencephalog. Clin. Neurophysiol. 4*, 443 (1952); J. M. Stroud, in *Information Theory in Psychology*, H. Quastler, Ed. (Free Press, Glencoe, Ill., 1955), p. 174; N. Wiener, *Cybernetics* (Wiley, New York, 1948), pp. 156–167.

3.6 Visual Perceptive Simultaneity and Masking of Letters Successively Presented*

PAUL FRAISSE

Under what temporal conditions are letters successively presented seen as simultaneous or successive? This problem has not received much attention. Using four dots or lights arranged in such a way as to form a diamond, Lichtenstein (1961) found that, when flashed successively, the four dots were perceived as forming the diamond if the total duration between the lighting of the first and fourth dot did not exceed 125 msec, variations in the temporal intervals having no effect within these limits. Results are not so precise when letters or words are used as stimuli; however, Hylan (1903) had noticed that six letters are viewed as simultaneous, whatever the order of presentation may be, provided the total duration does not exceed 80 msec. Stein (1928) showed that the letters of a word when flashed successively, in direct or in reverse order, were perceived in the same way as if the letters were presented simultaneously, provided that total duration of successive flashes did not exceed 100 msec.

* Reproduced by permission of *Perception & Psychophysics*, 1966, vol. 1, pp. 285–287.

The purpose of this work is to verify and render more precise these results, and particularly: (a) to compare the laws of this phenomenon with letters or dots in a geometrical pattern; (b) to compare the laws of perceptive integration to those of lateral masking (or metacontrast) between letters themselves, when we change the duration of the stimuli and of the interval.

Method

With a three channel tachistoscope (Scientific Prototype model) the subject is presented with a preliminary stimulus (followed by a light interval of the same luminance) after which a second follows.

Six-letter words of which letters 1-3-5 form a word and letters 2-4-6 another, were chosen. Example: F L E U R I formed with F E R and L U I. The first and the second words are respectively the first and the second stimuli. Letters are presented in such a way that in simultaneous presentation both stimuli are perceived as forming only one word. Capital

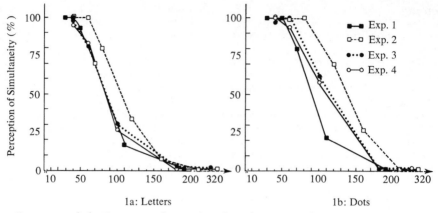

1a: Letters   1b: Dots

FIGURE 1a and 1b   Percentage of perception of simultaneity according to the total duration
(from the beginning of S_1 to the end of S_2).

letters are used (letters were 4 mm high and 3 to 4 mm thick). We used eight words of the same type as F L E U R I. Each subject was presented with two different words in order to neutralize the structural and frequency effects of the words.

For figurative material we used black dots in a diamond pattern divided into two stimuli (S_1: two vertical dots; S_2: two horizontal dots) and in an hexagon pattern divided into two triangles of 3 points each.

The durations of S_1, S_2, and the interval determined four experimental situations:

Experiment 1: $S_1 = S_2 = 15$ msec, with a varying interval from 0 to 320 msec.

Experiment 2: $S_1 = S_2$, varying simultaneously from 20 to 180 msec; interval $= 0$.

Experiment 3: S_1 varies from 20 to 320 msec; $S_2 = 20$ msec; interval $= 0$.

Experiment 4: $S_1 = 20$ msec; S_2 varies from 20 to 320 msec; interval $= 0$

In each situation there were eight different subjects (male and female students). The presentation order (figures or words) was counterbalanced in each situation. For four subjects the variable duration was presented first in increasing order and then in decreasing order; the inverse order was used for the other four. Words and figures were presented twice at each step of duration.

As a result of our experimental design (eight subjects by two orders—increasing and decreasing—by two presentations), we obtained 64 values for letters and figures.

The subject was asked to say: (a) whether or not he perceived the stimuli successively; (b) the letters viewed in each stimulus.

Results

We have classified the responses of the subjects according to two categories: simultaneous perception or successive perception, even in the case of the content of the stimuli being partly perceived, or the case of interference (letters from the second stimulus being given as ones of the first or inversely).

The results show that experimental situations are comparable only if the total duration of the stimulation, from the beginning of S_1 to the end of S_2, is taken into account. The longer the duration, the more often there is perception of succession (Figure 1a).

The phenomenon develops in the same way, whether or not there is an interval between the stimuli and whether or not the first stimulus is shorter, equal or longer than the second. It appears, however, that the situation where both stimuli have the same length, without an interval, is more favorable than the others.[1] Results with dots are the same (Figure 1b). This is true provided the duration of exposure of S_1

---

[1] A further experiment has confirmed that, when a total duration of 100 ms is used, simultaneity is always perceived more easily when S_1 is higher than S_2 and when there is no interval (Fraisse, 1968. L'intégration et le masquage de lettres présentées en succession rapide. *Année Psychol., in press*).

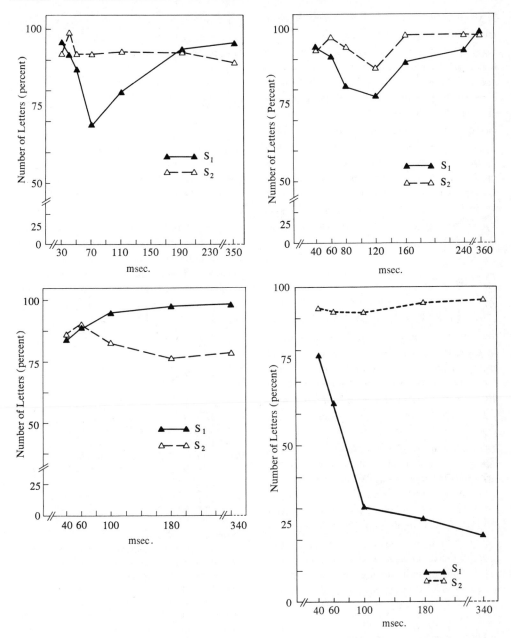

FIGURES 2, 3, 4, 5 Percentage of recognized letters according to the total duration from the beginning of S_1 to the end of S_2.

or S_2 is sufficient (here from 15 to 20 msec). We must add that individual differences are important though for any subject numerical values obtained with letters and dots are almost the same. It can be concluded that in the case of durations less than 80–120 msec simultaneity rather than succession will be perceived.

In order to study the masking effect we have taken the number of perceived letters belonging to the first or the second stimulus, irrespective of the order in which they were given by the subjects, whether forming a word or isolated, and whether or not perceptive simultaneity occurred.

The rate of perceived letters related to the total duration of presentation $S_1 + i + S_2$

is given in Figures 2, 3, 4, 5. Lateral masking effects are closely linked to the particular situations. In Experiment 1 (Figure 2) there is a maximum backward masking for a total duration of 70 msec, i.e., for a duration of 55 msec between the beginning of S_1 and the beginning of S_2. In Experiment 2 (Figure 3) the masking has the same nature with a maximum for a duration of 60 msec between the beginning of S_1 and beginning of S_2. In Experiment 3 (Figure 4), S_1 increases and there is a forward masking which increases with the duration of S_1. In Experiment 4 there is a backward masking which increases with the increase of duration of S_2.

Discussion

Visual perceptive simultaneity appears within the same temporal limits, be the stimuli letters or geometric figures. Results are not affected by the meaning of the stimuli. On the other hand, the relative duration of the stimuli and the interval play an almost insignificant role.

These results confirm those obtained by the above-mentioned authors and lend fresh support to the theses of those who believe in the existence of a psychological moment (Stroud, 1955; Lichtenstein, 1961; White, 1963).

However, specific modes of masking of the letters correspond to the diverse temporal conditions of the stimulation. We confirmed (a) the curve in U reported by Kolers (1962) and J. Blanc-Garin (1965), Weisstein and Haber (1965) and (b) an increasing effect of the masking when S_2 increased, S_1 being constant and an increasing forward masking when S_1 increased, S_2 being constant.

These phenomena of masking cannot be

[2] Our recent experiments show that the perception of simultaneity is better when forward and backward masking are minimum and counterbalanced, for a total duration of 100 ms.

explained as a result of the processes which determine perceptive simultaneity, even if they take place in the same scale of duration.[2]

Summary

Two sets of letters S_1 and S_2 when presented successively are perceived as simultaneous if the total duration of time from the beginning of S_1 to the end of S_2 is kept constant, whatever the duration of $S_{1'}$, $S_{2'}$ or the interval. The same law applies in the case of dots arranged to form geometrical figures. On the other hand, the phenomena of meta contrast with letters are modified when the relative duration of $S_{1'}$, $S_{2'}$, and the interval vary. Thus perceptive integration and masking depend upon different processes.

References

Blanc-Garin, J. Quelques problèmes posés par l'étude du métacontraste visuel. *Psychol. Franc.,* 1965, *65,* 147–154.

Blanc-Garin, J. Les relations temporelles dans le masquage latéral visuel. *Année Psychol.,* 1966, *66/2,* in press.

Hylan, J. P. The distribution of attention. I. *Psychol. Rev.,* 1903, *10,* 373–403.

Kolers, P. A. Intensity and contour effects in visual masking. *Vis. Res.,* 1962, *2,* 277–294.

Lichtenstein, M. Phenomenal simultaneity with irregular timing of components of the visual stimulus. *Percept. mot. Skills,* 1961, *12,* 47–60.

Stein, W. Tachistoskopisch Untersuchungen über das Lesen. *Archiv. ges. Psychol.,* 1928, *64,* 301–346.

Stroud, J. M. The fine structure of psychological time. In H. Quastler (Ed.), *Information theory in psychology.* Glencoe, Ill. The Free Press, 1955. pp. 174–207.

Weisstein, N., and R. N. Haber, A U-shaped backward masking function in vision. *Psychon. Sci.,* 1965, *2,* 75–76.

White, C. T. Temporal numerosity and the psychological unit of duration. *Psychol. Monogr.,* 1963, no. 575.

CHAPTER *4*

Reaction Time

4.1 Theories of the Psychological Refractory Period*

MARILYN C. SMITH

When two stimuli are presented in rapid succession, the reaction time (RT) to the second stimulus is typically prolonged compared with the RT to that stimulus when it is presented alone. This increase is maximal at the shortest interstimulus interval (ISI), and declines as the ISI is increased until at some value of ISI no further delay is encountered. This phenomenon has been studied using both continuous and discrete responses. Continuous responses are usually required in a tracking task: The S must keep his pencil on a moving target, and measurement of the delay in responding to changes in the direction of movement of the target is possible. Discrete responses are those most typically used: The S has two keys before him, and is told to press one key when the first stimulus comes on, the second key when the next stimulus comes on. In both cases, it is possible to vary the interval between the stimuli, hence varying the interval between the required movements. Surveys of such experiments can be found in several recent analytical reviews (Adams, 1964, 1966; Bertelson, 1966; Reynolds, 1964; Welford, 1960).

The delayed second RT (RT$_2$) suggests the presence of a limiting mechanism in the processing system, and various theories have been put forward to explain the nature of this

mechanism. This review attempts to state the various theories which have been proposed, and then examine their validity on the basis both of experimental findings and of logical consistencies. Because they are ad hoc theories, based on the finding that RT$_2$ declines as the ISI increases, they all "predict" this particular finding. Consequently, the various hypotheses must be judged on the basis of their other predictions.

General Method

Typically, Ss are presented with two stimuli in rapid succession and are required to make a key-press response to each stimulus. Because the main issues surround the *central* restraints in the processing of successive stimuli, attempts have been made to eliminate peripheral contributors to RT$_2$ delay. On the response side, the use of one hand has the complication of inertia in reactivating the same hand for the second response after it has completed the first response (Welford, 1959). The added delay of getting the mass in motion adds to RT$_2$ and artificially heightens the delay. Consequently, while some Es (Telford, 1931; Vince, 1948) employed only one hand for both responses, this is rare; in most studies, a different hand is employed for each response. Thus, for example, if two visual stimuli are employed, one on the left and one on the right, S would press the left key upon onset of the left light and the

* From: Marilyn C. Smith, "Theories of the Psychological Refractory Period," *Psychological Bulletin,* 1967, vol. 67, pp. 202–213. Copyright (1967) by the American Psychological Association, and reproduced by permission. The author is indebted to Wayne A. Wickelgren for his advice and assistance.

right key upon onset of the right light, using a different hand for the two responses.

On the sensory side, some Es have employed a visual-visual paradigm, some an auditory-auditory design, and others a visual-auditory paradigm. In all cases, Ss can clearly see the two stimuli, so that there is no question of delay due to perceptual interference effects such as masking. Using the visual-visual configuration, there is the possibility that some eye movement may be required from the position of Signal A to the position of Signal B, which might artificially inflate the delay effect. Probably the best arrangement is one in which the signals are visual and auditory, and where each signal receives a response by a different hand. Here there are no apparent contaminating peripheral effects for either stimuli or responses.

Proposed Theories

The explanations employed may be placed into three general categories. First, there is the theory that there is some physiological inhibitory effect of the first stimulus (s_1) upon the second (s_2)—the "central refractoriness" theory.

The second group of theories attribute the delay in RT_2 not to the influence of the first stimulus, which is considered to play the role of a warning signal initiating the foreperiod before presentation of the second stimulus, but to S's preparatory state, which is influenced by the values of ISI employed. These are referred to as "preparatory state" theories.

The final theoretical position is that somewhere in the arc of perception—response-selection—response-performance, there is a "single channel" which cannot process both stimuli simultaneously, with the result that the second stimulus must be "held in store" until after the processing of the first. These are the "single channel" theories.

CENTRAL REFRACTORINESS THEORY

Thorndike (1927), observing that Ss tended to avoid sequences of numbers in a task where they were instructed to randomly choose some number from 0 to 9 after the presentation of a word, suggested that the avoidance of sequences might be due to a "fundamental intrinsic unreadiness of a process to act again soon after it has acted." Such a possibility was given some support by the finding that this avoidance of sequences was greatly diminished when the interval between words was increased to 5 sec. Dodge (1927), commenting upon Thorndike's paper, suggested that this hypothesis could be tested by reducing interresponse times, arguing that "if various time intervals between stimuli could be used, a suppositious refractory phase in the barrier against repetition should theoretically be more apparent the nearer the responses approach each other in time."

The first germane experiments were done by Telford (1931). Telford presented successive auditory stimuli with ISIs ranging from .5 to 4 sec., and found that RTs were greatest following the shortest interval. He postulated that following some event in the chain of processes leading from the reception of the signal to the responding action, there is a central refractory state, analogous to that found in nerve fibres, but of much longer duration—up to about 1 sec. Telford called this the "psychological refractory period," a name now commonly applied to the general phenomenon of delay in RT_2 at short ISIs.

Let us examine some predictions of this theory:

1. The interval over which a delay in RT_2 should occur would be a fixed amount, equal to the value of the refractory period. Therefore, as the ISI is increased between the two stimuli, the delay in RT_2 should decrease, until at an ISI equal to or greater than the refractory period, there is no further delay.

While the delay in RT_2 does decline as the ISI is increased, the interval over which a delay occurs does not appear to be a constant, such as one could predict for excitation of nerve or muscle. The ISIs over which delays occur vary greatly depending upon the particular experimental conditions.

2. The delay in RT_2 should be unaffected by the uncertainty (i.e., amount of information) associated with the first stimulus, since speed

of conduction and resulting refractoriness should not be influenced by the number of alternatives from which the stimulus was selected.

Careful study of the delay in RT_2 as a function of the informational content of the first stimulus has not been done. The most relevant findings are those of Kay and Weiss (1961), who found that as the time uncertainty of the first stimulus was increased, by varying the range of foreperiods prior to the first stimulus, the delay in RT_2 also increased. This study will be presented in some detail under the discussion of preparatory state theories.

Thus, of the predictions made by the central refractoriness theory, only the prediction that there will be a delay in RT_2 which declines with increasing ISI has been substantiated by experimental data. Further, as there is no physiological evidence of refractoriness in any part of the nervous system for durations as long as those required, this theory does not seem to provide an adequate explanation.

PREPARATORY STATE THEORY

Many experimenters have argued that the prolonged second RT is in no way due to the influence of the first stimulus. Rather, they believe, delays in responding to the second stimulus can be explained along lines identical with those for explaining delays in responding to a single stimulus, namely, the range, frequency, or duration of the foreperiod preceding the stimulus. Preparatory state theories fall into two general categories:

Expectancy Theories. In a single RT study, Mowrer (1940) found that signals occurring before or after a modal or mean interval were reacted to relatively more slowly, and he explained this as being due to decreased expectancy at values other than the mean. Expectancy in this context means learning about the temporal relationships between events, and is the behavioral potential for "knowing" when a stimulus will occur and having a preparatory set for the response. Expectancy theorists, accepting the hypothesis that the mean ISI represents

the point of peak expectancy, explain the observed delay in RT_2 by stating that when the ISI between the two stimuli is randomly varied, as is usually done, Ss develop a high expectancy for the second stimulus (s_2) at the mean value of ISI. Consequently, when very short ISIs are presented, S's expectancy of s_2 is minimal, with the result that RT_2 is very high. As the ISI increases, the expectancy that s_2 will arrive momentarily increases, with a corresponding decline in RT_2.

The expectancy theory as applied to the psychological refractory period closely parallels the expectancy theory which has been proposed in the field of vigilance, and in some respects is indebted to the thinking on expectancy that has developed from vigilance research (Baker, 1959; Buckner & McGrath, 1963; Deese, 1955; Frankmann & Adams, 1962). In the vigilance situation there is a series of stimulus events stretched out over a long time period, with the ISIs statistically defined, just as they are in experiments on the psychological refractory period. The way in which expectancy is applied to the vigilance situation and its similarity to the notion of expectancy in the psychological refractory period may be seen from the following statement by Baker (1963):

> The expectancy hypothesis is a statement that the probability of detection of a signal in a vigilance task is greatest when the signal occurs after an interval which is equivalent to the mean of the ISI's preceding the interval in question: detection probability is low immediately after a signal, increases as the mean ISI of the preceding series is approached, and, if not reinforced by the occurrence of a signal, again decreases [p. 127].

One formulation of the expectancy theory as it applies to the psychological refractory period has been proposed by Elithorn and Lawrence (1955). In probability terms, they explained the delay as follows:

> At time 0 at the end of the foreperiod one of two responses will almost certainly be required and the probability of each stimulus response situation occurring then is approximately 0.5. The arrival of a single stimulus raises the probability of its own response to the region of 1.0, but at the same time it

causes the probability of the alternative situation to fall abruptly. Since the latter situation will arise sometime the probability that it will occur at the next time interval if it has not already occurred will increase with the passage of time until towards the end of the cycle this probability approaches unity. If, therefore, the observed RT to the second stimulus is inversely proportional to the hypothetical state of preparation, expectancy or probability of the appropriate response mechanisms, then it may be expected to be longer when this stimulus occurs shortly after the disjunctive situation. Similarly, it may be expected to approach that of a simple RT as ISI increases [p. 125].

Elithorn and Lawrence have, in addition, employed the auxiliary concept of inhibition of response. They argued that during the foreperiod preceding the first signal, S's expectancy that the stimulus may require a response by either hand causes increased excitability in both limbs. As soon as the first signal appears, the hand in which a response is not required is inhibited to prevent the occurrence of the wrong response. This inhibition dissipates during the ISI, and, together with heightened preparedness for the second response, results in declining RTs with the second hand as the interval increases. Thus, the delayed RT_2 can be explained as an interplay of inhibition and expectancy.

The theory makes the following predictions:

1. It is not the absolute but rather the relative value of the ISI which determines the delay in RT_2. If the majority of ISIs are small, so that S develops an expectancy for s_2 very soon after s_1, then delays should not be maximal at the shortest ISI.

Some support for this prediction of the expectancy theory is provided by Adams (1962), who varied the frequency of presentation of the shortest ISI (100 ms). He argued that if expectancy is an important variable, S should be more expectant for s_2 at short ISIs when a greater frequency of small intervals is used, and therefore there should be less delay in RT_2. His results support the expectancy view, in that overall RT_2 did decline in the group with greatest frequency of the smallest ISI. One could argue that since this was the most expected ISI,

RT_2 should have been fastest here. However, although the overall RT_2 latency declined, the RT to the signal at the shortest ISI (100 ms) was still greater than at any other ISI.

2. If the second stimulus were always given at some fixed period after the first (i.e., constant ISI), S should come to develop maximum expectancy at that value, and no further delays would be observed.

This prediction has not been supported. Since an expectancy theory states that the delay in RT_2 is due exclusively to subjective uncertainty about arrival times of the second signal, then if the ISI between signals is fixed, thus eliminating any uncertainty, no delay is predicted. In order to test this, Borger (1963) presented Ss with two stimuli, both either auditory or visual. His procedure was as follows: (a) ready click; (b) foreperiod (500 ms); (c) Signal 1; (d) ISI—fixed for any run of 30 presentations and varied between runs from 50 to 800 ms; (e) Signal 2. In addition to the "double runs," where S had to respond to two stimuli, there were also "single runs," in which S responded only to the second signal, the first being the same on every occasion and different from either of those normally given. During a single run, S removed his hand from the key corresponding to the first stimulus. Borger's results clearly do not support an expectancy theory, for even with ISI constant, there is a significant delay in RT_2 in the double runs. For single runs, however, RT_2 for short ISIs is no longer than for long ISIs. Thus, when S is required to respond to two stimuli, there is a delay in RT_2 at short ISIs, even if the interval between the two stimuli is fixed.

Borger's procedure of using blocks of fixed-length ISIs with the same Ss might be criticized on the grounds that it builds temporal expectancy within each block which may have some influence on subsequent blocks. However, similar results were obtained by Creamer (1963), who used an audiovisual task and assigned an independent group to each of five different ISI conditions (0, 100, 200, 400, and 800 ms). Creamer wanted expectancy out of the picture because it was his contention that delay in RT_2 could be produced by event uncertainty alone, even with complete time certainty. The delay function was plotted from the means of the independent groups. Once again, even with fixed ISIs, delays were found in RT_2. Delay was maximal at the shortest ISI and declined as the interval was increased.

3. Finally, Davis (1965a) has performed an experiment which suggests that the delayed second RT cannot be attributed solely to the statistical nature of the ISI series (i.e., range, duration, and frequency of the particular ISIs). He wanted to demonstrate that the effects are due mainly to the influence of the first signal, rather than the distribution of ISIs. Consequently, in one condition he eliminated the first signal altogether and substituted for it a "spontaneous" emitted response by S. The S pressed a key with his left hand whenever he chose; and at some interval following this, at the same ISIs used in the usual situation where two signals are presented, that is, 50 to 500 ms, a visual signal appeared to which S pressed a key with his right hand. The results were very clear. No delays were found in the RT, even with an ISI of 50 ms. This is in marked contrast to the large delay found in the second RT in experiments where S must respond to both stimuli. This would seem to support the theory that the delay is in some way influenced by the first signal.

It should be mentioned that the theoretical basis of this experiment has been criticized (Annett, 1966; Karlin, 1965) on the grounds that the initiation of the preparatory period may not necessarily begin with the observed efferent aspect of the response. Rather, it is possible that Ss do not emit the motor response until preparation for the signal is complete. In defending his position, Davis (1965b, 1966) has argued that if the period of preparation is begun prior to the occurrence of the spontaneous response, then the effective ISI period is increased:

> [Since] the effects of temporal uncertainty are known to increase with an increase in the range of intervals used . . . there should be a greater effect due to temporal uncertainty in the situation with the longer range of intervals (the spontaneous response situation) than in the situation with the

shorter range of intervals (the two-signal situation). Yet, results were in the opposite direction [1966, p. 180].

Based on the experimental findings reported here, an explanation of the delay in RT_2 solely in terms of S's expectancy of when the second stimulus will appear is not sufficient. Delays are observed even when S's expectancy is very high (Borger, 1963; Creamer, 1963), and no delays are observed when S does not have to select a response to a first stimulus, even though the set of ISIs employed is identical (Davis, 1965a).

Readiness Theory. A more satisfactory explanation of the delay in terms of preparatory set is given by the "readiness" theory (Poulton, 1950). Unlike expectancy theory, which accounts for the delay in terms of temporal learning, this theory states that Ss require a fixed period of time to prepare a response to a stimulus. Poulton (1950, p. 106) distinguished between expectancy, on the one hand, as delay which is "due purely to the subject not being ready for a response because he was not expecting to have to make it, and so had not prepared himself," and readiness, on the other hand, as delay which "was at least partly due to the subject not being *able* [italics added] to prepare himself." Thus, while the finding of delayed RT_2 with fixed ISI presents serious difficulties for a theory which bases the delay on temporal learning, it may still be handled by a readiness theory which states that even if S knows precisely when s_2 is coming, he requires a minimum period of time to prepare a response. With any interval shorter than this minimum, preparation will be less than optimum, and delays will be found. If s_1 is considered to be the warning signal for RT_2, then the ISI between s_1 and s_2 is analogous to the foreperiod, that is, the period between the warning signal and the stimulus in a single RT study. Evidence that delays occur in the single-reaction situation analogous to those found in the two-response situations would provide strong support for the theory that delays in RT_2 are due to lack of readiness.

Such support has been provided by Nickerson (1965). He performed a simple RT study employing a range of foreperiods similar to that used in the double-stimulation studies, that is, 100–900 ms. It was found that as the foreperiod between the stimulus and the warning signal (a visual signal similar to the first) was increased, simple RT was maximum at the shortest foreperiod and declined in a manner analogous to that found in situations where two reactions are required. Further, both the absolute and the relative duration of the foreperiod was found to be important. By varying the range of the foreperiods employed, he found that RT at a particular ISI was greater if that was the shortest ISI used than if the ISI fell in the middle of the series. This suggests that both expectancy and readiness may affect RT, since RT was found to decline both as the absolute and the relative duration of foreperiod increased. Thus, if S is completely ready (as in the Davis, 1965a, experiment, where S pressed a key to initiate the ISI), expectancy has no influence on RT. However, if S is not completely ready, then while readiness plays the predominant role, delay is also influenced to some extent by expectancy.

Finally, an experiment performed by Kay and Weiss (1961) suggests that the interval between the first and second stimulus is not the only determinant of the delay in RT_2. They wanted to show that the delays in RT_2 are similar to delays occurring when only a single reaction is required, and carried out an investigation specifically to compare simple and serial RT. The design of their experiment was as follows: (a) S pressed a ready key; (b) foreperiod of 1, 2, 3, or 4 sec; (c) Click 1; (d) ISI of 25–1000 ms; (e) Click 2. Eight conditions were employed. In Conditions 1 and 2, only the first click was given, and simple RTs were examined after regular and irregular foreperiods. However, we are more interested in the remaining six conditions of the experiment, where both clicks were given, with the foreperiod and ISI being varied either randomly or regularly. The S responded in some cases to both signals, in other cases only to one. The various conditions they employed

are shown in Table 1. It was found that in all cases RT_2 was maximal at the shortest ISI and declined as the interval was increased. At the shortest ISI, the mean RTs to the second signal for Conditions 3 through 8 were 155, 175, 189, 192, 244, and 265 ms, respectively. These results indicate that RT increases at the minimum ISI with the increasing uncertainty of the experimental conditions. Since RT increased in both the single- and double-response situations with increasing time uncertainty, Kay and Weiss concluded that "one possible explanation for the delay in responding to the second signal is along lines identical with those for explaining variability in the speed of responding to the first." However, although increasing uncertainty does lead to increased RT, there is a very important *quantitative* difference observed when S is required to make a response to the first stimulus, compared to the situation where no response to it is required, all other conditions being equal. Comparing RTs in Conditions 5 and 7 and in Conditions 6 and 8, RT was increased by 55 ms in the former when a response was required, and by 73 ms in the latter. Both these increases were significant.

TABLE 1

Summary of Conditions Employed by Kay and Weiss (1961)

Condition	Foreperiod	ISI	Signal Responded to
3	Regular	Regular	2
4	Regular	Irregular	2
5	Irregular	Regular	2
6	Irregular	Irregular	2
7	Irregular	Regular	1 & 2
8	Irregular	Irregular	1 & 2

On the basis of this study by Kay and Weiss, we might note that (a) the delay in RT_2 is significantly increased when Ss are required to make a response to s_1; and (b) the amount of delay is a function of the time uncertainty associated with s_1. In fact, RT_2 is greater if the first signal is irregular (Condition 5) than if the second signal is irregular (Condition 4). If increasing the time uncertainty of s_1 may be assumed to increase the time required to process the informaion associated with s_1, then this suggests that the delay in RT_2 is a function not only of the ISI, but of the processing time of the first stimulus. Such a view is further supported by the findings of Adams and Chambers (1962) and of Reynolds (1966) that with a constant ISI (time certainty), RT_2 is not delayed if the first response represents only a simple reaction (stimulus certainty). On the other hand, even with a constant ISI a delay *is* found if the first response represents a disjunctive or choice reaction. Consequently, the delay appears to be primarily a function of the type of response selection associated with the first stimulus, rather than the nature of the ISI series. This finding would support a "single channel" theory, discussed below.

SUCCESSIVE PROCESSING— "SINGLE CHANNEL" THEORIES

The final type of explanation proposed to account for this phenomenon is that somewhere in the central mechanisms there is a "channel" of limited capacity, which cannot attend to both response requirements simultaneously. Views differ as to where in the arc of sensory-input–response-selection–response-performance this limited capacity mechanism is to be found. Some hypotheses place it on the sensory side and others on the response side, but most believe that the limitation occurs at the response-selection stage. A brief summary of these theories follows.

Perceptual Delay. Broadbent (1958) has suggested that there may be a quantizing of perception into samples of about $\frac{1}{3}$ sec. He arrived at this figure on the basis of findings by Cherry and Taylor (1954), who showed that there was impairment in the understanding of speech when it was switched on and off at the rate of 3 cps. If this is taken as evidence that perception is quantized in units of about $\frac{1}{3}$ sec, then the delay on RT_2 is explained in the following way: When the first signal is given, S immediately closes his sample, and relays the information on for the

selection of a response. However, the next quantum will not be relayed for another $\frac{1}{3}$ sec. If the second signal arrives immediately after the first, it will have to wait until the $\frac{1}{3}$ sec has elapsed before it is relayed. It therefore follows that the longer the arrival of s_2 is delayed after the relaying of s_1, the less time it has to be held in store before being sent on. If it arrives after an interval greater than $\frac{1}{3}$ sec, there should be no delay at all.

The theory predicts the following:

1. If two stimuli arrive exactly simultaneously, they should be packaged in the same quantum, and no delay in responding to the second stimulus should occur.

This prediction is not supported by the data. Although some *E*s report less delay at 0 ms than at slightly larger ISIs (Elithorn & Lawrence, 1955; Marill, 1957), there are no reports of no delay at all, and most experimenters have found maximum delay with ISIs of 0 ms (Adams, 1962; Creamer, 1963; Davis, 1956; Reynolds, 1966).

2. Delays in RT_2 should be a function solely of the ISI between the two stimuli. The time required to select a response to s_1 should in no way influence the amount of time s_2 must be held in store.

This prediction appears to be contradicted by the findings of Kay and Weiss (1961), who found that the delay in RT_2 tended to increase with time uncertainty of the first stimulus. However, this problem has not been carefully studied.

3. Since the delay is caused by a perceptual process occupying a fixed time interval (the duration of the quantum), some constant value over which the delay exists should be found.

Though many experiments have been done on this question, no such fixed value has been found, and the delay appears to vary with the conditions of the particular experiment.

4. If the delay were due to a quantizing of perceptions, it would seem highly unlikely that perceptions from all modalities would be placed in the same unit. Thus, if the first stimulus were given in one modality, and the second in another modality, no delays in the transmission of the second response would be expected.

Davis (1957) tested this by presenting S with two successive stimuli, the first consisting of an auditory click, the second of a visual flash 50 to 500 ms after the first; the interval between the two stimuli was randomly varied. Once again, delays of the usual magnitude were found. This experiment tends to indicate that the delay is probably not on the sensory side of the arc.

Although this theory has the advantage of trying to explain the delay as the result of normal perceptual processes which can be demonstrated in other perceptual situations, such as Cherry and Taylor's auditory interference experiments, it does not appear to be supported by the present data.

Inhibition of Response. Other theorists believe that the delay occurs in the operation of the response mechanisms, rather than in the perceptual mechanism. Such a hypothesis was expressed by Reynolds (1964), who believes that in the double-stimulation situation, competing responses of the type described by Berlyne (1960) are elicited by the two stimuli. He described this as follows: "When events are uncertain, responses to both must be held in readiness to insure maximum efficiency of response to both. When either stimulus occurs, there well may be competing response tendencies which are associated with the other stimulus." The response more closely associated with a particular stimulus will overcome this competing response tendency. In order to explain the fact that it is the *second* reaction which is delayed, Reynolds postulated that "if one of the two responses available to S is not stronger than the other, then the response elicited by the first stimulus may become the 'prepotent' or dominant response." Reynolds emphasized that his theory has the advantage of being able, by training responses to specific stimuli previously unassociated with them, to operationally define a prepotent response— that response which has most often been associated with a particular stimulus—and hence to determine in advance which RT will be longer.

This theory makes the following predictions:

1. According to this theory, delays occur not in the selection of the response, but rather in its execution. Hence, if S never had to make an overt response to s1, no such competing responses should arise, and consequently there should be no delay in the reaction to the second stimulus.

Unfortunately, this problem has not been carefully investigated. Some indication that this is not so, however, is provided by the experiments of Nickerson (1965) and Kay and Weiss (1961). In both experiments, there was a delay on the simple RT to a stimulus even if no response was ever required to the first stimulus. In other words, when Ss had only one response to prepare, the response was delayed at short ISIs, even though no response was required to the first stimulus, and therefore no competing responses should have arisen. However, the magnitude of this delay was much smaller than the delay found when a response is required to the first stimulus. Therefore, while competing response tendencies cannot account for the entire delay, they may play some role in the double-response situation.

2. A response-competition theory would predict that the greater the similarity between the two responses required, the greater should be the tendency for response competition. For example, greater delays in RT_2 would be expected when both responses were manual than if one were verbal and the other manual.

Again, this problem has not been investigated.

Response-Selection Delay. A final single channel theory is that of response-selection delay, which states that selection of two responses cannot proceed simultaneously. Hence, when Ss are presented with two response tasks which must be performed in rapid succession, first one response is selected and then the other. During the selection of the first response, the second stimulus must be "held in store." The response selector or "decision mechanism," as it is referred to by proponents of this theory, is thus conceptualized as a single channel system, as opposed to a multichannel system which could simultaneously select many responses.

This theory has received considerable support (Craik, 1947, 1948; Davis, 1956, 1957,

1959, 1962, 1964, 1965a; Fraisse, 1957; Hick, 1948; Hick & Bates, 1950; Vince, 1948; Welford, 1952, 1959). Some of its assumptions have been listed by Welford (1959):

1. There are a number of sensory input mechanisms each capable of receiving data and storing it for a limited period of time, so that, for example, a short series of signals can be received as a unit.

2. There are a number of effector mechanisms containing both central and peripheral elements and capable of carrying out a series of actions, such as the press and release of a key or a series of taps, as a single unit.

3. Between these two elements there is a single channel decision mechanism which is of limited capacity in the sense that it takes a finite time to process information and can thus only deal with a limited amount of information in a given time. (Information is used here as a loose substitute for stimulus or signal, and not as it is defined in information theory.)

4. Sensory input data can be accumulated while the decision channel is occupied by dealing with previous data, and can be passed (together) to the decision channel as soon as it is free.

5. The decision channel can "issue orders" to the effector side for a series of responses, the execution of which can overlap with the decision channel's dealing with fresh input.

A possible mode of operation of this limited capacity mechanism can be conceptualized from some recent experiments on attention by Kristofferson (1965). He described attention as a limited capacity switching mechanism which is responsible for gating the flow of information. The information carried by each stimulus is considered to be transmitted in separate "channels," with the assumption that attention must be aligned with a channel before "read out" of the information can occur. If we assume that attention can be aligned with only one channel at a time, then the read out of the second channel will be delayed until attention is shifted to it.

Just when this attention shift can occur is not clear. Kristofferson believes that the attention mechanism has a fixed periodicity of M ms,

which is controlled by an internal generator whose physiological manifestation may be the alpha rhythm. Thus once attention is lined up with the first channel, it switches to the second channel M ms later, or at some multiple of M.

Such an attention-switching model may operate in one of two ways. One possibility is that attention is switched after some fixed interval following the initiation of the first response selection. Consequently, while the initiation of the second response selection is delayed, both can proceed simultaneously. Thus, provided the value of the fixed interval is not too long, some "multichannel" processing is possible.

On the other hand, attention may not switch until the first response selection is complete. If this is the case, response selections must occur sequentially. Since Kay and Weiss's findings suggest that the delay in RT_2 increases as the time required to process the first response is increased, it appears that the switch does not occur until after the first response has been selected—hence supporting the successive-response-selection model.

Given this assumed schema of operation, several authors have suggested formulas from which the magnitude of the delay in RT_2 can be calculated. Davis (1956, p. 25) suggested the following formulation:

If RT_1 = actual first reaction time
  RT_2 = predicted second reaction time
  RT_N = mean normal reaction time
   X = amount of delay, and
  ISI = interval between the two stimuli

then

$$X = RT_1 - ISI, \text{ for } RT_1 > ISI$$
$$X = 0, \text{ for } RT_1 < ISI, \text{ and}$$
$$RT_2 = RT_N + X$$

Therefore,

$$RT_2 = RT_N + RT_1 - ISI$$

A similar formula was suggested by Welford (1952). However, according to this model, no delay should occur at values of the ISI which are greater than the choice time for the first response. This, however, has not always been the case, and delays have been found at values of ISI as large as and larger than RT_1 (Davis, 1957; Telford, 1931; Vince, 1948). To account for this, Welford (1952) has added an additional assumption:

> If the stimuli fed back from a response are dealt with by the subject's central mechanisms in a similar way to stimuli given by the experimenter, we should expect that those fed back at the beginning of the response would "capture" the central mechanisms for a brief period, and that only when this period was over could any further stimuli from the response or any new stimulus given by the experimenter be attended to [p. 4].

In other words, the second reaction is delayed not only while the first response is being selected, but also while the proprioceptive feedback from the first response is being attended to.

Rather than introduce this feedback requirement, Davis (1957) has postulated that following the selection of a response, the central "single channel" may be refractory for a fixed period of time. He postulated that the refractory time may be about 100 ms. Unlike Telford, he does not believe the delay in RT_2 is totally the result of refractoriness after the passage of the first stimulus. Instead, he argued that while the delay is due to a single channel response selector, following the selection of a response there is a period of "refractoriness," adding an additional 100 ms. to the delay in RT_2.

Delays at values of ISI greater than the first RT are relatively easy to explain if an attention-switching model is accepted. According to such a model, some time may be required for the attention shift. Thus, the second response selection will be delayed not only by the time required for the first response selection, but by the interval required for attention shifting.

Let us now examine the predictions of a single channel response-selection model:

1. The delay in RT_2 should be a direct function of the time required to select the first response.

This question, as pointed out earlier, though an essential one for discriminating between so many of the theories, has not been systematically investigated. The only relevant experiment is that of Kay and Weiss, which would support this prediction, for as the time uncertainty of s_1, and thus perhaps the time required to select a response to it, was increased, the delay in RT_2 increased as well.

2. Since the delay in RT_2 is due to the necessity of first selecting a response to s_1, if no response selection is required to s_1, there should be no delay.

The data collected by Kay and Weiss (1961) and by Nickerson (1965) suggest that this is not so. Delays are still found in the response to s_2 after the presentation of s_1 even if no response is required to s_1. However, the delay is much greater when a response selection to the first stimulus is required.

3. If we assume that the single channel is limited only to the response-selection process, then the selection of the second response should be able to occur during the performance of the first response.

This question has not been carefully studied. Davis (1962) conducted an experiment to determine whether the actual performance of the first response was important in determining the delay in RT_2. Two sets of lights were displayed, each consisting of a left and a right neon bulb. For Display 1, either bulb in the first set came on. For Display 2, coming on 50 to 250 ms. after Display 1, again either the left or right bulb came on. The Ss were to respond only to Display 2, and were to ignore Display 1 (Sessions 2 and 3), or to report, after responding to Display 2, which light had been flashed in Display 1 (Sessions 4 and 5). Three Ss performed under a regular interval situation (intervals presented in blocks of 20) and three under a random interval situation.

In the regular interval group, no delay was encountered in the response. In the random interval situation, even when Ss were told to ignore the first display, there was some delay in reacting to the second display. However, this delay was much less than when S made a response to the first signal, and the delay was significant only at the shortest ISI. This led Davis to the belief that "the blockage caused by attention to a situation may not be as long as when an overt response to it has to be organized." Since the first signal could be identified without causing a delay in the response to the second, Davis suggested that the first stimulus was held in store and analyzed only after the response to the second display had been made. To explain the difference between the regular and random intervals, Davis postulated that if the S does not know when the second signal will come, he starts analysis of the first signal at once, so that the second signal will find the mechanism blocked.

Although Davis' results would seem to indicate that the prime delay in RT_2 is the result not of response selection to s_1 but of the performance of the first response, an important point should be noted. Under the no-response condition, Ss could have completely ignored the first stimulus or, as Davis suggested, delayed analyzing it until the second response had been selected. Therefore, this experiment has not really differentiated at all between relative delays in RT_2 as a function of whether a response was performed, but rather between relative delays when response selection is or is not carried out. To adequately test the effect of the performance of a response, response-selection times must be kept constant, even under conditions where no overt response is required.

The fact that delays in RT_2 are found with ISIs as long as or longer than RT_1 suggests that under some circumstances the single channel concept may apply to response performance as well as to response selection. For example, in some situations, attention may be required for the performance of a response and cannot shift to the second response selection until the first response has been performed.

Summary

Many experiments have been conducted to explain the delay occurring in the second of two successive reactions since this phenomenon was first described by Telford (1931).

The explanation that the delay is due to S's subjective uncertainty as to when the second stimulus will arrive, with expectancy increasing as the ISI is increased, does not seem adequate. This conclusion is based on the finding of Borger (1963) and Creamer (1963) that even when the ISI is kept constant the same delay curve is generated.

Similarly, the "readiness" hypothesis, which states that the delay is due to S requiring a fixed period of time to prepare himself for a response, cannot entirely explain the delay. Some portion of the delay may be due to readiness, for Nickerson (1965), studying simple reaction over a range of foreperiods similar to the ISIs typically employed in the double-response situation, found that RT varied inversely with the duration of the foreperiod. Since S did not have to select a response to the first warning signal, the delay in the RT to the second stimulus was clearly not due to the delay of response selection. However, the magnitude of the increase at the shortest ISI was very small when compared with delays when a response had to be selected to the first stimulus. Thus, while readiness appears to play some role, it is, in itself, not an adequate explanation. Rather, the majority of the experiments strongly suggest the presence of some limited capacity single channel in the system, most likely at the response-selection or decision stage.

The locus of this single channel may lie in the attention system. If we assume that selective attention is required for the facilitation or "boosting" of an S-R bond in order for response selection to occur, and that two S-R connections cannot be boosted simultaneously, then the delay in RT_2 is due to the necessity of waiting for attention to shift from the first response selection.

According to such a model, if the S-R bond for the first response selection is firmly established, so that no further boosting by the attention system is required, then attention should be immediately available for the second response selection. Consequently, no delay in RT_2 is expected in such a situation. Some support for this possibility is provided by the findings of Adams and Chambers (1962) and of

Reynolds (1966) that RT_2 is not delayed if the first response represents a simple, as opposed to a disjunctive, reaction. The model would also predict no delay in RT_2 if the first reaction is highly practiced. Further investigation along these lines is required.

References

Adams, J. A. Test of the hypothesis of psychological refractory period. *Journal of Experimental Psychology*, 1962, 64, 280–287.

Adams, J. A. Motor skills. *Annual Review of Psychology*, 1964, 15, 181–202.

Adams, J. A. Some mechanisms of motor responding: An examination of attention. In E. A. Bilodeau (Ed.), *Acquisition of skill*. New York: Academic Press, 1966. Pp. 169–200.

Adams, J. A., & Chambers, R. W. Response to simultaneous stimulation of two sense modalities. *Journal of Experimental Psychology*, 1962, 63, 198–206.

Annett, J. A note on Davis' repudiation of the expectancy hypothesis. *Quarterly Journal of Experimental Psychology*, 1966, 18, 179–180.

Baker, C. H. Toward a theory of vigilance. *Canadian Journal of Psychology*, 1959, 13, 35–42.

Baker, C. H. Further toward a theory of vigilance. In D. N. Buckner & J. J. McGrath (Eds.), *Vigilance: A symposium*. New York: McGraw-Hill, 1963. Pp. 127–154.

Berlyne, D. E. *Conflict, arousal and curiosity*. New York: McGraw-Hill, 1960.

Bertelson, P. Central intermittency twenty years later. *Quarterly Journal of Experimental Psychology*, 1966, 18, 153–163.

Borger, R. The refractory period and serial choice reactions. *Quarterly Journal of Experimental Psychology*, 1963, 15, 1–12.

Broadbent, D. E. *Perception and communication*. New York: Pergamon Press, 1958.

Buckner, D. N., & McGrath, J. J. (Eds.). *Vigilance: A symposium*. New York: McGraw-Hill, 1963.

Cherry, E. C., & Taylor, W. K. Some further experiments upon the recognition of speech with one and with two ears. *Journal of the Acoustical Society of America*, 1954, 26, 554–599.

Craik, K. W. J. Theory of the human operator in control systems. I. The operator as an engineering system. *British Journal of Psychology*, 1947, 38, 56–61.

Craik, K. W. J. Theory of the human operator in control systems. II. Man as an element in a control system. *British Journal of Psychology*, 1948, 38, 142–148.

Creamer, L. R. Event uncertainty, psychological refractory period and human data processing. *Journal of Experimental Psychology*, 1963, 66, 187–194.

Davis, R. The limits of the "psychological refractory period." *Quarterly Journal of Experimental Psychology*, 1956, 8, 24–38.

Davis, R. The human operator as a single channel information system. *Quarterly Journal of Experimental Psychology*, 1957, 9, 119–129.

Davis, R. The role of "attention" in the psychological refractory period. *Quarterly Journal of Experimental Psychology*, 1959, 11, 211–220.

Davis, R. Choice RTs and the theory of intermittency in human performance. *Quarterly Journal of Experimental Psychology*, 1962, 14, 157–166.

Davis, R. The combination of information from different sources. *Quarterly Journal of Experimental Psychology*, 1964, 16, 332–339.

Davis, R. Expectancy and intermittency. *Quarterly Journal of Experimental Psychology*, 1965, 17, 75–78. (a)

Davis, R. A reply to Dr. Lawrence Karlin. *Quarterly Journal of Experimental Psychology*, 1965, 17, 352. (b)

Davis, R. A reply to Dr. John Annett. *Quarterly Journal of Experimental Psychology*, 1966, 18, 180.

Deese, J. Some problems in the theory of vigilance. *Psychological Review*, 1955, 62, 359–368.

Dodge, R. A note on Professor Thorndike's experiment. *Psychological Review*, 1927, 34, 237–240.

Elithorn, A., & Lawrence, C. Central inhibition—Some refractory observations. *Quarterly Journal of Experimental Psychology*, 1955, 7, 116–127.

Fraisse, P. La période réfractaire psychologique. *Année Psychologique*, 1957, 57, 315–328.

Frankmann, J. P., & Adams, J. A. Theories of vigilance. *Psychological Bulletin*, 1962, 59, 257–272.

Hick, W. E. The discontinuous functioning of the human operator in pursuit tasks. *Quarterly Journal of Experimental Psychology*, 1948, 1, 36–51.

Hick, W. E., & Bates, J. A. *The human operator of control mechanisms*. London: Ministry of Supply, 1950. (Monogr. No. 17).

Karlin, L. Comments on "expectancy and intermittency." *Quarterly Journal of Experimental Psychology*, 1965, 17, 351.

Kay, H., & Weiss, A. D. Relationship between simple and serial reaction time. *Nature*, 1961, 191, 790–791.

Kristofferson, A. B. Attention in time discrimination and reaction time. Technical Report No. CR-194, 1965, National Aeronautics and Space Administration.

Marill, T. The psychological refractory phase. *British Journal of Psychology*, 1957, 48, 93–97.

Mowrer, O. H. Preparatory set (expectancy)—Some methods of measurement. *Psychological Monographs*, 1940, 52(2, Whole No. 233).

Nickerson, R. S. Response time to the second of two successive signals as a function of absolute and relative duration of intersignal interval. *Perceptual and Motor Skills*, 1965, 21, 3–10.

Poulton, E. C. Perceptual anticipation and reaction time. *Quarterly Journal of Experimental Psychology,* 1950, *2,* 99–112.

Reynolds, D. Effects of double stimulation: Temporary inhibition of response. *Psychological Bulletin,* 1964, *62,* 333–347.

Reynolds, D. Time and event uncertainty in unisensory reaction time. *Journal of Experimental Psychology,* 1966, *71,* 286–293.

Telford, C. W. Refractory phase of voluntary and associative responses. *Journal of Experimental Psychology,* 1931, *14,* 1–35.

Thorndike, E. L. The refractory period of associative prosesses. *Psychological Review,* 1927, *34,* 234–236.

Vince, M. A. Intermittency of control movements and the psychological refractory period. *British Journal of Psychology,* 1948, *38,* 149–157.

Welford, A. T. The "psychological refractory period" and the timing of high-speed performance: A review and a theory. *British Journal of Psychology,* 1952, *43,* 2–19.

Welford, A. T. Evidence of a single-channel decision mechanism limiting performance in a serial reaction task. *Quarterly Journal of Experimental Psychology,* 1959, *11,* 193–210.

Welford, A. T. The measurement of sensory-motor performance: Survey and reappraisal of twelve years' progress. *Ergonomics,* 1960, *3,* 189–230.

4.2 Effect of Luminance, Exposure Duration and Task Complexity on Reaction Time*

JAQUES KASWAN   STEPHEN YOUNG

A number of studies have shown that increasing luminance generally produces faster reaction times (RT) (Raab, Fehrer, & Hershenson, 1961; Teichner, 1954; Woodworth & Schlosberg, 1954), although at the brighter luminance values there is a decreasing effect on RT of equal logarithmic increments of luminance (Raab et al., 1961). Reaction times also become faster with lengthening exposure duration, but only within a narrow range of brief exposures (up to about 20 msec) and dim luminances (up to about 30 footlamberts [ftL.]) (Froeberg, 1907; Raab & Fehrer, 1962). At longer exposures, RT may not change at all (Raab et al.,

1961), or may increase slightly (Baumgart & Segal, 1942; Wells, 1913).

The above RT studies were limited to flash-detection situations. No data are available on how RT varies with luminance and exposure duration in more complex discrimination tasks. The main study reported here examines the effect of exposure duration and luminance on RT in a pattern-discrimination task, and a supplementary study examines the effect of these variables on RT in a figure-ground detection task. These two studies thus compare the effect of luminance and exposure duration on RT at two levels of task complexity.

Main Experiment

METHOD

Apparatus. All stimuli were presented in an electronic mirror tachistoscope, described in detail elsewhere (Kaswan & Young, 1963).

* From: Jaques Kaswan and Stephen Young, "Effect of Luminance, Exposure Duration and Task Complexity on Reaction Time," *Journal of Experimental Psychology,* 1965, vol. 69, pp. 393–394. Copyright (1965) by the American Psychological Association, and reproduced by permission. This study was supported by National Science Foundation Grant G-9589. Sally Haralson, Ruth Cline, and George Boroczi helped in running Ss and in data analysis. The generous availability of the facilities of the Western Data Processing Center were of substantial help in data analysis

Reaction times were obtained as part of another experiment (Kaswan & Young, 1963). The Ss were required to decide which of two patterns they were being shown, a line of evenly spaced dots (Ev) or a line of dots arranged in pairs (Pr). Three sets of paired and even patterns were used. Paired designs differed in that the distance between pairs was increased in the order $Pr_1 < Pr_2 < Pr_3$. The evenly spaced patterns were obtained by averaging the distance between and within pairs in the paired patterns, so that the distance between dots increased in the order $Ev_1 < Ev_2 < Ev_3$. In each session, Ss were shown only corresponding even and paired patterns, i.e., Ev_1-Pr_1; Ev_2-Pr_2; or Ev_3-Pr_3. Each of the five Ss had a total of 43 sessions. In each session, every design was presented under eight different exposure durations and eight luminances, by the method of constant stimuli. Exposure durations varied from 4 msec to 512 msec, in $\log_2$ steps. Luminance was varied in $\log_2$ steps from .09 mL. to 11.84 mL. The fixation field luminance was always equal to that of the stimulus field. Within a session each of the eight luminances was constant for a block of 16 exposures (every exposure duration for each pattern), for a total of 128 exposures for each session. The order of luminance blocks was randomized, with the restriction that the initial block was always in the brighter half of the range and that successive blocks were within two steps of each other. Pattern-exposure-duration combinations were randomized within each block, with each combination used only once within a block.

Approximately .5 sec before each exposure a warning signal was given with a manually operated buzzer, and S focused on the space between two horizontal edge markers on the fixation field. To respond, S was asked to hit, as quickly as possible, one of two microswitch keys located on either side of a finger rest. For three of the Ss, the key on the right side was associated with the evenly spaced designs; for two of the Ss this key was associated with the paired designs. The designs were not described verbally, either by S or by E, until the end of the study. If S saw absolutely no indication of a design during the exposure (i.e., not even a blurred line), he was instructed to hit either key, and then say the word "nothing." There was an interval of approximately 11 sec between exposures within blocks of exposures and 45 sec between each block, when intensity filters were changed.

Subjects. The Ss were five male college seniors who were paid for their participation. None had previous experience in perception experiments.

RESULTS

Figure 1a shows the mean RT for each pattern as a function of exposure duration, averaged across all luminances. Figure 1b shows the mean RT for each pattern at every luminance, averaged across all exposure durations. Each point in Figures 1a and 1b is based on correct responses from a total of 450 exposures. Only the RTs of correct responses were selected in the belief that these would most directly reflect differences in discrimination difficulty of these patterns.

Figures 1a and 1b show that, in general, RTs become faster with increases in duration and luminance, but exceptions occur at the longest duration and brightest luminance where there is some tendency for RT to become slower again.

Figures 1a and 1b also indicate an RT ordering of patterns which is similar to the ordering obtained for accuracy of identification (Kaswan & Young, 1963). With both accuracy and RT measures, the obtained ordering from lowest to highest accuracy and fastest to slowest RT was $Pr_1 < Pr_2 < Pr_3$ and $Ev_1 < Ev_2 < Ev_3$. Also, as for accuracy, RT to paired patterns tended to be slower than the RTs to comparable Ev patterns, except for the Ev_3-Pr_3 set, where RT to the two patterns was about the same, probably because these patterns were easily discriminated.

While RT reflects the order in which these patterns were accurately discriminated, variations in luminance appear to affect RT and accuracy differently. For accuracy, it was found that discrimination of the patterns depended largely on exposure duration and that variation of luminance had little effect on the level of

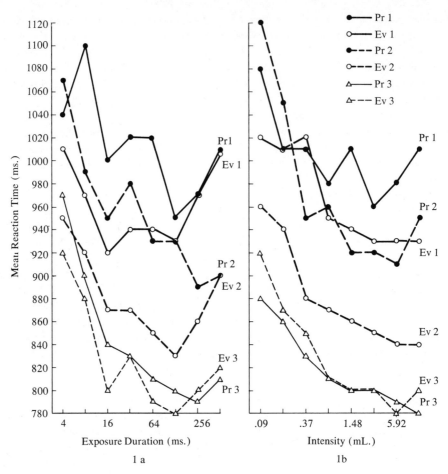

FIGURE 1   Mean reaction time for each pattern as a function of (1a) exposure duration averaged
over all luminance values for the main experiment and as a function of (1b) luminance averaged
over all exposure-duration values.

accuracy. Figure 1b shows, however, that RT was consistently and substantially affected by variations in luminance.

While Figures 1a and 1b show the "main effects" of exposure duration and luminance on RT, Figure 2 shows how these variables interact in their effect on RT. The parts of Figure 2 labeled a through h contain the results of the experiment described above. The parts of the figure labeled a' through h' report the results of the supplementary study which will be described later.

Each point in Figures 2a through 2h is a mean RT based on 340 responses, the result of combining correct, incorrect, and "nothing"

responses to all six stimuli by the five Ss. There was close similarity in the *form* of the curves for each pattern and each type of response, although incorrect and "nothing" responses were slower and more variable than correct responses. Figure 2 is therefore quite representative of the results. Vertical bars at representative points in each curve, indicating the standard error at each of these means, show that variability is small relative to the range of RT effects obtained as a function of luminance and duration. Only mean RTs from the sixth through the forty-first session are included. The first five sessions were eliminated because RT decreased over these sessions. During the

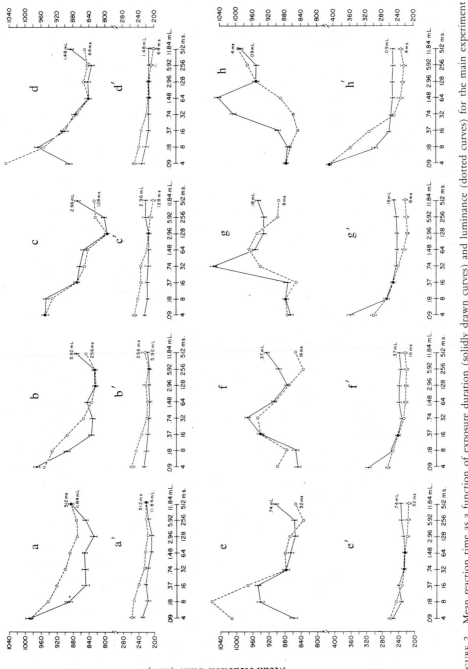

FIGURE 2 Mean reaction time as a function of exposure duration (solidly drawn curves) and luminance (dotted curves) for the main experiment (a through h) and the supplementary experiment (a' through h'). (Vertical bars through data points show the *SE* of the mean [see text]).

last two sessions, RT became very variable, perhaps because Ss anticipated the end of the experiment.

Each of the solid curves in Figure 2 shows the effect of exposure duration on RT under a different luminance parameter. The exposure-duration curve for the brightest parameter (11.84 mL.) is shown as the solid line in Figure 2a. Luminance values then become successively dimmer, with the solid curve under the dimmest parameter (.09 mL.) shown in Figure 2h. Solid curves are to be read against the exposure-duration scale shown on the abscissa (labeled "ms.") in each part of Figure 2. It is apparent that the exposure-duration-RT function changes with the level of luminance. As luminance parameters become dimmer (solid lines, Figure 2a to 2h), the slowest RT occurs at increasingly longer exposure durations. Thus, the slowest RT occurred at the 4-msec exposure under the 11.84-mL. luminance parameter (Figure 2a), at the 8-msec exposure under the 1.48-mL. parameter (Figure 2d), at about 16 msec under the .74-mL. parameter (Figure 2e), at 32 msec under the .18-mL. parameter (Figure 2g), and at 64 msec under the .09-mL. parameter (Figure 2h). This shift in the exposure duration for which the slowest RT occurred leads to a gradual inversion of the slope in the RT-exposure-duration function. At one extreme, under maximum luminance (11.84 mL., Figure 2a) RT became *faster* between 4 and 16 msec. At the other extreme, under minimum luminance (.09 mL., Figure 2h) RT became *slower* between 4 and 64 msec. Thus the slope of the RT function in Figure 2h is in the opposite direction to the slopes shown in Figures 2a, 2b, 2c, and 2d.

The curves drawn with dashed lines in Figure 2 show the effect of luminance on RT at each exposure-duration parameter. For example, the dashed curve in Figure 2a shows the effect of luminance on RT for the 512-msec parameter. Exposure-duration parameters (shown next to each curve) then become successively briefer, with the briefest (4 msec) for the dashed line in Figure 2h. These curves are to be read against the luminance scale (labeled "mL.") shown below the exposure-duration scale in each part of Figure 2.

The scales are arranged so that points directly above and below each other on the dashed and solid curves represent equal luminance-exposure-duration products. There is a tendency toward superimposition of the dashed and solid curves, indicating that changes in luminance and exposure duration generally have a similar effect on RT under these conditions. Figures 2d and 2e indicate, however, that the shift toward a reversal in the direction of the RT slope appears to occur a little later in the luminance curves (dashed lines) than in the exposure-duration curves (solid lines).

Since the shift in the direction of the slope of these curves occurred gradually with decreasing parameter values for both luminance and exposure duration, these results appear to constitute a reliable finding.

Figures 2a through 2h show that the present results differ in two major ways from RT findings in flash detection. One difference is that at low luminances (e.g., solid line, Figure 2h) RT becomes *slower* as exposure duration increases. The same effect was obtained for increases in luminance under brief exposure durations (e.g., dashed line, Figure 2h). At dim and brief parameter values previous studies found their most substantial RT variations in the *opposite* direction from those reported here. That is, RT tended to become *faster* with increasing exposure duration or increasing luminance, given, respectively, dim or brief parameter values.

A second difference between these results and previous findings relates to the difference in the size of the range of exposure durations and luminances affecting RT. As noted, Raab and Fehrer (1962) found that even at their dimmest luminance parameter (.3 ftL.), exposure durations longer than 20 or 25 msec had little effect on RT, whereas the range of effective luminance values was much wider (up to 3,000 ftL.). Figures 2a through 2h show, on the other hand, that exposure durations affected RT over a wide range (4–512 msec) at the dimmer luminance values.

The divergence of the present results from those previously reported may be due to at least two factors, task complexity and luminance condition. Luminance and exposure duration may affect RT differently when complex discriminations are involved as in the pattern-discrimination task used here, than in the much simpler visual task of flash detection. Another factor may be that luminance and exposure duration have a different effect on RT in flash detection than in a condition where the pre- and post-exposure fields are of the same luminance. Under constant luminance, as in the study reported above, the minimum function of luminance and exposure duration is to provide enough stimulus energy for the emergence of a detectable discrepancy in reflectance between figure and ground. In flash detection, the pre-exposure field is dark, so that the function of luminance and time is to provide sufficient light for the detection of a difference from the dark. In order to ascertain whether the findings obtained in the discrimination task can be attributed to the effect of task complexity or the constant luminance conditions used, a supplementary study was carried out.

Supplementary Study

In this study luminance and exposure-duration conditions remained the same as for the main experiment, but the task was simplified to a figure-ground detection. If the findings in the main study were largely the result of the luminance conditions used, similar results should be obtained in the supplementary study. If the results of the supplementary study turn out to be similar to those reported from flash-detection studies, then the results of the main study were probably due to complexity of discrimination.

METHOD

The tachistoscope, exposure duration, and luminance values were the same as in the main study. As in the main study, luminance of the fixation field equaled that of the stimulus field. The stimulus consisted of two $\frac{1}{2}$-in. black bars extending horizontally through the middle of the stimulus field, with a $\frac{1}{2}$-in. distance between the bars. The S's task was to press a single microswitch key as soon as he saw the stimulus. If he saw absolutely nothing, he was to say "nothing." A $\frac{1}{2}$-sec warning buzzer was fol-

lowed by one of three foreperiods (.5, 1, and 1.5 sec), after which the stimulus was presented. The buzzer-foreperiod-stimulus presentation cycle was controlled by Hunter timers. The cycle was repeated every 11 sec. Reaction times were recorded, using a Hewlit-Packard decade counter, to the nearest millisecond. Each of three Ss was given 21 replications of every exposure-duration-luminance-foreperiod combination. Exposure duration and foreperiod were randomized for each S in each session within each luminance. Luminance was varied in blocks as for the main experiment, except that each exposure duration occurred, in random order, three times (once for each foreperiod) before luminance was changed.

RESULTS

The results are shown in Figure 2a' through 2h'. Each point is a mean based on 54 exposures, combining results for the three Ss and the three foreperiods. Each S's longest RT for each exposure-duration-luminance-foreperiod combination was excluded from these results. The curves are plotted in the same way as those in Figures 2a through 2h. It is clear that the curves in Figures 2a' through 2h' slope in the direction reported for flash-detection studies and do not show the reversal in slope reported in the main study (Figures 2a through 2h). To the extent to which RT is affected, it always becomes faster with increases in luminance or exposure duration. The effect is most substantial at dim and brief exposures (Figures 2f' through 2h') and is in the *opposite* direction from that found for these parameters in the main study (especially Figures 2g and 2h).

The relative effects of exposure duration and luminance in the supplementary study also closely parallel the results of flash-detection studies. Raab and Fehrer (1962) reported that exposure durations longer than 5 msec produced little or no change in RT at luminance levels brighter than .3 ftL. (.32 mL.).[1] Similarly, in the present study, under the four brighter luminances, exposure duration had a negligible effect on RT as shown by the solid curves in Figures 2a' through 2d'. Raab and Fehrer also

[1] 1.0 ftL. = 1.076 mL.

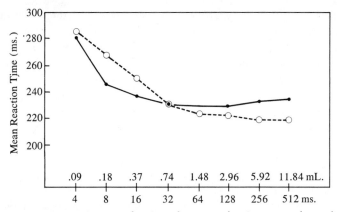

FIGURE 3 Mean reaction time as a function of exposure duration averaged over luminance (solid line, read against msec scale) and luminance averaged over exposure duration (dashed line, read against mL. scale).

found that exposure durations longer than 20 or 25 msec had little effect on RT at their dimmest luminance (.3 ftL.) which agrees with the present results where exposures longer than 16 msec had little effect on RT even at luminances as dim as .18 and .09 mL. (see Figures 2g' and 2h').

Again, as in the Raab and Fehrer study, the effect of luminance on RT extends over a wider range than the effect of exposure duration. As the dashed lines in Figures 2a' through 2d' show, RTs drop by from 40 to 60 msec with increasing luminance at the longer exposure parameters but, at the most, only about 20 msec with increasing exposure durations at the brightest luminance parameters (solid lines, Figures 2a' through 2d').

Figure 3 is comparable to Figures 1a and 1b, in summarizing overall effects of luminance and exposure duration on RT in the supplementary study. The solid curve shows the effect of exposure duration on RT averaged over luminance. For example, the mean RT, in Figure 3 for the 512-msec scale value (solid line), was obtained by averaging the eight RTs on the *dashed* curve in Figure 2a'. The dashed curve in Figure 3 shows the effect of luminance on RT averaged over exposure duration. Thus the mean RT obtained for the 11.84-mL scale value in Figure 3 (dashed curve) was obtained by averaging RT values for the eight points on the *solid* curve in Figure 2a'.

Figure 3 shows that the average change in RT *between* luminance or exposure-duration parameters is quite representative of the effect of each of these variables shown within Figures 2a' through 2h', where one parameter was always held constant. Thus the solid curve in Figure 3 shows that exposure durations longer than 16 msec have little or no effect in accelerating RT. Increase in luminance, on the other hand, appears to affect RT over a somewhat wider range, although the amount of this effect shown in Figure 3 seems negligible beyond 1.48 mL. The latter in no way contradicts Raab et al.'s finding that RT is affected by a very wide range of luminance values. Raab used as $\log_{10}$ scale which produced very large absolute luminance increments at the brighter levels. While our $\log_2$ scale allows a more sensitive assessment of RT changes at dimmer luminances, the $\log_{10}$ scale is probably more efficient in tapping RT changes at bright luminances, since both their data, and ours, indicate that, as luminance levels increase, greater increments in absolute brightness seem necessary to produce equivalent RT changes.

Discussion

The substantial similarity of the Raab and Fehrer findings and the results of our supplementary study indicate that the luminance conditions used (i.e., flash or constant illumination of fixation and exposure field) make little difference in how luminance and exposure duration affect RT. The similarity in the results of these studies is especially striking in view of the differences in apparatus and procedures used.

The results further suggest that the range of exposure durations affecting RT in a detection task is similar to the range affecting detection thresholds. Thus, in the supplementary study, exposure durations longer than 16 msec did not substantially affect RT (Figure 2a' through 2h'). Similarily, in a previous study, probability of detecting a single large dot under dim luminance (.09 mL.) was most affected at exposures briefer than 16 msec (Kaswan & Young, 1963).

The Raab *et al.* and our findings also indicate that RT in detection tasks is affected by a much wider range of luminance than exposure-duration values. This suggests that the effect of *luminance* in effecting minimum RT is different from the effect of luminance on "high criterion" detection thresholds (near 100% detection). The latter appears at least grossly determined by a reciprocal luminance-duration relationship (Bunsen-Roscoe "law"), whereas the *minimum* RT cannot be reached by increasing exposure duration to compensate for lower luminance (compare, for example, RTs to 300 ftL. and 3,000 ftL. flashes in the Raab papers).

The agreement with the Raab and Fehrer findings also indicates that the puzzling results of our main study—the reversal in the direction of RT slopes at dim and brief parameters and the extended effect of exposure duration and luminance on RT—were probably due to the complexity of the discrimination task and do not depend on the way in which luminance and exposure duration were varied.

In a previous study the authors suggested that luminance and exposure duration function differently in determining probability of detection and accuracy of pattern discrimination (Kaswan & Young, 1963). The present findings suggest a similar conclusion with regard to reaction time, since luminance and exposure duration clearly generate different RT functions in detection, as compared to pattern discrimina-

tion (compare Figures 2a through 2h with Figures 2a' through 2h'). The distinction between discrimination and detection may thus have more than semantic merit and warrants further investigation.

Summary

Reaction time to a pattern-discrimination task was found to be about equally affected by variation in exposure duration (4–512 msec) and luminance (.09–11.84 mL.). In a supplementary study of figure-ground detection, it was found that luminance affected RT to a greater extent than exposure duration. Further, it was found that luminance and exposure duration determined different RT functions in the 2 experiments. In the discrimination task there was a gradual shift in the relation of luminance and exposure duration to RT, from inverse at bright and long exposures, to direct at dim and brief exposures. In the detection task, RT was always inversely related to changes in luminance and exposure duration, to the extent to which RT was affected by these variables.

References

Baumgardt, E., & Segal, J. Facilitation et inhibition parametres de la fonction visuelle. *Annee psychol.,* 1942, *43,* 54–102.

Froeberg, H. The relation between magnitude of the stimulus and the time of reaction. *Arch. Psychol., N. Y.,* 1907, *25,* No. 8.

Kaswan, J., & Young, S. Stimulus exposure time, brightness, and spatial factors as determinants of visual perception. *J. exp. Psychol.,* 1963, *65,* 113–123.

Raab, D., & Fehrer, E. The effect of stimulus duration and luminance on visual reaction time. *J. exp. Psychol.,* 1962, *64,* 326–327.

Raab, D., Fehrer, E., & Hershenson, M. Visual reaction time and the Broca-Sulzer phenomenon. *J. exp. Psychol.,* 1961, *61,* 193–199.

Teichner, W. H. Recent studies of simple reaction time. *Psychol. Bull.,* 1954, *51,* 128–149.

Wells, G. R. The influence of stimulus duration on reaction time. *Psychol. Monogr.,* 1913, *15*(5, Whole No. 66).

Woodworth, R. S., & Schlosberg, H. *Experimental psychology.* New York: Holt, 1954.

4.3 Visual Reaction Time
and the Broca-Sulzer Phenomenon*

DAVID RAAB   ELIZABETH FEHRER
MAURICE HERSHENSON

If a brief light flash is followed by additional visual stimulation, it may appear less bright than if it had been flashed alone. The Broca-Sulzer phenomenon, metacontrast (e.g., Alpern, 1953; Stigler, 1910) and the Crawford effect (Crawford, 1947) are examples of such retroactive masking.

A theoretically important question that has received little systematic study concerns the behavioral effectiveness of a stimulus thus masked. Will overt responses to it be similar to the responses evoked by a less intense stimulus which phenomenally matches the masked one? This question was raised in 1942 by Baumgardt and Segal and led to an experiment in which reaction time (RT) was used as a measure of the Broca-Sulzer phenomenon.

This phenomenon, which has had ample verification, consists in the fact that the phenomenal brightness of a stimulus can be diminished by the unchanged continuation of the stimulus itself. Studies agree (e.g., Bills, 1920; Broca & Sulzer, 1902; Stainton, 1928) that the apparent brightness of a flash of light increases

with stimulus duration up to 50 to 100 msec, then decreases up to about 250 msec, after which flash duration has a comparatively negligible influence on apparent brightness. The overshooting effect is most marked with intense stimuli and is absent with weak ones. The method used in establishing the Broca-Sulzer phenomenon typically consists in matching the short duration test flash to a neighboring or surrounding light presented for several seconds.

The Baumgardt and Segal (1942) experiment was designed to determine whether differences in apparent brightness can be measured by RT. Specifically, they anticipated a shorter RT to a 50-msec flash than to a flash of 250 msec. It should be pointed out that Baumgardt and Segal assumed that the brightness differences that emerge with the Broca-Sulzer method derive purely from differences in stimulus duration. They therefore presented their light flashes unaccompanied by the comparison stimulus employed in the Broca-Sulzer procedure.

The stimulus used had a luminance of 1700 nits, (496 ft-L). The two durations were presented in blocks of 10 trials each, the blocks following each other in ABAB order. Of 31 comparisons between the means of successive blocks, all showed slightly faster (1 to 5 msec) RTs to the 50-msec flash. It is interesting to note that the published RTs were all less than the duration of the 250-msec stimulus and it is therefore obvious that the RT could not have

*From: David Raab, Elizabeth Fehrer, and Maurice Hershenson, "Visual Reaction Time and the Broca-Sulzer Phenomenon," *Journal of Experimental Psychology*, 1961, vol. 61, pp. 193–199. Copyright (1961) by the American Psychological Association, and reproduced by permission. This research was supported by grants from the National Science Foundation (G-6456) and from the National Institute of Neurological Diseases and Blindness (B-1028) and by funds provided by Brooklyn College. Edward H. Green of the Department of Physics gave generous assistance in the planning of the stimulus-generating equipment.

been affected by that part of the 250-msec stimulus that persisted after the reaction was completed.

A search of the literature yielded only one other study of the effect of a wide range of stimulus durations on RT to clearly suprathreshold visual stimuli. In 1913, Wells measured RTs to light flashes of the following durations: 12, 25, 64, 144, and 1000 msec. The intensity of the light cannot be determined accurately from the published report but was apparently well under 1 ft-L. Wells' data indicate that, in general, the 25- and 64-msec flashes yielded the fastest RTs. A series of studies by Chernikoff, Gregg, and Brogden (Chernikoff & Brogden, 1949; Chernikoff, Gregg, & Brogden, 1950; Gregg & Brogden, 1950a, 1950b) on the effect of stimulus duration on RT to auditory stimuli yielded congruent results. RT was found to increase as stimulus duration increased from 100 to 2400 msec.

Neither the Wells nor the Chernikoff et al. data can be explained on the basis of the Broca-Sulzer relation between stimulus duration and apparent brightness. Wells' light intensity was below that at which the Broca-Sulzer phenomenon can be demonstrated and no parallel to this phenomenon has been reported for audition. It seems more likely that the effect of stimulus duration on RT was mediated by attitudinal factors which could develop during a block of trials at the same stimulus duration (cf. Jarl, 1957; Johnson, 1923). Blocks of brief stimuli may arouse S to react as fast as possible, while longer lasting ones might encourage some relaxation of effort. This may also be the best explanation of Baumgardt and Segal's data even though their light intensity was sufficiently high to yield the Broca-Sulzer effect.

The present experiments have been designed to determine whether the Baumgardt and Segal findings are better explained on the basis of the Broca-Sulzer phenomenon or on the basis of attitudinal factors. In Exp. I, the stimulus durations were presented in random sequence in order to eliminate the possible effect of attitudinal factors which might develop during blocks of trials at the same duration. Thus, any advantage of the 50-msec flash could be attrib-uted to the Broca-Sulzer effect. Further, such an outcome would be good evidence that the latency of the response is correlated with perceived intensity, stimulus intensity being held constant. Three luminances, approximately 3000, 30, and 0.30 ft-L, were used. As the Broca-Sulzer phenomenon is apparent only with fairly intense stimuli, it was assumed that, if it does indeed affect RT, its effect should be most obvious with our most intense stimulus and absent with the weakest. Experiment II was designed to test the earlier findings that RT to a 50-msec flash is faster than RT to a 250-msec flash when stimuli of a given duration are presented in blocks of trials.

Experiment I

METHOD

Apparatus. The light source was a glow modulator tube (Sylvania R-1131C) mounted in a light-tight box with a circular aperture, 1 cm. in diameter, in front of the tube. The light was diffused over a ground glass plate placed 1 cm. in front of the lamp and bearing against the inside surface of the front of the box. All of the transilluminated glass was thus masked off except for the circular area in the aperture. This 1-cm. target, viewed binocularly from a headrest 50 cm. away, subtended 1° 10′ of arc.

The front side of the stimulus box measured 13 by 15.5 cm., and was painted black. The stimulus aperture at the center of this rectangle was surrounded by a ring, .75 cm. wide and 6.3 cm. in outer diameter, cut from a manila folder. This concentric ring served as a fixation device.

The apparatus was located in a sound proof room and was dimly illuminated from behind S's head by a diffuse circular source, 5.5 cm. in diameter, placed 160 cm. from the stimulus area. The luminance of this source was 22 ft-L. When illuminated by this source, the luminance of the black front surface of the stimulus box was too low to be measured by means of a Macbeth illuminometer. The fixation ring had a luminance of approximately 0.001 ft-L.

At all luminances studied, the target flash appeared far brighter than the ring and was the only transient visual stimulus.

The glow modulator tube was connected in series with the plate circuit of a triode-connected 6L6. The triode was biased beyond cutoff by means of a 45-v. battery and was pulsed into conduction by rectangular positive pulses from a set of Tektronix Pulse and Wave-Form generators. The current through the 6L6 (and glow tube) was adjusted to be 40 ma., and was monitored on an oscilloscope by means of a 10 ohm resistor in the cathode circuit of the 6L6. A regulated power supply furnished 350 v. dc.

A 2.7-megohm resistance, connected across the glow lamp, was found to yield optimum switching action. In addition, the driving pulses applied to the grid of the 6L6 were shaped to "over-volt" the glow modulator tube. With these arrangements, the tube could be pulsed once every 13 sec with latency of 50 μsec and jitter reduced to less than 10 μsec. Light output from pulse to pulse varied less than 0.5%.

Six generators were used to provide the six stimulus durations. The light pulse amplitudes were further monitored by means of a photocell and were adjusted to equality with an accuracy better than one percent. The six durations were preset and a six-position switch was employed to select each duration as required.

The flash durations used were 10, 25, 50, 100, 250, and 500 msec.

Three luminances covering a range of four log units were used. The highest was approximately 3000 ft-L as measured by a Macbeth illuminometer at the ground glass plate. The next was produced by inserting a Kodak filter, neutral density 2.00, between the tube and the ground glass plate. For the weakest light, an ND 3.00 and an ND 1.00 filter were used. All luminances were clearly suprathreshold.

Each trial began with a 1000-cycle warning tone lasting 1 sec., and was followed by a silent foreperiod of 0.5, 1.0, or 1.5 sec selected by means of a three-position switch. The light stimulus was presented (and the chronoscope started) at the end of this foreperiod. The whole sequence was presented once every 13 sec by means of Hunter decade interval timers.

RTs (measured from the onset of the stimulus pulse to S's depressing a normally closed telegraph key) were measured to the nearest millisecond by means of a Berkeley counter.

Subjects. The three authors served as Ss. Before the experiment proper began, each had undergone a training period of at least 10 hr.

Procedure. Each S served in 18 experimental sessions. Only one luminance was used in a given session. Each session consisted of four sets of 18 trials each in which each combination of the six durations and the three foreperiods appeared once in random order. Sessions for two Ss were in the sequence ABCCBACBAABC etc. (A, B, and C refer to the three flash luminances.) For the third S, this sequence was reversed. For each luminance-duration combination, there were 72 reactions for each S, 24 at each foreperiod.

After 5 min. of dark adaptation, eight practice trials were given before the recorded trials were run. A 2-min. rest period was given between Sets 2 and 3, i.e., after 36 recorded trials.

RESULTS

The mean RT for each S for each luminance-duration-foreperiod combination was computed after eliminating the longest and the shortest RT of the 24 at each combination. The means thus computed for each luminance-duration combination are based on 66 RTs, i.e., 72 minus 6. They are presented in Table 1 together with the combined means.

No effect of duration is apparent save possibly for the 10-msec duration of the weakest light which, on the average, yielded somewhat longer RTs than the other durations at this luminance. Phenomenally, this light appeared quite faint. For all Ss together, however, an analysis of variance showed that the six duration means did not differ significantly ($P >$ .05.) With the exception of this 10-msec light, both individual and combined mean RTs for the six durations at a given luminance were very similar and showed no consistent trends with duration. At the greatest luminance, where the effect of the Broca-Sulzer phenomenon

TABLE 1

Mean Reaction Times Classified by Flash Duration

FLASH LUMINANCE IN FT-L	S	FLASH DURATION IN MILLISECONDS						ALL RTs	
		10	25	50	100	250	500	Mean	SD
3000	EF	159.4	157.5	158.6	157.9	158.6	157.5	158.2	14.7
	MH	153.4	153.8	155.0	153.6	154.5	156.6	154.5	14.9
	DR	162.9	159.3	161.3	163.3	160.2	160.0	161.2	13.0
	Mean	158.6	156.9	158.3	158.3	157.8	158.0	158.0	14.6
30	EF	171.8	169.4	170.9	170.9	175.2	171.6	171.6	16.2
	MH	165.3	165.5	166.6	166.9	165.2	165.6	165.8	15.4
	DR	171.9	171.1	171.3	170.4	171.0	170.7	171.1	12.2
	Mean	169.7	168.7	169.6	169.4	170.4	169.3	169.5	15.1
0.30	EF	201.4	199.2	195.9	197.2	199.7	194.3	198.0	17.1
	MH	195.3	188.4	188.8	191.0	186.4	195.7	190.9	18.5
	DR	206.0	201.1	203.6	201.7	202.8	203.9	203.2	14.6
	Mean	200.9	196.2	196.1	196.6	196.3	198.0	197.4	18.0

Note—Each individual mean is based on 66 measures.

should be most apparent, the RTs to the 50- and to the 250-msec flashes were almost identical for each S. With the 3000- and the 30-ft-L lights, the 25-msec flash yielded (for the three Ss combined) a somewhat faster RT than any of the others, but the difference between the RT to the 25-msec flash and the longest of the remaining five RTs was only equal to the standard error of the difference (approximately 1.6 msec in both cases).

The data in Table 1 show clearly that luminance does affect RT. The RT to the 3000-ft-L light was, on the average, 12 msec faster than to the 30-ft-L light, and 39 msec faster than to the 0.30-ft-L light. As the standard error for each S's combined mean for a given luminance was less than 1 msec, these differences are highly significant for each S.

The effect of foreperiod on RT is shown in Table 2. In all cases, length of RT is inversely related to foreperiod duration. In fact, for the three Ss together, the difference in RT between the longest and shortest foreperiods was slightly greater than the difference between the 3000- and the 30-ft-L lights. For each S, at each of the three flash luminances, the difference between the 1.5-sec and the 2.0-sec foreperiod means was significant well beyond the .001

level. One S exhibited no difference between the 2.0- and the 2.5 sec foreperiod means. For each of the other two Ss, the means at each luminance for the 2.0-sec foreperiod were significantly longer than those for the 2.5-sec foreperiod, the six t's ranging from 2.14 to

TABLE 2

Mean Reaction Times Classified by Foreperiod Duration

FLASH LUMINANCE IN FT-L	S	FOREPERIOD DURATION		
		1.5 SEC	2.0 SEC	2.5 SEC
3000	EF	163.4	155.9	155.4
	MH	165.1	150.9	147.4
	DR	168.7	158.8	156.0
	Mean	165.7	155.2	152.9
30	EF	176.1	169.8	169.0
	MH	176.3	162.6	158.7
	DR	179.2	168.6	165.4
	Mean	177.2	167.0	164.4
0.30	EF	202.7	196.1	195.0
	MH	202.2	188.8	181.8
	DR	212.6	201.1	195.8
	Mean	205.8	195.3	190.9

Note.—Each individual mean is based on 132 measures. The σ_m of the individual means range between 0.87 and 1.68 msec.

4.14. The foreperiod effect found here is similar to that reported recently by Karlin (1959) and Klemmer (1956), both of whom showed that, over a given range of foreperiods, RT decreases with foreperiod length.

It is interesting to note that the effect of foreperiod on RT is independent of luminance level. Thus, for the three Ss together, the differences in RT between the shortest and medium foreperiods are 10.5, 10.2, and 10.3 msec, respectively, for the high, middle and low levels. The corresponding differences between the medium and long foreperiods are 2.3, 2.6, and 4.4 msec.

Experiment II

METHOD

Subjects. Fifteen undergraduates and one instructor, all naive in respect to the problem, served as Ss. The Ss were assigned at random to two groups of eight each, one a block and one a mixed group. Each S served in eight sessions.

Procedure: Block Group. In this experiment, only the 50- and 250-msec-flash durations of the 3000-ft-L light were used, as in the study of Baumgardt and Segal (1942). The two flash durations were presented in blocks of 18 trials each. Three foreperiods were used as in Exp. I. A daily session consisted of four such blocks in ABBA or BAAB sequence, these sequences being alternated on succeeding sessions in order to cancel any daily work curve effects. After 5 min. of dark adaptation, eight practice trials were given before the recorded trials of the first block were run. A 1-min. rest period separated successive blocks. The longest and the shortest RT of each block were discarded before block means were computed. The means for each flash duration for all eight sessions for a given S were thus based on 256 reactions.

Procedure: Mixed Group. A session consisted of four sets of 18 trials each. In each set, the 50- and the 250-msec flashes were presented nine times each in random order, three times

at each foreperiod. Otherwise, the procedure was identical with that of the block group. As each set contained only nine reactions to a given flash duration, the longest and shortest RTs were not discarded in computing the means. Each duration mean for an S for all eight sessions was therefore based on 288 RTs.

RESULTS

For the mixed group, flash duration had virtually no effect on RT. The data in Table 3 show almost identical RTs for the 50- and 250-msec durations. Moreover, no individual reacted significantly faster to either stimulus. The data are in complete agreement with those of Exp. I.

Two of the eight Ss of the block group reacted significantly faster to the 50-msec flash and five others reacted faster but not significantly so. Only one of the eight showed a reversal of this trend. A test of the significance of the eight differences yields a *t* of 1.92 which by a one-tailed test is significant at the .05 level for 7 *df*. By a sign test, 7 of 8 differences in the same expected direction is significant at the .04 level. Although the difference of 1.5 msec in RT in favor of the 50-msec flash is very small, it must be concluded that under block conditions of presentation, the briefer flash does yield faster RTs.

TABLE 3

Mean Reaction Times under Block and Mixed Presentations

	BLOCK GROUP				MIXED GROUP		
S	50 MSEC	250 MSEC	DIFF.	S	50 MSEC	250 MSEC	DIFF.
1	165.1	170.4	5.3*	1	166.4	167.6	1.2
2	165.3	168.9	3.6*	2	162.1	162.3	0.2
3	157.1	158.9	1.8	3	153.8	153.8	0.0
4	159.2	160.8	1.6	4	164.8	164.7	—0.1
5	169.5	170.4	0.9	5	174.5	174.3	—0.2
6	147.3	148.1	0.8	6	174.2	173.7	—0.5
7	185.5	186.0	0.5	7	176.8	176.1	—0.7
8	174.0	171.8	—2.2	8	186.8	185.1	—1.7
Mean	165.4	166.9	1.5	Mean	169.9	169.7	—0.2

* P < .01.

Discussion

The data of these experiments show that RT to distinctly suprathreshold light flashes is unrelated to flash durations between 10 tnd 500 msec when durations are presented in random order. Results showing faster RT to 50-msec flashes than to longer ones may, therefore, be attributable to attitudinal factors that can develop during blocks of trials. The fact that Ss in our block procedure showed smaller differences in RT to the two flash durations than those reported in previous studies may be due to the procedure we used. Our procedure differed from that of Wells and that of Chernikoff et al. in that we used varying foreperiods and a constant repetition rate whereas they used constant 2-sec foreperiods and a constant repetition rate. Baumgardt and Segal specify neither rate of stimulus presentation nor foreperiod duration. It is conceivable that attitudinal factors affecting RT are sensitive to procedural differences of this sort.

Our data give no support to the thesis of Baumgardt and Segal that short flashes are reacted to faster because they appear brighter.

Early in our experiments it became apparent that our method of stimulus presentation yielded a brightness-duration relation very different from that of Broca and Sulzer. According to the latter, the 50-msec flash should have appeared brighter than the longer flashes, especially when the stimulus luminance was high. Instead, we found that apparent brightness increased with stimulus duration up to the 500-msec flash for all three luminance levels. As this observation was so at variance with the Broca-Sulzer phenomenon, the following brief experiment was undertaken to measure apparent brightness as a function of flash duration by the method of single stimuli. It should be pointed out that this method is quite different from the one that has been used in all demonstrations of the Broca-Sulzer effect. It has previously been measured by matching the brief flash with a flash of much longer duration, exposed to an adjoining retinal area. In our experiment, there was no comparison stimulus. The flash was presented alone, as in the RT experiments, against a feebly illuminated and constant background.

Three undergraduate Ss were asked to rate the apparent brightness of the 3000-ft-L light on a 9-point scale, 9 representing very bright, 1 very dim, and 5 medium. The six flash durations at this intensity were presented in random order 24 times each. Although all Ss were aware that duration was a stimulus variable, none suspected that intensity was held constant throughout. Instead, they reported that the variation in intensity was far more apparent than the variation in duration, and they experienced little difficulty in assigning the ratings.

TABLE 4

Apparent Brightness Ratings of 3000-Ft-L Flash at Each Duration

S	FLASH DURATION IN MILLISECONDS					
	10	25	50	100	250	500
1	4.4	5.3	6.5	7.0	8.1	8.8
2	1.7	1.8	3.3	4.4	7.1	8.8
3	2.8	3.7	5.3	6.6	8.5	9.0
Mean	2.9	3.6	5.1	6.0	7.9	8.9

The mean ratings by each S appear in Table 4. As the intensity of the stimulus was at a level that should yield a pronounced Broca-Sulzer effect, it is obvious that this application of the method of single stimuli yielded results altogether at variance with the matching procedures that have been employed by previous investigators of this effect. It is very possible that the Broca-Sulzer effect occurs only when a test flash of short duration is presented adjacent to or surrounded by a patch of light of several seconds duration, and whose onset precedes that of the test flash by a number of seconds. It may, therefore, depend on interaction effects originating in other retinal areas instead of being a sole function of flash duration.

Our experiments have shown that the continuation of a light flash beyond the first 10 msec (over the range of stimulus levels studied here) does affect phenomenal brightness but not RT. The reaction latency was apparently determined within the first 10 msec of stimulation. Whether any other measure of response strength (such as force in the depression of the key) is correlated with phenomenal intensity cannot of course be answered on the basis of our data. In addition, it should be pointed out that our data give no answer to the question with which we began our investigations, namely, whether reaction time can be used as a measure of the Broca-Sulzer phenomenon. This phenomenon was not demonstrated under our conditions of stimulus presentation.

Summary

Previous studies of the effect of stimulus duration on RT have shown that RT increases as stimulus duration increases beyond approximately 50 msec. In Exp. I, in which six durations ranging from 10 to 500 msec were presented in random order, RT did not vary with stimulus duration. RT was, however, found to be a decreasing function of luminance and of foreperiod duration. In Exp. II, in which 50- and 250-msec flashes were presented in blocks of 18 trials each, a small but significant difference in favor of the briefer flash was found.

Our results suggest that attempts to explain the earlier findings on the basis of the Broca-Sulzer phenomenon are not justified. Instead, attitudinal factors that could develop when a given stimulus duration is presented repeatedly, as in the previous studies, are more likely to be responsible for the RT differences that have been reported.

An unsuccessful attempt to verify the Broca-Sulzer effect by the method of single stimuli indicates that this effect may require asynchronous stimulation of a neighboring retinal area. It was not observed in the absence of a comparison stimulus. Instead, phenomenal brightness increased with flash duration.

Under the range of conditions investigated, it is stimulus rather than apparent intensity that determines RT. The phenomenal brightness differences which were correlated with stimulus duration had no effect on reaction latency.

References

Alpern, M. Metacontrast. *J. Opt. Soc. Amer.*, 1953, *43*, 648–657.

Baumgardt, E., & Segal, J. Facilitation et inhibition parametres de la fonction visuelle. *Annee psychol.*, 1942, *43*, 54–102.

Bills, M. A. The lag of visual sensation in its relation to wave lengths and intensity of light. *Psychol. Monogr.*, 1920, *28*(5, Whole No. 127).

Broca, A., & Sulzer, D. La sensation lumineuse en fonction de temps. *CR Acad. Sci., Paris*, 1902, *134*, 831–834; *137*, 944–946, 977–979, 1046–1049.

Chernikoff, R., & Brogden, W. J. The effect of response termination of the stimulus upon reaction time. *J. comp. physiol. Psychol.*, 1949, *42*, 357–364. ·

Chernikoff, R., Gregg, L. W., & Brogden, W. J. The effect of fixed duration stimulus magnitude upon reaction time to a response terminated stimulus. *J. comp. physiol. Psychol.*, 1950, *43*, 123–128.

Crawford, B. H. Visual adaptation in relation to brief conditioning stimuli. *Proc. Roy. Soc. Lond.*, 1947, *134*, 283–302.

Gregg, L. W., & Brogden, W. J. The relation between duration and reaction time difference to fixed duration and response terminated stimuli. *J. comp. physiol. Psychol.*, 1950, *43*, 329–337. (a)

Gregg, L. W., & Brogden, W. J. The relation between reaction time and the duration of the auditory stimulus. *J. comp. physiol. Psychol.*, 1950, *43*, 389–395. (b)

Jarl, V. C. Method of stimulus presentation as antecedent variable in reaction time experiments. *Acta psychol.*, 1957, *13*, 225–241.

Johnson, H. M. Reaction-time measurements. *Psychol. Bull.*, 1923, *20*, 562–589.

Karlin, L. Reaction time as a function of foreperiod duration and variability. *J. exp. Psychol.*, 1959, *58*, 185–191.

Klemmer, E. T. Time uncertainty in simple reaction time. *J. exp. Psychol.*, 1956, *51*, 179–184.

Stainton, W. H. The phenomenon of Broca and Sulzer in foveal vision. *J. Opt. Soc. Amer.*, 1928, *16*, 26–39.

Stigler, R. Chronophotische Studien über den Umgebungskontrast. *Pflüg. Arch. ges. Physiol.*, 1910, *134*, 365–435.

Wells, G. R. The influence of stimulus duration on reaction time. *Psychol. Monogr.*, 1913, *15*(5, Whole No. 66).

4.4 Supplementary Report:
The Effect of Stimulus Duration and Luminance on Visual Reaction Time[*]

DAVID RAAB   ELIZABETH FEHRER

Raab, Fehrer, and Hershenson (1961) found that simple reaction time (RT) was independent of stimulus duration over the range of 10 to 500 msec. Luminance, on the other hand, was found to be an important determiner of RT. Since intensity rather than total energy (intensity times duration) determined RT, it is obvious that the critical duration (CD) for RT is 10 msec or less for the three luminance levels (3000, 30, and 0.3 ft-L) investigated.

The term critical duration has been borrowed from visual threshold studies, which have shown reciprocity (Bunsen-Roscoe law) up to a CD of approximately 100 msec, beyond which temporal integration ceases and the threshold is defined solely in terms of luminance.

It seemed worthwhile to determine the CDs in the mediation of RT for the luminances previously studied and the relation between RT and stimulus duration below these critical values. In the experiment to be reported, the six durations ranged from 0.5 to 20 msec, and thus overlapped the range used previously. Two additional intermediate luminances were included.

* From: David Raab and Elizabeth Fehrer, "Supplementary Report: The Effect of Stimulus Duration and Luminance on Visual Reaction Time," *Journal of Experimental Psychology,* 1962, vol. 64, pp. 326–327. Copyright (1962) by the American Psychological Association, and reproduced by permission. This research was supported by grants from the National Science Foundation (G-6456), and from the National Institute of Neurological Diseases and Blindness (B-1028) and by funds provided by Brooklyn College. The data were gathered by Carlos Goldberg and Naomi Maizel as part of an honors course.

Method

Target flashes were generated and RTs measured by the same equipment as that employed in our previous study. A single Tektronix wave-form generator provided the gating pulses for the glow modulator tube; pulse durations were switched between trials, as required.

In order to generate flashes having wave forms as rectangular as possible, the driving pulses were shaped to "overvolt" the glow modulator tube, and the tube itself was placed next to an ultraviolet source. With these arrangements, flash energy was found to be proportional to flash duration within 0.5 db. from 0.5 to 20 msec. The circular target, 1 cm. in diameter, subtended 1° 10′ of arc and was viewed binocularly.

Two senior honors students and the 2 authors served as Ss. Each S served in 30 experimental sessions. Computations are based on data of the last 25 sessions. Only one luminance was used in a given session; the five luminances were counterbalanced over test days for each S. Each session consisted of four blocks of 18 trials each, in which each combination of the six durations and three foreperiods appeared once in random order. Only the four longer durations could be explored for the 0.3 ft-L luminance, since this light was below foveal threshold when presented for 0.5 or 1 msec.

Each session began with 5 min. of dark adaptation. Four practice trials preceded the recorded trials. The four blocks were separated by 1-min. rest periods.

The 12 RTs obtained in a session for each of the six durations were reduced to 10 by discarding the longest and the shortest RT. Testing over 25 days (5 at each luminance) thus yielded means for each luminance-duration combination based on 50 trials.

Results and Discussion

Mean RTs for the 4 *Ss* combined are plotted in Figure 1. Each data point is thus based on 200 RTs.

For the two highest luminances, duration is unrelated to RT over the range studied. For the 30 ft-L flash, there was a 10-msec increase in RT when its duration was reduced from 5 to 0.5 msec. For the two lowest luminances, stimulus duration has a far more marked effect on RT, RT being obviously an accelerated function of flash briefness.

Our results show that the CD for moderately intense stimuli (3000 and 300 ft-L) is remarkably brief, being less than 0.5 msec. At 30 and at 3 ft-L, CD lies between 2 and 5 msec. For the weakest target, the CD lies between 10 and 25 msec. The present study shows a small decrease in RT as duration increased from 10 to 20 msec. In the previous study, a smaller de-

crease occurred between 10 and 25 msec, but there was no further decrease when this stimulus was prolonged beyond 25 msec.

These CDs for RT are far shorter than the 100-msec value previously reported for absolute threshold (e.g., Baumgardt & Hillmann, 1961) or the minimal value of 30 msec reported by Graham and Kemp (1938) for the incremental threshold at their highest background luminance. The three dependent variables, RT, RL, and DL, are thus differently related to stimulus duration, with the CD being obviously shortest for RT.

Although luminance differences are confounded with test days (i.e., only one luminance was studied in a given test session), the effect of luminance on RT is pronounced and is apparent at all durations studied. That RT decreases when luminance is increased is consistent with earlier findings (see Woodworth & Schlosberg, 1954). But the form of the relation between luminance and RT will depend on stimulus duration *unless* each stimulus duration is greater than the CD. In other words, our data could be replotted to display six different luminance-RT functions, one for each flash duration.

Our results show that although the overt response to a target flash may not appear until much later, the minimal latency of that response is determined very shortly after stimulus onset. The finding that increasing duration may cease to be effective long before the criterion response appears parallels the classical observation of this fact made by Hartline (1934). The fact that RT is determined by so brief a "package" of luminous energy is consistent with our earlier finding that RT is independent of the growth (with duration) of phenomenal brightness. In addition, it helps to explain why retroactive (metacontrast) masking of a flash does not affect its RT (Fehrer & Raab, 1962).

References

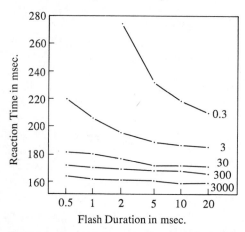

FIGURE 1   Reaction time as a function of stimulus duration. (The parameter is flash luminance in ft-L. Each data point is the mean for 4 *Ss*.)

Baumgardt, E., and B. Hillmann, Duration and size as determinants of peripheral retinal response. *J. Opt. Soc. Amer.*, 1961, *51*, 340–344.

Fehrer, E., and D. Raab, Reaction time to stimuli masked by metacontrast. *J. exp. Psychol.*, 1962, *63*, 143–147.

Graham, C. H., and E. H. Kemp, Brightness discrimination as a function of the duration of the increment in intensity. *J. gen. Psychol.*, 1938, *21*, 635–650.

Hartline, H. K. Intensity and duration in the excitation of single photoreceptor units. *J. cell. comp. Physiol.*, 1934, *5*, 229–247.

Raab, D.. E. Fehrer, and M. Hershenson, Visual reaction time and the Broca-Sulzer phenomenon. *J. exp. Psychol.*, 1961, *61*, 193–199.

Woodworth, R. S., and H. Schlosberg, *Experimental psychology.* (Rev. ed.) New York: Holt, Rinehart and Winston, Inc. 1954.

4.5 Choice Times and Detection with Visual Backward Masking[*]

ROBERT W. SEKULER

In a visual backward masking the detectability of one flash is reduced by a second flash which follows after a brief interval. Backward masking has been found to be a function of the temporal, intensive, and spatial relations between the first and second stimuli. Because the amount of masking varies along so large a number of well-explored stimulus dimensions, masking may be especially appropriate for studying signal detection. As in the classic detection situation (Swets, 1961) the second, or masking, flash may be thought of as adding noise to a signal contained in the first flash. There is another, equally important reason for studying detection within the masking context. It has been shown (Mackworth, 1963) that the information contained in a visual presentation may be available to a subject in the form of a visual image for as long as one second following the presentation. Because such an image is available it is impossible, under ordinary conditions, to specify the time at which a subject is actually using the information contained in the visual presentation. Even with tachistoscopic presentation it is difficult to determine how much time elapses between the onset of the effective stimulus and a subject's response. But this difficulty is diminished in backward masking because the information flash is quickly followed by a second flash, obliterating the image of the first.

In a previous experiment (Sekuler, 1965) a small test stripe contained in the initial flash of a two-flash masking sequence was omitted on varying proportions of trials. In addition to yes-no judgments the choice times associated with each response were also recorded. It was found that although incorrect "yes" responses were of longer latency than correct "yes" responses, there did not seem to be such a difference between correct and incorrect "no" responses. This curious asymmetry between the ways in which "yes" and "no" vary with response correctness led to the present study.

In the experiment to be described the test stripe in the first flash of each masking sequence was omitted on half the trials and both yes-no and choice-time data recorded for some 32,000 trials. A payoff structure with four different

* Reproduced by permission of *Canadian Journal of Psychology*, 1966, vol. 20, pp. 34–42. The research was done at the W. S. Hunter Laboratory of Psychology, Brown University, and was supported by a grant from the National Science Foundation (G-14314) to Harold Schlosberg. The report was prepared during the tenure of a Public Health Service Postdoctoral Fellowship at the Psychophysiology Laboratory of the Massachusetts Institute of Technology. The author is indebted to the late Harold Schlosberg for his encouragement and also to Trygg Engen, Richard B. Millward, and Wayne Wickelgren for their valuable suggestions.

matrices was used to control the subject's responses. In addition to the primary concern with reliability of the previous experiment, the present research should permit analysis of the effects of payoff structure upon choice times, a relation about which little is known.

Method

SUBJECTS

Ss were five undergraduates, four females and one male. All were naïve with respect to the purposes of the experiment. None had served in the previous study and each had acuity corrected to 20/20 or better.

APPARATUS AND PROCEDURE

Because stimulus conditions were identical to those of the previous experiment (Sekuler, 1965) only a brief description is provided here. A specially designed electronic projection tachistoscope was used to present stimuli. On each trial two flashes occurred. The initial flash was either an homogenous field containing a small dark test stripe or the same field without the test stripe. The second flash, spatially overlapping the first, always contained a pattern of alternating light and dark stripes. A fixation point of 1.5 minarc subtense was located in the centre of the target area. The second flash, 100 msec in duration, always followed the first by 40 msec. All luminances were held constant at the values previously reported.

A trial was initiated by S at the end of 0.5-sec auditory signal, the interval between trials being 5 sec. On each trial S used a telephone-type switch to signal his judgment of whether the test stripe had or had not been presented ("yes" and "no" respectively). The interval

between the onset of the first flash and S's response was measured to the nearest centisecond using a Standard Electric Corporation timer.

The test stripe was omitted on a randomly selected half of all trials within a session under the restriction that no more than seven consecutive trials be of the same type—stimulus present or absent. During a hemi-session the duration of the test stripe assumed a different value. Each S was tested with the same two stimulus durations though these values differed slightly among S's. Before the experiment five practice sessions were devoted to familiarizing S with the procedure and to the estimation of equally discriminable test stripe durations for each S. These test stripe durations, shown in Table I, were then used in the experiment.

Four payoff matrices were used to regulate the cost to S of incorrect responses. These are shown in Table II. S was informed that his responses would be weighted by the values of the cells in the matrix in effect for that session. For example, with Matrix 3 each correct response, "yes" or "no," carried a weight $+1$, each incorrect "yes" was weighted -3, while an incorrect "no" was only weighted -1. Ss were told that in addition to an hourly pay rate of $1.25, a $10 bonus would be given to

TABLE I

Test Stripe Durations Used for Each Subject

SUBJECT	DURATIONS (MSEC)	
1	3.0	4.0
2	3.5	4.5
3	4.0	5.0
4	4.0	5.0
5	4.0	5.0

TABLE II

Cost and Values of Response-Stimulus Contingencies in Payoff Matrices

	MATRIX 1		MATRIX 2		MATRIX 3		MATRIX 4	
	"YES"	"NO"	"YES"	"NO"	"YES"	"NO"	"YES"	"NO"
Stripe	$+1$	-1	$+1$	-1	$+1$	-1	$+1$	-3
No stripe	-1	$+1$	-2	$+1$	-3	$+1$	-1	$+1$

the single S receiving the highest point score after all responses had been weighted by the appropriate payoff structures. With the introduction of this bonus incentive Matrices 2 and 3 emphasized the cost of incorrect "yes," while Matrix 4 heavily penalized incorrectly responding "no." Matrix 1 was presumed neutral.

Order of testing with the two stripe durations was randomized for each S under the restriction that, over the 16 sessions, both durations appear equally often in each hemi-session in conjunction with each payoff matrix. Order of testing with matrices was randomized with the constraint that each matrix occur once in a block of four sessions. After an adaptation period S was carefully instructed about the matrix in effect for that session. Ss received no instructions about the speed with which they were to respond and when questioned after the experiment only one S claimed to have suspected that her choice times had been recorded.

A session consisted of 400 trials, 200 with each test stripe duration. A four-min. rest period intervened between hemi-sessions. During this period S confined his gaze to the target area. An auditory signal coincident with each correct response gave S immediate knowledge of results.

Results

For purposes of an analysis of variance, four categories of conditional responses were established: "yes" given that a stripe had appeared (Y/s), "yes" given no stripe (Y/n), "no" given that a stripe had appeared (N/s), and "no" given no stripe (N/n). A four-way analysis of variance was performed on the choice-time data. Mean choice times were entered in a Subject $\times$ Conditional response class $\times$ Matrix $\times$ Stripe duration analysis. The effect of matrix was significant at $p < .05$, $F(3, 12) = 4.408$, while for conditional response class effect $F(3, 12) = 6.908, p < .01$. The interaction between these two main effects was also highly significant, $F(9, 36) = 3.650$, $p < .01$. None of the other terms in the analysis approached significance, $p > .10$. In each case the appropriate interaction with subjects provided the error term. Figure 1 shows for

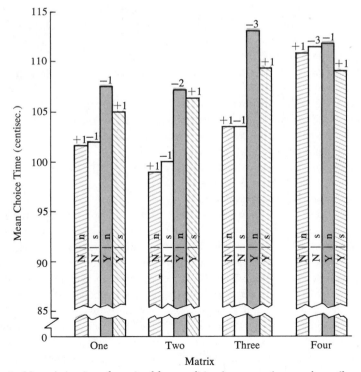

FIGURE 1   Mean choice times for each of four conditional response classes and payoff matrices.

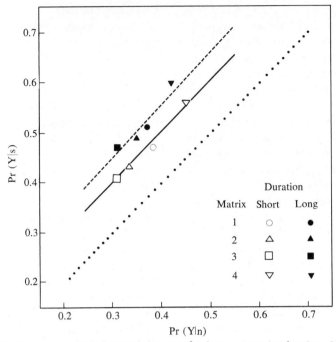

FIGURE 2   Receiver operating characteristic curves for the two test stripe durations. Lines fitted by eye; dotted line shows chance performance.

each response class and matrix the mean choice time averaged across subjects and the two stripe durations. The significance of the difference between selected points in Figure 1 was tested using a t based upon the error mean square. Mean choice times for incorrect "yes" (Y/n) are significantly greater ($p < .05$) than choice times for correct "yes" (Y/s) for every matrix except number 2. The differences between choice times for correct and incorrect "no" responses are non-significant ($p > .10$) for all matrices. In addition, "yes" choice times are significantly greater than "no" times for every matrix except 4, that matrix which was designed to emphasize the cost of incorrectly saying "no."

Receiver operating characteristic (ROC) curves were developed from the yes-no data after the suggestion of Swets (1961). The ROC curves for the group data are shown in Figure 2. It will be noted that the payoff structures used were not adequate to generate a substantial range of criterion shifts and that for either duration of test stripe the range of Pr

(Y/s) and Pr (Y/n) is only about 15 percent. This could be attributed to the paucity of the bonus relative to the guaranteed hourly wage. As in earlier studies of backward masking (Sekuler, 1965a) test stripe detectability increased with duration. This increase in detectability is refleced by the fact that in Figure 2 all four data points for the longer stripe duration lie above the corresponding points for the shorter stripe duration.

Discussion

The main finding of the previous study has been confirmed. Choice times for an incorrect "yes" are longer than for correct "yes." Times of "no" responses do not differ with response correctness. In addition, the effect of payoff structure is shown by the increase in "yes" choice times over matrices 1–3. The increase in penalty for incorrectly saying "yes" was expected to induce a higher criterion for "yes" response and according to some models of choice times (LaBerge, 1962; Myers & Atkinson, 1964) such a criterion change produces the observed lengthening of "yes" choice times. The results obtained under Matrix 4 are somewhat anomalous, however. While the heavy penalty for incorrect "no" did increase the "no" choice times, as might be expected, Matrix 4 also substantially increased "yes" times over the Matrix 1 baseline level. This may represent yet another kind of asymmetry between "yes" and "no" response systems. Even though penalties for incorrect "yes" affect "yes" and "no" choice times differentially (*viz.* matrices 2, 3), it seems that penalizing incorrect "no" responses pushes both response systems in the same direction—increasing both "yes" and "no" times.

It will be recalled that Matrix 1 was intended to be neutral with respect to "yes" and "no" response classes. Its neutrality is questioned by the fact that with Matrix 1 "yes" times are significantly greater than "no" times. This recalls the observation that subjects behave conservatively in reporting the occurrence of a stimulus increment in difference threshold experiments. Treisman proposed that social pressures force subjects in their everyday activities to keep their response criterion sufficiently high to minimize false positives, Y/n (1964; p. 30). Such behaviour, if carried over into the laboratory, might account for the response bias observed in the present experiment even with Matrix 1. The choice-time differences between Y/s and Y/n trials show that each subject responded differentially to the two stimulus states and, by definition, he was discriminating between them. The subject seems to set his criterion for "yes" responses above the point at which his choice times show him able to discriminate stripe-present from stripe-absent trials. This conservative criterion for "yes" responses probably resulted in a reduction of false positives.

Choice-time measures may be used in conjunction with a yes-no indicator to permit an analysis of the response strategy adopted by a subject. As an example, it has been suggested (Treisman, 1964; p. 30) that in certain circumstances a subject may use the following strategy: if during the period between stimulus onset and response, the criterion for "yes" is exceeded the subject responds "yes," otherwise he responds "no." Assuming independence between the motor portion of the response and the particular response selected, such a strategy ought to yield longer latencies for "no" responses than for "yes" responses. Data from the present experiment suggest that subjects were not using such a strategy.

There is no reason, however, to expect that the specific configuration of choice-time results obtained in the present experiment will be invariant over changes in experimental procedure which may themselves alter the relative utility of possible decision-making strategies. For example, the kind of strategy Treisman outlined may be particularly useful when the task is to detect a weak signal which is available to the subject for a relatively long observation period. In an experiment by Carterette, Friedman, and Cosmides (1965) subjects had to report the presence or absence of a weak tone embedded in white noise. The tone was omitted with varying probability and, when actually presented, it was terminated only by the subject's "yes"-"no" response. The results of Carterette, *et al.,* differ from those of the present experiment in two significant ways: (1) they found that better detection performance was associated with *slow* choice times; and (2) in many of their experimental conditions the mean times for "no" responses are longer than those for "yes" responses. Both of these findings can be explained in terms of the extended signal-observation period available to their subjects. Since the signal remained available until the subject responded, higher rates of detection could be achieved by taking advantage of the additional information provided in an extended observation. In addition, since the subject could extract additional information during the course of the observation interval it would be advantageous to use Treisman's strategy of waiting for the "yes" criterion to be exceeded and, if it were not, to respond "no." This would produce mean "no" times longer than mean "yes" times. The extended signal durations of Carterette, *et al.,* are in sharp contrast to the very brief period for which the signal was available to the subject in the backward masking situation of the present experiment. It will be of some interest to determine, in a single experimental context, how both signal duration and its dependence upon a subject's response time influence the obtained choice-time relation.

The constellation of choice-time results in the present experiment exerts severe constraints upon any proposed model of subjects' behaviour. One form which a model might take is suggested by the observing response interpretation outlined by Myers and Atkinson. Such a model would postulate that "associated with each response alternative is a tendency to approach or avoid that alternative. Further assume that the set of approach tendencies, and the order in which response alternatives are considered (or observed) determine the subject's choice on any trial . . ." (Myers & Atkinson, 1964, p. 197). If the order of consideration of alternatives leading to "no" and "yes" varied with payoff structure, the difference between mean "yes" and "no" times under matrices 1–3 might be explicable. For example, a subject attempting to limit false alarm rate might consider response alternatives in the order "no," "yes." The result would be mean "no" times shorter than "yes" times. If, in addition, the sensory basis for the "yes" response alternative were a function of stimulus intensity, the speed with which correct and incorrect "yes" responses occurred could differ in the manner of the present experiment. One possible form of appropriate hypothetical sensory mechanism has been proposed by McGill (1963, pp. 329–32). But data will have to be collected with a broader spectrum of payoff structures and stimulus presentation schedules before a firmer account of the underlying response strategy can be provided and the generality of the response asymmetries discussed herein may be gauged. Moreover, the behaviour of subjects under the apparently neutral payoff structure of Matrix 1 suggests that more attention ought to be given to biases which subjects bring to the experiment and to the possibility that such biases may indeed reflect the way in which extra-experimental experiences affect a wide range of signal detection and choice behaviours.

Summary

Choice response times and signal detection were studied in an experiment on visual backward masking. S made "yes" or "no" judgments of whether a test stripe had appeared in the first flash of each two-flash masking sequence. The test stripe was randomly omitted while the costs and values of "yes" and "no" responses were varied through four payoff matrices. For "yes" judgments, choice times for incorrect responses exceed those for correct responses. For "no" judgments, there was no difference between correct and incorrect choice times. It is shown that, when both choice times and yes-no data are available, the relations between the two sets of data may be used to dissect the underlying decision-making strategy used by the subjects.

References

Carterette, E. C., Friedman, M. P., & Cosmides, R. Reaction-time distributions in the detection of weak signals in noise. *J. Acoust. Soc. Amer.,* 1965, *38,* 531–42.

LaBerge, D. A recruitment theory of simple behavior. *Psychometrika,* 1962, *27,* 375–96.

McGill, W. J. Stochastic latency mechanisms. In R. D. Luce, R. R. Bush, & E. Galanter, Eds., *Handbook of Mathematical Psychology, 1,* 309–60. New York: John Wiley, 1963.

Mackworth, Jane F. The duration of the visual image. *Canad. J. Psychol.,* 1963, *17,* 62–81.

Myers, J. L., & Atkinson, R. C. Choice behavior and reward structure. *J. math. Psychol.,* 1964, *1,* 170–203.

Sekuler, R. W. Signal detection, choice response times, and visual backward masking. *Canad. J. Psychol.,* 1965, *19,* 118–32.

Sekuler, R. W. Spatial and temporal determinants of visual backward masking. *J. exp. Psychol.,* 1965, *70,* 401–6. (a)

Swets, J. A. Detection theory and psychophysics: a review. *Psychometrika,* 1961, *26,* 49–63.

Swets, J. A., Tanner, W. P., Jr., & Birdsall, T. G. Decision processes in perception. *Psychol. Rev.,* 1961, *68,* 301–40

Treisman, M. The effect of one stimulus on the threshold for another: an application of signal detectability theory. *Brit. J. statist. Psychol.,* 1964, *17,* 15–35.

CHAPTER 5

Visual Scanning and Searching

5.1 The Effect of Target Specification on Objects Fixated During Visual Search[*]

L. G. WILLIAMS

The subject of this paper is the search for targets in cluttered visual fields. The immediate experimental objective was to determine which things an observer fixates when he was provided with specific information about a target. These data will be used eventually to achieve a different goal—to develop a method for relating search time to characteristics of the target and of the background.

Which characteristics of targets are related to search time in cluttered fields? Green, McGill, and Jenkins (1953) found that under some conditions larger targets were located faster than small ones and that upright numbers were located faster than randomly oriented ones. Rhodes (1964) also found that larger targets were found more quickly than small ones. However, Baker, Morris, and Steedman (1960) found target size to be unrelated to search time, although they did find that compact targets were found relatively quickly.

Which characteristics of the background are related to search time? Numerosity is one such characteristic. Green, McGill, and Jenkins (1953), Boynton, Elworth, and Palmer (1958), McGill (1960), Baker, Morris, and Steedman (1960) and Williams and Borow (1963) have found that, with simple geometrical or alphabetical materials, search time is approximately proportional to the number of objects present in the display.

It is not simply the number of objects which is the important quantity, but rather the number of objects which are similar to the target. Green and Anderson (1956) and S. L. Smith (1962) have shown that for fields containing objects of different color, when the target's color is specified, search time is approximately proportional to the number of similarly colored objects in the field. In consonance with these results, Rhodes (1964) found that search time was negatively correlated with judged distinctiveness of the target's size and shape. S. W. Smith (1961) found search time was greater for fields containing objects more similar to the target in size, shape and contrast.

In sum, the above studies imply that search time depends on a relationship between the target and the background—namely, the similarities to the target of the various objects in the background.

The search act consists of a sequence of fixations which, in cluttered fields, typically fall on objects. It is hypothesized that the probability of a fixation falling on an object of a given class (for example, on objects of a given size or color or shape) is a function of the target specifications for that search task. Also, for a given search task, if the probabilities of fixating objects of each class are known, and if the numbers of objects of each class are known, then the search time distribution can be predicted. Although it is intuitively clear that this

[*] Reproduced by permission of *Perception & Psychophysics,* 1966, vol. 1, pp. 315–318. This work has been supported by the Engineering Psychology Branch Office of Naval Research, under Contract NONR 4774(00).

can be done, the mathematical details will be presented elsewhere.

The present study is a general attack on the problem of determining where S will fixate as a function of target specification. The specific question being asked was: when the target is specified in terms of its size, color, and/or shape, what proportion of S's fixations are on objects of each size, color, and shape?

Materials

Each search field contained 100 forms of a given size (about 2.8, 1.9, 1.3, or 0.8 degrees in visual extent), a given color (blue, green, yellow, orange, or pink), and a given shape (circle, semicircle, triangle, square, or cross). A different two-digit number, about 0.3 degrees in height, was printed within each form. The fields were displayed on a 1.22-meter square rear projection screen 1.72 meters in front of the subject. The screen subtended horizontal and vertical visual angles of 39 degrees. A typical field is shown in Figure 1.

Procedure

S's task was to locate a target defined by a specific two-digit number. He was also provided with varying amounts of information about the size, color, and shape of the target. Thus, S always knew the target number, either alone or along with one or more other characteristics.

The 35 mm slides from which the stimuli were projected were arranged in pairs. The first slide of each pair contained the target specification in the form of a two-digit number and a verbal description of the size, color, and/or shape in that order. For the four sizes, the terms very large, large, medium, and small were used. These instructions were then repeated in the center of the second, or search field, slide. Each trial lasted until S pressed a button indicating that he had found the target. The observer could present as many as 40 consecutive trials to himself by pressing a response button which controlled the slide projector, the auto-

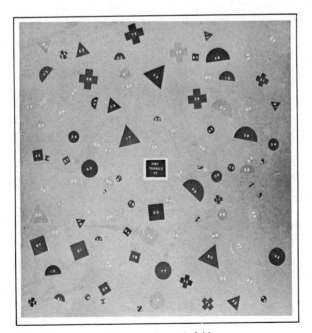

FIGURE 1   A search field.

matic camera, and associated apparatus which recorded the eye fixations. There were 200 different search trials per S, with a different search field being used for each trial.

Eye fixations were measured by the corneal reflection technique first used by Dodge and Cline (1901). In the procedure used in our laboratory, S's left eye was largely occluded. An infrared light source produced a virtual image in that eye, which was photographed through a magnification system. The eye fixation record for each trial consisted of a series of time exposures of 4 sec. duration.

Each S required two sessions of 2 to 3 hr. duration. Thirty male Ss from colleges and universities in the Minneapolis-St. Paul area took part in the experiment. All Ss possessed normal acuity and color vision as indicated by tests using a Titmus Professional Vision Tester prior to the experiment.

Results

The raw data consisted of the filmed records of the eye fixations. The records were transformed into tabulations of what Ss looked at during each trial by projecting each frame of film (containing about 13 fixations) on the search field, and by using correction procedures to reduce the error. The records from about one-sixth of the trials were not tabulated for two main reasons: the photographs were not in proper focus or the calibration photographs needed for tabulation were unsatisfactory.

Each fixation was tabulated as: (a) falling on a specific object in the field (61 percent); (b) at the center of the field containing the information about the target (2 percent); (c) between objects in the field (4 percent); (d) unscored (where the tabulator was not confident enough to classify the fixation into one of the above three categories, 29 percent); (e) a double fixation (when the fixation fell on the object which was just previously fixated, 3 percent). The above percentages are the approximate proportions of fixations within each category.

The accuracy of the eye movement measure-

ment procedure is not a completely determinate quantity, mainly because the ultimate criterion —where the observer was actually looking—is usually not independently known. A more detailed discussion of this question will be presented elsewhere. An indication of the accuracy of the technique used here is provided by the following procedure. When other Ss were instructed to look at specific objects in test fields equal in density to those used in the present study, the data tabulator's "relatively confident" object identifications were correct 95 or 98 percent of the time (depending on which of two alignment procedures he used). This should not be taken to suggest that 95 or 98 percent of the objects in Category a, above, were correctly identified, since in the calibration study just discussed *all* fixations were on objects, whereas in the present study it is presumed that only a fixed proportion were.

Fixation Data

The approximately 115,000 fixations that could be classified as falling on specific objects (Category a, above) will be the subject of discussion. These data will be treated separately for each type of instruction.

When only the two-digit number was specified, the fixations were unrelated to the color, size or shape of the objects in the field (Table 1, bottom row).

When only the color of the target (in addition to the two-digit number) was specified, there was a strong tendency to fixate objects of that color. When only the size was specified, the tendency to fixate targets of specified size was strong for the largest targets and moderate for the others. When only the shape was specified, the tendency to fixate objects of specified shape was slight.

When the color and size of the target were specified, Ss tended to fixate objects of the specified color just as when color alone was specified. Only when the target was specified to be of the largest size did Ss apparently also use size as a basis for fixation. Although the

TABLE 1

Proportion of Fixations on Objects Having the Specified Characteristics*

| | SPECIFIED CHARACTERISTICS | | | | | | | | | | | | | |
| | COLOR | | | | | SIZE (DEGREES OF VISUAL EXTENT) | | | | SHAPE | | | | |
SPECIFICATION	Bl	Gr	Ye	Or	Pi	2.8	1.9	1.3	0.8	Ci	Sc	Tr	Sq	Cr
Color	.61	.56	.59	.71	.60									
Size						.59	.29	.28	.35					
Shape										.26	.24	.24	.23	.29
Color + Size	.59	.65	.67	.66	.59	.52	.30	.30	.30					
Color + Shape	.64	.64	.66	.59	.59					.24	.26	.27	.24	.28
Size + Shape						.57	.30	.29	.35	.27	.25	.26	.24	.30
Color + Size + Shape	.54	.55	.55	.62	.54	.49	.31	.29	.28	.26	.28	.25	.26	.26
Number Only	.20	.20	.20	.18	.22	.25	.25	.26	.24	.20	.20	.20	.20	.20

* To illustrate, when color-plus-size was specified, then for yellow targets 67 percent of the fixations were on yellow objects. When color alone was specified, then for yellow targets 59 percent of the fixations were on yellow objects. The bottom row shows the proportion of fixations on objects of each characteristic indicated by the column label when only the two-digit number was specified.

proportions in Table 1 suggest that Ss also used other sizes as a basis for fixating objects, it is likely that those proportions are increased as a result of finding the target on the last fixation. To show this, assume that Ss used only color and completely ignored size. The number of fixated objects required to find these targets is usually small—a mean of about 18 objects. If let us say, 18 objects are fixated, and the first 17 objects are selected independently of size, then the expected number of specified size would, therefore, be

$$17 \times \frac{24}{99} + 1 = 5.12.$$

The proportion $5.12/18 = .28$ is of comparable value to those in the table for sizes other than the largest.

When the color and shape were specified, there was a strong tendency to fixate objects of specified color, and little or none (considering the argument in the last paragraph) to fixate objects of specified shape. When size and shape were specified, Ss fixated objects on the basis of both size and shape.

When color, size, and shape were specified, fixations were only related to color, the other information being ignored except when the target was also specified to be very large. The overall proportion of fixation on objects of the specified color is less here than for the color-plus-size condition. The statistical significance of this difference is high ($\chi^2 = 96.7$ with df = 1).

Another question of interest involves what S looks at when he does not look at objects having the specified characteristics. With the color specification there is no systematic tendency to look at any other color. However, with the size specifications, Table 2 shows that the likelihood of fixating an object depends on its similarity to the specified size. For three sizes, observers are most likely to fixate objects of specified size. For the "Large" specification the peak has shifted to the largest size. This

TABLE 2

Proportion of Fixations on Objects of Different Size for Each Size Specification

| SPECIFIED SIZE | SIZE OF FIXATED OBJECT | | | |
	VERY LARGE	LARGE	MEDIUM	SMALL
Very Large	0.59	0.24	0.11	0.07
Large	0.35	0.29	0.21	0.15
Medium	0.23	0.26	0.28	0.22
Small	0.13	0.20	0.31	0.35

may be a result of the specific words used in the instructions.

Search Times

The mean times required to find targets for the eight different specifications are shown in Table 3. As can be seen in the table, the specifications divide themselves into four classes: color specified, size but not color specified, shape but not color or size specified, and number only specified. The search times are increasingly greater for the four classes. These data correspond directly to the efficiency of looking as measured by the proportion of fixations on objects having the specified characteristics as shown in Table 1.

Discussion

The results can be summarized as follows: for a field containing objects differing widely in size, color, and shape, Ss selectively fixated objects much better on the basis of color than on size or shape. Further, when provided with information about two or three target characteristics, Ss generally fixated objects on the basis of a single characteristic, namely color if provided.

How should these data be interpreted? The search act consists of two main components—

TABLE 3

Mean Time To Find Target for Different Specifications.

SPECIFICATION	MEAN TIME (SECONDS)	NUMBER OF TRIALS
Color	7.6	455
Color and Size	6.1	463
Color and Shape	7.1	571
Color and Size and Shape	6.4	1178
Size	16.4	468
Size and Shape	15.8	457
Shape	20.7	461
Number Only	22.8	579

identification and acquisition. Identification is the classification of the foveally imaged object—this object is or is not the target. Acquisition is the selection of an object or point outside of the fovea to look at next. S's ability to selectively fixate objects on the basis of specific characteristics is, in fact, his ability to select objects in the extra-foveal field which are similar to the target as specified.

There are two alternative hypotheses about the process by which objects are acquired. One hypothesis is that the selection of each new object to fixate is a choice reaction task for the S. At any moment in time he is likely to be looking at a given object or point in the field. After having decided that that object is not the target, the next object is selected from the many visible ones in the extra-foveal field. The objects in the field can be seen with diminishing clarity with increasing distance from the fixation point. The hypothesis is that S makes a choice of one such object on the basis of the target specifications in at most about 300 msec (since he typically makes more than three fixations per second).

The other hypothesis is that S's percept of the total field is determined by the target specifications. When, for example, he searches for an orange target he perceives a patterning of orange objects on a background of other colored objects. He tries to look at different parts of this pattern until he comes to the target. Thus, when S searches for an orange square the figural structure consists of orange objects rather than orange square objects, simply because he is incapable of structuring the field in terms of both characteristics. S's ability to selectively fixate objects on the basis of any specific set of characteristics is determined by how well he can perceptually structure the field in terms of those characteristics. The data presented would suggest, for example, that in a field containing the five shapes used here, shape is a poor basis for such structure.

At this time the data do not conclusively support one of the hypotheses to the exclusion of the other. The author tentatively accepts the perceptual structuring hypothesis since the alternative has a major weakness with respect to the time constraints. Although up to 300 msec may be available for the choice reaction task, it is likely that only a fraction of this interval can actually be used since time is required for object identification and for eye movements. Since the simple reaction time for visual stimuli is about 180 msec (Woodworth & Schlosberg, 1960), it appears that there may be insufficient time for the hypothesized complex choice reaction.

Summary

When a person searches for a target in a cluttered visual field his eye fixations typically fall on objects. The effect of target specification on the probability of fixating different classes of objects was studied. For fields containing objects differing widely in size, color, and shape: a high proportion of searchers' fixations were on objects of a specified color, a moderate proportion of their fixations were on objects of a specified size, and a slight proportion of their fixations were on objects of a specified shape. When two or more target characteristics were specified, fixations were generally based on a single characteristic. It is proposed that the specification of a target creates a perceptual structure which the searcher explores. The study of visual fixations, in effect, is the study of the perceptual structure.

References

Baker, C. A., Morris, D. F., & Steedman, W. C. Target recognition on complex displays. *Hum. Factors,* 1960, *2,* 51.

Boynton, R. M., Elworth, C., & Palmer, R. M. Laboratory studies pertaining to visual air reconnaissance. WADC Tech. Rep. 55-304, Part III, Wright-Patterson Air Force Base, Ohio, April 1958.

Dodge, R., & Cline, T. S. The angle velocity of eye movements. *Psychol. Rev.,* 1901, *8,* 145.

Green, B. F., & Anderson, L. K. Color coding in a visual search task. *J. exp. Psychol.,* 1956, 51, 19.

Green, B. F., McGill, W. J., & Jenkins, A. M. The time required to search for numbers on large visual displays. MIT, Lincoln Laboratory, TR36, 1953.

McGill, W. J. Search distributions in magnified time. *Visual search techniques.* Washington: National Academy of Science - Nat. Res. Coun., 1960 (Pub. 712).

Rhodes, F. Predicting the difficulty of locating targets from judgments of image characteristics. Technical Documentary Report AMRL-TDR-64-19, Aerospace Medical Research Laboratories, Wright-Patterson Air Force Base, Ohio, March 1964.

Smith, S. L. Color coding and visual search. *J. exp. Psychol.,* 1962, 64, 434.

Smith, S. W. Time required for target detection in complex abstract visual display. Memorandum of Project Michigan 2900-235-R, Institute of Science and Technology, The University of Michigan, April 1961.

Williams, L. G., & Borow, Marion. The effect of rate and direction of display movement on visual search. *Hum. Factors,* 1963, 5, 139.

Woodworth, R. S., & Schlosberg, H. *Experimental psychology,* New York: Henry Holt and Company, 1960.

5.2 High-Speed Scanning
in Human Memory*

SAUL STERNBERG

How is symbolic information retrieved from recent memory? The study of short-term memory (1) has revealed some of the determinants of failures to remember, but has provided little insight into error-free performance and the retrieval processes that underlie it. One reason for the neglect of retrieval mechanisms may be the implicit assumption that a short time after several items have been memorized, they can be immediately and simultaneously available for expression in recall or in other responses, rather than having to be retrieved first. In another vocabulary (2), this is to assume the equivalence of the "span of immediate memory" (the number of items that can be recalled without error) and the "momentary capacity of consciousness" (the number of items immediately available). The experiments reported here[1] show that the assumption is unwarranted.

Underlying the paradigm of these experiments is the supposition that if the selection of a response requires the use of information that is in memory, the latency of the response will reveal something about the process by which the information is retrieved. Of particu-

lar interest in the study of retrieval is the effect of the number of elements in memory on the response latency. The subject first memorizes a short series of symbols. He is then shown a test stimulus, and is required to decide whether or not it is one of the symbols in memory. If the subject decides affirmatively he pulls one lever, making a positive response; otherwise he makes a negative response by pulling the other lever. In this paradigm it is the identity of the symbols in the series, but not their order, that is relevant to the binary response. The response latency is defined as the time from the onset of the test stimulus to the occurrence of the response.

Because they are well learned and highly discriminable, the ten digits were used as stimuli. On each trial of experiment 1, the subject[2] saw a random series of from one to six different digits displayed singly at a fixed locus for 1.2 seconds each. The length, s, of the series varied at random from trial to trial. There followed a 2.0-second delay, a warning signal, and then the test digit. As soon as one of the levers was pulled, a feedback light informed the subject whether his response had been correct. The trial ended with his attempt to recall the series in order. For every value of s, positive and negative responses were required with equal frequency. Each digit in the series occurred as a test stimulus with probability $(2s)^{-1}$, and each

* Science, August 5, 1966, vol. 153, pp. 652–654. Copyright © 1966 by the American Association for the Advancement of Science. Supported in part by NSF grant GB-1172 to the University of Pennsylvania. I thank D. L. R. Scarborough for assistance, and J. A. Deutsch, R. Gnanadesikan, and C. L. Mallows for helpful discussion.

[1] These experiments were first reported by S. Sternberg, "Retrieval from recent memory: Some reaction-time experiments and a search theory," paper presented at a meeting of the Psychonomic Society, Bryn Mawr, August 1963.

[2] Subjects were undergraduates at the University of Pennsylvania.

of the remaining digits occurred with probability $[2(10 - s)]^{-1}$.

Each subject had 24 practice trials and 144 test trials. Feedback and payoffs were designed to encourage subjects to respond as rapidly as possible while maintaining a low error-rate. The eight subjects whose data are presented pulled the wrong lever on 1.3 percent of the test trials.[3] Recall was imperfect on 1.4 percent of the trials. The low error-rates justify the assumption that on a typical trial the series of symbols in memory was the same as the series of symbols presented.

Results are shown in Figure 1. Linear regression accounts for 99.4 percent of the variance of the overall mean response-latencies.[4] The slope of the fitted line is 37.9 ± 3.8 msec per symbol;[5] its zero intercept is 397.2 ± 19.3 msec. Lines fitted separately to the mean latencies of positive and negative responses differ in slope by 9.6 ± 2.3 msec per symbol. The difference is attributable primarily to the fact that for $s = 1$, positive responses were 50.0 ± 20.1 msec faster than negative responses. Lines fitted to the data for $2 \leqslant s \leqslant 6$ differ in slope by an insignificant 3.1 ± 3.2 msec per symbol.

The latency of a response depends, in part, on the relative frequency with which it is required (3). For this reason the frequencies of positive and negative responses and, more generally, the response entropy (3), were held constant for all values of s in Experiment 1.

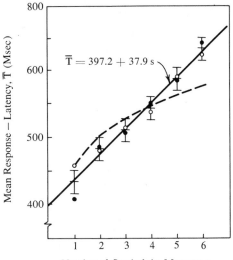

$$\overline{T} = 397.2 + 37.9\,s$$

Number of Symbols in Memory, s

FIGURE 1 Relation between response latency and the number of symbols in memory, s, in experiment 1. Mean latencies, over eight subjects, of positive responses (filled circles) and negative responses (open circles). About 95 observations per point. For each s, overall mean (heavy bar) and estimates of ± σ are indicated (4). Solid line was fitted by least squares to overall means. Upper bound for parallel process (broken curve).

However, the test-stimulus entropy (predictability) was permitted to co-vary with s.

Both response and test-stimulus entropies were controlled in Experiment 2, in which the retrieval process was studied by an alternative method similar to that used in more conventional experiments on choice-reaction time. In Experiment 1, the set of symbols associated with the positive response changed from trial to trial. In contrast to this varied-set procedure, a fixed-set procedure was used in Experiment 2. In each of three parts of the session, a set of digits for which the positive response was required (the positive set) was announced to the subject[2]; there followed 60 practice trials and 120 test trials based on this set. The subject knew that on each trial any of the ten digits could appear as the test stimulus, and that for all the digits not in the positive set (the negative set) the negative response was required. Each subject worked with nonintersecting positive sets of size $s = 1$, 2, and 4, whose composition was varied from subject to subject.

---

[3] These trials were excluded from the analysis. Three other subjects in experiment 1 (two in experiment 2) were rejected because they exceeded an error criterion. Their latency data, which are not presented, resembled those of the other subjects.

[4] For both experiments the data subjected to analysis of variance were, for each subject, the mean latency for each value of s. So that inferences might be drawn about the population of subjects, individual differences in mean and in linear-regression slope were treated as "random effects." Where quantities are stated in the form $a \pm b$, b is an estimate of the standard error of a. Such estimates were usually calculated by using variance components derived from the analysis of variance.

[5] The analyses of variance for both experiments provided a means of testing the significance of differences among slopes. Significance levels are .07 (experiments 1) and .09 (experiment 2), suggesting true inter-subject differences in slope; the population distribution of slopes has an estimated standard deviation of 8.0 msec per symbol.

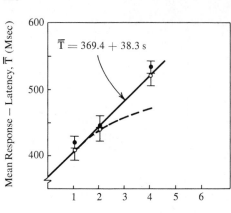

$$\overline{T} = 369.4 + 38.3 \, s$$

FIGURE 2 Relation between response latency and the size of the positive set, s, in experiment 2. Mean latencies, over six subjects, of positive responses (filled circles) and negative responses (open circles). About 200 (positive) or 500 (negative) observations per point. For each s, overall mean (heavy bar) and estimates of $\pm \, \sigma$ are indicated ([4]). Solid line was fitted by least squares to overall means. Upper bound for parallel process (broken curve).

Stimulus and response entropies were both held constant while s was varied, by means of specially constructed populations of test stimuli. Let $x_1, y_1, y_2, z_1, \ldots, z_4$ and $w_1, \ldots, w_3$ represent the ten digits. Their relative frequencies in the population were x_1, 4/15; each y, 2/15; each z, 1/15; and each w, 1/15. The three sequences of test stimuli presented to a subject were obtained by random permutation of the fixed population and assignment of x_1, the y_1, or the z_1 to the positive response. Thus, the population of test stimuli, their sequential properties, and the relative frequency of positive responses (4/15) were the same in all conditions.[6]

A trial consisted of a warning signal, the test digit, the subject's response, and a feedback light. Between a response and the next test digit, 3.7 seconds elapsed. As in Experiment 1, feedback and payoffs were designed to encourage speed without sacrifice of accuracy. The six

[6] A result of this procedure is that other factors in choice-reaction time were also controlled: stimulus discriminability ([4]); information transmitted ([3]); and information reduced, M. I. Posner, *Psychol. Rev., 71*, 491 (1964); P.M. Fitts and I. Biederman, *J. Exp. Psychol., 69*, 408 (1965).

subjects whose data are presented pulled the wrong lever on 1.0 percent of the test trials.[3]

The results, shown in Figure 2, closely resemble those of Experiment 1. A positive set in Experiment 2 apparently played the same role as a series of symbols presented in Experiment 1, both corresponding to a set of symbols stored in memory and used in the selection of a response. As in Experiment 1, linear regression accounts for 99.4 percent of the variance of the overall mean response-latencies.[4] The slope of 38.3 $\pm$ 6.1 msec per symbol is indistinguishable from that in experiment 1; the zero intercept is 369.4 $\pm$ 10.1 msec. In Experiment 2, the relation between latencies of positive and negative responses when $s = 1$ is not exceptional. Lines fitted separately to latencies of the two kinds of response differ in slope by an insignificant 1.6 $\pm$ 3.0 msec per symbol.

The linearity of the latency functions suggests that the time between test stimulus and response is occupied, in part, by a serial-comparison (scanning) process. An internal representation of the test stimulus is compared successively to the symbols in memory, each comparison resulting in either a match or a mismatch. The time from the beginning of one comparison to the beginning of the next (the comparison time) has the same mean value for successive comparisons. A positive response is made if there has been a match, and a negative response otherwise.

On trials requiring negative responses, s comparisons must be made. If positive responses were initiated as soon as a match had occurred (as in a self-terminating search), the mean number of comparisons on positive trials would be $(s + 1)/2$ rather than s. The latency function for positive responses would then have half the slope of the function for negative responses. The equality of the observed slopes shows, instead, that the scanning process is exhaustive: even when a match has occurred, scanning continues through the entire series. This may appear surprising, as it suggests nonoptimality. One can, however, conceive of systems in which a self-terminating search would be inefficient. For example, if the determination of whether or not a match had occurred were a slow operation that could not occur concurrently with scanning, self-termination would entail a long interruption in the scan after each comparison.

On the basis of the exhaustive-scanning theory, the zero intercept of the latency function is interpreted as the sum of the times taken by motor response, formation of the test-stimulus representation, and other unknown processes whose durations are independent of the number of symbols in memory. The slope of the latency function represents the mean comparison-time. The two experiments, then, provide a measure of the speed of purely internal events, independent of the times taken by sensory and motor operations. The average rate of between 25 and 30 symbols per second is about four times as high as the maximum rate of "subvocal speech" when the words are the names of digits (5). This difference suggests that the silent rehearsal (6) reported by subjects in both experiments should probably not be identified with high-speed scanning, but should be thought of as a separate process whose function is to maintain the memory that is to be scanned.

In view of the substantial agreement in results of the two experiments, one difference in procedure merits particular emphasis. A response in Experiment 1 was the first and only response based on a particular series, made about three seconds after the series had been presented. In contrast, the positive set on which a response was based in experiment 2 had been used on an average of 120 previous trials. Evidently, neither practice in scanning a particular series nor lengthening of the time it has been stored in memory need increase the rate at which it is scanned.

In accounting for human performance in other tasks that appear to involve multiple comparisons, theorists have occasionally proposed that the comparisons are carried out in parallel rather than serially (7, 8). (This perhaps corresponds to the assumption mentioned earlier that the momentary capacity of consciousness is several items rather than only one.) Are the present data inconsistent with such a proposal? Parallel comparisons that be-

gin and also end simultaneously (8) are excluded because the mean latency has been shown to increase with s. A process in which multiple comparisons begin simultaneously is more difficult to exclude if the comparison times are independent, their distribution has nonzero variance, and the response is initiated when the slowest comparison ends. A linear increase in mean latency cannot alone be taken as conclusive evidence against such a process. The magnitude of the latency increase that would result from a parallel process is bounded above, however (9); it is possible to apply the bound to these data.[7] This was done for the negative responses in both experiments, with the results shown by the broken curves in Figures 1 and 2. Evidently, the increase in response latency with s is too great to be attributed to a parallel process with independent comparison times.[8]

Other experiments provide added support for the scanning theory.[7] Two of the findings are noted here: (i) variation in the size, n, of the negative set ($n \geqslant s$) had no effect on the mean latency, indicating that stimulus confusability (4, 10) cannot account for the results of Experiments 1 and 2; (ii) variation in the size of a response-irrelevant memory load had no effect on the latency function, implying that the increase in latency reflects the duration of retrieval and not merely the exigencies of retention.

The generality of the high-speed scanning process has yet to be determined, but there are several features of Experiments 1 and 2 that should be taken into account in any comparison with other binary classification tasks (8, 11): (i) at least one of the classes is small; (ii) class members are assigned arbitrarily; (iii) relatively little practice is provided; (iv) high accuracy is required and errors cannot be corrected; and (v) until the response to one stimulus is completed the next stimulus cannot be viewed.

---

[7] S. Sternberg, in preparation.

[8] Exponentially distributed parallel comparisons (7) and other interesting theories of multiple comparisons (10) lead to a latency function that is approximately linear in log s. Deviations of the overall means from such a function are significant ($P < .03$) in both experiments.

Summary

When subjects judge whether a test symbol is contained in a short memorized sequence of symbols, their mean reaction-time increases linearly with the length of the sequence. The linearity and slope of the function imply the existence of an internal serial-comparison process whose average rate is between 25 and 30 symbols per second.

References

1. Melton, A W. *J. Verbal Learning Verbal Behavior* 2, 1 (1963).
2. Miller, G. A. *Psychology, the Science of Mental Life* (Harper and Row, New York, 1962), p. 47.
3. Garner, W. R. *Uncertainty and Structure as Psychological Concepts* (Wiley, New York, 1962).
4. Shepard, R. N. and J. J. Chang, *J. Exp. Psychol.* 65, 94 (1963); M. Stone, *Psychometrika 25*, 251 (1960).
5. Landauer, T. K. *Percept. Mot. Skills 15* (1962).
6. Broadbent, D. E. *Perception and Communication* (Pergamon, New York, 1958), p. 225.
7. Christie, L. S. and R. D. Luce, *Bull. Math. Biophys.* 18, 89 (1956); A Rapoport, *Behavioral Sci. 4*, 299 (1959).
8. Neisser, U. *Amer. J. Psychol. 76*, 376 (1963); *Sci. Amer. 210*, 94 (1964).
9. Hartley, H. O. and H. A. David, *Ann. Math. Stat. 25*, 85 (1954).
10. Welford, A. T. *Ergonomics 3*, 189 (1960).
11. Pollack, I. *J. Verbal Learning Verbal Behavior 2*, 159 (1963); D. E. Broadbent and M. Gregory, *Nature 193*, 1315 (1962).

5.3 Parallel versus Serial Processes in Multidimensional Stimulus Discrimination*

HOWARD E. EGETH

Although considerable effort has been devoted to the description of processes underlying discrimination along single dimensions, there have been few attempts to determine how these elementary processes may be combined when discrimination requires the consideration of more than one stimulus dimension. Despite the fact that they have not been amply studied by psychologists, discriminations among complex stimuli are far more common and important in our daily lives than simple discriminations. The present study is an effort to increase our understanding of complex discriminations by investigating in detail the fundamental task of deciding if two simultaneously presented multidimensional stimuli are identical or different when Ss have an incentive to respond both quickly and accurately.

The specific question which is dealt with in the present investigation is whether humans discriminate between multidimensional objects

* Reproduced by permission of *Perception & Psychophysics*, 1966, vol. 1, pp. 245–252. The study reported here is part of a dissertation submitted to the faculty of the Department of Psychology of the University of Michigan in partial fulfillment of the requirements for the Ph.D. degree. The research was supported by the Advanced Research Projects Agency, Department of Defense, and was monitored by the Air Force Office of Scientific Research, under Contract No. AF 49 (638)-1235 with the Human Performance Center, University of Michigan. The author held a National Science Foundation Fellowship while the research was being carried out. The generous help of J. D. Birch, P. M. Fitts, J. E. K. Smith, R. S. Tikofsky, and D. J. Weintraub is gratefully acknowledged.

by comparing them one dimension after the other (serial mode), or by comparing them on several dimensions simultaneously (parallel mode), or by comparing unitary representations of them without regard to their component dimensions (template mode). These three modes of information processing are of particular interest since there have been several recent attempts to assess their applicability to the task of pattern recognition as performed by both humans and computers (e.g., Uhr, 1963; Neisser, 1964; Sternberg, 1963). Each of these modes provides the basis for a class of models of the stimulus comparison process. Specific instances from these classes are discussed and, for each, behavioral predictions are made which may be tested against obtained data. In particular, the predictions which are made by each model regarding two important relations are stated to give a basis for comparison among the models. These relations are: (a) the function relating the time taken to determine that two objects are identical, i.e., "Same" reaction time (RT), to the number of relevant dimensions, and (b) the relation, for any given number of relevant dimensions, between the time required to determine that two objects are different ("Different" RT) and the number of relevant dimensions along which there are differences.

To facilitate the description of these models and their behavioral predictions, a set of three hypothetical two-valued dimensions (X, Y, Z) will be referred to occasionally. This set of independent dimensions, which may be used in constructing pairs of stimuli, has the characteristic that the two levels of X can be more quickly discriminated from one another than can the two levels of Y, which are, in turn, more discriminable than the values chosen for Z. The identical ordering of dimensions for "Same" RT also obtains.

In deriving predictions from all of the following models it is assumed that Ss are uninfluenced by the presence of irrelevant information. That is, it has been assumed that if a set of complex stimuli contains a dimension which is irrelevant to the judgment of "Same" vs. "Different," then Ss are capable of completely

filtering it. Although it is a simple matter to find instances in which irrelevant information (noise) cannot be ignored, there is evidence that, in reaction time experiments similar to the present one, Ss may filter irrelevant information. This evidence and the validity of the filtering assumption for the present experimental task are both treated in the discussion of the present experiment.

Serial Models. Serial models are characterized by the assumption that in determining whether two simultaneously presented multidimensional stimuli are the same or different, the two stimuli are compared dimension by dimension, one comparison after another. This assumption, in conjunction with the assumption that the comparison processes are independent, leads to the prediction that "Same" RT should increase with the number of relevant dimensions since a pair of stimuli must be found identical along every relevant dimension before a "Same" response can be made. Thus when all three dimensions (X, Y, Z) are relevant "Same" RT ought to be slower than the average of those three conditions in which two dimensions are relevant (X & Y, X & Z, Y & Z), and that average ought to be slower than the average of those three conditions in which only one dimension is relevant (X, Y, Z). In fact, it is a simple matter to show that as long as the same dimensions are used at each level of dimensionality (as in this example) the function relating mean "Same" RT to the number of relevant dimensions must be linear.

There are two attributes of serial models which are considered here, for the sake of simplicity, to be dichotomous. One attribute is concerned with whether "Different" judgments are made as soon as the two objects are found to differ on one relevant dimension (self-terminating comparisons), or whether every relevant dimension is examined on every trial regardless of the outcome of any comparison (exhaustive comparisons). The other attribute of serial models has to do with the order in which dimensions are compared. The two extreme cases considered here require Ss to use either a fixed order on every trial or a random order over a series of trials. Taken in combination, these two attributes result in four possible sub-classifications of serial models.

Since all serial models yield the identical prediction that "Same" RT must increase linearly with the number of relevant dimensions, only predictions concerning "Different" RTs are stated for each particular model. Serial/Exhaustive/Fixed order and Serial/Exhaustive/Random order both predict that for any given number of relevant dimensions, "Different" RT will be the same regardless of the number of relevant dimensions along which there are differences, since all dimensions are always compared. Thus, when Ss are dealing with two-dimensional stimuli, they ought to respond "Different" no faster when the pair of objects differs on both dimensions than when they differ on either one alone. These two models cannot be distinguished by the experiment proposed in this paper.

Serial/Self-Terminating/Fixed order and Serial/Self-Terminating/Random order both predict that for any given number of relevant dimensions, the greater the number which differ between two objects, the faster will be the average "Different" RT. This prediction is based simply upon the self-terminating assumption; on the average, the larger the number of dimensions which differ between two stimuli, the earlier will one of these differences be detected, whether the order of examination is fixed or random. These two models may be distinguished on the basis of another prediction about "Different" RTs. For example, when there are three relevant dimensions, an experiment can be arranged so that on certain trials there will be only one dimension along which there is a difference. Over a series of such trials, we can establish the mean "Different" RT separately for each dimension when it alone is different between the two stimuli. Assuming a fixed order of examination, the fastest of these RTs indicates the dimension which is interrogated first. This dimension is not necessarily the most discriminable one, it is simply examined before the others. (The fastest of the observed "Different" RTs will indicate the di-

mension that is interrogated first as long as the time required to judge that two stimuli are different is not substantially greater than the time required to judge that they are the same.)[1] With this RT as a standard, we may now inquire into the effect of having differences along one or more other dimensions in addition to the one that is interrogated first. If the process takes place in a fixed order, then adding more differences cannot reduce RT below the "standard," since, of course, none of the additional differences will be detected after the first one. In terms of the hypothetical set of dimensions introduced earlier, when X, Y, and Z are all relevant, if the "Different" RT when X alone differs between the two stimuli is shorter than the "Different" RTs when either Y or Z is alone different, then X must be interrogated first. Further, if Y and X, or Z and X, or even Y, Z, and X differ within a pair of stimuli, "Different" RT can be no faster than when X alone is different. However, assumption of a random order of comparisons from trial-to-trial leads to quite a different interpretation of the finding that differences along one of the dimensions (X) yield faster "Different" RTs than differences along either of the other two (Y or Z). The assumption of random order of comparisons obviously precludes the conclusion that X is consistently interrogated first, and implies that the observed mean "Different" RT when X alone is different is based in part on trials on which Y, or Z, or Y and Z are interrogated first. Thus, if Y and/or Z differ in addition to X, then the mean "Different" RT can be faster than when X alone is different since on those trials on which Y or Z happens to be examined first, the comparison process can terminate without having to reach X.

----

[1] Unfortunately, there is no direct evidence on this point in the present experiment, since the data concerning the two kinds of judgment times come from two different response systems, viz., the left and right hands. The task itself may impose response biases which could favor one response over the other, even though a payoff matrix was introduced to mitigate any such response preferences. It is for this same reason that no predictions were made that involved a comparison between "Same" and "Different" response times.

Parallel Models. Parallel models are characterized by the assumption that several comparisons may be made simultaneously. To make this presentation specific, the further assumptions are added here that these tests commence simultaneously and that irrelevant information is ignored. As with serial models there are two important dichotomous attributes of parallel models. First, parallel comparison processes may be either exhaustive or self-terminating. Secondly, the time required to make a comparison along a single dimension may be either constant over all trials or it may fluctuate somewhat from trial-to-trial, as would be the case if comparison times were distributed like a random variable. A word of explanation must be given concerning the implications of the assumption that comparison times are statistically distributed (for a more complete discussion see Rapoport, 1959). For example, consider a "Same" judgment; a correct decision hinges upon the outcome of as many tests as there are relevant dimensions. Therefore, a correct decision takes at least as long as the longest component. However, the mean of the longest time in a sample of statistically distributed times increases as the size of the sample increases, if there is any overlap at all among their respective distributions. Thus, the greater the number of relevant dimensions, the longer will be the mean time required to judge that two stimuli are "Same." Note that in the case of serial models it was not important to specify whether a comparison was of a fixed or a statistically distributed duration since predictions were based simply on expected values of a series (sum) of such processes.

In the section on serial models, it was important to know which single dimension gave rise to the fastest "Different" RT on those trials when, among several relevant dimensions, it alone was different. The same information is important for testing predictions from the parallel models. In addition, it is crucial to find out which dimension yields the slowest "Same" RTs. Of course, Ss can correctly respond "Same" on the basis of a single dimension only when there are no other relevant dimensions. Thus, for each dimension which is used in the conditions requiring multidimensional judgments, a separate condition must be run in which it is the only relevant dimension. From the results of these conditions, it is possible to determine how long it takes to judge that two stimuli are the same with respect to any given dimension. Predictions from the four sub-classes of parallel models follow.

Parallel/Exhaustive/Constant: For any number of relevant dimensions, "Same" RT should be equal to the "Same" RT when the single worst component is judged in isolation. Thus, if Z leads to a slower average "Same" RT than either X or Y when tested in isolation, then the mean "Same" judgments involving X and Z, Y and Z, or X, Y, and Z should be equal to the mean "Same" RT when Z is judged alone. Since the testing is assumed to be exhaustive, "Different" RT when several (but not necessarily all) relevant dimensions are different depends upon the relevant dimension which yields the slowest RTs: for those trials on which that dimension is "Same," the correct response ("Different") is limited by the "Same" RT obtained for that dimension; for those trials on which the "slowest" dimension happens to be "Different," the correct response is limited by the "Different" RT obtained for that dimension.

Parallel / Exhaustive / Distributed: Both "Same" and "Different" RTs will increase with the number of relevant dimensions. Differences along several relevant dimensions will not result in shorter RTs than a difference along the most discriminable of the relevant dimensions.

Parallel/Self-Terminating/Constant: For any given number of relevant dimensions, "Same" RT ought to be equal to "Same" RT for the least discriminable relevant component. Multiple differences will not result in faster RTs than a difference along only the most discriminable component dimension.

Parallel / Self-Terminating / Distributed: "Same" RT for complex stimuli ought to be longer than to the least discriminable component dimension. However, "Different" RT will be faster when there are differences along several dimensions (including the most discriminable one) than when there is a difference along only the most discriminable single dimension.

Template Models. The term "template" usually refers to a stored replica of a stimulus object. However, in the present context of comparing simultaneously presented stimuli it is probably worthwhile to ignore the notion that a template must be in memory. Rather, one might conceive of some process which replicates each of the two stimuli in a pair, and then makes an overall comparison between these two replicas. If there is a complete point-for-point match, then a "Same" response is made; if there is any mismatch at all, a "Different" response is made. This hypothesis leads to the prediction that "Different" responses should be equally fast regardless of the number of dimensions which actually are different. Furthermore, since tests are made on the basis of an overall comparison rather than from the combination of elementary tests on separate dimensions, it seems reasonable to predict that "Same" RT for multidimensional stimuli would never be slower than the "Same" RT to the single worst dimension. On the basis of these predictions, template matching seems very similar to the Parallel/Exhaustive/Constant model. Although the experiment reported in this paper cannot distinguish between these two models, they may be distinguishable on other grounds; they are both described here for completeness. (Of course, if they are both rejected on the basis of their common predictions, then it will not be necessary to find their distinguishing features.)

PREVIOUS RESEARCH

There have been several well conceived studies on the role of dimensionality in stimulus comparison. However, most of them have not used latency as a response measure, and thus offer little help in choosing among the models just presented (e.g., Shepard, 1964; and see Garner, 1962, for a review of the literature on absolute judgments of multidimensional stimuli).

Method

SUBJECTS

Six students at The University of Michigan were chosen from a large pool of persons who had volunteered to serve in psychological experiments for pay.

APPARATUS

The S sat at a table and looked directly into a Gerbrands two-field mirror tachistoscope which had a uniform light-gray background field. On the table in front of S was a panel with two response keys side-by-side labeled "Same" and "Different." The E gave a verbal "Ready" signal approximately 1 sec. before he initiated the stimulus presentation which was terminated by the depression of one of the two response keys. A printing timer made a record, accurate to the nearest millisecond, of the time between the onset of the stimulus and the depression of the response key.

TASK AND STIMULUS MATERIALS

There were seven conditions in the present experiment. Each was defined by the dimensions which were relevant to the "Same" or "Different" decision. These conditions were: Color (C), Form (F), Tilt (T), Color & Form (CF), Color & Tilt (CT), Form & Tilt (FT), and Color & Form & Tilt (CFT). Thus, for example, in FT, Ss were to respond "Same" whenever both stimuli were of the same form and tilt, and "Different" whenever form and/or tilt were different; color was irrelevant to the decision.

Pairs of stimuli were prepared on white index cards. A stimulus assumed one of two values on each of three dimensions: Form—square or circle; Color of form—vermillion or light blue, and Tilt of inscribed black line—45° left or right of vertical. The colors were from the Zip-a-tone Company series of adhesive papers; the other dimensions are illustrated in Figure 1. The outside diameter of the circle was 3/4 in. and the square was 5/8 in. on a side. Since there are eight possible stimuli resulting from

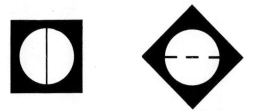

FIGURE 1   A stimulus pair illustrating differences along the dimensions of Form and of Tilt of inscribed line.

the combination of three independent binary dimensions, there are 64 possible pairs of such stimuli. The procedure used to keep the probabilities of "Same" and "Different" responses equal in every condition is outlined in the following three paragraphs.

One-Dimensional Stimuli. For any single dimension, half of the 64 possible pairs were "Same" and half "Different." One copy of each was made, and these, taken together, formed the deck (I) which was used for the three conditions involving single dimensions (C, F, & T).

Two-Dimensional Stimuli. Although half of the cards in Deck I can be categorized as "Same" and half as "Different" with respect to any single dimension, with respect to any pair of dimensions only one-fourth of the cards can be categorized "Same" while three-fourths are "Different." In order to keep the probabilities of the two types of responses equal in every condition, an additional deck had to be constructed for each of the three bidimensional conditions. These decks contained, in addition to the basic 64 cards of Deck I, enough replicas of cards which could be categorized "Same" with respect to the two relevant dimensions, so that half of the required responses would be "Same" and half "Different."

Three-Dimensional Stimuli. Only one-eighth of the cards in Deck I were "Same" with respect to all three dimensions. In order to keep the probabilities of the two types of response equal, another deck of cards was constructed for the tridimensional condition. It contained, in addition to the basic 64 cards of Deck I, enough replicas of cards which were "Same"

with respect to all three dimensions so that half of the required responses would be "Same" and half "Different." For every condition, there were more cards in the appropriate deck than there were trials; cards were selected for use by drawing at random, without replacement, from the pool of available cards.

PROCEDURE

Design. Three Ss were instructed to press the left key to indicate "Same" and the right key to indicate "Different," while the remaining three Ss were given the opposite response-assignment. All Ss served in one practice session and three experimental sessions. In each experimental session they participated in all seven conditions.

Three different orders of presentation of the seven conditions were constructed, and one of the three Ss from each of the two response-assignment categories served in each order. Each order had the following features: (a) the three one-dimensional conditions followed one another in a block, as did the three two-dimensional conditions; (b) the order of the one-, two-, and three-dimensional blocks formed a Latin square over the three days of practice; and (c) within the one- and two-dimensional blocks the order of particular conditions formed a Latin square over the three days of practice.

Each day, Ss received 30 trials in each of the one- and two-dimensional conditions, and 90 trials in the three-dimensional condition (CFT). Thus, each day, 90 trials were given at each level of dimensionality.

Practice Session. During the 1/2-hr. practice session Ss were first apprised of the payoff scheme, described below, which was to be used in the main experiment. They were then given 75 trials in a compatible two-choice reaction time task. On each trial an arrow was presented which pointed either left or right; they were to depress the key corresponding to the direction of the arrow. After each trial Ss were informed of their errors, and their RT. Following these trials, Ss received their response-assignment instructions. A series of 100 trials judging "Same" vs. "Different" with regard to pairs of letters—AA, AB, BA, BB—were given to insure that Ss were familiar with their particular response-assignment.

Experimental Sessions. The first experimental session began with a brief description of the stimuli and of the seven experimental conditions. The payoff scheme was reiterated and Ss were reminded of their response-assignment.

Before each condition, Ss were told which dimensions were relevant, and were given seven practice trials to insure that they understood the instructions.

There were 5-min. rest breaks between the blocks of one-, two-, and three-dimensional judgments, and 2-min. rest breaks between conditions within the one- and two-dimensional blocks. Also, there were two 2-min. breaks within the 90-trial three-dimensional condition.

Payoffs. Monetary bonuses and penalties were used to maintain fast, accurate responding. The base rate of pay was $1.00 per session. For every correct response which was equal to or faster than the arbitrary criterion of 450 msec S received 1¢, while for correct responses slower than 450 msec nothing was awarded. For every incorrect response, whether fast or slow, 5¢ was deducted from S's earnings—however, Ss were not allowed to earn less than the guaranteed base rate. Speed and accuracy feedback was given after every trial during the experiment.

Results and Discussion

In order to correct for an observed dependence of variance on mean in the present latency data and thus meet the assumptions of the analysis of variance model the dependent variable used was logarithm of reaction time.[2] Errors were excluded from the analysis, as were

[2] The reliability of the conclusion that "Different" RT decreases with the number of dimensions along which a pair of stimuli differ is attested to by the results of another experiment carried out by the author. Eighteen Ss made "Same" and "Different" judgments about pairs of four-dimensional stimuli. Again, the factor of number of dimensions of difference was a highly significant source of variance, $F = 24.42$, $df = 14/224$, $p < .001$. "Different" RT decreased regularly with increasing number of dimensions of difference.

unusually long times (RTs more than four standard deviations above the mean of a particular S's distribution of latencies in a given condition).

DIFFERENT RT AS A FUNCTION OF THE NUMBER OF DIMENSIONS OF DIFFERENCE

In the tridimensional condition, CFT, there are seven possible ways in which pairs of stimuli may differ (viz., they may differ along C, F, T, C & F, C & T, F & T, and C & F & T). The data from condition CFT, averaged over three sessions, were subjected to an analysis of variance. Response-assignment was the between-groups variable and the seven categories of "Different" stimuli formed the within-Ss variable. The results of this analysis indicated that the differences among the seven categories of "Different" stimuli were statistically significant, $F = 19.42$, $df = 6/24$, $p < .001$. Neither response-assignment nor the interaction of response-assignments with the within-Ss variable was a significant source of variance. In Figure 2 geometric mean "Different" RT is plotted as a function of the number of dimensions along which stimuli differed.

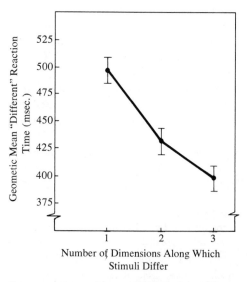

FIGURE 2   Geometric mean "Different" reaction time as a function of number of dimensions along which stimuli differ: [Experiment II] Condition CFT. (Vertical lines represent the respective 95 per cent confidence intervals.)

"Different" responses in the three bidimensional conditions were separated into those instances in which the stimuli differed along only one of the relevant dimensions and those instances in which they differed along both of the relevant dimensions. (In either case the data are averaged over series of trials in which the irrelevant dimension was "Same" or "Different" about equally often.) All six Ss had faster geometric mean "Different" RTs when there were differences along both relevant dimensions ($p < .05$).

Of the models considered in the introduction, only two are consistent with the data reported above, viz., Serial/Self-Terminating/Random order of interrogation and Parallel/Self-Terminating/Statistically distributed comparison times.[3]

It is possible, of course, that the use of data averaged over three days of practice may obscure changes in an S's mode of stimulus comparison which occur in that period of time. To test this possibility, data from condition CFT were analyzed in more detail.

For each S and each day of practice, "Different" responses in the tridimensional condition were classified according to the number of dimensions along which the stimuli differed (one, two, or three). The geometric mean RTs for each of these categories was calculated, and for each S on a day, the categories were ranked according to RT. For four of the six Ss the ranks on each day of practice were identical and indicated that "Different" RT was fastest when there were differences along all three dimensions and slowest when only one dimension differed (probability of identical order of three categories over three days for any single S, $< .03$). A fifth S showed the same pattern for the first two days, but reversed his rankings for one and two dimensions of difference on the last day ($p < .2$). For the sixth S, "Different" RT was consistently fastest when there were differences along all three dimensions; however, on two days, he reversed the

usual order for one and two dimensions of difference. Thus these data fail to indicate any major change in the stimulus comparison process over three days of practice. It is conceivable, of course, that Ss did switch from one of the two remaining models to the other; however, such a change presumably did not result in a differing ordering of the various categories of "Different" stimuli.

"SAME" RT AS A FUNCTION OF THE NUMBER OF RELEVANT DIMENSIONS

Mean log "Same" RTs were subjected to a three-way analysis of variance in which the seven conditions and three days of practice were within-S variables and response-assignment was the between-groups variable. Since the means of condition CFT were based upon three times as many observations as the means in the other conditions, a least-squares solution was required (Winer, 1962, p. 375ff). The results of this analysis indicated that the conditions were significantly different from one another, $F = 9.11$, df $= 6/24$, $p < .001$, and that practice led to a significant decrease in RT, $F = 21.77$, df $= 2/8$, $p < .001$. Response-assignment was the only other source of variance which approached significance, $F = 5.83$, df $= 1/4$, $.05 < p < .10$. None of the interactions among the three variables was statistically significant ($p > .10$). In particular, the failure to find an interaction between days and conditions indicated that these data do not permit the conclusion that different models are appropriate at different levels of practice.

Geometric means of "Same" RTs for the tridimensional condition and the three bidimensional and the three unidimensional conditions are given in Figure 3, along with the overall averages for the one-, two-, and three-dimensional conditions. Examination of the 95 percent confidence intervals for these overall averages indicates that the relation between "Same" RT and the number of relevant dimensions is reliably nonmonotonic, thus supporting none of the nine models proposed in the introduction.

It seems likely that the shape of the obtained function is reflecting other processes than com-

---

[3] The models developed in the introduction are based upon reaction time, not a logarithmic transformation of reaction time. Nevertheless, the general relations observed in the present experiment would be preserved by any reasonable monotonic transformation of these raw data.

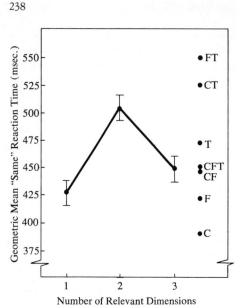

FIGURE 3 Geometric mean "Same" reaction time as a function of number of relevant dimensions: [Experiment II] (Vertical lines represent the respective 95 per cent confidence intervals). Points at the right represent the geometric mean "Same" reaction times for each of the seven conditions.

parisons among relevant dimensions. One possibility is that Ss adopted a lower "decision criterion" in condition CFT, i.e., that they were faster in this condition because they allowed themselves a higher error rate (see, e.g., Fitts, in press). In the present experiment, however, there is a *positive* correlation across conditions between speed and accuracy, and in particular the tridimensional condition had a somewhat lower error rate than any of the bidimensional conditions.

Another possible explanation of the nonmonotonic relation between "Same" RT and the number of relevant dimensions is loosely related to the Gestalt principles of perceptual organization. Since the comparison of stimuli when all three dimensions are relevant is a comparison of two whole figures, there is reason to think that such judgments ought to require less time than judgments which require the S to analyze the figures and compare components of the whole. This interpretation, although plausible, has the defect of leading to the prediction that tridimensional "Same" judgments ought to require less time than unidimensional

"Same" judgments, although the opposite obtained.

A third possible explanation of the relation between "Same" RT and dimensionality lies in a more thorough analysis of the Ss' task. Specifically, it should be pointed out that in order to make a correct response in the uni- and bidimensional conditions it is necessary to disregard information from irrelevant dimensions. There is considerable evidence that Ss can effectively ignore (filter) information from irrelevant dimensions in speeded tasks (Archer, 1954; Green & Anderson, 1956; Morin, Forrin, & Archer, 1961; Fitts & Biederman, 1965; Imai & Garner, 1965). Nevertheless, there is reason to believe that in the present experiment Ss did *not* ignore irrelevant information. If Ss were "filtering" irrelevant dimensions, then whether a pair of stimuli was "Same" or "Different" on these dimensions should have had no influence on the obtained RT. This null hypothesis was tested for the "Same" RT in the uni- and bidimensional conditions. Consider first the unidimensional conditions, each of which involved two irrelevant dimensions. "Same" RTs in each condition were separated into two (nonexhaustive) classes—those obtained when pairs of stimuli were the same on both irrelevant dimensions or when they were different on both. There were 18 possible comparisons made (6 Ss by 3 conditions), all of which indicated that unidimensional "Same" judgments were shorter when the stimuli were "Same" on both irrelevant dimensions. When the bidimensional conditions were analyzed in a similar way, 16 of 18 comparisons indicated that "Same" judgments were faster when the stimuli were the same with respect to the irrelevant dimension than when they were different. It is clear that Ss did not completely ignore the irrelevant dimensions. This finding has several implications for the analysis of the "Same" RT function shown in Figure 3. Firstly, since irrelevant dimensions did influence RT, then on at least some trials, Ss must have interrogated more dimensions than were logically necessary. This has the effect of making an observed uni- or bidimensional RT reflect more than the comparison times for the relevant dimensions. Secondly, since the error rate did not exceed

13% for any condition and since the function in question is based upon only correct responses, Ss must have in some way "suppressed" a tendency to respond on the basis of irrelevant dimensions, and it is plausible to think that this suppression took time. Therefore the RTs in the uni- and bidimensional conditions are not indicative of the times required to compare only relevant dimensions, and some other basis must be sought, in present data, to distinguish between the two models which still remain plausible.

ANOTHER BASIS FOR DISTINGUISHING BETWEEN SERIAL AND PARALLEL MODELS

The Parallel/Self-Terminating/Distributed model leads to the following prediction: Considering "Different" judgments made in the various conditions of the present experiment, the fastest ought to be in condition CFT on those occasions when all three dimensions are in fact different. The Serial/Self-Terminating/Random model leads to the prediction that the fastest "Different" judgments ought to be obtained in the best of the unidimensional conditions, since the model assumes that Ss can interrogate the single relevant dimension first and then stop. According to the latter model, in condition CFT, with all dimensions different, the S, of course, detects a difference no matter which dimension he interrogates first; however, on some proportion of trials he does so by examining first one of the less discriminable dimensions. Thus in the tridimensional condition, Ss ought not to be as consistently fast as they can be (in principle) in the best of the unidimensional conditions. These predictions were compared by determining the geometric mean "Different" RTs to identical types of stimuli (viz., different along all three dimensions) in conditions C and CFT. Five of six Ss were faster in condition C than in CFT, thus lending support to the serial model.

Although we have seen that Ss do not always completely ignore irrelevant dimensions, this does not necessarily invalidate the comparison just made. It should be clear that a prediction of the condition that ought to yield the short-est "Different" RTs may be valid as long as the assumptions on which it is based are not violated too severely. Just how severely were the assumptions of the two models violated? Although a quantitative index is not available, we may answer in the following way: They were enough in error to invalidate the assessment of the relation between "Same" RT and the number of relevant dimensions; however, they were sound enough to allow a meaningful interpretation to be drawn from the relation between "Different" RT and the number of relevant dimensions that differed between two stimuli. The crucial point in this argument is that the prediction of the condition yielding the shortest mean "Different" RT seems to require no more from the assumptions than did the prediction of the relation between "Different" RT and the number of dimensions of difference.

The results of the present experiment make it painfully clear that irrelevant dimensions of variation are not necessarily ignored at the command of the experimenter. It has already been pointed out that Ss in several previous experiments were able to filter irrelevant information. It is important to determine whether Ss in the present experimental situation could have filtered irrelevancies but chose not to do so, or whether the present conditions made filtering more difficult. Since all irrelevant dimensions were at other times relevant, it is a distinct possibility that implicit competing responses were engendered by irrelevant information (Hodge, 1959; Montague, 1965). However, Imai and Garner (1965) have demonstrated perfect filtering in a task in which irrelevant dimensions were also at other times relevant. This discrepancy is unresolved.

It seems clear that until more is known about the processing of irrelevant information it will be difficult, if not impossible, to achieve a good understanding of the processing of relevant information.

Summary

Although considerable effort has been devoted to the description of processes underlying discriminations along single dimensions, there have been few attempts to determine whether or how these elementary processes are combined when discrimination requires the consideration of more than one stimulus dimension. In the present experiment, Ss were required to indicate whether two simultaneously presented multidimensional visual stimuli were identical or different. The response measure was reaction time, and Ss had a monetary incentive to respond both quickly and accurately. It was concluded that the most appropriate model for this task is one that assumes that dimensions are compared serially, and that the order in which dimensions are compared varies from trial-to-trial. Further, when a pair differs along several dimensions, Ss do not necessarily examine every dimension before initiating the response "Different."

References

Archer, E. J. Identification of visual patterns as a function of information load. *J. exp. Psychol.*, 1954, *48*, 313–317.

Fitts, P. M. Cognitive aspects of information processing: III. Set for speed vs. accuracy. *J. exp. Psychol.*, in press.

Fitts, P. M., & Biederman, I. S-R compatibility and information reduction. *J. exp. Psychol.*, 1965, *69*, 408–412.

Garner, W. R. *Uncertainty and structure as psychological concepts*. New York: Wiley, 1962.

Green, B. F., & Anderson, L. K. Color coding in a visual search task. *J. exp. Psychol.*, 1956, *51*, 19–24.

Hartley, H. O., & David, H. A. Universal bounds for mean range and extreme observation. *Ann. math. Stat.*, 1954, *25*, 85–99.

Hodge, M. H. The influence of irrelevant information upon complex visual discrimination. *J. exp. Psychol.*, 1959, *57*, 1–5.

Imai, S., & Garner, W. R. Discriminability and preference for attributes in free and constrained classification. *J. exp. Psychol.*, 1965, *69*, 596–608.

Montague, W. E. Effect of irrelevant information on a complex auditory-discrimination task. *J. exp. Psychol.*, 1965, *69*, 230–236.

Morin, R. E., Forrin, B., & Archer, W. Information processing behavior: The role of irrelevant stimulus information. *J. exp. Psychol.*, 1961, *61*, 89–96.

Neisser, U. Decision time without reaction time: Experiments in visual scanning. *Amer. J. Psychol.*, 1963, *76*, 376–385.

Neisser, U. Experiments in visual search and their theoretical implications. Paper read at Psychonomic Society Meetings, Niagara Falls, October, 1964.

Rapoport, A. A study of disjunctive reaction times. *Behav. Sci.*, 1959, *4*, 299–315.

Shepard, R. N. Attention and the metric structure of the stimulus space. *J. math. Psychol.*, 1964, *1*, 54–87.

Sternberg, S. Retrieval from recent memory: Some reaction time experiments and a search theory. Paper read at Psychonomic Society Meetings, Bryn Mawr, August, 1963.

Sternberg, S. Estimating the distribution of additive reaction-time components. Paper read at Psychonomic Society Meetings, Niagara Falls, October, 1964.

Uhr, L. "Pattern recognition" computers as models for perception. *Psychol. Bull.*, 1963, *60*, 40–73.

Winer, B. J. *Statistical procedures in experimental design*. New York: McGraw-Hill, 1962.

5.4 Tendencies to Eye Movement and Perceptual Accuracy[*]

HERBERT F. CROVITZ WALTER DAVES

The present study deals with one possible role of sensory-motor factors in perception. While the movement of the eyes leads to new visual stimulation which may be relevant in perceiving, the neural activity responsible for an eye movement may itself play a role in perceptual integration whether or not an eye movement occurs and whether or not the sensory feedback effects of an eye movement are supplied to the locus of perceptual integration. This neural state tending to produce an eye movement and having a possible role in perceptual processing will be called a "tendency to eye movement."

The postulated process may be related to the process underlying the use of the term tendencies to eye movement as used perviously in psychology. For example, Woodworth (1938) cites a theory relating eye movements to the Müller-Lyer illusion which ". . . admits that actual movements do not occur in all cases, but assumes that a tendency to such movement is sufficient to give the impression of length" (p. 645). Recently the term has been used in perceptual theory by Gaffron (1950), Heron (1957), and Crovitz (1960).

In normal visual experience, perception may be affected by both the feedback supplied by eye movement and by the neural state which initiated the movement. Using a tachistoscope, however, when exposure time is shorter than the latency of eye movement, the eye movements which occur lead to the fixation of the blank post-exposure field. The *first* eye movement which occurs must be the result of the tendency to eye movement existing at the initiation of the movement. If, as assumed, there is a relationship between the tendency to eye movement qua neural state, and perception, a relationship should exist between some property of the initial eye movement, as an index of the tendency, and some property of perception. It would appear reasonable that a property in which a relationship could be shown would be the directionality of eye movement and perceptual accuracy; i.e., a congruence might be expected between the direction of the initial eye movement and the direction of the more accurate field.

Method

STIMULUS MATERIALS

The stimulus material[1] consisted of three sets of eight cards, each card with numerals appearing at 3°, 5°, and 7° of visual angle of both the left and right stimulus fields of a Gerbrands

[*] From: Herbert F. Crovitz and Walter Daves, "Tendencies to Eye Movement and Perceptual Accuracy," *Journal of Experimental Psychology,* 1962, vol. 63, pp. 495–498. Copyright (1962) by the American Psychological Association, and reproduced by permission. The authors are indebted to Karl Zener for his valued advice in the formulation and execution of this study; to Robert L. Green who made available part of the eye movement recording apparatus used, and to Paul G. Daston for critical reading of the report.

[1] The perceptual situation chosen was determined by requirements of a replication of an unpublished study on perceptual anisotropies and laterality done by Hilborn at Duke University. The present report, however, does not relate to the specifics of Hilborn's problem.

mirror tachistoscope. The tachistoscope was fitted with an eye aperture occluder such that the line of numerals across the whole field could be viewed binocularly or with the left or the right eye alone. Each set of eight cards used in the three viewing conditions (both eyes, left eye alone, right eye alone) had each of the numerals (2–9) in each of the six positions once. Otherwise the positions for the numerals were randomly selected. The numerals, executed in India ink using a Zephyr lettering kit, stood about ³⁄₁₆ in. high, and subtended a visual angle of about 30′.

PROCEDURE

Cards were presented in a fixed random order, binocular and monocular trials intermixed. On each trial S adjusted the eye aperture occluder according to E's instructions, viewing with both eyes, left eye alone, and right eye alone for a total of eight trials each. A constant exposure time of 100 msec was used, and since the latency of voluntary eye movements is somewhat longer than this (Woodworth, 1938) such post-exposure eye movements could not lead to fixation of a numeral.

RECORDING TECHNIQUES

An electro-oculograph technique was used to record initial postexposure eye movements. Eye movement potentials were amplified by a Grass Model III-D high efficiency EEG machine equipped with converter-demodulators (Grass Model CD-3) in order to provide dc voltage input to the pen. Electrodes were made of jeweler's "high fine" silver disks, 1 mm. thick by 8 mm. diameter, plated with silver chloride and encased in silver cups, in general agreement with the method suggested by Ford and Leonard (1958).

Electrodes were placed bitemporally for recording the horizontal components of the eye movements. A second channel was connected to the tachistoscope timer such that a sharp spike was produced on the moving paper record each time the stimulus field was flashed on and each time it was flashed off allowing for and leading to a check that the initial eye movement recorded began after the stimulus material flashed off. Paper speed was 30 mm/sec.

Before the electrodes were taped into position, the skin sites were washed with acetone and lightly sanded with fine grade sandpaper in order to reduce the resistance between the pair of electrodes. While the resistance was not measured directly (an extremely low voltage ohmmeter was not available and the phosphene effect of passing a current through the electrodes might have produced undue anxiety in the naive Ss) the resistance was considered sufficiently low when a calibration eye movement of 7° produced a pen deflection of at least 5 mm. on the eye movement channel with the gain setting used.

INSTRUCTIONS

The instructions to S were to fixate a centrally placed dot in the fixation field upon a "ready" signal, to refrain from moving his eyes until the stimulus appeared, to move his eyes to whatever numeral or numerals he pleased when the stimulus appeared.

The S was told to write on an answer sheet after each trial the numerals he had seen in the positions in which they had appeared.

SUBJECTS

Fourteen naive college students served as Ss.

Results

The data support the hypothesis that a congruence in direction exists between the initial postexposure eye movement and the more accurate field on trials in which there was both an eye movement and an accuracy difference between the fields. There were more congruent than noncongruent trials ($t = 5.05$, $P < .01$), and this relationship held for 13 of the 14 Ss (a binomial test giving $P < .01$).

This congruence also appears in each viewing condition individually. Table 1 presents the frequency of occurrence of trials with each combination of eye movement direction and accuracy difference for each viewing condition.

Disregarding perceptual accuracy, in both monocular sets of trials there are twice as many initial eye movements in the direction of the viewing eye than in the opposite direction; i.e.,

TABLE 1

Frequency of Occurrence of Each Combination of Accuracy Difference and Eye Movement Direction for Each Viewing Condition

VIEWING CONDITION	MORE ACCURATE FIELD	EYE MOVEMENT DIRECTION			
		RIGHT	LEFT	No.	TOTAL
	Right	30	3	10	43
	Left	2	32	7	41
Both eyes	Equal	5	14	9	28
	Total	37	49	26	
	Right	39	4	12	55
	Left	6	8	13	27
Right eye	Equal	8	11	11	30
	Total	53	23	36	
	Right	18	8	11	37
	Left	4	26	13	43
Left eye	Equal	3	17	12	32
	Total	25	51	36	

with right eye alone there are more initial eye movements to the right than to the left ($t = 4.12$; $P < .01$) and with left eye alone there are more initial eye movements to the left than to the right ($t = 5.36$; $P < .01$).

Scorable initial postexposure eye movements (in a latency range of from 150 msec to 1000 msec after stimulus onset) did not occur on about 30% of the trials. This can, in part, be attributed to the electro-oculograph method used. It was found to be subject to interference from eye blinks and occasional galvanic skin response potentials when such occurred in the latency range chosen.

Perceptual accuracy (defined as correct numeral reported in its correct location) was moderately high, with 52.9% of all reported numerals correct. However, *Ss* recorded only 35.8% of all reportable numerals.

Discussion

The results of the present experiment reveal a relation between relative accuracy of perception of numerals on either side of the fixation point and the direction of the initial post-exposure eye movement. The conditions of the experiment effectively precluded any visual feedback from eye movement which could lead to differential accuracy on the two sides of the field.

The significance of the present finding lies in the clear indication that other processes than visual feedback are significantly related to accuracy of report of visual material. However, the design of the study does not permit differentiation between the effects of tendencies to eye movements and the effects of possible kinesthetic feedback from the initial eye movement, a task for later empirical determination. Further, one explanation of the findings of a visual nature might lie in the possibility that the clearer perception of numerals on one side of the field, for whatever reason, might lead to an actual eye movement in that direction of relatively short latency. Congruence occurred on 85% of the trials in which the latency of initial post-exposure eye movements was from 150 to 175 msec. Whether such short latencies are consistent with an alternative explanation in terms of an underlying visual discrimination process is a question for more discriminating empirical determination.

The clear demonstration of an association between accuracy of report and eye movement direction urgently raises the need for clarification of the detailed ways in which tendencies to movement or other relevant variables may affect perception and calls for tests of alternative hypotheses. For instance, one problem is whether the motor tendency directly affects properties of the visual reaction itself or is more intimately related to the process of accurate report.

A secondary positive finding which also invites specific explanation is that initial postexposure eye movements tend to be made to the left when viewing with the left eye and to the right when viewing with the right eye. At a physiological level, the movement of the viewing eye is related to action of the external rectus muscle, and movements are made toward stimuli exciting nasal retina; while at a psychological level a possible relevant fact might be that S adjusted the eye aperture occluder and was "aware" that he viewed with a given eye alone, eye movements being in the direction away from the occluded aperture. Again an experimental determination between alternative explanations might give insight into the details of the process involved.

Regardless of ultimate explanation, the findings of the present experiment indicate the necessity of taking into account direction of initial postexposure eye movements as related to accuracy differences between the fields in tachistoscopic studies, and gives evidence that the presentation of stimuli at exposure times short enough to rule out fixation eye movements does not eliminate the possible effects of eye movements, or tendencies to eye movements, upon the subsequent report.

Summary

The direction of initial postexposure eye movements was studied in a tachistoscopic situation in which a row of numerals appeared across the visual field and no eye movement occurred until the cessation of stimulation. A congruence was found between the direction of the initial eye movement and the side of the visual field more accurately perceived. This finding supports the hypothesis that differential tendencies to eye movement are associated with differential accuracy. A secondary finding was that, in monocular viewing, there were more eye movements to the side of the viewing eye.

References

Crovitz, H. F. Patterns of relative localization of an odd element within a visual grouping as a function of laterality characteristics and tendencies to eye movement. Unpublished doctoral dissertation, Duke University, 1960.

Ford, A., and J. L. Leonard, Techniques for recording surface biolectric direct currents. *USN Electron. Lab. Rep.*, 1958, No. 839.

Gaffron, M. Right and left in pictures. *Art Quart.*, 1950, *13*, 312–331.

Heron, W. Perception as a function of retinal locus, and attention. *Amer. J. Psychol.* 1957, 70, 38–48.

Woodworth, R. S. *Experimental psychology.* New York: Holt, 1938.

5.5 Information and the Memory Span[*]

LESTER M. HYMAN   HERBERT KAUFMAN

The immediate memory span or the "span of attention" has been of interest to psychologists for many years. Traditionally, the immediate memory span has been reported in terms of the number of symbols (words, letters, numbers, figures, etc.) that Ss could correctly recall (Glanville & Dallenbach, 1929). Such researchers have found that for many types of symbols the number of items recalled is a constant, usually approximately equal to 7. In the past decade the number of bits of information in the symbols recalled has been reported along with the more traditional measurements of immediate memory span. A comparison of these measurements led Miller to the conclusion that, "the number of chunks of information is constant for immediate memory" (1956, p. 92).

Miller drew supporting evidence for his statement from experiments using sequential presentation of familiar visual symbols (Pollack, 1953; Hayes, 1952). The evidence from experiments using simultaneous presentation of familiar and unfamiliar visual symbols lends less compelling support to Miller's statement. Variables found to affect the span of immediate memory in the simultaneous presentation experiments include: the information load of the symbols (Glanville & Dallenbach, 1929), the number of symbols presented (Anderson & Fitts, 1959; Krulee, 1959), the identifiability of the symbols (Anderson & Fitts, 1959), and

time considerations in the stimulus presentation (Cherry, 1961). Sperling's use of a post-stimulus cueing technique has emphasized the importance of the period of time following stimulus presentation in extracting information from immediate memory (Sperling, 1960). Although stimulus-response compatibility has not been shown to affect memory span, Fitts and Switzer (1962) have shown it to be an important variable affecting information transmission in reaction time studies.

This study differs from previous studies in two ways. First, it allows for a comparison of the effects on immediate memory of relatively unfamiliar symbols differing in information load; second, it allows comparison of the effects of different message lengths (number of symbols per presentation) on immediate memory using unfamiliar symbols.

Method

STIMULI, APPARATUS AND SUBJECTS

Two sets of symbols were formed to give two "alphabets" differing in information content. The "low" information alphabet contained eight black geometric forms and was called the "F" alphabet. The forms used were triangle, star, heart, diamond, square, circle, T and X. Four colorings each of these eight forms yielded the 32 symbols of the "high" information or "CF" alphabet. The four colorings were

* Reproduced by permission of *Perception & Psychophysics,* 1966, vol. 1, pp. 235–237.

blue, red, green and copper. Messages were formed from each of the alphabets by random sampling with replacement. Messages composed of symbols from the "F" alphabet contained three bits of information per symbol while messages composed with symbols from the "CF" alphabet contained five bits of information per symbol. To allow overlap of both number of symbols per message and the total message information content, messages of four, six and eight symbols were constructed from the "F" alphabet and messages of four and six symbols were constructed from the "CF" alphabet. Fifty messages of each length for each alphabet were constructed. The symbols, ¾ in. high by ¾ in. wide were painted on 8½ x 11 in. white cards. Four-symbol messages appeared as one row of four characters with ¾-in. spaces between adjacent symbols. Six-symbol messages appeared as two rows of three symbols each and eight-symbol messages appeared as two rows of four symbols each. The messages were centered on the cards with ¾-in. spacing between rows.

The cards were presented in a two-field Gerbrands tachistoscope. The second field contained a center fixation point and was brightly lit to minimize after-images. Four graduate students in psychology served as volunteer Ss.

PROCEDURE

Prior to the first session the Ss examined all the symbols used in the experiment and chose a set of response symbols to use. All Ss agreed to use the symbols Δ, S, H, D, □, O, T, X to indicate the forms of presented figures and R, B, G, and C to indicate the color of the "CF" symbols. Responses were made on a grid containing boxes that corresponded to the number and positions of the symbols of the messages presented.

The Ss were seated at the tachistoscope in a darkened room and asked to fixate on the fixation point. They were told which set of symbols would appear and what message length would be shown. When the S said, "ready," a stimulus card was flashed on the screen for a brief period of time. The S was then given as much time as he wished to write down the symbols on the

response grid while a new message was readied for presentation. The procedure was repeated for the 50 messages of the message length and alphabet being presented. The presentation of the 50 messages of a given message length from a given alphabet constituted a session; a S sat through no more than one experimental session per day.

EXPERIMENTAL DESIGN

The experiment consisted of two parts. In the first part the Ss were exposed to the 4F, 8F, 4CF and 6CF messages. Each message was exposed for 500 msec. The Ss received each set of messages for four sessions, and the order of presentation of the different message types was balanced among the Ss. The order of messages within message types was randomized each time a message type was re-presented to a given S. During the second part of the experiment the Ss were exposed to the 6F, 8F, 4CF and 6CF messages, each message being presented for 100 msec. Each message type occurred three times and the order of appearance of conditions was again balanced among the Ss.

Results

NUMBER OF SYMBOLS RECALLED

Figure 1 presents the number of symbols correctly recalled as a function of session for the two alphabets averaged over message length and Ss. Responses to messages of different length were averaged when an analysis of variance showed no significant differences due to this variable ($F = .317$, $df = 1/12$, $p > .1$). Since the number of symbols correctly recalled was averaged over message length, each point on Figure 1 represents data from two sessions, one with the shorter and one with the longer messages. Each S sat for 28 sessions. An analysis of variance including data from all the 100 msec exposure sessions showed a highly significant difference between the number of symbols recalled from the two alphabets ($F = 90.25$, $df = 1/12$, $p < .001$).

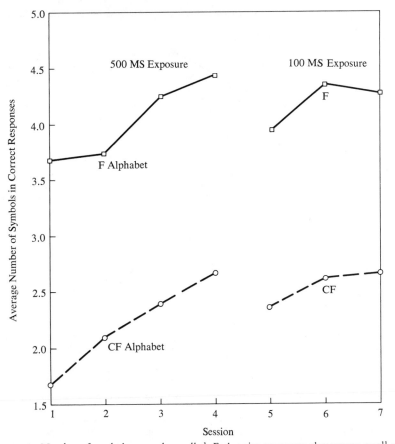

FIGURE 1   Number of symbols correctly recalled. Each point represents the average recall of 400 messages.

AMOUNT OF INFORMATION IN THE SYMBOLS RECALLED

Figure 2 presents the amount of information in the symbols correctly recalled for the two alphabets. As in Figure 1 the data are averaged over message length and Ss. Although there is some initial difference in the information in the symbols correctly recalled between the alphabets, this difference becomes negligible by the last session of the 500 msec exposure, and remains small over the remaining sessions. By the end of the last 500 msec exposure session all Ss had reached near perfect performance with the 4F messages. As a result the 4F messages were not presented during the shorter exposure time sessions. At the end of the experiment the Ss were given one additional session with the 4F messages at the 100 msec exposure time and their performance was still near perfect. An an-alysis of variance on the data from the 100 msec exposure time sessions showed no significant difference between the amount of information in the symbols correctly recalled for the two alphabets ($F = .395$, df $= 1/12$, $p > .1$).

Additional analyses were done to determine the effect of symbols recalled in incorrect posi-tions and of partial recall of the CF symbols. Again there were significant differences between the number of symbols recalled for the two alphabets and no difference in the amount of information in that recall.

Discussion

It would seem that under the conditions used in this experiment with the relatively unitary symbols presented, immediate memory

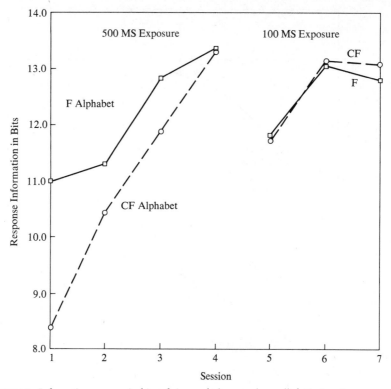

FIGURE 2   Information content in bits of the symbols correctly recalled. Each point represents the average of 400 messages.

is relatively constant for information and not constant for number of symbols. Since partially correct responses were possible and did occur, one possible explanation is that the symbols were not unitary and do not fall into the category of Miller's "chunks." This criticism is reasonable but cannot account for the constancy of information transmission found when partially correct responses were analyzed. An alternative explanation of the difference between the results of this experiment and the experiments on which Miller based his "chunking" hypothesis might be found in the human's ability to code stimuli. Simultaneous presentation of symbols minimizes the time available for an S to encode them. If the symbols are familiar and a set of responses available which have a high stimulus-response compatibility, Ss may still be able to encode them during the brief interval that a stimulus trace remains. There was evidence in the data from this experiment that some "fast" coding does take place. Many of the messages in both alphabets contained more than one instance of a given

symbol. An additional analysis showed that symbol recall and information transmission was greater as a fairly direct function of the number of repeated symbols in a message. Sequential presentation of a set of symbols offers the S a relatively large amount of time to encode visual stimuli into "chunks" containing larger amounts of information. Using the reasonable assumption that encoding information into "chunks" takes time, the results of this experiment are not necessarily inconsistent with Miller's "chunking" hypothesis but rather indicate a (temporal) bound on conditions under which the hypothesis holds. Corroborating evidence for this assumption has just become available from a recent study by Lamb (1966) which showed a perfect trade-off between information storage as a function of code redundancy and processing time. An experiment which compares the results of sequential and simultaneous presentation of unfamiliar symbols is planned as an additional test of the "coding time" explanation of the results found here.

Summary

Messages differing in number of symbols and symbol information load were presented tachistoscopically to 4 adult Ss. The messages were constructed by random drawing with replacement from an alphabet of 8 black form symbols and an alphabet of 32 colored form symbols. The number of symbols recalled varied as a function of alphabet; however, the information in recall was constant for all conditions. The number of symbols recalled and the information in recall was independent of message length.

References

Anderson, N. S., & Fitts, P. M. Amount of information gained during brief exposure of numerals and colors. *Readings for human engineering, concepts and theory.* University of Michigan, 1959, 12.5–1 to 12.5–8.

Attneave, F. *Applications of information theory to psychology.* New York: Holt, 1959.

Cherry, C. *On human communication.* New York: Science Editions Inc., 1961.

Fitts, P. M., & Switzer, G. Cognitive aspects of information processing. *J. exp. Psychol.,* 1962, *63,* 321–329.

Glanville, A. D., & Dallenbach, K. M. The range of attention. *Amer. J. Psychol.,* 1929, *41,* 207–236.

Hayes, J. R. M. Memory span for several vocabularies as a function of vocabulary size. *Quarterly Progress Report.* Cambridge, Mass: Acoustics Laboratory, Massachusetts Institute of Technology, Jan.-June, 1952.

Krulee, G. K. Information theory and man machine systems. *Readings for human engineering, concepts and theory.* University of Michigan, 1959, 12.1–1 to 12.1–9.

Lamb, J. C. Codes and human channel capacity. Unpublished Ph.D. thesis. University of Connecticut, 1966.

Miller, G. A. The magical number seven, plus or minus two. Some limits of our capacity for processing information. *Psychol. Rev.,* 1956, *63,* 81–97.

Pollack, I. The assimilation of sequentially encoded information. *Amer. J. Psychol.,* 1953, *66,* 421–435.

Sperling, G. The information available in brief visual presentations. *Psychol. Monogr.,* 1960, *74,* No. 11, 1–29.

5.6 Categorization Time with Categories Defined by Disjunctions and Conjunctions of Stimulus Attributes*

RAYMOND S. NICKERSON

In the classical choice-response-time (RT) experiment each of *n* stimulus alternatives is uniquely paired with one of *n* response alternatives, i.e., stimuli are paired with responses in a one-to-one fashion. Correct performance of the task depends on *S*'s ability to recognize which of the *n* alternative stimuli has occurred and to select and execute the appropriate one of the *n* possible responses. Recently several *E*s have used an RT paradigm which focuses attention on the process of stimulus categoriza-

* From: Raymond S. Nickerson, "Categorization Time with Categories Defined by Disjunctions and Conjunctions of Stimulus Attributes," *Journal of Experimental Psychology,* 1967, vol. 73, pp 211–219. Copyright (1967) by the American Psychological Association, and reproduced by permission. This is No. ESD-TR-65-565 of the Air Force Electronic Systems Division. Air Force Systems Command. This research was performed at the Decision Sciences Laboratory as part of Project 7682, Man-Computer Information Processing. Further reproduction is authorized to satisfy the needs of the United States Government. The author wishes to acknowledge the valuable assistance of Andrew Rinde who collected and helped to analyze the data for these studies.

tion as opposed to that of response selection. In this case stimuli are paired with responses in a many-to-one fashion, each of several stimuli being associated with a common response (Bricker, 1955; Fitts & Biederman, 1965; Morin, Forrin, & Archer, 1961; Nickerson & Fehrer, 1964; Pollack, 1963; Sternberg, 1963). The results obtained in this situation depend in large part on the nature of the perceptual-cognitive demands imposed by the categorization task. Some studies suggest that when a category is defined in terms of the physical properties of stimuli, the more properties that must be considered in the process of categorizing, the longer the categorization time (Fitts & Biederman, 1965; Nickerson & Fehrer, 1964; Posner, 1964).

In the study reported by Nickerson and Fehrer (1964) *S's* task was to decide whether a simple geometric figure was a member of a category which was defined by an inclusive disjunction of possible stimulus attributes. The category "green or triangle," for example, contained figures which were *either* green *or* triangular, or both. It was found that RT varied directly with the number of attributes which were *relevant* to the category criterion, and that for a given number of relevant attributes, RT was inversely related to the number of attributes with respect to which a stimulus *satisfied* the criterion.

The experiments described in this report may be considered an extension of the earlier study in several ways. In the earlier study, categories were defined by disjunctions of attributes, RTs were obtained only for positive cases (cases in which the stimulus did in fact belong in the defined category), and *Ss* were relatively unpracticed; in the present study both disjunctive and conjunctive criteria were used, RTs were obtained for both positive and negative cases, and performance measures were obtained over a range of practice.

The major theoretical impetus for these experiments was the question of sequential vs. parallel modes of information processing. Several researchers have felt this distinction to be a useful one to bring to bear on the problem of describing the human as an information

processing system (Christie & Luce, 1956; Neisser, 1961; Rapaport, 1959; Sternberg, 1963). A system is said to operate in sequence, at some level, if the elementary or component processes at that level occur in sequence, one at a time; it is said to operate in parallel if the component processes occur simultaneously. A hybrid system would be one whose mode of operation was neither completely sequential nor completely parallel. For example, some, but not all, of the component processes might occur simultaneously; or component processes might overlap in time with some minimum interval being maintained between starting times.

Clearly the question of sequential vs. parallel processing can be posed meaningfully only with respect to specific levels of activity of a system. In the context of research on human information processing the question has been asked with respect to such component processes as the comparing of an alpha-numeric character on an external visual display against a character represented in memory (Sternberg, 1963) or the testing of a character for such distinctive features as "roundness, angularity, the slopes of lines, and so on [Neisser, 1961]." In the present case, a component process may be conceived to be the determination of the presence or absence of an "attribute," as e.g., a specified size, color, or shape.[1] The process of deciding whether or not a stimulus is a member of a category defined by a combination of attributes may be viewed as composed of an appropriate set of more elementary processes, each of whose function is to determine the presence or absence of one of the relevant attributes. The question of interest is whether at the level of component processes thus conceived the performance of our *Ss* is more suggestive of a sequential or of a parallel processing mode.

---

[1] The word "attribute" is used in this report in a dual sense: (*a*) generically to denote dimensions of stimulus variability, i.e., size, color, shape, and (*b*) specially to denote states that a stimulus may assume with respect to particular dimensions, e.g., large, red, circle. It would be more precise to use one word to represent the former concept, and a different one to represent the latter; however, the use of "attribute" for both facilitates the discussion somewhat, and does not lead to any serious ambiguities.

General Method

Stimuli. Stimuli were simple geometric figures which varied with respect to three attributes: size, color, and shape. Specifically, the color was red, yellow, or blue; the shape was circle, triangle, or square; and the size was $\frac{1}{2}$, 1, or 2 in. in diameter (circles) or height (triangles and squares). All possible combinations were used, making a total of 27 perceptually distinct figures.

Task. In each of the experiments a *criterion* dichotomized the set of figures into two mutually exclusive and exhaustive subsets or *categories*. Only one of the categories was defined explicitly by the criterion; the other was simply the complement of the one defined. The task was described to S as that of deciding whether a figure belonged in the defined category, rather than as that of deciding in which of two complementary categories it belonged. Logically the two formulations are equivalent; the former was used because it seemed to represent a somewhat more natural statement of the task.

Category Criteria and Terminology. Categories were defined in terms of conjunctions and inclusive disjunctions of attributes, e.g., "large *and* red *and* circle," "large *or* red *or* circle." An attribute was *relevant* if it was referred to by the category criterion. A stimulus was said to *satisfy* a criterion with respect to a particular attribute if it had that attribute. A stimulus was called *"criterial"* if it belonged to the category defined by the criterion. Note that in the case of a disjunctive criterion a stimulus would be criterial if it satisfied the criterion with respect to *at least one* of the relevant attributes; in the case of a conjunctive criterion a stimulus would be criterial only if it satisfied the criterion with respect to *all* relevant attributes.

Concerning the number of attributes that must be considered in order to determine the criteriality, or noncriteriality, of a stimulus, the disjunctive and conjunctive criteria have an interestingly antipodal relationship. Where-as in the latter case all relevant attributes must be checked in order to determine that a stimulus is criterial, in the former all relevant attributes must be checked to determine that it is not. Conversely, with conjunctive criteria one need not, in general, check all relevant attributes to determine that a stimulus is not criterial; with disjunctive criteria one need not check all relevant attributes to determine that it is.

Procedure. Stimulus figures were presented one at a time in a Gerbrands tachistoscope. On each trial S initiated the stimulus exposure (and simultaneously started an electric timer) by pressing a foot pedal as soon as he wished after E signaled "ready." The exposure was terminated and the timer stopped by a press of either of two response keys. Pre- and post-exposure fields were light, of approximately the same intensity as the figure surround.

Experiment I

In Exp. I a category was defined either by a single attribute or by a disjunction of two or three attributes. The specific categories used are listed in Table 1. "Red," "large," and "circle" are abbreviated as R, L, and C, respectively.

TABLE 1

Category Criteria for Exp. 1

No. of Attributes Relevant to Criterion		
1	2	3
R	R or C	L or R or C
L	L or R	L or R or C
C	L or C	L or R or C

Since the locus of interest was the number of attributes relevant to a category criterion rather than the particular attributes involved, the three columns of Table 1 represent the three experimental conditions, and the three rows represent the counterbalancing of attributes over conditions.

METHOD

Half of the stimuli of each experimental run were criterial and half were not. In the case of two-attribute criteria, half of the criterial stimuli satisfied the criterion with respect to a single attribute only ($\frac{1}{4}$ with respect to one attribute, $\frac{1}{4}$ with respect to the other) and half satisfied it with respect to both. In the case of the three-attribute criteria, $\frac{1}{3}$ of the criterial stimuli satisfied the criterion with respect to a single attribute, $\frac{1}{3}$ with respect to two, and $\frac{1}{3}$ with respect to all three. In each case, each particular attribute, or combination, was represented an equal ($\pm$ 1) number of times.[2]

An experimental run consisted of 50 trials. The sequencing of criterial and noncriterial stimuli was determined by a random selection of five rows from Gellerman's table of trial orders (Stevens, 1951, p. 533).

The Ss were eight undergraduate female college students, each of whom had one run with each of the nine criteria listed in Table 1. Half of the Ss encountered the criteria in the order in which they are listed in the table, left to right, top to bottom. Half encountered them in the reverse order. (Because of a scheduling error, one of the Ss in the latter group encountered Cond. L last rather than as Run No. 6). Half of the Ss in each "order" group used the dominant hand, and half the nondominant hand, to press the "yes" key. Each S completed the nine runs within a period of 2 wk.

To assess the effects of practice on performance with the most complex task, three Ss were given an additional 27 runs with the three-attribute criterion. Each S used the same hand to press the "yes" key as she had in the main experiment; in two cases this was the dominant hand, and in one the nondominant. The Ss completed three runs a day for each of 9 successive working days. Procedural details were exactly as those of the three-attribute condition. The same stimulus cards were presented, but in a different order, on each run.

---

[2] The fractions reported in this paragraph are not quite accurate; however, the relative frequency of occurrence of the different types of stimuli were held as close to these proportions as the total number of trials per run permitted.

RESULTS

Figure 1 shows RT and percentage of errors as functions of the number of attributes satisfying the criterion with the number of attributes relevant to the criterion as the parameter. Each point on the RT graph represents a mean of 24 medians, each median representing the RTs of a single S from one experimental run and associated with the particular condition specified by the abscissa of that point on the graph. All RTs represent correct responses only.

Considering only the "yes" responses, with criteria involving more than a single attribute, RT decreased as the number of attributes which satisfied the criterion increased. This was invariably true of the summary scores of individual Ss, hence the trend may be considered statistically reliable ($p < .01$, sign test).

For a given number of attributes *satisfying* a criterion, the graph indicates that RT increased with the number of attributes *relevant* to the criterion. The summary scores of some Ss included exceptions to this rule. Although median RT (for individual Ss without exception was greater with a two-attribute than with a single-attribute criterion, it was not invariably greater with a three- than with a two-attribute criterion. However, L tests (Page, 1963) for those cases involving three-way comparisons (zero and one attributes satisfying criterion) and a sign test for the two-way comparison (two attributes satisfying criterion) showed the tendency for RT to increase with the number of attributes relevant to the criterion to be significant in each case ($L = 108$, $p = .01$, $L = 110$, $p = .001$ in the case of the L tests, $p < .05$ with the sign test).

Error rates were related to the experimental variables in much the same way as was RT, i.e., the relative frequency of errors tended to be high in those cases in which RT was long, and low when the latter was short. Perhaps the most striking feature of Figure 1b is the extremely high frequency of false negatives when the stimulus satisfies a multiattribute criterion with respect to only a single attribute.

Figure 2 summarizes the results of the second phase of the experiment, showing RT and percentage of errors as functions of the number of attributes satisfying the three-attribute criterion at different stages of practice. Each point on the RT graph represents the mean of 27 medians, one median per S per run. It would appear from the figure that both RT and error rate had stabilized fairly well by the end of the experiment. Moreover, the relationships obtained during the latter part of the experiment were very similar to those shown in the comparable curves of Figure 1.

Experiment II

Experiment II was similar to Exp. I except that the disjunctive categories listed in Table 1 were replaced by conjunctive categories involving the same attributes.

METHOD

With a conjunctive criterion a stimulus is criterial only if it satisfies the criterion with respect to all relevant attributes. Because of this fact, it will be somewhat more convenient to consider the relationship between stimulus and criterion in this case in terms of the number of relevant attributes with respect to which the stimulus *fails* to satisfy the criterion than in terms of the number of attributes with respect to which it satisfies it. It should be understood that a critical stimulus fails to satisfy the criterion with respect to zero attributes, whereas a noncritical stimulus fails to satisfy it with respect to one or more attributes.

In each experimental run half of the stimuli were criterial and half were not. With respect to the latter, control and counterbalancing procedures followed in this experiment were analogous to those followed in the case of criterial stimuli in Exp. I.

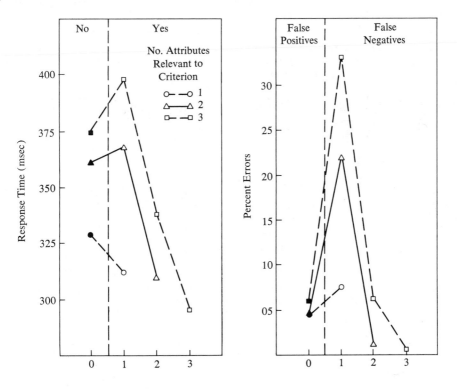

Number of Attributes Satisfying Criterion

FIGURE 1 Response time and percentage of errors as functions of the number of stimulus attributes satisfying disjunctive criterion with the number of attributes relevant to the criterion as the parameter. (Points on the RT graph are means of medians.)

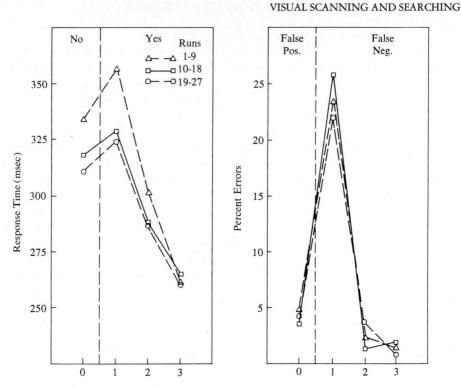

FIGURE 2   Response time and percentage of errors as functions of the number of stimulus attributes satisfying the three-attribute disjunctive criterion at different stages of practice. (Points on the RT graph are means of medians.)

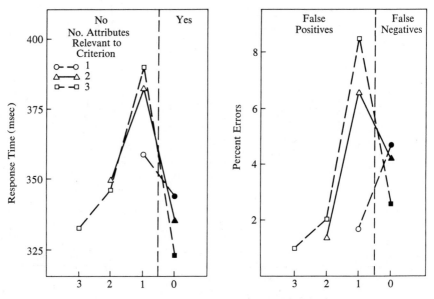

FIGURE 3   Response time and percentage of errors as functions of the number of stimulus attributes failing to satisfy conjunctive criterion with the number of attributes relevant to the criterion as the parameter. (Points on the RT graph are means of medians.)

The Ss were four female and two male undergraduate college students and two male laboratory employees. Procedural details were identical in all respects to those of the prior experiment.

Four Ss (all female college students) two of whom participated in the primary phase of Exp. II and two of whom did not, were given 27 runs under the three-attribute criterion condition. Two used the dominant hand, and two the nondominant hand, to press the "yes" key.

RESULTS

Figure 3 shows RT and percentage of errors as functions of the number of attributes failing to satisfy the criterion with the number of attributes relevant to the criterion as the parameter. Each point on the RT graph represents a mean of 24 medians, calculated as in Exp. I.

Considering only the "no" responses, with criteria involving two or three attributes, RT increased as the number of attributes failing to satisfy the criterion decreased ($p < .05$, sign test for two-way comparison, $L = 110$, $p < .001$ for three-way comparison).

With respect to the effect of the number of attributes relevant to the criterion, the results are rather less clearcut than were those of Exp. I. None of the RT differences was sufficiently consistent across Ss to be significant when assessed with the L test.

Error rates were generally much lower than in Exp. I, but as in that experiment they tended to be highest under those conditions in which RT tended to be longest.

Figure 4 shows RT and percentage of errors as functions of the number of attributes failing to satisfy the criterion at different stages of practice for the second phase of the experiment.

Discussion

In what follows we let r represent the number of attributes which are relevant to a criterion, and s or f to indicate the number with respect to which a criterion is satisfied, or fails to be satisfied by a stimulus; s and f will be used to describe the correspondence of stimuli to disjunctive and conjunctive criteria, respectively.

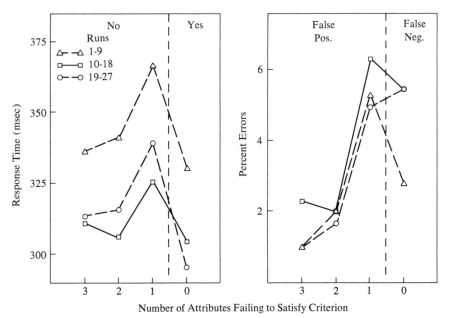

FIGURE 4   Response time and percentage of errors as functions of the number of stimulus attributes failing to satisfy the three-attribute conjunctive criterion at different stages of practice. (Points on the RT graph are means of medians.)

The results agree with those of Nickerson and Fehrer's (1964) earlier study in that with disjunctive category criteria positive RT varied directly with r and inversely with s. They go beyond the earlier results in showing (a) that the latter effect persisted after considerable practice, (b) that with conjunctive criteria negative RT varied inversely with f, (c) that this effect also tended to persist with practice, (d) that for $s = 0$ (noncriterial stimuli, disjunctive criteria) and $f = 0$ (criterial stimuli, conjunctive criteria) RT was shorter than would have been expected from an extrapolation of the results with $s \geqslant 1$ (criterial stimuli, disjunctive criteria) or $f \geqslant 1$ (noncriterial stimuli, conjunctive criteria), (e) that with both disjunctive and conjunctive criteria error rates were highest under those conditions in which RT was longest.

Suppose it is assumed (a) that the time required for the completion of a component process (determination of the presence or absence of a particular attribute) is a random variable, and (b) that the composite process is efficient in the dual sense that only relevant component processes are activated, and a decision concerning criteriality is not delayed after the combined outputs of the component processes are sufficient to warrant making it.

In the case of a sequential processing system, the composite time distribution for decisions involving n component processes would be the convolution of the individual component distributions, and decision time would tend to increase monotonically with the number of component processes required by the situation. In the present context, with disjunctive criteria the average number of component processes required would vary inversely with s for given r, and directly with r for given s; with conjunctive criteria the number of component processes would vary inversely with f for given r, and directly with r for given f.

In the case of a parallel processing system (a) for a decision which is contingent on the outcome of *any one* of n component processes the time distribution would be generated by considering all possible combinations of values (one taken from each of the component distri-

butions), selecting the smallest value from each combination and weighting it by the probability of occurrence of the combination; and (b) for a decision which is contingent on the outcome from *all* of n component processes, the distribution would be the distribution of largest values determined in an analogous way. For our present purposes it is sufficient to recognize that if the component distributions overlap to any degree, the mean of the composite distribution would be less than the least of the means of the component distributions in the first case, and larger than the largest of the component means in the second.

The first situation characterizes positive instances of disjunctive categories and negative instances of conjunctive categories, the number of component distributions from which a minimum value would be drawn being equal to s in the former case and to f in the latter. Hence decision time would be expected to vary inversely with s and f with disjunctive and conjunctive criteria, respectively. In both cases decision time should be independent of r for fixed s or f. Situation b is characteristic of negative instances of disjunctive categories and positive instances of conjunctive categories. The number of component distributions from which the maximum would be drawn is r, so decision time would be expected to increase with this variable in both of these cases.

Assumptions concerning the parameters of the component distributions would allow inferences concerning the expected values of the parameters of composite distributions; however, in this report our attention will be confined to the fairly gross implications mentioned above and summarized in Table 2.

With respect to the effect of the number of attributes satisfying (failing to satisfy) a criterion, both hypotheses lead to the same expectations. Considering only criterial (noncriterial) stimuli, the results with disjunctive (conjunctive) criteria were consistent with these expectations. However, the results obtained with noncriterial (criterial) stimuli and disjunctive (conjunctive) criteria pose a problem. For any given criterion, both hypotheses would predict that maximum decision times would be associated with these latter cases, and they were not. In connection with this point, it should be noted that with disjunctive criteria the frequency of false negatives was exceptionally high when criterial stimuli satisfied a multiattribute criterion with respect to only a single attribute; with conjunctive criteria the highest error rates—in this case false positives—were obtained when noncriterial stimuli failed by a single attribute to satisfy a multiattribute criterion. Any tendency to base decisions on insufficiently thorough analyses of stimuli would have the double effect of promoting high error rates under just these conditions and, as a result of luckily correct responses, of spuriously lowering RT for noncriterial (criterial) stimuli in the case of disjunctive (conjunctive) criteria. Whether the existence of such a tendency is sufficient to account for the results obtained is open to question; however, there is little doubt that it was a contributing factor. The relationship between error rate and the degree of correspondence between stimulus and criterion was similar to that obtained in another experiment (Nickerson, 1966), in which S's task was to decide whether a set of visually displayed English letters contained any items in common with a set of letters just committed to memory.

In this situation the frequency of false negatives tended to vary inversely with the number of items which the two sets (displayed and memorized) had in common, being especially high in the case of a single common item.

Concerning the effect of the number of attributes relevant to a criterion the two hypotheses do not lead to the same expectations. Specifically, the parallel processing hypothesis predicts that decision time will be insensitive to differences in this variable under certain conditions. In this regard, the results with disjunctive criteria appear to be consistent with the sequential, and incompatible with the parallel, hypothesis. The results with conjunctive criteria, however, are problematic for both hypotheses. In this case, none of the RT differences associated with differences in r were significant as assessed by an L test, i.e., this variable did not have a significant effect even under those conditions with respect to which both hypotheses agree that it should. It may be noted in fact that for criterial stimuli the RTs (Figure 3) are arranged in an order exactly opposite that which both hypotheses would predict. Although the differences were not statistically significant the same order was obtained in the scores of five of the eight Ss.

TABLE 2

Expected Relationship between Decision Time (DT) and r, s, and f

Type Criterion	Assumed Processing Mode	
	Sequential	Parallel
Disjunctive	Increase with decreasing s, for given r Max DT with noncriterial stimuli Increase with increasing r, for given s	Increase with decreasing s, for given r Max DT with noncriterial stimuli Independent of r, for given s $>$ 0 (criterial stimuli) Increase with increasing r, for $s = 0$ (noncriterial stimuli)
Conjunctive	Increase with decreasing f, for given r Max DT with criterial stimuli Increase with increasing r, for given f	Increase with decreasing f, for given r Max DT with criterial stimuli Independent of r, for given $f > 0$ (noncriterial stimuli) Increase with increasing r, for $f = 0$ (criterial stimuli)

Note.—r = number of attributes relevant to a category criterion, s = number of attributes with respect to which stimulus satisfies criterion, f = number of attributes with respect to which stimulus fails to satisfy criterion.

The results on the whole then are rather equivocal with respect to the question of sequential vs. parallel processing; some are consistent with both hypotheses, others are difficult to account for in terms of either. In retrospect it might be argued that decomposition of the categorization process into a set of attribute-detecting components is such a gross oversimplification that it is bound to lead to ambiguous results. However, it is clear that any process that would be capable of making the discriminations required in these experimental tasks would have to take cognizance, at least implicitly, of a sufficient number of attributes to determine membership, or nonmembership, in the categories defined. Furthermore, it is apparent from the data that the number of attributes that the situation required be attended to did in fact affect categorization time, even if not in a simple and entirely consistent way.

There is a procedural problem associated with this type of experimentation which may account in part for some of the apparent irregularities in the results. The problem stems from the implications which different category criteria have with respect to the control of variables other than those of immediate interest. For obvious reasons, E would like to structure the situation such that, for any experimental run (a) positive and negative cases occur with equal frequency, (b) no particular stimulus (unique combination of attributes) occurs more frequently than any other, and (c) the defining attributes of the criterion category are all in fact relevant (i.e., a simpler, but equally adequate, criterion cannot be substituted for the one given by E). Unfortunately, it is not always possible to satisfy all of these constraints simultaneously, given the tasks described above. The problem is most obvious when one considers the three-attribute conjunctive criterion. Suppose that in this case E decides to satisfy Constraints a and b. This can be done only by making every negative case an instance of the same stimulus (since the defined category contains only one member), but this would violate c, since S could find a single-attribute criterion which would work

as well as the three-attribute criterion provided by E. If, on the other hand, E decides to satisfy a and c then several different stimuli must occur as negative cases, whereas only a single stimulus is available for positive cases, and this violates b. Similarly, to satisfy b and c, one must violate a. In these experiments the convention was always to satisfy constraints a and c, which of course meant violating b. Analogous problems are encountered when one attempts to control the number of cases corresponding to each of the possible values of the variables s and f. The extent to which the results obtained are contingent on the particular compromises struck can be determined only by further research.

Summary

Ss were asked to decide as quickly as possible whether stimuli belonged to categories defined in terms of conjunctions or inclusive disjunctions of readily discriminated attributes, and to register their decisions by pressing 1 of 2 response keys. The independent variables of interest were the number of attributes which were relevant to a category criterion (r), and the number of attributes with respect to which a stimulus satisfied (s), or failed to satisfy (f), a criterion. It was found (1) that with disjunctive criteria positive RT varied directly with r and inversely with s, (2) that the latter effect persisted after considerable practice, (3) that with conjunctive criteria negative RT varied inversely with f, (4) that this effect also persisted with practice, (5) that negative instances of disjunctive categories and positive instances of conjunctive categories produced shorter RTs than would have been expected from an extrapolation of the results with positive and negative instances of disjunctive and conjunctive categories, respectively, (6) that with both disjunctive and conjunctive criteria error rates were highest under those conditions in which RT was longest. Implications of the results for the question of sequential vs. parallel processing modes were considered.

References

Bricker, P. D. The identification of redundant stimulus patterns. *J. exp. Psychol.,* 1955, *49,* 73–81.

Christie, L. S., & Luce, R. D. Decision structure and time relations in simple choice behavior. *Bull. Math. Biophys.,* 1956, *18,* 89–112.

Fitts, P. M., & Biederman, I. S-R compatibility and information reduction. *J. exp. Psychol.,* 1965, *69,* 408–412.

Morin, R. E., Forrin, B., & Archer, W. Information processing behavior: The role of irrelevant stimulus information. *J. exp. Psychol.,* 1961, *61,* 89–96.

Neisser, U. Time analysis of logical processes in man. *Proc. Joint West. Computer Conf.,* 1961, 579–585.

Nickerson, R. S. Response times with a memory-dependent decision task. *J. exp. Psychol.,* 1966, *72,* 761–769.

Nickerson, R. S., & Fehrer, C. E. Stimulus categorization and response time. *Percept. mot. Skills,* 1964, *18,* 785–793.

Page, E. B. Ordered hypotheses for multiple treatment: A significance test for linear ranks. *J. Amer. Statist. Ass.,* 1963, *58,* 216–230.

Pollack, I. Speed of classification of words into superordinate categories. *J. verbal Learn. verbal Behav.,* 1963, *2,* 159–165.

Posner, I. Information reduction in the analysis of sequential tasks. *Psychol. Rev.,* 1964, *71,* 491–504.

Rapaport, A. A study of disjunctive reaction times. *Behav. Sci.,* 1959, *4,* 299–315.

Sternberg, S. Retrieval from recent memory: Some reaction-time experiments and a search theory. Paper read at the Fourth Annual Meeting of the Psychonomic Society, Bryn Mawr, August 1963.

Stevens, S. S. (Ed.) *Handbook of experimental psychology.* New York: Wiley, 1951.

CHAPTER *6*

Sequential and Repetition Processes

6.1 A Research Strategy
for Studying Certain Effects
of Very Fast Sequential Input Rates
on the Visual System*

M. S. MAYZNER   M. E. TRESSELT
M. S. HELFER

The treatment of the visual system as an information processing system has recently become an important strategy for investigators working in the area of visual perception (e.g., Rosenblith, 1961). Such a strategy, which focuses on problems of visual information processing and related issues such as the "channel capacity" of the visual system, raises very basic and fundamental questions concerning the rate at which the visual system can process inputs, and such concern with the rate-handling capacity of the visual system immediately directs attention to the effects of input timing distributions on visual response mechanisms. Thus, Bartley (1959) in a review article suggests three forms of input timing distributions as being of central importance: "(a) single isolated stimuli; (b) paired stimuli, in which the two members of the pair are variously separated in time; and (c) trains of stimuli, often called intermittent stimulation. In intermittent stimulation, time intervals between stimuli may be varied, and the ratio between the stimulus (pulse) duration and the length of the cycle of intermittency may also be varied. These three forms of manipulation have turned out to be much more than empty differences in form of stimulation as will be seen later. The use of method (a) provides for a response from a resting system, at least as far as intended activation is concerned. Method (b) provides for the determination of the effect of the first stimulus on the second,

or otherwise stated, it provides for discovering how long it takes for the reacting system to complete its response and reassume status quo. Method (c) provides for still another aspect of the reacting system to become manifest. Since the optic pathway consists of a number of parallel channels, each with finite limits in the rate at which it can be reactivated, it is possible that, when a whole train of stimuli is delivered at a rate beyond which single channels can repeatedly respond, a redistribution of the relationships between repeated pulses and the responses to them occurs as stimulation progresses."

The major objective of the present paper is to briefly describe an experimental computer-based CRT display facility that seems particularly well-suited to study the type of temporal factors in vision Bartley has outlined and to discuss briefly some problems associated with research strategy when investigating such temporal factors with a computer-based display system. At the outset, it is important also to note that in addition to the temporal factors, Bartley discusses spatial factors and perhaps more importantly spatio-temporal factors need to be given explicit recognition in studying visual response mechanisms. For example, with Bartley's input timing distributions "b" and "c," the pair or train of stimuli which are separated in time may or may not also be separated in space; that is to say, the two stimuli of a pair may occur at the same location in space or at two different locations, and with a

* Reproduced by permission of *Psychonomic Monograph Supplements,* 1967, vol. 2, pp. 73–81.

train or string of stimuli; again, all may occur at the same spatial location or at many different locations.

In terms of previous research efforts, considerable work has been done with pairs of stimuli variously separated in time only or in time and space, e.g., see Raab's review (1963) on backward masking phenomena. Also, considerable work has been done on trains of stimuli with an extensive body of findings now accumulated on flicker, intermittent stimulation, and apparent movement, e.g., see Brown's chapter on "Flicker and Intermittent Stimulation" and Graham's chapter on "Perception of Movement" in *Vision and Visual Perception* (Graham, 1965) and White's (1963) monograph on temporal numerosity. However, the work on trains of stimuli has been concerned almost exclusively with very simple stimuli, i.e., typically light flashes, and has involved either a single spatial location, as most of the work on flicker, or at most a few different locations, as found in apparent movement studies. Little if any work has been done with trains of stimuli where the following three conditions obtain: (1) the stimuli are separate in time and space, (2) each individual stimulus is not merely a simple light flash, but a more complex configuration such as a line segment or some alpha-numeric symbol, and (3) the input string is relatively long (i.e., up to as many as 40 individual stimuli) and the input rate is very fast (i.e., in the range from 100 μsec per input up to 500 msec). The present paper shall be concerned exclusively with a systematic examination of these three conditions.

Two recent studies have started to examine longer stimulus trains, where the individual stimuli are separate in time and space, and are presented at relatively fast input rates. Thus, Julesz (1964) reports a study in which the sides of triangles, pentagons, and hexagons were presented cyclically in sequential or non-sequential order at various speeds or exposure durations. The sides were thin bright slits on a black background and exposure duration per side was set at approximately 200 msec (time between sides was set at zero) and gradually decreased until the polygon in question was

perceived as a single Gestalt. The times at which a single Gestalt was reported for the non-sequential order was very roughly about half of the time required for the sequential order. Julesz concludes, therefore, that "sequential presentation is easier to perceive than any departure from the sequential order."

In a similar type of study McFarland (1965) presented either the three sides or the three vertices of an equilateral line triangle sequentially. Sides or vertices were displayed for 10 msec each and time between sides or vertices was varied from 0 to 300 msec in 25 msec steps. Ss were required to report their perceptual experience in terms of three judgmental categories, namely, were the sides or vertices seen as (1) simultaneous, (2) overlapping, or (3) successive, and further, if the simultaneous judgment was given, the S also was instructed to report on whether the sides or vertices were joined to make a perfect triangle. The results showed that "as the time between sequential responses increases, both perception of simultaneity and joining show an initial rapid and linear decrease, and when sequential response is to side parts, both joining and simultaneity can be perceived over larger intervals than when sequential response is to angle parts."

Experimental Facility

Since it was desired to display sequentially at very fast input rates a long string of relatively complex stimuli (e.g., a string of 40 letters in adjacent spatial locations) maintaining precise control over the spatial and temporal characteristics of the display sequence, typical display devices such as projectors or tachistoscopes were not useful because of their inherent equipment limitations in generating long input strings at fast input rates, with precise control over spatio-temporal factors. It was decided, therefore, to employ a computer-based CRT display system which would provide extreme flexibility in precisely controlling the spatio-temporal characteristics of such display sequences and at the same time allow for very fast input rates.

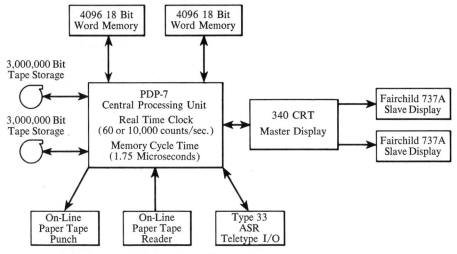

FIGURE 1   Block diagram of experimental computer-based CRT display facility.

This system consists of a high-speed online PDP-7 digital computer (manufactured by the Digital Equipment Corporation, Maynard, Mass.) having a memory cycle time of 1.75 μsec, 8K 18 bit words of core memory, 6 million bits of external tape storage, and an extended arithmetic element which allows for high-speed multiplication (average time 6.1 μsec), division (average time 9 μsec), shifting, and register manipulation. Coupled to and driven by the computer are three CRT display consoles. One display is a Master display (Type 340, modified to accommodate up to four slave displays), including a 64 alpha-numeric character set generator (Type 342) and a sub-routine interface (Type 347) which permits data display from arbitrarily located and non-consecutive display tables within the PDP-7 memory. Coupled to the 340 Master display are two Fairchild CRT slave displays (Type 737A, manufactured by the Fairchild Camera and Instrument Corporation, Clifton, N.J.). Figure 1 presents a block diagram of the experimental facility, Figure 2 is a picture of the two Fairchild displays (side by side) and the 340 Master display, and Figure 3 is a picture of the PDP-7 computer.

By using a digital computer to control the display of input sequences of a CRT display, one primarily is limited only by the memory cycle time of the computer and the display

generation time of the particular CRT being employed. In the present system, the PDP-7 computer, when appropriately programmed, will generate displays on the 340 Master display. Individual points may be plotted on a 238 mm square raster centered on the face of the display tube, consisting of a matrix of 1024 x 1024 separately programmable point locations. Thus by specifying appropriate point locations, one may display any type of geometric configuration one might care to generate. For purposes of the present paper, we shall be concerned primarily with the character mode of the 340 display system. In this programming mode one may specify for display any of the characters shown in Figure 4. The numbers under the characters represent the octal code of the character used in programming the character for display.

As may be seen, these alpha-numeric characters consist of a varying number of individual points and appear in Figure 4 as they appear on the 340 display. The electron beam which intensifies the individual points of these characters requires .5 μsec per point for intensification and 1.5 μsec per point for positioning. Thus, for example, the minimum time any character can be displayed is 2 μsec (.5 μsec + 1.5 μsec) times the number of points in the character. It should also be noted that the points of a particular character are intensified sequentially so that each character is generated in a sequential fashion. More specifically, if one programmed the 340 to display the character "1" for 1 msec, the electron beam would intensify or "paint" the individual points 50 times (i.e., 10 points x 2 μsec x 50 paints = 1000 μsec or 1 msec), or if one wished to display the characters "11111" simultaneously for 1 msec, the electron beam would intensify or "paint" the individual points of all five "ones" sequentially 10 times (i.e., 50 points x 2 μsec x 10 paints = 1000 μsec or 1 msec). This display technique is, of course, entirely different from the line scanning technique found in commercial TV display systems and allows one to precisely program character display times. Since the individual points of any display require 2 μsec for painting and positioning to the next point, the fastest display time will always be 2 μsec times the number of points in the display. On the other hand, if one wishes to display 1000 characters simultaneously—and let us assume for the 1000 characters 15000 points are needed—then 30 msec (2 μsec x 15000 points = 30 msec) must elapse before the electron beam will return to the first point, and thus the minimum display time would be 30 msec.

Since the plotting of many characters (i.e., 1000 or more) does begin to take relatively an appreciable amount of time, flicker will begin to appear on the display. To avoid this problem, the 340 display is coated with a P7 phosphor which has a very long decay time (on the order of many seconds) which greatly attenuates flicker when displaying a large number of characters. However, for the display application being discussed here, where precise timing of the display is required, the 340 with its P7 phosphor is totally unsatisfactory. Therefore, slaved to the 340 Master display are two Fairchild 737A display consoles (see Figure 2),

FIGURE 2   The two Fairchild displays and the 340 Master display.

FIGURE 3   The PDP-7 computer.

equipped with P24 phosphor whose decay times are on the order of a few μsec. These slave displays present exactly the same information programmed for display on the 340, but because of the decay time of the P24 phosphor, when the electron beam stops painting, the display, as far as the eye is concerned, is instantaneously dead, which allows for very precise timing of display input sequences. Such precise timing is, of course, not possible on the 340 display because of its long decaying phosphor. The points which make up the characters appear as bright spots of white light against the light green background of the CRT surface. Figure 5 shows a picture of the character set displayed on the Fairchild display. Direct interfacing of the PDP-7 computer to the Fairchild displays is not possible, since the character generator hardware involves the use of the 340 Master display.

The Fairchild display offers an effective display area of 224 mm x 280 mm, and X and Y axes gain and positioning controls also permit continuous changes in size and position of the input sequence on the display surface. For example, on the 340 Master display the characters shown in Figure 4 may be programmed in four sizes: namely, 8 mm wide x 12 mm high, or 4 mm x 8 mm, or 2 mm x 4 mm, or 1 mm x 2 mm. When these dimensions are expanded on the Fairchild display to maximum size, the values are 32 mm x 48 mm, 16 mm x 24 mm, 8 mm x 12 mm, and 4 mm x 6 mm, and when contracted to minimum size the values are 4 mm x 8 mm, 2 mm x 4 mm, 1 mm x 2 mm, and .5 mm x 1 mm. The smallest sizes (i.e., 1 mm by 2 mm and .5 mm x 1 mm) are not discriminable as characters but appear rather as small bright spots of high intensity light.

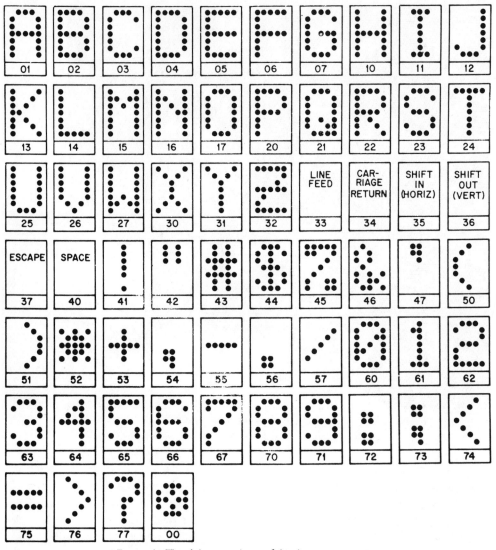

FIGURE 4   The alpha-numeric set of the character generator.

FIGURE 5   The character set as displayed on the Fairchild display.

Computer Display Program

In order to achieve the display capability desired (i.e., the sequential display of a long train of stimuli at very fast input rates), it was decided to write a general purpose display program, which would allow for considerable flexibility in specifying and entering display information, starting and stopping the display, altering information contained in the display, and allowing for a very wide range of input timing distributions to be examined. Therefore, a program was written that contains four basic display parameters which are specified by the E at the beginning of any display sequence. These four parameters are: (1) N, the number of alpha-numeric characters to be displayed (this may be any number from 1 to 40), (2) Content, the actual alpha-numeric characters to be displayed (these may be any of the characters shown in Figure 4), (3) Display order, the actual display sequence of the characters being displayed (with N characters, the number of possible different display orders is N!), and (4) Input timing distribution, the length of time each character is to be displayed and the inter-character times (both character times and inter-character times may vary from 100 μsec to 26.2143 sec in 100 μsec increments).

The present display program gives the E the capability of changing any one of these last three parameters without respecifying the others. If the E desires to change the number of alpha-numeric characters being presented, i.e., N, then he must respecify all four parameters. This particular feature of the display program was introduced to save on parameter "entry time" into the computer, since it allows the E to change only one parameter at a time keeping the other parameters fixed. Figure 6 is a flow chart showing the logic and essentials of the display program.

If we assume that the display program has already been loaded into the computer by means of the DECSYS tape units and that the program is ready to start executing, then the

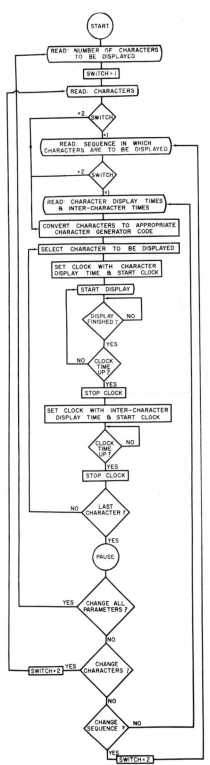

FIGURE 6   Flow chart of the computer display program.

following is a brief description of the procedure an E would go through to display, for example, the word "somersault" sequentially from left to right with each character being displayed for 5 msec and a delay of 10 msec between characters (i.e., inter-character times of 10 msec). All of the following parameter information is entered into the computer via the computer console teletype machine, as follows:

(1) The E types the number "10," since "somersault" has 10 letters. As already indicated this number may be any value from 1 to 40.

(2) The computer returns the carriage of the teletype machine and waits.

(3) E types "somersault."

(4) The computer returns the carriage and waits.

(5) E types the sequence of numbers 1, 2, 3, 4, 5, 6, 7, 8, 9, 10. This string of numbers represents the display order.

(6) The computer returns the carriage and waits.

(7) E types the sequence of numbers 50, 50, 50, 50, 50, 50, 50, 50, 50, 50 (note—50 beats = 5 msec). This string of numbers, one for each of the 10 letters in "somersault," represents the beats of a 10,000 cps computer clock, which is employed by the program to fix character display times and inter-character times. With this 10,000 cps clock, one beat of the clock represents 100 μsec, two beats represent 200 μsec, and 50 beats represent 5 msec (i.e., 50 x 100 μsec = 5 msec). Thus, this computer clock provides a display timing capability from 100 μsec (i.e., one clock beat, which is entered as the number "1" via the teletype console) up to 26.2143 sec (entered as the number "262,143") in 100 μsec increments. This upper limit of 26.2143 sec, which is $2^{18}-1$, is a result of the way in which the program was written, the clock frequency (i.e., 10,000 beats per sec), and the 18 bit word structure of the PDP-7 system. It is believed, however, that an input timing range extending from 100 μsec to 26 sec on 100 μsec in-

crements (for character times and inter-character times, all independently specifiable) provides all of the input timing flexibility one needs for the present research program.

(8) The computer returns the carriage and waits.

(9) E types the sequence of numbers 100, 100, 100, 100, 100, 100, 100, 100, 100. These nine numbers correspond to the nine inter-character times in a 10 character sequence (note—100 beats = 100 × 100 μsec = 10 msec).

(10) The computer displays the sequence of characters once and halts.

(11) E may redisplay the sequence by using the continue switch on the console of the computer. This may be done as often as desired.

Now if the E desires to change only the characters being displayed, say from "somersault" to "stochastic," he may do so by setting a particular accumulator switch on the computer console and typing "stochastic" (note that the new word "stochastic" must have the same number of characters as the old word "somersault"). The word "stochastic" now is displayed from left to right with the same times as were previously used for "somersault."

If the E next desires to change the sequence of display to a right to left order, he sets another accumulator switch and types the sequence "10, 9, 8, 7, 6, 5, 4, 3, 2, 1." The word "stochastic" is now displayed from right to left, i.e., the "c" is the first letter displayed followed by the "i," then the "t," "s," "a," "h," "c," "o," "t," and "s," using the same times. Any other display order may also be entered via the teletype, such as 7, 5, 9, 2, 1, 10, 4, 3, 8, 6, which with the word "stochastic" would mean "h" is the first letter displayed, followed by "c," "t," "s," "t," "c," "s," "i," "o," and "a," all letters being displayed, of course, in those letter positions in which they occur in the actual word. It should be noted that with 10 characters there are 10! or 3,628,800 different display orders possible, any one of which the E may insert, or if the sequence is 40 characters in length, then there are 40! different display orders possible, again, any one of which the E may choose to examine by inserting the appropriate 40 number sequence via the teletype console.

To change the display times and inter-character times, a third accumulator switch is set, and the new times are typed. For example, typing the sequence 50, 47, 140, 10, 70, 62, 12, 4, 31, 125, followed by 200, 125, 5, 300, 4, 61, 43, 1000, 12 causes (if the display order is still 7, 5, 9, 2, 1, 10, 4, 3, 8, 6 with the word "stochastic") the "h" to be displayed first for 5 msec, followed by a 20 msec inter-character delay, followed by the "c" for 4.7 msec, followed by a 12.5 msec inter-character delay, followed by the "t" for 14 msec, followed by a .5 msec inter-character delay time, etc. In addition, the E may start the entire program over again by setting still another accumulator switch, which permits one to change the number of characters being displayed (i.e., in the range from 1 to 40). When this change is made, values for the remaining three display parameters must again be reinserted via the teletype console.

For the most part, the program for displaying sequential information was written in Fortran II, which operates under control of the PDP-7 DECSYS supervisor programs. The only portion of the program written in assembly or machine language deals with the actual displaying of characters and the timing of the display. About 65% of the program is written, therefore, in Fortran. Three principal advantages result from using Fortran for this program. These are: (1) The experimental circumstances require a considerable amount of parameter information to be entered into computer memory via a teletype console, and Fortran offers an easy means of controlling the E-computer interaction through the use of Fortran input-output subroutines; thus all parameter information insertions and changes are affected via the Fortran I/O subroutines. (2) The use of Fortran greatly facilitates the writing of the sequential display program, as all I/O, logic, and translation to the character

generator codes are done in Fortran. (3) Fortran, because of its wide acceptance, is in itself a partial documentation of the program.

Research Strategy

With the experimental facility and computer display program outlined in the two previous sections, one is now equipped to study a variety of stimulus parameters and their effects on the visual response system. Since previous studies (Mayzner, Tresselt, & Cohen, 1966; Mayzner, Tressalt, Adrignolo, & Cohen, 1967) have already identified two possibly new effects (i.e., "sequential blanking" and "sequential displacement") employing the general approach outlined in this paper, this section will briefly discuss what stimulus parameters appear related to these effects.

Most generally, the research strategy we have adopted asks the question: "How does the visual system process a train of stimuli or inputs when (1) these inputs arrive sequentially in time, (2) occur at different locations in space, and (3) are displayed at varying input rates, from very fast to relatively slow?" With the present computer display program and CRT display facility, it is hoped some answers may be obtained to this question, and on the basis of preliminary findings, it would appear that the following seven stimulus parameters will require systematic study.

1. INPUT DISPLAY ORDER

This parameter refers to the display order in which a train or string of inputs are presented. For example, with five inputs, occurring in five immediately adjacent cell locations along a single horizontal line, 120 display orders are possible (i.e., 5!). Thus, if five adjacent cell locations are filled with the letters "c," "h," "a," "i," and "r" and the numbers 1, 2, 3, 4, and 5 are used to refer to the order in which these letters or imputs are displayed, then an order such as 12345 would mean "c" is displayed first (in the first cell location), "h" second (in the second cell location), "a" third (in the third cell location), "i" fourth (in the fourth cell location), and "r" fifth (in the fifth cell location); while an order such as 42513 would mean "i" is displayed first (in the fourth cell location), "h" is displayed second (in the second cell location), "r" is displayed third (in the fifth cell location), "c" is displayed fourth (in the first cell location), and "a" is displayed fifth (in the third cell location). As indicated in the previous section, the present computer display program presents characters along a single horizontal line in any one of 40 cell locations, and, unless otherwise stated, when reference is made to the display of inputs, this will refer to inputs displayed in immediately adjacent cell locations.

In two previous studies (Mayzner, Tresselt, & Cohen, 1966; Mayzner, Tresselt, Adrignolo, & Cohen, 1967) irregular display orders, such as 4̲2̲5̲1̲3, 7̲5̲9̲2̲1̲1̲0̲4̲3̲8̲6, and 1̲0̲, 18, 8̲, 15, 6̲, 17, 7̲, 3̲, 2̲, 1, 20, 1̲1̲, 19, 5̲, 16, 9̲, 14, 4̲, 12, 13, for 5, 10, and 20 input letter sequences were examined, and for display times ranging from 10 to 20 msec per letter and per interval between letters, approximately the first half of these inputs were not perceived (the "blanked" letter locations are underlined), and this phenomena was called "sequential blanking." A simulated picture of the sequential blanking effect for the word "somersault" with the display order 75921104386 is shown in Figure 7. The picture is simulated in the sense that the "blanked" letters (i.e., "o," "e," "r," "a," and "u") were specifically not displayed here to show the reader how the display actually appears to an observer when the appropriate input rate is actually employed. If regular display orders are employed, such as 1–5, 1–10, or 1–20, no elements are ever blanked. It was also discovered that with the letter sequence "somersault" and with a display order such as 13579246810, while no letters were blanked (unless letter size was very small), there was a marked spatial displacement of the second "s" away from the "r" to the right, and this phenomenon was called "sequential displacement." With the present computer display program, we will be able to examine any display order possible with strings from 2 to 40 characters in length.

Since the number of different display orders possible with N characters is N!, and exhaustive examination of all possible display orders for even N = 10 poses an unsolvable problem, as 10! = 3,628,800 different display orders. Therefore, the most reasonable research strategy would seem to be to examine exhaustively all possible display orders for N = 2 up to perhaps N = 6 and attempt to build with this data base a model that would hopefully predict the effects found with any longer sequences. If this proves to be impossible, then one would seem to be left with the task of examining display orders for longer sequences on a quasi-random basis attempting again to build a model which would predict what the effects of any display order might be, no matter what its length, or at least up to N = 40 (the capacity of the present computer display program).

2. INPUT DISPLAY RATE

This parameter refers to the rate at which a string of inputs are presented, or more specifically to the input timing distribution being examined. With the present computer display program, exposure time per character and time between characters may both be varied independently. In the previously cited work on "blanking" and "displacement" effects, it was found that if the shortest exposure times then available were employed (i.e., either 200 or 300 μ sec per character and per interval between characters), Ss perceived all stimulus elements, whether 5, 10, or 20 elements long, as occurring simultaneously, while the blanking and displacement effects occurred in the 10 to 20 msec range. The present program permits us to go as low as 100 μ sec per character and 100 μ sec between characters, and with these values, we find that a string of 40 Xs presented sequentially are clearly perceived as occurring simultaneously. With the range and timing flexibility of the present program where the time per char-

FIGURE 7   Simulated display of the word "somersault" (display order 75921104386) demonstrating the "sequential blanking" effect.

acter and inter-character times may all be specified separately and independently of one another, it will now be possible to assess the contribution of different input timing distributions to the perceptual process, in a manner that has never been possible in the past.

3. NUMBER OF INPUTS

This parameter refers to the number of inputs in the total input string. Here interest would focus on whether input length qua length plays any significant role in producing the effects observed to date.

4. CONTENT OR GEOMETRY OF INPUTS

This parameter refers to the actual content of the character being displayed in any given input location. In the findings previously discussed, input content qua content seemed to contribute nothing to the blanking and displacement effects that were observed, i.e., these effects occurred whether the characters being displayed were all the same letter, such as a string of Xs, a string of different letters, such as "chair" or "somersault," or a string of small line segments. However, examination of this parameter with the present program has already shown that content may play a very significant role. For example, in the range from 10 to 20 msec per character and time between characters, the following display order 75921104386 was examined with the following four content sequences: (a)----------, (b)//////////, (c)-/-//-//--, and (d)/-/--/--// (where the dashes and slashes are symbols 55 and 57, as shown in Figure 4). With content sequences (a) and (b) the first five elements displayed (which are underlined) were blanked; however, with sequences (c) and (d), which also should have shown blanking of these first five elements, no blanking occurred whatsoever, and all 10 elements were clearly perceived. Here then is evidence which strongly suggests that not only does display order and display input rate affect blanking, but that display content, with all other factors held constant, may also play a significant role in determining whether blanking will or will not occur.

5. & 6. INPUT SIZE AND INPUT INTENSITY

These parameters refer to the actual physical dimensions of any given input character and to its light or energy output. Size may be varied by appropriate controls on the Fairchild display or by programming as previously outlined. Since size of characters has been shown previously to produce either displacement or blanking (Mayzner, Tresselt, Adrignolo, & Cohen, 1967), this parameter requires systematic study. Unfortunately, as the size of a character is decreased on the Fairchild display, its intensity per unit area concomitantly increases as the points which make up each character are packed closer and closer together, and at present no easy method exists for separating or untangling these two effects. Intensity also may be varied indirectly by using an input character with few points, such as symbols 56 and 57 in Figure 4, or ones with many points, such as symbols 05 and 43. Careful systematic study of the effects of these two parameters probably should wait, however, until more precise and independent control of the appropriate stimulus dimensions is possible.

7. INPUT SPACING

This parameter refers to the spacing of inputs in the various cell locations along the horizontal display line. Since the program was written to accommodate up to 40 characters, 40 cell locations are available, and by using the space bar on the teletype one may, within the limits of 40 locations, have empty spaces between the characters. For example, the letters comprising the word "chair" may be displayed in five immediately adjacent cell locations or one may have one or more empty spaces between the letters. It has already been found, for example, with the word "chair" and the display order 42513, in which the letters "h" and "i" are blanked, if one keeps all factors constant except spacing, that "h" and "i" are no longer blanked if the input letters are spaced three input cell locations apart from one another. This finding suggests that blanking and perhaps displacement, as well, operates only over some given spatial distance—a result which obviously must be accounted for by any model which attempts to conceptualize the underlying visual response mechanisms.

Future Research Developments

The present experimental facility and computer display program, while making possible investigations of sequential perception that have not been possible heretofore, represents only a small fraction of the research potential that a computer-based CRT display system makes possible in the area of visual information processing. For example, the present display program allows only for the display of characters in a single horizontal line, while an obvious next extension would permit one to display characters sequentially in a 20 by 20 or even a 40 by 40 cell matrix,[1] and also allowing for the display of particular subsets of characters simultaneously, while preserving sequentiality between subsets, which would prove very useful in research on reading and language behavior, visual search, and short-term memory. For example, in research on reading and language behavior, if one displayed the words of a sentence sequentially from left to right (i.e., the normal reading order) versus some irregular order, at varying input rates (i.e., varying both word times and inter-word times, and in particular variations in inter-word times reflecting the grammatical structure of the sentence), a powerful technique might emerge for studying language processing mechanisms. Of equal interest also would be a program allowing for the sequential part presentation (i.e., line segments, angle segments, etc.) of simple and complex geometric shapes, such as, squares, circles, polygons, Necker cubes, etc., and, at the extreme, actual pictorial material, such as, outline faces, landscapes, etc. The whole domain of real and apparent movement also is susceptible to new and sustained investigation involving highly complex displays and input timing sequences. Finally, as the requirements for more complex displays and input timing distributions become critical, the single electron gun CRT will need to be replaced with multigun CRTs, also having a color capability, to allow for maximum flexibility in the generation of stimulus configurations for the study of visual information processing mechanisms.

Summary

The present paper describes an experimental computer-based CRT display facility, a computer display program, and a research strategy for studying how the visual system processes a train of stimuli or inputs when (1) these inputs arrive sequentially in time, (2) occur at different locations in space, and (3) are displayed at varying input rates, from very fast (i.e., 100 μsec per input) to relatively slow (i.e., 500 msec). Seven stimulus parameters believed critical to visual information processing mechanisms with sequential inputs are identified—namely, input display order, input display rate, number of inputs, content of inputs, input size, input intensity, and input spacing—and future research developments are briefly outlined.

References

Bartley, S. H. Central mechanisms of vision. In H. W. Magoun (Ed.), *Handbook of physiology*. Vol. 1. Washington, D. C.: American Physiological Society, 1959. Pp. 713–740.

Brown, J. L. Flicker and intermittent stimulation. In C. H. Graham (Ed.), *Vision and visual perception*. New York: Wiley, 1965.

Graham, C. H. Perception of movement. In C. H. Graham (Ed.), *Vision and visual perception*. New York: Wiley, 1965.

Julesz, B. Some recent studies in vision relevant to form perception. *Bell Tel. Lab. Rep.*, 1964.

McFarland, J. H. Sequential part presentation: A method of studying visual form perception. *Brit. J. Psychol.*, 1965, *56*, 439–446.

Mayzner, M. S., Tresselt, M. E., & Cohen, A. Preliminary findings on some effects of very fast sequential input rates on perception. *Psychon. Sci.*, 1966, *6*, 513–514.

Mayzner, M. S., Tresselt, M. E., Adrignolo, A. J., &

---

[1] Such a 40 x 40 cell matrix display program has just been completed.

Cohen, A. Further preliminary findings on some effects of very fast sequential input rates on perception. *Psychon. Sci.,* 1967, 7, 281–282.

Raab, D. H. Backward masking. *Psychol. Bull.,* 1963, 60, 118–129.

Rosenblith, W. A. (Ed.) *Sensory communication.* Cambridge, Mass.: MIT Press, 1961.

White, C. T. Temporal numerosity and the psychological unit of duration. *Psychol. Monogr.,* 1963, 77, No. 12 (Whole No. 575), 1–37.

6.2 *Repetition as a Determinant of Perceptual Recognition Processes**

RALPH NORMAN HABER

Three recent experiments were undertaken to explore some theoretical and methodological issues regarding the measurement of word recognition processes. One of these issues concerns a serious confounding which results from the use of the method of limits, a method that permeates nearly all of the research in this area. This method yields a perfect correlation between the number of presentations of the stimulus word and the duration (or intensity) of each presentation. To the extent that repetition alone, without any changes in duration of the stimulus, leads to an increase in perceptibility, then an important independent variable is being masked, and confused with other variables.

In these three experiments, the method of limits was replaced by a modified method of constant stimuli, so that each word was presented for a predetermined number of trials, but with no changes in duration between trials. In all cases, the intertrial interval was never less than 8 sec, during which time the subject reported what he had seen on the preceding trial.

* In W. Wathen-Dunn, J. Mott-Smith, H. Blum, and P. Lieberman (Eds.) *Models for the Perception of Speech and Visual Form.* Cambridge: MIT Press 1967, pp. 202–210. The three experiments reported in this paper were supported in part by a grant from the United States Public Health Service (MH-03244) to Yale University, where the research was completed. The author wishes to express his deep appreciation to Maurice Hershenson, with whom much of this work developed, and to Martha Breen, who assisted in the data collection in each of the experiments.

To study the effect of repetition, some of the words were presented for only one flash, others for two, and so forth, up to 25 presentations for some of the words. Duration was also varied, but never during the presentation of a word. Thus, some words were presented at 10 msec (i.e., all of the trials for that word would be at 10 msec), some at 15, 20, and so forth. In this way, the effects of repetition were assessed by comparing the number of letters perceived for different numbers of trials, holding duration constant. Likewise, the effects of duration were assessed by comparing the number of letters perceived for different durations, holding the number of presentations constant. For any given word, the subject would not know how many presentations he was to receive, so that he had no control over the number of trials. Therefore, he had to assume that each presentation might be the last one. This latter procedure partially corrects another methodological defect in the method of limits, in which the subject normally determines how many presentations he will receive, which he can shorten or extend by varying the quality of his report.

In addition to the separation of repetition and duration, a second major innovation was introduced into these experiments. The response indicator employed in nearly all studies on word recognition has been that of guessing the entire stimulus. Persistence in the use of this has continued in spite of serious criticisms raised by a number of authors (e.g., Garner, Hake, and Eriksen, 1956; Goldiamond, 1958). It is nearly impossible to reconstruct what the subject might have seen from what he guessed, since the latter places such reliance on the subject's previous knowledge, his expectations and hunches, and the ease with which he can take advantage of the redundancy in the stimulus. In place of guessing, in these experiments, the subject was always required to report the letters that he saw after each presentation. In this way, the indicator provided an index of the subject's perceptions, rather than his guesses.

With the changes described, these experiments can begin to assess the independent effects of duration and repetition on the perceptibility or clarity of the letters of words.

In other respects, these experiments were similar to most previous studies on word recognition. The stimuli were always seven-letter, three-syllable pronounceable words. In most conditions, they were English, whose frequencies were determined from the Thorndike-Lorge word counts (1944). For each study, the words were printed on long paper tapes, which were automatically centered and exposed, one line at a time, in one channel of a three-channel mirror tachistoscope, built by Scientific Prototype Mfg. Corp. A second background channel with two faint fixation lines was illuminated at 10 ft-L, except when the first channel was on.

On a signal from the experimenter, the subject pressed a switch which triggered the flash of the word. Immediately after each presentation, the subject reported the letters that he was sure he perceived. The subject was always told when trials for a new word would begin. The subject was scored as having perceived a word only if on the last presentation of the word he reported seeing all seven letters. No control over eye fixation was utilized, although the subject was cautioned not to initiate a flash unless he was fixated in the spot where the middle of the word would appear.

The first experiment (Haber and Hershenson, 1965) used 504 frequent English words, presented at five different durations, for from 1 to 25 trials each. Nine testing sessions of 1 hour each were required, with the first two being used to determine the duration values. These were specified for each of the 10 subjects separately, by finding the highest duration at which each subject rarely saw all seven letters on the first presentation. This base duration was approximately 15 msec for each subject. The other durations were then set 5 msec less and 5, 10, and 15 msec above this base value.

A marked effect of trials on the probability of seeing all seven letters of each word was found for the base duration and the two above it. The duration 5 msec below base (not shown) rarely permitted the subject to perceive any letters, regardless of the number of trials, whereas for the highest duration (not shown), the subject perceived all of the letters on the first or second trial.

The phenomenal reports of each subject indicated that the first few trials generally were blank (especially for the base duration), but with further presentations, first the beginnings of letters would appear, then whole letters, and often the entire word. The percept of the word that developed with repetition was not fuzzy or unclear, nor was it the result of a guess or

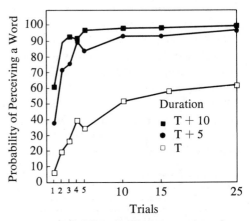

FIGURE 1   Probability of perceiving a word as a function of repetition trials (1 through 25) and duration (base, base plus 5 msec, and base plus 10 msec). (After Haber and Hershenson [1965].)

hunch. It assumed a clear status, so that the subject was never uncertain about his reports, even though he had been unable to see anything a few presentations earlier. Many subjects reported afterwards that they thought the duration or intensity of the stimulus was being increased between trials, and they were quite surprised to find that there had been no changes made.

This first experiment demonstrated that repetition alone increased the probability of seeing words, independent of any changes in the duration of the presentations. Further this effect was found for a relatively large range of duration of exposures. Thus, the ascending method of limits did appear to confound duration with repetition, since either of these manipulations alone produced increases in perceptibility. Further, it showed that the phenomenal percept of the letters increased steadily with repetition, suggesting a developmental process for the appearance of the percept. This effect was independent of the duration of exposure.

The second experiment (Hershenson and Haber, 1965) was designed to extend the previous findings to meaningless words. Half of the 288 words were selected from the same lists as in the previous study, whereas the other half were seven-letter, three-syllable (if pronounced by an English speaker) Turkish words. For these, the subjects could not use many of the overlearned hypotheses or guesses that he knew would work for English words. Ten subjects were used, each tested in six sessions, three for English words and three for Turkish. All words were assigned to one of three durations (15, 20, or 25 msec) and one of eight numbers of presentations (1, 2, 3, 4, 5, 10, 15, or 25). As in the previous experiment, the subjects reported the letters that he perceived on each trial.

Figure 2 shows that repetition increased the clarity of letters, regardless of whether the subject knew the meaning of the words. Thus, the repetition effect was demonstrated for words about which the subject could use very few of his hypotheses regarding redundancy

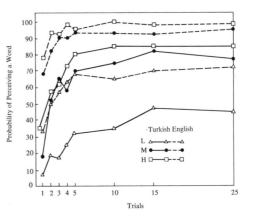

FIGURE 2   Probability of perceiving a word as a function of repetition trials, duration (low–15 msec; middle–20 msec; high–25 msec), and language (English and Turkish). (After Hershenson and Haber [1965].)

of the letters. Further, the rate of increase was similar for each language and duration. The relative perceptibility of letters of words from the two languages, as shown in Figure 2, was much greater for the letters of the English words. The subjects reported seeing more of the English letters on the first and each subsequent trial of English words as compared to corresponding trials for Turkish words, and these corresponding differences were massive. Meaning then seemed to play a role similar to duration in that both effected the initial perceptibility of the letters and the asymptotic performance, but not the rate of increase in accuracy over trials.

The third experiment (Haber, 1965) examined one aspect of meaning more directly. Only English words (totalling 576) were shown, evenly divided between rare and frequent. However, for half of the words, immediately preceding the first trial for each, the word was exposed for 5 sec whereupon the subject spelled it out loud. Then the regular trials commenced. In other respects the procedure was similar to the previous studies, though words were assigned to only one of two durations. Sixteen subjects were tested individually in nine 1-hr sessions each.

The major difference between this and previous studies was that for the words given

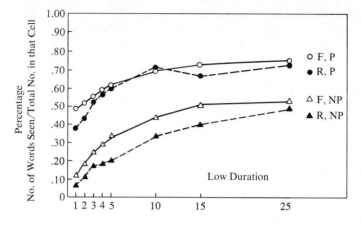

FIGURE 3   Probability of perceiving a word as a function of repetition trials, frequency of word (R-rare) and (F-frequent), and prior knowledge (NP-no prior exposure; P-prior exposure). (After Haber [1965].)

prior exposure, while the subject knew exactly what each of the letters would be, he still was required to report which letters he could see. This condition high-lighted most strongly the difference between having the subject guess the word rather than asking him to report the letters he saw. For the words given prior exposure, requests for guesses would be meaningless.

Figure 3 presents the results of the effects of repetition for the base duration, as a function of word frequencies, and prior exposure. (The higher duration is omitted to save space, though the pattern of results was quite similar.) Given prior exposure immediately before the trials of a word increased the probability of seeing its letters. A difference in perceptibility between rare and frequent words was also found, but only when no prior exposure was given. Since these data were collected using a clarity rather than a guessing indicator, they suggest that as long as the differential frequency of the words was not eliminated by prior exposure, that differential effected the clarity of the letters directly, not just the ability to guess the highly redundant ones, as Pierce (1963) among others, has suggested.

The most important result of this experiment, however, was the similarity in rates of development of the percept as a function of

any of the experimental variables. Specific prior exposure did not facilitate the rate of increase of seeing letters. It affected the amount of clarity—prior exposed words were seen more frequently—but not the rate of increase as a function of repetition.

DISCUSSION

The pattern of results from these three experiments suggests both methodological and theoretical revisions in thinking about word recognition processes. Methodologically, they point to a rejection of the method of limits as a technique for presentation of stimulus materials. Because an effect of repetition can be established independently of changes in duration or intensity, continued use of the method of limits would represent a confounding of these two classes of variables.

Theoretically these three experiments clearly indicate that repetition is an independent variable of recognition processes. The independence of repetition and duration needs to be qualified, however. If the duration is too brief, then repetition cannot bring the stimulus into a clear percept, regardless of the number of presentations. Likewise, repetition has no effect if the duration is so long that the entire percept is perfectly clear on the first presentation. However, near the lower end of the effective range, while a strong repetition effect is demonstrated, the asymptote for clarity does not approach 100%, regardless of the number of repetitions. When the duration is somewhat above the base value, while the initial presentation or two will result in only imperfect clarity, the function will eventually reach complete clarity.

These experiments were not designed to assess the relative importance of duration and repetition, but since these are the two variables confounded by the method of limits, a comparison of their effects was made. An attempt was made to determine whether perception was facilitated more by single presentations of long durations than by flashes of shorter durations but exposed for several trials. It was found that one long exposure was always superior to two or more shorter ones, summing to the same total, suggesting that duration accounted for more variance in clarity than did repetition. However, duration was varied in steps of 5 msec, a relatively coarse variation, which might have covered up sizable changes in repetitions. Therefore, this analysis should be repeated with durations varied in steps of a single msec. In this way, it might be that two flashes at 1 msec will be superior to one flash at 2 msec. In any event, a final conclusion awaits further research. Regardless of that outcome, however, the results from the three experiments already completed indicate clearly that repetition has a massive effect, increasing by over 50% the words in which all the letters are seen.

The intertrial interval in these experiments was never less than 8 sec, and sometimes a bit more if the subject was particularly slow in making a report. Haslerud (1964), in a replication of this design, reported that varying the intertrial interval systematically from 5 to 20 sec produced little significant change in the rate of development of the percept with repetition. This would suggest that further processing of the stimulus is not occurring during the intertrial interval, and that the size of the interval is not crucial as long as no interfering task is introduced.

Repetition is a variable of central importance in research on learning, and it is therefore somewhat surprising that it has not drawn much attention in perception. In part, this omission could stem from the assumed immediateness of perceptual experience. Even so, these results certainly indicate that repeated exposures of a stimulus help to bring its clarity up to strength. In this sense, perception of even highly familiar stimuli like words is not immediate at all, unless the initial presentation allows it to be.

In these experiments the effects of repetition are invariant over a number of quite different operations—duration, language, prior exposure, and frequency—operations that normally account for large portions of variance in most word recognition experiments. In these studies they account for variance in the level of clarity —each of them increases clarity—but they do not interact with repetition. They determine the clarity of the percept on the first presentation, and the ultimate clarity after many presentations, but seem to have little effect on the rate of increase in clarity with repetition.

This latter conclusion is supported by extensive curve fitting operations performed on the repetition functions from each condition in each of the three experiments. The fitting of a large number of different models was attempted and the only one that provided a fit to all of the data points was the negatively accelerated growth function: $P_n = A - q_1/n$, where P_n is the probability of seeing all of the letters of a word after the nth trial, A is the asymptote of the function after many trials, q_1 is the probability of not seeing all of the letters on the first trial, and n is the number of trials. The exponent of n was empirically not significantly different from 1.00 for each function, and hence does not appear in the equation. Since the starting probability (q_1) and the aysmptote (A) are highly related (r = + 0.85 over all conditions of all experiments), the relation of repetition to the probability of seeing the letters is specified by one parameter— the probability of seeing all of the letters on the first trial. Thus, the entire function in each condition can be generated by giving only one trial per word. This suggests that some weight can be attached to the conclusion that the effects of repetition cut across the other operations in these experiments, and is a highly stable effect.

Few models of perceptual behavior have incorporated repetition effects. While Hebb (1949) has built his cell-assembly model on repetition, he is concerned there primarily with the initial development of an assembly from novel stimulation in infancy and childhood, and has not discussed how repetition might affect already developed and organized assemblies. By extension, however, it is possible to apply the present results to his general theorizing. One possibility is that the degree of arousal of a fully developed and organized assembly mediates the perceptual experience of clarity—the more fully aroused an assembly corresponding to a stimulus, the greater the experienced clarity of the stimulus.

A number of variables would presumably determine the degree of arousal of an established assembly. Among these are: (a) Stimulus adequacy—the longer, or more intense, or more discriminable the stimulus, the greater the likelihood that it will arouse an assembly. This was shown in these experiments by the increase in clarity from stimuli at higher durations. Presumably the same effect could have been shown with changes in intensity, and that intensity and duration are related by the Bunsen-Roscoe Law (See Kahneman, 1967). (b) initial organization—the more organized the assembly prior to stimulation, the more likely it will be aroused by stimulation. Initial organization would presumably be a function of a number of variables, including the amount of prior experience with the specific stimuli (e.g., frequency of appearance of words in print, and meaningfulness of the stimuli), and prior knowledge or exposure of the stimuli. Finally, (c), given an initial organization and level of stimulus adequacy, repetition of stimulation should boost the arousal of the assembly. This does not refer to repetition building or constructing the assembly, but merely in getting it all going. In this way, a poorly organized assembly, hit with an inadequate stim-

ulus could still be brought to a high level of arousal by repetition of that stimulus. This is what happened, for example, in the second experiment with the low duration Turkish words, which achieved little clarity on the first trial, but which after repeated presentations over half of the Turkish words became perfectly clear. Also, as the present data indicate, there are lower limits to the inadequacy of the stimulus that can be overcome with repetition. Below some value of stimulus magnitude no increase in clarity can be achieved regardless of the number of repetitions. Finally, the present data suggest that the amount each repetition arouses an assembly is independent of the initial level of organization and stimulus adequacy, since neither of these parameters interacted with the rate of increase in clarity.

The extension of the Hebbian model is presented in this context, not because the data from these three experiments represent strict tests of the model, but because there is no comparable model to handle the effects of repetition. However, the model can provide considerable heuristic value to further research by suggesting the kinds of variables that should be investigated. The results of this further work can be used then to examine the adequacy of the model.

References

Garner, W. R., Hake, H. W., and Eriksen, C. W. Operationism and the concept of perception. *Psychol. Rev.,* 1956, *63,* 317–329.

Goldiamond, I. Indicators of perception; I. Subliminal perception, subception, unconscious perception: An analysis in terms of psychophysical indicator methodology. *Psychol. Bull.,* 1958, *55,* 373–411.

Haber, R. N. The effect of prior knowledge of the stimulus on word recognition processes. *J. exp. Psychol.,* 1965, *69,* 282–286.

Haber, R. N., and Hershenson, M. The effects of repeated brief exposures on the growth of a percept. *J. exp. Psychol.,* 1965, *69,* 40–46.

Haslerud, G. M. Perception of words as a function of delays between and summation of subliminal exposures. *Percept. mot. Skills,* 1964, *19,* 130.

Hebb, D. O. *The organization of behavior.* New York: Wiley, 1949.

Hershenson, M., and Haber, R. N. The role of meaning in the perception of briefly exposed words. *Canad. J. Psychol.,* 1965, 19, 42–46.

Kahneman, D. Temporal effects in the perception of light and form. In W. Wathen-Dunn (Ed.) *Proceedings of the symposium on models for the perception of speech and visual form,* Boston, 1964. Cambridge: M.I.T. Press, 1967. Pp. 157–170.

Pierce, J. Some sources of artifact in studies of the tachistoscopic perception of words. *J. exp. Psychol.,* 1963, 66, 363–370.

Thorndike, E. L., and Lorge, I. *A teacher's word book of 30,000 words.* New York: Teachers Collegs, Columbia University, 1944.

6.3 Rate of Presentation and Order of Recall in Immediate Memory[*]

MICHAEL I. POSNER

Introduction

Varying the rate of presentation of items for immediate recall serves two functions. First, it changes the time that an item must stay in store prior to recall and, secondly, it alters the time for rehearsal, association and other strategies to be brought into play. Thus Posner (1963) has suggested that increasing the rate of presentation will only show improved recall because of decreased time in store in tasks which tend to reduce the use of recall strategies.

A number of studies have manipulated time in store by varying the rate of presentation of aural sequences of digits for immediate recall. Conrad & Hille (1958) and Fraser (1958) have shown improved recall with increased rate of presentation. Many studies which appear to be similar have shown no differences or even

the opposite effect of rate (Calhoon, 1935; Fraisse, 1945; Peatman & Locke, 1934; Pollack, 1952). The Conrad & Hille (1958) study used several conditions in which the recall itself was rigidly paced but also contained a condition using unpaced recall which was superficially identical with those of Pollack (1952), yet the results were opposite. One reason for these discrepancies may involve the order in which subjects actually record the digits. As Mackworth (1962a) has pointed out, in a situation using written recall where only the final order need be correct some subjects will write down the last digits first. Conrad & Hille (1958), however, only tested unpaced recall after several conditions in which pacing forced the order of recall to match the order of presentation. These previous conditions may have set subjects to record the digits in the order received. On the other hand, studies finding opposite results to those of Conrad & Hille (1958) were run in groups and report no effort to control the actual order in which messages were recorded.

Since transformations of order involve a recall strategy which may be affected by rehearsal it is possible that allowing subjects to

* Reproduced by permission of the *British Journal of Psychology,* 1964, vol. 55, pp. 303–306. This study was supported in part by the Research Committee of the Graduate School of the University of Wisconsin with funds provided by the Wisconsin Alumni Research Foundation. Results of the study were presented at the Midwestern Psychological Association Meeting in May 1963.

record the digits in an order different from the presentation would be more beneficial at slow rates. The present study was designed, therefore, first to check whether order of recall interacts with rate of presentation in a manner which could cause these varying results and, secondly, to test the effect of rate upon recall with order fixed.

Method

Subjects. Twenty subjects were used in each of the main experiments and nine in the control group. All were students in introductory psychology courses of the University of Wisconsin and received course points for their participation.

Materials. Ten practice and forty regular series were recorded at each of two speeds, 30/min. and 96/min. Each series consisted of eight digits selected at random. The numbers in the series were recorded over white noise which served to reduce distractions from outside the experiment. There was a 20 sec. pause after each series.

Procedure. In Expt. I twenty subjects were run individually. They were randomly assigned to one of two groups. Group F received the series at the fast rate and group S at the slow rate. Subjects in each group performed two different tasks. In task O, after hearing all eight digits, the subjects repeated them back to the experimenter in the order presented. In task R they were required to present digits 5–8 first and then 1–4. To determine the order of the oral recall subjects said "blank" to indicate omitted digits. Within each group, half the subjects performed twenty series of condition O first and then, following 30 min. of an unrelated task, recalled twenty series in condition R; the other half did the reverse.

Expt. II was the same as described above except that the subjects heard the numbers through earphones instead of over a loudspeaker. In this experiment subjects wrote their recall on a score sheet which contained eight boxes per series clearly divided into two groups of four. During the practice series subjects were instructed to record the answers only in the way indicated by the particular condition being studied. Subjects were checked to be sure they followed this procedure.

Nine subjects were run in a group as a control. They listened to the digits played over the speaker, as in Expt. I, but they wrote the digits as presented rather than having to recall them. The subjects received 20 series at the slow speed followed by 20 at the fast speed.

Scoring. The basic score used was percentage of correct series. If any digit was incorrect the series was marked wrong. To compute serial position curves the number of correct digits at each position was computed. If any but the correct digit was inserted in a given position it was scored as an error.

Results

The basic results of the two experiments are shown in Table 1. The mean difference between the two tasks (R—O) is significantly higher at the slow speed in both studies. The results seem to show conclusively that the inverted recall of task R greatly improved performance at the slow speed while tending to have the opposite effect at the fast rate.

Looking at the differences in performance at

TABLE 1

Mean Percentage of Correct Series and Significance Tests

	FAST	SLOW	t
Task O			
Expt. I	51·5	29·5	2·13*
Expt. II	66·5	47	1·6
Task R			
Expt. I	52	50	0·2
Expt. II	59·5	60·5	0·08
Mean difference	0·5	20·5	2·26*
(R—O)	−7	13·5	3·14**

*P < 0·05; **P < 0·01.

the two rates, it is clear that if a reversal (task R) is required there are no differences between the two speeds. This is a frequent result of experiments which do not control order of recall. If, however, only the order condition is allowed, the fast speed appears to show better performance. In Expt. I the mean difference in recall between speeds is 22% ($P < 0.05$), while in the second experiment the difference is almost as great, 19·5%, but is not significant. Since this comparison is between independent groups at the two speeds the variability is quite high. However, the overall results seem to indicate that with the order condition required the fast rate is superior, as would be predicted by Conrad & Hille (1958).

To get a more complete idea of the effect of the transformation required in the reverse condition, Figure 1 shows the serial position curves for Expt. II. (The total possible error score for any one digit is 200.) Despite the use of oral recall, the serial position curves of Expt. I are virtually identical with those presented here. In the order condition recall at the fast rate is superior at every serial position, while in the reverse condition there is little difference between the two rates at any of the positions. It is clear that at both speeds prior recall of digits 5–8 improves performance at these positions, but at the fast rate this is accompanied by a much greater loss in retention at the first four positions than at the slow rate. This result would seem to agree with subjects' reports that, with presentation at the slow rate, rehearsal during the first four items preserves them during the subsequent presentation and recall of the last four. It may also be argued that reversal at the fast rate is difficult because of the problem of recognizing the fifth digit, but the serial position curves give no support to this explanation since the fifth digit at the fast rate is virtually errorless.

Two additional results should be briefly outlined. The increase in recall in all conditions of Expt. II over Expt. I seems to be explicable on the basis of the increased control over distraction which the earphones provided. It has also been shown previously that different types of responses may cause varying amounts of

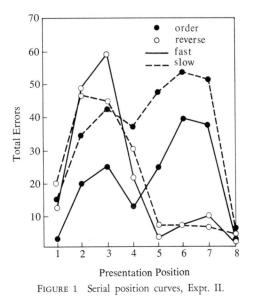

FIGURE 1   Serial position curves, Expt. II.

interference (Mackworth, 1962*b*). It is possible that written responses may cause less interference than oral responses. The control group was run to check the ability of the subjects to hear and record the digits when memory was not required. The results in terms of mean percentage of correct series were 98·3 for the slow rate and 95 for the fast rate. This indicates that whatever differences in ability to hear the series were present would not account for the superior performance at the fast rate found in the main studies.

Discussion

This experiment illustrates at least one reason for differences in results among studies of the effect of presentation rate upon immediate recall. If experiments do not control the order in which subjects actually record the responses they tend to show no great differences in performance between slow and fast rates. It is not surprising that the slow rate is actually superior in some studies, since recalling the last four digits first is not necessarily an optimal strategy and in free conditions even more successful transformations might be used. If, however, order of recall is controlled, this study agrees with those finding better recall at fast rates.

Mackworth (1962*a*) has also shown different serial order curves in her visual task with different orders of recall, although she does not report whether the subjects required to recall in order differed from her overall findings of improved recall with decreasing rate. Therefore it is not clear whether the findings presented in this paper also apply to a memory task with visual input.

Summary

University students attempted immediate recall of 8-digit series presented aurally. When subjects were required to report the digits in their presented order, the fast presentation rate (96 digits per minute) was superior to the slow rate (30 per minute). When subjects were required to report the last four digits, before giving the first four digits, this improved performance at the slow rate but not at the fast rate. These data resolve previous conflicting results and tend to support a decay factor in immediate memory.

References

Calhoon, S. W. (1935). A comparison of the ability to reproduce one syllable words auditorially presented. *J. Exp. Psychol. 18*, 621–32.

Conrad, R. & Hille, B. A. (1958). The decay theory of immediate memory and paced recall. *Canad. J. Psychol. 12*, 1–6.

Fraisse, P. (1945). Études sur la memoire immédiate. III. L'influence de la vitesse de présentation et de la place des éléments. La nature du présent psychologique. *Année psychol. 35*, 29–42.

Fraser, D. C. (1958). Decay of immediate memory with age. *Nature, Lond., 182*, 1163.

Mackworth, J. F. (1962*a*). Presentation rate and immediate memory. *Canad. J. Psychol. 16*, 42–7.

Mackworth, J. F. (1962*b*). The effect of the response upon the immediate memory span. *Canad. J. Psychol. 16*, 120–7.

Peatman, J. G. & Locke, N. M. (1934). Studies in the methodology of the digit span test. *Arch. Psychol., N.Y.,* no. 167.

Pollack, I. (1952). The assimilation of sequentially encoded information. Human Resources Lab., Memo Rt. No. 25, A.R.D.C. USAF.

Posner, M. I. (1963). Immediate memory in sequential tasks. *Psychol. Bull. 60*, 333–49.

6.4 Dichopic Summation of Information in the Recognition of Briefly Presented Forms[*]

WILLIAM A. CARLSON   CHARLES W. ERIKSEN

While binocular brightness interaction has been extensively studied (see Levelt, 1965, for a recent summary) little work has been carried out on binocular contributions to form perception. The present experiment was concerned with form identification under conditions where (a)

* Reproduced by permission of *Psychonomic Science*, 1966, vol. 5, pp. 67–68.

the form was presented to the right eye or to the left eye alone, (b) to corresponding retinal areas in both eyes simultaneously, and (c) to corresponding areas in the two eyes successively. By comparison of form identification accuracy under these conditions of presentation, the contribution of binocular viewing not only can be assessed but also whether the contribution depends upon simultaneity and further whether the gain from binocular viewing is greater than that to be attributed from two independent chances to perceive the form.

Method

The Ss were five patients at the Veterans Administration Hospital, Danville, and two staff members, screened for visual acuity. They had been further selected as being able to achieve the recognition criterion for forms presented to either eye alone at durations of 40 msec or less.

The apparatus consisted of a dichopic tachistoscope containing three fields. One field provided for an adapting luminance to both eyes and the right and the left eye viewing fields could be aligned by the use of front surface mirrors so as to produce a fused stimulus image when viewed by the two eyes. Field durations and sequencing were carried out by a Scientific Prototype Model GB tachistoscopic timer. The stimuli consisted of three five-sided nonsense forms constructed according to the method described by Attneave (1957). Both the right and left viewing fields contained a black-lighted fixation cross subtending .22 min. of angle which when viewed binocularly fused into a single image. Single forms were presented .5° below the fixation point and all stimulation was foveal. The forms were black, subtending .22° of angle on a maximum dimension, and were mounted on white matte finish plastic cards. The adapting field had a luminance of .68 mL and remained on continuously. Stimulation from either of the two viewing fields was superimposed upon the adapting luminance and the viewing fields themselves had a luminance of .29 mL.

Stimulation was activated by a trigger controlled by S. He was instructed to fixate the cross and when the image was clear and fused, to press the trigger which would initiate the stimulation sequence. Following a form presentation S was required to make a forced choice response among the three form alternatives which were displayed to one side of the tachistoscope in front of the S. Prior to begin-

ning the experimental trials all Ss were run for two practice sessions in order to become familiar with the forms and become adept at form recognition at brief durations. These practice sessions also served to establish an individual duration value (T) for the S which would yield above chance but less than 100% recognition for the forms presented to either eye alone. In the following four experimental sessions each S made 54 judgments for forms presented for duration T to the left eye alone, to the right eye alone, to the left eye for duration T followed immediately by stimulation to the right eye for duration T, to the right eye for duration T followed immediately by stimulation to the left eye for duration T, and to both eyes simultaneously for duration 2T. On those presentations where both eyes were stimulated the stimulation fell on corresponding retinal points.

Results

Table 1 shows the mean percent recognition accuracy for the six different methods of form presentation. Statistical tests show that stimulation of either eye alone is significantly poorer (p < .01) than any of the other four methods of presentation. Stimulation sequentially of the right eye and then the left eye or vice versa is not significantly different from stimulation of both eyes simultaneously. Stimulation of both eyes simultaneously for duration 2T was included as a control to insure that recognition accuracy on this task would improve by a

TABLE 1

Percent Correct Form Identifications as a Function of Conditions of Monocular and Binocular Viewing

MONOCULAR		DICHOPIC			
		SUCCESSIVE		SIMULTANEOUS	
RIGHT EYE	LEFT EYE	RIGHT TO LEFT EYE	LEFT TO RIGHT EYE	DURATION T	DURATION 2T
47.1	48.4	61.7	57.7	57.7	66.6

measurable amount when time increased. As can be seen from the table, this requirement has been met. Recognition accuracy for stimulation simultaneously of both eyes at duration 2T is significantly ($p < .01$) higher than recognition accuracy under any of the other five conditions.

Discussion

The results seem clear in showing that you get equal accuracy in form identification with equal energy entering the visual system. Forty msec of energy presented to each eye simultaneously yields essentially the same form identification accuracy as occurs when one eye is stimulated for 40 msec followed immediately by 40 msec of stimulation to the second eye. At first this would appear to be nothing more than another manifestation of time-intensity reciprocity but an interpretation in terms of the Bunsen-Roscoe effect would seem to rule out explanations of the latter as being localized in photo-chemical processes in the retina (Hartline, 1934). A central summation or integration of energy would seem to be required and would also be consistent with findings reported by Kahneman & Norman (1964).

In the present experiment there was no delay between the successive presentations to the two eyes. The finding of essentially the same identification performance with successive as opposed to simultaneous stimulation suggests a systematic exploration of the effects of introducing measured delays between the successive stimulations. However, with increasing delays summation effects may be obscured by a possible contralateral suppression. Bouman (1955) has reported that monocular stimulation results in raised thresholds in the other eye with latencies at least beyond 400 msec.

It is also possible that the present results do not reflect a true summation of information or energy. Instead, the gain in identification obtained from dichopic viewing, either simultaneous or successive, in the present experiment may be the result of two independent opportunities to perceive. An approximation of the level of performance to be expected on the basis of independence can be obtained in the following manner. An estimate of the number of times Ss failed to perceive the stimulus and guessed can be obtained from the percent of wrong responses (52%) which with an a priori probability of ⅓ correct guessing would be ⅔ of the total number of times he had to guess. Thus the S would have guessed a total of 78% of the trials. The probability that he failed to perceive the stimulus with either eye is then $.78^2$ or .61. Assuming ⅓ of these correct by chance and added to the 39% of trials in which he perceived the stimulus with either eye or both, the resulting hit rate for two independent chances is found to be 59%. This is not appreciably different than the values of 57% and 58% obtained for simultaneous and successive dichopic presentations.

It has been shown (Eriksen, 1966) that this method of computing independence will tend to overestimate the expected level. However, as an approximation it is quite close to the obtained values, so close that the possibility cannot be discarded that the gain from the dichopic viewing in the present experiment can be attributable to two independent chances to perceive rather than to a summation or integration of information in the visual system. Pirenne (1943) has previously reported that the dichopic detection of brief flashes fits a probability model of independence.

Summary

Visual form identification was studied under conditions where the forms to be identified were presented briefly to the right and left eyes alone, to the right and left eye simultaneously on corresponding areas, and to the right and left eye sequentially on corresponding areas. The results suggest the following conclusions: (1) successive stimulation of the two eyes is better than either eye alone if the stimulation falls on corresponding areas; (2) successive stimulation of corresponding areas is about identical to simultaneously stimulated corresponding areas; and (3) the amount of gain in identification accuracy resulting from stimulation to the two eyes was not greater than can be attributed to two independent opportunities to perceive.

References

Bouman, M. A. On foveal and peripheral interaction in binocular vision. *Optica Acta,* 1955, *1,* 177–183.

Eriksen, C. W. Independence of successive inputs and uncorrelated error in visual form perception. *J. exp. Psychol.,* in press.

Hartline, H. K. Intensity and duration in the excitation of single photoreceptor units. *J. cell. comp. Physiol.,* 1934, *5,* 229–247.

Kahneman, D., & Norman, J. The time-intensity relation in visual perception as a function of observer's task. *J. exp. Psychol.,* 1964, *68,* 215–220.

Levelt, W. J. M. Binocular brightness averaging and contour information. *Brit. J. Psychol.,* 1965, *56,* 1–13.

Pirenne, M. H. Binocular and uniocular thresholds of vision. *Nature,* 1943, *48,* 43–63.

CHAPTER 7

Microgenetic
and Ontogenetic Processes

7.1 Stabilization of the Retinal Image: A Review of Method, Effects, and Theory[*]

E. G. HECKENMUELLER

It has been known for some time that the eye is always in motion. Even under conditions where steady fixation is attempted, small, involuntary movements of the eye are always present. Knowledge of these movements has generated considerable experimentation in an attempt to understand their role in the visual process. This experimentation, most of which has been conducted within the past 12 years, has included investigations on both physiological and psychological levels. The questions which the experimentation has attempted to answer are: (*a*) What are the nature and extent of these involuntary eye movements? (*b*) What effect do these movements have on the visual process? A historical summary of the answers to the first question is presented by Ratliff and Riggs (1950), together with their own experimentation on the problem. Their results indicate that the involuntary movements consist of: a slow drift of the eye; a rapid, jerking movement (saccadic); and a small, rapid tremor superimposed on the drift. In view of the general nature of the methods which have been used in attacking the problem, the second question might better be stated as: What are the effects on the visual process of reducing or stopping the involuntary movements of the eye?

The purpose of this paper, therefore, is to summarize the attempts to answer this second question. The summary will proceed by considering: the methods of producing a stabilized image, the perceptual effects of a stabilized image, a summary of effects and comments, some relevant physiological evidence, and, the theoretical implications of the stabilized image phenomenon.

Methods of Producing a Stabilized Retinal Image

A summary of relevant studies gives an indication of the extent of the movements. The drift movements are of a magnitude of approximately 1 minute arc per second. The saccadic movements occur with magnitudes between 2 and 50 minutes of arc with an average somewhere around 5–6 minutes of arc. These saccades occur irregularly at intervals ranging from .2 to .5 second intervals. The small tremor movements occur with a magnitude of less than .5 minute of arc at a rate up to 150 cycles per second. An interesting finding regarding these tremor movements (Riggs and Ratliff, 1951) is that they are not coordinated between the two eyes in binocular fixation. So-called "corresponding points" on the two retinas, therefore, are not actually corresponding points.

* From: E. G. Heckenmueller, "Stabilization of the Retinal Image: A Review of Method, Effects, and Theory," *Psychological Bulletin*, 1965, vol. 63, pp. 157–169. Copyright (1965) by the American Psychological Association, and reproduced by permission. The author would like to thank W. N. Dember and R. J. Senter for their critical reading of this paper.

One effect of these involuntary movements, of course, is to keep the retinal image constantly in motion. It has been shown (Riggs, Armington, and Ratliff, 1954) that the retinal image is virtually stationary for exposures up to .01 second. Exposures as long as .10 second result in an average displacement of the retinal image of 25 seconds of arc which is approximately equal to the diameter of one foveal cone. In an exposure of 1.00 second, the average displacement is 3 minutes of arc. Thus a retinal image will traverse an average of 10 receptors during a 1.00-second exposure. The question then becomes one of stabilizing these movements to observe whether or not they are a necessary condition for normal vision.

One method of producing a stabilized image on the retina would be simply to stop the movements of the eye. The resulting discomfort and possible dire consequences to the subject, however, make this method the least likely of all. An alternate approach would be to present the visual stimulus in such a way that its image remains in the same position relative to the retina regardless of any movement of the eye. In other words, the visual stimulus must move with a direction and magnitude exactly opposite that of the eye movements so that the effect is one of cancelling out the movements so far as the retina is concerned. Many techniques have been developed to achieve this compensation, but all of them can be classified under one of the following three basic methods: methods in which the internal structure of the eye is imaged on the retina, methods which use an optical lever system, and methods in which the target is attached directly to the eye. Each of these methods, together with their variations, will be discussed in turn.

Internal Structure of the Eye

The first of these methods, those in which the internal structure of the eye is imaged on the retina, exploits well-known entoptic phenomena. For example, shadows of the retinal capillaries can be produced by moving a pinhole in front of the pupil while viewing a uniformly illuminated surface. Another type of entoptic phenomenon is known as "Haidinger's brushes" (Ratliff, 1958). These images have an hour-glass shape and can be seen by viewing a field of blue light through a polarizer. In all of these phenomena, the image which is being observed is a part of the eye structure itself and therefore remains stationary relative to the retina. The advantages of such methods are the very stable images which they afford and the absence of distortions (to be discussed later) which are sometimes introduced in methods using attachments to the eye. The disadvantages of these methods are mainly that the variety of targets which can be viewed is extremely limited and that there is no way to manipulate the degree of movement of the retinal image.

Optical Lever System

The second general class of methods involves the use of optical lever systems. These methods are fairly complex in design, but they are, in some ways, very versatile. They consist essentially of a system which projects the target on a small mirror mounted on a contact lens worn by the subject. The image is then viewed by the subject in one of two ways. Either the image from the mirror is directed onto a screen, or it is fed through a system of lenses focusing the image directly on the pupil. The latter method produces what is called a Maxwellian view. In both cases, the position of the image on the retina is made dependent on the position of the eye. As the eye moves, the mirror which is mounted to the contact lens worn on the eye also moves. Since the target is being projected from this mirror, then the target itself moves. The direction of eye movement is thus compensated for, but not the magnitude of movement. This is due to the difference in the angular displacement of the projected image relative to the angular displacement of the eye. By altering the length of the optical path through which the projected image reaches the eye, these differences in angular displacement can be exactly compensated. This alteration is accomplished through the use of suitably arranged mirrors and/or prisms placed in the optical path of the system (see Ratliff and Riggs, 1950, for a description of such a system).

A disadvantage of these systems is that the mirror from which the target is reflected is mounted in the contact lens on the temporal side of the pupil. The resulting geometry is such that only the eye movements in the horizontal direction can be compensated. An improved system was later developed (Clowes and Ditchburn, 1959) which alleviates this problem to a considerable degree. In this system, the mirror is mounted on a stalk which is attached to the contact lens. This type of mounting permits alignment of the mirror so that it is normal to the visual axis with the incidence of the light normal to the mirror. This arrangement allows for compensation in both the horizontal and vertical planes, and also compensates for slight translational movements of the head. The measurements by Clowes and Ditchburn indicate that 99.7% of the natural movements of the eye is eliminated.

An additional characteristic of these systems concerns the positioning of the subject's head. This is obviously an important consideration in such methods since any movement of the head naturally imposes additional movements on the eye. The usual technique for controlling the position of the head is to have the subject place his head against a rest while grasping a dental biting-board with his teeth.

The major advantages of these optical lever methods are the increased range of targets which can be used compared to the methods using entoptic phenomena, the capability of manipulating certain characteristics of the target, and the possibility of varying the degree of stabilization of the retinal image. Certain disadvantages are introduced, however, mainly as a result of the physical attachments on the eye which are required. These disadvantages would include slippage of the contact lens relative to the eye and the possibility of changes in the shape or movement of the lens especially when the eye engages in the relatively large flick movements. In addition, the torsional movements of the eye are not controlled which, among other things, limits the size of the field which can be used.

Targets Mounted Directly to Eye

The third general class of methods of producing a stabilized image consists of attaching the target directly to the eye. Ditchburn and Pritchard (1956) placed a calcite crystal, 6 millimeters in diameter, between two polaroid sheets and attached this to a stalk mounted on a contact lens. Illumination of the assembly produced interference fringes that resulted in the subject's seeing a pattern of rings. As the eye engaged in its involuntary motions, the target, being attached to the eye by way of the contact lens, moved with it, thus producing a stabilized image on the retina. This method yielded a large field, but the variety of targets was restricted.

A later step in the development of this method (Yerbus, 1957) was to mount a target onto a stalk which was attached to a high-power contact lens. The high-power lens, however, produced problems with regard to the quality of the retinal image. These problems were alleviated somewhat by improving the quality of the lens, but the lens also presented difficulties with regard to the subject's comfort. It was necessary to use a local anesthetic and also to tape back the eyelids of the subject.

Pritchard (1961a) presented a design which offered further improvements. A miniature light collimator was constructed and attached to a stalk on the contact lens. A target was inserted in the end of the collimator and was illuminated by a tiny grain-of-wheat light bulb. The resulting collimated light from the illuminated target thus appeared at optical infinity with the eye in a relaxed state. The advantages to this design are: stabilization of vertical, horizontal, and torsional movements over a large field is attained; focusing is required only when the system is constructed and none thereafter; anesthetics and retraction of the eyelids are not required; and the target can be changed during the experiment. The disadvantages compared to the optical lever systems are mainly that variations in the degree of stabilization cannot be achieved. It also possesses the other disadvantages to be discussed later which are associated with techniques involving physical contact with the eye.

Several investigators have used the techniques described under the third general class of methods of producing a stabilized image. Certain discrepancies which appeared among their results led Barlow (1963) to conduct a series of experiments designed to determine more precisely the amount of stabilization actually being achieved by the different methods. His study centered primarily on the problem of the slippage of the contact lens.

Barlow notes that two types of contact lens have been used in previous studies. One is the full-fitting type which covers the entire cornea. This type seats on the conjunctiva which is attached to the sclera only at the limbus. The second one is a suck-on type which seats near the limbus and is held in place by suction. The second type is, therefore, much less subject to slippage, although it does produce discomfort to the subject which can become quite painful with some of the more vigorous eye movements. By simultaneously comparing the stabilized images produced by each of these techniques with after-images which presented true stabilized images, Barlow was able to determine the amount of slippage of both types of lens. It was found that the full-lens type yielded an average movement of $\pm 3\frac{1}{2}$ minutes of arc while the suck-on type yielded an average of ± 40 seconds of arc with a maximum of about 2 minutes of arc.

Perceptual Effects of a Stabilized Image

A question might now be raised: if the normal perception of a target involves eye movements, what happens to the perception of a stabilized target in which eye movements have, in effect, been canceled? The first attempts to answer this question were undertaken inde-

pendently by Ditchburn working in England and by Riggs working in the United States.

Ditchburn and Ginsborg (1952) conducted a study in which they stabilized the image using an optical lever system. Stabilization was accomplished only in the horizontal plane, and the subject viewed the stabilized image projected on a screen. Ditchburn mentions that he had carried out preliminary experimentation in Dublin in 1945, but he was unable to repeat the experiment or to check on the degree of stabilization obtained. In the 1952 experiment, a circular patch of light covering a 1-degree visual field was presented as the target. The patch was divided vertically into two halves by making one half of the field either 30, 40, or 60% brighter than the other half. It was found that, after a few seconds of viewing, the demarcation line disappeared and the two halves appeared to be of equal brightness. This condition would persist for 2–3 seconds and would recur at intervals of about 1 minute. It was also observed that the contrast threshold was higher under the stabilized condition than it was under normal viewing conditions. Ditchburn proposed as a possible explanation that the eye recognizes the abnormality of the stabilized condition and temporarily makes an adjustment such as accommodation which would cause the image to reappear.

Riggs, Ratliff, Cornsweet, and Cornsweet (1953), also using an optical lever system, compared the effects as studied under three conditions of viewing: with eye movements compensated, with normal eye movements, and with exaggerated eye movements. The target consisted of a circular test field containing a fine, vertical line. Several different fields were used, each containing lines of different widths. These test fields were viewed as stabilized images (stabilization in the horizontal plane only) and were displayed inside a nonstabilized annulus which was also in the visual field. The subjects viewed the image for 1-minute periods and indicated the presence or absence of the vertical line by releasing a telegraph key. The results showed that, under the compensated condition, the vertical lines disappeared after a few seconds of viewing. After continued viewing, the lines would reappear and then fade out again, at a rate which was a function of the width of the line; that is, the finer the line, the less time it remained visible. Under the normal condition, fine lines disappeared and reappeared, but heavy lines remained constant, while under conditions of exaggerated motion, scarcely any lines disappeared.

In view of these findings, Riggs considered the possible function that the eye movements serve in the visual process. One function might be for purposes of acuity. The ability of the eye to make the increasingly finer brightness discriminations implied by acuity may be enhanced by eye movements. Another possibility arises from consideration of a physiological process proposed by Hecht (1937). This process hypothesizes that under conditions of constant illumination, the photoreceptor process in the retinal receptor cells reaches a stationary state in which opposing reaction rates become equal and the cells then fail to emit further neural impulses. Hartline (1940) mentions that few neural fibers respond to constant illumination—most fibers respond to "on-off" or "off" states of illumination only. Eye movements, then, might be required to maintain neural firing in general and may not be concerned primarily with acuity.

A second part of Riggs' study involved the same viewing conditions and the same targets, but the targets were presented for very brief durations so that disappearance did not occur and only the subject's ability to detect the lines was measured. Four exposure times were used: .034, .110, .213, and .472 second. The results indicate little difference in acuity as a function of stabilized, normal, or exaggerated viewing conditions. The stabilized condition was slightly superior at the shorter exposure times, and the exaggerated condition was better at .2-second exposures and over. The normal condition yielded results in between the other two conditions. Riggs' conclusion was that eye movements did not enhance acuity but rather seemed to function primarily to overcome loss of vision due to constant stimulation.

Ratliff (1952) conducted another study which also investigated the role of eye movements in visual acuity. A circular target with a grid of either vertical or horizontal striations was presented to the subject under normal viewing conditions. Records of the subject's eye movements were made by an optical lever arrangement in an attempt to correlate amount of movement with acuity. No evidence was found which would indicate an enhancement of acuity by eye movements; in fact, large amounts of tremor and drift were found to be detrimental to acuity.

Cornsweet (1956), again using an optical lever system with the same type of vertical-line target used previously, introduced a controlled rate of flicker in the illumination of the target. The rate of flicker was varied from .8 to 4.4 cycles per second. At the slower rates of flicker, the stabilized image remained visible for periods of time resembling those of normal viewing conditions. As the flicker rate increased, however, disappearance time increased until at 4.4 cycles per second the amount of time that the target was visible returned to values resembling those of the stabilized image. These results suggest that change in stimulation is at least one factor involved in maintaining perception of an image, and is consistent with the notion that the involuntary movements of the eye provide this change under normal conditions of viewing.

Using, as a measuring device, the phenomenon observed when flicker is imposed upon the target, Cornsweet then investigated the stimulus conditions which might initiate the involuntary drifts and saccadic movements of the eye. Three possible conditions which might trigger such movements seemed likely: the disappearance of the target, the displacement of the target from the retinal "center of best vision," or an inherent instability of the oculomotor system. The reasoning proceeded as follows: If the disappearance is the primary stimulus condition, then, as flicker rate increases, thereby increasing disappearance time, the eye movements should also increase. If, on the other hand, displacement is the stimulus condition, then stopping the image and thereby stopping displacement should decrease eye movements. If neither result is observed, the movements could be attributed to an inherent instability of the oculomotor system.

The results indicated that the drift movements of the eye are not influenced by either the disappearance or the displacement of the target. Drift movements might therefore be attributed to the instability of the oculomotor system. The saccadic movements, on the other hand, were not affected by disappearance, but they were affected by displacement of the target. This implies that saccadic movements are adjustive in function. The data indicate that the adjustments are corrective in both magnitude and direction. An interesting observation in this study is the finding that a fixation point must be provided if the corrective function is to be accomplished; otherwise the eye moves further and further away from the original position. This would suggest, as Cornsweet observes, that the saccadic movements are under visual rather than proprioceptive control.

Ditchburn and Fender (1955) also investigated the effects of flicker on the stabilized image. Using the improved type of optical lever system in which both horizontal and vertical movements are compensated, they varied the flicker rate from 0 to 60 cycles per second, and noted a gradual decrease in disappearance time up to approximately 20 cycles per second where the target remained visible for about 97% of the time or approximately equal to normal viewing conditions. The point of 20 cycles per second coincides with the critical flicker frequency under these conditions. As the flicker rate was further increased, a gradual increase in disappearance time occurred until, at 60 cycles per second, the visibility was about equal to that of a stabilized image.

The striking difference in these results compared to those obtained by Cornsweet (1956) should be observed. Cornsweet found a sudden increase in visibility at slow rates of flicker with a decrease up to 4.4 cycles per second, whereas Ditchburn found a gradual increase throughout the range of 0 to 20 cycles per second. One source of difference between the two studies lies in the method of producing flicker. Cornsweet flickered only the line within the visual field, while Ditchburn turned the entire field off and on.

A further finding by Ditchburn (Ditchburn and Fender, 1955) was that the brightness of the visual field under high flicker rates was greatly overestimated by the subject. A brightness of 10 millilamberts was estimated as high as 1,000 millilamberts. Ditchburn offers as a possible explanation the idea that the retina is receiving repeated strong bursts of impulses from the continued turning on of the light. This idea, however, does not seem to be consistent with the assumption that rapid flicker approximates steady illumination in which case the fibers should be incapable of repeated response. This inconsistency, together with the inconsistency with Cornsweet's data, presents a provocative problem for further research. Such research should bear importantly on the concept of changing stimulation as a factor in perception.

Krauskopf (1957) conducted a study in which the effects of retinal image motion on contrast thresholds were measured. An optical lever system with a Maxwellian view was used. The targets were vertical lines varying in width as follows: 10 seconds, 1, 4, and 8 minutes of arc. Various degrees of movement were induced in the targets by rotating one of the mirrors in the system. These movements were 1, 2, 5, 10, 20, and 50 cycles per second in frequency. The magnitude of the movements was also varied so that amplitudes of 30 seconds, 1, 2, and 4 minutes of arc were incorporated.

The results of these studies indicate that for all bar widths, lower contrast thresholds were obtained under high amplitude, low frequency motions than under stopped conditions. With narrow bars, high frequency motions raised thresholds relative to the stopped condition. Krauskopf observes that this suggests the disappearance of an image under stabilized viewing conditions is probably due to the removal of the low frequency components of normal retinal image motion. Frequencies below 10 cycles per second with an amplitude of 1 minute of arc or greater seemed particularly effective in maintaining target visibility. High frequency motions either have detrimental effects or, if the amplitude is less than 1 minute of arc, have no measurable effect at all. It would seem, therefore, that the drift and saccadic movements of the eye lower contrast thresholds while the small, high frequency tremor motions are ineffective so far as these thresholds are concerned.

A later study by Ditchburn, Fender, and Mayne (1959) makes necessary some qualification of these conclusions. Considering the suggestion of Marshall and Talbot (1942) that the most important characteristics of change in stimulation is the generation of "on" and "off" responses in the neural fibers. Ditchburn attempted to manipulate the degree of change by controlling the degree of the three types of eye movements. The improved model of the optical lever system as described by Clowes and Ditchburn (1959) was used together with an apparatus that could impose motion of any of the three types in any degree. The target was again a vertical black line.

It was found that the drift movements of the eye had some, but very little effect on visibility of the target. The saccadic movements produced a very sharp image, but the image would then fade out again. The tremor movements of the eye seemed to be a factor in maintaining vision, but their effects varied with different frequencies of the tremor. There also seemed to be important effects of the amplitude of the tremor movements as indicated by the finding that movements up to .3 minute of arc produced a decrease in the time in which the target remained visible, while movements that reached .3 minute of arc magnitude produced a sudden increase in visibility time.

Riggs and Tulaney (1959) regulated the extent of motion by varying the degree of compensation of eye movements. By means of an optical lever system, the ratio of the length of the viewing path to the length of the projection path was varied. A 2 : 1 ratio produced a stabilized image, and any deviation from this ratio introduced some degree of movement. The target was a circular path of light divided vertically into two halves of different brightnesses. This target was presented within a nonstabilized annular ring. The results show that as the degree of motion was increased, the amount of disappearance of the target decreased.

Using the same kind of bipartite field with the improved (Clowes and Ditchburn, 1959) type of optical lever system, Clowes (1961) studied the subject's ability to make brightness discriminations under conditions of exaggerated, normal, and stabilized movements of the retinal image. The ability to make such discriminations was found to increase as retinal image movement increased.

Keesey (1960), in another attempt to evaluate the effects of eye movement on visual acuity, used the improved (Clowes and Ditchburn, 1959) type of optical lever system with three different kinds of targets: a vernier offset between two vertical lines, a single line, and a grating. Seven exposure times were used in viewing each target. These exposure times varied from .020 to 1.280 seconds. No differences were found in acuity threshold values between the stabilized and the unstabilized conditions of viewing. The main factor seemed to be the exposure time, with threshold values decreasing to an asymptotic value as exposure time was increased. Acuity appears to be mainly a matter of discriminating spatial differences of intensity in the stimulation of the retina. For a given value of contrast, therefore, the ability to make such discriminations seems to be independent of the eye movements involved, and is primarily a function of exposure time.

Other findings of considerable interest were the observations (Pritchard, 1958; Pritchard and Vowles as cited in Pritchard, Heron, and Hebb, 1960) that the part of the image to which the subject's attention was directed remained in view longer than other parts, and that stimulation of other sensory modalities, such as a sudden noise or the operation of the telepgraph key used in recording, would cause regeneration of an image that had disappeared. Stabilization of a field containing three colors (Pritchard, 1961b) resulted in disappearance of the three colors after the first few seconds of viewing so that only three brightnesses were observed. With continued viewing, these three brightnesses gave way to an achromatic field of homogeneous brightness. These results are analogous to those of experiments that involve viewing colors in a Ganzfeld (Cohen, 1958).

Attention should also be given to some findings from experiments in which stabilization of the retinal image was complete or as near complete as possible. Such findings are those from studies in which the internal structure of the eye is imaged on the retina (Campbell and Robson, 1961; Doesschate, 1954). Campbell, for instance, found that the shadows or images viewed in this manner disappear in a few seconds and never return. Besides the problem of lens slippage, these methods also preclude effects due to changes in accommodation, pupil area variations, vignetting in the optical pathways, and changes in intraocular tension. Near-complete stabilization was also achieved by Yarbus (1957) using the suck-on type contact lens. Although some distortions occurred in image quality, the extremely stable image achieved produced the same kind of result mentioned above—that is, the target remained visible for about 3 seconds and then disappeared permanently.

Barlow (1963) presents a detailed phenomenological description of the events that follow stabilization of an image. He used the suck-on type of lens similar to that of Yarbus, but with improved image quality. The target was perceived with full clarity for 1 to 2 seconds which was followed by a loss of contrast and detail. The target then began to fluctuate for approximately 1 minute whereupon it disappeared, leaving a cloudy, indistinct field with a vague resemblance to the target contours. No further changes occurred as long as the conditions were not altered. If the image was moved such as by flicking the target mount, it was immediately regenerated, but sharp changes were produced only at the borders of the image with the area within the borders remaining unchanged. During the period of fluctuation, it was also observed that the regenerated image was never as good as the original in contrast and detail.

All of the studies which have been discussed thus far have investigated the effects of a stabilized image on the retina of one eye only. Several experiments have been reported on the effects of binocular stabilization.

Krauskopf and Riggs (1959) studied interocular transfer in the disappearance of stabilized images. Two optical lever systems were used, both with a projected target image. One system was used for each eye. A nonstabilized fixation field was also presented stereoscopically to both eyes. This fixation field consisted of an annular ring with a small dot in the center. Three conditions of stabilized viewing were used: the experimental condition, the control condition, and the test condition. In the experimental condition, a target consisting of a circular patch of light containing a small vertical bar in the left-hand side of the field was presented. This patch was presented within the annular fixation field to one eye only. In the control condition, the same kind of target was presented to the same eye except that now the vertical bar was positioned in the right-hand side of the field. In the test condition, exactly the same kind of target as the one used in the experimental condition was presented to the other eye. The sequence of presentation was, therefore, either the experimental condition for 30 seconds followed by the test condition for 30 seconds or control followed by test. These sequences resulted in the test bar's falling on either the same position of the retina in the second eye as compared to the first, or on a different position of the retina. The results indicate the disappearance of the stabilized image occurred significantly faster in the experimental condition as compared to the control. This demonstrates that the effects of the stabilized image are apparently transferred between eyes, thus supporting the idea that something other than purely retinal effects are at work.

In order to control for the possibility of the effect being due to afterimages, a separate set of experiments was run in which it was found that the subject failed to get an afterimage after 3 seconds of viewing. The effect of the transfer, however, lasted the full 30 seconds of viewing.

Krauskopf offers two possible explanations for the stabilized image phenomenon. One explanation would incorporate a neural mechanism involving centrifugal control of peripheral activity as proposed by Granit (1955). The other explanation suggests that some kind of neural adaptation is occurring in addition to the retinal photochemical adaptation process.

Cohen (1961) investigated the effects of contralateral visual stimulation on the disappearance of stabilized images. Three conditions of contralateral stimulation were used: a dark patch worn over one eye, half of a ping-pong ball placed over one eye to produce diffuse light, and a patterned stimulation produced by fixating a spot on the wall. Visibility of the stabilized image was found to increase in the order of contralateral stimulation presented above, thus offering further evidence in support of the idea that central factors are involved in the phenomenon.

Organization of the Disappearance Phenomenon

The emphasis of the studies cited thus far has been primarily on the disappearance and reappearance of a stimulus target which produces a constant stimulation of the retina. Several variables have been investigated in an attempt to discover the causal factors of this phenomenon. The question, it might be said, has been: Why does disappearance of an image occur under stabilized conditions of viewing? During the course of these studies, however, it was observed that not only does disappearance of the target occur, but it occurs in what seems to be an orderly fashion. For instance, in those studies in which a thin vertical line was viewed, the line not only disappeared, but it disappeared as a unit. The line did not gradually fade with first some parts disappearing and then others, but rather it followed an "all-or-none" principle—that is, it was either wholly visible or wholly invisible. These observations might be considered to present a second question: Why does the disappearance of a stabilized image occur in the way that it does? The following studies will present some attempts which have been made to answer this question.

Studies were conducted (Pritchard, 1961b; Pritchard, Heron, and Hebb, 1960) using a light-collimating system attached directly to the contact lens worn by the subject through which targets of varying shapes and complexity were projected. Many findings of interest were made. One general statement is that the length of time that a target remains visible is at least partly a function of the complexity of the figure. (Complexity here refers to an increase in the number of elements and/or an increase in meaningfulness.) A simple target such as a straight line may be visible only 10% of the total viewing time while a more complex figure might be visible 80% of the time. Second, a simple line vanishes completely as a unit and reappears the same way while the lines comprising a more complex figure behave independently of each other. Each separate element of the more complex figure, however, disappears and regenerates as a unit.

These two general principles of visibility as a function of complexity and the unitary action of elements are basic to the phenomenon. There are, however, other rules which the activity of the figures seems to follow. For instance, the profile of a face (a meaningful figure) will remain visible longer than an irregularly shaped curved line. If the profile is viewed alone, certain parts of the face appear and disappear as a unit; that is, the front of the face or the top of the head may remain visible while the rest disappears. A letter over which a jagged line has been superimposed will act independently of the jagged line in its disappearance, and will remain visible longer. While viewing a square, a common perception is one in which either the two horizontal or the two vertical lines appear and disappear together. Another aspect of the importance of linear organization can be seen while viewing a matrix of squares arranged in rows and columns. Whole rows or columns act together. Thus the entire matrix may disappear leaving a single row, column, or diagonal of squares remaining in view. Another illustration is the superiority of smooth, rounded figures (the "good" figures of Gestalt psychology) over jagged, irregular figures in maintaining visibility. A word such as "beer" when viewed may, due to fragmentation of the image, be seen as other words such as "peep," "peer," "be," or "beep." Finally, in considering field effects, it has been found that, while viewing a triangle and a circle placed side by side, the parts of the triangle and circle nearest to each other remain visible while the other parts disappear; or, if some other side of the triangle remains visible, an arc portion of the circle which is approximately parallel to that side also remains visible.

These field effects seem to be important aspects of the stabilized image phenomenon. An experiment was performed by Cohen (1961) in which two lines were presented to the subject with a separation between the lines of 25, 75, or 150 minutes of arc. One of the lines was presented as a stabilized image while the other was presented normally. It was found that an increase in separation produced a decrease in the amount of time that the stabilized line remained visible. Cohen suggests a field effect to account for this change in visibility as a function of distance.

These conclusions, however, require some modification in light of an experiment performed by Tees (1961). Two parallel lines (A and B) were presented with a diagonal line (C) positioned between them. The measurement of interest is the percentage of time that any given line (such as A) is accompanied by either of the other two lines (B and C) when disappearance occurs. It was found that Line A was accompanied by C 22% of the time and by B 73% of the time. If the only factor involved was a field effect, then such an effect should be stronger for the intervening line. Apparently a field effect is at work, but it must be more complex than previously supposed, or it must work in conjunction with some other mechanism.

A final observation (Pritchard, 1961b) should be mentioned regarding the activity of a "filled-in" figure, such as a blackened square, when presented as a stabilized image. Here it is ob-

served that disappearance of the square is gradual rather than sudden. The center portion of one of the sides will begin to fade with the fade-out spreading first toward the middle of the figure and then outwards toward the other sides. An important comment made by Hebb (1963) concerning this activity is that it demonstrates that a gradual fading can occur, thus strengthening the notion that the all-or-none type of activity observed with other figures is probably due to the failure of a system or systems.

Summary of Effects and Comments

The rather large number of effects associated with stabilization of the retinal image as presented in the preceding section can probably best be appreciated in summary. When the image of a visual target is stabilized on the retina, the image disappears and gives way to a homogeneous field. This condition remains so long as nothing else is changed. In most instances, however, the image will periodically reappear with a frequency determined by several factors. One of these factors is the degree of stabilization which is achieved. Any slippage of the contact lens, for instance, will cause the image to be regenerated. Assuming the amount of slippage to be constant, another factor which causes regeneration seems to be stimulation of another sensory modality. Also, if the attention of the subject is directed to a certain portion of the image, that portion will remain visible longer than others. The relative complexity of the image further determines the extent of disappearance, with more complex images remaining visible longer than simple ones. In addition, the disappearance of the image occurs in an all-or-none manner, and, in the case of more complex figures, seems to be subject to the classical Gestalt principles of organization.

Other important effects of a stabilized image were also discussed. As might be expected, any movement of the image once it has disappeared will result in restoration of the image. If the image is held stationary, the introduction of flicker in the illumination of the target enhances visibility depending on the rate of flicker. The apparent brightness of a stabilized image is greatly overestimated, and contrast thresholds were found to be considerably higher than in normal viewing conditions. A finding of considerable importance is the fact that, for exposure times sufficiently short to preclude disappearance of the image, visual acuity is apparently not affected by stabilization of the image.

These results imply that the involuntary movements of the eye are importantly related to the perception of a retinal image. In general, the low frequency, high amplitude components of these movements seem to be most effective. The effect of the movements seems to be primarily one of overcoming the loss of vision resulting from constant stimulation of the retina. Stated another way, the effect of the movements is to provide changing sensory stimulation of a spatial variety.

Finally, it was observed that the effects of a stabilized retinal image are transferred between eyes—that is, there are central as well as peripheral factors involved. This implies, at the very minimum, that neural adaptation processes are involved in addition to the photochemical adaptation processes of the retina.

As is always the case, observations which have been described are not exempt from some criticism. The criticism, however, does not reflect on the quality of the studies nor on the general nature of the results, but rather it is directed towards more precise quantifications in the effects which result from the many variables uncovered by the studies themselves. For instance, Barlow's (1963) discussion of the problems introduced by lens slippage does not invalidate the studies which were conducted, but simply means that the results must be considered as an expression of reduced image motion instead of stopped image motion. This implies further that studies in which motion was experimentally manipulated contain observations that resulted from the manipulated motions and motions due to slippage. Ideally, these effects should be separated.

Barlow also discusses other artifacts which can produce misleading results, but which either have been or can be controlled. Some of the factors include other possible sources of movement such as movement of the lens of the eye, pupil changes, and changes in accommodation. Retinal ischaemia (a local anemia produced by local obstacles to the arterial flow) and fading of vision due to distortion of the eyeball by the lens and increases in intraocular pressure are also possible factors, as are distortions in the image due to poor optical conditions (e.g., smearing of lens, corneal misting, etc.) The already present chromatic aberration of the eye may be even further increased by the use of short focus lens. If the entrance pupil to the eye is narrowed, the increase in diffraction which results mars resolution. A small pupil diameter also renders the eye more sensitive to transscleral light, thus reducing contrast in the image and mimicking fading. Finally, the quality of the image as seen through the contact lens must be carefully controlled by observing the image under conditions of natural eye movements.

Another problem for consideration would be the control of stimulation or lack of stimulation of the area of the retina not being subjected to the stabilized image. If there is any interaction between these areas and the area being stimulated, this control would seem to be quite important.

The knowledge that intersensory stimulation has effects on the visibility of the image introduces some methodological problems. In those studies using an optical lever system of stabilization, for instance, the use of a dental biting-board to control head movements may produce variations in the effects. The irritation which usually accompanies the wearing of the contact lens and the use of anesthetics are other sources of stimulation. In addition, the recording technique of pressing or releasing a telegraph key to signal the disappearance of the image is itself a source of stimulation known to effect visibility. A possible alternate method of recording might be to have the subject press the key after a given number of regenerations of the image and then compare these records with those obtained with individual regenerations recorded. A useful complementary recording technique might be the use of electroencephalogram records of the occipital alpha rhythm. If the alpha rhythm, which is suppressed under normal visual stimulation, recurs under conditions of stabilization of the retinal image, then the use of EEG recordings would not only be a valuable recording technique, but would also yield additional evidence regarding concomitants of the stabilized image phenomenon. Such a technique has been successfully used in experiments that involved viewing targets in a Ganzfeld (Cohen and Cadwallader, 1958).

Relevant Physiological Considerations

Electrophysiological studies have yielded much evidence concerning the structure of the visual system which is of particular interest so far as the stabilized image phenomenon is concerned. Since most of the evidence was obtained in animals, a cautious approach must be taken in extending such evidence to man. With this caution in mind, some of the findings of several investigators (Granit, 1955; Hubel, 1963; Kennedy, 1963) will be presented in synthesis.

The path from the retina to the cortex contains at least six different types of nerve cells. Three of these cells are the receptors, the bipolars, and the ganglion all of which are located in the retina. The other three are the cells of the lateral geniculate body, simple cortical cells, and complex cortical cells. All of these cell types are organized into receptive fields, the shape and structure of which differ for each type. Activity in each cell is either of an excitatory or an inhibitory nature and is produced by either the onset or offset of stimulation by light. If a large number of cells is subjected to stimulation, the differential excitatory and inhibitory activity from all of them summates to produce resultant "on" or "off" discharging systems. These resultant systems are superimposed upon a variable level of spontaneous

activity (noise) already present in the system, so that detection of the stimulus depends upon whether or not the resultant activity is above the noise level. When a group of cells is subjected to invariant stimulation, as is the case with a stabilized image, the inhibitory components exceed the excitatory and the resultant discharging system drops below the noise level, thus resulting in a cessation of neural firing. Either a movement of the image or a change in the noise level could produce detectable activity in the resultant discharging system.

The shape and structure of the receptive fields associated with the six different cell types suggest that each cell type may be specialized to evaluate only a limited number of dimensions of the visual stimulus. These dimensions include the frequency, intensity, pattern, orientation, position, and movement of the visual stimulus. Another possible effect of invariant stimulation, therefore (i.e., invariant on one or more of these dimensions), might be a loss of information concerning the dimensions in question. Thus, while complete invariance of stimulation would result in disappearance of an image, invariance on only a few dimensions might explain the ordered fragmentation of an image which is so typically observed.

Theoretical Implications of the Stabilized Image Phenomenon

The perceptual effects associated with the stabilized image phenomenon bear importantly on more general theories of perception. The ideas contained within some theories seem to be untenable in view of certain findings. Hebb (1963) discusses several of these ideas. The all-or-none disappearance of an image, for instance, makes unlikely any explanation by fatigue in independently functioning cells. Equally unlikely are explanations involving local areas of satiation, or those based on the activity of inhibitory cells. Fatigue or inhibition within the cells would require a precise coordination in time of thousands of cells to yield the sudden cessation of activity. Satiation effects would produce a fading of an image rather than the abrupt disappearance. Pritchard, Heron, and Hebb (1960) discuss as another unlikely explanation the idea of random fluctuation of thresholds in various parts of the visual field. Such random fluctuations could not account for the ordered activity which has been observed.

Two major theories that receive considerable support from the stabilized image phenomenon are Gestalt theory (Köhler, 1929) and cell-assembly theory (Hebb, 1949). In Gestalt theory, the notion of field effects can be applied to some of the organized activity which has been observed, such as the activity of adjacent figures (Pritchard, Heron, and Hebb, 1960). The holistic approach of Gestalt theory is also supported by the principles of closure, contiguity, and similarity which seem to be present in the organization of the disappearance of the stabilized image. On the other hand, cell-assembly theory finds support in the sudden, all-or-none kind of disappearance of separate elements, and also in the differential activity in meaningful versus meaningless figures. These observations make tenable the idea of specific assemblies of cells acting as perceptual elements that operate as a unit or not at all, and the idea that complex assemblies (i.e., meaningful) can remain active longer than less complex assemblies (i.e., meaningless). Both of these theories, however, have difficulty in explaining some effects. The work of Tees (1961), for instance, has demonstrated that, while Gestalt field effects may be present, they cannot completely account for the phenomenon found in the interaction between certain line patterns. Likewise, cell-assembly theory cannot account for the failure of angles to behave as separate elements, the completion noted in incomplete figures, and the nature of the disappearance of solid figures.

The stabilized image phenomenon also has relevance with respect to the role of learning in perception. The evidence indicates that some innate organization seems to be present but that this organization is modifiable as a result of experience. Although this view is certainly not new, it receives additional strong support.

A final consideration is related to the general notion of the role of changing stimulation in perception. Dember (1960) discusses this aspect of stimulus change with respect to the stabilized image phenomenon, and also relates it to findings of studies involving exposure to homogeneous fields and the phenomenon associated with the viewing of blurred images. The results of these studies all demonstrate that changing stimulation is necessary to both form and maintain a visual image.

Summary

A summary is presented of 3 basic methods used in reducing or stopping involuntary eye movements in order to produce a stable retinal image. This stabilization produces some degree of fading or disappearance of the target being viewed. Additional effects on such factors as acuity and contrast thresholds are considered, as well as the effects of such variables as exposure time, flicker, attention, meaning, and target complexity on the nature and extent of target disappearance. Some explanations for the phenomenon are presented, and the theoretical implications of invariant stimulation on the perceptual process are discussed.

References

Barlow, H. B. Slippage of contact lenses and other artifacts in relation to fading and regeneration of supposedly stable retinal images. *Quarterly Journal of Experimental Psychology*, 1963, *15*, 36–51.

Campbell, F. W., and J. G. Robson. A fresh approach to stabilized retinal images. *Journal of Physiology*, 1961, *158*, 1–11.

Clowes, M. B. Some factors in brightness discrimination with constraint of retinal image movement. *Optica Acta*, 1961, *8*, 81–91.

Clowes, M. B., and R. W. Ditchburn. An improved apparatus for producing a stabilized retinal image. *Optica Acta*, 1959, *6*, 128–133.

Cohen, H. B. The effect of contralateral visual stimulation on visibility with stabilized retinal images. *Canadian Journal of Psychology*, 1961, *15*, 212–219.

Cohen, W. Color perception in the chromatic Ganzfeld. *American Journal of Psychology*, 1958, *71*, 390–394.

Cohen, W., and T. C. Cadwallader. Cessation of visual experience under prolonged uniform visual stimulation. Paper read at American Psychological Association, Washington, D.C., 1958.

Cornsweet, T. N. Determination of the stimuli for involuntary drifts and saccadic eye movements. *Journal of the Optical Society of America*, 1956, *46*, 987–993.

Dember, W. N. *Psychology of perception.* New York: Holt, Rinehart and Winston, Inc., 1960.

Ditchburn, R. W., and D. H. Fender. The stabilized retinal image. *Optica Acta*, 1955, *2*, 128–133.

Dichburn, R. W., D. H. Fender, and S. Mayne. Vision with controlled movements of the retinal image. *Journal of Physiology*, 1959, *145*, 98–107.

Ditchburn, R. W., and B. L. Ginsborg. Vision with a stabilized retinal image. *Nature*, 1952, *170*, 36–38.

Ditchburn, R. W., and R. M. Pritchard. Stabilized interference fringes on the retina. *Nature*, 1956, *177*, 434.

Doesschate, J. T. A new form of physiological nystagmus. *Ophthalmologica*, 1954, *127*, 65–73.

Granit, R. *Receptors and sensory perception.* New Haven: Yale University Press, 1955.

Hartline, H. K. The receptive field of the optic nerve fibers. *American Journal of Physiology*, 1940, *130*, 690–699.

Hebb, D. O. *The organization of behavior.* New York: Wiley, 1949.

Hebb, D. O. The semiautonomous process: Its nature and nurture. *American Psychologist*, 1963, *18*, 16–27.

Hecht, S. Rods, cones, and chemical basis of vision. *Physiological Review*, 1937, *17*, 239–290.

Hubel, D. H. The visual cortex of the brain. *Scientific American*, 1963, *209*(5), 54–62.

Keelsey, U. K. Effects of involuntary eye movements on visual acuity. *Journal of the Optical Society of America*, 1960, *50*, 769–774.

Kennedy, D., Inhibition in visual systems. *Scientific American*, 1963, *209*(1), 122–130.

Köhler, W. *Gestalt psychology.* New York: Liveright, 1929.

Krauskopf, J. Effect of retinal image motion on contrast thresholds for maintained vision. *Journal of the Optical Society of America*, 1957, *47*, 740–747.

Krauskopf, J., and L. A. Riggs. Interocular transfer in the disappearance of stabilized images. *American Journal of Psychology*, 1959, *72*, 248–252.

Marshall, W. H., and S. A. Talbot. Recent evidence for neural mechanisms in vision leading to a general theory of sensory acuity. *Biological Symposium*, 1942, *7*, 117–164.

Pritchard, R. M. Visual illusions viewed as stabilized retinal images. *Quarterly Journal of Experimental Psychology*, 1958, *10*, 77–81.

Pritchard, R. M. A collimator stabilizing system. *Quarterly Journal of Experimental Psychology*, 1961, *13*, 181–183. (a)

Pritchard, R. M. Stabilized images on the retina. *Scientific American*, 1961, *204*(6), 72–78. (b)

Pritchard, R. M., W. Heron, and D. O. Hebb. Visual perception approached by the method of stabilized images. *Canadian Journal of Psychology*, 1960, *14*, 67–77.

Ratliff, F. The role of physiological nystagmus in monocular acuity. *Journal of Experimental Psychology*, 1952, *43*, 163–172.

Ratliff, F. Stationary retinal images requiring no attachments to the eye. *Journal of the Optical Society of America*, 1958, *48*, 274–275.

Ratliff, F., and L. A. Riggs. Involuntary motions of the eye during monocular fixation. *Journal of Experimental Psychology*, 1950, *40*, 687–701.

Riggs, L. A., E. C. Armington, and F. Ratliff. Motions of the retinal image during fixation. *Journal of the Optical Society of America*, 1954, *44*, 315–321.

Riggs, L. A., and F. Ratliff. Visual acuity and the normal tremor of the eyes. *Science*, 1951, *114*, 17–18.

Riggs, L. A., F. Ratliff, J. C. Cornsweet, and T. N. Cornsweet. The disappearance of steadily fixated visual test objects. *Journal of the Optical Society of America*, 1953, *43*, 495–501.

Riggs, L. A., and S. U. Tulaney. Visual effects of varying the extent of compensation for eye movements. *Journal of the Optical Society of America*, 1959, *9*, 741–745.

Tees, R. C. The role of field effects in visual perception. *Undergraduate Research Projects in Psychology, McGill University*, 1961, *3*, 87–96.

Yarbus, A. L. A new method of studying the activity of various parts of the retina. *Biofizika*, 1957, *2*, 165–167.

7.2 Variation of Spontaneous Ocular and Occipital Responses with Stimulus Patterns[*]

JOHN C. ARMINGTON   KENNETH GAARDER
AMY M. L. SCHICK

Considerable attention has been devoted to improving methods of stimulating and recording the human electroretinogram (ERG), the major aims being to elicit photopic activity from more localized and specifiable retinal areas. The purpose of this article is to describe a newly developed recording procedure which has proved to have several advantages over previous methods, and to illustrate some of its properties.

This new technique makes use of many successful aspects of earlier methods, and, in fact, is closely related to the moving-stimulus method developed by Riggs, Johnson, and Schick.[1,2] With their method, the subject views a stimulus grid of alternate bars of different wavelength or intensity. The bars are abruptly displaced periodically so that the areas which are occupied by one set of bars at one moment are occupied by the other set during the next interval and *vice versa*. The stray light from this moving pattern tends to be constant and does not produce transient responses. The light falling within the stimulus field is not constant, however; it produces small responses which can be detected using computerized procedures. Their method almost completely eliminates the scotopic-response components due to stray-light stimulation of the periphery, leaving only the response from the stimulus areas.

The method to be described here also makes use of a striped field but introduces an important new feature. Under certain viewing conditions, the eye makes frequent small saccadic movements when the subject is fixating on a stationary pattern, which provide discrete changes of retinal stimulation.[3-5] Stabilized-image studies have shown that these changes of stimulation are necessary to maintain vision.[6,7] In view of this, it is reasonable to suppose that bursts of activity would be found in the visual system, associated with these movements.

Gaarder *et al*,[8] have shown that involuntary saccadic movements are followed by electrical responses in the occipital cortex, hereafter referred to as visual evoked responses, which may be detected with electrodes mounted on the occipital scalp. The subjects looked at the center

* Reproduced by permission of the *Journal of the Optical Society of America*, 1967, vol. 57, no. 12, 1534–1539. Paper presented at the 1967 Spring meeting of the Optical Society in Columbus, Ohio. This research was partially supported by U.S. Army Contract DA-49-193-MD-2978.

[1] L. A. Riggs, E. P. Johnson, and A. M. L. Schick, *J. Opt. Soc. Am.* 56, 1621 (1966).

[2] E. P. Johnson, L. A. Riggs, and A. M. L. Schick, *Vision Res.*, Suppl. No. 1, 75 (1966).

[3] F. Ratliff and L. A. Riggs, *J. Exptl. Psychol.* 40, 687 (1950).

[4] R. M. Steinman, R. J. Cunitz, G. T. Timberlake, and M. Herman, *Science* 155, 1577 (1967).

[5] K. Gaarder, *Nature* 212, 321 (1966).

[6] L. A. Riggs, F. Ratliff, J. C. Cornsweet, and T. N. Cornsweet, *J. Opt. Soc. Am.* 43, 495 (1953).

[7] R. W. Ditchburn and B. L. Ginsborg, *Nature* 170, 36 (1952).

[8] K. Gaarder, J. Krauskopf, V. Graf, W. Kropfl, and J. C. Armington, *Science* 146, 1481 (1964).

of a stationary stimulus field which was either a small circular spot of light or a larger field of light containing small dark spots. A beam of light that was reflected from a mirror mounted on a contact lens worn by the subject, was used to track the eye movements. Each saccade which exceeded a certain magnitude triggered an average-response computer which sampled the immediately following portion of the brain potential record. The amplitude and latency of the resulting responses were shown to vary with stimulus luminance.

The present experiment had several specific aims. The first was to determine whether responses initiated by spontaneous saccadic displacements of the retinal image could be recorded at the eye. It would be possible for electrical activity at the retinal level to be of such low amplitude that it could not be detected although there was a prominant response at the brain. For example, Tepas and Armington,[9] using conventional flash procedures, found that weak stimuli could produce definite evoked responses at the cortex even though the electroretinogram was too small to be seen.

Assuming that this was successful, the second aim was to begin to investigate the relation between the magnitude of ERG responses produced in this manner and different aspects of the stimulus situation. In the Gaarder et al.[8] study of evoked responses, as mentioned above, stimulus luminance was found to be a relevant factor. The data also suggested that the spatial distribution or pattern of the stimulus might be important. It is clear that some stimulus patterns in combination with saccadic eye movements of a given magnitude and direction would produce larger changes of stimulation and hence, would be expected to elicit larger responses than others. The striped field was chosen to permit control of the amount of change of stimulation. The width of the stripes in the pattern as well as its luminance was varied.

ERG responses and evoked responses from the visual cortex were recorded simultaneously, in order to compare the results at the two sites and to provide data relevant to questions raised by Gaarder et al.[8] This comparison is particularly relevant in view of the method used for elicitation of the responses. Several authors[10, 11] have described "central intermittency" or "cortical excitability cycles" in the cortex. As the responses in this situation are paced by spontaneous movement of the eyes, the cortical potentials might indicate some sort of gating effects not evident at the retinal level. In this regard, it would be pertinent to compare results obtained in this situation with those obtained with the Riggs et al. method,[1] in which the stimulus is moved. When the stripe width is approximately equal to the size of the eye movements, the retinal effects of the two stimulation methods are similar. Differences of the results would be attributable to the correlation of the responses with spontaneous eye movements in the present method.

Apparatus and Procedure

APPARATUS

The apparatus for this experiment consisted of three main parts: a stimulator for presenting grating stimuli to the eye, an eye-movement recording system for detecting saccades, and a two-channel electrophysiological recording system. Stimulus light from a tungsten-ribbon filament was transmitted to the eye through a conventional optical system. One of a series of grids consisting of vertically oriented, alternating opaque and transparent bars of equal width was mounted within the field stop of the system so as to be presented in Maxwellian view. Six grids were used, subtending visual angles of 1.5, 4.5, 9, 13, 30, and 40 min per cycle. Interchangeable neutral density filters could be inserted in the light path behind the grid. The filament image at the pupil was 1.5 mm in diameter.

The stimulus appeared to the subject as a steady vertical grid pattern within a circular

[9] D. I. Tepas and J. C. Armington, Vision Res. 2, 449 (1962).

[10] P. Bertelson, J. Exptl. Psychol. 18, 153 (1966).

[11] H. Gastaut, A. Roger, J. Corriol, and R. Naquet, Electroenceph. Clin. Neurophysiol. 3, 401 (1951).

13.2° field. A small black fixation spot appeared in the center of the middle bright bar of the stimulus field. The maximum luminance of the bright bars was 7300 trolands. There was a constant luminance ratio of 63 to 1 between the bright and dark bars.

The eye-movement detector was similar to that described by Krauskopf et al.[12] In its original application, the device produced an infrared image upon the limbus of the subjects' eye. The light reflected from this image re-entered the movement detector and was delivered to a photocell. If the eye moved to one side, more of the image fell upon the iris, less infrared light was reflected back to the photocell, and its electrical output dropped. If the eye moved to the other side, more infrared was reflected to the photocell, and its output increased. Thus, the output of the photocell provided an indication of the horizontal position of the eye. The present experiment required that the subject wear a contact lens to record the electrical response from the eye. Reflections from the front of the lens prevented the eye-movement detector from working reliably. To avoid this difficulty, the infrared image was focused upon a black-and-white paper flag mounted on the electrode stalk of the contact lens. Lateral displacement of the flag provided an indication of eye movement. The flag was oriented so that the system responded to the horizontal component of eye movement. To ensure stable recording, the subject's head was firmly fixed to the eye-movement system with a biting board and a head rest. A patch was worn over the nonstimulated eye.

The electrical signal from the eye-movement detector was amplified and then taken to a trigger unit which provided a positive pulse whenever a horizontal saccadic eye movement occurred. The pulses triggered an average-response computer. The computer thus began its sweep upon the occurrence of a saccadic eye movement.

Potentials from the eye were obtained with an electrode mounted on the same contact lens

used to record eye movements. The reference electrode for eye recordings was attached to the skin on the cheek under the opposite eye. The amplified signals from the eye were delivered to the input terminals of the first computer channel. Potentials from the occipital area were obtained with a bipolar placement on the midline. One electrode was over the inion and the other was about 5 cm above. This signal was amplified and delivered to the second channel of the computer. The computer averaged the activity in these two channels during the interval of 15 to 265 msec after the onset of successive saccades. When 100 samples had been summed, the result was written out on an $x-y$ plotter. An upward deflection of the average recording from the eye occurred when the electrode on the contact lens was positive with respect to the electrode on the cheek. An upward deflection in the other channel indicated that the anterior occipital electrode was positive with respect to the one over the inion.

PROCEDURE

The subject's eye was aligned with the apparatus, and the stimulus luminance was set at one of the test values. After about 10 min, recording was started. Records were made for the grids presented consecutively in a random order with a 1-min rest between each presentation. The presentations were repeated in a different order so that two readings were obtained for each grid size. The luminance was then changed to a new value and the entire procedure was repeated. Two or three luminances were tested in a single session. The same luminances were tested again in a later experimental session. The retinal illuminance produced by the bright bars ranged from 7300 to 1 td. One subject was tested at intervals of 0.3 and 0.4 log units. The other two subjects, who provided confirmatory data, were tested at 1.0 log-unit intervals over the same range. Several control sessions were performed with the pupil and lens immobilized with 1% Mydriacyl and additional electrodes mounted on the face around the eyes. These experiments were designed to test the possibility of eye-movement artifacts.

[12] J. Krauskopf, V. Graf, and K. Gaarder, *Am. J. Psychol.* 79, 73 (1966).

Results

Responses were found from the eye as well as from the brain. An example of each is shown in Figure 1. The upper trace is a recording obtained from the eye electrodes of subject JCA. Note that the eye movement was followed by a positive and then a negative deflection. This pattern was also typical of the other subjects, although in some instances their positive components were less prominent. Occasionally these could not be clearly discerned, and only the negative components could be measured. The two double arrows indicate how the responses were measured.

The occipital responses were quite similar for all subjects; the example shown at the bottom of Figure 2 may be taken as representative. Its measurement also is indicated by a double arrow.

Series of response waves recorded from the eye are shown in Figure 2 for three of the grids over the luminance range. The coarsest and finest grids and one giving large responses (13

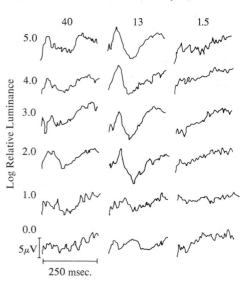

FIGURE 2   Responses from the eye for various combinations of grid size and test luminance.

min/cycle) were chosen to show the range of the results. Examination of the various waves shows that the chief effects are on the amplitude of the responses rather than on their waveform. The largest responses were seen with middle-grid finenesses and with stimuli of high to moderate luminance. At the lowest luminances, little response could be observed for any grid. The response was comparatively low at high luminances for the finest or for the coarsest grid.

Responses recorded simultaneously from the scalp electrodes are presented in Figure 3 for the same stimulus parameters. Again, the most noticeable effects are those upon the amplitudes of the responses. The same conditions which resulted in the most conspicuous responses at the eye did so with this electrode placement.

The waves in both of these figures show considerable variability. The number of responses averaged was quite small for this kind of work; the greatest responses were still of low amplitude relative to the biological noise.

A graph of response amplitude as a function of luminance for one subject is shown in Figure 4. All of the data shown were obtained with the 13-min/cycle grid. The three curves represent

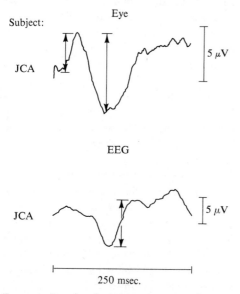

FIGURE 1   Samples of spontaneous responses from the eye (ERG) and the brain (EEG) showing activity recorded from 15 to 256 msec following eye movements. The double arrows indicate the amplitude measures used for further treatment of the data.

two measures of the ERG responses and one of the evoked visual potential, as illustrated in Figure 1. The three curves are clearly similar in form. The response measures increase with increasing luminance over the lower part of the range. At moderate luminance values all three of the curves level off, and further increases of luminance do not produce greater responses. The negative wave of the ERG reaches a higher plateau than the positive wave. The plateau for the evoked potentials is highest of all. The luminance curves for the other grid sizes were similar in form to these, but the plateaus were correspondingly lower, due to the decrease of change of stimulation. As mentioned earlier, the variability of the measures is considerable; this is particularly evident when the over-all level of response magnitude is low, as for the ERG positive wave. The general form of the curves and the similarity between them is clear, however. It is interesting to note that the occipital responses under the conditions of this experiment were more stable than those from the eye.

The effect of grid size is shown in Figure 5. In order to provide more reliable estimates, the data for the flat portion of the luminance curves, between 2 and 5 log units, were averaged

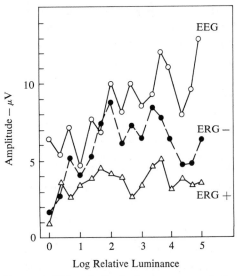

FIGURE 4 Effect of stimulus luminance on response amplitude for the positive and negative waves from the eye (ERG+, ERG−) and for the visual evoked potential (EEG).

for each grid value. These average response amplitudes are plotted as a function of grid fineness, which was expressed log min/cycle. Graphs are presented for the same three response components used in Figure 4. The three curves are similar in form. The vertical displacement represent their differences of amplitude. All three curves attain their maxima at the same fineness. The least responses occur with

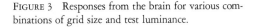

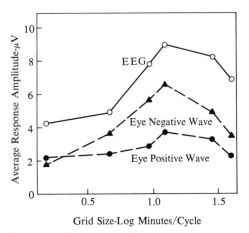

FIGURE 3 Responses from the brain for various combinations of grid size and test luminance.

FIGURE 5 The effect of grid size upon the amplitudes of the three response components.

the finest grids; response magnitude also drops off for coarse grids, but it does not become as small as with the fine grids.

Discussion

Electrophysiological studies of the visual system have employed transient stimulation almost without exception. It is well recognized that the discharge of the eye is strong when a stimulus light is first turned on, but that it drops off markedly with continuing stimulation. The saccadic eye movements of the human eye negate this decrease of response by providing frequent displacements of the retinal image and accompanying changes of stimulation. A response of the retina is to be expected following each saccade, and this, in turn, should pace the activity of later stages of the visual system.

This paper shows that electrical responses following spontaneous eye movements can be recorded at the eye as well as at the cortex and describes some of their properties. Control experiments provided evidence that the response at the eye was not a movement artifact.[13] These were carried out by comparing the activity recorded from electrodes placed at different positions about the eye where they would be sensitive to eye movement with the activity obtained with the contact-lens electrode. The lens and pupil were immobilized with 1% Mydriacyl to rule out the possibility that the potentials at the eye were generated by their activity. Responses from the contact lens electrode were virtually unchanged by these procedures; the 13-min/cycle grid still produced the largest signals. No consistent response activity could be detected from the electrodes situated to respond to eye movement. Since this response is under stimulus control, both with respect to stimulus luminance and grid fineness, it would seem to represent true visual activity.

The waveform shown in the top row of Figure 1 and in Figure 2 is similar to that of electroretinograms produced by external movement of the stimulus pattern. The positive component is not always prominent. It should be noted, however, that in some experimental situations the electroretinogram has appeared as low-amplitude negative fluctuation.[14-16] Thus, although direct evidence is lacking, it appears reasonable to assume that the response at the eye is an aspect of the electroretinogram.

The size of an eye movement relative to the fineness of the stimulus grid determines the effective change of retinal stimulation. If the stripe width is adjusted so that the eye moves through an angle equal to one-half of the angle subtended by a cycle of the stimulus grid, the positions on the retina which were occupied by bright bars before the saccade will be exactly filled by black bars after the movement and *vice versa*. Such movements will produce a maximal change of retinal stimulation. If the stripes subtend a much larger angle than that of the average eye movement, their image will shift only a small amount relative to their width, and the only change will occur along the edges. This represents a much smaller net change of stimulation. Very small stripes, particularly those approaching the limit of the eye's resolution, will also produce little over-all change of stimulation. Thus, if all eye movements were of exactly the same size, it would be anticipated that some stimulus grids would produce large responses and others small ones or none at all.

The small involuntary saccades have been shown to be consistent in amplitude. Their median amplitude, depending upon stimulus conditions, ranges from a small value up to 6 or 7 min of arc.[3, 17] Since successive eye movements vary about this central value, however, very coarse or fine grids would be expected to produce small average responses, while grids of moderate angular extent would be more effective. Of all the grids used in the present

[13] J. A. Michael and L. Stark, *Electroenceph. Clin. Neurophysiol. 21*, 478 (1966).

[14] J. C. Armington, D. I. Tepas, W. J. Kropfl, and W. H. Hengst, *J. Opt. Soc. Am. 51*, 877 (1961).

[15] K. T. Brown, K. Watanabe, and Murakami, Cold Springs Harbor Symposia on Quantitative Biology XXX, 457 (1965).

[16] P. Gouras, *J. Physiol. 187*, 455 (1966).

[17] J. Krauskopf, T. N. Cornsweet, and L. A. Riggs, *J. Opt. Soc. Am. 50*, 572 (1960).

experiment, the 13° and 9° finenesses most closely corresponded to the size of an average eye movement. As has been seen, responses were obtained with these grids. Thus it appears that response magnitude in this situation is determined by the amount of change of stimulation. If the apparatus were adjusted to limit closely the range of eye-movement sizes used to trigger the computer, the curves in Figure 5 might be sharper, the response magnitudes more critically related to the fineness of the grid, and less variable.

The similarity of form of the luminance functions for the ERG and evoked potential is of interest. The cortical potentials should represent a direct transformation of the retinal data if the effects are due solely to visual excitation at both loci. The agreement between the sets of data lends support to this thesis. Another way to rule out the possibility of higher-order neural effects at the cortical level would be to compare data obtained with this method with similar data using the moving-stimulus method. When the fineness of the stationary grid used in the present method is adjusted so that the angle subtended by one stripe width is equal to the average eye-movement size, the stimulus change on the retina is the same as that produced with the moving-stimulus method. Data obtained with the two methods should therefore be comparable; any differences seen would be caused by the correlation of responses in the present method with eye movements.

The effectiveness of the method of recording spontaneous ERG's can now be evaluated. One advantage of this method is that the total amount of light entering the eye does not change during the recording period. The stray light outside of the image area tends to be constant and unfluctuating, and thus ineffective for producing transient visual responses. The observed response is from the limited retinal area on which the stimulus is imaged. This is also a feature of the moving-stimulus method developed by Riggs and his associates.[1, 2] A second advantage of this method is that it can result in an improved signal-to-noise ratio. With conventional methods of response averaging, only the activity elicited by external stimulus changes is summed. Responses to spontaneous eye movements appear as nonstimulus-locked fluctuation of the background against which signals are recorded and they therefore add to the variability. This method is designed to study these spontaneous responses, and eliminates this source of variability.

A potentially important feature of this method is that responses are produced naturally rather than by manipulating the stimulus. In this sense, this method is complementary to stabilized-image work, which is directed at the properties of vision when eye movements are counteracted. Experiments with stabilized images have demonstrated the necessity of spontaneous eye movements for maintained vision. This method allows examination of responses which result from these movements.

Summary

Stabilized-image experiments have demonstrated that the changes of retinal stimulation which are produced by spontaneous eye movements are necessary to maintain vision. They suggest the hypothesis that each saccadic eye movement is followed by electrophysiological response. This report describes a method for recording such responses at the eye and at the brain and summarizes some of their properties. Steadily illuminated gratings of selected degrees of coarseness are used as stimuli. Activity from the eye and the occipital scalp is fed to an average-response computer which is triggered by involuntary saccadic eye movements. The amplitudes of the responses obtained at both recording sites are dependent upon stimulus luminance and grating pattern. Very fine or very coarse gratings are less effective than those of moderate spatial frequency.

7.3 Stimulus Exposure Time, Brightness, and Spatial Factors as Determinants of Visual Perception*

JAQUES KASWAN   STEPHEN YOUNG

Previous evidence suggests that when visual stimuli are presented at very brief exposure times (ET) they are seen as less differentiated than at longer ETs (Bender, 1938; Flavell & Dragnus, 1957; Kaswan, 1958). This effect has been interpreted to indicate that perception develops and becomes differentiated as a function of increasing ET—a process termed "microgenesis" by Flavell and Dragnus (1957).

Systematic investigation of this differentiation process requires the specification of the spatial stimulus parameters along which such differentiation may occur. Following previous work (Kaswan, 1958), variations in distance between dots arranged in a line are considered the relevant parameter in the present study. The specific measure of this parameter can be best illustrated with the stimuli used. When the distance between alternate dots is varied by a constant amount, pairs (Pr) of dots are generally perceived (see Pr designs, Table 1). The *difference* in distance between

pairs *relative* to that within pairs is considered the spatial stimulus parameter relevant to perceptual differentiation. This parameter will be called relative spatial distance (RSD). Since the distance between pairs increases from Design Pr1 to Pr2 to Pr3 while the distance within pairs remains constant, these designs should reflect increasing facilitation of perceptual differentiation. In the evenly spaced (Ev) designs, the absolute distance between dots increases from Design Ev1 to Ev2 to Ev3, but the distance between dots within each design remains constant. Evenly spaced designs are therefore considered homogeneous with respect to variations in distance.

The assumption that less spatial differentiation is seen with decreasing ET implies that differences in spacing within a Pr design will be seen less frequently as ET is decreased. Thus, when Ss are shown a Pr design with an Ev design as the alternative, the Pr design should be more often reported as Ev as ET is decreased. Since the perception of homogeneous spacing presumably occurs first in time, a high level of accuracy should be found for Ev designs even when ETs are brief. Thus, the difference in accuracy between Ev and Pr designs should be maximal at short ETs and should decrease as ET becomes longer. Further, the greater the relative spatial differences (RSD) between components in a design, the briefer should be the ET required to make it appear evenly spaced. Accordingly, it is assumed that the amount of time required for correct discrimination of a

* From: Kaswan and Young, "Stimulus Exposure Time, Brightness, and Spatial Factors as Determinants of Visual Perception," *Journal of Experimental Psychology,* 1963, vol. 65, pp. 113–123. Copyright (1963) by the American Psychological Association, and reproduced by permission. This study was supported by a grant from the National Science Foundation (G-9589). Part of the data contained in this paper was presented at the 1961 American Psychological Association meetings. The authors would like to express their appreciation to George Boroczi for helping to run Ss. The generous availability of the facilities of the Western Data Processing Center was of substantial help in data analysis.

Pr design should increase in the order Pr3, Pr2, and Pr1.

It is conceivable that the proposed interaction of ET and RSD is not specifically a function of time but of the total energy of stimulation, which would involve as parameters both ET and degree of illumination. In fact, the evidence points to considerable reciprocity of intensity (I) and ET in the determination of perceptibility, as illustrated by the Bunsen-Roscoe law (e.g., Hunter & Sigler, 1940). This study is designed to explore the possibility of such reciprocity for stimuli whose components vary in relative spatial distance (RSD).

Method

Subjects. Five paid male Ss ranging from 21 to 29 yr. of age, were used in the experiment. The Ss were UCLA seniors and graduate students and had some sophistication in psychology, but none had any conception of the purpose of the experiment. One S had minimal previous experience with tachistoscopic presentation. All Ss had at least 20/30 uncorrected vision.

Apparatus. An electronically timed tachistoscope was constructed for the experiment from a design similar to one used by Smith, Spence, and Klein (1959). Briefly, this instrument uses timed gating circuits and a logic system to provide for sequential presentation and independent timing of the fields. The apparatus was modified by the addition of a 1450-v. dc, 230-ma. full wave selenium power supply which was heavily loaded to provide 30 ma. of relatively pure direct current to each of the fields. Each field contained two vertically mounted 8-in. 4500°-K mercury argon lamps coated with magnesium tungstate and other short decay phosphors which were manufactured by the Aristo Corporation. With these improvements, it was found that a rectangular light pulse, with rise and decay times of approximately 250 μsec. could be obtained at exposure times as low as .004 sec. A switching system was added to allow rapid selection of the experimental exposure times. Continuous monitoring and calibration of the light output of the tachistoscope were obtained with a photomultiplier input to an oscilloscope. The photomultiplier was located directly below the eyepiece.

Two fields were used, a fixation field and a stimulus field. Semiopaque field stops in both fields provided an 8-in. square field with a discrete but minimally contrasting border. The two fields were matched for color and an unattenuated intensity of 11.84 mL. measured with a Spectra brightness spot meter (Photo Research Corporation). Intensity was attenuated by insertion of neutral density filters directly in front of the eyepiece, so that light output from the two fields was always identical.

Both the fixation and stimulus field were 40 in. from the eyepiece. A chin rest and close fitting face mask were used to insure minimal head movement. All viewing was binocular.

The fixation field contained two horizontal $\frac{1}{4}$-in. black dashes on a flat white surface located so that they would fall just inside the border and an equal distance on either side of the stimulus when the two fields were superimposed.

Stimuli. Six stimuli were used (see Table 1). Each contained a single horizontal line of $\frac{1}{16}$-in. diameter black dots centrally located on flat white cards. The maximum visual angle subtended by a line of dots was 10° to either eye. Two basic linear arrays of dots, one evenly spaced and one paired, were used. Three paired patterns were obtained by successively doubling

TABLE 1

Critical Dimensions of Stimulus Patterns

	PATTERN DESIGNATION	NUMBER OF DOTS	LENGTH OF LINE (CM.)	DISTANCE CM.* BETWEEN PAIRS	DISTANCE CM.* WITHIN PAIRS
SET					
1	Ev1	16	16.5		1.1
	Pr1	16	16.5	1.2	1.0
2	Ev2	16	17.7		1.2
	Pr2	16	17.7	1.4	1.0
3	Ev3	14	18.2		1.4
	Pr3	14	18.2	1.8	1.0

*For Ev patterns: distance between dots.

an increment in the distance between pairs. Corresponding evenly spaced patterns were obtained by spacing dots the average of the distance between and within pairs in the paired patterns. The dimensions of the stimuli are given in Table 1.

Procedure. The experiment began with two practice sessions in which Ss were shown only Designs Ev3 and Pr3 (Table 1). Each design was presented at eight different ETs at each of eight I's using the method of constant stimulus. The ETs were successively doubled from .004 sec. to .512 sec., thus ranging from -8 to -1 $\log_2$ sec. Intensities were successively halved from the maximum luminance of 11.84 to .093 mL., thus ranging from 3.5 to -3.5 $\log_2$ mL. In each session, eight I blocks of 16 exposures each (each ET for each design), were presented for a total of 128 exposures. The order of I blocks was randomized with the restraint that the initial block was always in the brighter half of the I range and that successive blocks were always within two ordinal I steps of each other. These restraints were intended to minimize dark adaptation problems. Design-ET combinations were randomized within each block with the restraint that each combination was used only once in each block of 16.

The Ss were first shown either the Ev3 or Pr3 design and told to hit one of the two microswitch keys, located on either side of a finger rest, as quickly as possible whenever this design was presented. They were then shown the other design and instructed to respond with the other key. A warning signal was given approximately .5 sec. before each exposure with a manually operated buzzer in response to which S was asked to focus between the edge markers of the blank field. For 3 of the Ss the key on the right side was associated with the Ev design, for 2 of the Ss this key was associated with the Pr design. The designs were never verbally described by either Ss or E until the end of the study. If S saw absolutely no indication of a design during an exposure (i.e., not even a blurred line), he was instructed to hit either key and then say the word "nothing" (NO). There was an interval of approximately 11 sec. between ex-

posures within a block of 16 exposures and 45 sec. between each block when I filters were changed.

The experimental sessions were like the practice sessions. Each S was given one of the three Ev-Pr sets at each session, with the sequence of sets randomized, but all three sets were given before one was repeated. Each S had 43 sessions of 45 min. each, spaced over a 3-mo. period, with from three to five sessions per week. Each S thus received 13–15 replications of each I-ET-design combination, so that a total of almost 28,000 responses was recorded for the 5 Ss combined.

Results

RSD-ET Relations. The relevant results are shown largely in Figures 1a and 2a. Percent correct values were obtained by dividing the number of correct responses by the combined number of correct and incorrect responses, excluding NO responses. There was a total of approximately 560 exposures for each point in Figures 1 (a and b) and 2 (a and b) so that the N for each point can be computed by subtracting the product of 560 and the percent NO responses from 560 and treating the resulting number as the denominator for computing percent correct responses. The curves shown in Figure 1 (a and b) were obtained by fitting cubic equations to the data, using the method of least squares.

Figure 1a shows the percent correct responses for each design as a function of ET averaged over all I's and Ss. As expected, the percent correct responses at each ET decreased from Design Pr3 to Pr2 to Pr1, and accuracy to Pr designs increased as a function of ET.

Figure 2a examines the functional equivalence of the effect of RSD and ET on accuracy which was expected from the assumption of the interaction of spatial differentiation and ET. To facilitate this comparison, the Pr designs were constructed so that RSD increases from Pr1 to Pr2 to Pr3 on the same log basis as do I and ET. Thus, as can be seen from Table 1, the difference obtained by subtracting the dis-

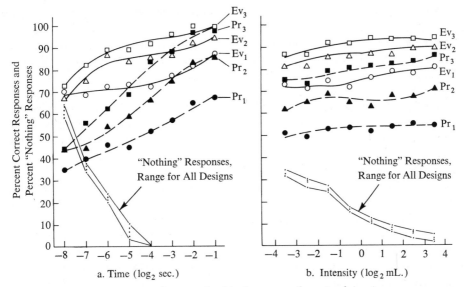

FIGURE 1 Percent correct and percent "nothing" responses for each of the six patterns as a function of exposure time (a) and as a function of intensity (b). (Curves fitted with cubic equations.)

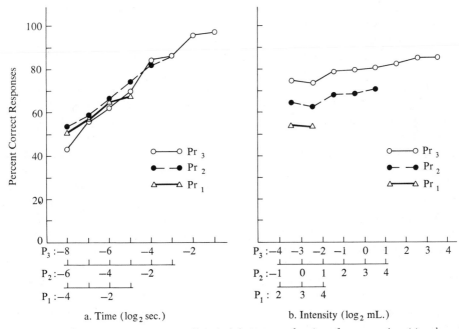

FIGURE 2 Percent correct responses for paired designs as a function of exposure time (a) and intensity (b). (Distributions are plotted at values of time and intensity which give the closest approximation to $D \times ET = k$ and $D \times 1 = k$, respectively.)

tance between pairs from that within pairs is 2 mm., 4 mm., and 8 mm. for Designs Pr1, Pr2, and Pr3, respectively. Accordingly, these differences, which are the values of RSD for these designs, increase on a log2 scale. The considerable superimposition of curves in Figure 2a was obtained by transposing the Pr design curves from Figure 1a, but taking the initial data point at .004 sec. ($\log_2 = -8$), .016 sec. ($\log_2 = -6$), and .064 sec. ($\log_2 = -4$) for Pr3, Pr2, and Pr1, respectively. Thus, RSD and ET do not show a one-to-one relationship, but the results indicate that when ET is quadrupled (e.g., .004 sec. to .016 sec.) for each successive halving of RSD (e.g., Pr3 vs. Pr2) a RSD-ET equivalence is approached in terms of percent correctly perceived.

Figure 1a also shows the overall effect of ET on Ev designs and permits a comparison of results for each set of Ev-Pr designs (i.e., Ev1 vs. Pr1; Ev2 vs. Pr2; Ev3 vs. Pr3). As expected, accuracy to the Ev design of a given set was greater than accuracy to the Pr design in that set, especially at short ETs. Contrary to expectations, however, the curves for Ev designs tend to follow the order of accuracy for Pr designs and show a definite growth function, especially at short ETs. Since discrimination of Ev designs was presumed to temporally precede discrimination of Pr designs, there was no reason to expect that Ev designs should ever be seen as paired. Occasional errors would be ascribed to confusion, such as accidentally hitting a wrong key, which should be independent of ET or I so that Ev design accuracy curves were expected to be horizontal and superimposed. In spite of this deviation from expectations, the maximum differences in accuracy between Ev and Pr designs of each set still occurred at brief ETs as postulated by the differentiation hypothesis.

RSD-I. Figure 1b gives percent correct responses for each design as a function of I averaged over all ETs and Ss. It is clear from the horizontal curves that changes in I had little effect on accuracy so that the ordinal relations between designs reflect primarily the average effect of ET shown in Figure 1a.

It is obvious that the relationship found for ET and RSD as shown in Figure 2a cannot be obtained for I and RSD since the I curves shown in Figure 1b are parallel and nonoverlapping and, therefore, cannot be superimposed by an I scale shift.

It was found, however, that by transposing the Pr curves in Figure 1b and taking initial

data points at .093 mL. ($\log_2 = -3.5$), .74 mL. ($\log_2 = -.5$), and 5.92 mL. ($\log_2 = 2.5$) for Pr3, Pr2, and Pr1, respectively, a constant difference of about 5% was present between all remaining data points of the three designs as shown in Figure 2b. This finding suggests that, while I, unlike ET, cannot compensate for decreases in spatial differentiation, I does have a slight effect on discriminability in a regular relationship to RSD.

I-ET Relations. Figure 3 (a and b) shows I-ET interactions most clearly. Percent correct responses were again based on the ratio of incorrect to the sum of correct and incorrect responses, excluding NO responses. There was a total of approximately 210 exposures at each point of these two graphs. The number of NO responses can be seen in Figure 4 and can be used to compute the actual N at each point of Figure 3 (a and b). Standard deviations at individual points ranged in percent from 1.45 at 11.84 mL. and 8 msec to 8.51 at .09 mL. and 8 msec for Ev designs and from 2.35 at 5.43 mL. and 8 msec to 7.84 at .18 mL. and 4 msec for Pr designs. The median SD for Ev designs was 2.37%, and for Pr designs it was 3.36%. Standard deviations at each point were estimated by $\sqrt{PQ/N}$, where P = percent correct responses, Q = percent incorrect responses, and N = sum of correct and incorrect responses.

The bottom scales of these figures are constructed to show the effect of ET within each I, going from the brightest I at the left to the dimmest I at the extreme right with ET increasing from left to right within each I block. Results are shown with solid lines. It is clear that the increase in accuracy as a function of ET at each I block is about the same. The scales on the top of Figure 3 (a and b) were constructed to show the effect of I within each ET, with the longest ET at the extreme left, and the shortest ET at the extreme right. Intensities increase from left to right within each ET block, and results are plotted with dashed lines. Both figures, but especially Figure 3b, show that ET is the limiting factor for accuracy, since given long ETs (extreme left) changes in I had no effect, and at the briefest ET (extreme right)

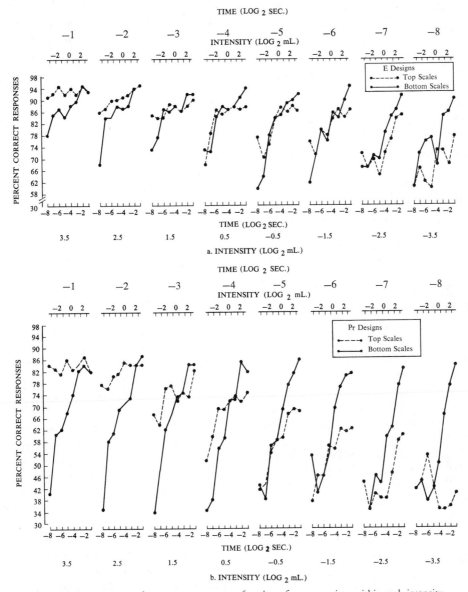

FIGURE 3 Percentage of correct responses as a function of exposure time within each intensity (solid lines) and as a function of intensity within each exposure time (dashed lines). (Each distribution is plotted to permit comparison of complementary I-ET log units, so that if $1 \times T = k$, solid and dashed lines should be superimposed. Data for Ev designs are shown in a, data for Pr designs are in b.

accuracy was not improved by increasing I. At intermediate block values, the effect of ET was always greater than that of I, especially for Pr designs (Figure 3b). These results held for all designs, although the average magnitude of accuracy shifted as a function of RSD (see Figure 1a).

Figure 3 (a and b) was also constructed to assess possible 1-ET reciprocity, since points on dashed and solid lines represent equal I-ET products (i.e., $\log I + \log t = k$). Thus, for example, the first point at the extreme left of each graph in the solidly drawn curves represents the accuracy of discrimination at the brightest I and the fastest ET. The complementary point on the curve drawn with dashes reflects the accuracy of discrimination at the longest ET and dimmest I. By the nature of this method of graph construction, two points in each block are always superimposed, since they are the same I-ET combinations. It is only when both ET and I are intermediate values that anything approaching I-ET reciprocity can be discerned. This tendency toward reciprocity appears somewhat greater for Ev (Figure 3a) than for Pr designs (Figure 3b).

In addition to greater I-ET reciprocity, accuracy for Ev designs also changed over a narrower range than that for Pr designs. Further, while indications of I-ET reciprocity are absent at extreme blocks, some effect of I on accuracy is present even at the fastest ET for Ev but not for Pr designs.

In order to help evaluate the effect of I and ET on discrimination independent of spatial distance variables, a supplementary experiment was carried out with the same Ss on completion of the main study. They were shown either a centrally located 10-mm. black dot or a blank field, and required to indicate what was shown by depressing one of two keys corresponding to the stimuli. Each of the 5 Ss was given two exposures of each stimulus at each of the I-ET values used in the main study, so that there was a total of 10 exposures of each I-ET combination for each stimulus for all Ss combined. The results are shown in Table 2. It is clear that

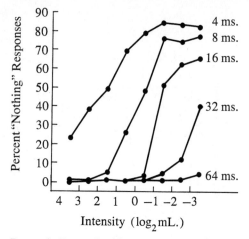

FIGURE 4   Percent "nothing" responses as a function of exposure time and intensity.

errors to the dot predominate and are concentrated at dim and fast exposures.

NO Responses, S, and Practice Effects. Figure 1 (a and b) indicates that the frequency distributions of NO responses are about the same for all designs. An analysis af variance comparing total frequency of NO responses for each design yielded an $F(5, 20) = 2.31, p > .05$. Figure 4 shows the frequency of NO responses for each ET as a function of I. Since the NO responses occurred with almost exactly the same frequency for all designs only the combined curves for Pr designs are shown here. Each point is based on 210 responses. It is clear that NO responses were concentrated at short and dim exposures. Since the single dot in the supplementary study was also rarely seen at these exposures, it is probable that NO responses can generally be accepted at face value. No ETs above .064 sec. are shown since there was only a total of three NO responses above that point. It is interesting to note that when successively longer ET curves in Figure 4 are shifted back about two log units along the I scale, for each log unit of ET the curves are superimposed within a range of about 10% in accuracy. This indicates that when accuracy of perception is disregarded some I-ET reciprocity is obtained.

Tables 3 and 4 combine the eight I and eight ET values into brighter and dimmer and faster

TABLE 2

Errors to Blank (B) and Dot (D) Stimuli as a Function of I and ET

ET (SEC.)	L (ML.)					
	.09		.19		.38	
	D	B	D	B	D	B
.004	9	0	8	1	7	0
.008	7	1	5	1	1	0
.016	1	1	0	0	0	0

Note.—Total errors to all other ET-I combinations not shown were 2 (D) and 8 (B).

TABLE 3

Number of Correct and Incorrect (N) and Percent Correct Responses as a Function of S, Intensity, and Exposure Time for Ev Designs

		EXPOSURE TIME										
		FAST ET (.004–.032 SEC.)						SLOW ET (.064–.512 SEC.)					
		Ev1		Ev2		Ev3		Ev1		Ev2		Ev3	
INTENSITY	SUB-JECT	N	%	N	%	N	%	N	%	N	%	N	%
	AP	164	87	173	90	217	77	254	71	211	87	213	99
	CW	238	73	217	84	226	84	240	94	221	95	223	99
Bright (1.94–11.84 mL.)	LP	176	79	183	89	180	94	209	82	229	94	254	100
	JH	199	61	168	71	206	75	239	85	195	92	253	92
	GF	196	76	183	89	191	90	228	83	205	90	225	98
Quadrant mean		(N = 195; % = 81.6)						(N = 227; % = 91.0)					
	AP	90	79	83	87	66	80	214	77	221	88	225	96
	CW	213	62	197	62	200	71	240	85	222	95	225	98
Dim (.09–.74 mL.)	LP	88	77	89	84	75	83	205	76	228	92	257	95
	JH	93	43	59	61	77	69	230	76	194	86	243	91
	GF	117	80	104	85	125	88	213	68	210	87	223	95
Quadrant mean		(N = 112; % = 75.6)						(N = 223; % = 86.8)					

TABLE 4

Number of Correct and Incorrect (N) and Percent Correct Responses as a Function of S, I, and ET for Pr Designs

		EXPOSURE TIME										
		FAST ET (.004–.032 SEC.)						SLOW ET (.064–.512 SEC.)					
		Pr1		Pr2		Pr3		Pr1		Pr2		Pr3	
INTENSITY	SUB-JECT	N	%	N	%	N	%	N	%	N	%	N	%
	AP	176	24	174	31	170	70	223	58	220	79	224	98
	CW	234	58	215	79	220	85	259	82	226	97	226	99
Bright (1.48–11.84 mL.)	LP	177	40	184	55	214	78	207	63	219	84	249	97
	JH	198	59	132	71	202	83	242	57	189	68	256	89
	GF	204	33	187	24	189	30	224	50	211	72	227	85
Quadrant mean		(N = 192; % = 54.8)						(N = 227; % = 76.6)					
	AP	91	37	110	32	69	62	224	49	231	73	226	92
	CW	190	53	195	64	198	66	237	73	221	95	225	97
Dim (.09–.74 mL.)	LP	81	30	90	53	81	64	211	58	228	78	261	87
	JH	74	51	59	63	66	85	239	57	192	69	256	96
	GF	124	23	103	19	120	13	224	49	206	55	219	68
Quadrant mean		(N = 107; % = 47.4)						(N = 227; % = 73.2)					

and slower halves, respectively, and give the total number of correct plus incorrect responses (N) and the percent correct responses for each S for each design at each combination of I and ET. While the principal purpose of these tables was to present individual differences, they also provide a more convenient but less detailed comparison than graphic presentations of N and percent correct responses to changes in the three stimulus parameters. As can be seen most clearly from the overall quandrant means, the role of I is much more important for N than for percent correct responses. While the accuracy and number of responses varied considerably from S to S, the effects of RSD, I, and ET were usually in the same direction for each S as that shown in the combined data (Figure 1, a and b).

In order to assess practice effects, each S's 40 sessions were divided into quartiles, according to the chronological order of sessions to see if an increase in percent correct responses could be found from the first through the fourth quartile. The obtained $F(3, 12) = .11$ ($p > .05$) indicated no change in accuracy with practice. In fact, percent correct in the first and last quartile was about the same. This indicates that the initial practice sessions provided sufficient warm up for this task.

Discussion

The results of this study provide clear evidence that, for the stimuli used here, perception occurs largely as a result of spatial differentiation over time. This was shown not only by the increase in accuracy to Pr designs as a function of ET, but also by the increase in accuracy as a function of increasing RSD (Pr1, Pr2, Pr3), so that ET and RSD tended to have functionally equivalent effects on accuracy (Figure 2a). Emphasis on RSD is important, since increases only in the absolute distance between dots (Ev1 < Ev2 < Ev3), resulted in accuracy curves which tended to be parallel to each other and to the abscissa, so that, unlike the Pr design curves, the Ev design curves could not be superimposed.

The finding of a much greater effect of ET than I on accuracy of discrimination in these stimuli (Figure 3, Tables 3 and 4), is in accord with findings of Leibowitz and Bourne (1956) for the effect of I and ET on shape constancy. When shape judgments were plotted as a function of increasing I with the fastest ET (.01 sec.) as the parameter, the resulting curve was quite flat and very close to the law of retinal image. When shape judgments were plotted as a function of increasing ET with the dimmest luminance (.01 mL.) as the parameter, there was a regular, seemingly linear, increase toward shape constancy. The authors note that constancy tended to be destroyed by decreases in stimulation because constancies presumably depend on the presence in the visual field of stimuli in addition to the discriminative stimulus which cannot be discriminated at low energy levels. While the nature of these "additional" stimuli was not specified, it is clear that ET played a more decisive role than I in making such stimuli effective for shape constancy.

While the stimuli used in this study cannot be considered directly analogous to those involved in shape constancy, it seems reasonable to consider RSD as indicating characteristics of the designs "additional" to the dots for the perception of groupings, in the same sense in which size and distance may be additional cues for size constancy. The essential point is that the relation among stimuli is critical for the response in both cases.

The NO responses or the converse—the sum of accurate and inaccurate responses—are analogous to responses in a detection task, where only the identification of the presence or absence of a stimulus is considered. Under these conditions I was found to be a more critical stimulus variable than it was in response accuracy. Further, since there were about the same number of NO responses for all designs, detection was shown to be independent of spatial relations. These findings are in line with the results of other studies showing I-ET reciprocity for such detection tasks as dot numerosity (Hunter & Sigler, 1940), grating acuity (Graham & Cook, 1937), absolute threshold (Graham & Magaria, 1935), and "frequency of seeing" studies (Liebowitz, Myers, & Grant, 1955a, 1955b). While it might appear that dot numerosity identification might require more complex discrimination than merely identifying the presence of a stimulus, Schlosberg's (1948) formulation indicates that it is possible to predict the Hunter and Sigler results fairly well by considering the contribution of each dot to the discrimination as an independent event, reducing the problem essentially to a set of detection tasks. The Leibowitz et al. (1955a) study supports this formulation for small numbers of dots, as does a recent study by Restle, Rae, and Kiesler (1961).

These considerations suggest that a two-phase temporal process may occur in the perception of complex displays. The first phase presumably involves only the detection of the presence or absence of stimuli and depends on the total energy of stimulation (I × ET). When the task requires that different stimuli be related to each other, or where, as in this study, the spatial relations among elements within a stimulus array are relevant, the ET required for detection is insufficient for accurate identification. Once the presence of stimuli has been detected, a second phase, discrimination, follows. In this phase, the amount of *additional* ET required for accurate discrimination appears to depend on the amount of spatial differentiation in the design (see Figure 2a).

Acceptance of this formulation requires a revision of the usual conception of I and ET as reciprocal up to some critical ET (e.g., Boynton, 1961, p. 740). The present findings and the pertinent literature noted above suggest that reciprocity fails to hold even at ETs in the millisecond range when perceptual accuracy depends on the relational characteristics of stimuli. Also, it is important to note that no postulation of cognition such as counting or thinking, need be presumed in the temporal development of discrimination for these orders of magnitude since enough information is obtained within 64 msec to result in better than 70% accuracy for P designs at all but the two dimmest intensities (see Figure 3b). Even higher accuracy was obtained for Ev designs within this ET limit (Figure 3a). Since cortical transmission times

are probably much slower than 64 msec (Lansing, Schwartz, & Lindsley, 1959), cognitive evaluation of the stimuli may occur after the *cessation* of the exposure and prior to the response, but this is not likely to play a role in the ET-RSD relationship, which largely determines the information for such evaluation.

Considering I-ET relations to be more critical for detection than for accurate discrimination of more complex displays suggests a reason why greater I-ET reciprocity was found for Ev than Pr designs (Figure 3). Since no differential spatial cues need to be taken into account for the identification of these designs, Ev design identification is probably closer to, and more likely to overlap with the detection phase of perception, as is also indicated by the briefer ETs necessary for identification of Ev than of Pr designs.

Summary

In a forced choice task, 5 Ss chose between linear displays of dots arranged in pairs or evenly spaced presented at 8 exposure times ranging from .004 to .512 sec. and 8 intensities ranging from .09 to 11.84 mL. Intensity had little effect on accuracy. Accuracy was largely a function of exposure time and, for paired designs, the amount of relative spatial distance between to within pairs of dots. Detecting the presence or absence of stimuli was a joint function of exposure time and intensity and independent of relative spatial distance. The findings support the assumption that perception becomes differentiated over time, and indicate that relative spatial distance can be used as a stimulus measure of differentiation. A 2-phase process of the temporal development of perception is proposed.

References

Bender, L. A visual motor gestalt test and its clinical use. *Amer. Orthopsychiat. Ass. res. Monogr.*, 1938, No. 3.

Boynton, R. M. Some temporal factors in vision. In

W. A. Rosenblith (Ed.), *Sensory communication.* New York: Wiley, 1961. Pp. 739–755.

Flavell, J. A., & Dragnus, J. A. A microgenetic approach to perception and thought. *Psychol. Bull.,* 1957, *54,* 197–217.

Graham, C. H., & Cook, C. Visual acuity as a function of intensity and exposure time. *Amer. J. Psychol.,* 1937, *49,* 654–661.

Graham, C. H., & Margaria, R. Area and the intensity-time relation in the peripheral retina. *Amer. J. Physiol.,* 1935, *113,* 299–305.

Hunter, W. S., & Sigler, M. The span of visual discrimination as a function of time and intensity of stimulation. *J. exp. Psychol.,* 1940, *26,* 160–179.

Kaswan, J. W. Tachistoscope exposure time and spatial proximity in the organization of visual perception. *Brit. J. Psychol.,* 1958, *49,* 131–138.

Lansing, R. W., Schwartz, E., & Lindsley, D. B. Reaction time and EEG activation under alerted and nonalerted conditions. *J. exp. Psychol.,* 1959, *58,* 1–7.

Leibowitz, H. W., & Bourne, L. E., Jr. Time and intensity as determiners of perceived shape. *J. exp. Psychol.,* 1956, *51,* 277–281.

Leibowitz, H. W., Myers, N. A., & Grant, D. A. Frequency of seeing and radial localization of single and multiple visual stimuli. *J. exp. Psychol.,* 1955, *50,* 369–374. (a)

Leibowitz, H. W., Myers, N. A., & Grant, D. A. Radial localization of a single stimulus as a function of luminance and duration of exposure. *J. Opt. Soc. Amer.,* 1955, *45,* 76–78. (b)

Restle, F., Rae, J., & Kiesler, C. The probability of detecting small numbers of dots. *J. exp. Psychol.,* 1961, *61,* 218–222.

Schlosberg, H. A probability formulation of the Hunter-Sigler effect. *J. exp. Psychol.,* 1948, *38,* 155–167.

Smith, G. J. W., Spence, D. P., & Klein, G. S. Subliminal effects of verbal stimuli. *J. abnorm. soc. Psychol.,* 1959, *59,* 167–176.

7.4 Binocular Summation in the Perception of Form at Brief Durations*

CHARLES W. ERIKSEN   THOMAS S. GREENSPON JOSEPH LAPPIN   WILLIAM A. CARLSON

The superiority of binocular viewing in a detection situation seems well established (Collier, 1954; Matin, 1962; Pirenne, 1943; Shaad, 1935; Wolf & Zigler, 1963) although the basis for this superiority is still a matter of controversy. Some view binocular vision as essentially two monocular systems working together. From

* Reproduced by permission of *Perception & Psychophysics,* 1966, vol. 1, pp. 415–419. This investigation was supported by Public Health Service research Grant MH-1206 and a Public Health Service Research Career Program Award K6-MH-22014. The authors wish to acknowledge their appreciation to Roy M. Hamlin, Research Psychologist, and other members of the staff at the Danville Veterans Administration Hospital where pilot studies were carried out for this experiment.

this viewpoint the increased sensitivity in brightness thresholds that occurs with binocular regard can be attributed to the gain accruing from two independent chances to detect the target. Pirenne (1943) seems to have been the first to apply an independence probability model to binocular threshold data, and he concluded that the reduction in binocular over monocular thresholds was no greater than could be attributed to two independent detectors.

More recent work by Collier (1954) and Matin (1962) has shown that the gain in binocular detection is greater than can be attributed to independent detectors. Instead, their data suggest a summative process from the two eyes. Levelt (1965), a recent exponent of an interactionist or summative theory of binocular vision, has advanced a theory of brightness interaction in which total brightness depends upon a weighted average of the luminance contributions from each eye where the weights add to a constant. Further, the weighting assigned to the input from each eye is in part dependent upon contour information provided to that eye.

The present experiment is concerned with the contribution of binocular vision to form identification at brief durations and low luminance. Nearly all of the experimetal work on interocular summation has been concerned with brightness but there is reason to expect that a study of the interaction or possible summative role of the two eyes in form identification might yield different results as well as extend our general knowledge of binocular vision. Levelt's (1965) as well as Bouman's (1955) work has suggested that contour information is processed differently in binocular vision than is brightness and an assessment of the effects of binocular vision on form identification would seem to be a necessary step in the process of understanding such binocular phenomena as rivalry and suppression.

Method

Subjects. Six Ss, four males, served as paid volunteers. They were selected on a basis of their having essentially similar form identification functions in each of their eyes. They also represented a relatively homogeneous group in terms of exposure duration necessary to obtain above-chance identification accuracy for the three forms employed.

Apparatus. A dichopic viewing system was constructed and was used along with programmer, timers and lamp driver from a Scientific Prototype Model GA three-field tachistoscope. The optical system is shown schematically in Figure 1. Stimuli mounted on white plastic cards could be presented in the stimulus card holders in the right and left eye stimulus fields and were frontlighted by two Sylvania F-4G5/-

CWX bulbs which in turn were pulsed and programmed by the Scientific Prototype equipment. A light-proof baffle (B) obscured all but a circle of 2° of angle diameter of the stimulus display. This circular field was reflected off front surface mirrors (M) back through a beamsplitting mirror (BS) and then through tubes made of black construction paper which terminated at the viewing hood.

The S rested his head on a hood visor to help maintain a constant position and viewed the displays through the black tubes. The diameter of these tubes was such that the ends of the tubes exactly coincided with the 2° diameter circular holes in the baffles in the stimulus compartments. Luminance from the adapting field, diffused through milk glass, was reflected from

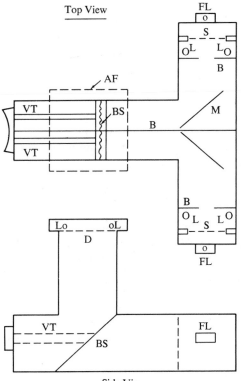

FIGURE 1 Schematic top and side views of the dichopic viewing system. The major parts and construction are as follows: (a) FL—fixation light sources; (b) S—stimulus holders; (c) L—Sylvania F4 T5/ CWX lamps; (d) B—light proof baffles; (e) M—front surface mirrors; (f) BS—beam splitter; (g) AF—adaptation field; and (h) VT—viewing tunnels.

the beam splitter (BS) to the S's eye. Fixation for both the right and left eye fields was a back-lighted "X," .12° of angle, which was obtained by a solid black card positioned immediately behind the stimulus card but having the "X" cut out of it. Light for the "X" was provided by GE 44 bulbs in the back of the stimulus compartments. The "X" was visible to the S with a stimulus card in place by means of a circular hole cut in the center of the stimulus card that positioned over the luminous "X." The luminance of the fixation point was such that it was clearly visible against the background adapting field luminance.

The stimuli were the capital letters A, T and U, obtained from Paratype No. 11316, 18-point Futura bold and subtended .12° of visual angle. They occurred at the corners of an imaginary 1° square centered on the "X" fixation point. The letters were mounted on white vinyl cards and had approximately 96% contrast. The fixation point was on constantly. Both stimulus fields and the adapting field had a constant luminance of .3 mL.

Procedure. Before participating in the experimental sessions each S was given two practice sessions during which he identified the three letters presented under dichoptic conditions. Here the same letter was presented to the two eyes on corresponding retinal areas simultaneously. During the last practice session an exposure duration was determined for each S that yielded 70 to 75% identification accuracy. This duration is referred to hereafter as time T. All Ss achieved the criterion at exposure durations in the range of 20 to 25 msec (mean = 23).

Following the practice sessions each S served for one session on each of six experimental days. During each session S received four blocks of 24 trials except for the last session where only two blocks of trials were run. There were 11 experimental conditions that were randomly distributed into the available blocks. The 11 conditions were: (a) stimulus presented to the right eye alone at time T; (b) left eye alone at time T; (c) right eye at time 2T (twice the exposure duration for the S that was used in conditions a and b); (d) left eye at time 2T;

(e) right and left eye simultaneously on corresponding retinal areas at time T; (f) right eye followed immediately by stimulation to left eye, each eye for time T; (g) left eye followed immediately by stimulation to right eye on corresponding areas, each eye for time T; (h) right eye followed immediately by left eye stimulation each for time T on noncorresponding heterolateral retinal areas; (i) left eye followed immediately by stimulation to right eye each for time T on noncorresponding heterolateral areas; (j) right eye followed by left eye on noncorresponding homolateral areas; and (k) left eye followed immediately by right eye on noncorresponding homolateral areas.

The stimuli appeared randomly in the four corners of the imaginary square except for the noncorresponding homo- and heterolateral conditions. For the unfused homolateral conditions the two occurrences of the letter on a trial were on the same side of the square, one in the upper corner and one in the lower corner. For the heterolateral unfused condition the two occurrences of the letter were either on the two bottom corners or the two upper corners.

In order to control for luminance summation-contrast reduction effects (Eriksen, 1966a) during the conditions of successive stimulation, a letter was exposed to one eye while the other eye remained dark, then the reverse occurred. The adapting field remained off during the entire stimulation sequence. For single eye stimulation one eye was presented a letter while the other eye received darkness; then the other eye received a blank illuminated field while the first eye received a dark period. For the fused simultaneous condition both eyes were simultaneously stimulated with the letter form and followed by a period of darkness equal to the exposure duration before return of the adapting field luminance. For the unfused conditions the sequence of stimulation was the same as for the monocular conditions.

Before each trial, on a ready signal from E, S fixated the "X" in each field and when they were fused and the "X" appeared sharp and clear, he triggered a stimulation. Upon completion of the stimulation the S gave a forced-choice response from among the three possible letters along with a confidence rating as to his certainty of his judgment. Numbers 1, 2 and 3 were used to reflect his confidence with 1 indicating very certain and 3 a guess.

Results and Discussion

The data were first analyzed for a possible sequential order effect of right eye to left eye or left eye to right eye in the three conditions involving successive stimulation under dichopic conditions. The percent correct form identifications under fused successive, unfused homolateral and unfused heterolateral were analyzed in a three-way classification analysis of variance (conditions, right-left or left-right eye sequence, and Ss). The only significant effect was that attributable to conditions (F = 8.7, df = 2/10, p < .01) which reflected a superiority of the fused condition over the two unfused conditions. The lack of a significant S effect was anticipated since the exposure duration for each S had been adjusted to yield essentially comparable performance over Ss on the basis of the S's performance during the practice sessions. The sequence order variable and its interactions gave F ratios of less than 1.

In Table 1 the percent correct forced-choice form identifications are shown by Ss for each of the eight main experimental conditions.

Average values are also shown in Table 1. In view of the lack of significant or suggestive effects attributable to right-left or left-right stimulation sequence, the data obtained under these two sequences of stimulation for the fused successive and the unfused homo- and heterolateral conditions have been pooled.

Of major interest in Table 1 is the percent correct form identifications under the two fused and the two unfused dichopic conditions. As is seen, both the successive and the simultaneous fused conditions are superior to either of the unfused conditions. The significance of the differences was evaluated by a two-way classification analysis of variance (conditions and Ss). The differences between the four conditions were significant beyond the .01 level (F =9.6, df = 3/15). None of the other effects approached significance. Comparison of the four condition means with each other revealed that the fused successive and the fused simultaneous conditions differed from both the unfused conditions at beyond the .01 level. There was no significant difference between the two unfused conditions, but there is a suggestion that for fused dichopic stimulation successive is superior to simultaneous. However, this difference did not attain significance (p > .10).

While presenting the same form either simultaneously or successively on corresponding retinal areas is superior to presentation to noncorresponding areas, the latter conditions show

TABLE 1

Percent Correct Form Identification by Ss and Experimental Viewing Conditions

| | MONOCULAR | | | | DICHOPIC | | | |
| | RIGHT EYE | | LEFT EYE | | FUSED | | UNFUSED | |
SUBJECTS	TIME T	TIME 2T	TIME T	TIME 2T	SIMULTANEOUS	SUCCESSIVE	HOMOLATERAL	HETEROLATERAL
MN	38	83	46	79	63	69	62	59
SH	58	75	44	96	69	70	66	66
JM	54	98	43	92	79	81	59	69
CE	44	96	57	98	78	86	68	58
JC	71	92	46	88	71	82	60	63
WL	48	92	73	94	75	74	65	72
	313	536	309	547	435	462	380	387
Mean	52	89	52	91	73	77	63	64

considerable gain in identification over that obtained by presentation to either eye alone. It is tempting to conclude that the performance under stimulation of corresponding retinal areas for the fused conditions represents a binocular summation process whereas the stimulation to noncorresponding or unfused areas represents the gain over monocular stimulation attributable to two chances to perceive or identify the form. However, other possibilities must be considered. Performance under the unfused dichoptic conditions might also represent a binocular interaction. The obtained level of performance could represent some summative process which is not as great as when the dichoptic stimulation is on fused areas. Alternatively, it is possible that the poorer performance for the unfused relative to the fused conditions may represent an inhibitory process operating interocularly for stimuli that do not fall on corresponding points. This latter alternative would require an extremely short latency for the inhibitory process since stimulus durations were on the order of 20 to 25 msec.[1]

Interpretation becomes clearer if we can compute or determine what the level of performance would be if the two eyes behaved as independent perceptual units. Previous models, in attempting to compute the level of performance to be expected from independent chances, have followed Pirenne (1943) which is unfortunate since Pirenne made a serious error which overestimates the level of performance to be expected on the assumption of independence. He used the formula

$$P_1 + P_2 - P_1 P_2$$

where P_1 and P_2 refer to the probabilities of detection in the separate eyes under monocular stimulation. This formula is correct when applied to such events as coins or dice, but psychophysical detections or hit rates involve a guessing component, particularly if a forced-choice procedure is employed. Thus, the percent correct form identification in the present experiment for left eye stimulation represents not only the number of times S perceived the form but also the number of times he guessed correctly when he did not perceive it.

The problem involved in computing the level of performance to be expected with independent chances has been discussed elsewhere (Eriksen, 1966b) along with models that provide a more appropriate prediction based on the independence assumption.[2] A close approximation to the level to be expected from independent systems can be obtained by correcting the monocular hit rates for guessing. Let P_R and P_L be the monocular hit rates for the right and left eyes respectively. Then $1 - P_L$ is the percent of incorrect responses for the left eye. With an a priori probability of a correct guess being $1/3$, then $3/2$ of $1 - P_R$ and $3/2$ of $1 - P_L$ would lead to an estimate of the total percent of the time that S guessed for the re-

---

[1] There is some evidence that such short latencies of inhibition are not probable, even within one eye, Barlow, FitzHugh and Kuffler (1957) present such evidence as an incidental finding in a study on the relationship of Ricco's law within one retinal ganglion cell receptive field of the cat. As the area of a circular stimulus to an RF increases, threshold for firing of the ganglion cell drops, until a critical diameter is reached. At this point the threshold rises again due to the inclusion of an inhibitory annulus in the stimulated area. This relationship was true for stimulus flashes of 380 msec but did not hold when the flash was only 7 msec; in this case the threshold tended toward an asymptote. The authors ascribe this to either a differential latency for inhibition and excitation or to a kind of inertia effect in which inhibition must build up over a longer period of time. With the added complication that central mechanisms involve, it can be seen that interocular inhibition probably has a reasonably long latency.

[2] The assumption that there are only two kinds of trials, those where S perceives and those where he guesses, is an oversimplification. Eriksen (1966b) has presented a more elaborate model based upon several states of partial information in the S following a stimulus presentation. These states are estimated via the S's confidence rating associated with each judgment. A two-state model such as described above will tend to overestimate the hit rate for two independent chances to perceive if the number of different information states existing in the S is greater than two. Confidence judgments were obtained from Ss in the present experiment but an error was made in allowing the Ss to distribute the confidence range over the entire range of experimental conditions. As a consequence the Ss used their high confidence judgments for the fused and unfused dichoptic conditions where more information was obtained and a higher confidence existed. Judgments on the monocular conditions were almost invariably given a confidence rating of "guess."

spective monocular presentations. If we let G_R and G_L represent the total percent of guess trials for monocular presentations to the respective eyes, then for a dichopic presentation $1 - G_RG_L$ is the percent of times the S would correctly perceive the form with one eye or the other or both. This value must then have added to it the number of correct guesses that occur on the occasions when S fails to perceive the form with either eye. Thus the percent correct form identifications to be expected if the eyes behaved as independent systems is given by

$$1 - G_RG_L + 1/3G_RG_L$$

This two-state model was applied to the data of the present experiment. Each S's monocular hit rates were used to compute what the hit rate should be based on two independent chances to perceive. These predicted values were then averaged through the six Ss and gave a predicted hit rate of 66%. This value agrees very closely with the values of 63 and 64% obtained under the two unfused dichopic conditions. As expected, the direction of error is toward overestimation.

The close agreement between the hit rates for the unfused dichopic conditions and the value predicted from the model for independence are strongly suggestive that the gain in the nonfused conditions over monocular stimulation represents what could be expected from two independent opportunities to perceive the stimulus. The superiority of the fused over the unfused dichopic conditions then represents an actual interocular summation process. This conclusion is reinforced by the fact that the above model for independence has been shown in several other perceptual situations to produce close predictions of the effects of independent opportunities to perceive (Eriksen, 1966b; Eriksen & Lappin, 1965; Eriksen & Lappin, in press).

While there seems to be a genuine summative effect in form identification, the summation does not appear to be complete. This can be seen by comparing the dichopic fused conditions with the monocular time 2T conditions.

In these four conditions the energy entering the visual system is the same and in the case of the dichopic fused successive condition the energy is distributed over the same time span as for the monocular 2T conditions. (The time 2T conditions are monocular stimulations at twice the exposure durations of the time T conditions.) For all Ss monocular stimulation in either eye at time 2T yields appreciably greater form identification than that obtained for the dichopic fused conditions. This failure to obtain complete dichopic summation might be attributed to inertia-like effects involved in the activation of the individual sensory receptor cells in the separate eyes. It also may reflect a basic contour development time such as reported by Kahneman (1965) which has to be duplicated in the separate eyes in the case of dichopic stimulation. There is also the possibility of uncorrelated nystagmic movements in the two eyes that lead to occasional trials on which the stimulations do not fall exactly on corresponding areas. This latter possibility could be ruled out using stabilized image techniques.

It is apparent from the data that there is no difference for the dichopic unfused stimulation whether the stimuli falling on noncorresponding areas follow homolateral or heterolateral pathways. If the two stimulations fall in the nasal retina of one eye and the temporal retina of the other both stimulations go to the same brain hemisphere as opposed to the case where both stimulations fall on the nasal or on the temporal retinas in the separate eyes. One might have anticipated a difference in these two methods of unfused stimulation on the basis of correlated sensitivity or alternatively, "noise" within the separate hemispheres. Failure to find a difference between homo- and heterolateral stimulation suggests that the noise or sensitivity is as uncorrelated within a hemisphere as across hemispheres. This is consistent with previous findings that have indicated that for stimulations in the fovea at least a degree or more apart, perceptual system error is uncorrelated at a given moment in time (Eriksen, 1966a; Eriksen, Munsinger, & Greenspon, 1966; Eriksen & Lappin, in press).

Summary

Visual form identification at brief durations was studied under: (a) monocular presentation; (b) dichopic presentation where the same form was presented successively on noncorresponding areas; and (c) dichopic presentation where the same form was presented on corresponding areas simultaneously and successively. Form identification for noncorresponding area dichopic presentation was at the level to be expected from 2 independent chances to perceive. Both simultaneous and successive dichopic presentation on corresponding areas gave identification accuracy significantly above the level predicted by the assumption of independence. However, the binocular summation was not complete. When the same amount of energy entering the visual system in a binocular presentation was given in a monocular stimulation, the latter condition gave significantly better identification.

References

Barlow, H. B., FitzHugh, R., & Kuffler, S. W. Change of organization in the receptive fields of the cat's retina during dark adaptation. *J. Physiol.*, 1957, *137*, 338–354.

Bouman, M. A. On foveal and peripheral interaction in binocular vision. *Optica Acta*, 1955, *1*, 177–183.

Collier, G. Probability of response and intertrial association as functions of monocular and binocular stimulation. *J. exp. Psychol.*, 1954, *47*, 75–83.

Eriksen, C. W. Temporal luminance summation effects in backward and forward masking. *Percept. & Psychophys.*, 1966a, *1*, 87–92.

Eriksen, C. W. Independence of successive inputs and uncorrelated error in visual form perception. *J. exp. Psychol.*, 1966b, *72*, 26–35.

Eriksen, C. W., & Lappin, J. S. Internal perceptual system noise and redundancy in simultaneous inputs in form identification. *Psychon. Sci.*, 1965, *2*, 351–352.

Eriksen, C. W., & Lappin, J. S. Independence in the perception of simultaneously presented forms at brief durations. *J. exp. Psychol.*, in press.

Eriksen, C. W., Munsinger, H. L., & Greenspon. T. S. Identification versus same-different judgment: An interpretation in terms of uncorrelated perceptual error. *J. exp. Psychol.*, 1966, *72*, 20–25.

Kahneman, D. Exposure duration and effective figure-ground contrast. *Quart. J. exp. Psychol.*, 1965, *17*, 308–314.

Levelt, W. J. M. Binocular brightness averaging and contour information. *Brit. J. Psychol.*, 1965, *56*, 1–13.

Matin, L. Binocular summation at the absolute threshold of peripheral vision. *J. Opt. Soc. Amer.*, 1962, *52*, 1276–1286.

Pirenne, M. H. Binocular and uniocular thresholds of vision. *Nature*, 1943, *48*, 43–63.

Shaad, Dorothy. Binocular summation in scotopic vision. *J. exp. Psychol.*, 1935, *4*, 391–413.

Wolf, E., & Zigler, M. J. Effects of uniocular and binocular excitation of the peripheral retina with test fields of various shapes on binocular summation. *J. Opt. Soc. Amer.*, 1963, *53*, 1199–1205.

CHAPTER *8*

Encoding, Rehearsal, Storage, and Retrieval

8.1 Nature of the Effect of Set on Perception*

RALPH NORMAN HABER

When a perceiver is given instruction to attend to only one of several attributes of a stimulus, he is able to report his perception of that attribute more accurately than he would be able to otherwise. Külpe, in 1904, first documented this effect experimentally, and, since then, a number of investigators have replicated the basic finding. The operations have typically involved either instructing the subject (S) as to which attribute he should attend, or providing S with a set of alternatives, from which the stimulus has been drawn. However, the same process is implied by implicit instructions emanating from S himself, such as would occur when a hungry man is looking for food. The experimental demonstration requires that the set cannot be satisfied by peripheral mechanisms such as eye movements or scanning of the stimulus to locate the relevant attributes, since, otherwise, the phenomena would not be as interesting.

This paper is not a general review of the effects of set on perception, although such a review is badly needed to bring Gibson's (1941) discussion up to date. Rather, the topic here is an examination of the two basic hypotheses that have been used to interpret set effects. As these issues were not so clearly developed at the time of Gibson's review, little reference can be made to his paper.

At least two basic and dissimilar interpretations have been suggested to explain the effects of set on perception. The older one, favored by Külpe and most of the investigators following him, including the "New Look" theorists in perception, appeals to a perceptual enhancement or "tuning" hypothesis (Dember, 1960; Postmast, 1963), whereby attending to a particular attribute of a stimulus results in a clearer and more vivid perception of that attribute—it stands out more. By the same token, the incidental attributes are not as clear and do not stand out. Thus, the perceptual tuning hypothesis places the locus of the effect of set in the perceptual system itself, occurring while the stimulus is being viewed.

The alternative hypothesis is that set has no effect on perception itself, but only on some aspects of the memory trace or on responses to that perceptual experience. Several varieties of this "response" hypothesis have been proposed: (a) The set facilitates relevant responses by S, increasing the probability that S can identify the stimulus in his report; (b) the set causes S to report the emphasized attributes first, before memory of the stimulus fades, thus allowing those attributes to be reported more accurately; (c) the set modifies the organization of the memory trace, so that the important attributes are remembered more accurately.

* From: Ralph Norman Haber, "Nature of the Effect of Set on Perception," *Psychological Review*, 1966, vol. 73, pp. 335–351. Copyright (1966) by the American Psychological Association, and reproduced by permission. Partial support for this research was provided by a grant from the United States Public Health Service (MH 03244) to the author at Yale University, where this work had been completed. I am most appreciative to Thomas Natsoulas and Maurice Hershenson for their many valuable comments on the manuscript.

The two basic hypotheses have wider application in perception and memory than just to problems of set. Behind them lies specification of one of the most difficult distinctions in any analysis of perceptual behavior. The tendency has been to assume that just because S was reporting immediately what he had perceived he was therefore performing a "perceptual" task. There is a crucial difference between reporting one's experience and reporting the attributes of stimuli that one remembers seeing. One task is perceptual, while the other deals with a memorial process. These must be conceptually differentiated, even if they may function similarly, and even if they proceed originally from the same sensory base. There are innumerable experiments that fail to make this distinction, and much of the controversy among perceptual theories results directly from this confusion. The two hypotheses under discussion in this paper reflect the distinction being proposed. To provide evidence relating to either or both of these requires that operational definitions be made for measurement of perceptual experience directly, or that deductions from these hypotheses specify operations in terms of memory alone that will still permit inferences concerning perceptual experience. As the present discussion will amply illustrate, neither of these conditions is well met in practice, though abundant data are available regarding both of these hypotheses.

Needless to say, the earliest experiments (e.g., Külpe, 1904; Rubin, 1913; Wilcocks, 1925; Yokahama, reported in Boring, 1924) were not designed to separate these two basic hypotheses, even though the hypotheses were discussed as alternative explanations for the various results.

Külpe's (1904) stimuli were groups of letters varying in color and location. Prior to most presentations, S was given a set to note only one of the several attributes of the stimulus: the number, position, or color of the letters, or the overall figure formed by the letters. For the remaining stimuli, no specific set was given. After the presentation, S was instructed to report the attributes as best he could, with no order specified. If he left any out, the experimenter (E) questioned him on those. Külpe found the S was more accurate in reporting the attribute for which he had paid attention prior to the presentation and was less accurate in reporting the others. Külpe suggested that the attention instructions facilitated the clarity of the percept.

Wilcocks (1925), responding to a criticism of Külpe by Rubin (1913), extended Külpe's method to include a memory variable. Wilcocks argued that if the reports of attributes after the presentation were in an uncontrolled order, it is possible that S might have forgotten some of them by the time he was questioned. Therefore, Wilcocks randomly arranged the order of reporting the attributes, though, in other respects, his experiment was similar to Külpe's. He found in general that accuracy was poorer the later an attribute was reported. Even so, he found that when order of report was controlled, the report of the attended-to attribute was more accurate than that of the unattended-to ones. Thus, while a memory variable was shown to be operative, it seemed to be independent of the enhancement effect. Therefore, Wilcocks concluded that Külpe's basic finding was replicated and could not be reduced to a memory process. Likewise, he accepted Külpe's interpretation of this process as perceptual enhancement.

Chapman (1932) used similar figures, where S could either count the letters, locate their positions, or name them. Instructions to attend to only one of these attributes were given in some sessions 4 seconds prior to the stimulus exposure, and in the remaining session 2 seconds following the exposure, in both cases by means of an illuminated display. Chapman's results showed that accuracy of report was higher when the attention instruction was given before the stimulus exposure, as compared to afterwards. Comments made by Ss indicated that the attended-to attribute was perceived more clearly during the actual exposure of the stimulus. They felt they did worse in the aftercondition because they had to keep too many things in mind. However, the comments also suggested that Ss' memory of the stimulus was affected by the type of set given. In the prior condition, they indicated that the memory for the irrelevant attributes faded and became indistinct. Thus, Chapman concluded that attention instructions given prior to the exposure both enhanced the perception of the stimulus itself during its actual exposure and, further, started in motion a differential forgetting process, where the relevant attribute was maintained in memory more accurately and for a longer time.

The evidence regarding the effect of set reviewed to this point supports a perceptual tuning hypothesis, primarily on the basis of Ss' postexperimental introspective comments. They report that the set-for attributes are clearer, stand out more, fade less rapidly, and the like. Support for at least one of the response hypotheses is also found, based on before-after differences, order of report effects, as well as introspective comments regarding fading memory. In light of the importance of an S's report of his perceptual experience, the comments regarding experience in these experiments must be given weight, even though they were not collected in any systematic or complete fashion nor subjected to any content analysis, and even though S was given no pretraining on the categories to use in his report. (See Postman, 1963, for a discussion of these criteria to be used for the evaluation of introspective reports in perceptual research.)

While an S in this type of experiment might be confident that he noticed changes in the perceptual characteristics of the stimulus as his set changed, no converging operations (Garner, Hake, and Eriksen, 1956) sufficient to demonstrate the validity of those reports were employed. Introspectively, it might be very difficult for an S to differentiate a rapidly fading memory, for example, from an image that was perceptually less clear. Unless experiments are designed to guarantee that S can make this distinction introspectively (and the ones just reviewed clearly do not offer such a guarantee), they cannot provide unequivocal evidence regarding either of these two hypotheses. Therefore, this evidence can be considered only suggestive support for the perceptual tuning hypotheses, as well as providing some evidence

for at least one of the versions of the response hypothesis.

The New Look in perception, beginning after World War II, accepted this evidence, however, as offering strong support for the perceptual tuning hypothesis (Bruner, 1957a, 1957b). A number of experiments were then reported that seemed to provide further support for this hypothesis, including ones by Neisser (1954), Postman and Bruner (1949), Bruner and Postman (1949), Krulee, Podell, and Ronco (1954), Green and Anderson (1956), Ross, Yarczower, and Williams (1956), Hoisington and Spencer (1958), to name only a few. For example, Postman and Bruner (1949) showed that if S was given a multiple set of alternatives (e.g., one of two stimulus words will be either a food or a color word—report only that one), he had higher recognition thresholds than if a single set was given (e.g., one of two stimulus words will be a food word —report only that one). Thus, they argued that since the recognition thresholds were manipulated by the set, the set had actually changed the perceptual characteristics of the stimulus.

Neisser (1954) presented Ss a list of words to study, indicating that some of them would later be shown tachistoscopically. He did in fact show some of the original words, but, in addition, exposed some that were homonyms of other words on the list. He found no facilitation of the homonyms, even though the original words were reported more rapidly. Since a word and its homonym require the same response, but only the original word was facilitated, he concluded that the presentation of the actual word prior to exposure must have made the word itself stand out perceptually.

Bruner and Postman (1949) gave Ss the set to expect to see normal playing cards, but in fact showed them cards in which the colors and suits did not agree (e.g., black hearts). While many Ss apparently ignored the incongruity and reported the cards as they would normally appear (e.g., red hearts or black clubs or spades), a few Ss reported seeing "compromise" perceptions (e.g., brown or purple hearts). These latter responses have been interpreted as supporting a perceptual hypothesis, since no response facilitation could be expected for a category such as purple hearts that S had never seen before.

Bruner (1957b) has offered an intriguing suggestion regarding the relationship between the two hypotheses under discussion. He proposes that perceptual experience (the concern of the first hypothesis) is the result or end product of categorization (the concern of the second hypothesis). Thus, an object is experienced or perceived *only after* it has been properly classified—that is, responded to. Prior to its identification, the perceptual experience of a stimulus is blurred and indistinct. In the present context, then, if the perceiver has a set which facilitates classification of the stimulus, it also then facilitates the clarity of its percept.

Bruner and Potter (1964) present some evidence relevant to one aspect of this notion. They show S a common, everyday object extremely out of focus and then gradually increase the focus until it is perfectly clear. During the period of increasing focus, S is required to give a running commentary of what he thinks the picture contains, from which the point of correct identification can be determined. They found that if the focus increases very slowly, so that S has extensive viewing during which he cannot correctly classify the stimulus, he requires a greater amount of focus before correct identification occurs. From this the authors argued that the extent to which S misclassifies the picture during the very fuzzy presentations prolongs the time before he can see it clearly. Presumably, during this time, S is testing his classifications against the fuzzy image, and he has to reject the wrong classifications he made before he can concentrate on testing correct ones. Only after he tries and checks the correct one does he come to see the picture clearly.

Obviously, this kind of experiment, interesting as it is, cannot provide much evidence for as complex a position as Bruner is espousing here. He has to make too many additional assumptions to have a clear-cut analysis. A somewhat more relevant, though still indirect, test of this notion was reported by Hershenson and Haber (1965). These authors had previously found that the clarity of letters of words increased markedly if they were flashed several times, even when on the first flash S could see none or few of the letters (Haber, 1965a; Haber and Hershenson, 1965). However, the rate of increase in clarity for Turkish words was slightly faster than that for English words. It was assumed that S would be less likely to misclassify what he knew was a Turkish word from only partial information, since he knew it would be a totally unfamiliar word. Therefore, this result was interpreted to imply that when S made incorrect anticipatory classificatory responses for the English words, this slowed down the development of their clarity.

Even given these kinds of data, Bruner's notion faces serious theoretical problems on other counts, as, for example, how one can see something that is novel when he cannot classify it correctly. Therefore, until more than this meager and indirect evidence is available, little else can be said for this version of a linkage between the two processes.

An independent line of research, originally led by Ames (e.g., 1951), has provided the basis of the Transactionalist theory of perception. In this context, many demonstrations were created to show how an S's assumptions based on past experience or knowledge directly affect his perceptual experience. In one of the most striking of these, a physically rotating trapezoidal-shaped window appears to oscillate back and forth, and to be rectangular in shape. This is a very powerful perceptual experience, experienced by nearly every viewer, so that it is difficult to explain in terms of any kind of response process. Haber (1965b) has recently shown that if Ss are given extensive experience with the apparatus and knowledge of the theory behind the illusion, their perceptual experience changes so the majority of Ss report seeing the nonillusory rotation of the trapezoidal figure. Numerous other examples of these demonstrations can also be used to support the effects of S's assumptions (set) on his perceptual experience directly, in ways suggesting that response processes are inoperative.

Shortly after the beginnings of the New Look, strong interest was revived in alternative interpretations involving response and memory processes. Many of the New Look experiments were scrutinized for evidence of these processes or for faults in design. Accompanying this methodological concern was the new development in theorizing about methods of research in perception. The most important single paper in this regard is by Garner *et al.* (1956). While not taking sides with respect to these two hypotheses, Garner *et al.* point out quite persuasively the inadequacy of nearly all previous research to decide among the interpretations of the effects of set, as well as motivation and implicit instructions, on perception. They suggest several nonperceptual interpretations of these patterns of results and present the concept of converging operations as an experimental design to provide tests between the two hypotheses. They are particularly concerned with the possibility that the set limits the number of alternatives from which S must make his response, thus increasing the probability that the correct response will be made, independent of any perceptual enhancement. Eriksen (1958, 1960, 1962) has continued this position, arguing that nearly all research in this area has failed to differentiate the two hypotheses satisfactorily, and that since from his point of view the response interpretations are more parsimonious, there is no evidence to support a perceptual interpretation. His position has received added support from a number of recent studies.

Lawrence and Coles (1954) argued, along with Chapman (1932), that a perceptual tuning hypothesis has to predict that a set given before the stimulus, as compared to one given afterwards, will provide greater facilitation of report. They go further and suggest a dual hypothesis: Perhaps perceptual enhancement does occur if a prior set is given, but, when given afterwards, facilitation could be due to some selectivity in the memory process. If this were true, then an experiment like Chapman's would not distinguish between the purely perceptual and the dual hypothesis, since they might both be correct.

Lawrence and Coles (1954) used pictures of single familiar objects, with the set administered by projecting on the screen, either immediately before or after the stimulus exposure, the names of four alternatives for the stimulus. The alternatives were very similar to one another for some trials, while on others they were quite discrete. One group of Ss had no alternatives at all; this served as a control on the use of the alternatives.

The results showed that giving alternatives of either type increased the accuracy of recognition of the stimuli, as compared with the no-alternative control group. Hence, the effect of set was demonstrated. However, alternatives given after the exposure were just as useful as those given before (which stands in contrast to Chapman's before-after difference).

This failure to replicate Chapman's before-after difference was not considered crucial, since the equality may have been due to perceptual enhancement from the before set and memory selection from the after set—the two processes just balancing each other. However, they also failed to find any interaction between the before-after sets and the type of alternatives (similar or discrete). They had argued that a perceptual hypothesis would predict no difference between the two types of alternatives when they are given before the presentation, since the correct alternative would stand out whether other alternatives were similar or not. On the other hand, since the after set could not affect enhancement, it must affect memory, which should show a differential effect of the two types of alternatives—discrete ones being more effective in facilitating correct recognition than similar ones. Failure to find evidence in support of this prediction (discrete alternatives consistently facilitated recognition more than similar ones for both before and after sets) led Lawrence and Coles (1954) to reject any form of the perceptual tuning hypothesis, and to argue that the effect of set was via some selective facilitation of memory processes.

By implication, Lawrence and Coles provided a possible explanation for Chapman's before-after difference—the one they failed to replicate. Under the assumption that the entire effect of set is caused by memory and response processes, the earlier the set is given, the greater the opportunity it will have to provide facilitation of these processes. Thus, even if there is no perceptual tuning, administering the set prior to the exposures gives S just that much more time to organize his memory. Sets given after the stimulus presentation have to act on an already fading memory trace and are at a disadvantage compared to a set given before the trace has weakened. As the delay between the exposure and the set increases, the superiority of the prior alternatives should increase. Since Chapman had a longer delay than Lawrence and Coles, this slight time difference may have accounted for the different outcome in the two experiments.

An interrelated group of studies by Long, Reid, and Henneman (1960), Long, Henneman, and Garvey (1960), and Reid, Henneman, and Long (1960) has used a model of set as a response limiter, similar to Garner et al.'s (1956) notion, whereby set "increases perceptual accuracy by increasing the probabilities of certain responses and decreases the probabilities of others in the various response classes [Long, Reid, and Henneman, 1960, p. 554]." Most of their experiments used single letters as stimuli, degraded in clarity, with set manipulated by giving S a group of alternative letters, of which the stimulus letter would be one. The alternatives were given either before or after the exposure. They found that decreasing the number of alternatives increased the accuracy, regardless of whether the alternatives were given before or after the exposure. From this they concluded, as did Lawrence and Coles (1954), that set was acting on the selection of responses, and not on perception itself. Greater accuracy was also found if the alternatives were drawn from an exclusive subset rather than from the entire alphabet. Further, they showed that set effects could be produced by restriction of the categories (rather than alternatives) into which the stimulus might fall. This is somewhat similar to the Postman and Bruner (1949) finding, but was found to be true regardless of whether the restriction was given before or after the stimulus. This greatly weakens Postman and Bruner's contention that restriction of category affects the perception of the stimulus itself. All of these findings are consistent with a response-limiting interpretation of set.

However, Long, Reid, and Henneman (1960) also found and replicated several before-after differences. One was found when only two alternatives were provided, so that being told the stimulus was one of two particular letters before the flash helped S report the letter more accurately than if such a set was given 1 or 2 seconds after the flash. Another before-after difference occurred in an auditory version of their experiments, when four alternatives were presented either before or after the stimulus letter was spoken in noise. Finally, when two degraded letters were presented and S was asked which of the two was a specific alternative, they found that specifying the search letter before the presentation facilitated correct discrimination, as compared to a later specification.

Each of these findings is inconsistent with the response interpretations of set, and it is not clear how they might be explained other than by some form of perceptual enhancement. The Lawrence and Coles' explanation—that the earlier the set is given, the greater its opportunity to facilitate memory processes—will not work, since it should follow that the greater the number of alternatives, the greater the effect of an earlier set. "Increasing the alternatives implies that the number of discriminating characteristics between them become more restrictive, and thus are more likely to be lost in the trace [Lawrence and Coles, 1954, p. 213]." However, these findings, inconsistent with a response interpretation, occurred primarily with a few alternatives, and no before-after differences were found with larger number of alternatives.

In a different line of research, Taub (1965), following the work of Teichner, Reilly, and Sadler (1961) and Teichner and Sadler (1962), presented an array of letters to S, asking him to report all of them. The number of letters in the array, the exposure duration, and the relative value of each of the letters (set) were varied. Value was manipulated by assigning points for correct reports of letters, with differential value attached to letters from the first and second half of the alphabet. Taub found that value affected accuracy (a set effect), but primarily through a reduction in accuracy of the low-valued letters, rather than an increase in the high-valued ones. This occurred in spite of the finding that the first letter reported from an array was most likely to be one of high value.

Taub's (1965) experiment is most relevant to the issues of this discussion because of the similarity of a prediction he makes to the Lawrence and Coles' (1954) similar-discrete difference presented earlier:

> . . . if a major selective process in perception was involved, then the size of the difference between high- and low-value letters should vary inversely with length of exposure. That is, a perceptual set, which would make the higher value categories easier and quicker to identify (Bruner, 1957), would occur at those conditions where there is little time to detect and discriminate between the categories, but have little effect at longer exposures where all letters would be equally discriminable. Predictions from a selective recall point of view would be the opposite. That is, as exposure time increases and the rate of memory loading decreases, Ss would have more time to selectively code the categories which are detected. Thus, a selective memory process explanation would predict increasing differences in response to value as exposure time increases [p. 142].

Since Taub found unequivocal evidence that increasing exposure time increased the differences in accuracy between high- and low-value words, he rejects a perceptual tuning explanation in favor of some variety of the memory hypothesis—especially a selective-recall one. However, Taub used relatively long exposure durations (500–2,500 milliseconds), so that visual searching clearly occurred for the longer presentations. Therefore, his data are equivocal with respect to this issue, since S has opportunity to seek out the high-value items if given sufficient time, and this would imply nothing about the effects on perception at all. Thus, it appears that, while the prediction is relevant, it requires a presentation time considerably shorter than Taub used to test it adequately.

A different type of experiment was reported by Lawrence and LaBerge (1956) in which they were concerned with the response hypothesis of a fading memory. The stimuli were pairs of cards from the Wisconsin Card Sorting Task, with an attention-instruction set given only before the exposures, by indicating the relative value for each attribute correctly reported. For one group of Ss, all three attributes (number, color, shape) received equal value; for another, one attribute was always emphasized by offering 100 times as much money as each of the other two attributes. All three attributes had to be reported, but S determined the order. A third group, with equal set, had the order in which the three attributes were to be reported controlled and varied from trial to trial.

When the emphasis and equal conditions were compared, they found that the effect of set appeared to increase accuracy for the attended-to attribute and decrease it for the other two. They also found that the decrement from first to third report under the equal condition was about the same magnitude as the difference between the critical and incidental attributes in the emphasis condition. While they did not measure the order of report when unequal attention instructions had been given, Lawrence and LaBerge (1956) argued that the set effect could have been entirely determined by the order in which S reported the attributes. That is, if, whenever one attribute was critical, S always reported that one first, then the accuracy of the critical attribute would be higher because it had been reported first.

Thus, Lawrence and LaBerge suggest that no assumption need be made about reorganization of memory or changes in response probabilities, but only that all memory for the stimulus is slowly fading. Whatever is reported first will be more accurate than later-reported items. This hypothesis is very similar to one Wilcocks (1925) tested but rejected. Lawrence and LaBerge cannot test this in their data since they did not measure the preferred order of report when the attention instructions made one attribute critical.

This test was provided in experiments by Harris and Haber (1963) and Haber (1964a). The same stimulus materials and procedures for inducing sets were used, but each S was tested under all set conditions, including a forced order of report specified by E on half of the trials, and a free order on the other half. S could report the stimulus in whatever order he chose (though he had to indicate the one he used). Under forced order of report, when just the first attribute reported was analyzed, if that first report was of a critical attribute, it was more accurately reported than if it was of an incidental one. The same was true for the second and third reports. Thus, Lawrence and LaBerge (1956) were incorrect when they argued that the set effect could be explained in terms of order of report. Holding order of report constant, the set effect was still obtained. Harris and Haber (1963) did find that some Ss reported the critical attributes first if they were allowed to choose their own order of report. But even granting this, it did not account for the set effect. Thus, this simpler hypothesis of Lawrence and LaBerge was shown to be inadequate.

While the findings of Harris and Haber (1963) and Haber (1964a) indicated that fading memory coupled with a varying order of report could not explain the set effect, they did discover what may be a more explicit determiner of set—namely, the encoding processes by which S translates the percept of the stimulus into memory. Some pilot work had indicated that nearly all Ss spontaneously encoded this type of stimulus into words and silently rehearsed the message repeatedly until all of the attributes had been reported. Further, with these stimuli, it was found that Ss used one of two dissimilar strategies to accomplish this encoding. Some Ss encoded it by separating the stimulus into objects on the left and right (e.g., one red triangle, three blue stars). The remaining Ss encoded it by separating the stimulus into its three dimensions (e.g., red blue, triangle star, one three). The order of the dimensions in this latter Dimensions code could of course be varied without disturbing the strategy, while the former Objects coding strategy has its order of encoding fixed by the rules of English syntax.

To investigate the effects of differential coding strategy on perception, Harris and Haber (1963) and Haber (1964a) trained Ss to use one of the two coding strategies. In both of these experiments, an effect of set and of order of report was found. (Emphasized dimensions were reported more accurately than unemphasized dimensions, holding order of report constant, and the dimensions reported first were more accurate than those reported later.) However, both of these effects strongly interacted with coding strategy. So strongly, in fact, that nearly all of these effects were accounted for by the performance of those Ss using the Dimensions code. Thus, those Ss who used the Objects code, based on English syntax, were not significantly more accurate on the emphasized, as compared to the unemphasized, dimensions. Further, regarding the order of report effect, as shown in the replication study (Haber, 1964a), the difference between the early and later reported dimensions was smaller for those Ss using the Objects code than for those using the Dimensions code. Finally, Ss using the Objects code had a greater overall accuracy of report, regardless of condition.

It seems clear therefore that the set and order of report effect can in large part be explained by the operations of the coding strategies themselves. These results suggest that the set effect stems as much from a change in the initial organization of the memory of the stimulus produced by the strategy by which S encodes the stimulus, rather than from a facilitation of contact with an already organized memory or through the effects of a fading memory or through the changes in the probability of the correct response being available.

However, the results on coding strategy do not indicate the reasons for the differences between these two coding strategies. To assess these, Haber (1964b) conducted a third study, using the same stimuli, strategy-training procedures, and set manipulation, but requiring S to verbalize his encoding and rehearsal of the encoded stimulus so it could be tape-recorded. Each S was instructed to begin talking immediately after the flash with his verbal encoding of the stimulus, and to repeat this encoding over and over for 20 seconds.

Haber found that Ss using the Objects code could begin encoding considerably faster and complete encoding more rapidly than Ss using the Dimensions code. Thus, the two strategies differed sharply in the speed with which they could translate the stimulus into memory. If there is some after-image or short-term memory of the stimulus, lasting perhaps several hundred milliseconds beyond its offset (Averbach and Coriell, 1961; Mackworth, 1963; Sperling, 1960), then the strategy that can translate this image into memory most rapidly is more likely to have that encoding based on a good image that will allow it to be more accurate. In this way, one can account for the difference in overall accuracy between the strategies. Similarly, if one strategy encodes slower than the other, then presumably the items it encoded last would be poorer in accuracy, which would suggest that the order of report effect could also be accounted for by the differences in the speed of encoding. Finally, it was found that the Dimensions coders nearly always encoded the critical dimension first, while the Objects coders always followed the same order—that of English syntax. Thus, the set variable can also be explained by the differential speed of encoding. If the attributes encoded first are always the critical ones, leaving the others to be encoded later from a rapidly fading image of the stimulus, it is not surprising that the critical attribute is reported more accurately. This does not depend upon order of *report,* as Lawrence and LaBerge thought, but on order of *encoding.*

The two strategies also differed in the frequency of errors made after the initial encoding, with transpositions, intrusions, and omissions occurring significantly more frequently during the rehearsal process in the Dimensions code. This could further account for the order of report effect—the items reported later would be based upon a rehearsed encoding that had undergone some erroneous change. This would be true whether S was reporting the stimulus attributes in an order he chose or in one forced upon him by the experiment.

This experiment suggests, then, that the coding strategies differ in two important ways: the speed of encoding, and the resistance to errors during rehearsal. It further suggests that these two differences could account for both the effect of set and the effect of the order of report in the experiments by Lawrence and LaBerge

(1956). Harris and Haber (1963), and Haber (1964a), as well as by implication some of the earlier experiments discussed above. For example, the study by Neisser (1954) can now be explained in terms of encoding, without having to make any assumptions about the nature of the percept. This alternative explanation suggests that while the response given to the homonyms NO and KNOW is identical, the encoding of those two words into memory would be quite different. One reason for the difference could be that encoding is faster for words one expects to see. Thus, encoding of the unexpected KNOW begins later, takes longer, and therefore uses a progressively more degraded trace. While there has been no direct test of this explanation, it seems reasonable that the more prepared S is for what he will see, the more likely it is that he will have an appropriate strategy and category available in which to encode the stimulus.

It should be noted that variation in encoding is not the only nonperceptual interpretation of the Neisser (1954) experiment and of experiments similar to it. Since Neisser's Ss are in a guessing situation, where they must guess the word from presumably only fragments of the letters given perceptually (at least on the first few flashes), they will have more success guessing those words they were given a set to see (e.g., NO will be easier to guess than its homonym KNOW, which they had not experienced in the preliminary training). This interpretation has been used by Eriksen and Browne (1956) in a related type of study. It says nothing about increased clarity of the stimulus caused by the prior set, but only that such a set may facilitate guessing of the correct word when only a few pieces of it are seen perceptually.

The encoding analysis advanced above is a more specific hypothesis about the outcome of the Neisser experiment than the more general guessing one. It attempts to specify the translation of the visual image, as it is generated on the retina by the stimulus, into some kind of memorial trace or persistence after the stimulus terminates. While the visual image may persist for a brief time after the stimulus offset, in the form of a short-term memory, it is crucial that perceptual theory take into account the processes that occur after that short-term memory has faded. Since it is obvious that memory for stimuli persists long after the stimulus (and any attendant short-term memory and afterimages) has terminated, no perceptual theory can be complete without cognizance of this persistence of memory.

Specifically, the encoding explanation being discussed here suggests that most visual stimuli are remembered by being encoded into previously learned linguistic units, usually words. This encoding takes place while the stimulus (or its brief short-term memory) is still present, and whatever has not been encoded after the stimulus has faded is entirely lost and not available in permanent memory. This is not to deny that a few Ss may use some nonlinguistic code, especially for nonlinguistic stimuli. However, certainly with respect to the kinds of materials of greatest interest to psychologists, encoding into words is the most probable basic strategy.

Variation in the adequacy of encoding can presumably depend upon a number of variables. The experiments reported above on encoding of Wisconsin Card Sorting Task concept cards suggest that when a number of highly familiar dimensions of a stimulus must be encoded quickly, accuracy of encoding depends upon whether S has at his disposal a strategy that lends itself to rapid coding, preferably without having both to learn the code as well as perform the encoding operations. Thus, using a highly overlearned syntax for the order of encoding is preferable to one for which S must think about what should be encoded next.

In many perceptual experiments, the problem is not one of speed of encoding familiar dimensions, but of encoding degraded and often unpredictable stimuli. For example, a typical trial of a word-recognition experiment presents S with a fragmentary flash which first has to be maintained in memory and then that memory compared with possible alternatives of what the original stimulus must have been. If S has no adequate way of maintaining the fragments in memory, he will not be able to test any hypotheses about the stimuli once it terminates.

Thus, in most perceptual situations, two sources of variation are present—the adequacy of encoding a visual image, often imperfect, into memory, and the success of guessing what stimulus gave rise to those remembered fragments. To take an extreme though not too uncommon instance, stimuli for which S has no code for translaton into memory are notoriously difficult to remember, even though S may perform perfectly on simultaneous discriminations with such stimuli. That is, he can make all of the appropriate responses to the stimulus while it is present, but cannot reconstruct it after it terminates. Most people experience this difficulty in describing colors, tastes, odors, and feelings from recollection. It is usually suggested that they do not have the appropriate words or other codes with which to maintain them in memory. These examples represent instances of excellent matching between the stimulus and prior experience, but very poor encoding of the stimulus into memory. Thus, short-duration presentations or delayed responses would show poor performance. One exception to this is found for those few people with eidetic imagery (see Haber and Haber, 1964) who are capable of maintaining a nearly perfect visual image of the stimulus for many minutes. These eidetic perceivers seem to do little if any encoding of the stimulus while the image persists, so that once it fades their memory of the stimulus is little better than that of more typical individuals.

Evidence relating to this specific distinction between encoding the percept and then matching the resultant memory to prior knowledge is very sparse, though it is beginning to accumulate. For example, McKinney (in press), by presenting single letters continuously and asking S to report changes or fragmentation in the percept of the letter, found that if the letter was embedded in a series of other letters which S was labeling as letters, much less change was reported than if it was embedded in a series of geometric designs for which no labels were suggested. Thus, the stability of the percept is increased when the object can be labeled (an operation probably equivalent to encoding).

Hintzman (1965), following work by Conrad (1964), presented lists of 8 symbols, selected so that matched pairs of them would be auditorily confusable (e.g., 2 with Q, 3 with T, etc.). Analyses of errors showed that auditory confusions were far greater than chance, suggesting that Ss were maintaining these symbols in memory by some type of auditory encoding and rehearsal. This was explicitly found when, for the half of trials on which white noise was used to prevent S from hearing his own thoughts, S produced overt rehearsal. However, Hintzman also reports that some Ss did not use rote aural encoding, but rather attempted to classify the string of symbols (e.g., to make up a mathematical formula). Such Ss made few aural confusions. Thus, the nature of the coding adopted by S determined the pattern of errors made. This, of course, was a situation where the symbols from which each presentation was drawn were well known in advance. Hence the matching of an encoded memory to prior experience was presumably perfect, with all of the variance in the encoding of that memory.

Gruber, Kulkin, and Schwartz (1965) presented a paired-associate learning task in which half of the Ss were instructed to attempt to form a visual image between the two members of each pair. These Ss had higher recall scores for all exposure durations, ranging from 1–24 seconds. Here, again, it would seem that aids for encoding of perceptually presented familiar material increase the accuracy of its encoded representation in memory.

The investigation and manipulation of coding variables in general in the study of perceptual and cognitive processes is becoming more extensive and is playing a far greater role in theory than 5–10 years ago. Much of the impetus for this has been Miller's (1956) paper on coding effects in information processing, although scattered work was reported before (e.g., Fitts, 1954; Pollack, 1952). More recently, however, a number of important experimental and theoretical papers have applied encoding processes to a wide range of perceptual data and problems (e.g., Broadbent, 1958; Conrad, 1964; Glanzer and Clark, 1962, 1963; Mackworth, 1963; Miller, Galanter, and Pribrim, 1960; Sperling, 1963).

The three studies on coding strategies by Haber have shown the importance of coding processes in the investigation of the effects of set. They suggest the possibility that many of

the effects of set on reports of perception can be explained by differential encoding processes. Many studies have reported that the emphasized attribute of a stimulus can be reported more accurately than other attributes, irrespective of when the instruction for emphasis is given. However, in the Haber studies, this finding is dependent upon the nature of the encoding strategy—only one type of strategy will produce this emphasis-set effect. Similarly, only one type of strategy leads to an order of report effect. Thus, whether attention instructions (and restriction of alternatives) will lead to a set effect may depend upon whether S's encoding strategy is susceptible to such a manipulation.

An alternative possibility is that on the trials when the set is given to S, he changes his strategy so as to maximize the payoff from the set. In the Haber experiments, only a few Ss varied their strategies from condition to condition—too few to provide any kind of analysis of their performance. But this is a very likely possibility, particularly if the various set conditions make quite different demands upon Ss' reports. Since the studies by Haber are the only ones that have shown this higher-order dependency of set on encoding, further research will be needed before these possibilities can be analyzed successfully.

Conclusions

Evidence on the effects of set has been reviewed with respect to two basically different hypotheses—set enhances the percept of the stimulus while S is actually viewing it; set facilitates report of the stimulus without affecting its percept.

At least three varieties of nonperceptual hypotheses were discussed: (*a*) response-limiting or response-probability changes, (*b*) order of report changes coupled with a fading memory, and (*c*) reorganization of the memory process itself. The second alternative does not seem to be a necessary condition for the production of set effects, since even when order of report is controlled the effects of set are still found without loss in magnitude. The supporting evidence for the response-probability interpretation is extensive, in that the magnitude of the set effect varies with the manipulation of the probabilities of responses or limitations on responses. The third alternative, reorganization of the memory process mediated by S's coding strategy, is strongly supported in the results of three studies by Harris and Haber (1963) and Haber (1964a, 1964b). Further, Haber's interpretations of those results suggests that the response-probability explanation may be reduced to memory reorganization (encoding), so that only one nonperceptual hypothesis may be needed.

While this review then suggests a narrowing of the number of nonperceptual alternatives, it provides less resolution to which of the two basic hypotheses is correct. The problem of analysis is still very complex—many of the experiments discussed provided clear-cut evidence for response or memory explanations, but without simultaneously demonstrating a lack of a perceptual effect. That is, finding evidence in favor of one hypothesis does not disprove the other, since they are not incompatible, only alternative. There is no reason to doubt that both may be correct and occurring together.

It is likely that a set effect created by differential value (e.g., Harris and Haber, 1963; Külpe, 1904; Lawrence and LaBerge, 1956) is mediated primarily or perhaps totally by characteristics of S's coding strategy. However, even with this, the Harris and Haber (1963) and Haber (1964a, 1964b) experiments do not rule out perceptual changes, since they had no converging operations sufficient to separate percept from coding effects. Their argument took the form that the set effect was present only in Ss using one type of strategy and not in Ss using another—therefore the set effect must have been due to properties of the strategy. Further, when the strategies themselves were examined, temporal and interference processes were found that were sufficient to account for the differential set effects between the two strategies, though again, this does not rule out perceptual effects completely.

So what conclusions does this evidence permit? Most Ss feel an increase in perceptual clarity occurs under appropriate set conditions, though their reports give no guarantee that they can really distinguish felt clarity from a better memory. On the other hand, there is no reason to doubt their reports either. Just because the evidence supporting response processes is clear does not imply that perceptual enhancement does not occur. Further, Bruner and Postman's (1949) finding of compromise perceptions and the strength of the trapezoidal illusion, to pick just two examples, make it difficult to doubt that at least some kinds of sets affect perception directly.

Therefore, this review must conclude inconclusively with respect to a choice between the two hypotheses. Some evidence exists to support each of them, and some exists which favors one over the other. But there is none that supports one while disproving the other. The issue is still crucial in perceptual theory, and obviously much more very careful research is needed. There is adequate demonstration now of the effects of set on both perception and responses. It still remains to show the conditions under which each will occur.

Summary

To explain the effects of set on reports of perceptual experience 2 hypotheses are elaborated —set enhances the percept directly, or set facilitates responses and memorial organization of the perceptual experience that itself was uneffected by the set. Extensive research is reviewed that is relevant to each of these hypotheses, especially studies that attempt to differentiate them.

References

Ames, A., Jr. Visual perception and the rotating trapezoidal window. *Psychological Monographs,* 1951, 65(7, Whole No. 324).

Averbach, E., and E. S. Coriell. Short-term memory in vision. *Bell System Technical Journal,* 1961, 40, 309–328.

Boring, E. G. Attribute and sensation. *American Journal of Psychology*, 1924, *35*, 301–304.

Broadbent, D. E. *Perception and communication.* New York: Pergamon Press, 1958.

Bruner, J. S. Neural mechanisms in perception. *Psychological Review*, 1957, *64*, 340–358. (a)

Bruner, J. S. On perceptual readiness. *Psychological Review*, 1957, *64*, 123–204. (b)

Bruner, J. S., and L. Postman. On the perception of incongruity: A paradigm. *Journal of Personality*, 1949, *18*, 206–223.

Bruner, J. S., and M. C. Potter. Interference in visual recognition. *Science*, 1964, *144*, 424–425.

Chapman, D. W. Relative effects of determinate and indeterminant Aufgaben. *American Journal of Psychology*, 1932, *44*, 163–174.

Conrad, R. Acoustic confusions in immediate memory. *British Journal of Psychology*, 1964, *55*, 75–84.

Dember, W. *The psychology of perception.* New York: Holt, 1960.

Eriksen, C. W. Unconscious processes. In M. R. Jones (Ed.), *Nebraska symposium on motivation: 1958.* Lincoln: University of Nebraska Press, 1958. Pp. 169–226.

Eriksen, C. W. Discrimination and learning without awareness: A methodological survey and evaluation. *Psychological Review*, 1960, *67*, 279–300.

Eriksen, C. W. Figments, fantasies and follies: A search for the subconscious mind. In C. W. Eriksen (Ed.), *Behavior and awareness.* Durham: Duke University Press, 1962. Pp. 3–26.

Eriksen, C. W., and C. T. Browne. An experimental and theoretical analysis of perceptual defense. *Journal of Abnormal and Social Psychology*, 1956, *52*, 224–230.

Fitts, P. M. The influence of response coding on performance in motor tasks. In J. Macmillan (Ed.), *Current trends in information theory.* Pittsburgh: University of Pittsburgh Press, 1954. Pp. 169–226.

Garner, W. R., H. W. Hake, and C. W. Eriksen. Operationism and the concept of perception. *Psychological Review*, 1956, *63*, 317–329.

Gibson, J. J. A critical review of the concept of set in contemporary experimental psychology. *Psychological Review*, 1941, *38*, 781–817.

Glanzer, M., and W. H. Clark. Accuracy of perceptual recall: An analysis of organization. *Journal of Verbal Learning and Verbal Behavior*, 1962, *1*, 289–299.

Glanzer, M., and W. H. Clark. The verbal loop hypothesis: Binary numbers. *Journal of Verbal Learning and Verbal Behavior*, 1963, *2*, 301–309.

Green, B. F., and L. K. Anderson. Color coding in a visual search task. *Journal of Experimental Psychology*, 1956, *51*, 19–24.

Gruber, H. E., A. Kulkin, and P. L. Schwartz. The effect of exposure time on mnemonic processing in paired-associate learning. Paper read at Eastern Psychological Association, Atlantic City, April 1965.

Haber, R. N. A replication of selective attention and coding in visual perception. *Journal of Experimental Psychology*, 1964, *67*, 402–404. (a)

Haber, R. N. The effects of coding strategy on perceptual memory. *Journal of Experimental Psychology*, 1964, *68*, 257–362. (b)

Haber, R. N. The effect of prior knowledge of the stimulus on word recognition processes. *Journal of Experimental Psychology*, 1965, *69*, 282–286. (a)

Haber, R. N. Limited modification of the trapezoid illusion with experience. *American Journal of Psychology*, 1965, *78*, 651–655. (b)

Haber, R. N., and R. B. Haber. Eidetic imagery: I. Frequency. *Perceptual and Motor Skills*, 1964, *19*, 131–138.

Haber, R. N., and M. Hershenson. The effects of repeated brief exposures on the growth of a percept. *Journal of Experimental Psychology*, 1965, *69*, 40–46.

Harris, C. S., and R. N. Haber. Selective attention and coding in visual perception. *Journal of Experimental Psychology*, 1963, *65*, 328–333.

Hershenson, M., and R. N. Haber. The role of meaning in the perception of briefly exposed words. *Canadian Journal of Psychology*, 1965, *19*, 42–46.

Hintzman, D. L. Classification and aural coding in short-term memory. *Psychonomic Science*, 1965, *3*, 161–162.

Hoisington, L. B., and C. Spencer. Specific set and the perception of subliminal material. *American Journal of Psychology*, 1958, *71*, 263–269.

Krulee, G. K., J. E. Podell, and P. G. Ronco. Effect of number of alternatives and set on the visual discrimination of numerals. *Journal of Experimental Psychology*, 1954, *48*, 75–80.

Külpe, O. Versuche uber Abstraktion. *Berlin International Congress of Experimental Psychology*, 1904, 56–68.

Lawrence, D. H., and G. R. Coles. Accuracy of recognition with alternatives before and after the stimulus. *Journal of Experimental Psychology*, 1954, *47*, 208–214.

Lawrence, D. H., and D. L. LaBerge. Relationship between recognition accuracy and order of reporting stimulus dimensions. *Journal of Experimental Psychology*, 1956, *51*, 12–18.

Long, E. R., R. H. Henneman, and W. D. Garvey. An experimental analysis of set: The role of sensemodality. *American Journal of Psychology*, 1960, *73*, 563–567.

Long, E. R., L. S. Reid, and R. H. Henneman. An experimental analysis of set: Variables influencing the identification of ambiguous visual stimulus-objects. *American Journal of Psychology*, 1960, *73*, 553–562.

Mackworth, J. F. The relation between the visual image and post-perceptual immediate memory. *Journal of Verbal Learning and Verbal Behavior*, 1963, *2*, 75–85.

McKinney, J. P. Verbal meaning and perceptual stability. *Canadian Journal of Psychology*, 1966, in press.

Miller, G. A. The magical number seven, plus or

minus two: Some limits on our capacity for processing information. *Psychological Review,* 1956, *63,* 81–97.

Miller, G. A., E. Galanter, and K. Pribrim. *Plans and the structure of behavior.* New York: McGraw-Hill, 1960.

Neisser, U. An experimental distinction between perceptual processes and verbal response. *Journal of Experimental Psychology,* 1954, *47,* 399–402.

Pollack, I. The assimilation of sequentially encoded information. *HumRRO Research Laboratory Memo Report,* 1952, No. 25.

Postman, L. Perception and learning. In S. Koch (Ed.), *Psychology: The study of a science.* Vol. 5. New York: McGraw-Hill, 1963. Pp. 30–113.

Postman, L., and J. S. Bruner. Multiplicity of set as a determiner of behavior. *Journal of Experimental Psychology,* 1949, *39,* 369–377.

Reid, L. S., R. H. Henneman, and E. R. Long. An experimental analysis of set: The effect of categorical restriction. *American Journal of Psychology,* 1960, *73,* 568–572.

Ross, S., Y. Yarczower, and G. M. Williams. Recognition thresholds for words as a function of set and similarity. *American Journal of Psychology,* 1956, *69,* 82–86.

Rubin, E. Bericht uber experimentelle Untersuchungen der Abstraktion. *Zeitschrift für Psychologie,* 1913, *63,* 386–397.

Sperling, G. The information available in brief visual presentations. *Psychological Monographs,* 1960, *74*(No. 11, Whole No. 498).

Sperling, G. A model for visual memory tasks. *Human Factors,* 1963, *5,* 19–31.

Taub, H. A. Effects of differential value on recall of visual symbols. *Journal of Experimental Psychology,* 1965, *69,* 135–143.

Teichner, W. H., R. Reilly, and E. Sadler. Effects of density on identification and discrimination in visual symbol perception. *Journal of Experimental Psychology,* 1961, *61,* 494–500.

Teichner, W. H., and E. Sadler. Effects of exposure time and density on visual symbol identification. *Journal of Experimental Psychology,* 1962, *63,* 376–380.

Wilcocks, R. W. An examination of Külpe's experiments on abstraction. *American Journal of Psychology,* 1925, *36,* 324–341.

8.2 Word-Frequency Effect and Response Bias*

D. E. BROADBENT

During the past 15 years or so, very much research interest and effort have been occupied with the comparison of the perception of words which are common in ordinary language on the one hand, and those which are uncommon on the other. The fact that common words are, other things being equal, more easily perceived

* From: D. E. Broadbent, "Word-Frequency Effect and Response Bias," *Psychological Review,* 1967, vol. 74, pp. 1–15. Copyright (1967) by the American Psychological Association, and reproduced by permission. Thanks are due to Margaret Gregory for conducting the experimental work discussed in this paper, and to the British Medical Research Council for support. Some of the concepts were presented in outline form in a presidential address to the British Psychological Society in April 1965.

is perhaps only a special case of the general influence of probability on perception. From the time of the classic experiments on distortion in perception and remembering, such as those of Bartlett (1932), it has been common ground to most psychologists that a probable event is easily perceived. The useful feature of the word-frequency effect is that it allows quantitative studies, which are almost impossible in the case of most other similar phenomena met in everyday life. It is hard to put a number to the probability of perceiving a man in a bowler hat in the City of London, as opposed to Manhattan. Consequently it is difficult to test any precise theory of perception choosing as stimuli pictures of men in bowler hats. In the case of words, however, we can to some extent describe the relative probabilities of different words in quantitative form. They thus provide a convenient special tool for investigating the general question of probabilistic effects in perception.

In very recent years, a number of writers on the word-frequency effect have considered the possibility that the effect is due to a response bias, rather than to some feature of the input of information to the organism. Unfortunately, the term response bias is itself ambiguous. There seem to be at least four different senses in which the term has been used, each implying a different definition of it. Definitions have not, however, usually been given, and the term has been used as self-explanatory. It seems worthwhile, therefore, to distinguish these possible definitions. As will be seen, when this is done the experimental evidence suggests that three of the definitions are inadequate as explanations of the word-frequency effect. The fourth, however, is very adequate. This fourth sense, admittedly, is not the one which has been most frequently used in the past. Thus it is not very surprising that several authors have concluded that response bias was not an adequate explanation (e.g., Brown & Rubenstein, 1961; Zajonc & Nieuwenhuyse, 1964).

A convenient starting point for the modern interest in response bias may be taken as the paper of Goldiamond and Hawkins (1958), who showed that when a tachistoscope was flashed at experimental subjects (Ss) without any word actually being presented, and when the responses were scored as if some particular word had indeed been present, they were scored as being more accurate in identifying those words which had in a preliminary experiment been more frequently presented. Since there could be no sensory component in this experiment, the effect could legitimately be described as response bias. In addition, it seems that the presentation of a fixed set of alternatives between which S has to choose, rather than an open-ended type of test, markedly reduces the word-frequency effect (Pierce, 1963; Pollack, Rubenstein, & Decker, 1959). Thus the effect certainly depends upon an adjustment of the

organism which can be fairly rapidly effected, and which is not inherent in the nature of the stimulus. The use of the term "artifact" by Pierce shows that such a process of adjustment is not to all ways of thinking a genuinely perceptual effect at all. In brief, however, all the following different possible hypotheses seem to be consistent with the phenomena so far cited; each of them implies a different definition of "response bias."

PURE GUESSING

On this model, S perceives a proportion of the stimuli correctly, and guesses on some or all of the remaining trials. If his guesses are more frequently common words rather than uncommon words, he might by chance score some correct responses on common words which would enhance his apparent performance.

SOPHISTICATED GUESSING

A more complex model is one in which, even when a stimulus word has not been correctly perceived, the information which has arrived at the senses nevertheless rules out some English words as being impossible, and leaves a restricted set of alternatives as still consistent with what has been heard. If now S chooses at random out of this restricted set, but with a bias towards the more probable words, he will, just as in the simple model, score some correct answers on common words by chance.

OBSERVING RESPONSE

In attempting to identify the word which has been presented, S may adjust his sense organs or his central mechanisms so as to maximize the effects of stimuli which he expects, at the cost of being badly adjusted to detect improbable stimuli. This might be described as a kind of "observing response" model: Its predictions will of course be closely similar to those of a view which regards the word-frequency effect as purely perceptual with no response component. However, this view does make it clear that the perceptual effect depends upon the adjustment of the observer and so may be less in forced-choice situations. It is therefore included as a possible variety of "response bias" theory, despite its similarity to nonresponse theories. It is worth noting, however, that evidence inconsistent with this theory may also exclude a "pure perception" view of the effect.

CRITERION BIAS IN DECISION

Lastly, the situation might be viewed as analogous to a statistical decision, in which the stimulus presented provides evidence pointing to a greater or lesser extent to each of the words in S's vocabulary. If S were biased in such a way as to accept a smaller amount of evidence before deciding in favor of a probable word rather than an improbable word, the word-frequency effect would be obtained. This last approach is probably the least used of the four, but it is nevertheless the one which the present paper will attempt to support.

To clarify the differences between the models, let us think of the following hydraulic analogy. Let us suppose a vast array of test tubes, each partly full of water, and each corresponding to a word in the language. The choice of one tube corresponds to perception of a word, and the probability of choice of any tube is greater when the water level in it is higher.[1]

On Model 1, presentation of a stimulus has no effect on the water levels, but all "high-frequency" tubes start off with more water than "low-frequency" tubes. Thus a high-frequency choice is more probable.

On Model 2, presentation of a stimulus raises the water level in a small proportion of tubes. This subsample includes the correct tube, but that tube receives no more water than each of the others in the subsample. Choice is effectively restricted to the few tubes selected by the stimulus: Within these few, a high-frequency choice is more probable because the initial level in that class of tubes was higher.

On Model 3, presentation of a stimulus adds more water to the correct tube than to any other. This additional amount is itself greater when the tube is "high-frequency" than when it is low, perhaps because funnels are fitted to that class of tube to catch every possible drop. Correct choices of such tubes will therefore be more frequent even if the initial difference in levels is small or absent.

On Model 4, presentation of a stimulus again adds more water to the correct tube than to any other, but the additional amount is the same whatever the class of tube involved. Since, however, the initial level in high-frequency tubes is greater, a high-frequency choice is more probable.

The following points should be noted. First, the four models differ largely in the way in which the effect of the stimulus combines with that of the class of response. Second, response bias corresponds in Models 1, 2, and 4 to an initial difference in water level; while in Model 3 it may do so but also corresponds to a difference in the change of level produced by a stimulus. Third, in Models 3 and 4 the presence of a real stimulus, no matter how faint, always increases the probability of a correct perception.

Detailed Implications of these Theories

PURE GUESSING

This sense of "response bias" has been clearly stated by Dember (1960, p. 287), and is that which one would naturally infer from the papers of Goldiamond and Hawkins (1958) and Pierce (1963). (Throughout this paper it should be remembered that previous authors may have been *opposing* the value of response bias in their use of the term, and also may have changed their usage in later references.)

This simple theory implies that if

P_c = apparent score correct

p_c = truly perceived

p_F = probability of apparently correct response by guessing in the absence of a stimulus

then $P_c = p_c + (1 - p_c) \, p_F$.

---

[1] To be precise, the level of water in a tube shall be proportional to the logarithm of the probability of choice of that tube, as will appear later. Furthermore, in Models 1 and 2 there may also be occasions when the presentation of a stimulus determines a correct choice perfectly, with no probabilistic element. These occasions, however, are independent of word frequency and can be ignored for the moment.

We may define "response bias" in this case as the difference in p_F between common and uncommon words: If p_c is the same for all words, a greater p_F for common words would give a greater P_c for those words. But this model immediately involves us in ridiculous impossibilities. For example, even if no guesses of uncommon words are made at all, it means that S has a very high probability of guessing a common word correctly by chance. In an experiment to be reported later, there is a difference of approximately .2 in the probability of correctly perceiving a common as opposed to an uncommon word, and this means that the probability of guessing a common word completely correctly must be greater than .2. Since, however, this can be shown for more than five common words, the model is manifestly absurd. The word-frequency effect is much too large to be explained by supposing that the listener simply picks a word out of his whole vocabulary of common words whenever he fails to perceive correctly.

In addition, this model of perception is inconsistent with the effect on P_c which can be produced by presenting a fixed vocabulary of possible words and varying the size of this vocabulary. If pure guessing were the explanation of the improved performance which is shown with a smaller vocabulary, then the gain in correctly perceived words should always be smaller than the increase of probability of a completely random choice turning out correct. Thus a reduction in vocabulary size from 100 words to 50 should produce an improvement in performance of, at maximum, .01: but this is considerably less than that actually attained.

Lastly, even if the foregoing reasons are not regarded as sufficient to exclude this model, it makes the following prediction which, as we shall see, turns out to be unjustified. Suppose we examine the errors which each S makes and divide them into common and uncommon words. Now when the stimulus word itself is common, some of the occasions when S guesses a common word will be scored as correct answers and not as errors. But if the stimulus was in fact a common word, naturally

TABLE 1

Guessing Theories of Word-Frequency Effects

S's PERFORMANCE		
TRUE PERCEPTION X%	HIGH FREQUENCY GUESSES Y% ($= a + b$)	LOW FREQUENCY GUESSES Z%

APPARENT SCORE IN EXPERIMENT			
	CORRECT	HF ERROR	LF ERROR
HF stimulus	X + a	b	Z
LF stimulus	X	a + b	Z

none of the guesses of uncommon words can possibly be scored by the experimenter as correct, and all of them appear on the answer sheet as errors. When, however, the stimulus is an uncommon word, the situation is reversed, and every guess of a common word is entered as an error. It may even be the case that an occasional guess taking the form of an uncommon word does turn out to be correct, and thus there may even be fewer recorded uncommon errors in this case than when the stimulus is a common word. Certainly, however, there will be more recorded errors of common words. If, therefore, we examine the error words and divide them into those words which are common in the language and those which are not, the ratio of occurrence of the former to the latter should be greater if the actual stimulus was uncommon than if the stimulus was common. (See Table 1.) The effect must be a substantial one, if the word-frequency effect itself is large, since the entire advantage of the common words is derived from the fact that some common guesses are not scored as such. This prediction therefore serves as a test of this type of model.

SOPHISTICATED GUESSING

This theory is much less clearly absurd than the previous one. It has been upheld by Solomon and Postman (1952), Newbigging (1961), J. T. Spence (1963), and Savin (1963), among others. Brown and Rubenstein (1961) also used a formulation of response bias which is in some ways of this type. (The latter authors, however, found that the effect was too large for a model of this type. They contended that the number of responses, including error responses, which were of the same frequency class as the stimulus, was larger than it would be by chance, and they consequently suggested that S was receiving some information from the stimulus about the extent to which the actual word was common or uncommon.)

The theory can be represented by an equation closely similar to that for the previous case, namely

$$P_c = p_c + (1 - p_c) \, p_F \times \frac{N}{n};$$

where

N = total number of words in listener's vocabulary

n = number of words still possible after reception of a stimulus.

Response bias is defined as previously, as the difference in p_F between common and uncommon words. This would be perfectly capable of giving rise to a word-frequency effect of the magnitude actually observed, since the additional term $\frac{N}{n}$ could well be substantial enough to make the word-frequency effect considerably larger than the pure random probability of guessing a particular high-frequency word out of all those in the English language. For similar reasons, this model is capable of dealing with the large improvement in performance which occurs when the vocabulary of possible words is known and is small. Recently Stowe, Harris, and Hampton (1963) have produced a version of this model which predicts an exponential relationship of the form

$$P_c = p_F{}^{1/K}$$

and have presented data fitting such an equation.

It may be added that a similar type of model can be used to account for the large improvement in performance which occurs when a few words of context are given before a somewhat noisy stimulus word. In such a case, the listener may be able to say correctly what the target word is on quite a high proportion of occasions, even although he has quite a low chance of doing so with either of the two sources of information by itself. Empirically, this effect also can be fitted by an exponential relationship (Pollack, 1964; Rubenstein & Pollack, 1963; Tulving, Mandler, & Baumal, 1964).

Leaving aside the support or criticism which earlier papers provide for this model, it will be clear that it makes a prediction similar to the model previously discussed. That is, for common stimulus words some of the apparently correct answers were in fact guesses, and therefore there should be fewer common words among the errors to such stimulus words than there should be to uncommon stimulus words.

OBSERVING RESPONSE MODEL

This view has been most baldly stated by Broadbent (1958, p. 54) for the case of perceptual defense rather than the word-frequency effect. It would naturally arise, however, from a motor theory of speech perception (Liberman, Cooper, Harris, & MacNeilage, 1963), and is included among a number of other mechanisms by Bruner (1957, p. 138). The essential feature of this third class of theories is that the input to the perceptual mechanism is regarded as flowing disproportionately from those characteristics of the stimulus which are especially indicative of common words. For example, peripheral or central adjustments might orient the system towards receiving acoustic cues relevant to the distinction between P and D, and not those cues relevant to the distinction between X and Z. Since the former letters, and perhaps their corresponding phonemes, are more common than the latter, this might give more accurate perception of common words. A number of well-known experiments show adjustment towards selective perception of some inputs rather than others (Broadbent, 1958). However, such a theory would not imply the same predictions as Models 1 and 2 concerning errors. One might on the contrary expect that detection of the *absence* of common phonemes would be especially efficient, as well as that of their presence. Thus common words would not occur often as errors, compared with their occurrence as correct responses.

In support of this analysis, one may cite an experiment on division of attention which has been analyzed by the techniques of signal- detection theory (Broadbent & Gregory, 1963). The experiment involved a man listening for a tone in noise in one ear, while he either memorized six digits arriving at the other ear, or else ignored them to concentrate upon the tone. Using signal detection theory, it is possible to calculate, from true and false responses in a psychophysical situation, a parameter (d') which can broadly be described as signal-noise ratio, and it was shown that concentration of attention upon one sensory channel improved this ratio. Thus the general prediction of the third theory would be that the parameter corresponding to signel-noise ratio, in a detection theory analysis, should be greater for common than for uncommon words: Response bias is here defined as a difference in d'.

RESPONSE BIAS AS A CRITERION PLACEMENT

This view has been most clearly stated by Goldiamond (1962) but is consistent with other lines of theorizing such as Treisman (1960) and Broadbent and Gregory (1963).

Signal detection theory, which has been briefly mentioned above, is now widely familiar (Swets, 1964). In brief, the basic suggestion is that some process varies randomly within the nervous system about a mean which is shifted in value by the arrival of a signal. In the case of yes-no detection of a single signal, some critical level of the process has to be exceeded for detection of the signal to occur, and it is obviously possible to produce a high rate of detections either by a large shift in the mean value of the process when the signal occurs, or else by a low value of the critical level. In the

latter case, there will (other things being equal) be large numbers of false alarms. Nevertheless, a low critical level may be rational if signals are very probable, and it has been shown experimentally that the changes in performance produced in psychophysical situations by changes in the probability of a signal appear to correspond to changes in the criterion level. They do not correspond to changes in d', the shift of the mean value of the internal process which is produced by a signal.

The latter parameter is the one which was mentioned in the last section as corresponding to signal-noise ratio, and it would appear therefore that experiments on the detection of simple tonal signals of different probability lead us to a prediction diametrically opposed to the one derived from the previous model. If one could analyze the perception of speech on the basis of signal detection theory, this model would suggest that the word-frequency effect would correspond to a difference in the critical level necessary for a word to be perceived.

The perception of speech involves choice from many alternatives rather than the simple yes-no detection of a signel. Signal-detection theory has been extended to the forced-choice case, and when the resulting mathematics are applied to experiments on the perception of words drawn from known vocabularies of different sizes, the magnitude of the effect is satisfactorily explained without needing to suppose any change in the parameter corresponding to signal-noise ratio (Swets, 1964, p. 609). There thus appears to be a reasonable case for examining the word-frequency effect using the methods of signal-detection theory, and attempting to decide which of the crucial parameters is changed when common words are perceived rather than uncommon ones.

Unfortunately, it is difficult, using the methods of signal-detection theory, to handle the case in which a number of different responses (decision outcomes) have different degrees of bias attached to them. Accordingly, a fresh analysis has been made using a procedure suggested by Luce (1959), and this will now be explained. It should be emphasized that the method suggested by Luce derives from a different axiomatic approach from the earlier signal-detection theory, but the present author does not intend to support one set of axioms or the other. The two calculations lead to approximately similar conclusions in most instances, but in the present case the method of Luce is considerably more convenient.

The Analysis of Multiple Choice Situations with Varying Biases

The normal analysis of the forced-choice situation, from the point of view of signal detection, is to suppose that there are a number of different variables, equal to the number of alternative choices, and each varying normally and with unit variance about a mean which is zero for all alternatives except the correct one. For the correct alternative, the mean value is d'. On each trial, one sample is drawn from each of the resulting distributions, and the largest value determines the alternative which is chosen for response. The correct response, therefore, clearly has the greatest probability of occurrence, but there is some chance that one of the other alternatives may, through ill fortune, reach a high value when the correct alternative happens to have taken on a low value.

Biases are introduced into the situation by supposing that some alternatives have a mean which is greater than zero even before a stimulus arrives and are shifted by a further amount d' if the appropriate stimulus occurs.

Let us start by taking the case of a two-alternative forced-choice decision. In this case, we have two normal distributions, each with unit variance, and one of which has mean zero while the other has mean d'. If a sample is drawn from each distribution, the difference between these samples is itself distributed normally with mean d'. Thus if the two processes are named x and y, and if we take the difference x — y, there will be two resulting distributions, one with mean + d' when x is correct, and the other with mean — d' when y is correct. If now we decide in favor of one

alternative whenever x — y is positive, and the other when x — y is negative, we obtain a percentage of correct answers which can be calculated from the properties of the normal distribution, and which is convertible to d' by published tables.

By adopting a decision rule which changes from one alternative to the other when x — y equals zero, we have taken a situation of zero bias. It would of course be equally possible to adopt the rule that we decide in favor of one alternative when x — y is greater than or equals C, and in favor of the other alternative when x — y is less than C. This would introduce a bias in favor of one alternative or the other, which would be precisely analogous to the criterion setting adopted in the yes-no case.

The approach adopted by Luce (1959) depends upon the following valuable approximation. If we have a process of the type already mentioned, normally distributed with zero mean, and if there is some critical value of the process at a value C, then to a reasonable approximation

$$\log \frac{P_F}{P_S} = KC$$

where

P_F = probability that process will not attain C

P_S = probability that process will exceed C

K = a constant, which may be eliminated by using appropriate units for scaling the value of the process.

This approximation allow us to work out very simply the consequences of a two-alternative decision, such as the one considered above. Thus if

mean of distribution corresponding to Alternative 1 correct = log a
mean of distribution corresponding to Alternative 2 correct = — log a
Criterion level = + log V (i.e., a bias in favor of Alternative 2),

TABLE 2

Relative Strengths of Four Responses in the Presence of Each of Four Stimuli, to Illustrate the Notation

	RESPONSES			
STIMULI	1	2	3	4
1	$\alpha_1 V_1$	V_2	V_3	V_4
2	V_1	$\alpha_2 V_2$	V_3	V_4
3	V_1	V_2	$\alpha_3 V_3$	V_4
4	V_1	V_2	V_3	$\alpha_4 V_4$

then when Alternative 1 is presented

$$\frac{\text{Probability of Response 1}}{\text{Probability of Response 2}} = \frac{a}{V},$$

and when Alternative 2 is presented

$$\frac{\text{Probability of Response 1}}{\text{Probability of Response 2}} = \frac{1}{aV}.$$

This analysis can now be extended to the case of more than two alternatives, by use of the principle that the relative probabilities of any two alternatives are unaffected by the presence or absence of other alternatives. In the case of speech, this principle appears in general to be approximately valid, as has been shown by Clarke (1957). We may therefore draw up a table in which the columns represent responses and the rows stimuli; within each row, the ratio of the numbers in any two columns represents the ratio of the probabilities of those two responses when the stimulus appropriate to that row has been presented.

That is, the entries in the table correspond to the quantities a and V of the example already given. For the four-choice case, see Table 2. Notice that each response may possess a different bias, and in addition that the effect of the correct stimulus may be different for each of the possible stimuli.

Turning now to the word-frequency effect, let us consider for simplicity two classes of words, one consisting of high-frequency words and the other of relatively low-frequency words. Again for simplicity, we may suppose that each of the former possesses a constant response bias V relative to each of the latter. Table 3 shows a section of the table for this situation. There would of course be many other possible responses, some of them lying outside the two frequency categories altogether, but, as already argued, this would not affect the relative probabilities involved. The probability of responding with any one particular erroneous word is of little practical use. It is, however, of interest to consolidate all the error responses in the high frequency class with which we are concerned, which we may suppose to contain N_H different words, and also those in the low-frequency class, which we may suppose to contain N_L different words. Table 4 illustrates this change.

Table 4 will hold both for Model 3 and for Model 4: Model 3 holds if $\alpha_H > a_L$, and Model 4 holds if $a_H = a_L$ and $V > 1$.

To clarify the meanig of the table, let us consider a few illustrative predictions from it. Suppose $\alpha_H = \alpha_L = 1$, that is, no stimulus effect occurs at all (the Goldiamond and Hawkins situation). Let us also put $N_H = N_L = 4$,

TABLE 3

Relative Strengths of the Correct Response and of Each of Two Errors, in the Case of Speech Perception with Common and Uncommon Stimuli

STIMULUS	CORRECT RESPONSE	ONE PARTICULAR HIGH FREQUENCY ERROR	ONE PARTICULAR LOW FREQUENCY ERROR
High frequency	$\alpha_H V$	V	1
Low frequency	α_L	V	1

TABLE 4

Final Table of Relative Strengths for Correct Responses and for Two Types of Incorrect Response, in the Case of Speech Perception Considering All Words in the Language

STIMULUS	CORRECT RESPONSE	ERRORS OF HIGH FREQUENCY	ERRORS OF LOW FREQUENCY
High frequency	$\alpha_H V$	$(N_H\text{-}1)V$	N_L
Low frequency	α_L	$N_H V$	$N_L\text{-}1$

that is, consider a small fixed vocabulary like that of Goldiamond and Hawkins in which no responses occur outside the vocabulary. Then if $V > 1$, say $V = 4$, the probability of a correct response to an HF stimulus is

$$\frac{4}{4 + 3 \times 4 + 4} = .2$$

while the probability of correct response to an LF stimulus is

$$\frac{1}{1 + 4 \times 4 + 3} = .05.$$

Thus the Goldiamond and Hawkins effect will occur.

In the same situation, suppose a stimulus of moderate strength is applied, so that $a_H = a_L = 6$. Assuming Model 4, then correct HF response have probability

$$\frac{24}{24 + 12 + 4} = .6$$

and correct LF responses have probability

$$\frac{6}{6 + 16 + 3} = .24.$$

Notice that the difference in probability of the two types of correct response becomes greater when a stimulus is present, an effect which has sometimes been regarded as excluding a response-bias interpretation. On the other hand, if the stimulus is exceedingly strong, $a_H = a_L = 400$, the difference in correct responses becomes slight again.

HF correct responses then

$$= \frac{1600}{1600 + 12 + 4} \cong .99.$$

LF correct responses then

$$= \frac{400}{400 + 16 + 3} \cong .95.$$

In other words, with a strong stimulus prior biases are effectively overruled, and one perceives what is really present.

While these implications of the analysis help one to understand it, the two main questions are whether the facts of perception are consistent with this analysis rather than with Model 1 or 2; and, if this analysis is appropriate, whether Model 3 or 4 is the more nearly correct. To test these questions, two further predictions may be drawn from Table 4, for the case when N_H and N_L are large.

1. On Models 3 and 4, the ratio of errors of high frequency to errors of low frequency will be approximately constant, whatever the frequency class of the stimulus, provided that N_H and N_L are large. This is quite contrary to the prediction of the two guessing models, since, as already indicated, these models cannot allow large values of N_H and N_L.

2. If, for each class of stimulus, we divide the correct answers by the errors which were of the correct frequency class, we obtain for the high-frequency stimulus $\alpha_H/(N_H - 1)$, and for the low-frequency stimulus $\alpha_L/(N_L - 1)$. Dividing one of these ratios by the other thus gives us $\alpha_H/\alpha_L \times (N_L - 1)/(N_H - 1)$. If we can determine N_L/N_H by some independent means, then if the two ratios are equal, this implies that $\alpha_H = \alpha_L$. This in turn means that the

"observing response" class of interpretation (Model 3) is not valid. It will also exclude purely perceptual theories of the effect. In that event, the response bias V must count for the entire word-frequency effect that is present.

An Illustrative Experiment

MATERIALS

Two lists of 60 monosyllabic words and one of 60 disyllabic words were prepared. Each list was prepared as follows. A group of 20 high-frequency words and another group of 20 low-frequency words were selected, new groups being used for each list. The list of 60 was then compiled by drawing words at random from the two groups of 20 subject to the restrictions that each word occurred at least once and not more than twice, that there were equal numbers of high-frequency and low-frequency words and also that not more than three successive words were drawn from the same frequency group.

The high-frequency words all had frequencies of at least 100 occurrences per million words (AA in the Thorndike-Lorge, 1944, count). They were selected by taking the first monosyllable or disyllable, as appropriate, on every tenth page of the Thorndike-Lorge word count. The low-frequency words had frequencies of not less than 10 and not more than 49 per million. (That is, they were in fact within the vocabulary of all normal adults.) They were selected by a similar procedure, the first word being selected on a different page from the first high-frequency word. Proper names, words suspected of having very different frequencies in English and American usage, and words beginning with a vowel were excluded from both the high-frequency and the low-frequency groups; also excluded from the low-frequency group were words having homonyms with higher frequencies.

The lists were recorded on one channel of a twin-channel Ferrograph recorder, each word being preceded by a serial number which served as a ready signal; a gap of about 12 seconds

elapsed between successive words. Electronically generated wide-band noise was recorded on the second channel. The tape was played back with the outputs from both channels fed into a single external loudspeaker. The gain levels were adjusted so that the speech was reproduced at comfortable listening level (mean peak readings of 83 db. re .0002 dynes/cm^2). The noise level was set by trial-and-error in preliminary experiments to allow about 30% correct responses in an open-ended situation while not resulting in perfect performance in a forced-choice: in fact the S/N ratios that resulted were in the region of 0 db.

All Ss were British housewives from the Applied Psychology Research Unit panel between the ages of 20 and 50.

PROCEDURE

(a) *Monosyllables.* The Ss were tested in groups. One group of 12 Ss heard List 1 of monosyllables and a second group of 12 on a subsequent occasion heard List 2. Six Ss of each group gave forced-choice responses while the other six gave open-ended responses. The "forced-choice" Ss were given two matrices, one with the 20 high-frequency words corresponding to the rows and the other with the 20 low-frequency words. (They were not informed of the difference in frequency between the two lists.) The columns of each matrix were numbered to correspond with the test number on the tape. They were told that each test word, according to its number, would be a member of one of the lists and that they should respond by ticking in a cell on the appropriate matrix, also that they should avoid leaving blanks. The Ss making open-ended responses were told that all the words were monosyllables and that they should write down whatever word they thought that they had heard even if they were unsure about it. However, blanks were allowed if S was really uncertain.

In order to avoid confusion arising from Ss losing their places and not being sure what serial number of response they should be completing (the numbers were given on the tape but were heard against the background of noise) the experimenter presented each number visually while the corresponding signal was being heard.

(b) *Disyllables.* The procedure for the list of disyllables was similar. Two groups, one of 11 and the other of 13, heard the same list on separate occasions; five Ss made open-ended responses in one group and seven in the other, the remaining Ss in each case making forced-choices. The Ss were informed that all the words would have two syllables.

SCORING

For each S in the open-ended condition six scores were taken: (*a*) the number of correct high-frequency responses, (*b*) the number of wrong high-frequency responses (of the same number of syllables as the stimulus) made to high-frequency stimuli, (*c*) the number of wrong low-frequency responses made to high-frequency stimuli, (*d*) the number of correct low-frequency responses, (*e*) the number of wrong high-frequency responses made to low-frequency stimuli, (*f*) the number of wrong

low-frequency responses made to low-frequency stimuli. A high-frequency response was any response word having a frequency of 100 or more per million. A low-frequency response was any response word having a frequency of between 10 and 49 per million. Responses having a number of syllables different from the stimulus words were not included.

Those Ss who were presented with disyllables made a fair number of incorrect responses which consisted of a stem (usually high-frequency) followed by a common suffix, for example, "camp-ing." Such responses were not counted as high-frequency or low-frequency errors if the stem word was within the correct frequency limits because these words are not given as such in the Thorndike-Lorge word book. They could not, therefore, have been included in the sample count made to establish the relative numbers of high-frequency and low-frequency words, nor sampled as stimuli. Whether for generating stimuli, classifying responses, or counting vocabulary size, the Thorndike-Lorge count was always used as the criterion.

TABLE 5
Monosyllables

STIMULUS	PERCENTAGE CORRECT	HIGH-FREQUENCY ERRORS	LOW-FREQUENCY ERRORS
High-frequency	32.50[A]	32.25[C]	15.83[E]
Low-frequency	12.77[B]	41.67[D]	19.17[F]

Note. $\frac{A \times F}{C \times B} = 1.512$. From Thorndike and Lorge: $\frac{\text{No. of LF monosyllables}}{\text{No. of HF monosyllables}} = 1.42$.

TABLE 6
Disyllables

STIMULUS	PERCENTAGE CORRECT	HIGH-FREQUENCY ERRORS	LOW-FREQUENCY ERRORS
High frequency	32.77[A]	9.73[C]	6.67[E]
Low frequency	11.11[B]	9.17[D]	14.44[F]

Note. $\frac{A \times F}{C \times B} = 4.38$. From Thorndike and Lorge: $\frac{\text{No. of LF disyllables}}{\text{No. of HF disyllables}} = 5.39$.

SAMPLING COUNT TO ESTABLISH THE RELATIVE NUMBERS OF HIGH-FREQUENCY AND LOW-FREQUENCY WORDS

On page 5 and every subsequent fifth page throughout the book (41 pages in all) a count was made of the numbers of (*a*) high-frequency monosyllables, (*b*) high-frequency disyllables, (*c*) low-frequency monosyllables, (*d*) low-frequency disyllables occurring on that page. Proper names other than American place names were included in the count because several of the Ss had given proper names among their responses.

Results

FORCED-CHOICE

This condition was included in order to confirm that the percentage of correct responses was indeed similar for the high-frequency and low-frequency words in these particular tape recordings, and therefore that the random sampling of stimuli had not resulted in one class of words being acoustically superior in intelligibility. Preliminary studies had raised a suspicion that this can happen with nonrandom samples such as PB lists, but in the present case it did not and the two classes of words were equally intelligible.

OPEN-ENDED

The percentages of responses in each of the six categories of interest are shown in the tables. It will be noticed (*a*) that the word-frequency effect is markedly present, amounting to a difference in probability of correct response of about .2; (*b*) the errors of high frequency are, in the experiment on monosyllables, in a constant ratio to the errors of low frequency, regardless of the nature of the stimulus.[2] In the case of disyllables, there is some sign that low-frequency errors are more common to a

low-frequency stimulus: this difference is not quite significant, being due to eight Ss out of the 12 tested, and will be discussed later. It is, in any case, in the wrong direction as far as the guessing models are concerned. Thus these data clearly disprove the two guessing models; (*c*) in both experiments, the ratio of correct responses to errors of the appropriate frequency class, when compared for high- and for low-frequency stimuli, gave approximately the correct prediction of the relative number of words in the frequency classes according to the Thorndike-Lorge word count. The difference from the correct value is not, in fact, significant. If we work out the value for each individual S, then among the group receiving monosyllables seven Ss gave an estimate larger than that from the Thorndike-Lorge and five Ss gave a smaller estimate, while among the group receiving disyllables the numbers were five and seven. Thus it appears that there is no difference between high-frequency and low-frequency words in the quantity corresponding to d' in signal-detection theory: The entire word-frequency effect is due to Model 4.

Conclusion and Limitations

The considerable number of experiments already in the literature on this topic have not provided data analyzed in this way. Consequently they do not assist us in deciding whether Model 4 explains the word-frequency effect in all cases, or whether the experiment cited is in some way peculiar. However, the experiment appears reasonably representative, and the author has been unable to find any feature of earlier results which Model 4 is unable to explain. Therefore, until some data are analyzed in this way and give contrary results, it would seem simplest to hold that Model 4 has been operative in all experiments on word frequency. This means

---

[2] My attention has been drawn by Harris Savin to the prediction of Model 2 that errors to an HF stimulus will occur disproportionately often to those stimuli which happen to be very similar to other words of high frequency, and this will oppose the prediction tested here. We have therefore, reanalyzed the data, weighting errors from each stimulus inversely by the total number of errors to that stimulus, but the results are unchanged. It will of course be evident that Models 2 and 4 are in some ways very similar, so that supporters of the former may be happy to regard the latter as a modification of it.

(*a*) that the effect is not due to biased guessing on trials when the stimulus has left correct and incorrect words equally probable,

(*b*) that the effect is not due to an increase of the stimulus contribution to correct perception of high-frequency words, but

(*c*) that the effect is due to a prior bias in favor of common words, which combines with sensory evidence favoring the objectively correct word.

It may be worth noting certain changes in conditions which might be expected to alter the pattern of results. For example, small values of N_H and N_L will tend to produce data which do not exclude Models 1 and 2. This is because the difference between N_H and $N_H - 1$ will then become important, so that the relative number of errors which are common words will increase if the stimulus is uncommon. We have found this to apply to forced-choice experiments, and also to visual rather than auditory ones. In the visual case, errors usually have several individual letters in common with the stimulus, and this restricts the effective size of N_H and N_L. One would expect a similar pattern of results with an auditory experiment at high signal-noise ratios.

Experiments showing this feature would, however, merely fail to disprove Models 1 and 2; they would not be evidence against Model 4. It is more important to consider cases in which Model 4 might be found insufficient.

One such case might be that in which unwillingness to respond at all becomes a major factor. Absence of response was allowed in our experiment, and so long as S does not use this possibility too often, the various ways in which it might be included in the mathematics do not differ much in the predictions they produce. Some (not all) of them might, however, require adjustment of Model 4 to fit data in which absence of response was common.

Perhaps more important is the possibility that stimulus words may carry information about their frequency class. As already indicated,

Brown and Rubenstein (1961) concluded this, although providing data inconsistent with Model 3. Their conclusion is dependent, however, upon the particular assumptions implicit in their equations, and from our present point of view there is no need to accept it. Our results on monosyllables positively oppose it. There was, however, an insignificant tendency among disyllables for errors to be more common in the frequency class of the objective stimulus. Furthermore, the phenomenon of the "descent of the median" (Pollack, 1962) makes it seem likely that error frequencies sometimes change with the population of words presented. Therefore, although there is no positive evidence on this point, it may be that Model 4 may in some situations require modification by increasing V for HF stimuli.

Many, including the author, may regret the exclusion of any perceptual filtering or observing response mechanism. As some consolation we might postulate that such a mechanism could only become operative if relatively few cues were involved, that is, if N_H and N_L were small either through the use of a small vocabulary or through a powerful context. However, attempts in Cambridge to find such an effect have so far failed completely.

The supporters of a purely perceptual effect might rather consider that the use of the term response bias is perhaps misleading when it is applied to a model of the present type. It will be clear that the bias which has been postulated is not something which affects only the final overt response of writing down or uttering the word, but rather a bias applied to some central event, which may or may not occur following the delivery of a stimulus at the sense organs. The author would not think that a response bias in this sense can be described as an artifact. Rather it is a particular part of the perceptual mechanism. The term response bias is also objectionable because it suggests a kind of peripheralist theory which is now clearly unsatisfactory. Nevertheless, the bias which appears in the present model would explain results such as those of Goldiamond and Hawkins and the reduction of the word-frequency effect in forced-choice situations, and these are the phenomena which have given rise to the usual use of the term response bias. It is to be hoped that many of those who oppose the usefulness of the concept in its sense of pure or sophisticated guessing may nevertheless welcome its appearance as a parameter in a theory of perception based upon signal-detection theory.

Summary

Many recent investigators have studied "Response Bias" theories of the perception of common vs. uncommon words. 4 different classes of theory are distinguished, and it is demonstrated that 3 of them are inconsistent with previously published and fresh data. The 4th sense of response bias, however, leads to the prediction that bias on correct responses may be greater than that on errors, and is very accurately consistent with the data. This is the sense of response bias as analogous to the bias of a criterion in a statistical decision.

References

Bartlett, F. C. *Remembering*. Cambridge University Press, 1932.

Broadbent, D. E. *Perception and Communication*. London: Pergamon Press, 1958.

Broadbent, D. E. and M. Gregory. Division of attention and the decision theory of signal detection. *Proceedings of the Royal Society*, Ser. B. 1963, *158*, 222–231.

Brown, C. R., and H. Rubenstein. Test of response bias explanation of word-frequency effect. *Science*, 1961, *133*, 280–281.

Bruner, J. S. On perceptual readiness. *Psychological Review*, 1957, *64*, 123–152.

Clarke, F. R. Constant-ratio rule for confusion matrices in speech communication. *Journal of the Acoustical Society of America*, 1957, *29*, 715–720.

Dember, W. N. *The psychology of perception*. New York: Holt, 1960.

Goldiamond, I. Perception. In A. J. Bachrach (Ed.), *Experimental Foundations of Clinical Psychology*. New York: Basic Books, 1962, Pp. 280–340.

Goldiamond, I., and W. F. Hawkins. Vexierversuch: The log relationship between word-frequency and recognition obtained in the absence of stimulus words. *Journal of Experimental Psychology*, 1958, *56*, 457–463.

Liberman, A. M., F. S. Cooper, K. S. Harris, and P. F. MacNeilage. Motor theory of speech perception. (*Proceedings Speech Communication Seminar, Stockholm*, 1963) *Journal of the Acoustical Society of America*, 1963, *35*, 1114. (Abstract).

Luce, R. D. *Individual Choice Behavior*. New York: Wiley, 1959.

Newbigging, P. L. The perceptual redintegration of frequent and infrequent words. *Canadian Journal of Psychology*, 1961, *15*, 123–132.

Pierce, J. Some sources of artifact in studies of the tachistoscopic perception of words. *Journal of Experimental Psychology*, 1963, *66*, 363–370.

Pollack, I. Incorrect responses to unknown messages restricted in word frequency. *Language and Speech*, 1962, *5*, 125–127.

Pollack, I. Interaction of two sources of verbal context in word identification. *Language and Speech*, 1964, *7*, 1–12.

Pollack, I., H. Rubenstein, and L. Decker. Intelligibility of known and unknown message sets. *Journal of the Acoustical Society of America*, 1959, *31*, 273–279.

Rubenstein, H., and I. Pollack. Word predictability and intelligibility. *Journal of Verbal Learning and Verbal Behavior*, 1963, *2*, 147–158.

Savin, H. B. Word-frequency effect and errors in the perception of speech. *Journal of the Acoustical Society of America*, 1963, *35*, 200–206.

Solomon, R. L., and L. Postman. Frequency of usage as a determinant of recognition threshold for words. *Journal of Experimental Psychology*. 1952, *43*. 195–201.

Spence, J. T. Contribution of response bias to recognition thresholds. *Journal of Abnormal and Social Psychology*, 1963, *66*, 339–344.

Stowe, A. N., W. P. Harris, and D. B. Hampton. Signal and context components of word recognition behavior. *Journal of the Acoustical Society of America*, 1963, *35*, 639–644.

Swets, J. A. (Ed.) *Signal detection and recognition by human observers*. New York: Wiley, 1964.

Thorndike, E. L., and I. Lorge. *The teacher's word book of 30,000 words*. New York: Teachers College, Columbia University, Bureau of Publications, 1944.

Treisman, A. M. Contextual cues in selective listening. *Quarterly Journal of Experimental Psychology*, 1960, *12*, 242–248.

Tulving, E., G. Mandler, and R. Baumal. Interaction of two sources of information in tachistoscopic word recognition. *Canadian Journal of Psychology*, 1964, *18*, 62–71.

Zajonc, R. B., and B. Nieuwenhuyse. Relationship between word frequency and recognition: Perceptual process or response bias? *Journal of Experimental Psychology*. 1964, *67*, 276–285.

8.3 Familiarity of Letter Sequences, Response Uncertainty, and the Tachistoscopic Recognition Experiment*

D. J. K. MEWHORT

Since Cattell's classic studies of tachistoscopic recognition, it has been known that subjects can report more letters from a tachistoscopic display composed of words than from one composed of random letter sequences (Woodworth & Schlosberg, 1954, p. 101). In a modern investigation of the problem, Miller, Bruner, and Postman (1954) have shown that the phenomenon is not unique to words but can be obtained by varying the familiarity of letter patterns within pseudo-words.

The explanation usually offered to account for this phenomenon involves the argument that a subject makes use of extra sources of information when dealing with familiar material, but is unable to do so when dealing with unconnected letters. Words and other familiar letter sequences provide a number of cues which presumably permit the subject to supply unperceived letters. For example, one may guess a word on the basis of its overall shape and thus report letters correctly without identifying each one separately. According to this explanation then, the subject fills in unavailable material with whatever the context, in terms of his experience with language, tells him ought to be

* Reproduced by permission of the *Canadian Journal of Psychology*, 1967, vol. 21, pp. 309–321. This research was supported in part by the Defence Research Board of Canada Grant No. 9401–26 to M. P. Bryden. The author wishes to thank M. P. Bryden for his encouragement and assistance in connection with this research, and A. O. Dick, G. E. MacKinnon, P. Merikle, and R. V. Thysell for their helpful comments. Some of these data were reported in a paper read at the Eastern Psychological Association meeting, Boston, April 1967.

correct. With randomly obtained letter sequences language habits are not a good guide, but for familiar patterns the chances are good that letters supplied will correspond to what was actually in the tachistoscopic display.

This kind of response bias (or response uncertainty: Garner, 1962, pp. 35–8) theory seems to be widely held and has received considerable indirect support from studies in which, for example, subjects have read incomplete or incorrectly spelled words (Woodworth & Schlosberg, 1954, pp. 102–5) and from studies correlating the recognition threshold with variables such as word frequency (Goldiamond & Hawkins, 1958; Solomon & Howes, 1951). Other explanations have been suggested. For example, Miller, Bruner, & Postman (1954) have argued that there is a limit to the amount of information which is available in a tachistoscopic exposure. Familiar letter sequences contain less information per letter than unfamiliar materials. Thus, although the same amount of information is processed, the subject will report more letters from familiar sequences than from unfamiliar ones. In their experiment, 8-letter pseudo-words were constructed to represent various levels of approximation to English. Sequences least like English (termed 0-order approximations to English) were constructed by selecting successive letters according to a table of random numbers. For the other sequences, the selection of successive letters was constrained to match the statistical nature of English. For example, 4-order approximations were constructed to reflect the relative frequency in English of letter quadruples. In such pseudo-words, the average amount of information per letter is inversely related to the order of approximation to English. Miller *et al.* presented these pseudo-words tachistoscopically and found that the number of letters identified increased both with an increase in exposure duration and with an increase in the order of approximation to English. To take into account differences in information per letter of the various approximations to English, Miller *et al.* weighted the mean recognition scores by a factor proportional to the average information per letter for each order of approximation. The weighted recognition scores for the redundant sequences, i.e., the higher order approximations, matched those of the 0-order sequences. This relation has been shown to hold over a wide range of exposure durations and luminances (Mewhort & Tulving, 1964).

Baddeley (1964) has re-interpreted the Miller, Bruner, & Postman (1954) experiment in terms of short-term memory factors. He suggested that the subject perceives all of each letter sequence unambiguously but is less able to remember the low redundant materials. To demonstrate this, he presented the same material at a duration long enough to ensure that the subject could see all of each letter sequence. Under these conditions, the relation between order of approximation to English and accuracy of identification paralleled that found by Miller *et al.* Baddeley argued, on the basis of this experiment, that highly redundant sequences are easier to encode (i.e., "chunk"; Miller, 1956) and hence, that sequential redundancy has its effect on recognition performance in terms of memory.

Both Baddeley and Miller *et al.* agree that there is a limit to the amount of information processed and that more material (but the same amount of information) in a highly redundant sequence can pass this limit. Baddeley's point is that the limitation is not a perceptual one but is a matter of short-term memory. Furthermore, both would agree that the response-bias explanation is inadequate. However, neither Miller *et al.* (1954) nor Baddeley (1964) offers any

evidence against the "filling in" explanation outlined earlier. Miller *et al.* argue convincingly that some letters contain more information than others (because of their context) and that a constant amount of information is processed. They leave open, however, the question of how the subject makes use of the context in order to vary the amount of information that each letter contains. To specify that performance is better measured in terms of information units rather than letter units does not specify the way in which the subject deals with familiarity. Baddeley's data show that memory factors are likely to be important but they, like Miller, Bruner, & Postman's, are consistent with the view that the sequential constraint built into the higher order approximations simply permits the subject to "fill in" a letter which he has forgotten.

The present experiment was designed to check on the adequacy of the response-bias theory as a first step in discovering how subjects make use of familiar letter structure in the tachistoscopic recognition task. The logic of the experiment is as follows: suppose that a subject is shown a large display but is asked by means of a post-exposure cue to report only a part of it. If the familiarity of letter sequences has its effects in terms of output processes such as response bias, then the familiarity of material which a subject stores but which he does *not* report should have no effect on the identification of whatever material he does report.

Method

SUBJECTS

The 32 Ss serving in this experiment were undergraduates fulfilling a course requirement in introductory psychology at the University of Waterloo.

APPARATUS

The materials were presented binocularly in a Gerbrands 2-field mirror tachistoscope. The tachistoscope was programmed to switch from the pre-exposure field containing a fixation point, to the exposure field, and then back to the pre-exposure field. The luminance of the 2 fields was approximately 4 foot-lamberts. The duration of the exposure was 100 msec. The mechanical timer of the tachistoscope was calibrated against an electronic one. A tone of either 250 or 1000 c.p.s. was provided by a tone generator connected to a loudspeaker. The tone sounded for 1.03 sec and was programmed to occur either simultaneously with, or 400 msec after, the offset of the exposure field. The tone was controlled by the mechanical timer of the tachistoscope.

MATERIALS

Sixteen 8-letter pseudo-words from the list provided by Miller *et al.* (1954) were used. Eight were low redundant (0-order approximation to English) and eight were high redundant (4-order approximation to English). These pseudo-words were divided into two sets, each having four of 0-order and four of 4-order approximation to English. For both sets, the pseudo-words were prepared on white cards with Letraset Instant Lettering (No. 287, 18 point Grotesque monotype) in upper case letters. The pseudo-words were arranged in two rows per card, in all combinations (low/low, low/high, high/low, high/high) of low redundant and high redundant sequences. Pairing of the words was arranged according to a 4 × 4 Graeco-Latin square such that each pseudo-word appeared in both rows twice: once paired with a pseudo-word of the same order of approximation; once with a pseudo-word of the other order of approximation. The pseudo-words are presented in Table 1.

Under the conditions of this study, the visual angle subtended by each letter was approximately 28 min. In terms of visual angle, the rectangular display comprising the two pseudo-words was approximately 4° 12′ long and 1° 29′ high.

DESIGN

The experiment was a $2^5 \times 4$ factorial experiment with three variables manipulated between Ss and three within. On each of the eight trials, each S was shown tachistoscopically *two* pseudo-words and was required to identify let-

ters from *one* of them. The pseudo-words, either 0-order or 4-order approximations to English, were arranged in two horizontal rows. The variables manipulated within Ss were: (*a*) the order of approximation to English of the row to be reported; (*b*) the order of approximation of the other row (i.e., the row not required); and (*c*) the row required (top or bottom).

The materials were divided into two sets. Half the Ss were required to report the top row of the first set of materials and the bottom row of the second. The other half reported the top row of the second set and the bottom row of the first. This procedure defines a dummy between-Ss variable. In addition, each S viewed all the materials in only one of four arrangements (see Table 1). The four arrangements constitute four levels of a second between-Ss dummy variable. These dummy variables were introduced as a result of the counterbalancing procedures used when pairing the pseudo-words, and as a control for any potential differences between pseudo-words of the same order of approximation to English. Instructions to S indicating which row he was to report were provided post-exposurally by means of an auditory cue. The cue was delayed for one-half the Ss. Thus, the three between-Ss variables were the two dummy variables and the delay of the auditory cue.

PROCEDURE

All Ss viewed eight cards, each displaying two pseudo-words. After the exposure, a tone of either 250 or 1000 c.p.s. was presented. The low tone (250 c.p.s.) indicated that S should attempt to report the letters from the bottom row while the high tone (1000 c.p.s.) instructed report of the top row. On four trials the top row was required, and on the other four trials the bottom one was required. In both cases, S reported two 4-order sequences; one was paired with a 0-order sequence and one with a 4-order sequence. They also reported two 0-order sequences similarly paired. The four trials requiring the top row were randomly mixed among the four requiring the bottom row. A different random sequence was used for each S. A fixation point, provided in the pre-exposure

TABLE 1
Stimulus Materials

ARRANGEMENT	SET 1				SET 2			
	LOW/LOW	LOW/HIGH	HIGH/LOW	HIGH/HIGH	LOW/LOW	LOW/HIGH	HIGH/LOW	HIGH/HIGH
1	YRULPZOC	DLEGQMNW	MOSSIANT	VERNALIT	WXPAUJVB	CVGJCDHM	LYMISTIC	FAVORIAL
	OZHGPMTS	POKERSON	GFUJXZAQ	RICANING	VQWBVIFX	OTATIONS	MFRSIWZE	PREVERAL
2	DLEGQMNW	YRULPZOC	RICANING	POKERSON	CVGJCDHM	WXPAUJVB	PREVERAL	OTATIONS
	GFUJXZAQ	VERNALIT	OZHGPMTS	MOSSIANT	MFRSIWZE	FAVORIAL	VQWBVIFX	LYMISTIC
3	GFUJXZAQ	OZHGPMTS	VERNALIT	RICANING	MFRSIWZE	VQWBVIFX	FAVORIAL	PREVERAL
	YRULPZOC	MOSSIANT	DLEGQMNW	POKERSON	WXPAUJVB	LYMISTIC	CVGJCDHM	OTATIONS
4	OZHGPMTS	GFUJXZAQ	POKERSON	MOSSIANT	VQWBVIFX	MFRSIWZE	OTATIONS	LYMISTIC
	DLEGQMNW	RICANING	YRULPZOC	VERNALIT	CVGJCDHM	PREVERAL	WXPAUJVB	FAVORIAL

TABLE 2
Mean Number of Letters Correctly Reported

	ORDER OF APPROXIMATION OF THE ROW NOT REPORTED							
	0-ORDER				4-ORDER			
	ORDER OF APPROXIMATION OF THE ROW REPORTED							
	0-ORDER		4-ORDER		0-ORDER		4-ORDER	
	Top	Bottom	Top	Bottom	Top	Bottom	Top	Bottom
0-delay	3.37	2.93	3.68	3.00	3.56	3.18	5.18	4.18
400-delay	2.62	2.56	3.43	2.68	3.25	2.18	4.12	4.62
Mean	3.00	2.75	3.55	2.84	3.40	2.68	4.65	4.40

field, appeared equidistant between the two rows and centred between the fourth and the fifth letters of the two pseudo-words.

Ss were instructed to report the letters required verbally in any order that they found convenient; E recorded the letter responses in the order that S reported them. Ss were instructed that the pseudo-words were "not English which one might find in a dictionary" but which "might occasionally look as if they should be English words." In addition, it was made clear that "look as if they should be English words" did not mean that English words had been mis-spelled, or altered, but meant that the letter sequences composing each pseudo-word were familiar without copying a known word. All Ss were asked after each trial which row had been required: there were no mistakes.

Before participating in this experiment, Ss were given fifty practice trials involving recognition of a different set of 8-letter, 0-order, pseudo-words. These trials virtually eliminated any practice effect in this experiment.

SCORING

For the data which follow the responses were scored as if the letters had always been taken from the row requested. This scoring procedure is arbitrary: if S is shown, for example, VERNALIT and DLEGQMNW, and responds with an "L," it is impossible to determine from which row the letter has been taken. These cases were rare; indeed, when analysis parallel to that which follows was performed assuming that such letters had been taken from the "wrong" row, the results were substantially the same.

Results

A six-way analysis of variance was performed to check on the dummy variables. This analysis showed no effects attributable to either of these variables or interactions with them. Since these variables were of no interest and were generated by the counterbalancing procedure, the data were collapsed across them and re-analysed. The data are summarized in Table 2 and a sum-

TABLE 3
Analysis of Variance of Letters Correct from the Correct Row

SOURCE	MEAN SQUARE	df	F
Total	2.872	255	
Between			
Delay (D)	21.391	1	3.50*
error	6.107	30	
Within			
Reported (R)	25.000	1	13.35**
R.D.	1.563	1	
error	1.873	30	
Not reported (NR)	39.063	1	25.68***
NR.D	.062	1	
error	1.521	30	
Row (Rw)	23.766	1	13.47***
Rw.D	.015	1	
error	1.765	30	
R.NR	13.141	1	7.25**
R.NR.D	.765	1	
error	1.812	30	
R.Rw	1.000	1	
R.Rw.D	.250	1	
error	2.099	30	
Rw.NR	1.000	1	
Rw.NR.D	.563	1	
error	3.056	30	
R.NR.Rw	.766	1	
R.NR.Rw.D	2.640	1	
error	1.812	30	

$*.05 > p < .10$ $**p < .025.$ $***p < .005.$

mary of the second (4-way) analysis of variance appears in Table 3. This analysis indicates several large and reliable effects:

Delay of Cue. The mean numbers of letters correct for the 0-delay and the 400-delay conditions were 3.64 and 3.06 respectively. The difference is just short of statistical reliability ($p < .10$) at the conventional level. The presence of a strong trend, together with the fact that delay of cue stimulus has been found to be a reliable effect in other experiments (e.g., Dick, 1967; Dick & Bryden, 1966), suggests that the trend be considered a reliable one. However, while increasing the delay of the extra-exposure cue reduced overall performance, there were no interactions involving delay which approached significance.

The Row Reported. More letters were correctly reported from the top row (mean number correct: 3.66) than from the bottom row (mean number correct: 3.05). These data are consistent with two interpretations. On the one hand, subjects may have ignored the fixation point and simply looked at the top row. This does not seem likely: when questioned after the experiment the subjects reported that they had not ignored the bottom row. Also, if the subjects had ignored the bottom row, one would expect a difference in the number of intrusion errors from the two rows. No reliable difference was found. On the other hand, the superiority of the top row may reflect the order in which the material is processed. Although the exposure duration is too brief to permit the subject to refocus his eyes during the tachistoscopic exposure, there is some evidence that the subject deals with alphabetic material in "reading order," that is from top-to-bottom and left-to-right (Bryden, 1967). According to this interpretation, the top row is easier because the subject deals with it first.

The Familiarity of the Material Reported. The mean number of letters correct when reporting 0-order and 4-order approximations were 3.04 and 3.66 respectively.

The Familiarity of the Material Not Reported. The mean number of letters correctly reported when 0-order sequences were stored but not reported was 2.96. The corresponding mean of 4-order sequences was 3.74. These data indicate that effects of familiarity of letter sequences involve more than a change in the subjects' guessing efficiency when responding. If familiarity simply permitted a subject to fill in letters not seen in the manner outlined earlier, the familiarity of sequences at which the subject never guesses ought to be irrelevant. Hence, the data provide straightforward evidence that "filling in" on the basis of language habits and other output-uncertainty interpretations do not account for the effects of familiarity.

The Interaction of the Kind of Material Reported with That Not Reported. This interaction is illustrated in Figure 1. The redundancy of the row reported is relatively more important when the redundancy of the row not reported is high. Similarly, the effect of the redundancy of the row not reported is relatively unimportant unless the redundancy of the row reported is high. A point of interest in this figure concerns the effects of the familiarity of the letter sequence reported when the sequence not reported is of 0-order approximation. Although "guessing" does not provide a complete explanation, it might, nevertheless, be an important contributor. If this were so, one would expect the slope of this function to be large and positive. It is apparent from Figure 1 that this is not the case. This interaction can be interpreted in terms of the information available in the tachistoscopic display. When a low redundant sequence is reported and paired with another one not reported, the tachistoscopic display contains a maximum amount of information. On the other hand, when the subject is shown two high redundant sequences, the amount of information in the display is at a minimum. A

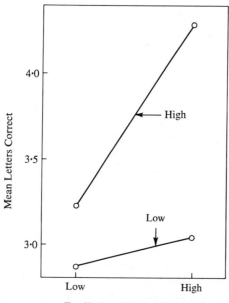

FIGURE 1   Mean number of letters correctly reported as a function of the order of approximation to English of the row reported and of the row not reported.

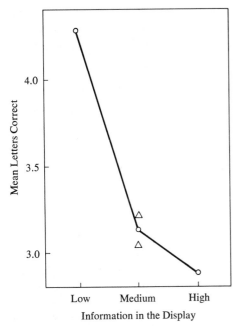

FIGURE 2   Mean number of letters correctly reported as a function of the information in the display as a whole. This figure shows the same data presented in Figure 1 recast by pooling the cases in which an S reports a sequence of one order of approximation paired with a sequence of the other order.

middle point is provided by the case in which the subject reports one kind of sequence paired with the other. Figure 2 shows the recognition performance as a function of the amount of information in the display. For this figure, the cases in which the subject reports a low redundant sequence while it is paired with a high one, or reports a high redundant sequence paired with a low one, have been averaged to provide a middle point. These data are orderly: performance is a monotonic decreasing function of the amount of information in the display. The data, plotted in Figure 2, could well have been taken from an experiment in which the subjects recognized letters from pseudowords of three orders of approximation to English. Recasting the data in this way shows that it is the information in the display as a whole and not only that part which the subject must report which determines the level of performance.

Discussion

The data presented have shown that a response-bias model does not account for the effects of familiarity in the tachistoscopic recognition task. Language habits do not simply alter the subject's guessing efficiency or his response criterion (Green & Swets, 1966) but also represent a fixed bias on the way in which alphabetic material is processed during recognition.

There is considerable evidence demonstrating the importance of short-term memory factors in the tachistoscopic recognition task (e.g., Averbach & Coriell, 1961; Smith & Carey, 1966; Sperling, 1960). It appears that there is no limit to the amount of information which is initially available from the tachistoscopic display but that most of this information (especially spatial information; Dick, 1967) is lost before it can be encoded into memory. In Figure 2, it was shown that performance could be predicted from the average information per letter of the display as a whole. Assuming that all of the information was initially available as Sperling (1960) and Averbach and Coriell (1961) suggest, it follows that the difference in performance on 0- and 4-order materials reflects a limited capacity memory process. Hence, the question of how the subject makes use of context or familiarity must be answered in terms of memory factors.

A memory system can be conceived following the analogy of computer technology in terms of three operations: input, storage, and output (cf. Melton, 1963). Preliminary to asking how memory is sensitive to familiarity and context, it is important to know where, in terms of input, storage, or output, it is sensitive. By considering each to be responsible in turn, it is possible to construct several models, all of which account for the superior retention of familiar materials. The present data appear to be inconsistent with both storage and output models.

According to an output model, familiar and unfamiliar materials are not differentiated in memory until the subject attempts to retrieve them. In the present experiment, however, when the material retrieved was held constant, performance depended on material not retrieved. This relation suggests than an output model cannot account for all the present data. A storage model suggests, on the other hand, that the differentiation between familiar and unfamiliar material takes place in the time interval between input to memory and retrieval from it. One implication of this model is that the greater the time material must be retained, the greater the differentiation which is made by the memory system between familiar and unfamiliar materials. In the present experiment, this critical time interval was controlled by delaying the post-exposure auditory cue. The data indicate that, while delaying the cue and thus lengthening the retention interval did reduce overall performance, the interaction predicted by the storage model did not appear. Thus, the only model consistent with the data is an input model. Unfortunately, locating the part of a conceptual memory system responsible for familiarity effects does not specify how memory makes use of familiarity. For example, it may be that familiar materials can be put into storage in such a way that they are more accessible (Tulving & Pearlstone, 1966). On the other hand, more of the familiar material may be put into storage than of the unfamiliar.

The difference between 0- and 4-order pseudo-words is based on a left-to-right ordering of the letters. The familiar materials are familiar only when read in a left-to-right order. This fact suggests that the encoding process sensitive to familiarity must take into account the relative spatial information attached to each letter. The sequential processing (scanning) implied earlier could well serve to differentiate the relative spatial information. Locating a sequential processing mechanism during input in this way has two important implications. First, more material from the top row ought to be reported than from the bottom row (*supra,* 315). Secondly, while the order of processing is important to the efficiency with which material is encoded, once encoded, order

of processing no longer affects accuracy of report (although order of report presumably does; Bryden, 1967). This second implication can also be checked against the data: in addition to sequential processing, a second time-dependent loss was postulated in order to explain the effect of delaying the post-exposure cue. If both had the effect of simply increasing the total time in storage, it would be reasonable to assume that these two time-dependent losses ought to add. If this were so, there should have been an interaction between the row reported and the delay of the post-exposure cue: the difference between the top and the bottom rows ought to have been larger when the post-exposure cue was delayed. This interaction did not appear.

Placing a sequential mechanism during input is consistent with the finding that performance as a function of the length of time material was retained is independent of the kind of material. The encoding mechanism is a classification mechanism. The kind of material determines either how much material is encoded or the kind of encoding that takes place; it is not important once the material has been encoded. It is also consistent with Mewhort's (1966) finding that spacing letters is more harmful to 4-order sequences than to 0-order sequences.

Two words of warning should be added. The present data are concerned with a manipulation of familiarity within pseudo-words. When actual words are used, it is reasonable to suppose that some of the encoding processes are short-circuited. Also, the material was not kept in the memory for very long: the longest time between the onset of the exposure and the offset of the partial report cue was only 1.5 seconds. If material is retained in storage longer, rehearsal and other storage factors may become increasingly important.

Summary

Ss shown paired pseudo-words (either 0-order or 4-order approximation to English) for 100 msec. were instructed post-exposurally to identify letters from one of the pseudo-words.

Approximation to English not only of the pseudo-words reported, but also of those *not reported,* affected accuracy of identification. Delaying the post-exposure instruction cue 400 msec reduced performance equally for both kinds of material. It appeared that S processes all the material, not just that reported, and that a limited capacity system, rather than output uncertainty (response bias) is required to explain the superior recognition of familiar materials.

References

Averbach, E., & Coriell, A. S. Short-term memory in vision. *Bell Sys. tech. J.,* 1961, *40,* 309–28.

Baddeley, A. D. Immediate memory and the "perception" of letter sequences. *Quart. J. exp. Psychol.,* 1964, *16,* 364–7.

Bryden, M. P. A model for the sequential organization of behaviour. *Canad. J. Psychol.,* 1967, *21,* 37–56.

Dick, A. O. Short-term memory for several stimulus attributes. Paper read at meeting of Eastern Psychological Association, Boston, 1967.

Dick, A. O., & Bryden, M. P. Short-term memory for familiar and unfamiliar material. Paper presented at meeting of Eastern Psychological Association, New York, 1966.

Garner, W. R. *Uncertainty and structure as psychological concepts.* New York: Wiley, 1962.

Goldiamond, I., & Hawkins, W. F. Vexierversuch: the log relationship between word-frequency and recognition obtained in the absence of stimulus words. *J. exp. Psychol.,* 1958, *56,* 457–63.

Green, D. M., & Swets, J. A. *Signal detection theory and psychophysics.* New York: Wiley, 1966.

Mewhort, D. J. K. Sequential redundancy and letter spacing as determinants of tachistoscopic recognition. *Canad. J. Psychol.,* 1966, *20,* 435–44.

Mewhort, D. J. K., & Tulving, E. Sequential redundancy, illumination level, and exposure duration as determinants of tachistoscopic recognition. Paper presented at meeting of Canadian Psychological Association, Halifax, 1964.

Melton, A. W. Implications of short-term memory for a general theory of memory. *J. verb. Learn. verb. Behav.,* 1963, *2,* 1–21.

Miller, G. A. The magical number seven plus or minus two: some limits on our capacity for processing information. *Psychol. Rev.,* 1956, *63,* 81–97.

Miller, G. A., Bruner, J. S., & Postman, L. Familiarity of letter sequences and tachistoscopic identification. *J. gen. Psychol.,* 1954, *50,* 129–39.

Smith, F., & Carey, P. Temporal factors in visual information processing. *Canad. J. Psychol.,* 1966, *20,* 337–42.

Solomon, R. L., & Howes, D. H. Word-probability, personal values, and visual duration thresholds. *Psychol. Rev.,* 1951, *58,* 256–70.

Sperling, G. The information available in brief visual presentations. *Psychol. Monogr.,* 1960, *74,* No. 11 (Whole No. 498).

Tulving, E., & Pearlstone, Zena. Availability vs accessibility of information in memory for words. *J. verb. Learn. verb. Behav.,* 1966, *5,* 381–91.

Woodworth, R. S., & Schlosberg, H. *Experimental psychology.* New York: Holt, Rinehart, & Winston, 1954.

8.4 Rehearsal and Decay in Immediate Recall of Visually and Aurally Presented Items*

M. C. CORBALLIS

Waugh (1960) has suggested that the primacy effect typically found in short-term serial memory may occur because subjects rehearse earlier items more extensively than later ones. Reynolds and Houston (1964) have provided some support for this "cumulative rehearsal" hypothesis in a study of memory for nonsense syllables following a single learning trial. When they instructed subjects to rehearse right through the list each time a new syllable appeared, the primacy effect was about the same as for a control group who were not given specific rehearsal instructions; the primacy effect was much reduced, however, when subjects were given rehearsal instructions which should have precluded cumulative rehearsal. In this study, presentation was slow (one syllable every 4 seconds) and recall was tested 45 seconds after presentation by a serial anticipation method.

The present study was designed to test the hypothesis for memory more typically classed as short-term, that is, memory for digit series, tested by immediate recall. Two presentation conditions were compared, one (Condition D) in which interdigit intervals were long initially but were gradually decreased within series, and one (Condition I) in which interdigit intervals were initially short but were gradually increased

within series. The total time to present the digits in each series was the same under each condition. The hypothesis of cumulative rehearsal would predict better recall under Condition I, in which there was more time later in the series to rehearse both early and late digits, than under Condition D, in which there was less time for rehearsal later in the series. On the other hand, if subjects rehearse each item as it comes and do not rehearse an item after the next has appeared, as implied by associative chain theories of serial memory (e.g., Hull, et al., 1940), there should be no difference between the two conditions.

These predictions may be complicated by the possibility that the short-term memory trace decays fairly rapidly over time (Brown, 1958). Assuming equal rehearsal under the two conditions, the decay hypothesis would predict better recall under Condition D than under Condition I, the reverse of the prediction from the cumulative rehearsal hypothesis. This follows because under Condition D the digits were presented, on the average, nearer in time to the recall period than the corresponding digits presented under Condition I.

Two experiments are reported here. The two conditions were presented visually in the first experiment and aurally in the second. Several authors have suggested that there may be important differences between visual and auditory modalities in the processing of information for short-term serial recall (Conrad, 1964; Mackworth, 1964; Sperling, 1963).

* Reproduced by permission of the *Canadian Journal of Psychology,* 1966, vol. 20, pp. 43–51. The research reported in this paper was supported by a grant (No. 9425-10) from the Defence Research Board of Canada to Dr. Dalbir Bindra. The author wishes to thank Miss Thelma Loveless for assistance in running the second experiment.

Method

EXPERIMENT 1

Subjects. Ss were 24 high school students who volunteered to act as subjects for a variety of psychological experiments during the summer vacation. There were 14 boys and 10 girls; their ages ranged from 14 to 17 years.

Apparatus and Material. Digits were projected by means of a multiple-stimulus projector, designed to project any of the digits 0 through 9, or either a red or a green flash, onto a black screen measuring 1½ in. by 2 in. The projector was connected to a stepper, pre-programmed to select series of nine digits. Each series was preceded by a green flash, which served as a ready signal, and was followed by a red flash, which was the signal for S to repeat the digits. There were two programmes, A and B, each consisting of 13 series of 9 digits each. The digits within each series were randomly selected with the restriction that no digit could appear twice in any one series. Presentation timing was controlled by tone signals, recorded on tape. The output from the tape recorder was amplified and fed into the stepper. Presentation times of digits and intervals between them were thus determined by, respectively, durations of, and intervals between, successive tone signals. There were two sequences of tone signals, representing decreasing (D) and increasing (I) conditions respectively, each capable of projecting either programme A or programme B. Both sequences projected the first series of 9 digits at a regular presentation speed of 50 digits/min., each digit being projected for 0.6 sec. This first series constituted a practice trial. For the remaining 12 series each digit was projected for 0.3 sec., and the intervals between succesive digit onsets were as follows:

> *Condition D:* 1.9, 1.7, 1.5, 1.3, 1.1, 0.9, 0.7, and 0.5 sec.
> *Condition I:* 0.5, 0.7, 0.9, 1.1, 1.3, 1.5, 1.7, and 1.9 sec.

Total time to project each series was 9.9 sec. for each condition. For all series, including the practice series, the green flash was projected for 1.0 sec beginning 2.0 sec before the onset of the first digit, and the red flash was projected for 1.0 sec beginning 1.0 sec following the offset of the last digit. These timing characteristics are illustrated in Figure 1.

Procedure. Each S was tested individually and received both conditions. Half the Ss (7 boys and 5 girls) received Condition D followed by Condition I (DI group), and the other half received Condition I followed by Condition D (ID group). Within each group programmes A and B were counterbalanced, 6 Ss receiving A followed by B and 6 receiving B followed by A. Ss were instructed to call out

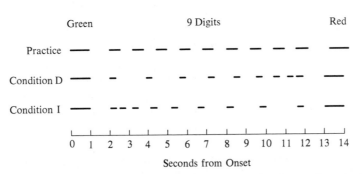

FIGURE 1 Diagram showing timing of digit and signal presentations for practice series, Condition D and Condition I, in Experiment 1. Horizontal bars represent "on" periods for visual stimuli.

the digits, after the red flash had appeared, in the order in which they had been presented. Projection was stopped after the practice series, then run continuously through the remainder of the series in each condition. Ss were informed that they had 9 sec in which to repeat each series; 9 sec after offset of each red flash the green flash appeared to signal a new series. Between conditions there was a rest pause of 2–3 min. S's responses were recorded on tape.

Scoring. Four measures of recall were used. (1) *Total number correct:* the number of digits correctly reported was counted for each series. Reported digits were scored correct if they corresponded to a digit actually presented, except that if a particular digit was reported more than once it could be counted only once. No account was taken of order of recall. (2) *Initial sequence:* the number of digits reported correctly and in the correct order was counted from the beginning of the list until the first error or omission. For example, if the actual sequence was 71269-4385, and S reported 71263485 his initial sequence score would be 4. (3) *Final sequence:* the number of digits reported correctly and in the correct order was determined by counting *backwards* from the final digit until an error or omission was reached. In the example given under (2) above, S's final sequence score would be 2. If S failed to report the final digit, his score would be 0. (4) *Tau scores:* as a measure of the extent to which Ss were able to report the digits in the correct order, Kendall's tau (Kendall, 1948) was calculated between the order of report of correct digits and the order of presentation of those digits. If any digit was omitted in response, it was also omitted from the presented series, and the remaining digits re-ranked accordingly, prior to calculation of tau. If a particular, correct digit was repeated in response, that serial position was chosen which maximized tau for the series and the other or others were disregarded. In the example given under (2) above, S would receive a tau score of 0.93. This measure was included following the suggestion of Conrad (1959) that order recall is independent of content recall.

EXPERIMENT 2

Subjects. Ss were 12 men and 12 women from an introductory psychology class. Their ages ranged from 17 to 21 years.

Apparatus and Material. The numbers 1 through 10 were recorded on tape. They were then re-recorded many times on a second tape to form a pool of spoken numbers. These numbers were excised from the tape and spliced together in a new order to form two programmes, each consisting of 13 series of nine numbers each. These programmes consisted of the same numbers as programmes A and B except that the digit 0, whenever it occurred in the visual programmes, was replaced by the number 10 on the tape. "Ten" was preferred to "zero" because it is a shorter, crisper word, less likely to encroach on the succeeding number when intervals between numbers were short. Ready and repeat signals in the auditory programmes consisted of 1000-c.p.s. tone signals spliced in before and after each series. Four tapes were made up in this way, two for each programme. For each programme there was a decreasing (D) and an increasing (I) condition, in which the intervals between successive digit onsets were the same as in the corresponding conditions in Experiment 1. The ready signal tone was sounded for 0.5 sec beginning 1.5 sec before the onset of the first spoken number in each series, and the repeat signal was sounded for 0.5 sec beginning 1.3 sec after the onset of the last digit in each series. There was an interval of 9 sec between series for S to repeat the numbers.

Procedure. The procedure was entirely analogous to that used in Experiment 1, half the Ss receiving Condition D then Condition I (DI group), and the other half Condition I then Condition D (ID group). Again, programmes A and B were counterbalanced within each group of 12 Ss. The tapes were played over a speaker, and S's responses were recorded on tape. Instructions to S were, in effect, the same as in Experiment 1.

Scoring. The scoring procedure was the same as in Experiment 1.

Results

For each subject, scores on each of the four recall measures were summed over the 12 series presented under each condition in each experiment. These summed scores were subjected to analyses of variance for Latin square design. Separate analyses were carried out for each recall measure. Independent variables were presentation conditions (D *vs.* I), first *vs.* second sessions, and groups (DI *vs.* ID).

CONDITION D VS. CONDITION I

Experiment 1 (visual presentation) gave clear evidence in favour of the cumulative rehearsal hypothesis. Condition I resulted in significantly higher total number correct ($p < .05$) and significantly higher final sequence scores ($p < .05$). Initial sequence scores were slightly higher for Condition I, but the difference was not significant. Experiment 2 (aural presentation) failed to provide convincing evidence in favour of the cumulative rehearsal hypothesis. Total number correct was the only measure which favoured Condition I over Condition D, and

the difference was significant on a one-tailed test only (one-tailed $p < .05$). The other three scores did not yield significant differences.

Figure 2 shows serial position curves for Conditions D and I in both experiments. Number of correct responses, regardless of their serial position in response, were counted for each serial position of presented digits, and summed over subjects, sessions, and series within sessions. This figure illustrates the superiority of Condition I, in Experiment 1 especially, and shows that this superiority was confined mainly to recall of the last three digits. Another point of interest is that the recency effect was much more pronounced for aural than for visual presentation.

Table 1 shows mean initial and final sequence scores for Conditions D and I in both experiments. Again, it is of interest that the final sequence scores were markedly higher for aural than for visual presentation.

SESSIONS

In both experiments there was evidence for a practice effect, resulting in better recall in the second session than in the first. In Experiment 1, the difference was significant for total number correct ($p < .001$), initial sequence scores ($p < .01$), and final sequence scores ($p <$

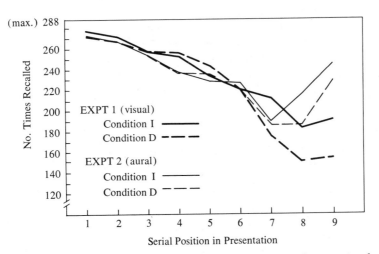

FIGURE 2 Number of times digits were recalled in each serial position of presentation, for each condition and each experiment. The maximum possible score for each condition was 288.

TABLE 1

*Mean Initial Sequence and Final Sequence Scores for Each
Condition in Each Experiment*

	EXPERIMENT 1 (VISUAL)		EXPERIMENT 2 (AURAL)	
	CONDITION D	CONDITION I	CONDITION D	CONDITION I
Initial sequences	3.62	4.03	3.85	3.75
Final sequences	0.77	1.39	2.38	2.37

.05). In Experiment 2, it was significant for total number correct ($p < .001$) and initial sequence scores ($p < .01$).

DI GROUP VS. ID GROUP

In both experiments the DI group gave somewhat higher scores than the ID group. In Experiment 1 the difference was significant ($p < .05$) for initial sequence scores, and in Experiment 2 it was significant ($p < .05$) for tau scores. The difference was more apparent for the three recall measures (initial sequences, final sequences, tau scores) which depended on correct ordering of digits in response, than for total number correct, which was defined independently of order of recall. The difference may therefore be one of ordering the digits rather than one of recalling what digits were presented. It may be interpreted as an interaction between conditions (I and D) and sessions. Table 2 shows average tau scores for each condition, in each session, for the two experiments. Initial sequence scores and final sequence scores showed very similar trends.

Discussion

The results of Experiment 1 support the hypothesis that subjects tend to rehearse cumulatively when presentation is visual; moreover, the superiority of Condition I which favoured cumulative rehearsal, over Condition D which did not, was confined to the digits presented late in the series. Inspection of the serial position curves (Figure 2) suggests in fact that it was the last three digits which were better recalled under Condition I. Indeed rehearsal may have been cumulative during presentation of the first six digits in *both* conditions, since there appeared to be no difference in recall of these digits even though it took longer to present them under Condition D than under Condition I. If rehearsal were cumulative, no special advantage would attach to the long *initial* interdigit intervals in Condition D. Subsequent to presentation of the sixth item, however, there would be considerably more time for cumulative rehearsal under Condition I than under Condition D. It seems likely, then, that supe-

TABLE 2

*Mean Tau Scores for Each Condition in Each Session,
for Both Experiments*

	EXPERIMENT 1 (VISUAL)		EXPERIMENT 2 (AURAL)	
	CONDITION D	CONDITION I	CONDITION D	CONDITION I
First session	.880	.757	.901	.820
Second session	.768	.873	.830	.881

rior recall of the last three digits under Condition I resulted because these digits were more likely to be rehearsed under this condition than under Condition D.

Experiment 2, however, failed to provide convincing evidence that subjects rehearse cumulatively when presentation is aural, although there was some suggestion that recall was slightly better under Condition I than under Condition D. It is likely, however, that rehearsal, especially cumulative rehearsal, is more restricted when presentation is aural than when it is visual. There is evidence that rehearsal is essentially verbal in character, and that auditory confusions arise, presumably from verbal rehearsal, even when presentation is visual (Conrad, 1964). If, as Sperling (1963) suggests, a primary function of verbal rehearsal in visual memory tasks is to convert information from visual to auditory storage, then it follows that rehearsal should be less necessary when presentation is auditory in the first place. Moreover, the possibility of auditory confusions should be even greater for aural than for visual presentation, since subjects might be expected to make auditory confusions not only within the rehearsed items, but also between rehearsed items and items being aurally presented. This would be especially true if rehearsal were cumulative, in which case the item being rehearsed at any point need not be the item just presented. It is plausible, then, to suppose that subjects do not rehearse cumulatively when presentation is aural, or at least not to the extent they do when presentation is visual.

The most striking difference between results of Experiments 1 and 2, however, was the much more pronounced recency effect in Experiment 2. This is evident both in the serial position curves shown in Figure 2 and in the final sequence scores given in Table 1. Assuming that the recency effect reflects retention of items in short-term storage even though they were not rehearsed (Waugh, 1960), this finding supports Sperling's (1963) notion that auditory short-term storage is more effective and lasts longer than visual. However the slight recency effect for visual presentation under both conditions

suggests that subjects may have occasionally retained the last digit at least in purely visual storage.

The results provide no direct support for decay theory, which, as noted in the Introduction, would predict better recall under Condition D than under Condition I. It is possible to argue, however, that the results are indirectly consistent with decay theory since the results of Experiment 1, especially, demonstrate the importance of rehearsal, and it is often maintained (e.g., Broadbent, 1958) that the function of rehearsal is to prevent decay. It is also possible, however, that the function of rehearsal is to strengthen storage against the effects of interference, rather than of decay. One feature of the present results favours an interference rather than a decay interpretation. In both experiments the difference between recall of the last digit and recall of the penultimate digit was roughly the same, within modalities, whether the interval between presentation of these digits was 0.5 sec. (Condition D) or 1.9 sec. (Condition I)—see Figure 2. This supports Mackworth's (1964) conclusion that not much decay occurs during presentation of items, and is more in line with the theory (Waugh & Norman, 1965) that availability of a particular item in short-term storage depends on how many items have been presented subsequent to that item rather than on how long the item has been in storage.

The lower scores for the ID group compared with the DI group may reflect different strategies employed by subjects in the different groups, since the difference was not specific to one or other condition; that is, the lower scores for Condition I in the first session persisted in the second session when the conditions were reversed. The difference was apparent only for those measures which depended to some extent at least on the order in which the digits were reported. It is possible, then, that subjects in the ID group may have adopted a different ordering strategy from that adopted by subjects in the DI group, even though subjects in both groups were instructed to report the digits in the order presented. Posner (1964) has reported an experiment suggesting that there is a tendency in short-term serial memory, especially marked when presentation is slow, to record later items before earlier ones in response. A similar tendency may have operated in the ID group in the present experiment. Note that the lowering of tau scores for the ID group, in Experiment 2 particularly, does not reflect early recording of late digits due simply to early omissions, but reflects rather a genuine re-ordering of digits; that is, a tau score of less than one for any series necessarily means that at least one digit was reported *before* another digit which it originally followed in the presented series. Any tendency to record late items before early ones lends further support to the notion that later items may be held in short-term storage but not rehearsed; since this storage is unstable, there would be some advantage in responding with these items as early as possible, before they are lost through interference or decay. Further research is required on this point, however.

Summary

Immediate recall of 9-digit series was compared under two conditions, one (Condition I) in which interdigit intervals were short at first but were gradually increased within series, and one (Condition D) in which intervals were long at first but gradually decreased. Twenty-four Ss received both conditions in each of two experiments; presentation was visual in the first experiment and aural in the second. Recall was better for Condition I in Experiment 1 supporting a hypothesis that Ss rehearsed cumulatively during visual presentation of digits. Experiment 2 failed to show any consistent difference between conditions. A recency effect was more marked for Experiment 2 than for Experiment 1, suggesting that short-term storage of unrehearsed digits is more effective in auditory than visual modality, but there was little evidence within modalities to support decay theory.

References

Broadbent, D. E. *Perception and communication.* London: Pergamon, 1958.

Brown, J. Some tests of the decay theory of immediate recall. *Quart. J. exp. Psychol.,* 1958, *10,* 12–21.

Conrad, R. Errors of immediate memory. *Brit. J. Psychol.,* 1959, *20,* 349–59.

—— Acoustic confusions in immediate memory. *Brit. J. Psychol.,* 1964, *55,* 75–84.

Hull, C. L., Hovland, C. I., Ross, R. T., Hall, M., Perkins, D. T., & Fitch, F. B. *Mathematico-deductive theory of rote learning.* New Haven: Yale University Press, 1940.

Kendall, M. G. *Rank correlation methods.* London: Griffin, 1948.

Mackworth, Jane F. Auditory short-term memory. *Canad. J. Psychol.,* 1964, *18,* 292–303.

Posner, M. I. Rate of presentation and order of recall in immediate memory. *Brit. J. Psychol.,* 1964, *55,* 303–6.

Reynolds, J. H., & Houston, J. P. Rehearsal strategies and the primacy effect in serial learning. *Psychon. Sci.,* 1964, *1,* 279–80.

Sperling, G. A model for visual memory tasks. *Hum. Factors,* 1963, *5,* 19–31.

Waugh, Nancy C. Serial position and the memory span. *Amer. J. Psychol.,* 1960, *73,* 68–79.

Waugh, Nancy C., & Norman, D. Primary memory, *Psychol Rev.,* 1965, *72,* 89–104.

8.5 Acoustic Factors
versus Language Factors
in Short-Term Memory*

R. CONRAD   P. R. FREEMAN
A. J. HULL

Introduction

One of the reasons why Ebbinghaus thought so highly of nonsense syllables was the belief that they would be free from meaning and the effects of language experience; memory could thus be studied uncontaminated by verbal habit. That the assumption was false has long been recognised, and for 40 years or more no verbal learning experiments have used nonsense syllables without controlling for association value or meaningfulness, and more recently Underwood & Schulz (1960) have shown that pronunciablility is also an important determinant of ease of learning letter groups. These measures, though without doubt reliable predictors, are limited by the fact that norms are required before they can be used, that such norms are only available for certain types of letter sequence (e.g. CVCs, CCCs etc.), and that the norms are based on consensus of opinion which needs to be laboriously determined for each type of letter sequence.

In 1958 Miller reported that ease of recall or letter sequences was a function of letter se-

quence redundancy thus including, probably, most of the earlier measures in one which obviates the need for independently established norms, and which can be applied to any length of sequence. Di Mascio (1959) reported that even single letter frequency was related to memorizability, and Underwood & Schulz (1960) reported significant correlations between ease of learning single leters as response terms in paired-associate learning, and frequency of occurrence in English. Baddeley (1964) showed that a simple-to-use approximation to second order letter sequence redundancy, which he called predictability, was a highly effective predictor of ease of learning, and since it was based on published tables of diagram frequency (Baddeley, Conrad & Thomson, 1960) required no prior testing.

Baddeley, Conrad & Hull (1965) measured the predictability of 40 6-consonant sequences and obtained a highly significant correlation with ease of short-term memorizing. But when second-order effects were partialled out, a Di Mascio (1959) single-letter frequency measure did not correlate significantly with ease of memorizing.

Coming at verbal learning from an angle completely different from that based on language habits of the kind referred to, Conrad (1962, 1964) showed that when consonant sequences are memorized for short-term recall after visual presentation, memory errors correlate highly with listening errors in a conven-

* Reproduced by permission of *Psychonomic Science*, 1965, vol. 3, pp. 57–58. This article was written while the senior author (R. Conrad) held a position of Visiting Scientist at the Human Performance Center, Department of Psychology, University of Michigan. This post was supported by the Advanced Research Projects Agency, Department of Defense, and monitored by the Air Force Office of Scientific Research under Contract No. AF 49(638)–1235.

tional intelligibility test for spoken consonants. This result suggested that another factor in determining the ease with which a letter sequence could be learned, would be the acoustic confusability of the letters within the sequence. This prediction was confirmed by Conrad & Hull (1964) who in the same study showed that when acoustic confusability was held constant, information in the sequence was of minor importance.

However, these measures of acoustic confusability confounded predictability (letter-sequence effects), while the Baddeley, Conrad & Hull (1965) study of predictability confounded effects of acoustic confusability. The present study was carried out in an attempt to get independent estimates of the effects of these parameters.

Method

Using all consonants except Z, 40 6-letter sequences were randomly generated with the sole constraints that no letter appeared more than once in a sequence, and letters occurred equally often in each serial position. Sequences were presented letter by letter for immediate recall by means of frame by frame film projection at a rate of 80/min. Unlimited time for written recall was allowed. Ss were 45 paid housewives.

When the sequences had been generated to meet the above constraints, the probability of acoustic confusion was calculated for each sequence from the table of listening data given by Conrad (1964). Similarly the predictability for each sequence was calculated from the table of diagrams of the English language in Baddeley, Conrad & Thomson (1960). The rank correlation between the two measures was .18 ($p > .2$).

Results

The measure of recall was simply the number of letters in a sequence wrong for the particular serial position. The mean number of errors per subject/sequence was 1.51 (range:

.54–3.33). The error data were fitted significantly well (F = 19.23, df: 2/37) by the function: $Y = .895\ X_0 + .059\ X_1$, where Y = errors. X_0 = probability of acoustic confusion, X_1 = predictability. The acoustic similarity component is significant at the .001 level, the predictability component is significant at the .02 level.

Since letters occurred equi-probably in each serial position, the total number of errors per letter was taken as an index of ease of memorizing letters. The product-moment correlation between frequency with which a letter was wrongly recalled and frequency of listening error (Conrad, 1964) was .75, $p < .001$. When language frequency was correlated with the frequency with which a letter was incorrectly given as response in the memory task, the product-moment correlation was .09. When language frequency was correlated with frequency of the letter being wrongly recalled, the correlation was again about .09.

Discussion

It seems adequately shown that for short-term storage of consonant sequences, encoding of presented material depends much more on what the individual letters sound like, than on the frequency with which they have previously been met in the course of using language. Single-letter frequency seems irrelevant to the task and the results sharply qualify the SPEW hypothesis of Underwood & Schulz (1960) which asserts that the availability of verbal units as responses in new associative connections depends on the frequency with which they have previously been experienced. However, when the index of experience is based on higher order sequence relationships it does become more important for memory. Nevertheless, Conrad (1963) has shown that when letter sequence redundancy is very high and relatively homogeneous, as with common words, the acoustic properties of the word still dominate. S's encoding strategy is probably dependent on the time he has available for it.

Summary

Forty five Ss recalled 6-consonant sequences immediately after leter by letter visual presentation. The main, factor contributing to ease of recall was within-sequence acoustic confusability. Language habits were relatively unimportant. Single-letter language frequency was unrelated to recall; second order effects made a small but significant contribution.

References

Baddeley, A. D. Immediate memory and the "perception" of letter sequences. *Quart. J. exp. Psychol.,* 1964, *16,* 364–367.

Baddeley, A. D., Conrad R., & Hull, A. J. Predictability and immediate memory for consonant sequences. *Quart. J. exp. Psychol.,* 1965, *17,* 175–177.

Baddeley, A. D., Conrad, R., & Thomson, W. E. Letter structure of the English language. *Nature,* 1960, *186,* 414–416.

Conrad, R. An association between memory errors and errors due to acoustic masking of speech. *Nature,* 1962, *193,* 1314–1315.

Conrad, R. Acoustic confusions and memory span for words. *Nature,* 1963, *197,* 1029–1030.

Conrad, R. Acoustic confusions in immediate memory. *Brit. J. Psychol.,* 1964, *55,* 75–84.

Conrad, R., & Hull, A. J. Information, acoustic confusion and memory span. *Brit. J. Psychol.,* 1964, *55,* 429–432.

Di Mascio, A. Learning characteristics of nonsense syllables: A function of letter frequency. *Psychol. Rep.,* 1959, *5,* 585–591.

Miller, G. A. Free recall of redundant strings of letters. *J. exp. Psychol.,* 1958, *56,* 485–491.

Underwood, B. J., & Schulz, R. W. Meaningfulness and verbal learning. New York: Lippincott, 1960.

CHAPTER 9

Attention

9.1 Selective Attention: Perception or Response?*

ANNE TREISMAN   GINA GEFFEN

Introduction

The characteristics of human selective attention have recently been explored in some detail, typically by experiments requiring subjects to respond selectively to one of two or more simultaneous speech messages. When the two messages come from different sources, subjects can repeat one back very efficiently, but can usually report nothing of the verbal content of the other (Cherry, 1953), apart from a few highly important or relevant words (Moray, 1959, Treisman, 1960). If we ask the subject specifically to recall single target words presented to one ear, his ability to repeat the words on the other ear is totally disrupted at the times when the target words occur (Mowbray, 1964). This limit to performance is clearly not due to a shortage of ears or mouths, since either message can be clearly heard, and since the verbal responses required are successive not simultaneous. But we can still ask whether the limit to our capacity for perceiving speech arises on the perceptual or on the response side of the brain's central communication channel. Can we only analyse and identify half the incoming words or can we only organize memory

storage and response for one of the two messages?

Broadbent (1958) favours the perceptual hypothesis and suggests that a "selective filter" in the brain rejects the unwanted message before its content is fully analysed. Deutsch and Deutsch (1963) prefer the explanation that all stimulus inputs are fully analysed and that selection is made only to determine responses and memory. Reynolds (1964) gives a similar account in terms of competition between responses and assumes that the second message in Cherry's type of experiment is "not a potent elicitor of responses" except when it contains the subject's own name or other highly relevant signals. One obvious way of separating response from stimulus competition is to ask for two different responses from one and the same stimulus and to compare this with the same two responses made to two different simultaneous stimuli. The experiment we shall describe was an attempt to throw more light on the nature of the limit to human speech transmission and on the level at which it occurs.

To test how far attention is a feature of perception rather than of response, we can compare the same response made to an attended and an unattended message. To test how far the limit affects the performance of responses, we see what interference a second response to the same stimulus causes in the performance of a primary response. We can combine these two problems into one experimental test by

* Reproduced by permission of *Quarterly Journal of Experimental Psychology,* 1967, vol. 19, pp. 1–17. We should like to thank the Medical Research Council for supporting this research, Mr. C. Turner who helped carry out a pilot experiment, and Dr. M. Treisman for his helpful criticisms.

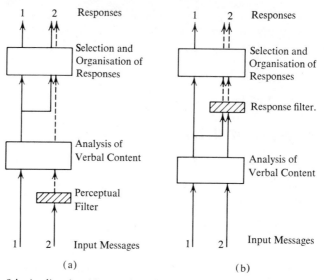

FIGURE 1 Selective listening (a) assuming a limit to perceptual capacity and (b) assuming a limit to response capacity.

presenting two messages and requiring two responses, one of each being given priority by the instructions. The primary message and response are chosen (on the basis of previous findings) to occupy most of the limited capacity available to the subject. The primary response is made to the primary message only and the other response to both messages. Both are made immediately the stimulus is given, so no memory limits are involved in determining performance. The two hypotheses are illustrated in Figure 1.

Figure 1a assumes a perceptual limit, with a "filter" reducing the perceptual analysis of message 2, but no limit to the responses which can be made to perceived signals. Response 2 is therefore made much more efficiently to message 1 than to message 2. Figure 1b assumes that the two messages are perceived equally well, but that only one response can be efficiently performed. Response 2 is therefore equally inefficient to message 1 and to message 2. In this experiment, the two responses to the primary message are made to the same stimulus, which must have been correctly perceived if either response is made correctly. Any reduction in the efficiency of the primary response produced by the second response to the primary message must therefore be due to

response rather than stimulus competition. In the experiment to be reported, the two messages were prose passages, played one to each ear of the subject over headphones. The subject attended to one of the two (the primary message) and repeated it back continuously as he listened to it (the primary response). The secondary response, which was made to both messages, was to tap with a ruler whenever a particular target word was heard in either message.

The main aim was to compare perceptual and response competition in the selective listening task, but it is of interest also to explore the nature of the limit in more detail: (1) What effect will verbal characteristics of the target words have on performance? Since Broadbent put forward his filter theory of selective attention in 1958, it has generally been assumed that the main limit in selective attention is determined by the information content of the messages. We can compare three ways of varying the information content of the target words: (a) varying their transition probability (this was done by fitting the target words into the verbal context of the passage or inserting them at random points); (b) varying the number of target words by using members of large or small ensembles (for example comparing "any digit" with the single word "Boat"); (c) increasing the linguistic or semantic ambiguity without changing the number of phonetic patterns by using words with several meanings (e.g. "Fit") or several homophones (e.g. "Right, Rite, Write, Wright"). These variables might have different effects on perceptual and on response competition. If the hypothesis of limited *perceptual* capacity is correct, some clear differences should also emerge between target words in the primary and secondary message with respect to these linguistic variables. For instance if the secondary message is filtered out before analysis of its verbal content, we should not expect changes in context or meaning to affect performance. The subject would react to the target words, if at all, simply as particular speech sounds.

(2) If the responses compete, what is the nature of the competition? If two responses are made to the same stimulus (for example the verbal response of repeating the target word and the manual response of tapping to it), are they determined at the same stage of perceptual analysis, or is the manual response triggered simply by recognition of the speech sound before its syntactic and semantic role in the sentence is analysed? When one states that a word has been "perceived" one is not making an all-or-nothing assertion: it may be that no stimulus reaching our nervous system is ever fully classified in all possible ways. We probably analyse chiefly those features relevant to the particular response we wish to make. If we assume that speech perception is a hierarchical process, in which categorizations may be made at a number of different levels, such as the physical sound, the phonemic pattern, the word, the syntactic structure and the semantic interpretation, it may be possible for different responses to be selected and programmed at different stages in the sequence rather than all being dependent on its completion. In the present experiment the particular acoustic pattern of the target words could have been sufficient signal for the tapping response, but the repeating response probably required a higher level of analysis, since subjects were repeating the whole passage rather than isolated words. Other experiments have shown that they can

only do this efficiently, at the speed we used, when they make use of the general contextual redundancy, implying some recognition of syntax and meaning. If this redundancy is reduced, the repeating response breaks down (Moray and Taylor, 1958). If the tapping and repeating responses do not interfere, this might be due to their being "cued" at different points in the perceptual sequence. This suggestion was not tested directly, but the results give some indications which will be examined in the discussion.

(3) We investigated the effect of stimulus-response compatibility on attention. Can one, by choosing a response which is closely related to the stimulus, bypass the usual limited capacity decision channel? In reaction time tasks there is now considerable evidence (Leonard, 1961; Mowbray, 1960; Davis, Moray and Treisman, 1961; Broadbent and Gregory, 1962) that the more compatible, overlearned, natural and automatic the relation between stimulus and response, the less effect is produced by increases in information content. The subject appears to function as a multichannel system in which decisions are taken in parallel rather than sequentially. Would the same be true of selective listening tasks? Moray and Jordan (1966) suggest that compatibility may be equally important here.

(4) Finally we hoped to compare the effects of auditory noise and of inattention on the perception of speech. Broadbent and Gregory (1963) and Treisman (1960, 1964) suggested that the perceptual filter mediating selective attention might "attenuate" unwanted messages rather than block them completely. If the effect of inattention is to reduce the signal-to-noise ratio of all but the selected message, one might expect the resultant behaviour to resemble that produced by an external masking noise.

Method

Apparatus and Stimulus Materials. Two Ferrograph twin-track tape-recorders were used. The experimental messages were presented on one tape-recorder and the responses were recorded on one track of the second while the primary message was re-recorded on the other track. The messages were presented dichotically to subjects through a pair of Brown moving-coil headphones, and both responses were recorded through a microphone. The prose passages were all extracts from "Lord Jim" by Conrad, some of them modified slightly to allow target words to be inserted in context. Both were recorded by the same woman speaker. The primary message started two or three words before the secondary one and they finished together; each was 150 words long and lasted about 1 min. Three target words were inserted in each passage of every part at random points, with the restriction that none occurred in the first or last 10 words or within less than eight words of another target word in either the same message or the competing message on the other ear. The intensities of these target words were measured using a Marconi valve volt-meter, and were later correlated with the subjects' performance.

Four different tape-recordings were used. The first three were essentially similar, in that each used the same five classes of target words and they were designed to test the same theoretical points. However each recording used a different set of prose passages and different examples of each class of target word, in order to control for accidental differences in difficulty of particular words or passages. The target words used in these three tapes are given in Table 1, together with descriptions of the variables being investigated. Each type of target word was given in context in two passages (e.g. "her big clear *eyes* would remain fastened on us . . .") and out of context in two other passages (e.g. "waste ground interspersed *check* with small patches of . . ."). In each condition (e.g. "Hot" in context) there were therefore six target words in the primary messages (three in each of two passages) and six in the corresponding secondary messages. These recordings were used to investigate the following variables, and to compare their effects on perception of and response to the target words: (1) transition probabilities from the verbal context; (2) ensemble size of the target words; (3) variety of possible meanings of target words all sharing the same phonetic form; (4) different grammatical forms of the target words; (5) stimulus-response compatibility.

The fourth tape-recording included the following target words:

(i) "From" and "But," each in and out of context, to compare the efficiency of responses to functional, non-lexical words with those to the nouns and adjectives of the first three recordings.

(ii) "Right" in context; homophones of "Right" (i.e. "Write," "Rite" and "Wright") in context; "Right" in the primary message with homophones of "Right" in the secondary message. There are two main questions: firstly would the homophones be any more difficult than the single word, that is would they function as several different target words in the same way as the digits, colours or parts of the face, or could they all be treated as a single, target, speech sound. Secondly, would subjects find it difficult to avoid tapping to homophones when instructed to tap only to "Right," indicating that the tapping response was initiated at some stage before the meaning was analysed? Both answers should help to locate the stage in perceptual analysis at which the tapping response was initiated, and to show whether this differed for attended and unattended message.

(iii) "Hot" in context in two primary messages paired with "Hot" out of context in the secondary messages, and two pairs with the reverse arrangement. In all other conditions the target words were either in context on both ears or out of context on both. The context of the primary message could therefore conceivably facilitate perception of target words in the secondary message as well. For example when the target word was "Hot," the passage might be about a parched and sweating man under a blazing sun in the desert. This restricted subject-matter could generally lower thresholds for perception of "Hot" in either passage. Pairing target words in context on one ear with target words out of context on the other controls for this possibility and ensures that any effect of context is restricted to the passage in which the target word itself occurs in context.

General Procedure. All subjects except the control groups were treated as follows. They were given some practice trials at repeating back one of two simultaneous speech passages, until they were doing this fluently, and also some practice at tapping to target words (not those used in the experiment proper). They were then given the experimental passages with the primary one always on the right ear, and were asked to repeat back this passage, keeping their attention fixed on the right ear. They were told before each pair of passages what the target word would be (e.g. "Hot in context" or "any colour out of context") and they were asked to tap if ever they heard this target word in either ear; they were not to shift their attention to the secondary message, since we were interested in seeing whether they heard it *despite* the fact that they were attending to something different. It was emphasized that if they shifted their attention, they would miss some words of the primary passage and so fail in the primary task. They were asked, after each passage in which they tapped to a word in the secondary message, whether they felt they had shifted their attention in order to hear the word or whether it had "just come through" while they were attending to the right ear message. They seemed quite able to distinguish these two cases, as shown in the results. Cases in which they had shifted before hearing the target word were not included in the results, since the secondary message had effectively become the primary message for those few moments.

The first passages containing each type of target word were presented in different random orders, and the second passages in the reverse order, to counterbalance any effects of practice or fatigue. The experiments lasted about 1½ hr. with a 10-min. break in the middle. Subjects were questioned about which conditions seemed most difficult, and were also asked whether the loudness of the two passages remained approximately equal throughout.

Further differences in the procedure adopted for control groups are given in the following section on subjects and design.

Subjects and Design of Experiments. The volunteer subjects were undergraduates at Oxford University (none reading Psychology); they were paid four shillings an hour. Their hearing was approximately equal in both ears and each subject equated the loudness of the tape-recordings in the two ears for himself before starting the experiment. They were divided into a number of different groups.

Group A, consisting of 42 subjects, was used in Experiment 1, to investigate the variables summarized in Table 1. Fourteen subjects were tested with each of the first three tape-recordings, following the general procedure described above. Since they all had essentially the same conditions, their results were analysed together.

Group B, consisting of nine subjects, was used in the masking Experiment 2. Each of the same Group A passages was presented singly, masked by noise, and the subjects were asked simply to tap whenever they heard one of the target words. Thus their attention was focussed on the single message and the single response of tapping to target words. Each primary and secondary message in each of the

TABLE 1

Target Words Used to Test the Main Experiment Variables

VARIABLE	HIGH STIMULUS INFORMATION	ADJECTIVE, ONE MAIN MEANING	NOUN, ONE MAIN MEANING	SEVERAL MEANINGS	HIGH STIMULUS-RESPONSE COMPATIBILITY
Group A	Any Digit	Tall	Boat	Right	Tap
Group B	Any Colour	Hot	Trees	Fit	Tap
Group C	Any Part of the Face	Tired	Night	Point	Tap

first three tape recordings was heard by three of the subjects in Group B. The signal-to-noise ratio was adjusted in a pilot experiment to give approximately 50 percent correct responses.

Group C, comprising 11 new subjects, was used in Experiment 3, in order to clarify some points arising from Experiment 1. They followed the same procedure as Group A but were given the new target words and passages of the fourth tape-recording.

Finally Group D, a further 10 subjects, was used in Experiment 4 to check on the effect of cerebral dominance. Since all other subjects attended to the right ear and tapped with the right hand, there might have been some cerebral asymmetry favouring the primary message. Group D followed the same procedure as Groups A and C, and heard the third tape-recording from Experiment 1, but one primary message containing each type of target word

was played to the right ear and one to the left. Each passage of a pair was repeated by half the subjects when on the right ear and by half the subjects when on the left. All target words on the right ear were tapped to by the right hand and all target words on the left ear by the left hand.

Results

Correct Responses. The recorded responses were analysed as follows: counts were made of the target words correctly tapped to, the number of target words receiving both tapping and repeating responses, the number of target words receiving only one of the two responses and the number receiving neither response. These were converted to percentages and are given in Tables 2 and 3. Analyses of variance

TABLE 2

Percentage of Target Words Receiving Verbal or Manual Response*

TARGET WORD		DIGITS, COLOURS, PARTS OF FACE		RIGHT, FIT, POINT		TALL, HOT, TIRED		BOAT, TREES, NIGHT		BUT, FROM (GROUP C)		TAP	MEAN	
IN OR OUT OF CONTEXT		IN	OUT	IN	OUT	IN	OUT	IN	OUT	IN	OUT	OUT	IN	OUT
Primary message	Repeat	92.2	55.2	97.0	68.5	95.9	68.1	98.1	68.5	95.5	75.0	68.5	95.9	67.1
	Tap	88.9	67.4	93.3	84.4	95.6	85.2	95.1	90.7	75.8	81.9	93.3	89.7	91.9
Secondary message	Tap	8.5	2.6	3.7	7.8	15.6	8.1	14.8	9.9	4.5	6.1	7.8	9.4	6.9

* All results are from Groups A, B and C except for target words "But" and "From" which are results from Group C.

TABLE 3

Percentage of Target Words in Primary Message Receiving Both, One or Neither Response

TARGET WORDS	DIGITS, COLOURS, PARTS OF FACE		RIGHT, FIT, POINT		TALL, HOT, TIRED		BOAT, TREES, NIGHT		BUT, FROM, (GROUP C)		TAP
IN OR OUT OF CONTEXT	IN	OUT	IN	OUT	IN	OUT	IN	OUT	IN	OUT	OUT
Both responses	87.3	51.1	92.1	66.6	94.4	65.9	95.1	67.9	75.8	69.0	67.8
One response	7.1	20.4	6.0	19.7	2.6	21.5	3.1	23.5	19.6	18.8	26.3
Neither response	5.6	28.5	1.9	13.7	3.0	12.6	1.8	8.6	4.6	12.2	5.9

TABLE 4

Percent Tapping Responses to "Right" and Its Homophones

Target Word	1. Right (correct)	2. Homophones (correct)	3. Homophones (incorrect)	4. Right (correct in primary message); Homophones (incorrect in secondary message)
Primary message	91	94	30	88
Secondary message	5	8	3	8

were carried out on the number of correct tapping responses for all subjects in Group A together. One analysis was made on all conditions except the nouns and the target word "Tap." The other analysis was made just on the "Tap" and "Tall, Hot or Tired" out of context conditions (since "Tap" was never given in context). The main points which emerged are as follows:

(1) An overwhelming majority of tapping responses was made to the primary message rather than the secondary one, a mean of 86.5 percent. compared with 8.1 percent. This strongly indicates a perceptual limit in selective listening.

(2) The target words in the primary message which fitted into the verbal context received more responses than those occurring at random points, ($p < 0.001$, *V.R.* = 31.7, *d.f.* 1,41). In the secondary message the difference was also significant, though slighter ($p < 0.025$, *V.R.* = 6.5, *d.f.* 1,41). Here it was due mainly to the specific, lexical words, and was in fact reversed for the words of many meanings. A possible explanation here is that the facilitation was due to the context of the primary message. This would explain why context favoured only the specific lexical words and not the function words or the words of many meanings, since these did not restrict the general theme of the primary message. When target words in context on one ear were paired with target words out of context on the other ear, the effect of context on the secondary message disappeared. Group C made 14 percent correct tapping responses to "Hot" out of context and 15 percent to "Hot" in context. This confirms that part at least of the facilitating effect of verbal context

in other conditions was due to the related subject-matter of the primary message. Moreover, a later experiment (not yet published) using the same task has shown no effect at all of verbal context in the secondary message. This reinforces our belief that the apparent facilitation here is an artefact.

(3) There were some signfiicant differences between the different types of target words in both primary and secondary messages. The classes of words (digits, colours and parts of the face) received significantly fewer responses than the single words, particularly when they were out of context. A Scheffé test showed that the difference was significant, $p < 0.001$ for both primary and secondary messages. The words with many meanings were as easy to tap to as the words with one main meaning in the primary message, but they were more difficult in the secondary message. This latter finding is surprising in the light of other results, particularly of Group C's experiment with the homophones of "Right." These are given in Table 4. In Condition 1, subjects were presented with and asked to tap only to "Right"; in Condition 2, they were presented with any of the four homophones, "Right," "Write," "Rite" and "Wright" and were asked to tap to any of them. This condition proved no more difficult than the first, with either primary or secondary message. In Condition 3, they were asked to tap only to "Right" but were presented only with its homophones, and in Condition 4 they were again asked to tap only to "Right," but while only "Right" was presented in the primary messages only its homophones were included in the secondary messages. Condition 3 shows that subjects could successfully discriminate and

avoid about two-thirds of the incorrect homophones in the primary message. However in the secondary message they tapped to as many of the incorrect homophones in Conditions 3 and 4 as they did to the correct words in Conditions 1 and 2. They could not therefore have heard the verbal context which differentiated the four homophones. Given this proof that the homophones were not identified as such, we can see no obvious explanation for the relative difficulty of "Right" and its homophones in the secondary message compared with the single adjectives and nouns.

(4) Differences in grammatical form only affected performance taking the extreme comparison of lexical items versus functional parts of speech. The nouns and adjectives gave identical results, but "From" and "But" evoked fewer tapping responses when they were *in* context. However they were *repeated* just as efficiently as the nouns and adjectives.

(5) The target word "Tap" in the primary message received significantly more tapping responses than the adjectives "Tall," "Hot" or "Tired" out of context ($p < 0.05$, $V.R. = 4.61$, $d.f. = 1, 41$), but in the secondary message the difference disappeared.

We return to these results in the Discussion, where we try to relate them to the problems raised in the Introduction.

Interference. The next result we analysed was the amount of interference with the repeating response caused by the target words in the primary and secondary messages. We compared the interference in those cases where the subject tapped correctly to the target word and in the cases where he failed to tap. For this purpose,

the words of the primary message were divided into four categories: (i) the target words in the primary message, or the words in the primary message which coincided with target words in the secondary message; (ii) the three words preceding these; (iii) the five words succeeding them; (iv) all other words. The percentage of these classes of words which showed errors or omissions in repeating was calculated separately for the occasions when subjects tapped and when they failed to tap and separately for target words in the primary and in the secondary message. On analysis of variance, no significant difference in interference emerged due to differences in the target words used, so the results given in Table 5 are the mean percentages over all the target words.

The table shows that tapping to target words in the primary message interfered slightly with the repeating response both to the target word itself and to the succeeding five words, a mean of about 11 percent. errors compared with about 7 percent. to the other words. (The variance due to which words were being repeated—target, three before, five after or other words—was significant, $p < 0.01$, $V.R. = 21.32$, $d.f. = 3, 6$.) Tapping to target words in the secondary, unattended message, however, was considerably more disruptive, causing over 30 percent. errors and omissions in repeating the words coincident with or succeeding them in the primary message. (Here the variance ratio was significant, $p < 0.001$, $V.R. = 29.90$, $d.f. = 3, 6$.) In an overall analysis of variance including both primary and secondary message and excluding "other" words (which were common to both) the difference in interference with the primary and secondary message was significant ($p <$

TABLE 5

Interference with Repeating Response Caused by Target Words

	PERCENT ERRORS AND OMISSIONS WHEN TAPPED				PERCENT ERRORS AND OMISSIONS WHEN MISSED TAPPING		
CLASS OF WORD	3 BEFORE	TARGET	5 AFTER	OTHER WORDS	3 BEFORE	TARGET	5 AFTER
Primary message	6.2	11.1	10.8	7.4	20.0	76.5	19.1
Secondary message	19.2	36.8	31.8	7.4	7.0	8.3	7.0

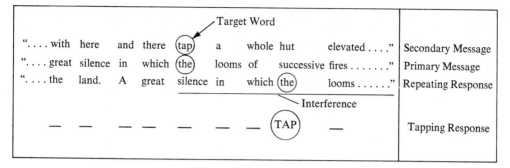

FIGURE 2   Interference with repeating three words preceding target caused by target word in secondary message.

0.001, $V.R. = 156.9$, $d.f. = 1, 4$). When subjects missed tapping, the results were reversed. In the primary message 76.5 percent. target words which received no tapping response also failed to be repeated, as did about 20 percent. of the neighbouring words. Two explanations are possible: either these words were simply not perceived, or the two responses competed so strongly that neither could be made overtly. Perhaps the most interesting point is that missed target words in the secondary message caused no increase whatever in interference with the repeating response, strongly suggesting that they were not identified at all. This is consistent with a perceptual limit to subjects' capacity which was fully occupied by receiving the primary message.

A possible difficulty with this interpretation is the high proportion of errors and omissions in repeating the three words before the secondary target, when this received a tapping response (a mean of 19.2 percent. per word). Two explanations are possible: (1) it might be due to shifting of attention, so that the secondary message was actually functioning as primary message on those occasions where the target word was heard. (2) Since the mean ear-voice lag in repeating is three words, the subjects' attention might have remained on the primary message until the target word occurred, but its occurrence somehow erased the three previous primary message words or prevented the repeating response, perhaps by causing a subsequent shift of attention (see Figure 2). To decide whether subjects had switched their attention

before the target word occurred, we counted the omissions and errors in the preceding words, six to three before the target. The interference here was 8.2 percent. which does not differ significantly from the 7.4 percent. of the "other words." (This contrasts with 59.3 percent. errors and omissions on each of the same words on those few occasions where the subject reported shifting his attention before hearing the target word.) It seems then that the 8.1 percent. of secondary target words which received a tapping response were perceived despite the subjects' lack of attention, but that once these words had "got through" they interfered with repeating responses and perception of the following few words of the primary message.

Latencies.   The response latencies for tapping and repeating were measured for the first nine subjects in Group A who received each of the three tape-recordings. We counted the number of primary message words intervening between the target word and the response, which had been recorded simultaneously on the second track of the tape-recorded results. For comparison the latency of the repeating response to a number of non-target words was also measured; in each case the word selected occurred five before the target word. The mean latencies are given in Table 6.

To get some further indication whether the two responses were being organized simultaneously or successively, the latencies of each individual pair of responses to the same target word were subjected to t tests and to product-moment correlations. The t tests showed significant differences for only 11 out of 27 subjects; six showed shorter tapping than repeating latencies and five showed the opposite. The mean correlation over the different subjects was $r = 0.80$ ($d.f. = 1100, p < 0.001$).

Masking Experiment. The mean percentage of target words detected by Group B in the masking experiment was 55 percent for the primary message and 52 percent for the secondary message. These do not differ significantly, so there appears to have been no bias in the actual tape-recording favouring the primary message. Does external noise have an effect similar to that of inattention? The numbers of taps to each target word in the attention experiment were correlated with those in the masking experiment. Correlating the taps for each occurrence of each target word in the two conditions, the overall correlation was $r = 0.39$ for the primary messages ($d.f. = 154, p < 0.001$) and $r = 0.18$ for the secondary message ($p < 0.05$). However, part of this correlation might have been due to the independent variables of verbal context and particular target words, both of which might affect the attention and the masking scores in the same way. When the correlations were calculated separately for each type of target word in and out of context and then averaged, the mean r for the primary message was still significant ($r = 0.27, d.f. = 138, p < 0.01$), but for the secondary, unattended message it was completely insignificant ($r = -0.06$). The intensity, clarity or whatever other factors increase intelligibility under masking were also somewhat helpful in increasing tapping responses to target words in the attended message, but seem to have had no effect in facilitating detection of unattended

words. The same conclusion emerged from the objective measures of intensity: the difference in intensity between target words and other words did not correlate at all with the number of tapping responses they evoked (the values of r for the different target words in the first recording were 0.00, 0.26, 0.15, -0.08 and 0.46 for the primary message, and 0.12, -0.06, -0.32, -0.06, -0.20 for the secondary message). None of these correlations is significant. This was rather a surprising result, which will be discussed later.

Cerebral dominance. Finally we come to the results for the control Group D, relating to cerebral dominance and left-right asymmetry. Table 7 gives the mean percentages of correct tapping responses in the different conditions for the left and right ears. On analysis of variance, the difference between left and right ear target words was completely insignificant for the primary message, but target words on the left ear in the secondary, unattended message received significantly more taps than those on the right ear ($p < 0.025, d.f. = 1, 18, V.R. = 7.67$). The difference is mainly due to the passage containing "Tired," in context, and the interaction between target words and left-right difference was significant ($p < 0.025, d.f. = 2, 18, V.R. = 6.23$). This shows that the choice of left ear for the unattended message in the main experiment was, if anything, favouring responses to the secondary target words, probably because the primary task of repeating was easier for messages on the right ear and so left more spare capacity for the secondary task.

The efficiency of the repeating response also showed differences between left and right ear messages. The percentage of errors and omis-

TABLE 6

Response Lags, Measured in Words

RESPONSE	TAPPING	REPEATING TARGET WORD	REPEATING WORD 5 BEFORE TARGET
Primary message mean	2.9	3.1	3.2
Secondary message mean	3.0		

sions in repeating the "other words" (i.e. not target, three before or five after) was 10.0 percent for the left ear and 6 percent for the right. This difference was significant on analysis of variance ($p < 0.01$, $V.R. = 19.0$, $d.f. = 1, 9$). There was no significant increase in left-right asymmetry when subjects repeated the target words, the three before and the five after.

Discussion

PERCEPTUAL OR RESPONSE LIMIT?

Our first aim was to discover how far attention is limited by a restriction on perceptual capacity and how far it is limited by the number of responses which can be simultaneously organized. The difference in tapping responses to primary and secondary messages gives the answer, which overwhelmingly favours a perceptual limit with a filter selecting before the two messages are fully analysed, as in Figure 1a rather than 1b. Since both stimulus and response are identical for the primary and secondary message, it is difficult to argue for a difference in importance, in response load or in response bias, and the result seems best explained on the assumption that the secondary target words are much less likely to be identified than the primary ones. There is also some degree of response competition shown by the number of occasions when one response to primary target words was given but not the other (about 19 percent.). But in this task the response competition is much less dramatic than the perceptual competition.

Lawson (1966) has recently repeated this experiment with an interesting difference in the task and very different results. Instead of words as her signals to tap, she used brief tones or pips. The difference between responses to the primary and secondary messages almost completely disappeared. It seems that analysis of simple physical signals precedes both the selective filter and the analysis of verbal content in the perceptual sequence, that the bottleneck in attention arises chiefly in speech recognition, where of course the information load is usually much higher. To confirm the belief that the verbal content of the secondary message in the present experiment was not being analysed, we find no evidence whatever of interference from secondary target words when these received no tapping response.

On the other hand, in those cases where the subject did tap to the target word in the secondary message, this caused significantly more interference with the repeating response than tapping to the primary message, (more than 30 percent. errors or omissions on each of the target and five succeeding words compared with 11 percent. for primary target words). In both cases the same two responses are made; the only difference is that there are two words to identify when the target is in the secondary message and only one when it is in the primary message. Thus the difference in interference again supports the hypothesis of a perceptual limit. Two further points support the idea that most of the secondary message was not perceived: (1) the fact that the verbal context of the target words probably does not facilitate

TABLE 7

Effect of Left-Right Differences on Tapping Responses

| | | Tap | | Parts of Face | | Point | | Tired | | |
			In Context	Out	In	Out	In	Out	Mean
Primary message	Left	90.0	90.0	80.0	93.3	90.0	93.3	86.7	89.0
	Right	93.3	90.0	76.7	86.7	96.7	96.7	96.7	91.0
Secondary message	Left	10.0	10.0	6.7	6.7	3.3	33.3	16.7	12.4
	Right	0.0	10.0	10.0	3.3	0.0	6.7	6.7	5.2

responses as it does in the primary message; (2) subjects' failure to distinguish the homophones of "Right" in the secondary message. The only verbal factor we expected would have an effect on taps to the secondary message was the information content of the classes of words compared to the single words, since these would impose a greater load on the limited perceptual capacity. This did affect performance: the classes of words received significantly fewer tapping responses than the single words with one main meaning.

Stimulus Variables in Primary Message. In contrast, many of the stimulus variables affected perception of the primary message (as shown by the number of target words receiving at least one of the two responses). The verbal context had a marked effect increasing both tapping and repeating responses. Increased size of the target word ensemble led to significantly poorer performance, decreasing the percent. correct and increasing the latency, particularly when the target words were out of context. When they were in context, the difficulty due to increased ensemble was almost cancelled out by the high transition probabilities. These findings confirm once again that our perceptual capacity is limited at least partly by the information content of stimuli presented. In this experiment, however, the information limit was shown only when the class of target words included different phonetic patterns and not when its members varied only in meaning. The two stimulus variables which also affected responses directly where the predictable or random insertion of target words in the context of the passages and the grammatical difference between lexical and function words. The proportion of target words receiving one response but not the other was much higher for target words out of context (24.7 percent. compared with 8.2 percent.). Here we have a dissociation between the two ways of increasing information—increasing the size of the ensemble and decreasing the transition probability. The former appears to affect only the word's chance of being correctly perceived, while the latter affects also the selection of responses. For the

function words in context, there were abnormally few tapping responses compared with other grammatical classes of target words. The relevance of these differences is discussed below.

ORGANIZATION OF TWO COMPETING RESPONSES

The third problem raised in the Introduction is the relation between two competing responses made to the same perceived signal. At what stage in the sequence of perceptual decisions are the responses selected, and does this affect the degree to which they interfere with one another? The present results give no conclusive answers to these questions, but they may give some indications.

Firstly we compared the latency of the tapping and the repeating responses to the primary target words. The mean latency of the tapping response was shorter, by about 80 millisec, but *t* tests on the pairs of latencies to individual target words showed significant differences for only 11 out of 27 subjects. The correlation between the two latencies was high for nearly all subjects, which makes it unlikely that the word was being analysed by two independent systems for the two separate responses. The result gives little evidence either for or against serial programming of the tapping and repeating responses.

Secondly we compared the characteristics of the primary target words which affected the repeating and the tapping responses, to get some indication of the stage in the perceptual sequence at which each was initiated. Table 2 shows that they followed a similar pattern on the whole. Both responses were worse with classes of words than single words, but not with words of many meanings or homophones. This could be taken as evidence that both responses are initiated together before the meaning is analysed. However an alternative explanation is possible: since the different meanings of "Fit," "Point," "Right" and its homophones are only brought out when the words are in context, any resultant decrement due to the increased ensemble of meanings might be cancelled out by facilitation from the verbal context. Even the digits, colours, etc., were only about 5 percent. worse than the single words, when they were in context. Further evidence about the tapping response comes from the condition where tapping to homophones was incorrect: when subjects were asked to tap only to "Right" they tapped mistakenly to 30 percent. of the homophones in the primary message, compared with 94 percent. when the homophones were correct. In this case, subjects were certainly identifying the meaning of two-thirds of the target words and tapping to the speech sound for one-third. However this condition differed from the others in that the instructions to avoid tapping to homophones stressed the importance of analysing meaning before tapping. Thus the 30 percent. mistaken taps may be more significant than the 64 percent. of homophones avoided.

The variable which causes the most striking divergence between the tapping and the repeating responses is the verbal context. While the lack of context severely impaired the repeating response, reducing the correct words by 29 percent., the decrement for the tapping response was only 8 percent. When words were out of context, tapping was consistently better than repeating. This suggests that the tapping response was not dependent on the same high level of analysis as the repeating response. While subjects relied on the verbal context to give the meaning of target words before they could repeat them back, this was not essential for the tapping response. On the other hand the tapping response was facilitated a little by the verbal context; the improvement of 8 percent. was statistically significant. Two explanations are possible: either the tapping response was made, in some cases at least, to the verbal unit rather than the speech sound, or the effect was entirely due to the greater ease of repeating words in context, which left more spare response capacity for tapping.

The only other points in Table 2 at which the two responses diverge are the target words "From" and "But," which in context are much worse at evoking a tapping than a repeating response, and the target word "Tap" where the tapping response is much better, presumably because of the high stimulus-response compatibility. On the assumption that the tapping response is triggered by the speech sound, we might explain the difficulty of "From" and "But" in context by saying that the speech sounds are less distinct: with sentence intonation, these function words will seldom carry as much stress as the lexical items. If we assume full verbal analysis, the explanation may be that "From" and "But" are not perceived as distinct functional units in the same way as the lexical words, but simply as part of the syntactical unit or phrase in which they occur. The repeating response could mirror the whole phrase, while the tapping response required the subject to isolate the particular words "From" or "But" within the phrase. In this case the verbal context actually makes the tapping response more difficult.

In conclusion then, we have no convincing proof either that the responses are always organized successively or that they are always initiated at the same point in the perceptual hierarchy from speech sound to meaning. However, any tests which were not entirely ambivalent favoured the alternative of serial programming at different levels of analysis: the slightly shorter latency for tapping, the much greater difficulty of repeating than of tapping to words out of context and the failure to identify a third of the homophones before tapping, all suggest that the tapping response was triggered at a lower level than the repeating response. Any evidence which might suggest simultaneous organization can also be explained in a way consistent with serial organization. If the serial hypothesis is correct, it might account for the relative lack of response competition found in this experiment.

STIMULUS-RESPONSE COMPATIBILITY

The third question raised in the Introduction was how far compatibility of stimuli and responses might allow them to bypass the limited capacity of selective attention. The result differed for the primary and the secondary messages: while the target word "Tap" in the primary message received significantly more and quicker tapping responses than the corresponding adjectives "Tall," "Hot" and "Tired" out of context, in the secondary message there was no difference at all. This is quite consistent with the model of selective attention controlled by a perceptual filter. Stimulus-response compatibility can be interpreted as the high conditional probability of a particular response given a particular stimulus—a reduction in response but not stimulus uncertainty. One would therefore expect it to affect subjects only once the target word had been identified: it might then be expected in the primary, attended message to facilitate the tapping response rather than the repeating response, which it does, and perhaps also to decrease the response competition, which it does not (tapping to the target word "Tap" caused if anything more interference with the repeating response than the other target words). If we are right that little of the secondary, unattended message is being perceived, the target word "Tap" should gain little benefit from its compatible response.

NATURE OF PERCEPTUAL FILTER

The last point to discuss is the nature of the perceptual "filter" which so drastically reduces recognition of the secondary message. The subjects did hear a few of the target words from the secondary message, but showed no evidence of hearing anything more. Treisman (1960, 1964) suggested a modification of Broadbent's original model, based on an analogy with the signal detection theory of sensory thresholds (Tanner and Swets, 1954). If the filter reduced the signal-to-noise ratio of unattended messages rather than blocking them completely, words which were highly important or relevant to the subject might still be perceived despite this attenuation, provided that the criteria for detecting them were sufficiently low. This would have the biological advantage that unattended messages could be monitored for any important signals, without at the same time much increasing the load on the limited capacity available for speech recognition. Broadbent and Gregory (1963) measured changes in signal strength and criterion when the subject was attending to and away from a tone masked by noise and obtained results consistent with this suggestion. It explains how in the present ex-

periment subjects were able to hear about 8 percent. of the unattended target words, when told in advance what these would be.

However a point which seems at first sight unexpected is the lack of correlation between the particular words which were detected in the attention and in the masking experiments. If the filter has the effect of reducing the signal-to-noise ratio of unattended messages, one might expect some parallel with the effects of an external masking noise, in that those features of target words which made them likely to survive the one would also make them likely to survive the other. However there is an important difference between these conditions which might explain the lack of correlation: in the attention experiment subjects are occupied with the primary message, and the degree of attenuation of the secondary message affected by the filter may vary with the load on attention imposed by the primary message. This will probably fluctuate from moment to moment, with the predictability or difficulty of the words, the rate at which they are spoken and so on. If so the signal-to-noise ratio of unattended words will fluctuate randomly in relation to particular target words and this random variation may swamp any correlation with the effects of the constant external noise used in the masking experiment.

Another prediction from this model of the attention process is that there should be some false positives, related in sound to the target words in the unattended message. There were a few of these: subjects tapped to a total of 11 non-target words in the whole experiment (compared to 232 target words detected), and all of them were similar sounds such as "both" for "boat," "light" for "night," "at" for "but" (except one which was "face" for "any part of the face," a semantic error). It is not possible to work out an exact false positive rate, since one does not know the number of words at risk. As a very rough guide, excluding the passages with digits, colours or parts of the face, there were an average of 7.6 words per passage which shared two phonemes with the target word, as did all the actual false positives made. This would give a false positive rate for all passages with single target words, of 0.17

TABLE 8

Changes in Signal Strength and Decision Criterion in the Different Experimental Conditions

	MASKING (PRIMARY MESSAGE MASKED BY NOISE, PRIMARY RESPONSE)	INATTENTION (SECONDARY MESSAGE, SECONDARY RESPONSE)	ATTENTION (PRIMARY MESSAGE, SECONDARY RESPONSE)
d'	2.0	1.8	4.2
β	5.1	34	30

percent. compared to a hit rate of 11.2 percent. In the masking experiment the corresponding rates are 3.4 percent. false positives and 58.3 percent. hits, assuming that the same mean of 7.6 words per passage are at risk. Finally for the primary message in the attention experiment, the rates are 0.19 percent. false positives and 89.7 hits.

It is tempting to look up the corresponding values given by signal detection theory for d', the signal strength, and β, the criterion, in each of these tasks. However the assumptions underlying this use of signal detection measures are questionable: (1) we assume a central continuous dimension of evidence determining perception of particular target words, along which the actual target and "noise" words vary in similarity; (2) we assume that their distributions on the similarity dimension are normally distributed, overlapping and with approximately equal variance; (3) we take a rather arbitrary number of 7.6 for the set of "noise" words in any passage; (4) finally we have pooled the results for all subjects and all target words in the hit and false positive rates given above. (It seems reasonable to exclude the digits, colours and parts of the face, since the criteria may well differ where a class of different sounds must be detected and where a single sound is the target.) These assumptions mean that little weight can be given to the absolute values for d' and β, but since the assumptions are constant for all three conditions, it may be worth looking at the directions in which the values change as we change the task variables. On the general model we suggested, for the masking condition we should expect a low d' (because of the added noise)

and a relatively low criterion (since this is the subject's only task); for the secondary message in the attention task, we predict a low d' (due to the reduction in signal-to-noise ratio introduced by the filter) and a relatively high criterion (because tapping to target was a secondary task competing with the primary repeating response); finally for the primary message in the attention task we expect a high d' (since the message is unmasked and receiving full attention) and again a high criterion (because tapping is the secondary response). Table 8 gives the values of d' and β obtained. They are quite consistent with the predictions.

Summary

Does our limited capacity in selective listening tasks arise primarily in perception or in response organization? To examine this, subjects were given two dichotic messages, one primary and one secondary, and had to make two different responses: the primary response was to "shadow" the primary message; the secondary response was to tap on hearing certain target words in either message. Since the secondary response was identical for the two messages, any difference in its efficiency with the two messages must be due to a failure in perception of the secondary message. Any interference between the primary and secondary responses (repeating and tapping) to target words in the primary message must be due to a limit in performing simultaneous responses, since if either was correctly performed the target word must have been perceived. The results clearly showed that the main limit is perceptual.

Various target words were used to investigate the nature of the perceptual and response limits. Factors investigated were (1) the information content of the target words, (2) their range of meanings, (3) their grammatical class, and (4) the compatibility between stimuli and responses. A relative lack of response competition was found, which might be due to successive organization of the two responses at different stages in the perceptual sequence. The results were interpreted in terms of signal detection theory and the effects of reduced signal-to-noise ratio produced by inattention were compared with those produced by an external masking noise.

References

Broadbent, D. E. (1958). *Perception and Communication.* London: Pergamon.

Broadbent, D. E., and Gregory, M (1962). Donders' b- and c- reactions and S–R compatibility. *J. exp. Psychol., 63,* 575–8.

Broadbent, D. E., and Gregory, M. (1963). Division of attention and the decision theory of signal detection. *Proc. Roy. Soc. B., 158,* 222–31.

Cherry, E. C. (1953). Some experiments on the recognition of speech with one and with two ears. *J. accoust. Soc. Amer., 25,* 975–9.

Davis, R., Moray, N. P., and Treisman, A. M. (1961).

Imitative responses and the rate of gain of information. *Quart. J. exp. Psychol., 13,* 78–89.

Deutsch, J. A., and Deutsch, D. (1963). Attention: some theoretical considerations. *Psychol. Rev., 70,* 80–90

Lawson, E. A. (1966). Decisions concerning the rejected channel. *Quart. J. exp. Psychol., 18,* 260–5

Leonard, J. A. (1961). Choice reaction time experiments and information theory. In Cherry, E. C. (Ed.) *Information Theory,* London: Butterworths, pp. 137–46.

Moray, N. (1959). Attention in dichotic listening: affective cues and the influence of instructions. *Quart. J. exp. Psychol., 11,* 56–60.

Moray, N., and Jordan, A. (1966). Practice and compatibility in two-channel short term memory. *Psychon. Sci., 4,* 427–8.

Moray, N., and Taylor, A. (1958). The effect of redundancy in shadowing one of two dichotic messages, *Language & Speech, 1,* 102–9.

Mowbray, G. H. (1960). Choice reaction times for skilled responses. *Quart. J. exp. Psychol., 12,* 193–9.

Mowbray, G. H. (1964). Perception and retention of verbal information presented during auditory shadowing. *J. accoust. Soc. Amer., 36,* 1459–64.

Reynolds, D. (1964). Effects of double stimulation: Temporary inhibition of response. *Psychol. Bull., 62,* 333–47.

Tanner, W. P., Jr., and Swets, J. A. (1954) A decision-making theory of visual detection. *Psychol. Rev., 61,* 401–9.

Treisman, A. M. (1960). Contextual cues in selective listening. *Quart. J. exp. Psychol., 12,* 242–8.

Treisman, A. M. (1964). Selective attention in man. *Brit. Med. Bull., 20,* 12–6.

9.2 Attention:
Some Theoretical Considerations[*]

J. A. DEUTSCH   D. DEUTSCH

There has, in the last few years, been an increase in the amount of research devoted to the problem of attention, which has been summarized

in Broadbent's (1958) important work. Whilst psychologists have been investigating the behavioral aspects of attention, suggestive evidence has also been found by neurophysiologists. We feel that it would be useful at this

[*] From: J. A. Deutsch and D. Deutsch, "Attention: Some Theoretical Considerations," *Psychological Review,* 1963, vol. 70, pp. 80–90. Copyright (1963) by the American Psychological Association, and reproduced by permission. This work was wholly supported by Grant M-4563 from the National Institute of Mental Health, National Institutes of Health,

United States Public Health Service and Grant G 21376 from the National Science Foundation. We are grateful to D. E. Broadbent, K. L. Chow, D. A. Hamburg, and F. Morrell for helpful comment and discussion.

time to consider the theoretical implications of some of this research.

Our paper is divided into three parts. In the first we consider some of the behavioral findings on attention. In the second a system is proposed to account for various features of this behavior. Although we do not consider it necessary to identify a system of this type with particular neural structures (see Deutsch, 1960) since a machine embodying such a system would also display the behavior we wish to explain, we do, however, venture some tentative hypotheses concerning the neural identification of the proposed system.

Behavorial Considerations

However alert or responsive we may be, there is a limit to the number of things to which we can attend at any one time. We cannot, for instance, listen effectively to the conversation of a friend on the telephone if someone else in the room is simultaneously giving us complex instructions as to what to say to him. And this difficulty in processing information from two different sources at the same time occurs even if no overt response is required. This phenomenon of selective attention has been investigated in a number of experiments. The most important of these deals with the processing of information emitted simultaneously by two separate sound sources (Broadbent, 1954; Cherry, 1953; Spieth, Curtis, & Webster, 1954). Two problems arise from the results of such experiments. The first is how different streams of information are kept distinct by the nervous system, and how a resultant babel is thereby avoided. The second is why only one of the messages (once it has been kept distinct and separate) is dealt with at any one time. A proposed solution to the first problem, based on experiments in which two messages were fed simultaneously one to each ear, was that the messages were kept distinct by proceeding down separate channels (such as different neural pathways). Nor was it difficult for Broadbent (1958) to extend such a notion to other cases. It had been shown in numerous

experiments that we are enabled to listen to one of two simultaneous speech sequences while ignoring the other, by selecting items for attention which have some feature or features in common, such as their frequency spectra (Egan, Carterette, & Thwing, 1954; Spieth et al., 1954) and their spatial localization (Hirsch, 1950; Poulton, 1953; Webster & Thomson, 1954). It was supposed that relatively simple mechanisms were responsible for segregation according to these categories, though the principles of their operation were not made clear.

Broadbent's (1958) answer to the second problem, of how one message is admitted to the exclusion of others, followed from the notions we have already considered. It was proposed that there was a filter which would select a message on the basis of characteristics toward which it had been biased and allow this message alone to proceed to the central analyzing mechanisms. In this way, messages with other characteristics would be excluded and so the total amount of discrimination which would have to be performed by the nervous system would be greatly decreased. Whole complex messages could be rejected on the sole basis of possessing some simple quality, and no further analysis of them would occur.

However, it seems that selection of wanted from unwanted speech can be performed on the basis of highly complex characteristics. For instance, Peters (1954) found that if an unwanted message is similar in content to the wanted one, it produces more interference with the adequate reception of the latter than if it is dissimilar to it. This shows that the content of the two messages is analyzed prior to the acceptance of one and rejection of the other. Gray and Wedderburn (1960) have also found that when speech was delivered to subjects in both ears simultaneously, such that a meaningful sequence could be formed by choosing syllables or words alternately from each ear, the subjects reported back the meaningful sequence rather than the series of words or syllables presented to one ear or the other. Treisman (1960) presented two messages, one to each ear, and subjects were asked to repeat what they heard on one ear. The messages were switched from one ear to the other in the middle and it was found that subjects tended to repeat words from the wrong ear just after the switch. "The higher the transition probabilities in the passage the more likely they were to do this" (Treisman, 1960).

Other evidence, indicating that complex discriminations would be required of the filter, has been produced by experiments concerning the selection of novel stimuli, for which function Broadbent (1958) assumes the filter to be responsible. Sharpless and Jasper (1956), studying habituation to auditory stimuli in cats, found that habituation, both behavioral and EEG, was specific not only to the frequency of sound presented, but also to the pattern in which a combination of frequencies was presented. Evidence for human subjects is presented by Sokolov (1960) and Voronin and Sokolov (1960), who report that when habituation has been established to a group of words similar in meaning but different in sound, then arousal occurred to words with a different meaning. Behavioral data on the arousal of curiosity in rats upon the presentation of novel visual patterns are reported by Thomson and Solomon (1954).

Such evidence as the above would require us, on filter theory, to postulate an additional discriminative system below or at the level of the filter, perhaps as complex as that of the central mechanism, to which information was assumed to be filtered.

Howarth and Ellis (1961) have presented an ingenious experimental argument to show that the same discriminatory mechanism functions in normal perception and when, on filter theory, the discrimination would have to be performed at the level of the filter. The case they put forward is as follows. Moray (1959) had shown that if a subject is listening selectively to one channel and ignoring the other, calling his name on the rejected channel will on a certain proportion of instances cause him to switch his attention to this channel. This was explained by assuming that the subject's name had a higher priority for the filter than the message to which he had been attending. Oswald, Taylor, and Treisman (1960) in a well-controlled

experiment reported that during sleep a subject tends to respond selectively to his own name. Howarth and Ellis (1961) went on to show that the subject's name has a significantly lower threshold than other names when the subject is required to listen normally and there is masking by noise. After analyzing quantitatively their results and those obtained by Oswald et al. and Moray, they (Howarth & Ellis, 1961) conclude that,

> There is, therefore, a very impressive amount of agreement among these three very different experiments concerning the relative intelligibility of one's own name. It seems an obvious conclusion to suppose that the same pattern-analyzing mechanism is required to account for behavior during dichotic listening or during sleep

as during ordinary listening under noise. Thus although Broadbent's (1958) filter theory provides an ingenious explanation of the selection of messages by means of simple and few discriminations, such as which ear is being stimulated, it becomes less attractive as an explanation of those cases where complex and many discriminations, discussed above, are needed.

If we may identify levels in filter theory with neural levels, then there is also evidence against a two-level system to account for novelty and habituation on neurological grounds. Sharpless and Jasper (1956) found that specificity of habituation to tonal pattern was destroyed by bilateral regions of cortex concerned with audition. It is known from other work (Goldberg, Diamond, & Neff, 1958) that sound pattern discrimination is a cortical function. On the other hand, frequency specific habituation was maintained with Sharpless and Jasper's lesions and it has been shown that frequency discrimination can be taught to animals without these cortical areas (Goldberg et al., 1958). This shows, first, that the level at which habituation occurs is not the same for both pattern and tone, and second, that the destruction of the level which is essential to normal functioning also destroys an animal's ability to habituate. This renders it plausible to assume that the mechanism responsible for habituation is not on a different level from that responsible for other learning and discrimination.

Theoretical Considerations

This review of the behavioral evidence leads us to the probable conclusion that a message will reach the same perceptual and discriminatory mechanisms whether attention is paid to it or not; and such information is then grouped or segregated by these mechanisms. How such grouping or segregation takes place is a problem for perceptual theory and will not concern us here. We may suppose that each central structure which is excited by the presentation of a specific quality or attribute to the senses, is given a preset weighting of importance. The central structure or classifying mechanism with the highest weighting will transfer this weighting to the other classifying mechanisms with which it has been grouped or segregated.

The main point with which we are concerned is the following. Given that there is activity in a number of structures, each with a preset weighting of importance, how might that group of structures with the greatest weighting be selected? Or, in behavioral terms, how might the most important of a group of signals be selected? Any system which performs such a function must compare all the incoming signals in importance. This could be done by comparing each incoming signal continuously to every other incoming signal and deciding which is the most important by seeing which signal has no other signal which exceeds it in the physical dimension by which "importance" is represented. But a small amount of reflection will suffice to show that such a system is very uneconomical. Each possible incoming signal must have a provision in the shape of numerous comparing mechanisms, through each of which it will be connected to all other possible signals. So that as the number of possible signals increases, the number of mechanisms to compare them all against each other will increase at an enormous rate. If the same comparing mechanisms are to be shared by pairs of signals then the time to reach a decision will increase out of all bounds.

However, there is a simpler and more economical way to decide that one out of a group of entities is the largest. Suppose we collect a group of boys and we wish to decide which is the tallest. We can measure them individually against each other and then select the boy in whom this comparison procedure never yielded the answer "smaller." This is like the system outlined above. The decision smaller will be made in this case when we lower a horizontal plane or ruler down on the heads of two boys. The boy whose head is touched by this instrument is declared to be larger and the other boy smaller. But such a procedure is cumbersome because there are many pairs of boys and we must scan through many records of individual boys before we can select the tallest. We could, of course, argue that a simpler solution would be to use an absolute measure of height, such as a ruler with feet and inches inscribed on it. But this procedure is not really simpler. Each boy must be compared against the ruler, and then the measurements themselves must be compared against each other in much the same way as the boys were to decide on the larger and smaller in each couple.

If we are simply interested in finding the tallest boy, then an alternative procedure may be used. Suppose we collect our group below our board which is horizontal and travels lightly up and down, and then ask all our group to stand up below it. Then the boy whose head touches the board when the whole group is standing up will be the tallest boy in the group. If then we call him out, the board will sink until it meets the head of the next tallest individual. If we introduce some other boys into the group, then if there is a taller boy in this group the board will be raised until it corresponds to his height. In such a system only the tallest individual will make contact with the board, and so he will himself have an immediate signal that he is the tallest boy.

Now suppose that instead of boys, we have signals, not varying in height, but in some other dimension (which we may continue to call "height") which corresponds to their importance to the organism. Suppose that each signal as it arrives is capable of pushing up some "level" up to its own "height" (the height determined by its importance), then the most

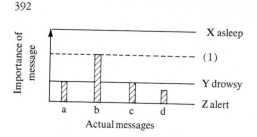

FIGURE 1 Diagram to illustrate operation of proposed system. (The interrupted horizontal line—1—represents the "level" of importance in the specific alerting system which is raised and lowered according to the incoming messages. The solid horizontal lines represent levels of general arousal. At X, the organism is asleep and none of the actual messages produce alerting. At Y, the organism is drowsy and only some incoming messages produce alerting. At Z, the organism is awake. All messages could be alerted to, but the specific alerting system allows only b to be heeded.)

important signal arriving at any particular time will determine this level, analogous to the horizontal board in our example. It will then be the case that any signals which arrive then or after and are of lesser importance and so of smaller height will be below this level. However, if the signal of greater height ceases to be present, then the level will sink to the height reflecting the importance of one of the other signals which is arriving.

If we suppose that only signals whose height corresponds to the height of the level switch in further processes, such as motor output, memory storage, and whatever else it may be that leads to awareness, we have the outline of a system which will display the type of behavior we associate with attention. Only the most important signals coming in will be acted on or remembered. On the other hand, more important signals than those present at an immediately preceding time will be able to break in, for these will raise the height of the level and so displace the previously most important signals as the highest.

So far we have omitted any discussion of the role of general arousal in selective attention. Without such arousal, usually (but not invariably, Bradley & Elkes, 1953; Gastaut, 1954) indicated by characteristic patterns on the electroencephalogram, awareness of and behavioral responsiveness to peripheral stimulation are absent. Some degree of general arousal is thus necessary for attention to operate. Furthermore, individuals when aroused will attend to any incoming message, provided that it is not concomitant with a more important one, whereas when asleep they will only respond to very "important" messages, such as a person's own name (Oswald *et al.,* 1960) or, in the case of a mother, the sound of her infant crying. And when drowsy, though responsive to a larger range of stimuli than when asleep, subjects will tend to "miss" signals which they would notice when fully awake.

The system which takes this into consideration is schematically represented in the diagram above (Figure 1). Any given message will only be heeded if the horizontal line (Y) representing the degree of general arousal meets or crosses the vertical line, the height of which represents the "importance" of the message. Whether or not alerting will take place then depends both on the level of general arousal and on the importance of the message. Attention will not be paid to Message b though it is the most important of all incoming signals, when the level of general arousal is low (Position X). When the level of general arousal is at Z, which is very high, attention could be paid to all the signals a, b, *c*, d, and e. In fact, attention is paid only to b as a result of the operation of the specific alerting mechanism.

Further, it is supposed that a message will increase the level of general arousal in proportion to its importance and for various lengths of time in proportion to its importance, so that messages which would not have been heeded before will command attention if they follow in the wake of a more important message.

The mechanism whereby the weighting of importance of messages is carried out is given by Deutsch's (1953, 1956, 1960) theory of learning and motivation, and will be only briefly summarized here, since it is not the main point of the paper. It is assumed that on exposure to a succession of stimuli, link-analyzer units responsive to these stimuli will be connected together. Certain primary links, when stimulated by physiological factors, generate excitation, and this is passed on from link to link along the connections established by experience. Each link-analyzer unit will receive excitation depending first, on the state of the primary links to which it is connected, either directly or indirectly, and second, on the "resistance" of such a connection, which is determined by past learning. It is assumed that the amount of such excitation arriving at a link-analyzer unit determines both its threshold of excitability by incoming stimuli (leading to an increased readiness to perceive a stimulus whether it is there or not) and the ranking of importance of such a stimulus (e.g., Lawrence, 1949, 1950). We should predict from this theory an inverse correlation between the attention-getting or distracting value of a stimulus when attention is being paid to another, and its threshold (regarded as the likelihood of its being reported by a subject when he is asked to say what he perceives). We should also expect that stimuli which have a high importance weighting should more often be mistakenly perceived when similar stimuli are present.

Neurophysiological Correlates

We may ask how the suggested system would fit what is known of the physiological substrate of attentive behavior. One of the salient features of the system as proposed is that it assumes that all sensory messages which impinge upon the organism are perceptually analyzed at the highest level. It would therefore be of relevance to discuss the group of neurophysiological experiments the results of which have been claimed to demonstrate a neural blockage of "rejected" messages at the lower levels of the primary sensory pathways. Hernández-Peón, Scherrer, and Jouvet (1956) showed that the evoked response at the dorsal cochlear nucleus to clicks was reduced by the presentation of "distracting" olfactory and visual stimuli. A similar effect was found in the visual pathways (Hernández-Peón, Guzman-Flores, Alcarez, & Fernandez-Guardiola, 1957). Stimulation of the reticular formation could produce similar results, and it was supposed

that such stimulation was treated as the presentation of a distracting stimulus. It has also been demonstrated by various workers (e.g. Galambos, Sheatz, & Vernier, 1956; Hernández-Peón & Scherrer, 1955) that responses to auditory clicks recorded from the dorsal cochlear nucleus (as well as other placements) diminish with repetition. Habituation to photic stimuli has been demonstrated for the retina (Palestini, Davidovich, & Hernández-Peón, 1959) and for the olfactory bulb (Hernández-Peón, Alcocer-Cuaron, Lavin, & Santibañez, 1957). It was therefore proposed that during inattention to a signal (either by distraction or habituation) information concerning this signal was blocked at the level of the first sensory synapse by means of "afferent neuronal inhibition." Recently, however, evidence has been produced indicating, at least for the visual and auditory pathways, that such changes in the evoked potential were due to peripheral factors, and represented simply a decrease in the effective intensity of the stimulus. Hugelin, Dumont, and Paillas (1960) report that when the middle ear muscles were cut stimulation of the reticular formation would not cause a diminution in the amplitude of the evoked responses. They report further that such contractions of the middle ear muscles which result from reticular stimulation produce a mean diminution of microphonic potentials of less than 5 decibels. The reduction in sensation brought about by these means therefore appears unimportant. Naquet, Regis, Fischer-Williams, and Ferrandez-Guardiola (1960) found that if the size of the pupil were fixed by local application of atropin the evoked potential recorded from placements below the cortex demonstrated a consistent amplitude.

The above findings do not, however, apply to changes in the cortical evoked response during distraction or habituation. Moushegian, Rupert, Marsh, and Galambos (1961) found that in animals in which the middle ear muscles had been cut, cortical evoked responses to clicks still demonstrated diminution during habituation and distraction, and amplification when the clicks were associated with puffs of air to the face. Naquet, in the experiment quoted above, reports that application of atropin to the pupil did not prevent a variation in cortical evoked responses, which diminished during desynchronization and were enhanced during synchronization of electrical rhythms, also changing in morphology.

Reports of changes in cortical evoked responses during habituation and distraction are many and varied, and it would be impossible in this space to describe the field in detail. Certainly disagreement exists over what occurs as well as over its interpretation. For instance, Horn (1960), recording flash evoked responses in the visual cortex of cats when resting, and when watching a mouse, found that the responses were reduced in amplitude when the cat was watching the mouse; when it ignored the mouse, responses remained of high amplitude. Further, after a series of tone-shock combinations, it was noted that the evoked response to flash was reduced after a series of tones only if there was "some visual searching component in the cat's response to the acoustic stimuli." Horn argues that attenuation of evoked responses in the cortex might be correlated with *greater* sensitivity in the appropriate region, rather than signifying a reduction in incoming information. However, other recent experimenters continue to maintain that evoked responses diminish in amplitude when attention is *not* being paid to the test stimulus. Garcia-Austt, Bogacz, and Vanzulli, (1961) recorded scalp visual evoked responses in human subjects (who were able to give introspective reports) during presentation of flash stimuli. They report,

> When the stimulus is significant and therefore attention is paid to it, the response is relatively simple and widespread. When, on the other hand, the stimulus is not significant and no great attention is paid to it, the response is reduced, complex, and localized.

It would seem that changes in the evoked potential at the cortex do indeed take place during habituation and attention shifts; but that what those changes exactly are, and what they represent, is not yet clear.

We should indeed expect, on the above theory of attention, changes in the cortical evoked potential when attention is being paid to a stimulus, reflecting the activation of various processes, such as motor output and memory storage. Pertinent to this assumption is the discovery by Hubel, Henson, Rupert, and Galambos (1959) of what they term "attention" units in the auditory cortex. By the use of microelectrodes implanted in unanesthetized and unrestrained cats, they obtained records from units which responded only when the animal was "paying attention" to the sound source. These attention units appeared to be both interspersed amongst the others and segregated from them. We may venture to interpret these results by supposing that the units in question formed part of the systems, discussed above, responsible for the appropriate motor response to stimulation or the committing of items to memory, and so forth, or that they lay on the pathway to these systems. Thus they would be inactive even if impulses evoked by auditory stimulation were reaching the cortex, provided that the animal was not also attending to the stimuli.

There is another theoretical assumption for which we might reasonably seek a neurophysiological counterpart. We suppose that a selection of inputs from a variety of sources takes place by comparison with a fluctuating standard. This implies the existence of an undifferentiated structure with widespread connections with the rest of the central nervous system. We are tempted, on account of the evidence for the diffuseness of its input, to identify the brain stem reticular formation as this particular structure. Potentials may be evoked throughout this structure by excitation of various sensory systems (French, Amerongen, & Magoun, 1952; Starzl, Taylor, & Magoun, 1951), and various cortical structures (Bremer & Terzuolo, 1954; French, Hernández-Peón, & Livingston, 1955). Occlusive and facilitatory interaction between responses evoked in the reticular formation from very different sources have further been observed (Bremer & Terzuolo, 1952, 1954; French et al., 1955). Single unit studies demonstrating a convergence of input from several sources have also been reported (Amassian,

1952; Amassian & De Vito, 1954; Hernández-Peón & Hagbarth, 1955; Scheibel, Scheibel, Mollica, & Moruzzi, 1955). A similar conclusion, that the reticular formation is capable of acting as a nonspecific system, can be based on neuroanatomical evidence. Scheibel and Scheibel (1958) state on the basis of their extensive histological study:

> the degree of overlap of the collateral afferent plexuses is so great that it is difficult to see how any specificity of input can be maintained, rather it seems to integrate and vector a number of inputs.

We have also postulated that the fluctuating level correlates with states of arousal. Again the brain stem reticular formation seems well suited to fulfill this function. Its importance in the regulation of states of arousal has been demonstrated both through work involving lesions (Bremer, 1935; French, 1952; French & Magoun, 1952; Lindsley, Schreiner, Knowles, & Magoun, 1949) and stimulation of this structure (Moruzzi & Magoun, 1949; Segundo, Arana, & French, 1955). Recently Moruzzi (1960) has shown that the lower brain stem may play an important role in the initiation of sleep. It also seems likely that the thalamic reticular system is involved in the regulation of states of arousal. Large bilateral lesions of the anterior portion of this system may produce coma analogous to that produced by lesions of the midbrain (French *et al.,* 1952) although the depth of coma so produced is less profound. Stimulation of portions of this system has also been shown to produce either sleep or arousal depending on the parameters of stimulation (Akimoto, Yamaguchi, Okabe, Nakagawa, Nakamura, Abe, Torii, & Masahashi, 1956; Hess, 1954).

The work of Adametz (1959), Chow and Randell (1960), and Doty, Beck, and Kooi (1959), who demonstrated that with different operational techniques and with assiduous nursing care massive lesions of the mid-brain-reticular formation need not produce coma, should, however, be considered. Chow, Dement, and Mitchell (1959) found also that massive lesions in the thalamic reticular system need not produce coma. Until reasons for these discrepant results are found we must regard our conclusions as to the role of the reticular system in attention as tentative.

Whatever the explanation of the findings on lesions in the reticular formation may turn out to be, it seems that, if we are right, some diffuse and nonspecific system is necessary as a part of the mechanism subserving selective attention. Such a system should be found to have afferent connections from all discriminatory and perceptual systems. Through these connections it should be influenced to take up a variety of levels; the level at any one time corresponding with the level of the "highest" afferent message from the discriminatory mechanisms. On its efferent side such a nonspecific system should again be connected with all discriminatory and perceptual mechanisms. Through such connections it would signal to them its own level. If this level of the nonspecific system was above that of a particular discriminatory mechanism, no registration in memory or motor adjustment would take place, if such a discriminatory mechanism was stimulated. Consequently, only that discriminatory mechanism being activated whose level was equal to that of the diffuse system would not be affected. In this way the most important message to the organism will have been selected.

Summary

The selection of wanted from unwanted messages requires discriminatory mechanisms of as great a complexity as those in normal perception, as is indicated by behavioral evidence. The results of neurophysiology experiments on selective attention are compatible with this supposition. This presents a difficulty for Filter theory. Another mechanism is proposed, which assumes the existence of a shifting reference standard, which takes up the level of the most important arriving signal. The way such importance is determined in the system is further described. Neurophysiological evidence relative to this postulation is discussed.

References

Adametz, J. H. Rate of recovery of functioning in cats with rostral reticular lesions. *J. Neurosurg.*, 1959, *16*, 85–98.

Akimoto, H., Yamaguchi, M., Okabe, K., Nakagawa, T., Nakamura, I., Abe, K., Torii H., & Masahashi, I. On the sleep induced through electrical stimulation of dog thalamus. *Folia psychiat. neural. Jap.*, 1956, *10*, 117–146.

Amassian, V. E. Interaction in the somatovisceral projection system. *Proc. Ass. Res. Nerv. Ment. Dis.*, 1952, *30*, 371–402.

Amassian, V. E., & DeVito, R. V. Unit activity in reticular formation and nearby structures. *J. Neurophysiol.*, 1954, *17*, 575–603.

Bradley, P. B., & Elkes, J. The effect of atropine, hyoscyamine, physostigmine and neostigmine on the electrical activity of the brain of the conscious cat. *J. Physiol.*, 1953, *120*, 14–15.

Bremer, F. Cerveau isolé et physiologie du sommeil. *CR Soc. Biol., Paris*, 1935, *118*, 1235–1242.

Bremer, F., & Terzuolo, C. Rôle de l'écorce cérébrale dans le processus physiologique du réveil. *Arch. int. Physiol.*, 1952, *60*, 228–231.

Bremer, F., & Terzuolo, C. Contribution à l'étude des mécanismes physiologiquès du maintien de l'activité vigile du cerveau. Interaction de la formation réticulée et de l'écorce cérébrale dans le processus des réveil. *Arch. inter. Physiol.*, 1954, *62*, 157–178.

Broadbent, D. E. The role of auditory localization in attention and memory span. *J. exp. Psychol.*, 1954, *47*, 191–196.

Broadbent, D. E. *Perception and communication.* London: Pergamon, 1958.

Cherry, E. C. Some experiments on the recognition of speech with one and with two ears. *J. Acoust. Soc. Amer.*, 1953, *25*, 975–979.

Chow, K. L., Dement, W. C., & Mitchell, S. A., Jr. Effects of lesions of the rostral thalamus on brain waves and behavior in cats. *EEG clin. Neurophysiol.*, 1959, *11*, 107–120.

Chow, K. L., & Randell, W. Learning and EEG studies of cats with lesions in the reticular formation. Paper read at the first annual meeting of Psychonomics Society, Chicago, 1960.

Deutsch, J. A. A new type of behaviour theory. *Brit. J. Psychol.*, 1953, *44*, 305–317.

Deutsch, J. A. A theory of insight, reasoning and latent learning. *Brit. J. Psychol.*, 1956, *47*, 115–125.

Deutsch, J. A. *The structural basis of behavior.* Chicago: Univer. Chicago Press, 1960.

Doty, R. W., Beck, E. C., & Kooi, R. A. Effect of brain-stem lesions on conditioned responses in cats. *Exp. Neurol.*, 1959, *1*, 360–385.

Egan, J. P., Carterette, E. C., & Thwing, E. J. Some factors affecting multi-channel listening. *J. Acoust. Soc. Amer.*, 1954, *26*, 774–782.

French, J. D. Brain lesions associated with prolonged unconsciousness. *AMA Arch. Neurol. Psychiat.*, 1952, *68*, 727–740.

French, J. D., Amerongen, F. K., & Magoun, H. W. An activating system in brain stem of monkey. *AMA Arch. Neurol. Psychiat.*, 1952, *68*, 577–590.

French, J. D., Hernández-Peón, R., & Livingston, R. B. Projections from cortex to cephalic brain stem (reticular formation) in monkey. *J. Neurophysiol.*, 1955, *18*, 74–95.

French, J. D., & Magoun, H. W. Effects of chronic lesions in central cephalic brain stem of monkeys. *AMA Arch. Neurol. Psychiat.*, 1952, *68*, 591–604.

Galambos, R., Sheatz, G., & Vernier, V. G. Electrophysiological correlates of a conditioned response in cats. *Science*, 1956, *123*, 376–377.

Garcia-Austt, E., Bogacz, J., & Vanzulli, A. Significance of the photic stimulus on the evoked responses in man. In Delafresnaye (Ed.), *Brain mechanisms and learning.* Oxford: Blackwell, 1961. Pp. 603–626.

Gastaut, H. The brain stem and cerebral electrogenesis in relation to consciousness. In Delafresnaye (Ed.), *Brain mechanisms and consciousness.* Springfield, Ill.: Charles C Thomas, 1954. Pp. 249–283.

Goldberg, J. M., Diamond, I. T., & Neff, W. D. Auditory discrimination after ablation of temporal and insular cortex in cat. *Federat. Proc.*, 1957, *16*, 47–48.

Goldberg, J. M., Diamond, I. T., & Neff, W. D. Frequency discrimination after ablation of cortical projection areas of the auditory system. *Federat. Proc.*, 1958, *17*, 216–255.

Gray, J. A., & Wedderburn, A. A. I. Grouping strategies with simultaneous stimuli. *Quart. J. exp. Psychol.*, 1960, *12*, 180–184.

Hernández-Peón, R., Alcocer-Cuaron, C., Lavin, A., & Santibañez, G. Regulación centrifuga de la actividad électrica del bulbo olfactorio. Punta del Este, Uruguay: Primera Reunión Cientifica de Ciencias Fisiólogicas, 1957. Pp. 192–193.

Hernández-Peón, R., Guzman-Flores, C., Alcarez, H., & Fernandez-Guardiola, A. Sensory transmission in visual pathway during "attention" in unanaesthetized cats. *Acta neurol. Lat.-Amer.*, 1957, *3*, 1–8.

Hernández-Peón, R., & Hagbarth, K. Interaction between afferent and cortically induced reticular responses. *J. Neurophysiol.*, 1955, *18*, 44–55.

Hernández-Peón, R., & Scherrer, H. Habituation to acoustic stimuli in cochlear nucleus. *Federat. Proc.* 1955, *14*, 71.

Hernández-Peón, R., Scherrer, H., & Jouvet, M. Modification of electric activity in cochlear nucleus during "attention" in unanaesthetized cats. *Science*, 1956, *123*, 331–332.

Hess, W. R. The diencephalic sleep centre. In J. F. Delafresnaye (Ed.), *Brain mechanisms and conscious-*

ness. Springfield, Ill., Charles C Thomas, 1954. Pp. 117–136.

Hirsh, I. J. The relation between localization and intelligibility. *J. Acoust. Soc. Amer.,* 1950, *22,* 196–200.

Horn, G. Electrical activity of the cerebral cortex of the unanesthetized cat during attentive behavior. *Brain,* 1960, *83,* 57–76.

Howarth, C. I., & Ellis, R. The relative intelligibility threshold for one's own name compared with other names. *Quart. J. exp. Psychol.,* 1961, *13,* 236–239.

Hubel, D. H., Henson, C. O., Rupert, A., & Galambos, R. Attention units in the auditory cortex. *Science,* 1959, *129,* 1279–1280.

Hugelin, A., Dumont, S., & Paillas, N. Tympanic muscles and control of auditory input during arousal. *Science,* 1960, *131,* 1371–1372.

Lawrence, D. H. Acquired distinctiveness of cues: I. Transfer between discriminations on the basis of familiarity with the stimulus. *J. exp. Psychol.,* 1949, *39,* 770–784.

Lawrence, D. H. Acquired distinctiveness of cues: II. Selective association in a constant stimulus situation. *J. exp. Psychol.,* 1950, *40,* 175–188.

Lindsley, D. B., Schreiner, L. H., Knowles, W. B., & Magoun, H. W. Behavioral and EEG changes following chronic brain stem lesions in the cat. *EEG clin. Neurophysiol.,* 1949, *1,* 455–473.

Moray, N. Attention in dichotic listening: Affective cues and the influence of instructions. *Quart. J. exp. Psychol.,* 1959, *11,* 56–60.

Moruzzi, G. Synchronizing influences of the brain stem and the inhibitory mechanisms underlying the production of sleep by sensory stimulation. *Int. J. EEG clin. Neurophysiol.,* 1960, Suppl. No. 13, 231–256.

Moruzzi, G., & Magoun, H. W. Brain stem reticular formation and activation of the EEG. *EEG clin. Neurophysiol.,* 1949, *1,* 455–473.

Moushegian, G., Rupert, A., Marsh, J. T., & Galambos, R. Evoked cortical potentials in absence of middle ear muscles. *Science,* 1961, *133,* 582–583.

Naquet, R., Regis, H., Fischer-Williams, M., & Fernandez-Guardiola, A. Variation in the responses evoked by light along the specific pathways. *Brain,* 1960, *83,* 52–56.

Oswald, I., Taylor, A., & Treisman, M. Discrimination responses to stimulation during human sleep. *Brain,* 1960, *83,* 440–453.

Palestini, M., Davidovich, A., & Hernández-Peón, R. Functional significance of centrifugal influences upon the retina. *Acta neurol. Lat.-Amer.,* 1959, *5,* 113–131.

Peters, R. W. Competing messages: The effect of interfering messages upon the reception of primary messages. *USN Sch. Aviat. Med. res. Rep.,* 1954, Project No. NM 001 064.01.27.

Poulton, E. C. Two-channel listening. *J. exp. Psychol.,* 1953, *46,* 91–96.

Scheibel, M. E., & Scheibel, A. Structural substrates for integrative patterns in the brain stem reticular core. In H. H. Jasper, L. D. Proctor, R. S. Knighton, S. Roberts, W. C. Noshay, C. William, and R. T. Costello (Eds.), *Reticular formation of the brain.* Boston: Little, Brown, 1958. Pp. 31–55.

Scheibel, M. E., Scheibel, A., Mollica, A., & Moruzzi, G. Convergence and interaction of afferent impulses on single units of reticular formation. *J. Neurophysiol.,* 1955, *18,* 309–331.

Segundo, J. P., Arana, R., & French, J. D. Behavorial arousal by stimulation of the brain in monkey. *J. Neurosurg.,* 1955, *12,* 601–613.

Sharpless, S., & Jasper, H. Habituation of the arousal reaction. *Brain,* 1956, *79,* 655–678.

Sokolov, E. N. Neuronal models and the orienting reflex. In Mary A. B. Brazier (Ed.), *The central nervous system and behavior: Transactions of the third conference.* New York: Josiah Macy, Jr. Foundation, 1960. Pp. 187–276.

Spieth, W., Curtis, J. F., & Webster, J. C. Responding to one of two simultaneous messages. *J. Acoust. Soc. Amer.,* 1954, *26,* 391–396.

Starzl, T. E., Taylor, C. W., & Magoun, H. W. Collateral afferent excitation of reticular formation of brain stem. *J. Neurophysiol.,* 1951, *14,* 479–496.

Thompson, W. R., & Solomon, L. M. Spontaneous pattern discrimination in the rat. *J. comp. physiol. Psychol.,* 1954, *46,* 281–287.

Treisman, A. M. Contextual cues in selective listening. *Quart. J. exp. Psychol.,* 1960, *12,* 242–248.

Voronin, L. G., & Sokolov, E. N. Cortical mechanisms of the orienting reflex and its relation to the conditioned reflex. *Int. J. EEG clin. Neurophysiol.,* 1960, Suppl. No. 13, 335–346.

Webster, J. C., & Thomson, P. O. Responding to both of two overlapping messages. *J. Acoust. Soc. Amer.,* 1954, *26,* 396–402.

9.3 Selective Attentiveness
and Cortical Evoked Responses
to Visual and Auditory Stimuli*

PAUL SPONG   MANFRED HAIDER
DONALD B. LINDSLEY

In a previous study (1) we demonstrated that the magnitude of visually evoked responses was correlated with fluctuations in attentiveness during a prolonged visual vigilance task. In contrast, the study reported here was concerned with short-term attentiveness to either click or flash stimuli presented alternately. Average evoked potentials were recorded from visual and auditory areas while subjects attended to stimuli within one of the two sense modalities and ignored those in the other. Three methods of inducing and maintaining attentive sets were compared.

Thirteen subjects performed under all three experimental conditions: vigilance, key-pressing, and counting. Under all conditions, alternating clicks and flashes were presented 1 second apart. For the *vigilance condition,* the subjects were instructed to perform, during one-half of the experiment, a vigilance task in one modality, and to ignore stimuli presented in the other modality; they were instructed to reverse the procedure during the other half of the experiment. Thus, when subjects were performing the visual vigilance task, attending to flashes rather than clicks, they received bright flashes (intensity 15 lam) requiring no response, and occasional dim flashes (9 lam) which required the pressing of a key. The purpose of this task

was to ensure that attention was paid to all flashes. The clicks which alternated with the flashes during the visual vigilance task were all of the same intensity (400 μbar) and were ignored by the subject. When subjects were performing the auditory vigilance task, attending to clicks rather than flashes, they were required to press a key in response to occasional weak clicks (100 μbar) interspersed among the more numerous louder clicks (400 μbar). Flash stimuli alternating with the clicks during the auditory vigilance task were all of the same intensity (15 lam) and were to be ignored.[1]

For the *key-pressing condition,* during one-half of the experiment the subjects pressed a key after each stimulus in one sense modality; in the other half they did the reverse. Stimulus intensity was held constant under this condition (flashes, 15 lam; clicks, 400 μbar). For the *counting condition,* the subjects were instructed to attend to either flashes or clicks but were required to count each stimulus in the modality in which they were attending and to press a key after each 50 stimuli. Stimuli in the other sense modality were to be ignored. Stimulus intensity was held constant and was the same as for the key-pressing condition.

In each half of the experiment with subjects under the vigilance condition, 330 flashes and 330 clicks were presented. During the visual

* *Science,* April 16, 1965, vol. 148, pp. 395–397. Copyright © 1965 by the American Association for the Advancement of Science. Supported by NASA contract NsG-623 and NSF grant GB-1844; also aided by ONR, contract Nonr 233 (32). One of us (M.H.) was a USPHS international postdoctoral research fellow (FF-534).

[1] Flash intensity measured by Spectra Brightness Spot Meter (Photo Research Corporation) at various flash rates and extrapolated; click intensity measured in microbars, a calibrated condenser microphone being used (Brüel and Kjaer type 4134).

vigilance task, 30 of the flashes were dim, and during the auditory task 30 of the clicks were weak. Under each of the other conditions 300 flashes and 300 clicks were presented during each half of the experiment. Each half of an experimental session lasted approximately 10 minutes with a 5-minute rest period between halves. Visual flash stimuli were produced by Grass PS-1 photostimulators and were diffused by means of a 10- by 12-cm flashed-opal glass screen located at the end of a viewing tube 30 cm from the subject's eyes. For bright stimuli one of the photostimulators was set at intensity 4, and for dim stimuli the other was set at intensity 4 with an additional filter. Auditory stimuli were generated by a Grass S-4 stimulator and were relayed to the subject by Permoflux PDR-8 cushioned earphones.

The electroencephalogram was recorded on a Grass model 6 electroencephalograph and an Ampex FR-1300 frequency-modulated tape recorder, from three scalp locations: occipital, temporal, and vertex. The occipital electrode was sited approximately 2.5 cm above the inion and 2.5 cm to the right of the midline at O_2; the temporal electrode, midway between C_6 and T_4; the vertex electrode at C_z. These letter designations are according to the 10-20 electrode system of the International Federation of Electroencephalographic Societies (2). In each case the reference electrode was placed on the left earlobe.

Time-averaging of the cortical responses to the 300 flash and 300 click stimuli, presented while the subjects were performing the visual and auditory tasks under each experimental condition, was accomplished by means of a Mnemotron computer of average transients. Responses to flashes and clicks were averaged separately from all three recording sites, but data reported here deal only with flash responses recorded from the occipital area and click responses from the temporal area.

Evoked potentials to flash or click stimuli recorded from the scalps of human subjects over the visual and auditory areas, respectively, consist of a complex sequence of waves. Despite this complexity and a certain amount of variability, there exists within subjects and between subjects a fairly regularly identifiable pattern of waves, the peaks and troughs of which we have identified in Figure 1 as *a, b, c, d,* and *e.* Of these, the second negative peak (*d*) is usually the most prominent component and has a surprisingly constant latency for a given set of stimulus conditions. The latency of peak (*d*) for a flash stimulus recorded over the visual area is approximately 160 msec; the latency of peak (*d*) for a click stimulus recorded over the auditory area is approximately 110 msec. In this study, the magnitude of the wave defined as (*c-d-e*) constituted the principal criterion for comparing the evoked potentials elicited under the different experimental conditions. The long latency and diffuse cortical representation of this wave suggests that it is a secondary potential (3), perhaps related to the nonspecific sensory system.

Figure 1 presents characteristic data from two of the 13 subjects studied under each of the three experimental conditions. Under the vigilance condition, when subjects were attending to the flash stimuli (visual vigilance task), the amplitude of the visually evoked response (VER) to flashes, recorded from the occipital area, was much greater than when subjects were attending to the click stimuli (auditory vigilance task). Similarly, when subjects were attending to the click stimuli (auditory vigilance task), the amplitude of the auditory evoked response (AER) to clicks recorded from the temporal area, was greater than when subjects were attending to flashes (visual vigilance task). All 13 subjects in the experiment showed VER and AER differences between tasks of the type illustrated in Figure 1. Basically similar data were obtained when the subjects were under the key-pressing condition: here also the VER and AER amplitudes were greatest when subjects were attending to stimuli in the corresponding sense modality. Thus, when subjects were performing the visual key-pressing task (pressing the key after each flash), the amplitude of the VER's to flashes was greater than when the subjects were pressing the key after each click. Again, all 13 of the subjects showed VER and AER differences between attentive and inattentive conditions of the kind illustrated in Figure 1. Data obtained with the subjects under the counting condition were

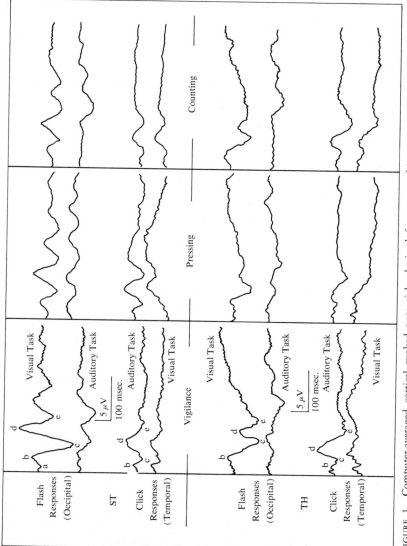

FIGURE 1 Computer-averaged cortical evoked potentials obtained from two subjects (ST and TH) in response to flashes and clicks. The potentials were recorded from the occipital and temporal areas while the subjects performed visual and auditory tasks under three experimental conditions: vigilance, key-pressing, and counting. Flashes alternated with clicks throughout. Each trace is the averaged evoked response to 300 stimuli. Analysis time, 500 msec. In the upper left-hand section, the major peaks and troughs of the visual and auditory evoked responses are identified by letters *a* to *e*; the amplitude of the wave defined by *c-d-e* is the principal differentiating criterion. Recordings: right occipital and temporal areas to left ear; negativity upward.

equivocal. Six subjects showed differences of the kind found under the other two conditions; three subjects showed no differences; and four subjects showed differences in the opposite direction. As we will explain below, counting may be a task which divides rather than focuses attention.

These data indicate that when attentiveness is effectively manipulated between sense modalities, the amplitude of cortical evoked responses in a given sense modality varies according to whether or not the subject is attending to stimuli in that or another modality. It is important to note that subjects in this experiment were required to be alert for relatively short periods of time (10 minutes). This contrasts with the situation in the experiment we reported previously (1), in which subjects performed a vigilance task lasting nearly 2 hours. Attentiveness inevitably fluctuated considerably during performance of that prolonged task, as subjects were usually highly alert at the beginning and much less so at the end. It remained an open question, therefore, whether changes in the cortical evoked responses with changes in attentive state would occur in a continually alert subject. Data obtained under the conditions of the present experiment allow us to state unequivocally that, even in an alert subject, changes in evoked responses occur which are related to the subject's attentive state.

Several other workers have examined the effect of selective attentiveness on cortical evoked responses in humans (4–8). Their results have been varied and therefore inconclusive, perhaps because of the varied procedures employed in establishing attentive sets. For example, van Hof et al. (4) reported that attending to flash stimuli by counting them had no effect on the amplitude of the evoked responses to the flashes. On the other hand, Jouvet (5) and Garcia-Austt et al. (6) reported that counting flash stimuli enhanced the amplitude of the VER. In contrast, Callaway et al. (7) recently reported that patients showed a decrease in AER amplitude while attending to bursts of tone. The procedures used by the various investigators suggest that the method by which an attentive set was established may have been

an important determinant of the findings in a particular experiment. In our experiment, the vigilance and the key-pressing tasks were effective in enhancing cortical evoked responses, whereas the counting task was relatively ineffective. Counting, rather than focusing attention on relevant stimuli, may be distracting because of the necessity of keeping track of the number of stimuli counted. In most of the studies cited above, a counting task was used to elicit attentiveness. The equivocal results obtained may have been because of this.

Our results seem to indicate conclusively that when an attentive set is established by making subjects perform a perceptual discrimination which requires close attention to every stimulus, the amplitude of the cortical evoked responses varies with the attentive set of the subject.

Summary

Cortical evoked responses to flashes and clicks were recorded from human subjects performing visual or auditory tasks under three conditions of selective attentiveness. The subjects were required to attend to the flashes and to ignore alternating clicks, or vice versa. Responses to flashes recorded from the occipital area were larger when attention was directed toward visual stimuli, and responses to click stimuli recorded from the temporal area were larger when attention was directed toward auditory stimuli.

References

1. M. Haider, P. Spong, D. B. Lindsley, Science 145, 180 (1964).
2. H. H. Jasper, Electroencephalog. Clin. Neurophysiol. 10, 371, (1958).
3. P. Buser and M. Imbert, in Sensory Communication, W. A. Rosenblith, Ed. (Wiley, New York, 1961).
4. M. W. van Hof et al., Acta Physiol. Pharmacol. Neerl. 11, 485 (1962).
5. M. Jouvet, Psychol. Franc. 2, 254 (1957).
6. E. Garcia-Austt, J. Bogacz, A. Vanzulli, Electroencephalog. Clin. Neurophysiol. 17, 136 (1964).
7. E. Callaway, R. T. Jones, R. S. Layne, Arch. Gen. Psychiat. 12, 83 (1965).
8. H. Davis, Science 145, 182 (1964).

Index of Names

Index of Subjects

413